Why You Need this New Edition
6 good reasons why you should buy this latest edition of *Theories of Development*

1. A revised chapter on ethology suggests new ways in which the study of other species provides insight into human development.

2. This new edition gives additional attention to several theorists' views of children's play—an aspect of development that is endangered in contemporary schools and society.

3. A new summary of Lawrence Kohlberg's seventh stage reveals his concern with spiritual issues not addressed in his standard six stages of moral development.

4. The chapter on Noam Chomsky's theory includes a new section on scientists' attempts to teach language to chimpanzees. This section features Sue Savage-Rumbaugh's work with the bonobo species.

5. The chapter on learning theory describes the behavioral treatment of autism in greater detail and indicates a new direction this treatment is taking.

6. The Epilogue updates ways in which the standards movement stifles young children's development.

PEARSON

SIXTH EDITION

THEORIES OF DEVELOPMENT

Concepts and Applications

WILLIAM CRAIN

*The City College
of the City University of New York*

Boston   Columbus   Indianapolis   New York   San Francisco   Upper Saddle River
Amsterdam   Cape Town   Dubai   London   Madrid   Milan   Munich   Paris   Montreal   Toronto
Delhi   Mexico City   Sao Paulo   Sydney   Hong Kong   Seoul   Singapore   Taipei   Tokyo

Executive Editor: *Jeff Marshall*
Editorial Director: *Craig Campanella*
Editor in Chief: *Jessica Mosher*
Associate Editor: *LeeAnn Doherty*
Editorial Assistant: *Courtney Elezovic*
Marketing Manager: *Nicole Kunzmann*
Director of Marketing: *Brandy Dawson*
Executive Marketing Manager: *Jeanette Koskinas*
Production Editor: *Karen Mason/Pat Torelli*
Manufacturing Manager: *Evelyn Beaton*
Manufacturing Buyer: *Debbie Rossi*
Cover Administrator: *Kristina Mose-Libon*
Editorial Production and Composition: *Laserwords Private Limited, Chennai*

Credits and acknowledgments borrowed from other sources and reproduced, with permission, in this textbook appear on pages xi–xii or on the appropriate page within the text.

This is a special edition of an established title widely used by colleges and universities throughout the world. Pearson published this exclusive edition for the benefit of students outside the United States and Canada. If you purchased this book within the United States or Canada you should be aware that it has been imported without the approval of the Publisher or the Author.

Many of the designations by manufacturers and sellers to distinguish their products are claimed as trademarks. Where those designations appear in this book, and the publisher was aware of a trademark claim, the designations have been printed in initial caps or all caps.

10 9 8 7 6 5 4 3 2 1

**Prentice Hall
is an imprint of**

ISBN-10:   0-205-00862-3
ISBN-13: 978-0-205-00862-9

To Ellen, Adam, Tom, and Sally

CONTENTS

This sixth edition of *Theories of Development* is fundamentally similar to the earlier editions. Its purpose, once again, is to introduce students to a variety of theorists, giving special attention to those who have contributed to that distinctly developmental perspective that began with Rousseau. The book focuses, that is, on writers who help us understand how development might arise from our inner promptings and spontaneous interests and how we might view the world differently at various stages of life.

This new edition updates several chapters. I have most substantially revised Chapter 3 on ethology—a revision that reflects my growing conviction that the study of other species casts considerable light on human development. In addition, several chapters give greater attention to children's play. At a time when education policymakers are so willing to sacrifice children's free, creative play for the sake of higher test scores, it's important to see how great developmental theorists recognized the value of play.

The updated Instructor's Manual, which includes test questions, is available for download from the Instructor's Resource Center at *www.pearsonhighered.com/IRC*.

Over the years, many people have contributed to this book. I offer special thanks to my wife Ellen. As always, she provided unwavering support and valuable insight. I also am deeply indebted to our children, Adam, Tom, and Sally. It was initially by watching them that I became so impressed by the growth process that I decided to write this book about it. Our children are grown now, but they continue to offer support and ideas that mean a great deal to me.

This new edition has benefited from critical readings and suggestions by Jonathan Lang, Borough of Manhattan Community College; Robert Markowitz, University of West Florida; Stephanie Shine, Texas Tech University; Deborah Thomas, Washington State Community College; and Sandra Triebenbacher, East Carolina University.

I am grateful, finally, to those who have given permission to quote from various sources:

- The first stanza of Emily Dickinson's poem, "Growth of Man like Growth of Nature," appears on page xv and is reprinted by permission of the publishers and the Trustees of Amherst College from *The Poems of Emily Dickinson*, Thomas H. Johnson, ed., Cambridge, Mass.: The Belknap Press of Harvard University Press. Copyright © 1951, 1955, 1979, 1983 by the President and Fellows of Harvard College.

- Carol Haber granted permission to reprint in Chapter 2 excerpts from Louise B. Ames, "Don't Push Your Preschooler," *Family Circle Magazine*, December, 1971.
- Holistic Education Press gave permission to reproduce in Chapter 3 material from my article, "Is Children's Play Innate?" which appears in the Summer 2010 issue of *Encounter: Education for Meaning and Social Justice*.
- Excerpts in Chapter 12 are taken from *Childhood and Society* by Erik H. Erikson. Copyright © 1950 © 1963 by W.W. Norton & Company, Inc., renewed © 1978, 1991 by Erik H. Erikson. Used by Permission of W.W. Norton & Company, Inc.
- Excerpts in Chapter 13 were reprinted and edited with the permission of The Free Press, a Division of Simon & Schuster, Inc., from *The Empty Fortress: Infantile Autism and the Birth of the Self* by Bruno Bettleheim. Copyright © 1967 by Bruno Bettelheim. Copyright renewed © 1995 by Ruth Bettelheim, Naomi Pena, Eric Bettelheim. All rights reserved.
- Henry Holt and Company granted permission to reproduce lines from my 2003 book, *Reclaiming Childhood*. This material appears in the Epilogue.

Credit for the use of illustrations and other material is given within the text.

William Crain

Growth of Man like growth
Of Nature
Gravitates within,
Atmosphere and sun confirm it
But it stirs alone.

Emily Dickinson

Introduction

We all have assumptions about the nature of development. We commonly assume, for example, that children's development is in our hands—that children become what we make them. We think it is our job to teach them, to correct their mistakes, to provide good models, and to motivate them to learn.

Such a view is reasonable enough, and it is shared by many psychologists—by those called learning theorists and by many others as well. Psychologists use more scientific language, but they too assume that parents, teachers, and others structure the child's thought and behavior. When they see a child engaging in a new bit of behavior, their first guess is that it has been taught. If, for example, a 2-year-old girl shows an intense interest in putting objects into place, they assume someone taught her to do this, for she is a product of her social environment.

There is, however, another tradition in psychology—a line of developmental theorists beginning with Jean-Jacques Rousseau—that looks at children differently. These writers are less impressed by our efforts to teach or otherwise influence children. Instead, they are more interested in how children grow and learn on their own. These scholars, whose ranks include Arnold Gesell, Maria Montessori, and Jean Piaget, would wonder if this 2-year-old's interest in ordering objects might not be a spontaneous one—something she has begun entirely by herself. Her concern for order might even be greater than that of those around her. For just as children, at a certain stage, develop an inner urge to stand and walk, they may also develop a spontaneous need to find order in their environment.

If we follow a child around, taking the time to observe the child's natural tendencies, we find that the child has many spontaneous interests. A $1\frac{1}{2}$-year-old may become fascinated by a ball, a puddle of water, or a mound of sand—things that can be touched, felt, and acted on. The child may examine and play with such objects for long periods of time. Such interests may be so intense and so different from our own that it is unlikely they are the product of adult teachings. Rather, the

1

developmental theorists think, children have an inner need to seek out certain kinds of experiences and activities at certain times in life.

The writers in the developmental tradition do not agree on every point, and they have studied different aspects of people's lives. Nevertheless, they share a fundamental orientation, which includes this interest in inner growth and spontaneous learning.

The developmentalists' concerns have been practical as well as theoretical. Montessori, for example, became dissatisfied with the standard educational method, whereby teachers try to direct children's learning by rewarding their correct answers and criticizing their mistakes. This practice, Montessori thought, undermines children's independence, for children soon turn to the teacher, an external authority, to see if they are right. Instead, she tried to show that if we observe children's spontaneous interests, we can provide tasks on which they will work independently and with the greatest concentration, without external direction or motivation. For, she thought, an inner force prompts children to perfect their capacities at each developmental stage.

In many other ways, writers with a strong developmental orientation have contributed to a new understanding of childhood and the years that follow. Unfortunately, however, their writings have not received the full consideration they deserve. Their emphasis on spontaneous development has often struck psychologists as too romantic or too radical. Piaget, to be sure, has found a wide audience, but often a very skeptical one.

There is one place where the developmentalists' concerns are seriously expressed. This is in humanistic psychology. Maslow and the humanists have drawn heavily upon developmental ideas. But the humanists have usually done this in a very implicit way, without recognizing how much they owe to earlier developmental contributions.

This book, then, is devoted to an appreciation of some of the outstanding developmental theorists. We will discuss the theorists who have followed closely in the footsteps of Rousseau, along with other theorists, including ethologists and psychoanalysts, who share a developmental outlook. We will discuss their concepts and some of the practical implications of their work. We will also review the first orientation I mentioned—that of the learning theorists, who help us understand behavior from a more environmental perspective. We will not cover learning theory in the depth it deserves, for this book is primarily concerned with the developmental tradition. But we will try to get a flavor of the learning theorists' ideas. In the chapter on Vygotsky, in addition, we will look at a pioneering attempt to integrate strong developmental and environmental perspectives. In the conclusion, we will discuss the ways in which developmental theorists have anticipated and advanced humanistic ideas and insights.

CHAPTER 1

Early Theories: Preformationism, Locke, and Rousseau

The two great pioneers in child psychology were John Locke and Jean-Jacques Rousseau. Locke was the father of environmentalism and learning theory; his heirs are scientists such as Ivan Pavlov and B. F. Skinner. Rousseau began the developmental tradition in psychology; his followers include Arnold Gesell, Maria Montessori, Heinz Werner, and Jean Piaget. Both Locke and Rousseau made radical departures from an earlier outlook called preformationism.

PREFORMATIONISM

For centuries, people seem to have looked on children as fully formed miniature adults. The French historian Philippe Ariès (1914–1984) described how this view was predominant during the Middle Ages. Medieval paintings and sculptures, for example, routinely portrayed children—even newborns—with adult body proportions and facial characteristics. The children were distinguished only by their size. It was as if the children had arrived preformed in the adult mold (Ariès, 1960, pp. 33–34).

In medieval social life, too, Ariès argued, children were treated like adults. When they were 6 or 7 years old, they were typically sent off to other villages to begin working as apprentices. They learned carpentry, farming, domestic service, weaving, and other crafts and trades on the job. The child lived as a boarder in a master's house and often worked alongside other apprentices who were much older than he or she. No one paid much attention to the child's age, for the child had basically entered adult society. The child wore the same clothes, played the same games, and participated in the same festivals as the grownups

(Ariès, 1960, pp. 71–72, 411). "Wherever people worked," Ariès said, "and also wherever they amused themselves, even in the taverns of ill repute, children mingled with the adults" (p. 368).

Ariès acknowledged that younger children—before the age of 6 or 7—were treated differently. People recognized their need for protection and care. But on the whole, Ariès suggested, people were indifferent to children's special characteristics. No one bothered to study, for example, the infant's developing speech or motor development; and when artists included children in their paintings, they depicted even newborns as miniature adults.

Some historians have challenged Ariès's views. Because medieval written documents are sparse, it's difficult to evaluate all the disagreements, but historians such as Barbara Hanawalt (1986) and Shulamith Shahar (1990) have gathered enough evidence to indicate that Ariès was sometimes prone to overstatement. It appears that apprenticeships, while common, were not as universal as Ariès claimed, and that 6- and 7-year-olds sometimes entered the adult workplace more gradually than Ariès implied. Still, by the age of 12 or so, most children were carrying out adult responsibilities, and I believe that Ariès's critics have done more to qualify Ariès's accounts than to refute them.

Moreover, other sources have shown that the image of children that Ariès highlighted—that of the child as a little adult—has been prevalent throughout the ages. This image is perhaps most evident in preformationistic theories in embryology. For centuries, many scientists believed that a tiny, fully formed human, or homunculus, is implanted in the sperm or the egg at conception (see Figure 1.1). They believed that the human is "preformed" at the instant

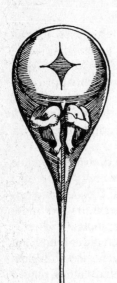

FIGURE 1.1
Drawing by Hartsoeker (1694) of a fully formed human in the sperm.
(Reprinted in Needham, 1959, p. 206.)

of conception and only grows in size and bulk until birth. Preformationism in embryology dates back at least to the fifth century B.C.E. and is found in scientific thinking throughout the ages. As late as the 18th century, most scientists held preformationist views. They admitted that they had no direct evidence for a fully formed homunculus, but they argued that this was only because it is transparent or too small to see (Balinsky, 1981, p. 11; Needham, 1959, pp. 34–35, 91, 213–222).

As we look back on the "little adult" views of the past, it's easy to regard them as quaint and antiquated. But we often lapse into the same thinking today, as when we expect young children to be able to sit as still as we can in social settings, or when we assume that their thinking is the same as ours. For example, I was recently standing in a supermarket checkout line and heard a mother next to me upbraid her toddler for having put several items that he liked into the shopping cart: "You know I can't afford those things," the mother said, as if the toddler had an adult knowledge of grocery budgets. We are vulnerable to an adult egocentrism and assume that even young children think as we do, even if our attitude isn't as dominant as it once was (Ausubel, 1958, p. 24).

In embryology, preformationism gave way during the 18th century, when microscopic investigations showed that the embryo developed in a gradual, sequential manner. In European social thought, preformationism began to decline earlier, in the 16th century, accompanying changes in the occupational world.

During the Middle Ages, most of the occupations—such as farming, carpentry, domestic service, metal work, and weaving—required skill, but the adults believed that 6- and 7-year-olds could begin learning them on the job. Children, therefore, were able to mix in with adults. After 1500 or so, the occupational world showed clear signs of change. With the invention of the printing press, the growth of commerce and market economies, and the rise of cities and nation-states, the occupational world began to take on a "white-collar" look. New opportunities arose for merchants, lawyers, bankers, journalists, and government officials—occupations that required reading, writing, and math. The members of a rising middle class saw that they could advance their families' fortunes by providing their children with the academic instruction that these new occupations required. This new demand for education sparked a tremendous growth of schools in 16th- and 17th-century Europe (Crain, 1993).

The upshot was that growing numbers of parents (especially in the middle class) were no longer willing to send their children off to work at the age of 6 or 7 years. Parents wanted their children to go to school first. Parents began keeping their children in school at least until they were 12 years old, and often until they were well into their teens. Thus the growth of schools gave the child a new status. The child was no longer someone who was ready for the adult world, but someone who had to be kept apart from it while undergoing an extensive education. The child was seen less as a little adult and more as a future adult (Ariès, 1960, pp. 329, 412).

LOCKE'S ENVIRONMENTALISM

Biographical Introduction

As the rising middle class pursued new opportunities, it challenged the traditional feudal order. The middle class no longer accepted a society in which everyone's place was predetermined by birth. It sought a brighter future, pinning great hopes on education to bring it about. In so doing, it helped usher in the modern way of life.

But the feudal regime wasn't about to just hand over its authority. It imposed economic regulations and waged an ideological war. It accused the new middle class—the bourgeoisie—of selfishly abandoning loyalty, honor, and the old ways.

In these battles, those seeking change drew inspiration from the intellectuals of the 18th-century Enlightenment, such as Denis Diderot and Nicolas de Condorcet. These writers argued that if people could rid themselves of the authoritarian state and church, people could live freely and democratically, and science, technology, and education would produce great progress for all. These writers, in turn, drew heavily on the late-17th-century theories of the British philosopher John Locke (1632–1704).

Writing in language that was refreshingly clear and sensible, Locke rejected the widespread belief that there are vast, innate differences among people. Instead, Locke argued, people are largely shaped by their social environments, especially by their education. Locke then showed how this happens and how education could be improved. To many Enlightenment thinkers, Locke's writings were full of wonderful possibilities. If one could change people's environments and education, one could produce an egalitarian, democratic society (Gay, 1969, pp. 511–516).

Locke was born in the village of Somerset, England. His father, a small landowner, was the first to instill in him a belief in democracy. Locke attended the Westminster School and Oxford University, but found both plagued by the pedantic lessons so prevalent in his day. Although he seems to have been a rather shy boy, he frequently became so bored and restless in class that he preferred to talk to his classmates rather than pay attention to the instructor (Pheardon, 1952, p. vii; Quick, 1880, p. xx; Sahakian & Sahakian, 1975).

Still, Locke did well enough at Oxford to gain appointments at the university tutoring Greek and moral philosophy. For a while, Locke had trouble deciding on his future. A devout Christian, he thought he might become ordained in the Church of England, but he decided to study medicine instead, primarily so he could learn about the natural sciences. He assisted a note-worthy chemist, Robert Boyle, and was deeply impressed by the scientific method and its reliance on empirical evidence. As a physician, Locke successfully treated Lord Ashley, later the Earl of Shaftesbury; became Shaftesbury's friend and personal secretary; and also tutored his grandson. His association with Shaftesbury, however, eventually proved troublesome. When Shaftesbury was imprisoned for criticizing the king, Locke was forced to flee England and find asylum in Holland. There, Locke wrote a series of letters to his friend Edward Clark, offering advice on the upbringing of Clark's son. These letters inspired Locke's most important work on education, *Some Thoughts Concerning Education* (1693). After the successful Revolution of 1688, Locke returned to England and saw the publication of two other great books. The first was his *Essay Concerning Human Understanding* (1690), which established him as the father of empiricism in philosophy and learning theory in psychology. His other great book was *Two Treatises on Government* (1689), which set forth many of the central ideas in the U.S. Constitution (Lamprecht, 1928; Russell, 1945).

Locke's View of Development

The starting point of Locke's theory was his refutation of the doctrine of innate ideas. Prior to Locke, many philosophers held that some ideas, such as mathematical truths and beliefs in God, are innate, existing in the mind prior to experience. Locke argued that observations of children will show that these ideas are not present from the beginning and that they are learned. He said it is more accurate to think of the child's mind as a blank slate, and whatever comes into the mind comes from the environment. We might consider

> the mind to be, as we say, white paper void of all characteristics, without any *ideas*. How comes it to be furnished? . . . Whence has it all the materials of reason and knowledge? To this I answer, in one word, from *experience*; in that all our knowledge is founded, and from that it ultimately derives itself. (1690, vol. 1, bk. 2, sec. 2, emphasis in original)

Locke did qualify this statement a bit. He noted that although most of a person's knowledge comes from the environment, a person also can learn, in time, by reflecting on his or her own thinking and beliefs (1690, vol. 1, bk. 2, chap. 1). Locke also acknowledged that there are some innate differences among individuals (1693, sec. 1).

But on the whole, Locke said, it's the environment that molds the mind. And the environment's influence, Locke emphasized, is especially powerful in the child's early years. This is when the child's mind is most pliable, when we can mold it as we wish. And once we do so, its basic nature is set for life (1693, secs. 1, 32).

Precisely how does the environment exert its effects? First, many of our thoughts and feelings develop through *associations.* Two ideas regularly occur together, so we cannot think of one without simultaneously thinking of the other. For example, if a child has had bad experiences in a particular room, the child cannot enter it without automatically experiencing a negative feeling (Locke, 1690, vol. 1, bk. 2, chap. 33, sec. 15).

Much of our behavior also develops through *repetition.* When we do something over and over, such as brushing our teeth, the practice becomes a natural habit, and we feel uneasy when we have failed to perform it (Locke, 1693, sec. 66).

We also learn through *imitation.* We are prone to do what we see others do, so models influence our character. If we are frequently exposed to silly and quarrelsome people, we become silly and quarrelsome ourselves; if we are exposed to more noble minds, we too become more noble (1693, sec. 67).

Finally, and most important, we learn through *rewards* and *punishments.* We engage in behavior that brings praise, compliments, and other rewards; we refrain from those actions that produce unpleasant consequences (sec. 54).

These principles, Locke believed, often work together in the development of character. For example, a little girl is likely to hang up her clothes if she sees her parents hang theirs up, through imitation. After she hangs up her clothes a few times in succession, this good trait becomes a habit, and this habit becomes all the stronger if she receives some praise or compliment for it.

The previous example illustrates the usefulness of Locke's ideas for bringing up a child. Let us now look more closely at his views on education.

Locke's Educational Philosophy

Locke thought of education broadly, as the formation of the child's character as well as academic learning. In fact, he gave greater weight to character development, so we will consider this first.

Self-Control.   Locke said the main goal of education is self-control: "It seems plain to me that the principle of all virtue and excellency lies in a power of denying ourselves the satisfaction of our own desires, where reason does not authorize them" (1693, sec. 38).

To instill self-discipline, we first should tend to the child's physical health. When the body is sick and weak, one has little ability to control its demands. Accordingly, Locke advised us to give children plenty of exercise so their bodies will become strong, and he suggested that children play outdoors in all seasons so they will learn to endure the hardships of all kinds of weather (secs. 1–16, 33).

If children are to acquire discipline, we must be firm with them from the start. Many parents coddle their children and give in to their every whim; the parents think that such indulgence is all right because their children are still small. But the adults fail to realize that early habits are difficult to break. Children who find that they can get whatever they want, simply by asking or crying out, never unlearn this bad habit. So parents should never reward children when they desire things they do not need. Children should learn that they will get favorable results only when they ask for things that their parents consider appropriate (secs. 38–40).

The Best Rewards and Punishments. From the beginning, then, we should pay close attention to how we reinforce our children's behavior. We should reward only reasonable behavior, never behavior that is unreasonable or self-indulgent.

The use of rewards and punishments, however, is a tricky matter. Not all rewards and punishments produce desirable effects. Locke was especially opposed to the use of *physical punishment*. In the first place, its use establishes undesirable associations. If a child is beaten or chastised for letting her mind wander during reading lessons, she will not only associate pain with mind wandering, but with the sight of books as well. Further, physical punishment is often ineffective. The child submits while the rod is in sight, but just as soon as the child sees that no one is looking, she does whatever she wants. Finally, when physical punishment does work, it usually works too well. It succeeds in "breaking the mind; and then, in the place of a disorderly young fellow, you have a low-spirited moped creature" (sec. 51).

Similarly, not all kinds of rewards are desirable. Locke opposed the use of money or sweets as rewards because their use undermines the main goal of education: to curb desires and to submit to reason. When we reward with food or money, we only encourage children to find happiness in these things (sec. 52).

The best rewards are praise and flattery, and the best punishment is disapproval. When children do well, we should compliment them, making them feel proud; when they do poorly, we should give them a cold glance, making them feel ashamed. Children are very sensitive to approval and disapproval, especially from their parents and those on whom they depend. So we can use these reactions to instill rational and virtuous behavior (sec. 57).

We also can strengthen the effectiveness of our approval and disapproval by pairing these reactions with other consequences. For example, when a little boy asks politely for a piece of fruit, we give it to him, and we also compliment him on his politeness. In this way, he learns to associate approval with agreeable consequences and thus becomes more concerned about it. Alternatively, when he breaks something he likes, we add a look of disappointment in him, so he will come to associate our disapproval with negative consequences. Through such practices, we deepen the child's concern for the opinions of others. Locke said that if you can make children "in love with the pleasure of being well thought on, you may turn them as you please, and they will be in love with all the ways of virtue" (sec. 58).

Small Steps.   Locke was concerned that children acquire many fears. For example, children are initially attracted to animals, but when one hurts a child's finger, she associates the sight of the animal with pain and fears all animals of the same species. Locke wanted children to grow up to be brave adults, so he recommended a method for eliminating fears. He didn't advise adults to just rush in and try to break the child of fears, but to eliminate them by "gentle degrees" (sec. 115). If a child fears a chicken, we should first let someone else sit beside the chicken at some distance from the child, until the child can watch the animal without fear. Then we should slowly and gradually bring the child closer to the chicken, making sure the child can observe the chicken without anxiety. Finally, we let the child touch the chicken while the chicken is held by another, until the child herself can handle the animal comfortably.

Rules.   Most parents set down all kinds of rules and then punish their children when they disobey them. This practice is basically useless. Children have great difficulty comprehending and remembering rules in the abstract, and they naturally resent getting punished for failing to comply with a rule that they could barely keep in mind. As an alternative to commands, Locke suggested two procedures.

First, since children learn more from example than precept, we can teach them much by exposing them to good models. Children will eagerly model their behavior after that of a virtuous person, especially when we compliment them for doing so (sec. 68).

Second, Locke suggested that, instead of issuing commands, we have children practice the desired behavior. For example, instead of instructing children to bow whenever they meet a lady, it is better to give them actual practice in bowing, complimenting them each time they bow correctly. After repeated practice, they will bow as naturally as they breathe, without any thought or reflection, which is essentially foreign to them anyway (sec. 66).

Children's Special Characteristics.   Locke's discussion of the futility of teaching rules that exceed a child's understanding introduced something new into his system. Before this, he had written as if the child's mind were a lump of clay that we could mold in any way we wished. Now, however, he was saying that children have their own cognitive capacities that set limits on what we can teach. He also suggested that children have temperaments peculiar to their age, such as a liking for noise, raucous games, and gaiety, and he added that it would be foolish to try to change their natural dispositions (sec. 63). Thus Locke seemed to admit that children are not blank slates after all. As various scholars have pointed out (e.g., Kessen, 1965, pp. 59, 72; Russell, 1945, p. 606), Locke was not above a certain amount of inconsistency. If he had insights that contradicted his basic environmentalism, the inconsistency didn't trouble him.

Academic Instruction.   Locke was upset by the academic instruction of his time, which forced children to spend long hours a day struggling with material that made no sense to them. Locke pointed out that instruction is most effective when children enjoy it. He suggested that children could learn many things, such as reading letters and words, through games (secs. 148, 150). Locke also recommended that instruction be arranged in steps, so children could thoroughly master one topic before going on to the next, and he wanted children to see the order and usefulness of their studies (secs. 180, 195).

Locke acknowledged that children will dislike some of the lessons that adults consider necessary for their future. In these cases, the teacher should try to ease the children through them. Certainly the teacher should avoid physical punishment or strong verbal rebukes. Harsh discipline simply makes the child fearful, and a teacher can't do much with a fearful child. As Locke put it, "'Tis as impossible to draw fair and regular characters on a trembling mind as on shaking paper" (1693, sec. 167). It is better to rely on the kinds of rewards and punishments discussed earlier—praise and disapproval.

In an interesting passage (secs. 118–119), Locke emphasized the need to take advantage of the child's natural curiosity. Children, he said, learn for the sake of learning; their minds seek knowledge like the eye seeks light. If we simply listen to their questions and answer them directly, their minds will expand beyond what we would have imagined possible. In fact, Locke attributed such power to the child's natural curiosity that it makes one wonder about his general thesis. If the child's curiosity is so powerful, why do we need to use external rewards and punishments for learning? Perhaps they are necessary in the training of the child's character, but it may be that children will develop their intellectual powers through intrinsic curiosity alone. But if Locke saw such a possibility, he didn't say anything about it, and in the end he reverted to his environmental thesis. When children reason clearly, we should compliment and flatter them. In this way, we teach them to reason (sec. 119).

Evaluation

As a psychologist, Locke was far ahead of his time. His principles of learning—the principles of association, repetition, modeling, and rewards and punishments—all have become cornerstones of one or another version of modern learning theory. His thoughts on changing behavior by "gentle degrees" is fundamental to some of the most contemporary thinking in the field. We shall see the extent to which Locke anticipated modern thinking in later chapters.

Locke's ideas on education, in addition, are pretty much those of the contemporary educator. Most teachers use rewards and punishments, such as praise, grades, and criticism, to motivate children to learn. Most enlightened teachers are also aware of the influence of models and the need to proceed in arranged steps and are opposed to physical punishment.

Most modern educators even share Locke's inconsistencies. Although they believe it is necessary to shape or mold the child through rewards and punishments, they also recognize that such social influences are not all-powerful. They are sensitive to the child's readiness to learn different things, and they recognize that children learn best when they are spontaneously curious about a particular subject. Nevertheless, like Locke, educators are not prepared to rely too heavily on children's intrinsic motivation to learn on their own. Teachers believe it is up to them, the adults, to teach children the right things. They do not really believe children would learn what they should without external inducements such as praise and grades. In general, they share Locke's view that education is essentially a socialization process. The child learns to gain adults' approval, and in this way the child learns what he or she needs to know to become a useful and virtuous member of society.

ROUSSEAU'S ROMANTIC NATURALISM[1]

Biographical Introduction

We have now reviewed two early conceptions of development. We have discussed the preformationist view, which considered the child as a miniature adult. We also have looked at the views of Locke, who argued that children are like empty containers that are filled by adult teachings.

The true developmentalist position is different again. Its first forceful expression is found in the work of Jean-Jacques Rousseau (1712–1778). Rousseau agreed with Locke that children are different from adults, but he made the point more positively. Children are not empty containers or blank slates but have their own modes of feeling and thinking. This is because they grow according to nature's plan, which urges them to develop different capacities and modalities at different stages.

Rousseau believed that it is vital for us to give nature the chance to guide the child's growth. Unlike Locke, he had no faith in the powers of the environment, especially the social environment, to form a healthy individual. Well-socialized adults, he felt, are far too dependent on the opinions of others. They have forgotten how to see with their own eyes and to think with their own

---

[1]This heading is suggested by Muuss (1975, p. 27).

minds; they see and think only what society expects them to. So, instead of rushing in to teach children to think in the "correct" ways, we should allow them to perfect their own capacities and to learn in their own ways, as nature intends. Then they will learn to trust their own powers of judgment.

Rousseau's beliefs, especially his faith in nature as opposed to societal influences, sparked the Romantic movement in the history of ideas. At the same time, his belief in a natural ground plan for healthy growth ushered in the developmental tradition in psychology.

Rousseau's revolt against society grew out of his personal life. He was born in Geneva, the son of a watchmaker and a beautiful, sentimental mother who died giving birth to him. For the first 8 years of his life, he was raised by his father and an aunt. He said his father was devoted to him, but he added that his father never let him forget he had caused his mother's death (Rousseau, 1788, p. 5). His aunt also was kind, but she refused to let him play in the street with the other children. Rousseau therefore spent most of his time reading, and by the age of 7 he had read every novel in his mother's library.

When Rousseau was 10 years old, his father got into a bitter dispute and had to flee Geneva to avoid prison. For the next 6 years, Rousseau was shuttled through several homes. He rarely got along with his masters, who often humiliated him, intensifying his already timid and self-conscious nature. He told, for example, of wanting to buy some pastry but of being afraid to enter the shop because he imagined that acquaintances would spot him and laugh at him (1788, p. 36). His main relief came from fantasies, in which he imagined himself in the heroic situations he had read about. He also engaged in a good deal of stealing and cheating.

When Rousseau was 16 he began the life of a vagabond. He traveled about, trying to earn what money he could, but he was never successful. His main talent, he found, was winning the favors of older women. He was not exactly a Don Juan—he was very timid when it came to sex—but he did get several ladies to take care of him.

At the age of 29, Rousseau invented a new system of musical notation, which he took to Paris. It was poorly received, and he was deeply disappointed. Still, his efforts to publish the system brought him into contact with some of the great minds of the 18th-century Enlightenment—people such as Diderot, Voltaire, and Condorcet. Rousseau even contributed some articles (mostly on music) to Diderot's *Encyclopedia*. But even among such creative and courageous thinkers—who were frequently arrested for their writings—Rousseau felt like an outsider. For one thing, he felt too shy to participate in the witty and clever dialogue of the Paris salons and social life. Moreover, Rousseau was developing a viewpoint that differed from that of other Enlightenment intellectuals. He, too, rejected dogmatic authority, but he didn't share their optimistic belief in progress. In some ways, Rousseau believed, people in the modern metropolis were worse off than ever. They were so busy making a good impression and saying the right things that they had no thoughts or feelings of their own (Berman, 1970; Cranston, 1982, pp. 163–164, 217–221; Rousseau, 1788, pp. 267–268, 346, 354).

At the age of 33, Rousseau's personal life underwent a major change. He took up with an illiterate servant girl named Thérèse, with whom he spent the rest of his life. She gave birth to five children, but Rousseau placed them all in a state foundling home. He said that he later realized his action was wrong, but at the time he did not have the money to raise them, and he felt that if he did they would wind up living a life as miserable as his own (Rousseau, 1788, p. 367).

Rousseau's first major literary success came at the age of 37, when he entered an essay contest that asked whether the arts and sciences had contributed to the betterment of morals. Rousseau argued in the negative and won the prize (Rousseau, 1750). During the next several years, he wrote several essays and books, the most important of which are *The Social Contract* (1762a) and *Emile* (1762b). *The Social Contract* opens with the famous line, "Man is born free, and everywhere he is in chains." That is, humans are naturally good and could live happily according to their spontaneous passions, but they are enslaved by social forces. This book describes a better society. *Emile* is Rousseau's main book on child development and education. It is titled after the fictitious boy whom Rousseau proposed to tutor according to nature's plan for healthy development.

In the course of his writings, Rousseau challenged the feudal state and church. He considered himself a devout Christian, but he argued against uncritical conformity to religious authority. As a result, officials in Paris tried to arrest him and those in Geneva barred him from the city, and he spent many of his last years in exile, paranoid and miserable. When Rousseau died, he was buried in the French countryside, where his body remained until after the French Revolution, which his writings had helped inspire. His remains were then triumphantly removed to Paris and placed in the Pantheon.

Many people have found Rousseau so deficient as a man that they have refused to take his ideas seriously, especially on education. How can a man who abandoned his own children to an orphanage have the audacity to prescribe the right upbringing for others? However, it sometimes takes one who has lived on the outside of the conventional social order to create a radical vision. Rousseau said that he was "thrown, in spite of myself, into the great world, without possessing its manners, and unable to acquire or conform to them" (1788, p. 379). He believed his only legitimate response was to rail against society and to seek, in its place, a different vision of how life might unfold. He tried to show how the healthiest development might come not from society's influence, but from nature. In so doing, Rousseau became the father of developmental psychology.

Rousseau's Theory of Development

Childhood has a special place in the sequence of human life, yet we know nothing about it. This is because we are so exclusively concerned with the child's future—with the things the child will need to know to fit into adult society. Even "the wisest writers devote themselves to what a man ought to know, without asking themselves what a child is capable of learning. They are always looking for the man in the child, without considering what he is before he becomes a man" (Rousseau, 1762b, p. 1).

When we take the time simply to observe children, we find that they are very different from us. "Childhood has its own ways of seeing, thinking, and feeling" (Rousseau, 1762b, p. 54). This is according to nature's design. Nature is like a hidden tutor who prompts the child to develop different capacities at different stages of growth (p. 181). Her product might not be an individual well trained to fit into a social niche, but rather a strong, complete person. If we wish to aid nature in this process, we must first learn all we can about the stages of development. Rousseau believed there are four main stages.

Stage 1: Infancy (birth to about 2 years).   Infants experience the world directly through the senses. They know nothing of ideas or reason; they simply experience pleasure and pain (p. 29). Nevertheless, babies are active and curious and learn a great deal. They constantly try to touch everything they can, and by doing so they learn about heat, cold, hardness, softness, and other qualities of objects (p. 31). Infants also begin to acquire language, which they do almost entirely on their own. In a sense, they develop a grammar that is more perfect than ours; they employ grammatical rules without all the exceptions that plague adult speech. Pedantically, we correct their mistakes, even though children will always correct themselves in time (p. 37).

Stage 2: Childhood (about 2 to 12 years).   This stage begins when children gain a new independence; they can now walk, talk, feed themselves, and run about. They develop these abilities, too, on their own (p. 42).

During this stage, children possess a kind of reason. But it is not the kind that deals with remote events or abstractions. Rather, it is an intuitive reason that is directly tied to body movement and the senses. For example, when a girl accurately throws a ball, she demonstrates an intuitive knowledge of velocity and distance. Or when a boy digs with a stick, he reveals an intuitive knowledge of leverage. However, thinking is still extremely concrete. A child can be taught about a globe, with all the countries, towns, and rivers. But when asked, "What is the world?," he is likely to say, "A piece of cardboard" (p. 74).

Stage 3: Late Childhood (about 12 to 15 years).   This third stage is a transitional one between childhood and adolescence. During this period, children gain an enormous amount of physical strength; they can plow, push carts, hoe, and do the work of adults (p. 128). They also make substantial progress in the cognitive sphere and can, for example, do relatively advanced problems in geometry and science. Still, they are not yet disposed to think about purely theoretical and verbal matters. Instead, they can best exercise their cognitive functions through concrete and useful tasks, such as farming, carpentry, and mapmaking.

During the first three stages, children are by nature *presocial*. That is, they are primarily concerned with what is necessary and useful to themselves and have little interest in social relationships. They enjoy working with physical things and learning from nature; the world of books and society is foreign to them. Even as late as the third stage, between 12 and 15 years, the model for the child's life should be Robinson Crusoe, a man who lived alone on an island and who became self-sufficient by dealing effectively with the physical environment (p. 147).

Stage 4: Adolescence.   Children become distinctly social beings only at the fourth stage, which begins with puberty. Rousseau said that puberty begins at age 15, somewhat later than we would date it today. At this time, the child undergoes a second birth. The body changes and the passions well up from within. "A change of temper, frequent outbreaks of anger, a perpetual stirring of the mind, make the child almost ungovernable" (p. 172). The young person, who is neither child nor adult, begins to blush in the presence of the opposite sex, for he or she is dimly aware of sexual feelings. At this point, the youngster is no longer self-sufficient. The adolescent is attracted to and needs others.

The adolescent also develops cognitively. He or she can now deal with abstract concepts and takes an interest in theoretical matters in science and morals.

These, then, are Rousseau's four stages, which he believed unfold in an invariant sequence according to nature's plan. His stages, especially adolescence, would seem to emerge more slowly than we would expect today, and this might partly reflect a genuine historical difference. Rousseau, however, also believed that the true course of human development is slower than we ordinarily recognize. We are always looking at children as if they were already adults, whereas nature would have children take the time to develop the capacities and interests of childhood (p. 181).

Rousseau also proposed that these stages *recapitulate* the general evolution of the human species. Infants are similar to the earliest "primitives," who dealt with the world directly through their senses and were concerned only with pleasure and pain. The next two stages of childhood parallel the "savage" era, when people learned to build huts, make tools, fish, trap, and utilize other skills. People formed loose associations with others, but they still were largely self-sufficient.

Adolescence, finally, parallels the beginning of true social life. Historically, social existence began with the division of labor. As work became specialized, people could no longer produce all they needed by themselves. Thus they had to rely on others. As they became increasingly immersed in society, they became the slaves of conventions and social approval. Even savages, to be sure, were somewhat concerned with the opinions of others, but this concern deepened as people became embedded in social life. As a result, modern individuals no longer think for themselves. "The savage," Rousseau said, "lives within himself; the sociable man, always outside himself, knows how to live only in the opinion of others" (Rousseau, 1755, p. 179).

Rousseau's Educational Method

Rousseau thought we were most fulfilled as savages, but he realized that those days are gone forever. Still, we do not need to become the weak conformists that we presently are. Nature will continue to guide children's development along the road to independence. Under its urging, children will spontaneously perfect their capacities and powers of discrimination by dealing with physical things, without adult teaching. So, if one follows nature's guidance, it should be possible to bring the child to adolescence with an independent mind. Then, when the young person does enter the social world, he or she can cope effectively with it.

Rousseau told how this would happen in the case of Emile, his imaginary pupil.

Emile's Education. Rousseau would have a basic faith in Emile's capacity to learn much on his own, from nature's inner promptings. For example, as an infant Emile would have a strong urge to explore the world through his senses. Accordingly, Rousseau would remove all harmful objects from the house and let Emile explore it. If Emile wished to inspect an object, Rousseau would bring it to him. No adult guidance would be necessary (Rousseau, 1762b, pp. 31, 35).

At the same time, Rousseau would not permit Emile to rule over him. He would bring Emile an object when Emile had a genuine need to learn about it, but never when Emile simply had a capricious desire to have his tutor do his bidding (p. 52).

Emile also would learn to walk and talk on his own. Rousseau would never push or correct his pupil. Such practices only make children timid and anxious. They begin looking to others for correction and thereby lose their independence (pp. 39–40).

As Emile moved into the second stage, that of childhood, he would have an urge to run, jump, shout, and play. Rousseau would never check these activities, for Emile would be following nature's inner prompting to develop his body through vigorous exercise. Rousseau would not, like many adults, always be saying, "Come here, go there, stop, do this, don't do that" (p. 82), for Emile would then turn to his tutor for guidance and "his own mind would become useless" (p. 82).

Rousseau would present various lessons, but only those that fit Emile's age. Since children at this stage are developing their senses, Rousseau would suggest games such as finding one's way in a completely dark room, thus developing the sense of touch (p. 98). Because children do anything that keeps them moving freely, he would take advantage of this impulse to help Emile learn to judge heights, lengths, and distances. He would point to a cherry tree and ask Emile to select a ladder of the proper height. Or he would suggest that they cross a river, and ask Emile which plank would extend across the banks (p. 105).

In all such lessons, Emile would be able to judge his successes by himself. Emile could see for himself if he had chosen a plank that was large enough to extend across the river. He could make this judgment because the lesson corresponds to his current capacities. It requires only the use of his senses. There is nothing in the lesson that is beyond his grasp, nothing that would force him to turn to his tutor for help (p. 141).

Rousseau said that each stage "has a perfection, a ripeness, of its own" (p. 122). We are used to thinking about a "grown man," but it is no less pleasing to consider a "grown child," and to look at Emile at age 10 or 12.

> His face, his bearing, his expression speak of confidence and contentment; health shines in his countenance. . . . I see him keen, eager, and full of life. . . . His manner is free and open. . . . [He excels] at running, jumping, raising weights, estimating distances, inventing games. . . . He will not be so stupid as to go ask other people about what he sees; he will examine it on his own account. . . . His ideas are few but precise, he knows nothing by rote and much by experience. . . . So do not expect set speeches or studied manners from him, but just the faithful expression of his thoughts and the conduct that springs from his inclinations. (pp. 122–126)

To most observers, Emile will be simply a rough, happy boy, but raised in concert with nature he will have "reached the perfection of childhood" (p. 126).

During the third stage, that of late childhood, Emile's maturing cognitive powers would enable him to learn mathematics and science, but he would reason effectively in these spheres only in connection with concrete activities. Accordingly, Rousseau would encourage him to think about mathematical problems that naturally emerged in the course of activities such as farming and carpentry. Rousseau would provide only minimal guidance and, again, he would never correct Emile's mistakes. His goal would not be to teach Emile the right answers but to help him learn to solve problems on his own.

> Let him know nothing because you have told him, but because he has learned it for himself. Let him not be taught science, let him discover it.

If ever you substitute authority for reason he will cease to reason; he will be a mere plaything of other people's thoughts. (p. 131)

Only at adolescence would Emile begin reading many books and receive his introduction into the larger social world. By this time he would have developed an independent nature, and with his new capacities for theoretical reasoning, he could judge society at its true worth (p. 183).

Comparison with the Usual Practices.　Rousseau, then, would encourage Emile to perfect his capacities at each stage, according to nature's own schedule, and he would never present anything that Emile could not judge for himself. Rousseau's method would differ radically from that of most educators.

Most schools are not content to treat children as children, with their own needs and ways of learning. Instead, they try to instill adult knowledge as quickly as possible. As a result, they present many lessons that exceed the child's understanding. For example, they give lessons in history, geography, and mathematics that have nothing to do with the child's direct experience and assume a capacity for reasoning that the child lacks. As children struggle with such lessons, they find learning a miserable experience. And not only this. Because they cannot fully comprehend what the adult is saying, they are forced to take things on faith, to accept answers simply because the adult has explained them to be true. They have no recourse but to ask their parents or teachers, "Did I get the right answer here?" "Is this right?" They thereby learn to depend on others and cease to think for themselves.

When children are asked to learn things that exceed their grasp, they become lazy and unmotivated. To motivate them, teachers use threats, bribes, disapproval, and flattery. They try to get children to learn in order to win the adult's approval. Such procedures only reinforce the child's dependency on the approval of others (p. 54).

Rousseau said that his own method, in contrast, would be "merely negative" (p. 57). That is, he would exercise Emile's body and senses but keep his mind idle as long as possible. He would shield Emile from all opinions until his capacity for reasoning had developed, at which point he could judge them for himself. At the age of 12 or 15 years, Emile would appear ignorant in the conventional sense. He would know nothing of society or morals and have no precocious knowledge to display. But he would have learned to judge everything according to his own experience. He therefore would be capable of real thinking (pp. 127, 170).

Rousseau anticipated the impatience others would have with his advice. It would seem as if he were failing to prepare the child for the future. How could we be certain that the child would know what was necessary when the time came? Rousseau's reply was that societies change so rapidly that it is really impossible to predict what knowledge will be useful. But more importantly, our obsession with the future contains the greatest of all traps; in our hurry to teach children what we think they will need, we present lessons that exceed their understanding and force them to turn to us for help. Rousseau wanted us to slow down and give children a chance to learn in ways that come naturally to them and to learn on their own (pp. 141, 157).

Evaluation

Rousseau introduced several key ideas into developmental theory. First, he proposed that development proceeds according to an inner, biological timetable. For the first time, we have a picture of development unfolding fairly independently from environmental influences. Children are no longer simply shaped by external forces, such as adult teachings and social reinforcements. They grow and learn largely on their own, according to nature's plan. Today we would call this plan *biological maturation*.

Second, Rousseau suggested that development unfolds in a series of stages, periods during which children experience the world in different ways. Children differ from adults not because they are blank slates that will gradually take on adult teachings; rather, at each stage, the child's patterns of thought and behavior have their own unique characteristics.

Third, Rousseau proposed a new philosophy of education, one which we would today call *child centered*. He said, "Treat your scholar according to his age" (p. 55), by which he meant we should fit our lessons to the child's particular stage. In this way, children will be able to judge matters according to their own experience and powers of understanding.

All three of these ideas have become central tenets of many developmental theories; this is shown in the following chapters. At the same time, though, many developmental theorists would disagree with parts of Rousseau's theory. Many would argue, in particular, that the child is not nearly as asocial as Rousseau suggested. For example, modern ethologists point out how babies become strongly attached to their caretakers. This attachment, they say, is genetically governed; it has evolved because proximity to parents has enhanced babies' chances for survival (see Chapter 3 in this book). Actually, Rousseau was aware of such attachments (p. 174), but he conveniently ignored them when outlining his overall theory. He wanted children to learn to reason on their own, apart from society's corrupting influences, and he therefore declared that nature intends for them to live apart from the social world, even if he knew better.

When Rousseau argued that we should protect children from society, he had particular concerns in mind. He saw adults teaching children social manners and beliefs before children have the ability to judge them according to their own powers of reasoning. In this process, adults make children the slaves of social conventions.

But contemporary psychology includes developmentalists (e.g., Kohlberg, Chapter 7 in this book) who prize independent thinking as much as Rousseau did, but who believe, nevertheless, that children can make their way through the social world. They believe that children will form social and moral theories on their own, fairly independent of adult teachings. Furthermore, if children think long and hard about social problems, they will reach stages that transcend conventional modes of social thought. So it may be that children can live in the social world without being undone by it.

All the same, it was Rousseau who introduced the crucial question into modern developmental and humanistic thinking: Can inner growth lead to ways of experiencing and feeling that can stand up to the crushing pressure of social conformity?

CHAPTER 2

Gesell's Maturational Theory

BIOGRAPHICAL INTRODUCTION

Rousseau believed behavior unfolds according to nature's inner plan or timetable. Today we would call this process *biological maturation*, and the person who did the most to initiate the study of maturation was Arnold Gesell (1880–1961).

Gesell grew up in Alma, Wisconsin, a small town on the bank of the upper Mississippi River. In an autobiographical account, he described an almost idyllic midwestern childhood, in which "hills, valley, water and climate concurred to make the seasons distinct and intense in my home town. Each season had its own challenges and keen pleasures, accentuated by the ever-changing, yet enduring river" (Gesell, 1952a, p. 124). Gesell used similar language to describe the beauty he saw in the growth process, with "its seasons and sequences" (Gesell & Ilg, 1943, p. 57). This is not to say, however, that Gesell was merely a gushing romantic. He studied children's development with painstaking observation. To increase his knowledge of the underlying physiological processes, he went to medical school at the age of 30, even though he already had a Ph.D. and had been working successfully as a psychologist. In his 50 years at the Yale Clinic of Child Development, he and his colleagues engaged in incredibly extensive and detailed studies of the neuromotor development of babies and children. They developed behavior norms that are so complete that they still serve as a primary source of information for pediatricians and psychologists today. Gesell also developed one of the first tests of infant intelligence (Gesell & Amatruda, 1941) and was one of the first researchers to make extensive use of film observations.

Gesell also wrote on child rearing, advocating a child-centered approach. He was the best known "baby doctor" in the early 1940s, until

Dr. Benjamin Spock published his famous book in 1946. Nevertheless, Spock was partly influenced by Gesell.

PRINCIPLES OF DEVELOPMENT

The Concept of Maturation

The child's growth or development, Gesell said, is influenced by two major forces. First, the child is a product of his or her environment. But more fundamentally, Gesell believed, the child's development is directed from within, by the action of the genes. Gesell called this process *maturation* (Gesell & Ilg, 1943, p. 41).

An outstanding feature of maturational development is that it always unfolds in fixed sequences. This can first be seen in the developing embryo, where, for example, the heart is always the first organ to develop and function. Soon afterward, the rapidly differentiating cells begin to form the central nervous system—the brain and the spinal cord. The development of the brain and the head, in turn, begins before the other parts, such as the arms and the legs. This order, which is directed by the genetic blueprint, is never violated.

Similarly, sequential development continues after birth. For example, just as the head develops early in the embryo, it also takes the lead in early postnatal development. Babies first have control over their lips and tongues, then gain control over their eye movements, followed by control over the neck, shoulders, arms, hands, fingers, trunk, legs, and feet. In both prenatal and postnatal development there is a head-to-foot (cephalocaudal) trend (Gesell, 1946, p. 339).

As babies grow, they learn to sit up, to stand, to walk, and to run, and these capacities, too, develop in a specific order. They emerge with the growth of the nervous system, which itself is directed by the genes.

Children, of course, vary in their *rates* of development. They do not all stand up and walk at the same age. Nevertheless, they all proceed through the same sequences. Moreover, individual differences in growth rates, in Gesell's view, are largely controlled by the internal genetic mechanism (Gesell, 1945, p. 161).

As indicated, the effects of maturation are contrasted with those of the environment. In prenatal development, this means that maturation is distinguished from aspects of the internal environment, such as the embryo's temperature and the oxygen it receives from its mother. These environmental factors are certainly vital—they support proper growth—but they play no direct role in the sequential unfolding of structures and action patterns. This is the work of the maturational mechanism.

Once the baby is born, she enters a different kind of environment. It is not only an environment that meets the child's physical needs but also a social and cultural environment that tries to induce the child to behave in the proper ways. Gesell said that the child clearly needs the social environment to realize his or her potentials, but he also argued that socializing forces work best when they are in tune with inner maturational principles (Gesell & Ilg, 1943, p. 41).

Gesell was particularly opposed to efforts to teach children things ahead of schedule. Children will sit up, walk, and talk when they are ready, when their nervous systems have sufficiently matured. At the right moment, they will simply begin to master a task, from their own inner urges. Until then, teaching will be of little value, and may create tensions between caretakers and children.

Some evidence for the maturational position on teaching has come from studies with identical twins. For example, Gesell and Thompson (1929) gave one twin practice at such activities as stair-climbing and the grasping and manipulation of cubes. This twin did show some skill superior to that of the other, but the untrained twin soon caught up, with much less practice. And he did so at about the age at which we would expect him to perform the various tasks. Apparently, then, there is an inner timetable that determines the readiness to do things, and the benefits of early training are relatively temporary. The question of early stimulation is controversial, but it does seem that our efforts to speed up early motor development produce only small effects (De Hart, Sroufe, & Cooper, 2004, p. 145; Zelazo, Zelazo, & Kolb, 1972).

Maturation, then, refers to the process by which development is governed by intrinsic factors—principally the genes, which are chemical substances contained within the nucleus of each cell (see Figure 2.1). The genes determine the sequence, timing, and form of emerging action-patterns.

However, the mechanisms by which the genes work are complex. Even today, not everything is completely understood. We know that the genes do not work in isolation from one another, and they respond to outside signals. Some signals come from other parts of the nucleus and from the cell's cytoplasm (see Figure 2.1). Other signals come from outside the cell (Campbell & Reece, 2005, pp. 362, 420). So even when describing the action of the gene, we must consider its external environment. Nevertheless, we can still think of

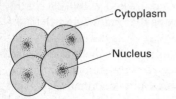

FIGURE 2.1
A group of cells. The nucleus contains chromosomes, which contain genes.

maturation as the process by which the genes direct development, albeit in conjunction with environmental factors.

So far, I have primarily been illustrating maturational growth with early motor behavior, which was Gesell's main scientific focus. However, Gesell believed that maturation governs the growth of the entire personality. He said, for example,

> [The child's] nervous system matures by stages and natural sequences. He sits before he stands; he babbles before he talks; he fabricates before he tells the truth; he draws a circle before he draws a square; he is self-ish before he is altruistic; he is dependent on others before he achieves dependence on self. All his capacities, including his morals, are subject to the laws of growth. (Gesell & Ilg, 1943, p. 11)

The Study of Patterns

Gesell said that when we study growth we should not just measure things in quantitative form but should examine patterns. A pattern may be anything that has a definite shape or form—for example, an eyeblink. But what is most important is the patterning process, the process by which actions become organized (Gesell & Ilg, 1943, pp. 16–17).

We find good illustrations of the patterning process in the case of babies' vision. At birth, babies' eyes are apt to rove around aimlessly, but after a few days or even hours babies are able to stop their eyes and look at objects for brief periods. They can stop their eyes and stare "at will" because a new patterned connection has been made between the nerve impulses in the brain and the tiny muscles that move the eyes (pp. 17–18).

By the age of 1 month, babies can usually regard a ring that is dangled before them and then follow it through an arc of about 90°. This ability implies a new organization—that between the eye muscles and the grosser muscles that rotate the head (p. 19).

Patterning continues to widen when babies organize their eye movements with their hand movements, when they look at what they hold. By 4 months, babies can usually look at a rattle that they have been holding. "This is a significant growth gain. It means that eyes and hands are doing team work, coming into more effective coordination. Mental growth cannot be measured in inches and pounds. So it is appraised by patterns" (p. 19).

Still, hand-eye coordination is by no means complete at 4 months. For some time, the eyes will be in the lead. At 4 months, for example, babies can often "pick up" a 1-inch cube or even a small candy pellet with their eyes; that is, they can focus intently on the cube or pellet and consider it from slightly different angles. But they cannot yet grasp it with their hands. Babies may be seen looking at the cube and then looking at their hands, as if they have an idea of grasping the cube, but they simply cannot do it. The nervous

(a) Four months:
    sees but cannot contact.

(b) Six months:
    palmar grasp.

(c) Ten months:
    pincer grasp
    (index finger and thumb).

Figure 2.2
Developments in hand-eye coordination.
(From A. Gesell, *An Atlas of Infant Behavior*, Vol. 1, New Haven,
CT: Yale University Press, 1934. By permission.)

system has not yet sufficiently grown. It is not until 6 months that babies are usually able to pick up the cube with a crude palmar grasp, and not until 10 months that they can pick up the cube or a pellet with a pincer grasp, with opposing thumb and index finger (see Figure 2.2). Hand-eye coordination develops slowly—it becomes gradually more organized and comes to include more differentiated or refined movements.

Other Principles of Development

Gesell's observations suggested several other principles of growth. We will consider three: reciprocal interweaving, functional asymmetry, and self-regulation.

Reciprocal Interweaving. Humans are built on a bilateral basis; we have two hemispheres of the brain, two eyes, two hands, two legs, and so on. Our actions, too, have a dualistic quality, as when we either flex or extend our limbs. *Reciprocal interweaving* refers to the developmental process by which two tendencies gradually reach an effective organization. For example, in the development of handedness, the baby first uses one hand, then both together again, then prefers the other hand, then both together again, and so on, until he or she ultimately reaches one-handed dominance. This back-and-forth quality of preferences suggests the metaphor of weaving, hence the term "reciprocal interweaving." Gesell showed how reciprocal interweaving describes the patterning of many behaviors, including visual behavior and crawling and walking (Gesell, 1946, pp. 342–349).

Gesell also believed that reciprocal interweaving characterizes the growth of the personality. Here, we see the organism integrating introverted and extroverted tendencies. For example, the child who was self-composed at age 3 turns inward at $3\frac{1}{2}$, becoming timid and unsettled. This period of introversion is followed by a swing to extroversion at age 4, and the two tendencies finally become integrated and balanced at 5. Cycles such as this begin in infancy and continue at least until age 16. The organism temporarily loses its equilibrium as it expands into new inner or outer realms, but it then reorganizes itself at new levels (Gesell, Ilg, & Ames, 1956, pp. 16–20).

Functional Asymmetry.   Through the process of reciprocal interweaving, then, we balance the dualities of our nature. But we rarely achieve perfect balance or symmetry. In fact, a degree of asymmetry is highly functional; we are most effective when we confront the world from an angle, favoring one hand, one eye, and so on.

The infant's asymmetric tendency is seen in the *tonic neck reflex*, a reflex Gesell discovered in humans. Gesell noted that babies prefer to lie with their heads turned to one side, and when they do so they automatically assume the tonic neck reflex posture. They extend the arm on the side to which the head is turned (as if looking at the hand) and flex the other arm behind the head. The tonic neck reflex posture looks very much like the basic stance of a fencer (see Figure 2.3). This reflex is dominant during the first 3 months after birth

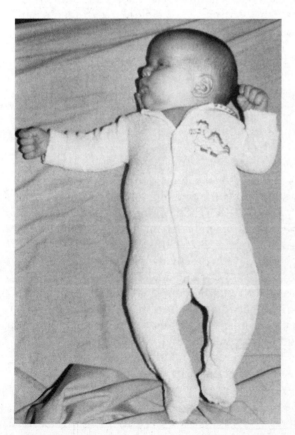

FIGURE 2.3
The tonic neck reflex.

and then eclipses, with new developments in the nervous system (Gesell, 1946, pp. 349–354).

Self-Regulation.   Gesell believed that intrinsic developmental mechanisms are so powerful that an organism can, to a considerable degree, regulate its own development. In one series of studies, he showed how babies can regulate their cycles of feeding, sleep, and wakefulness. When the babies were permitted to determine when they needed to nurse and sleep, they gradually required fewer feedings per day and stayed awake for longer periods during the daytime. Progress did not follow a straight line; there were many fluctuations, including regressions. But the babies did gradually work out stable schedules (pp. 358–364).

Gesell also wrote about self-regulation from a slightly different angle, focusing on the organism's capacity to maintain an overall integration and equilibrium. Growth, of course, also involves disequilibrium. As we just saw, infants' sleeping and feeding patterns frequently fluctuate. We also saw comparable fluctuations in the development of the personality, where periods of stability are followed by periods of instability as children enter new introverted or extroverted phases. Tensions arise when children venture into new unknowns. But self-regulatory mechanisms are always at work, ensuring that the organism never goes too far in one direction before it catches its balance, consolidating its gains before moving forward once again.

Because of intrinsic self-regulating processes, children sometimes resist our efforts to teach them new things. It is as if something inside tells them not to learn too much too soon. The integrity of the organism must be preserved.

Individuality

We have now reviewed many of Gesell's ideas about growth. One general issue, however, needs to be discussed. This is the problem of individuality. Gesell strongly believed in the uniqueness of each child. Unfortunately, however, his position was obscured by the way in which he summarized his findings. For example, he wrote about the child at ages 2, $2\frac{1}{2}$, 3, and so on, as if we could expect all children at each age to behave in exactly the same way. He did warn that he was using age norms only as shortcut devices (Gesell & Ilg, 1943, pp. 60–61), but he never indicated the actual amount of individual variation that does occur at each age, so individuality did often become lost in his writings.

Gesell's actual position, as mentioned, was that all normal children go through the same *sequences*, but they vary in their *rates* of growth. He also suggested that growth rates might be related to differences in temperament and personality. In an interesting discussion (pp. 44–45), Gesell presented three hypothetical children—one who grows slowly, one who grows rapidly, and one who grows irregularly—and suggested how each growth style might show up in a variety of personal dispositions. Child A, who grows slowly, might be generally slow and cautious, able to wait, even-tempered, and generally wise about life's problems. Child B, who develops rapidly, might be quick-reacting, blithe and happy, up and at it, and generally bright and clever. Child C, who develops irregularly, might sometimes be overcautious and sometimes undercautious, be moody, have trouble waiting, and show flashes of brilliance. Gesell believed that each individual temperament and growth style makes different demands on the culture, and that the culture should try to adjust to each child's uniqueness.

PHILOSOPHY OF CHILD REARING

According to Gesell, child rearing should begin with a recognition of the implicit wisdom of maturational laws. Babies enter the world with an inborn schedule, which is the product of at least 3 million years of biological evolution; they are preeminently "wise" about their needs, and what they are ready and not ready to do. Thus parents should not try to force their children into any preconceived pattern but should take their cues from the children themselves.

On the topic of feeding, for example, Gesell strongly advocated demand feeding—feeding when the baby indicates a readiness—as opposed to feeding by any predetermined schedule. He wrote,

> There are two kinds of time—organic time and clock time. The former is based on the wisdom of the body, the latter on astronomical science and cultural conventions. A self-demand schedule takes its departure from organic time. The infant is fed when he is hungry; he is allowed to sleep when he is sleepy; he is not roused to be fed; he is "changed" if he fusses on being wet; he is granted some social play when he craves it. He is not made to live by the clock on the wall, but rather by the internal clock of his fluctuating needs. (Gesell & Ilg, 1943, p. 51)

As parents suspend their ideas about what the baby "ought" to be doing—and instead follow the baby's signals and cues—they begin to appreciate the baby's inherent capacity for self-regulated growth. They see how the baby regulates her own cycles of feeding, sleep, and wakefulness. A little later, they see how the baby learns to sit up, creep, and crawl on her own, without pushing and prodding. Parents begin to trust the child and the growth process.

Gesell emphasized that the first year is the best time for learning to respect the child's individuality (p. 57). Parents who are alertly responsive to the child's needs during infancy will naturally be sensitive to the child's unique interests and capacities later on. They will be less inclined to impose their own expectations and ambitions on the child and more inclined to give the child's individuality a chance to grow and find itself.

Gesell believed that parents need, besides an intuitive sensitivity to the child, some theoretical knowledge of the trends and sequences of development. In particular, they need to realize that development fluctuates between periods of stability and instability. This knowledge fosters patience and understanding. For example, the parent will be helped by the knowledge that $2\frac{1}{2}$-year-olds go through a troubled period during which they can be very obstinate. Knowing this, the parent will not feel an urgent need to stamp out this behavior before it is too late. Instead, the parent will be able to deal with the child more flexibly, and perhaps even enjoy this child who so intently tries to establish her independence (pp. 197, 296).

One of Gesell's followers, Louise Bates Ames (1971), offered parents the following advice:

1. Give up the notion that how your child turns out is all up to you and there isn't a minute to waste.
2. Try to appreciate the wonder of growth. Observe and relish the fact that every week and every month brings new developments.
3. Respect his immaturity. Anticipate the fact that he will, in all likelihood, need to creep before he walks, express himself with single words before he talks in sentences, and say "No" before he says "Yes."
4. Try to avoid thinking always in terms of what comes next. Enjoy, and let your child enjoy each stage he reaches before he travels on (pp. 108, 125).

So far, Gesell's philosophy sounds like one of extreme indulgence and permissiveness. One might ask, "Doesn't this attitude lead to spoiling?" "Won't children start becoming bossy, always wanting their own way?"

Gesell's answer was that, of course, children must learn to control their impulses and get along with the demands of their culture. However, he argued that children best learn to do this when we pay attention to their own maturing ability to tolerate controls. For example, with respect to feedings, the baby at first should not be made to wait too long. "The most vital cravings of the infant have to do with food and sleep. These cravings have an individual, organic nature. They cannot be transformed or transgressed" (Gesell & Ilg, 1943, p. 56). But a little later—by 4 months or so—the baby's gastrointestinal tract no longer dominates life as it did before, and the baby's less intense and less frequent cries tell the parent that she is now able to wait for feedings.

Later on, developments in language and an increased time perspective help children delay immediate gratification. At $2\frac{1}{2}$ years, they do not need their juice immediately because they understand when the parent says, "Pretty soon." At 3 they may understand, "When it's time." And by 4, they want to help prepare the meals themselves. The culture, then, can ease children into its fabric by gearing itself to children's own maturing readiness to tolerate controls (p. 54).

Thus Gesell believed that alert caretakers can achieve a reasonable balance between maturational forces and enculturation. But it is clear that Gesell wanted the culture to do most of the adjusting. Enculturation, he said, is necessary, but our first goal should not be to fit the child into the social mold. This is the aim of authoritarian regimes. In democracies we prize autonomy and individuality, qualities that have their deepest roots in the biological impulse toward optimal growth (p. 10).

Enculturation takes place in the school as well as in the home. Schools teach children the skills and habits they will need as adult members of society. But teachers, like parents, should not think so exclusively in terms of cultural goals that they overlook the manner in which the child grows. For example, although our culture values accurate work, teachers need to recognize that children are naturally less precise at one age than another. Vigorous, unstable 6-year-olds are error prone, whereas more stable 7-year-olds readily take to drills and perfectionistic work. Accordingly, the developmentally minded teacher will not force 6-year-olds to learn in a way that runs counter to their nature, but will save drills for the time when the child benefits from them (Gesell & Ilg, 1946, pp. 374–381).

At the same time, it is not enough to adjust techniques to each age or grade; for children also vary widely in their growth rates, as well as in their special talents. Accordingly, teachers need to gear their work to the individual child's state of readiness and special abilities. At present, most schools do not do this. They overemphasize uniform achievement standards, such as grade-level reading scores, thereby ignoring children's need to grow according to their own timing and to develop their unique potentials. Schools, of course, do need to teach standard cultural skills, but in a democracy their first task is to help children develop their full personalities. To do this, they must let children guide them, just as children themselves are guided by a biological ground plan for optimal growth (pp. 388–392).

EVALUATION

In Gesell's hands, Rousseau's idea of an inner developmental force became the guiding principle behind extensive scholarship and research. Gesell showed how the maturational mechanism, while still hidden, manifests itself in intricate developmental sequences and self-regulatory processes. Gesell indicated that there are good reasons to suppose that development follows an inner plan.

Nevertheless, most contemporary psychologists would consider Gesell's maturational position too extreme. Most psychologists acknowledge the role of maturation but nevertheless believe teaching and learning are much more important than Gesell claimed. They believe the environment does more than merely support inner patterning; it also structures behavior. For example, although children cannot learn to throw a ball or play a piano before attaining some level of neuromotor maturation, they also acquire such behavior patterns through teaching and reinforcement. Still, it is largely because of Gesell's work that even the most ardent learning theorists take some notice of inner maturational processes.

The most frequently voiced criticisms of Gesell center on his manner of presenting age norms. As mentioned, his norms imply too much uniformity and give us no idea of how much variation to expect at any given age. Moreover, Gesell's norms were based on middle-class children in a university setting (Yale) and may not apply perfectly in other cultural contexts.

In recent years, Gesell's age norms have been challenged by research focusing on newborns (babies under 1 month of age). Newborns, it now seems, have many surprising capacities. Under the right conditions, they can visually follow moving objects for short distances, can reach for objects, and can discriminate among shapes, colors, sounds, tastes, and odors. They can imitate movements such as tongue-protrusions and they exhibit a walking reflex (Fogel, 2009, pp. 247–249, 221; McFarlane, 1981). In light of such findings, the developmental picture provided by Gesell seems too slow. Newborns now appear to be "a lot smarter" than anyone thought, and researchers are finding remarkable qualities of babies' minds in the following few months as well (Lipsitt, 1971; Siegler & Alibali, 2005, p. 180). Indeed, researchers sometimes make it sound as if babies are so advanced that they are really little adults, as the preformationists said.

These new findings are important, but they must be viewed with caution. In the first place, many of the newborn's advanced competencies, including visual following and hand-reaching, are very fragile and difficult to elicit. Experimenters must sometimes wait for hours and even days for babies to demonstrate them (Als, 1978; Bower, 1982, p. 169; Fogel, 2009, p. 227; MacFarlane, 1981).

Furthermore, some precocious abilities, including reflexive walking, reaching, and imitation, ordinarily disappear after a month or two. Some of these, to be sure, may be maintained by exercise (Bower, 1982), but they ordinarily seem to drop out as behavior comes under the control of higher cortical centers. Then, when they do reappear, they have a much more voluntary appearance (Hofer, 1981, pp. 120–123). Thus some of the early, precocious capacities are only temporary. Perhaps they are vestiges of our evolutionary past, of a time when we developed much more rapidly than we now do.

In any case, the new research on newborns at most supplements, rather than directly contradicts, the developmental picture Gesell provided. Contemporary pediatricians and infant specialists still consider Gesell's norms of great value, using them to help determine what babies should be able to do at various ages.

Gesell also provided a coherent philosophy of child rearing. We should not, he said, try to force children into our predetermined designs, but should follow their cues as they express basic biological forces of growth. The research findings bearing on Gesell's position have often been ambiguous (Caldwell, 1964), but some interesting studies do support him (Appleton, Clifton & Goldberg, 1975). In a particularly impressive study, Bell and Ainsworth (1972) asked what happens when parents respond promptly to their babies' cries (rather than acting on their own ideas about when it is all right for them to cry). The clear finding was that responsiveness does not lead to spoiling. On the contrary, by the age of 1 year these babies, in comparison to babies of less responsive parents, cried less and were more independent. They enjoyed being held, but if the mother put them down they did not cry or protest but happily ventured off into exploratory play. They might check back on the mother's presence from time to time, as is natural at this age, but they were basically quite independent. Apparently, then, when babies' signals are heeded, they become confident that they can always get help when needed and therefore can relax and venture forth on their own.

There also is some evidence, though only impressionistic and anecdotal, that things can go very wrong when Gesell's principles are excessively violated. This evidence comes from the study of schizophrenic patients, whose childhood experiences often seem precisely the opposite of those that Gesell recommended. These patients seem to have felt, as children, that their own natural impulses and desires counted for little, or threatened others, and that they were forced to fulfill others' predetermined images and expectations (Laing, 1965; R. White, 1963). I would like to illustrate the point with a brief description of a 9-year-old boy whom I saw for a psychological evaluation. The boy found life very frightening and probably was on the verge of psychosis. The parents had not wanted a child—they were in their 40s and the mother had a number of physical ailments that made it taxing for her to care for him. Consequently, she wanted a good, well-disciplined boy—an adult, really—who would cause her no trouble. She tried to toilet-train him at 6 months of age, long before he showed any readiness to participate in the process. And when he began walking and vigorously exploring the world at 1 year, she became distressed; he was becoming a nuisance and "getting into things." She even perceived his behavior as abnormal. Because of her circumstances, then, she practically reversed Gesell's advice: She had a fixed image of the good child she wanted and was unable to accept and follow her son's natural inclinations. As a result, the boy developed an intense fear that any action he might take, unless approved by his parents beforehand, was extremely dangerous. He did not trust himself or his natural impulses.

There is some evidence, then, in support of Gesell's position—that it is desirable to respond to children's cues and inclinations as they follow an inner, biological schedule. But there also is evidence that might argue partly against Gesell. In particular, research by Baumrind (1967, 1989) suggests that independent, self-reliant, and mature children have parents who demand a great deal of them. Baumrind thinks these parents set tasks that are within their children's abilities, and to this extent the parents follow Gesell's recommendations. But these parents also seem more demanding and controlling than Gesell might have thought necessary.

Perhaps philosophies such as Gesell's will never be completely proven or refuted by empirical evidence alone; too much may depend on one's own values. All the same, it would seem that we have much to gain by listening to Gesell. Although it is true that we must control, direct, and instruct our children to some extent, we usually seem to be in quite a hurry to do these things. What seems more difficult for us is to take the time to watch, enjoy, and appreciate our children as we give them a chance to do their own growing.

CHAPTER 3

Ethological Theories: Darwin, Lorenz and Tinbergen, and Bowlby and Ainsworth

Ethology is the study of animal and human behavior within an evolutionary context (Lorenz, 1981, p. 1). The person most identified with modern evolutionary theory is Darwin.

DARWIN AND THE THEORY OF EVOLUTION

Biographical Introduction

Charles Darwin (1809–1882) was born into a distinguished English family. His grandfather, Erasmus Darwin, was a renowned physician, poet, and philosopher, and his father also was a prominent physician. Young Darwin, in contrast, seemed headed for no great heights. As his father once said, "You care for nothing but shooting, dogs, and rat-catching, and you will be a disgrace to yourself and your family" (Darwin, 1887, p. 28).

Darwin studied medicine for a while, and then began studying for the Anglican clergy at Cambridge, but he was generally bored and his grades were uneven. Still, he made a favorable impression on some of his professors at Cambridge, especially those who shared his fascination with nature and wildlife. One professor, John Henslow, recommended Darwin for the position of naturalist on the worldwide voyage of the H.M.S. *Beagle,* the voyage on which Darwin made observations that eventually led to his theory of evolution.

As Darwin examined fossils and variations among living species, he concluded that the various species had a common ancestor, and newer species either had died out or had changed to meet the requirements of their changing environments. If this conclusion were correct, then the common theological view on the origin of the species must be wrong; the species had not been created in a fixed and perfect form, but had evolved. Although the idea of evolution had been expressed before, its plausibility deeply distressed Darwin. It caused religious doubts in his mind and he knew it would shock others (Gruber, 1981). He wrote to a friend that it was "like confessing a murder" (Murphy, 2007).

Darwin wanted to make sure the evidence supported his theory, and he didn't publish it until 17 years after he first sketched it out on paper (Carroll, 2009, p. 43). In fact, he wouldn't have published it then had he not learned that Alfred Wallace was going to publish a similar theory. Since the theory was going to be made public anyway, Darwin wanted partial credit for it. Upon the recommendation of their colleagues, Darwin and Wallace presented their theory in 1858 under joint authorship. A year later, Darwin published his great work, *The Origin of Species.* Darwin continued developing his theory the rest of his life, and, despite the bitter reactions it produced, he became widely recognized for his monumental achievements. When Darwin died, he was buried in Westminster Abbey, next to Isaac Newton.

The Theory of Natural Selection

As mentioned, Darwin was not the first to propose a theory of evolution. In Darwin's day, biologists had been debating the views of Jean Baptiste Lamarck, who proposed that evolution occurred through the inheritance of acquired characteristics. For example, giraffes stretched their necks to reach the leaves on high trees and then passed along their lengthened necks to the next generation. Lamarck's theory, however, turned out to be wrong.

In the Darwin-Wallace theory, no new characteristics need be acquired during an individual's lifetime. In essence, Darwin's theory is as follows. Among the members of a species, there is endless variation; and among the various members, only a fraction of those who are born survive to reproduce. There is a "struggle for existence" during which the fittest members of a species live long enough to transmit their characteristics to the next generation. Over countless generations, then, nature "selects" those who can best adapt to their surroundings—hence the term *natural selection* (Darwin, 1859, chaps. 3 and 4).

Darwin asked us to consider, for example, the situation of wolves (p. 70). During seasons when prey is scarce, the swiftest and strongest wolves have the best chances for survival. They are therefore more likely than the others to live long enough to reproduce and pass on their traits—today we would say their genes—to the next generation. After many such seasons, the traits of speed and strength will become increasingly prevalent in the population of the species.

Evolution usually seems to occur extremely slowly, revealing noticeable changes only after numerous generations. Consequently, we do not usually get a chance to see evolution at work in any simple way. However, biologists did have such an opportunity in England in the mid-1800s. In Manchester, there were numerous white moths that blended in well with the white trees in the area, making it difficult for birds to spot and kill them. Among the moths, there were a small number of dark ones (the products of mutations), who were easily detected by the predators. Consequently, only a few dark moths lived and reproduced. But when industrialization took place, coal smoke darkened the trees, making the white moths easy prey. Now the dark ones had the best chance of surviving long enough to reproduce, and over the next 50 years their number increased from less than 1% to 99% (Ehrlich & Holm, 1963, pp. 126–130).

The Case of Humans

In *The Origin of Species* (1859), Darwin discussed evolution but barely mentioned the evolution of humans. The topic was too incendiary. He waited to address it in a book he published 12 years later, *The Descent of Man* (the first edition was published in 1871; the second edition in 1874). In that book he firmly argued that our species is not separate from others—not the act of a special creation, as almost everyone believed. Rather, humans and other species descended from common ancestors. Long ago, Darwin speculated, humans and apes branched off from a common ape-like animal. At an even more distant time, humans and other mammals probably evolved from an amphibian, and before that, from aquatic life forms. Sharing common ancestors, we and other living species are all related. We are part of one extended family. There are, of course, differences among species. But if we look with an open mind, we see similarities between ourselves and other species—similarities that bear the stamp of our common heritage (1874, pp. 160, 629–632).

We see, for example, that we are like other animals on the physical level. Our bones are similar to those of animals as diverse as monkeys, bats, and seals, and "so it is with our muscles, nerves, blood vesicles, and internal viscera" (p. 6).

Darwin also observed that early human embryos are highly similar to the embryos of other animals. This fact, too, suggests common ancestry (p. 25). The strongest argument of this kind was made by Ernst Haeckel, who, in the late 1860s, proposed that *ontogeny recapitulates phylogeny*. That is, the development of an individual organism (ontogeny) repeats in an abbreviated way the evolutionary history of its species (phylogeny). The human embryo goes through phases when it looks like a fish, then an amphibian, and so on, recapitulating the ancient evolutionary history of our species. This proposition has raised considerable skepticism, and it would be wrong to say that the human embryo ever resembles the *adult* forms of other species. However, it does resemble the *early* forms (Thain & Hickman, 1994, p. 67).

Darwin also discussed how some physical structures he called "rudiments," such as our tailbone, reveal our descent from earlier forms (1874, p. 23). But Darwin's most innovative proposal was that evolutionary continuity is seen in the *behavioral* realm, in the areas of reason and emotion. He challenged the long-held Western view that reason and emotion are exclusive to our species.

Darwin recognized that humans developed rational thought to a higher degree than other species. Because our species is physically weaker and slower than many others, we had to rely on intelligence and inventions (including tools) to survive (1874, p. 65). But humans didn't develop intellectual powers out of the blue. These capacities emerged gradually, in the course of our evolutionary past, and intelligence is evident in the many animals who share our ancestry.

Darwin told, for example, about a bear in captivity who could not reach a piece of bread floating in some water. So the bear dug a ditch to the water, which resulted in the bread sailing down the ditch to him (p. 79). This certainly required creative thinking. Darwin said the more that naturalists study the behavior of any particular animal, the more intelligent they find the animal to be (p. 77).

Other species also share our capacity for rich emotional lives. Many animals, for example, express joy, which is most apparent when the young members of other species, such as puppies, kittens, and lambs, are at play. Like human children, they happily frolic about (1874, p. 70).

Darwin was especially interested in the moral emotions, the concern for others. He recognized that human morality differs from that of other animals. We bring greater intellect to moral issues and reflect more on them (1874, p. 115). But Darwin suggested that many animals have developed the fundamentals of morality, the building blocks on which human morality was built.

The members of many species want their companions near them, send out warning calls in times of danger, and sometimes come to one another's aid. To illustrate, Darwin (1874, p. 104) told the story of a troop of baboons moving through a valley and up a hill. While some of the baboons were still in the valley, a pack of dogs attacked. Hearing the attack, some of the older males came down from the hill and roared so ferociously that the dogs drew back. By the time the dogs resumed their attack, all the baboons had climbed out of danger—except for one. This 6-month-old baboon was still below and called loudly for help. He was surrounded by the dogs. "Now one of the largest males, a true hero, came down again from the mountain, slowly went to the young one, coaxed him, and triumphantly led him away—the dogs being too much astonished to make an attack" (Darwin, 1874, p. 104).

Darwin's emphasis on mutual aid and altruism has puzzled scholars because he also wrote about the "struggle for existence" which includes competition among individuals within a species (1859, chap. 3). For example, male deer engage in combat in the spring (1874, p. 531). These battles ensure that the strongest males, rather than the frail ones, transmit their characteristics to the next generation. But Darwin also believed in the importance of helpful behavior for *group survival*. Those groups of animals (including humans) who banded together and looked out for one another must have had a better chance of surviving (1874, pp. 124, 137).

In summary, Darwin emphasized the continuities between our species and other species, in both physical characteristics as well as cognitive and emotional characteristics. He did not suggest that animals share all our emotions, and certainly not all our cognitive powers, but he did say that no sharp line separates the minds of humans from other animals. After two lengthy chapters on this topic in *The Descent of Man* (1874), Darwin concluded that the "various emotions and faculties . . . of which man boasts may be found in incipient, or even sometimes in well-developed form in the lower animals" (p. 130).

Evaluation

Contemporary biologists generally consider Darwin's theory to be correct in its broad outline. Biologists agree with Darwin that there is enormous variation within species, and that species change because only some members survive long enough to reproduce and pass their traits on. But Darwin didn't understand the mechanisms underlying variation and the transmission of traits. It was only after the work of Gregor Mendel and others that we began to understand how these activities are performed by the genes. In other ways, Darwin was far ahead of his time. His thoughts on group selection, for example, have only recently received serious consideration from eminent biologists (Wade, 2009).

Darwin believed, as we have seen, that natural selection applies not only to physical characteristics (such as coloring) but also to various kinds of behavior. Thus Darwin opened the way to ethology—the field in biology that studies animal behavior from an evolutionary perspective. We will now review some of the ideas of modern ethologists and then look at the applications of these ideas to the study of human development.

MODERN ETHOLOGY: LORENZ AND TINBERGEN

Biographical Introduction

Konrad Lorenz (1903–1989) is often called the father of modern ethology. He did not necessarily make more discoveries than other ethologists, but his bold, vivid, and often humorous writing style did much to call attention to this new field.

Lorenz was born and raised in Austria. His father was a prominent physician who wanted Lorenz to become a doctor too, so Lorenz dutifully earned a medical degree. However, he never lost his boyhood enthusiasm for the study of nature and wildlife, and he next studied zoology at the University of Vienna, earning a Ph.D. in this field. Lorenz began his studies in ethology in the early 1930s, when he became convinced that one can see the landmarks of evolution in the innate behavior patterns of animals just as surely as in their physical characteristics (Lorenz, 1981, p. 101). He made many of his observations on his own large Austrian estate, where numerous species of wild animals freely roamed.

Niko Tinbergen (1907–1988) worked quietly in Lorenz's shadow. Despite this, ethologists consider his work equally substantial. Tinbergen was born in the Hague, the Netherlands, and like Lorenz was fascinated by animals and wildlife as a boy. In school, Tinbergen's work was erratic; he did well only in subjects that interested him, and he struck many of his teachers as a lazy youngster whose primary enthusiasm was for sports. Nevertheless, Tinbergen went on to earn a Ph.D. in biology at the University of Leiden in 1932 and began doing brilliant ethological studies. His research was interrupted during World War II when the Germans put him in a prison camp for protesting the dismissal of Jewish professors at the university. During his imprisonment, Tinbergen wrote on ethology as well as writing stories for children. After the war he became a professor at Oxford. In 1973 Tinbergen and Lorenz, along with a third eminent ethologist, Karl Von Frisch, won the Nobel Prize in physiology and medicine (Baerends, Beer, & Manning, 1975).

Methodological Approach

Ethologists are convinced that we can understand an animal's behavior only if we study the animal in his or her natural setting. Only in this way can we watch an animal's behavior patterns unfold and see how they serve in the adaptation of the species. We cannot, for example, understand why birds build nests where they do unless we see how such behavior protects the species from predators in the natural environment. Psychologists who only study animals in their laboratories miss out on a great deal. In such captive situations, many species do not even reproduce, and one frequently has no opportunity to observe their nesting, mating, territorial, or parental behavior.

When ethologists study a new species, their first step is simply to get to know the species as well as possible. That is, the ethologist engages in *naturalistic observation;* the ethologist observes an animal's characteristic behavior and then compares the behavior with that of other species. Only after ethologists have gathered a great deal of descriptive material do they attempt experiments to test their ideas or try to formulate general laws.

Instinctive Behavior

Ethologists are interested in instincts. In everyday language, we casually refer to any unlearned behavior as "instinctive" or as an "instinct," but ethologists consider instincts as a special class of unlearned behavior.

An instinct, in the first place, is *released by a specific external stimulus*. This is the case, for example, in the rescuing behavior of the chicken. The hen appears to respond any time her chicks are in danger, but a closer examination reveals that she is actually reacting to a very specific stimulus—the chicks' distress call. This point has been demonstrated in an experiment by Brückner (cited in Tinbergen, 1951, p. 34). When chicks were tied to a post and hidden behind a screen, the mother still rescued them because she heard the distress calls. When, however, the screen was removed and the struggling chicks were covered by a glass enclosure—so the hen could see her chicks in trouble but could not hear them call—she ignored them. She needed to hear the specific distress call.

Similarly, a specific stimulus releases the tendency to fight in the male three-pronged stickleback fish (Tinbergen, 1951, p. 48). In the spring the adult male establishes a territory, builds a nest, and courts females. He also develops a bright red spot on his belly. When other sticklebacks enter his territory, he may or may not fight—depending on the sight of a specific stimulus, the red spot on the invader's belly.

If a pregnant female enters his territory, his behavior is different. When he moves toward her, she tilts her body upward, exposing her full belly, and this stimulus causes him to go into a zigzag dance. This dance is a signal for her to approach, and when she does, he returns to the nest. Once there, his behavior signals her to enter. This intricate ritual continues until the eggs are fertilized, with each component of the ritual governed by a specific releasing stimulus (pp. 48–50).

Specific releasing stimuli also determine the reactions of the young to their parents. For example, a young jackdaw bird will follow its parent into the air only when the parent takes off at a certain angle and speed (Lorenz, 1935, pp. 157–161).

Instincts also are *species-specific*, which means particular behavior patterns are found only in members of a specific species. There may be some overlap; for example, we may see young birds in several species following a mother in single file. But on close inspection, there are distinctive differences in the following or in the way the parent's behavior releases following in each species (Lorenz, 1935, p. 157).

In addition, instinctive behaviors always include some *fixed action pattern*, some stereotyped motor component. Fighting gestures, courtship behavior, and modes of following always contain some fixed aspect.

Not every part of an instinct, however, must be of a fixed nature. For example, peregrine falcons engage in free flight when searching for prey. There is no rigid pattern to their search; they glide around in various areas where past experience has taught them to look. But once they spot their prey (e.g., a starling bird), their actions do become stereotyped. Their swoop and their manner of catching their prey constitute a fixed action pattern (Lorenz, 1952a, p. 306).

The fixed action pattern also has an underlying *drive component*, an inner urge to engage in the instinctive behavior. Consequently, if the behavior has not been released for a long time, the drive behind it can build up to the point that less specific stimuli will suffice, as when males court females who lack the specific releasing stimuli. In some cases, the internal pressure for release builds up to such a high pitch that the fixed action pattern goes off "in a vacuum" (Lorenz, 1963, pp. 52–53).

Finally, instincts, as the products of evolution, have some *survival value*. However, as Freedman (1971) observes, it is often all too easy to create plausible-sounding explanations of a behavior's adaptive value. What is really needed is research on the question. For example, Tinbergen (1965) wondered why herring gulls remove their young's egg shells after hatching. After all, this requires them to spend time away from the nest, endangering their young. He hypothesized that the glistening of the shells in the sun attracts predators, and he conducted an experiment to see if this were so. He scattered some egg shells in one area and found that, in fact, predators investigated this area much more than a comparable area lacking the shells.

As mentioned earlier, ethologists distinguish instincts from other kinds of unlearned behavior. Ethologists have given the most attention to the differences between instincts and reflexes (Hess, 1962). Instincts may contain reflexes, but instincts also may be more complex. For example, the stickleback's zigzag dance must involve many reflexes. Also, a reflex, such as an eyeblink, can be released by many stimuli—wind, noise, dust, bright lights, and so on. There does not seem to be a specific external releaser.

Imprinting

In many instances, an animal's responsiveness to specific releasers is innate or inborn. But in many other instances, the animal is born with a gap in his or her knowledge. The animal is innately equipped with all the patterns of an instinct but lacks some information about the releasing stimulus. When this information is filled in during an early critical period, the process is called *imprinting*.

Many species of young birds and mammals enter the world with incomplete knowledge about the stimuli that will release their following response. It's as if a gosling, for example, were to say, "I know I have an instinct to follow, I know I'm supposed to get into single file, and I know something about the releaser—it's my mother when she departs. But what does she look like?" This is the information the gosling acquires when she follows the first moving object she sees during an early critical period. Ordinarily, this object is the real mother, but when orphan

Greylag goslings were raised by Lorenz, they took him for their "mother." They energetically followed him about in single file wherever he went, ignoring other geese (see Figure 3.1). They had imprinted on him (Lorenz, 1935, p. 124).

FIGURE 3.1
These goslings have imprinted on Lorenz.
(Thomas D. McAvoy/Time & Life Pictures/Getty Images.)

Although Lorenz was not the first to observe imprinting, he was the first to state that it occurs during a *critical period*. This means the young animal will form an attachment to an object only if she is exposed to and follows that object during a specific time early in life. If the young animal is exposed to an object before or after the critical period, no attachment is formed. And once the critical period has passed, it may be impossible to induce the animal to attach itself to another kind of object (p. 127).

Lorenz found that species differ with respect to the range of objects on which they will imprint. Greylag goslings seem to imprint on almost anything that moves (some even have imprinted on boats). Mallard ducklings, in contrast, are more finicky. Lorenz found that they would imprint on him only if he stooped below a certain height and made a quacking sound as he moved about. Mallards, then, have an innate schema of certain aspects of the proper parent—the parent must move, be of a certain height, and make a certain sound. Imprinting only fills in the rest of the visual pattern (Lorenz, 1935, p. 135; 1952b, pp. 42–43).

Once imprinted on a mother-figure, goslings, ducklings, and other young birds follow the mother the best they can, but they occasionally become separated or fall behind. They then search for the mother while uttering "lost piping" calls (which vary somewhat from species to species). When a mallard mother hears the piping, she sounds a loud guiding call, and if the duckling still cannot reach her, she turns back and fetches the straggler. When she reaches the duckling she utters a greeting, and she and her duckling exchange joyful sounds (Lorenz, 1935, pp. 176–177; 1981, p. 276).

Imprinting can determine not only the following response in the young but later social behavior as well. In particular, early imprinting can affect later sexual preferences, as Lorenz also learned from personal experience. One of his neighbors hand-raised an orphan jackdaw bird that imprinted on humans, and when this bird reached sexual maturity he courted Lorenz. He attempted to seduce Lorenz in typical jackdaw fashion, by inserting crushed worms into Lorenz's mouth. When Lorenz shut his mouth, the bird put the worms into his ear. This bird, then, having been exposed only to humans during his early life, focused on humans as the objects of his later sexual advances. The critical period for sexual imprinting may differ from that for parental imprinting, but it too occurs very early, long before sexual behavior actually emerges (Lorenz, 1935, p. 132; 1937 p. 280; 1952b, pp. 135–136).

Lorenz found that among Greylag geese, the attachment of adult "lovers" is as strong as young ones' attachment to their parents. When adult geese lose sight of a partner, they search frantically. "The goose moves about restless by day and night, flying great distances and visiting all places where the partner might be found, uttering all the time the penetrating trisyllabic long-distance call" (1963, p. 208). If the goose's partner is lost forever, the goose appears grief-stricken and loses all confidence.

So far, we have been discussing the formation of social attachments, parental as well as sexual. Imprinting-like processes also can govern other kinds of learning, including the learning of territorial maps, food preferences, and songs. In pioneering research Marler and Tamura (1964) found that white-crowned sparrows in the San Francisco area learn aspects of their songs during an early critical period. The birds don't learn the entire song—the basic structure is inborn—but they pick up "regional dialects" during the critical period (so, for example, the birds sing differently if they grew up in Berkeley instead of Sunset Beach). Other researchers have uncovered similar findings with respect to numerous species of songbirds around the world (Ball & Hulse, 1998).

Nevertheless, most research on imprinting has focused on the forma-tion of social attachments, especially on the early following response. Some of this research has raised questions about some of Lorenz's initial formulations. For instance, Lorenz (1935) initially proposed that parental imprinting is always supraindividual. That is, he believed the young imprint on a particu-lar species of parent but not on an individual parent. But other ethologists observed that young animals do imprint on individual parents (Bateson, 1990), and Lorenz modified his position (Lorenz, 1965, p. 57).[1]

Other research, especially that conducted in laboratories, has questioned Lorenz's view of the critical period as completely fixed. If, in particular, one initially rears a bird in conditions of sensory deprivation, one can slow neural development and extend the critical period (Bateson, 1991). Some researchers therefore prefer the term *sensitive period* to *critical period*, suggesting greater flexibility in the boundaries (Maestripieri, 2001).

Several ethologists have looked for the conditions associated with the boundaries of the critical or sensitive period. In large part, the *beginning* seems to be ushered in by inner, maturational promptings; the young animal spon-taneously searches for a parent on which to imprint. This search has an urgent quality (Bateson, 1991). Lorenz said the Greylag gosling behaves as if she feels very lonely; the gosling utters her lost piping call and looks for somebody to follow (1981, p. 280).

Hess (1962, 1973) gathered evidence that the critical period *ends* with the onset of the fear response. Once the young animal starts showing fear, she avoids any new or strange object and wants to stay near her imprinted par-ent. Even laboratory researchers who look for ways of extending the critical period (e.g., Bateson, 1991) recognize the importance of fear in bringing the period to a close.

Imprinting occurs in many birds and mammals (including sheep, deer, and buffalo) that live in groups, move about soon after birth, and are

---

[1]Sexual imprinting, in contrast, usually seems to determine only the species that the young will later court, not the particular member of the species. One can only be sure that the young will not court its imprinted parent; this is somehow excluded (Lorenz, 1935 p. 132).

under strong predator pressure. In these species, imprinting ensures that the animal will follow an escaping parent in times of danger (Freedman, 1974, p. 19). It also enables the young to form a special bond with a particular parent.

But imprinting may also occur, if more slowly, in other species, including primates such as chimpanzees. Young chimpanzees do not show much concern over whom they are with until they are about 3 or 4 months old. Then they develop a marked preference for their mother (or foster parent) and become distinctly wary of other adults. After this, they stay fairly near her, returning to her from time to time, and if she should signal that she is about to depart, they rush over and climb aboard. Thus chimps clearly attach themselves to a particular adult during a certain period in life (Bowlby, 1982, pp. 190, 196). A similar process may occur in human children, as we shall discuss momentarily.

Evaluation

Ethology was primarily developed in continental Europe, and it took some time for it to be accepted in the United States. During the 1950s, 1960s, and 1970s, U.S. psychologists widely criticized it for ignoring the role of the environment and experience.

In a prominent study, Bernard Riess (1954) showed that rats deprived of experiences with sticks failed to show the nest-building instinct. Such experiments, however, miss the ethologists' point. Ethologists recognize that instincts have evolved because they have been adaptive within certain environments and that instincts need the right environment to develop properly. The environment is important. All that ethologists claim is that instinctive behaviors have a large innate component and that, given the environment to which the instinct is preadapted, the instinct will emerge without elaborate conditioning or learning.

Ethologists have produced many insights with respect to nonhuman species, but they generally have been slow to apply these insights to humans. I suspect that they fear intense resistance if they talk about humans and other animals in the same breath. They would be told that humans are different from other species, that human behavior is more determined by culture and learning. There is a degree of truth to this, but I believe the resistance more fundamentally stems from the centuries-old belief that our species is simply too magnificent to be associated with "lowly" animals (Balcombe, 2006, pp. 25–27). In any case, let us now consider a great, pioneering effort to apply ethological insights to human development—the work of Bowlby and Ainsworth.

BOWLBY AND AINSWORTH ON HUMAN ATTACHMENT

Bowlby

Biographical Introduction

John Bowlby (1907–1990) was born in London, the son of an upper-class English family. In his interpersonal relations, Bowlby maintained an old-fashioned British reserve, but his career was hardly traditional. He taught in two progressive schools for children, received psychoanalytic training when it was still new, and in 1936 became one of the first British psychiatrists to work in the area of child guidance.

Early on, Bowlby became concerned about the disturbances of children growing up in understaffed orphanages and nurseries, where the caretakers couldn't provide the children with much emotional interaction. The children frequently showed an inability to form intimate and lasting relationships with others. It seemed to Bowlby that the children were unable to love because they missed an opportunity to form a solid attachment to a mother figure early in life. In 1948 the World Health Organization commissioned Bowlby to pull together the research evidence on such institutional deprivation, which he summarized in his 1951 report, *Maternal Care and Mental Health.* The report produced widespread interest in the effects of institutional upbringing.

But Bowlby's greater interest was in another group of children—toddlers who had formed firm attachments to their parents and then went into the hospital for a period of one to several weeks. Bowlby and his coworkers began gathering information on these toddlers' experiences in the late 1940s and early 1950s. At the time, most hospitals kept parents off the children's wards. Hospital staff believed that parents would disrupt routines and spread infections. But when parents dropped off their children at the hospitals, the children became extremely upset. For days, the toddlers cried loudly and searched for their parents. They kept asking, "Where's my Mummy?" After a while they became more subdued, as if in a state of mourning, but they continued to yearn for their parents. With Bowlby's support, a young coworker, James Robertson, worked feverishly to convince hospitals to allow parents to stay with their children. In 1952, Robertson produced a film, *A Two-Year-Old Goes to Hospital,* to show the suffering of a little girl named Laura. She was a very pretty girl who was exceptionally self-controlled, but her emotions broke through. She tried in vain to escape the hospital and get back home, and she became increasingly miserable, sobbing to herself when alone. She kept crying,"I want my Mummy. Where has my Mummy gone?"

For a long time most medical professionals refused to take such observations seriously. They came up with alternative explanations for the children's havior, such as the possibility that Laura wasn't properly brought up. People tended to believe that children should act more maturely. But Bowlby, feeling that the toddlers' distress was natural, searched for a theoretical perspective that could shed light on his impression. His answers came from ethology (Bowlby, 1980, chap. 1; 1982, pp. 25–28; Karen, 1994, chap. 6).

Theory of Attachment: Overview

Earlier, we saw how young birds imprint on their parents and then follow them about. If the babies should lose contact, they utter distress calls. Bowlby pointed out that such behavior is common in a wide variety of animals. Of course, not all species are physically capable of following their parents soon after birth. But they initially have other ways of maintaining contact with the parent. A young infant chimpanzee, for example, clings to the adult. Bowlby called actions such as following, crying out, and clinging—actions that maintain proximity to a parent—*attachment behaviors.* He said attachment behaviors became part of an animal's instinctive nature because they proved highly adaptive. A young animal who lacked the urge to maintain proximity to the mother—a youngster who was content to remain apart from her—would have become relatively easy prey (Bowlby, 1982, pp. 180–190; 1973, pp. 57–59).

Bowlby stated that similar attachment behaviors occur in human babies. Human babies, too, want to be close to their mothers. As soon as they can crawl, babies try to follow their mothers, and they become upset when separated. They cry out and redouble their efforts to regain contact. Bowlby said we should consider attachment behaviors in humans to be in the same category as those in other species. In our species, like others, attachment behaviors became part of our biological equipment because they helped the young survive, providing protection from predators (1982, p. 183).

Today, the mention of predators might sound odd. Greater dangers are posed by automobiles and industrial chemicals, but Bowlby asked us to consider our *environment of adaptedness,* the basic environment in which we evolved. He believed that anthropological data provide a pretty good picture of human life beginning about 2 million years ago, when our ancestor *Homo habilis* began using crude stone tools. Throughout nearly all of the subsequent 2 million years, our ancestors probably moved about in small groups, searching for food and risking attacks by large predators. When threatened, humans cooperated to drive off the predators and to protect the sick and young. The largest humans fended off the predators while the young followed their mothers to a safer position behind them (1982, pp. 58–64). If a toddler lacked the urge to follow the mother, he or she became "a more or less easy meal for a lurking leopard or a pack of hunting dogs" (Bowlby, 1973, p. 143).

During this huge span of time, attachment behavior undoubtedly acquired some of the characteristics we see today. But Bowlby also believed that human attachment behavior began evolving earlier, in ancestors we shared with other animals (Bowlby, 1982, pp. 59, 183).

As we saw earlier, Lorenz and others advanced the concept of imprinting to describe a process by which attachment to a parent can develop. Bowlby suggested that a kind of imprinting also occurs in human children, although it develops more slowly than in other animals. It certainly develops more slowly than in birds, and even more slowly than in chimpanzees and gorillas.

Briefly, human imprinting develops along the following lines. In the first months of life, babies cannot actively crawl after a departing parent, but they have other signals and gestures for keeping the parent close. One way is to cry. The cry is a distress call; when the infant is in pain or is frightened, she cries and the parent is impelled to rush over to see what is wrong. Another attachment behavior is the baby's smile; when a baby smiles into a parent's eyes, the parent feels love for the baby and enjoys being close.

Initially, babies' social gestures are largely indiscriminate. For example, they will smile at any face or cry for any person who leaves their sight. But between about 3 and 6 months of age, babies narrow their responsiveness to a few familiar people, develop a clear-cut preference for one person in particular, and then become wary of strangers. Soon after this, they become more mobile, crawling about, and they take a more active role in keeping their principal attachment figure nearby. They monitor this parent's whereabouts, and any sign that the parent might suddenly depart releases following on their part. The whole process—focusing on a principal attachment figure whose departure then releases following—parallels imprinting in other species. This attachment figure, usually a parent, is incredibly important to the young child, and the child wants to stay in proximity to the parent.

In his writings, Bowlby used the ethological terms *instinct* and *imprinting* in a purposely loose sense. He wanted to show that these concepts apply to human behavior in a general way, not as extremely precise, detailed definitions (1982, pp. 136, 220). Nevertheless, Bowlby felt that these ethological concepts provided the powerful explanations he had been looking for. He said that when he first learned about them, in the 1950s, it was a "eureka" experience (Karen, 1994, p. 90). In particular, he understood why toddlers like Laura (in James Robertson's film) become so shaken when separated from their parents. As a product of evolution, the human child has an instinctual need to stay close to the parent on whom she has imprinted. This need is built into the very fiber of the child's being. So when the toddler loses contact with the parent, the toddler tries to find the parent and cries out with distress calls. The child isn't being "babyish"; she is simply engaging in natural behaviors that have brought safety to young humans for millions of years. Without these behaviors, it's unlikely that human populations would have survived. If, despite the child's efforts, she cannot regain contact with the parent, the child's anxiety becomes intense. On some level, the child may feel she will die.

Let us now look at the phases through which babies normally develop their attachment to caretakers.

Phases of Attachment

Phase 1 (birth to 3 months): Social Gestures with Limited Selectivity.
Within a few days after birth, infants have some capacity to discriminate
among people. They prefer their mothers' voices, odors, and faces to those of
other people (Fogel, 2009, pp. 121, 240–241, 244). But during the first 3 months
babies' selectivity is often limited. Much of the time, they respond to everyone in the same ways, as we shall see as we review their social gestures.

The most endearing early gesture is the *social smile*. Social smiles begin
at 3 or 4 weeks of age and are usually directed at a high-pitched human voice.
Beginning at 6 to 8 weeks of age, babies' smiles become brighter and more
energetic and are primarily directed at a visual stimulus—the face (Bowlby,
1982, pp. 283–286; Fogel, 2009, p. 286).[2] One can tell when visual smiles are
about to start. About a week beforehand, the baby starts to gaze intently at
faces, as if studying them. Then the baby breaks into open smiles (Figure 3.2).
This is often an electrifying moment in a parent's life; the parent now has

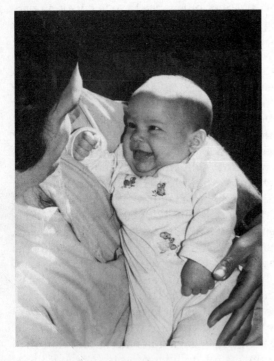

FIGURE 3.2
The sight of a baby smiling into
one's eyes stirs love and fosters
attachment.

---

[2]Actually, babies begin smiling right after birth. They emit eyes-closed smiles, usually
as they fall off to sleep. But these smiles are not yet social; they are not yet directed at people
(Freedman, 1974, p. 178).

"proof" of the baby's love. The sight of one's baby looking deeply into one's eyes and smiling causes a feeling of love to well up from within. (Even if you are not a parent, you might have had a similar feeling when any baby smiled at you. You cannot help but smile back, and you think that you and the baby share a special bond.)

Actually, until 3 months or so, these smiles aren't selective. Babies will smile at any face, even a cardboard model of one. The main stipulation is that the face be presented in the full or frontal position. A profile is far less effective. Also, a voice or a caress is a relatively weak elicitor of smiling during this stage. It seems, then, that the baby's social smile is released by a fairly specific visual stimulus (Bowlby, 1982, pp. 282–286; Freedman, 1974, pp. 179–181, 187; Fogel, 2009, p. 286).

In Bowlby's view, smiling promotes attachment because it maintains the proximity of the caretaker. When the baby smiles, the caretaker enjoys being with the baby; the caretaker "smiles back, 'talks' to him, strokes and pats him, and perhaps picks him up" (Bowlby, 1982, p. 246). The smile itself is a releaser that promotes loving and caring interaction—behavior that increases the baby's chances for health and survival.

At about the time that babies begin smiling at faces, they also begin *babbling* (and cooing and gurgling). They babble primarily at the sound of a human voice and, especially, at the sight of a human face. As with smiling, babbling is initially unselective; babies will babble when almost any person is around. The baby's babbling delights the caretaker, prompting the caretaker to talk back. "Babbling, like smiling, is a social releaser [that] has the function of maintaining a mother-figure in proximity to an infant by promoting social interaction between them" (p. 289).

Crying also results in proximity between caretaker and child. It is like a distress call; it signals the baby needs help. Babies cry when they are in pain, hungry, cold, or experience discomfort. They even cry when a person at whom they had been looking leaves their field of vision, although during the first weeks the particular person in question matters little. Babies also will permit almost any person to quiet them through rocking or by attending to their needs (pp. 289–296).

Proximity also is maintained by the baby's *holding on*. The newborn is equipped with two holding responses. One is the grasp reflex; when any object touches the baby's open palm, the hand automatically closes around it. The other is the Moro reflex, which occurs either when babies are startled by a loud noise or when they suddenly lose support (as when one holds their head from underneath and then suddenly lets it drop). Their response is to spread their arms and then to bring them back around the chest. The action looks as if the baby were embracing something (see Figure 3.3). In earlier times, Bowlby thought, these reflexes served the purpose of keeping hold of the parent who carried them about. If, for example, a mother saw a predator and suddenly ran, the chances were that the baby had a grasp of some part of her with the hand

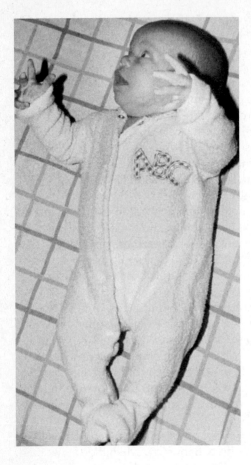

FIGURE 3.3
The Moro reflex: A startled baby
exhibits an embracing action.

(see Figure 3.4). And if the baby lost hold, he or she would embrace the mother again (p. 278).

Babies also are equipped with *rooting* and *sucking* reflexes. When their cheek is touched, they automatically turn their head to the side from which the stimulation came and then "root" or grope until their mouth touches something, which they then suck. The rooting and sucking reflexes obviously aid breast-feeding, but Bowlby also regarded them as attachment patterns because they bring the baby into interaction with the mother (p. 275).

Phase 2 (3 to 6 months): Focusing on Familiar People. Beginning at about 3 months, the baby's behavior changes. For one thing, many reflexes— including the Moro, grasp, and rooting reflexes—drop out. But more importantly for Bowlby, the baby's social responses begin to become much more selective. Between 3 and 6 months, babies gradually restrict their smiles to familiar people; when they see a stranger, they simply stare (Bowlby, 1982,

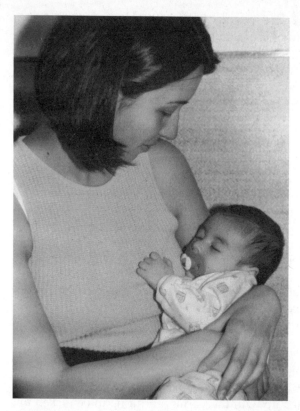

FIGURE 3.4
With her grasp reflex, this month-old baby has a hold on
her mother's shirt.

pp. 287, 325). Babies also become more selective in their cooing and babbling;
by the age of 4 or 5 months, they make these sounds only in the presence of
people they recognize (p. 289). Also, by this age (and perhaps long before),
their crying is most readily quieted by a preferred figure. By age 5 months,
finally, babies begin to reach for and grasp parts of our anatomy, particularly
our hair, but they do so only if they know us (pp. 279, 300).

   During this phase, then, babies narrow their responsiveness to familiar
people. They usually prefer two or three people—and one in particular. They
most readily smile or babble, for example, when this person is near. This
principal attachment figure is usually the mother, but it doesn't have to be.
It can be the father or some other caretaker. Babies seem to develop the
strongest attachment to the one person who has most alertly responded to
their signals and who has engaged in the most pleasurable interactions with
them (pp. 306–316).

Phase 3 (6 months to 3 years): Intense Attachment and Active Proximity-Seeking.   Beginning at about 6 months of age, the infant's attachment to a particular person becomes increasingly intense and exclusive. Most notably, infants *cry out* when the mother figure leaves the room, demonstrating *separation anxiety*.

Observers have also noted the intensity with which the baby *greets* the mother after she has been away for a brief time. When she returns, the baby typically smiles, reaches to be picked up, and when in the mother's arms, hugs her and crows with delight. The mother, too, displays her happiness at the reunion (1982, pp. 295, 300).

The new exclusiveness of the baby's attachment to a parent is also evident at about 7 or 8 months when the baby exhibits a *fear of strangers*. This reaction ranges from a slight vigilance to outright cries at the sight of a stranger, with the stronger reactions usually occurring when the baby feels ill or is in an unfamiliar setting (pp. 321–326).

But babies are not restricted to the expression of strong emotions. By 8 months, they can usually *crawl* and therefore can begin to *actively follow* a departing parent. Babies will make the most concerted efforts to regain contact when a parent departs suddenly rather than slowly, or when they are in unfamiliar surroundings (pp. 256–259). (See Figure 3.5.)

Once infants can actively follow a parent, their behavior begins to consolidate into a *goal-corrected system*. That is, babies monitor the parent's whereabouts, and if the parent starts to leave, they urgently follow, "correcting" or adjusting their movements until they regain proximity. When they get near the parent, they typically reach up with their arms, gesturing to be picked up. When held, they calm down again (p. 252).

Babies, of course, often move away from attachment figures as well as toward them. This is particularly evident when they use the caretaker as a *secure base from which to explore*. If a mother and her 1- or 2-year-old child enter a park or playground, the child will typically remain close for a moment or two and then venture off to explore. However, the child will periodically look back, exchange glances or smiles with her, and even return to her from time to time before venturing forth once again. The child initiates brief contacts "as though to assure himself that she is still there" (p. 209).

Using the mother as a secure base, babies and toddlers are happy explorers. Although they periodically monitor the mother's presence, they are comfortable investigating things at some distance from her. But this situation can quickly change. If, when a child glances back at the mother, she seems inaccessible (or, more threatening yet, seems ready to depart) the child will hurry back to her. The child also will rush back if he or she is frightened by some event, such as a loud noise. In these circumstances the child will want close physical contact and may require a good deal of comforting before he or she will venture away from the mother once again (Bowlby, 1988, p. 62; 1982, pp. 257–259, 373).

FIGURE 3.5
An 8-month-old baby struggles to follow her mother.

By the end of the first year, an important variable is the child's general *working model* of the attachment figure. That is, the child has begun to build up, on the basis of day-to-day interactions, a general idea of the caretaker's accessibility and responsiveness. So, for example, a 1-year-old girl who has developed some general doubts about her mother's availability will tend to be anxious about exploring new situations at any distance from her. If, in contrast, the girl has basically concluded that "my mother loves me and will always be there when I really need her," she will explore the world with more courage and enthusiasm. Even so, she will occasionally monitor her mother's presence, for her need for her mother is vital (Bowlby, 1973, pp. 203–206; 1982, pp. 354, 373).

Phase 4 (3 years to the end of childhood): Partnership Behavior. Prior to the age of 2 or 3 years, children are concerned only with their own need to maintain a certain proximity to the caretaker; they do not yet consider the caretaker's plans or goals. For the 2-year-old, the knowledge that mother or father is "going next door for a moment to borrow some milk" is meaningless; the child simply wants to go, too. The 3-year-old, in contrast, has some under-standing of such plans and can visualize the parent's behavior while he or she is away. Consequently, the child is more willing to let the parent go. The child begins acting more like a partner in the relationship. Still, there are limits on the amount of physical separation 3-year-olds can tolerate, for they still have a great need for the parent's care.

Attachment as Imprinting

Now that we have examined the child's attachment in some detail, we are in a position to appreciate Bowlby's thesis that attachment follows a course sim-ilar to imprinting in animals. Imprinting, you will recall, is the process by which animals learn the releasing stimuli for their social instincts. In particu-lar, young animals learn which moving objects to follow. They begin with a willingness to follow a wide range of objects, but this range quickly narrows, and at the end of the imprinting period they usually will follow only the mother. At this point the fear response limits the ability to form new attach-ments. The sensitive period for imprinting has ended.

In humans, we can observe a similar process, although it develops much more slowly. During the first weeks of life, babies cannot actively follow objects through locomotion, but they do direct social responses toward people. They smile, babble, hold on, cry, and so on—all of which keep people close. At first, babies direct these responses toward anyone. However, by 6 months of age they have narrowed their attachment to a few people and one in particular. They primarily want this person near. At this point they become afraid of strangers, and, as they learn to crawl, they follow their prin-cipal attachment figure whenever she departs. They have imprinted on a particular person; it is she who releases following.

Institutional Deprivation

Early in his career, Bowlby was struck by the inability of many institution-ally reared children to form deep attachments later in life. He called these individuals "affectionless characters"; such individuals use people solely for their own ends and seem incapable of forming loving, lasting ties to others. In his 1951 World Health Organization report, Bowlby speculated that they lacked the opportunity to form an early relationship with a mother-figure (Bowlby, 1965).

The conditions in many institutions do seem unfavorable for the for-mation of intimate human ties. In many institutions, babies receive care from several nurses who can meet their physical needs but who have little time to interact with them. Frequently, no one is around to heed the babies' cries, to return their smiles, to talk to them when they babble, or to pick them up when they desire. Consequently, it is difficult for the baby to establish a strong bond with any particular person.

When writing his report, Bowlby had not yet read about imprinting, but he intuitively felt that there is a sensitive period for forming the first, vital attachment. Bowlby never seemed perfectly confident about the age when the sensitive period ends, but his writings suggest it ends with the appearance of fear responses, as in other species (1982, pp. 222–223). If so, the sensitive period might end at 8 or 9 months, the age by which babies ordinarily have shown a fear of separation (6 months) as well as a fear of strangers (8 or 9 months). If the baby hasn't formed an attachment by this age, the baby may have missed the sensitive period for developing bonds in general.

The most relevant recent research has looked at institutionalized children in Romania. In 1989, political turmoil forced many babies into extremely understaffed orphanages. Many caring families in the United Kingdom adopted children in the orphanages, and researchers have followed the children's progress up to the age of 11 years. It appears that babies adopted prior to the age of 6 months escaped social deficits. In contrast, about a quarter of the children who were adopted between the ages of 6 and 42 months exhibited social deficits, such as shallow relationships with others. Thus the watershed appears to be 6 months, when the initial fear response (separation anxiety) ordinarily emerges (Dozier & Rutter, 2008).

On the basis of this finding, Mary Dozier and Michael Rutter (2008, pp. 707–708) suggest there may be a genetically programmed period, ending at 6 months, for the normal attachment to a parental figure. If the baby does not form a bond with a parental figure by this age, subsequent relationship problems can occur. But Dozier and Rutter acknowledge that more research is needed on this topic.

Separations

Although Bowlby was interested in early institutional deprivation, he was much more interested in cases where the child forms a normal attachment and then suffers a separation. This was the kind of separation illustrated by James Robertson's 1952 film, *A Two-Year-Old Goes to Hospital*. Bowlby and Robertson (Bowlby, 1980, chap. 1; 1982, chap. 2) proposed that when separations are forced on 1- to 3-year-olds, and last from one to several weeks, the child's behavior typically goes through three stages.

First, children *protest*. They cry and scream for their mother. They search for her and are alert to any sight or sound indicating she is present after all. Sometimes they insist their mother is coming soon, ignoring what they've been told. During this phase, the children usually reject all forms of substitute care.

Second, they go through a period of *despair*. They become quieter and less active, and appear to be in a deep state of mourning. But although their hopelessness deepens, they continue to look for their mother.

Finally, a stage of *detachment* sets in. During this period, the child is livelier and may accept the care of nurses and others. The hospital staff may think the child has recovered. However, all is not well. When the mother returns, the child seems not to know her; the child turns away from her and acts as if he has lost all interest in her. The reactions are probably a defense against further disappointment.

Fortunately, most children do reestablish their tie to the mother after a while. But this is not always the case. If the separation has been prolonged or is repeated, the child may give up on people altogether. The result here, too, is an "affectionless character," a person who no longer cares for others in any deep way.

Attachment and Separation through the Life Cycle

Although Bowlby wrote primarily about attachment in childhood, he believed that attachment is important throughout the life cycle. Adolescents break away from parental dominance, but their attachment to parents persists; adults consider themselves independent, but they seek proximity to loved ones in times of crisis; and older people find that they must increasingly depend on the younger generation. In general, Bowlby said, being alone is one of the great fears in human life. We might consider such a fear silly, neurotic, or immature, but there are good biological reasons behind it. Throughout human history, humans have best been able to withstand crises and face danger with the help of companions (Bowlby, 1982, p. 207; 1973, pp. 84, 143, 165).

In his writings on adult attachment, Bowlby emphasized how people provide each other with a secure base of support. You will recall that such behavior begins early. When, for example, a 1- or 2-year-old goes to a new park with a caretaker, the child uses the caretaker as a base from which to explore. Knowing that the caretaker is available if needed, the child enthusiastically explores the surroundings. Bowlby suggested that similar behavior characterizes the healthiest adult partnerships (1979, pp. 204–205). Each partner knows he or she has an unwavering backup, someone who can be trusted to provide emotional support and assistance when needed. Knowing that support will be there, individuals have the courage to venture forth and meet life's challenges. Secure bases of support also are provided by relatives and friends. Bowlby said, "All of us, from the cradle to the grave, are happiest when life is organized as a series of excursions, long or short, from a secure base provided by our attachment figure(s)" (1988, p. 62).

Because attachments are vital throughout life, separations and losses can cause personal upheaval. This is evident, for example, when a person loses a parent, goes through a divorce, or becomes a widow. Attachment researchers have most thoroughly studied cases of widowhood, and they have found that the reactions of the bereaved display many similarities to those of children who suffer separations. Most dramatically, the bereaved also search for the lost person.

"I walk around searching," said one widow. "I go to the grave . . . but he's not there." Others feel drawn to the old haunts they and their loved ones used to frequent, as if they might find their loved ones there. Sometimes they call out for the deceased. "Oh Fred, I do need you," shouted one widow during a research interview, before bursting into tears (Bowlby, 1980, p. 90). A 1993 study found that a full year after a spouse's death, 63% of the respondents sensed that their spouse was with them at times (Shaver & Fraley, 2008, p. 51). Sometimes the bereaved think they see their deceased partner on the street or hear the partner moving about the house at night (Bowlby, 1980, p. 89). This desperate searching reminds one of the adult geese described by Lorenz (1963, p. 208).

Many friends and professionals see the behavior of bereaved adults as irrational. They tell them to pull themselves together, to face reality, and to focus on the future instead of dwelling on the past. Bowlby's view was different. He suggested that in the course of evolution, an urge to find missing loved ones became a powerful part of our biological makeup. Underlying the urge is the assumption that "all losses are retrievable"; hoping for the impossible, we keep searching (Bowlby, 1979, p. 86). And because the drive to reunite with loved ones is natural, it should be respected, even when it might strike us as unrealistic. To be helpful, we should give bereaved individuals a chance to talk freely about their feelings and wishes. Research indicates that this opportunity facilitates a healthy readjustment (Bowlby, 1979, pp. 86, 97, 100–101).

Bowlby gave attachment theory its start, but much of its progress—as well as its current popularity—owes to the work of his colleague Mary Ainsworth.

Ainsworth

Biographical Introduction

Mary D. S. Ainsworth (1913–1999) grew up in Toronto and at the age of 16 entered the University of Toronto. There, she was impressed by the psychological theory of William Blatz, who emphasized how parents may or may not provide children with security. Ainsworth felt Blatz's ideas helped her understand why she was a bit retiring in social settings. She stayed on at the university to earn a doctorate and taught psychology for a few years. In 1950 she married Len Ainsworth, and the couple went to England, where she answered a newspaper ad for a research assistant to John Bowlby. Thus began a 40-year collaboration. In 1954 Len accepted a position teaching in Uganda, and Ainsworth used her two years there to go to the villages near Kampala to make careful, naturalistic observations of how babies become attached to their mothers (Karen, 1994). This research, later published in her 1967 book, *Infancy in Uganda*, sketched out the phases of attachment that Bowlby outlined in his writings. Ainsworth's Uganda research also described how babies use the mother as a secure base from which to explore. Indeed, Bowlby (1988) credited Ainsworth with discovering infants' secure-base behavior. And, taking a first stab at a groundbreaking formulation, she described three patterns of attachment—three different forms the attachment process may take among individual babies.

After arriving in the United States from Africa, Ainsworth began a study of 23 middle-class babies and their mothers in Baltimore. The Baltimore study, which was more elaborate than the Uganda study, replicated and expanded the Uganda findings on the patterns of attachment and stimulated a tremendous amount of research on the topic.

Patterns of Attachment

In the Baltimore study, Ainsworth and her students observed the babies and their mothers in their homes for the first year of the babies' lives, visiting them for about 4 hours every 3 weeks. When the infants were 12 months old, Ainsworth wanted to see how they would behave in a new setting, so she brought them and their mothers to a playroom at Johns Hopkins University. She was particularly interested in how the babies would use the mother as a base from which to explore and how they would react to two brief separations. In the first separation, the mother left the baby with a stranger (a friendly female graduate student); in the second, the baby was left alone. Each separation lasted 3 minutes, but was shortened if the baby showed too much distress. The entire procedure, which lasts 20 minutes, is called the Strange Situation. Ainsworth and coworkers (Ainsworth, Bell, & Stanton, 1971; Ainsworth, Blehar, Waters, & Wall, 1978) observed three patterns.

1. Securely Attached Infants.   Soon after entering the playroom with the mother, these babies used her as a base from which to explore. When the mother left the room, however, their exploratory play diminished and they sometimes became visibly upset. When the mother returned, they actively greeted her and remained close to her for a moment or two. Once reassured, they eagerly ventured forth to explore the environment once again.

When Ainsworth examined the earlier home observations of these children, she found the mothers had typically been rated as sensitive and promptly responsive to their babies' cries and other signals. The mothers had been lovingly available when the babies needed comforting. For their part, the babies cried very little at home and used the mother as a base from which to explore in the home as well.

Ainsworth believed these infants demonstrated the healthy pattern of attachment behavior. The mother's day-in and day-out responsiveness had given the baby faith in the mother as a protector; her simple presence in the Strange Situation gave the child the courage to actively explore the surroundings. At the same time, the child's responses to the mother's departure and return in this new environment revealed the baby's strong need for proximity to her—a need that has had enormous survival value throughout human evolution. This pattern has been found to characterize about 65% of the 1-year-olds evaluated in the Strange Situation in U.S. samples (Goldberg, 1995; van IJzendoorn & Sagi-Schwartz, 2008).

2. Insecure-Avoidant Infants.   These infants appeared quite independent throughout the Strange Situation. As soon as they entered the room, they rushed off to inspect the toys. Although they explored, they didn't use the mother as a secure base, in the sense of checking in with her from time to time. They simply ignored her. When the mother left the room, they didn't become upset, and they didn't seek proximity to her when she returned. If she tried to pick them up, they tried to avoid her, turning their bodies away or averting their gaze. This avoidant pattern has been found in about 20% of the infants in U.S. samples (Goldberg, 1995; van IJzendoorn & Sagi-Schwartz, 2008)

Because these infants display such independence in the Strange Situation, they have struck many people as exceptionally healthy. But when Ainsworth saw their avoidant behavior, she guessed they were suffering from some degree of emotional difficulty. Their detachment reminded her of children who had experienced painful separations.

The home observations supported Ainsworth's guess that something was wrong. The mothers had been rated as relatively insensitive, interfering, and rejecting. And the babies often seemed insecure. Although some were very independent in the home, many were anxious about the mother's whereabouts.

Ainsworth's overall interpretation, then, was that when these babies entered the Strange Situation, they suspected they couldn't count on their mother for support and they therefore reacted in a defensive way. They adopted an indifferent, self-contained posture to protect themselves. Having suffered so many rejections in the past, they attempted to block out their need for their mother to avoid further disappointment. And when the mother returned from the separation episodes, they refused to look at her, as if denying any feelings for her. They behaved as if they were saying, "Who are you? Am I supposed to know you?—you who won't help me when I need it" (Ainsworth, Bell, & Stanton, 1971, p. 47; Ainsworth et al., 1978, pp. 241–242, 316).

Bowlby (1988, pp. 124–125) speculated that this defensive behavior can become a fixed and pervasive part of the personality. The child becomes an adult who is overly self-reliant and detached, a person who can never let down his or her guard and trust others sufficiently to form close relationships.

3. Insecure-Ambivalent Infants.

In the Strange Situation, these infants were so clingy and preoccupied with the mother's whereabouts that they hardly explored at all. They became extremely upset when the mother left the room, and they were markedly ambivalent toward her when she returned. At one moment they reached out for her; at the next moment they angrily pushed her away.

In their homes, these mothers had typically treated their babies in an inconsistent manner. The mothers had been warm and responsive on some occasions but not on others. This inconsistency had apparently left the babies uncertain whether the mothers would be there for them when called on. As a result, they usually wanted to keep the mother close at hand—a desire that intensified greatly in the Strange Situation. These babies became very distressed when the mother left the playroom, and they urgently tried to regain contact with her when she returned, although they also vented their anger toward her. The ambivalent pattern is sometimes called "resistance" because the children not only desperately seek contact but resist it. This pattern usually characterizes 10 to 15% of the 1-year-olds in U.S. samples (Goldberg, 1995; van IJzendoorn & Sagi-Schwartz, 2008).

Disorganized/Disoriented Infants.

For some time, researchers found that some children's Strange Situation behavior didn't fit perfectly into the three types. In the late 1980s, Mary Main and Judith Solomon examined 200 anomalous cases and saw that many of the children exhibited peculiar behavior, especially when the mother returned to the room. For example, they walked toward the mother, but with their faces averted, or they froze in a trance-like state. It seemed that the children were at a loss as to how to act because they wanted to approach their mother but were afraid to do so. To classify such behavior, Main and Solomon proposed a fourth category, *Disorganized/Disoriented,* and subsequent research sometimes includes it. The category generally captures about 14 to 24% of children in the samples. Research on the causes of such fearful behavior points to the possibility of physical abuse (Lyons-Ruth & Jacobvitz, 2008).

Follow-Up Studies.

If the Strange Situation taps fundamental differences among children, it should predict differences in their later behavior. A number of studies have found that the infants classified as securely attached in the Strange Situation have continued to behave differently from the others in childhood and adolescence. On cognitive tasks, the securely attached children have scored higher on measures of persistence and self-reliance. In social settings, such as summer camps, they have received higher ratings on friendliness and leadership. Infant attachment alone doesn't determine all later behavior, of course. Other factors, such as ongoing family support, have an effect. But a secure attachment in infancy gets the child off to a good start (Weinfield et al., 2008).

Ainsworth reported that secure attachment was the product of maternal sensitivity to children's signals and needs. This finding is theoretically important because ethologists believe children have built-in gestures that must be heeded for development to unfold properly. Ainsworth's finding has been replicated by other investigators with great consistency. In addition, intervention programs that increase mothers' sensitivity to their children's cues do promote more secure attachments. At the same time, the estimated relationship between maternal sensitivity and secure attachment is often more modest than attachment theorists would like to see. So there is a need for more exploration of the variables that foster secure attachment (Belsky & Fearon, 2008). There also is a need to clarify the role of fathers in the attachment process.

Marinus van IJzendoorn and Abraham Sagi-Schwartz (2008) have led efforts to test the cultural universality of Ainsworth's first three patterns. They report that the Strange Situation produces the same three patterns in various parts of the world, including Israel, Africa, Japan, China, Western Europe, and the United States. In all the samples, secure attachment is the dominant type, but there also are differences. The U.S and Western European samples contain the highest percentages of avoidant children. Perhaps the West's cultural emphasis on independence leads parents to rebuff babies' needs, and the babies defend themselves with avoidant behavior.

Working Models in Children and Adults.   Attachment research has been moving forward at a rapid pace, and one of the most popular topics is that of internal working models. Bowlby, you will recall, conceived of the working model as the child's expectations and feelings about the attachment figure's responsiveness. Because the working model involves internal mental events, it is difficult to investigate in infancy; we cannot interview babies about their thoughts and feelings. But after the age of 3 years or so, research becomes feasible. Bretherton, Ridgeway, and Cassidy (1990) found that 3-year-olds could complete stories about an attachment situation. They could provide endings, for instance, to a story about a child who fell and hurt her knee while taking a walk with her family. As predicted, the securely attached children, compared to the others, most frequently depicted the parents in their story endings as responsive and helpful (saying, for example, that a parent will put a bandage on the child's knee).

Adults, too, have developed thoughts and feelings about attachment, and their attitudes undoubtedly influence the way they treat their children.

Mary Main and her colleagues (Main et al., 1985; Main & Goldwyn, 1987) interviewed mothers and fathers about their own early memories in an Adult Attachment Interview. Focusing on the openness and flexibility of the parents' responses, Main developed a typology that has proven to correlate quite well with children's classifications in the Strange Situation (Hesse, 2008). Main's types include:

> *Secure/autonomous* speakers, who talk openly and freely about their own early experiences. These parents tend to have securely attached children. Apparently the parents' acceptance of their own feelings goes hand-in-hand with an acceptance of their infants' signals and needs.
>
> *Dismissing of attachment* speakers, who talk as if their own attachment experiences are unimportant. These parents tend to have insecure-avoidant children; the parents reject their own experiences in much the same way that they reject their infants' proximity-seeking.
>
> *Preoccupied* speakers, whose interviews suggest that they are still struggling, inwardly or outwardly, to win their own parents' love and approval. It may be their own neediness that makes it difficult for them to respond consistently to their infants' needs. (Main & Goldwyn, 1987)

Following the introduction of the Disorganized/Disoriented category of infant attachment, researchers have looked for a corresponding pattern in the Adult Attachment Interview. Investigators have found that parents of Disorganized/Disoriented children sometimes exhibit lapses in consciousness and logical thinking (Lyons-Ruth & Jacobvitz, 2008). These lapses might be associated with outbursts that generate fear in their babies, but this is merely conjecture at this time.

Several studies have found that when parents are interviewed prior to the birth of their babies, their interview classifications correlate with their babies' attachment behavior in the Strange Situation at 1 year of age. Generally, the overlap is about 70%. However, it has been more difficult to find an adult interview classification that predicts the Disorganized/Disorganized infant category (Main, 1995, p. 446).

Practical Applications of the Bowlby/Ainsworth Endeavor

Institutional Care.   Bowlby and his colleagues have had a tremendous impact on child care issues.

Bowlby's 1951 World Health Organization report significantly raised awareness with respect to emotional deprivation in orphanages. This does not mean that countries have consistently taken steps to provide more loving care, but Bowlby did a lot to bring attention to the problem.

Bowlby, together with James Robertson, also battled against the hospital practice of separating toddlers and young children from their parents. On this front, Bowlby and Robertson had great success. True, health care professionals initially resisted his recommendations to allow parents to room-in with their children. But in the 1970s rooming-in did become a common hospital practice. Most hospitals now allow parents to stay with their children (Karen, 1994, chap. 6).

Day Care.   As increasing numbers of U.S. mothers work outside the home, families are turning to day care for assistance, and they are placing their children in day care settings at younger and younger ages. Indeed, day care for infants (children under 12 months of age) is already quite common.

To some extent, day care has become a political issue. Some people argue that day care supports a woman's right to pursue a career. Others lobby for day care because it enables economically disadvantaged parents to work and make more money. Nevertheless, Bowlby (Karen, 1994, chap. 22) and Ainsworth (1973, p. 70) have raised questions about it. Does early day care prevent a baby from forming a bond with her parents? What are the emotional effects of daily separations from the parents in the first few years of life?

The research on such questions is still ongoing but it is clear that even young infants who attend day care for several hours a day become primarily attached to their parents, not to their day care providers (Clarke-Stewart, 1989).

But research does raise the possibility that children who spend a great deal of time in day care can suffer some ill effects. A major study by the National Institute of Child Health and Human Development (NICHD) found that the more time young children spend in day care up to the age of 4 1/2 years, the more likely the children are to display aggressive and disobedient behavior (2003). The NICHD generally found these effects to occur regardless of the quality of the day care (whether or not the settings provided lots of nurturance and individual attention). However, a more recent study found the relationship between time in day care and aggressive behavior to be modest, and high-quality day care diminished the adverse effects (McCartney et al., 2010). Still, taken as a whole, the research evidence is sufficient to raise concerns.

In a sense, the search for quality day care really reflects wider problems in contemporary societies, as Bowlby (1988, pp. 1–3) and Ainsworth (Karen, 1994, p. 415) tried to indicate. In earlier village societies, parents could take their children to work with them in the fields or in the shops, and parents received a good deal of child care assistance from grandparents, aunts and uncles, teenagers, and friends. There was also time for games and socializing with the children. In today's hectic world, the situation is different. Parents usually live apart from their relatives and must raise their children alone, and parents often come home from work too exhausted to be very responsive to their children. Although quality day care may seem desirable, what parents really need are new occupational and social arrangements that permit them to spend considerably more relaxed and enjoyable time with their children.

A Child-Centered Approach to Child Rearing.

Bowlby (1982, p. 356) said that parents as well as professionals repeatedly asked one basic question: Should a mother always meet her baby's demands for her presence and attention? The fear is that too much attention will lead to spoiling.

The Bowlby/Ainsworth position is the same as Gesell's. Evolution has provided infants with signals and gestures that promote healthy development, and it is wisest to respond to them. As parents, we should follow our impulse to go to our babies when they cry, to return their smiles, to talk back when they babble, and so on. Infants are biologically prepared to guide us with respect to the experiences they need, and our relationships with them will develop most happily when we follow their cues.

As indicated, this position is buttressed by the research of Ainsworth and others. Parents who respond sensitively and promptly to their infants' signals tend to produce babies who, at 1 year of age, are securely attached. In home settings, these babies cry less than other babies and are relatively independent. They seem to have developed the feeling that they can always get the parents' attention when necessary, so they can relax and explore the world. Such infants do, to be sure, monitor the parents' whereabouts; the attachment system is too strong to ever completely shut down. But even in new settings, they do not worry excessively about the mother's presence. Instead, they use her as a secure base from which to explore. They venture away from her to investigate the surroundings, and even though they glance back at her and perhaps return to her from time to time, it is not long before they venture forth once again. "The picture," Bowlby said, is "that of a happy balance between exploration and attachment" (1982, p. 338).

Parents, Bowlby said, can in fact produce a spoiled or overmothered child. But they do not accomplish this by being too sensitive and responsive to the baby's signals. If we look closely, we see that the parent is taking all the initiative. A parent might insist on being close to a child, or showering the child with love, whether the child wants it or not. The parent is not taking his or her cues from the child (p. 375).

In recent years, many parents have found a new way to be intrusive. They provide their infants and toddlers with all kinds of early stimulation, from flash cards to computers, in an effort to accelerate their children's intellectual development. Ainsworth believed that such parental behavior is unhealthy because it takes too much control away from the child (Karen, 1994, p. 416).

Parents can be more helpful, Ainsworth and Bowlby say, by giving children opportunities to pursue their own interests. Parents can frequently do this simply by being available to the child, by providing the child with a secure base from which to explore. When, for example, a young girl wants to climb some large rocks, or wade into the ocean surf, the parent's presence is necessary for the sake of the child's safety and to help out if called on. But the child doesn't want or need the parent's supervision or instructions. All she needs is the parent's patient availability. This alone gives her the assurance she needs to boldly try out new activities and explore the world on her own.

EVALUATION

Darwin argued that humans share many emotions and cognitive capacities with other species, reflecting our common ancestry. Darwin's position was revolutionary at the time, and it still meets with resistance today. Many scientists believe that our species is vastly different from and superior to other animals (Balcombe, 2006, pp. 25-27). Despite this sentiment, Bowlby emphasized the similarities between attachment behavior in humans and other animals. When a human child follows her mother and cries out when separated, the child is engaging in behavior similar to that of ducklings, goslings, fawns, young monkeys and chimpanzees, and numerous other young animals.

Adopting this perspective, Bowlby cast children's behavior in a new light. Prior to Bowlby, people often saw the child's need to stay close to a parent as merely babyish and immature. But Bowlby suggested that it became part of our species' innate make-up because it served the same adaptive function as in other species: It provided children with protection. If human children had lacked the need to maintain proximity to their parents, many of them would have died.

If a need is part of an organism's biological nature, it is important that the need be met. If we meet a child's need for nutritious food, the child grows up healthier than if the need is frustrated. Bowlby, Ainsworth, and their colleagues have tried to show that the same principle applies to attachment. When caregivers are available in case their children need them, and are responsive to their children's cries and other attachment gestures, the children develop well. They are relatively independent at 1 year of age and generally approach life with courage and initiative in the years that follow. To be sure, all the evidence isn't overpowering, but it's largely consistent with the Bowlby/Ainsworth position.

This does not mean that everyone agrees with the Bowlby/Ainsworth viewpoint. Jerome Kagan (1984) has argued that Ainsworth ignores the role of innate temperament. Kagan says that the avoidant infants, for example, ignore the mother in the Strange Situation not because they are defending themselves against rebuffs but because they are innately fearless. However, attachment theorists have mounted a good deal of evidence suggesting the patterns of attachment cannot be reduced to innate temperament (Vaughn, Bost, & van IJzendorn, 2008).

As attachment theory moves forward, I hope writers will clarify the relationship between attachment and love. Bowlby (1979, p. 130) and others (see Feeney, 2008) sometimes write as if all the nuances of love can be reduced to the attachment model. This is doubtful. Love can include sexual desire, perceptions of beauty, and a host of feelings and fantasies that extend beyond attachment, which is more limited to one's faith in another's support. True, attachment and love can overlap, but we need clear discussions of when this overlap occurs and when it does not.

Nevertheless, attachment theory has produced great insights. Moreover, Bowlby's general approach, which centers on the continuity of human behavior with that of other animals, can be applied to other areas. I will conclude by suggesting how this approach can deepen our understanding of children's play.

Extending Bowlby's Approach: The Case of Play

Play, especially free, physically active play, is endangered today. Educational policymakers believe children should be doing more important things—namely, mastering academic skills. Schools have therefore largely eliminated play from kindergartens (Miller & Almon, 2009). Many schools also have eliminated or reduced recess in the elementary grades. Parents, too, are often willing to sacrifice play for early academic instruction, which they believe will give their children a jump-start on future success.

But is children's play expendable? Or is it an innate need that must be respected for children to develop fully?

First, let us consider play in nonhuman species. One of the remarkable facts about play is that it is ubiquitous in mammals, especially young mammals. We see it in young chimps, monkeys, cats, dogs, wolves, sheep, goats, rats—every mammal one can think of. Play also is common in birds. Even octopuses have been seen at play (Balcombe, 2006).

What's more, the animals appear to be innately driven to play. If you have observed kittens or puppies, I bet this has been your impression. I was recently struck by the play of a baby goat, Boomer, who was born on the farm animal sanctuary my wife Ellen and I founded. Within 10 days after birth, Boomer scampered about and performed jumping stunts. He climbed on rocks and tried jumping down, forward and backward, spinning in different directions before he landed. When he ran about, he periodically leapt into the air and threw his legs out in new ways. All the while, his mother kept an eye on him but she never intervened. I had never seen the other goats (all adults) engage in such antics. Boomer clearly hadn't learned his maneuvers from the others. He was inwardly motivated to perform them.

Scholars have entertained various hypotheses on the adaptive value of play. One key possibility is that play develops the capacity to improvise and therefore enables animals to handle unexpected events. If Boomer had to jump from a rock to escape a predator, he would have a number of acrobatic alternatives at his disposal (Spinka, Newberry, & Bekoff, 2001).

What, then, are the implications for humans? In evolutionary theory, the fact that play is found in all other mammals is highly significant. It suggests that the human need to play didn't just develop in our species' unique cultural or evolutionary history, after we branched off from other species. Rather, the need to play, like much of our physical structure, is rooted in the ancestry we share with other mammals.

Moreover, play in human children probably has served a similar adaptive function—the development of the capacity to improvise. To be sure, human children don't just run, jump, and engage in physical play like other young animals do. Human children also make use of symbolic fantasy, as when they use sticks to represent people and create imaginary scenarios. But the urge to improvise—and to create and to imagine—has undoubtedly helped our species survive, and the urge may be an evolutionary continuation of a similar drive in other young animals.

If the human child's play expresses an innate urge or need, we should see consequences of permitting, rather than frustrating, it. Several studies suggest that preschool play enhances cognitive capacities such as problem solving and creativity, as well as the ability to see things from others' perspectives (Hirsh-Pasek et al., 2009; Taylor & Carlson, 1997). When children are deprived of play, they seem to become depressed and stressed out, but more research is needed to document this possibility (Ginsburg, 2007).

Additional evidence that play is an innate drive comes from George Eisen's (1990) little-known account of children in the ghettos and in the concentration camps of the Holocaust. One might suppose that hunger, anguish, and terror would have completely suppressed their desire to play, but this did not happen. Summarizing the diaries and reports of victims, Eisen says, "Play burst forth spontaneously and uncontrollably without regard to the external situation" (1988, p. 66). Lacking manufactured toys, the children made their own—out of mud, snow, rags, and bits of wood. When a skeptical interviewer asked a little girl how she could have played in Auschwitz, her face lit up and she said, "But I played! I played with nothing! With the snow! With the balls of snow!" (p. 72).

In the Lodz ghetto, children played games with cigarette boxes, which became treasures. One observer wrote, "Children's eyes beg for those boxes, children's hands reach out for them" (Eisen, 1988, p. 69). Hanna Levy-Haas, an inmate of the Bergen Belsen concentration camp, concluded that children's yearning for play is an "instinctual impulse." "I feel," she wrote, "it is an urge that springs from the soul of the children themselves" (pp. 60–61).

It seems quite possible, then, that the child's urge to play is just as innate in the human child as in other animals. If so, educational policymakers who ignore it ignore a fundamental and creative aspect of our species.

CHAPTER 4

Montessori's Educational Philosophy

BIOGRAPHICAL INTRODUCTION

Most of the developmentalists we discuss in this book had ideas on education, but only Maria Montessori dedicated herself to the actual teaching of children. Montessori (1870–1952) was born in the province of Ancona, Italy. Her father was a successful civil servant with traditional ideas on the role of women in society. Her mother, in contrast, hoped that Montessori would go as far as she could in life. It was this hope that took hold. It is said that when Montessori was seriously ill as a 10-year-old, she told her anxious mother, "Don't worry, Mother, I cannot die; I have too much to do" (Kramer, 1976, p. 28). At the age of 26, Montessori became the first woman physician in Italy's history.

Montessori's first professional interest was in mental retardation. She was impressed by the extent to which institutionalized children with this diagnosis hungered for experience; she felt they might be teachable if the right methods were used. She read as much as she could find on mental retardation and education in general and found that her own intuitions had guided an earlier line of educators, including Johann Heinrich Pestalozzi, Edouard Séguin, and Friedrich Froebel—educators who had worked in the spirit of Rousseau. Their writings helped convince Montessori that we cannot simply begin teaching children with developmental delays the things we think they ought to know, such as reading and writing. This will lead only to frustration. Instead, we must first simply observe the children and take note of their natural tendencies and spontaneous interests. Then we will be in a position to take advantage of the children's own natural inclinations and ways of learning. For example, Séguin found that children with developmental delay, like typically developing children at younger ages, are most interested in objects that stimulate their senses and permit physical activity. Accordingly, he gave them objects to place in different-sized holes, beads to thread, pieces of cloth to button and lace, and other concrete and useful tasks (Kramer, 1976, p. 61).

Montessori followed Séguin's approach, using many of his materials and trying out new materials of her own. To her delight, this new approach worked, and she ventured to teach more difficult matters, including reading and writing, in the same way. Since the children with developmental delay seemed to learn best by touching and feeling objects, she gave them wooden script letters that they liked to run their hands over again and again. By such methods, she taught many of the children to read and write as skillfully as typical school children of the same age.

During her work with the children with developmental delay, Montessori worked closely with another physician, Dr. Giuseppe Montessano, with whom she had a love affair. The result was a son, Mario. Montessori and Montessano never married, apparently because his parents objected (Kramer, 1976, p. 92). At that time in Italy, news of an illegitimate child would have ruined her career, so she followed the advice of her friends and secretly sent Mario to a wet nurse in the country. She did continue to visit her son, who later became an important educator in the Montessori movement. Nevertheless, the episode threw Montessori into a crisis, which she weathered by deepening her Catholic faith.

In 1907 Montessori took over responsibility for educating children who lived in a tenement in the slums of San Lorenzo, a section of Rome. There, she established a school for over 50 extremely poor children—the sons and daughters of unemployed laborers, beggars, prostitutes, and criminals. In this school—called the Casa dei Bambini, or Children's House—Montessori continued to develop her ideas and techniques, and she was so successful that by 1913 she was one of the most famous women in the news. It seemed that her ideas were about to change the course of education throughout the world. However, her ideas apparently turned out to be too radical for the educational mainstream, and within 5 years she was all but forgotten except by a small band of followers. It was not until the 1960s that her work once again began to catch the attention of psychologists, educators, and the general public (Kramer, 1976; Lillard, 1972).

THEORY OF DEVELOPMENT

Although Montessori's interests were more practical than theoretical, she did develop a definite theoretical position, one that owed much to Rousseau. She argued that we are wrong to assume that children are whatever we make them, for children also learn on their own, from their own maturational promptings (Montessori, 1936a, p. 22; 1949, pp. 17, 223). And, like Rousseau, she argued that children often think and learn quite differently from adults (Montessori, 1936b, p. 69).

A central component of Montessori's theory is the concept of *sensitive periods*. Sensitive periods are similar to critical periods; they are genetically programmed blocks of time during which the child is especially eager and able to master certain tasks. For example, there are sensitive periods for the acquisition of language and for the beginning use of the hand. During these periods, the child works with all her might at perfecting these abilities. And, "if the child is prevented from enjoying these experiences at the very time when nature has planned for him to do so, the special sensitivity which draws him to them will vanish, with a disturbing effect on development" (Montessori, 1949, p. 95).

The Sensitive Period for Order

During the first sensitive period, which takes place primarily during the first 3 years, the child has a strong need for order.[1] As soon as children can move about, they like to put objects where they belong; if a book or a pen is out of place, they resolutely put it back. And even before this, they often become upset at the sight of something out of order. Montessori told, for example, of a 6-month-old girl who cried when a visitor put an umbrella on the table. The girl looked at the table and cried for some time. She became calm only when the mother, with a flash of insight, put the umbrella on the rack where it belonged (Montessori, 1936b, p. 50).

To us, such reactions, which are quite common, seem silly. This is because the adult need for order is on a different plane. For the adult, order provides a certain measure of external pleasure, but for the young child, it is essential. "It is like the land upon which animals walk or the water in which fish swim. In their first year [infants] derive their principles of orientation from their environment which they must later master" (p. 53).

The Sensitive Period for Details

Between 1 and 2 years of age, children fix their attention on minute details. For example, they detect small insects that escape our notice. Or, if we show them pictures, they seem to disregard the main objects, which we consider important, and focus instead on tiny objects in the background. This concern for details signals a change in children's psychic development. Whereas they were at first attracted to gaudy objects and brilliant lights and colors, they are now trying to fill in their experience as completely as possible. To adults, the small child's concern for the minutest details is perplexing. It is further evidence that a child's "psychic personality is far different from our own, and it is different in kind and not simply in degree" (Montessori, 1936b, p. 69).

---

[1]Montessori was rather vague about the ages of her sensitive periods, so the ages listed in this chapter are not definite.

The Sensitive Period for the Use of Hands

A third sensitive period involves the use of the hands. Between about 18 months and 3 years of age, children are constantly grasping objects. They particularly enjoy opening and shutting things, putting objects into containers and pouring them out, and piling objects up (Montessori, 1936b, p. 83). During the next 2 years or so, they refine their movements and their sense of touch. For example, 4-year-olds enjoy identifying objects by touching them with their eyes closed—a game that has far greater interest for the child than the adult (Montessori, 1948a, pp. 127, 229).

The Sensitive Period for Walking

The most readily visible sensitive period is for walking. Learning to walk, Montessori said, is a kind of second birth; the child passes from a helpless to an active being (Montessori, 1936b, p. 77). Children are driven by an irresistible impulse in their attempts to walk, and they walk about with the greatest pride as they learn how.

We frequently fail to realize that walking, like other behaviors, means something different to the child than it does to us. When we walk, we have a destination in mind; we wish to get somewhere. The toddler, in contrast, walks for the sake of walking. For example, the child may walk up and down the staircase, over and over. The child does not walk to get somewhere, but to "perfect his own functions, and consequently his goal is something creative within himself" (p. 78).

The Sensitive Period for Language

A fifth sensitive period—and perhaps the most remarkable one of all—involves the acquisition of language. What is remarkable is the speed with which children learn such a complex process. To learn a language, children must learn not just words and their meanings, but a grammar, a system of rules that tells them where to place the various parts of speech. If, for example, we say, "The tumbler is on the table," the meaning we give those words derives from the order in which we say them. If we had said, "On tumbler the is table the," our meaning would have been hard to grasp (Montessori, 1949, p. 25). The rules underlying grammars are so elusive and abstract that linguistic scholars are still trying to understand them in a formal way. Yet children master them without much thinking about it. If a child is exposed to two languages, the child masters them both (p. 111).

Because the child's ability to grasp language is so great, Montessori concluded that the child must be endowed with a special kind of language receptivity or "mechanism" (p. 113). This mechanism is very different from anything in the mental life of the older child or the adult. Whereas we learn a second language with great deliberation, consciously struggling to memorize rules regarding tenses, prefixes, modifiers, and so on, the child absorbs language *unconsciously.*

From Montessori's descriptions, the child's language acquisition sounds very much like a kind of imprinting. At a certain critical time—from the first few months of life until $2\frac{1}{2}$ or 3 years—children are innately prepared to absorb sounds, words, and grammar from the environment. "The child *absorbs* these impressions not with his mind, but with his life itself" (p. 24). Sounds create impressions of incredible intensity and emotion; they must set in motion invisible fibers in the child's body, fibers that start vibrating in the effort to reproduce those sounds (p. 24). We adults can hardly imagine what this experience is like, except perhaps by recalling the feeling we get when we are profoundly moved by a symphony, and then imagining a similar feeling that is several times stronger. This particular sensitivity for language comes into play during the first 3 years or so, and then is gone.

Montessori suggested that because language acquisition is governed by innate, maturational factors, children develop language in the same stages no matter where they grow up (p. 111). For example, they all proceed from a stage of babbling to a stage where they begin speaking words. Next, they enter a stage in which they put two-word sentences together (e.g., "Boy go"), and there follows a period in which they master increasingly complex sentence structures.

These stages, Montessori emphasized, do not emerge in a gradual, continuous manner. Instead, there are several times during which the child seems to be making no progress, and then new achievements come in explosions. For example, the child bursts out with a number of new words, or suddenly masters a set of rules for forming parts of speech, such as suffixes and prefixes, in a sudden explosion (p. 114).

Between the ages of about 3 and 6 years, children no longer absorb words and grammar unconsciously, but they still are in the general sensitive period for language. During this time they are more conscious of learning new grammatical forms and take great delight in doing so (see Figure 4.1).

FIGURE 4.1
Some early sensitive periods.

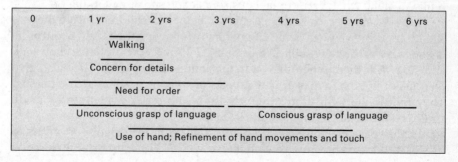

By the time the child is 5 or 6, then, and is ready for the traditional school, the child has already learned to talk. "And all this happens without a teacher. It is a spontaneous acquisition. And we, after he has done all this by himself, send him to school and offer as a great treat, to teach him the alphabet!" (p. 115). We are also so presumptuous as to focus on the child's defects, which are trivial in comparison to the child's remarkable achievements. We see how adults assume that what they teach the child amounts to everything and how they grossly underestimate the child's capacity to learn on her own.

EARLY EDUCATION IN THE HOME

At various sensitive periods, then, children are driven by an inner impulse to independently master certain experiences. The goal of education is to assist this process. Since children do not ordinarily enter nursery or Montessori schools until they are 2 or 3 years old, parents and caretakers are really the first educators.

To be of help, we do not necessarily need a formal knowledge of child psychology. What we need is a certain attitude. We need to realize that it is not our job to direct our children's learning, for we must, above all, respect their efforts at independent mastery. We must have faith in their powers of inner construction. At the same time, we do not have to simply ignore or neglect our children. What we can do is give them the opportunities to learn what is most vital to them. We can watch for their spontaneous interests and give them the chance to pursue them.

For example, Montessori (1936b, p. 49) told about a nurse who pushed her 5-month-old girl in the carriage through the garden. Each day, the girl was delighted to see a white marble stone cemented to an old gray wall. Apparently the girl took pleasure in her discovery that the stone was in the same place; she was developing her sense of order in the world. In any case, the nurse, noting the girl's interest, stopped each day to permit the child to look at the sight. The nurse did not just push the girl along at her own pace, but let the infant's spontaneous interest guide her. She was not teaching the child in the ordinary sense, but she was behaving like the ideal teacher. She was giving the baby the opportunity to make whatever spontaneous connection she was working on.

To take another example, parents can help their children during the sensitive period for walking. Some parents enjoy following their child about as he or she masters this new skill. These parents follow their children as they walk and stop with them when they stop to examine new sights. They also give their children time to master new aspects of walking, such as stair-climbing. They follow their children's own rhythms and enjoy watching the pride children take in mastering new skills (chap. 11).

Other parents, however, fail to give their children full opportunities to master walking on their own and in their own way. Some try to teach the child to walk—a practice that probably gives the child the sense that his or her own efforts are inadequate. Or parents fail to realize what walking means to the child; they assume the child, like themselves, wants to get somewhere. So they pick up their children and carry them, or push them in strollers, so as to reach their destination more rapidly. Or parents become afraid of where the child's walking may lead, so they surround the child with safeguards, such as playpens (chap. 11).

Children, of course, do eventually learn to walk, but the parental reactions affect the children's feelings about their inner rhythms and independence. In one case, they gain the feelings of freedom and pride that come from mastering an important skill on one's own. In the other case, they find that their own efforts at mastery produce negative reactions. The result may be a lingering inhibition with respect to one's inner promptings. It is possible that later athletic ability and physical grace are related to the manner in which children first learn to walk.

Once the child can walk easily, she can venture outdoors and explore the natural settings around her. Montessori was deeply impressed by the extent to which nature invigorates the child. Hiking with parents through parks or meadows or climbing hills, 2-year-olds show amazing energy and stamina; they happily cover distances the adults wouldn't have imagined possible. Natural settings also stimulate the young child's powers of observation. While on a walk, the child will frequently stop to examine a brook, an animal, or a fallen branch for long stretches of time, completely absorbed in quiet contemplation. When young children are given opportunities to freely explore and study nature, they become happy and serene. Contact with nature seems to fulfill a vital emotional need (Montessori, 1948a, chap. 4).

THE MONTESSORI SCHOOL

When children are about $2\frac{1}{2}$ years old, they can enter a Montessori school. There, they learn in the same class with children up to age 6 or so—approximately the same age range as in Montessori's Children's House. Increasingly, Montessorians are opening schools so that children can continue with Montessori's more advanced methods—sometimes even through high school. But the ages are still mixed (e.g., 6 to 9) because Montessori found that children enjoy this arrangement.

Independence and Concentration

The goal of education in the Montessori school is the same as that in the home. The teacher does not try to direct, instruct, drill, or otherwise take charge of the child; instead, the teacher tries to give the child opportunities for *independent* mastery. The assumption is that if the school environment contains the right materials—those that correspond to the children's inner needs at various sensitive periods—the children will enthusiastically work on them on their own, without adult supervision.

To create the right environment, Montessori first spent considerable time simply observing children's behavior with respect to various materials. She then retained those that the children themselves told her were the most valuable to them. They told her this in a rather dramatic way; when they came across materials that met deep, inner needs, they worked on them with amazing *concentration*.

Montessori first became aware of the child's capacity for concentrated effort when she saw a 4-year-old girl in the Children's House working on cylinders. That is, the girl was placing different-sized cylinders in the holes of a wooden frame until she had them all in place (see Figure 4.2). Then she would take them out again, mix them up, and start over. All the while she was oblivious to the world around her. After she had repeated this exercise

FIGURE 4.2
A boy works on wooden cylinders.
(St. Michael's Montessori School, New York City, Haledjian photo.)

14 times, Montessori decided to test her concentration. She had the rest of the class sing and march loudly, but the girl simply continued with her work. Montessori then lifted the girl's chair—with the child in it—onto a table. But the girl merely gathered up her cylinders in her lap and kept on working, hardly aware of the disturbance. Finally, after 42 repetitions, the child stopped on her own, as if coming out of a dream, and smiled happily (Montessori, 1936b, p. 119).

After that, Montessori observed the same phenomenon on countless occasions. When given tasks that met inner needs at sensitive periods, the children worked on them over and over. And when they finished, they were rested and joyful; they seemed to possess an inner peace. It seemed that children were achieving, through intense work, their true or normal state; Montessori therefore called this process *normalization* (Montessori, 1949, p. 206). She then made it her goal to create the most favorable environment for this kind of concerted effort.

Free Choice

In preparing her environment, Montessori tried to suspend her own ideas about what children should learn and to see what they selected when given a free choice. Their free choices, she learned, usually led to work on the tasks that most deeply engrossed them. For example, she noticed that the 2-year-olds, when free to move around in the room, were constantly straightening things up and putting them in order. If, for example, a glass of water slipped from a child's hands, the others would run up to collect the broken pieces and wipe the floor (Montessori, 1936b, p. 121). What she observed was their need for order. Accordingly, she altered the environment so they could fulfill this need. She made small washbasins so the children could wash their hands and brushes; she made small tables and chairs so they could arrange them just right; and she lowered the cupboards so they could put their materials away where they belonged. In this way, activities of daily living became part of the curriculum. All the children enjoyed these activities, but the 2-year-olds took them the most seriously. They constantly inspected the room to see if anything was out of place. For them, ordering the environment met the deepest inner need (Montessori, 1948a, p. 48).

Today, the core Montessori materials are largely set, but the teacher still relies heavily on the principle of free choice. Each child goes to the cupboard and selects the apparatus that she wants to work on. The teacher has faith that the children will freely choose the tasks that meet their inner needs at the moment.

Although the teacher permits free choice, the teacher will from time to time introduce a new task to a child who seems ready for it. This is done most delicately. The teacher presents the material clearly and simply and then steps back to observe the child's behavior. The teacher watches for concentration and repetition. If the child does not seem ready for the new task, it is put aside for another day. The teacher must be careful to avoid giving the impression that the child "ought" to learn a particular task; this would undermine the child's ability to follow her own tendencies. If the child does begin to work actively on the material, the teacher moves away and lets the child work independently (Lillard, 1972, pp. 65–68).

The teacher's attitude, Montessori said, is essentially a passive one—that of an observer (Montessori, 1936a, p. 39). He or she spends most of the time simply watching the children, trying to guess each one's particular needs and state of readiness.

Rewards and Punishments

The Montessori teacher, then, is not so much a director but a follower. It is the child who leads the way, revealing what she most needs to work on. In this, the Montessori teacher behaves very differently from the typical teacher, who has set goals for the children and tries to take charge of their education.

The typical teacher often finds that children lack enthusiasm for the things they are asked to learn. The teacher therefore relies heavily on external rewards and punishments—praise, grades, threats, and criticism. Yet these external inducements often seem to backfire. Quite often, children become so concerned with external evaluations—so afraid of getting wrong answers and looking stupid—that they cannot concentrate deeply on their work. Driven by such pressure, they will learn a certain amount of material, but they can easily come to dislike school and the learning process (Holt, 1964; Montessori, 1948a, p. 14).

Equally damaging, external evaluations rob children of their independence. Children soon begin looking to external authorities, such as the teacher, to know what they should do and say. Montessori felt that authorities use rewards and punishments primarily to make the child submissive to their will. Like Rousseau, she wondered how a child who becomes anxious about external approval will ever learn to think independently or will ever dare to criticize the conventional social order (Montessori, 1948a, pp. 14–18).

Thus rewards and punishments have no place in the Montessori classroom. Montessori teachers trust that if they pay attention to children's spontaneous tendencies, they can find the materials on which children will work intently on their own. The children will do so out of an inherent drive to perfect their capacities, and external inducements will become superfluous.

The traditional teacher often justifies reward and criticism as necessary because children need to know when they are right or wrong. Montessori agreed that children need to learn from their errors, but she did not want the children to have to turn to adults for this information. Accordingly, she developed many materials with a built-in *control of error*. For example, the cylinders, which teach spatial dimensions, have this control. If a child has not put each cylinder in the proper hole, there will be one cylinder left over. When children see this, their interest is heightened. They then figure out how to correct the matter on their own.

Gradual Preparation

Montessori found that children cannot learn many skills all at once. For example, 4-year-olds often desperately want to learn to button their coats and tie their own shoes, as a consequence of their natural urge toward independence, but these tasks are too difficult for them. They lack the fine motor skills.

To deal with such problems, Montessori developed materials that would enable the children to learn skills in steps, at levels they could master. In the case of shoe-tying, she developed a large tying frame (see Figure 4.3) so the children could practice the correct tying pattern with grosser muscle movements (Montessori, 1948a, p. 93). She also utilized the principle of indirect preparation (p. 224). That is, she gave them unrelated tasks, such as cutting vegetables (see Figure 4.3) and holding a pencil, through which they could simultaneously perfect their dexterity. Then, when the children decided to attempt to tie their own shoes, they could readily do so, for they had gradually mastered all the necessary subskills.

Reading and Writing

I have mentioned, by way of illustration, some of the tasks that are part of the Montessori method (e.g., the cylinders and the exercises of daily living). We cannot review every component of the Montessori curriculum in this book, but I will indicate how Montessori approached one important area: reading and writing.[2]

Montessori found that if one begins at the age of about 4 years, children will learn to read and write with great enthusiasm. This is because they are still in the general sensitive period for language. They have just mastered language unconsciously and are now eager to learn all about it on a more conscious level, which reading and writing permit them to do. If, in contrast, one waits until the age of 6 or 7 years to teach written language, the task is more difficult because the sensitive period for language has already passed (p. 276).

Four-year-olds usually master writing before reading. This is because writing is the more concrete and sensory activity and therefore better suits the young child's style of learning (p. 233). Still, one cannot teach writing all at once. If one asks 4-year-olds to make a sound and write it, they will be unable to do so; one must introduce writing through a series of separate preparatory exercises.

---

[2]For a summary of the method for teaching arithmetic, see Montessori, 1948a, chaps. 18 and 19.

FIGURE 4.3
Children at work on a tying frame and an exercise of daily living.
(St. Michael's Montessori School, New York City, Haledjian photo.)

First, the child is shown how to hold a pencil and then practices drawing by staying within outlines. Children love to practice drawing as precisely as possible, for they are in the sensitive period for precise hand movements. They also have been mastering hand-eye coordination through exercises of daily living, such as cutting vegetables, pouring water, and polishing silver.

In another exercise, children trace their fingers over sandpaper letters that are pasted onto blocks of wood (see Figure 4.4). For example, they make the "m" sound and trace it as they do so. The letters are written in script, rather than print, because children find the movements of script freer and more natural. Through this exercise, then, they learn to make the movements of the letters. They love repeating this exercise, for they are still in the sensitive periods for learning about sounds and refining their sense of touch. Frequently they like to close their eyes and trace the letters with their fingers

FIGURE 4.4
A girl works on sandpaper letters.
(St. Michael's Montessori School, New York City, Haledjian photo.)

alone. Six-year-olds, in contrast, derive no particular pleasure from the sandpaper letters, for they have already moved out of the sensitive period for touch. The letters, incidentally, have a built-in control of error, since the child can tell when her finger has strayed off the letter and onto the wood because the wood feels different (p. 229).

In a third exercise, children are given a moveable alphabet that permits them to form the letters of words. For example, they look at a picture of a cat, sound out the letters, and then make the word with the letters. This, too, they repeat endlessly, out of their spontaneous interest in the elements of spoken language (pp. 234–237).

Through these and other separate exercises, then, children learn the various skills involved in writing. When they finally put these skills together and begin to write letters, there usually follows an "explosion of writing." They will write all day long (p. 239).

Writing paves the way for reading. Through writing, children form a muscular and visual memory of the letters and words and therefore can recognize them. Consequently, the 5- or 6-year-old who has learned to write can usually learn to read with very little help from the teacher (Lillard, 1972, p. 122). Children often say that nobody taught them to read at all. Montessori did aid the process, though. Her essential method was to show a word printed on a card, ask the child to sound it out, and then ask the child to sound it out more quickly. In most cases, children rapidly catch on and begin reading words on their own.

During the entire preparatory period for writing and reading, the children do not even look at a book. Then, when they first pick a book up, they can usually begin reading it immediately. Consequently, they avoid all the frustrating experiences that children so often associate with books. There follows an "explosion of reading." Children delight in reading everything they see (Montessori, 1948a, p. 253).

The sensitive care with which Montessori prepared each small step is impressive. The exercises are arranged so that each comes easily to the child, for each corresponds to the child's natural way of learning. Montessori noted that her method contrasts sharply with that of most teachers, who simply give children lessons and then spend most of their time criticizing them for their mistakes. Criticism, Montessori felt, is humiliating and pointless. Instead of criticizing, which only tears down, the teacher should figure out ways of helping children build their skills (Montessori, 1949, p. 245).

Misbehavior

We have emphasized how Montessori teachers prize the child's independence—how they avoid imposing expectations on the child, or even praising or criticizing the child. This is true with respect to *intellectual* work. *Moral* misconduct is another matter. Children are not permitted to abuse the materials or their classmates.

In the Montessori school, respect for the materials and for others usually develops quite naturally. The children know how important the work is for themselves, so they respect the work of the other children. If they do bother a child who is in deep concentration, the child usually insists on being left alone in such a way that they automatically respect this wish. Sometimes, though, the teacher must intervene. Montessori (1948a, p. 62) recommended isolating the child for a moment. In this way, the child has a chance to see the value of the work for others and to sense what he or she is missing. The child will then begin constructive work without any further prompting.

In general, the Montessori view of discipline is different from that of most teachers, who think that it is their job to gain control over the class. They shout: "I want everyone in their seats!" "Didn't you hear what I just told you?" "If you don't behave this instant you won't go out for recess!" The Montessori teacher is not interested in such obedience. Real discipline is not something imposed from without, from threats or rewards, but something that comes from within, from the children themselves as they "pass from their first disordered movements to those that are spontaneously regulated" (p. 56).

Misbehavior, in Montessori's view, usually indicates that the children are unfulfilled in their work. Accordingly, one's task is not to impose one's authority on the children but to observe each child more closely, so one will be in a better position to introduce materials that will meet his or her inner developmental needs. The teacher expects a certain amount of restlessness and distracted behavior during the first days of the year, but once the children settle into their work they become so absorbed in it that discipline is rarely a problem.

Nature in Education

So far I have described Montessori education as if it occurs completely indoors. Actually, Montessori believed that even though children go to school, they still need rich contact with nature outdoors. In making this point, she believed she was bucking a modern trend. Modern societies devalue nature. They have built artificial indoor environments that make us feel so safe and comfortable, we don't realize the extent to which we have lost our connection to the soil, plants, wildlife, and the elements. We do not realize how much our lives have become impoverished because of this loss, and, more tragically, we overlook the importance of nature for children (chap. 4).

The child, Montessori said, has a stronger affinity for nature than we do and benefits more fully from rich contact with it. In natural settings, children spontaneously become quiet and watchful, developing strong powers of patient observation. They also benefit emotionally. The sight of a flower, an insect, or an animal fills the child with joy and wonder, and as the child contemplates such things, she develops a love of life (pp. 70–71).

Box 4–1   Two 6-Year-Old Boys' Views on School Matters

Note the differences in the role of the teacher in the minds of these two children.

1. Who taught you to read?
    Regular School Child: "My teacher."
        Montessori Child: "Nobody, I just read the book, and to see if
                                 I could read it."

2. Do you get to work on anything you want?
    Regular School Child: "No. But we can go to the bathroom any-
                                 time we want. But we're not allowed to go
                                 to the bathroom more than four times."
        Montessori Child: "You can work on anything you want."

3. What would happen if you bothered another kid who was working?
    Regular School Child: "I'd get in trouble from the teacher."
        Montessori Child: "He'll just say, 'Please go away, I'm busy.'"
                                 (What would you do?) "I'd just go away,
                                 'cause I don't want to bother someone
                                 working."

Montessori didn't commit herself to the precise ages at which the child is especially attuned to nature, but she suggested that this special sensitivity lasts at least until adolescence (Montessori, 1948b, p. 35). In any case, she believed it is terrible that modern life separates children from nature so thoroughly that their powers of observation and feelings of love for the world just wither away.

In cities, it is particularly difficult to bring children into contact with untamed nature, so Montessori relied on gardening and animal husbandry, which she introduced in the Children's House (ages 3 to 6) and continued to provide in the elementary school years (Montessori, 1909, chap. 10; 1948a, p. 75). These activities help children develop several important virtues. One is responsibility. Without any prodding, children diligently and lovingly water seedlings and care for animals. Children also learn patient foresight. They see how plants grow in their season and learn to wait for life to unfold according to its own timing. Finally, children strengthen their feeling for nature. As they help things live and grow, they develop the sense that they are a part of living creation, a part of something much larger than themselves. They grow spiritually.

Fantasy and Creativity

Montessori was critical of attempts to enrich children's fantasy lives through fairy tales, fables, and other fanciful stories. She saw fantasy as the product of a mind that has lost its tie to reality (Montessori, 1917, p. 255).

Montessori's position on fantasy would appear to contradict one of her most basic tenets—namely, that we should follow children's natural inclinations. She acknowledged that children have a natural bent toward fantasy. As she put it, the child's "mentality differs from ours; he escapes from our strongly marked and restricted limits, and loves to wander in the fascinating worlds of unreality" (p. 255). But she wanted to help the child overcome these tendencies. When we read children fairy tales or tell them about Santa Claus, we only encourage their credulity. When they hear these stories, furthermore, their basic attitude is passive; they simply take in the impressions we give them. They believe fantastic things because they have not yet developed their powers of discrimination and judgment. And it is just these powers that they need to build.

Montessori did recognize the uses of a creative imagination, such as that possessed by the artist. But the artist's creativity, she maintained, is always tied to reality. The artist is more aware of forms, colors, harmonies, and contrasts than we are. If we wish children to become creative, then, we must help them refine such powers of discrimination (pp. 250–251).

When it came to drawing, for example, Montessori recognized that children have a strong inner urge to draw, but she didn't encourage their "free drawing." Instead, she tried to help them discriminate among forms and colors through activities such as filling in insets and cutting colored paper. Montessori didn't actually suppress children's free drawing, but her own goal was to enhance children's powers of observation and discrimination (Montessori, 1948a, chap. 20).[3]

Elementary and Secondary Education

Montessori is best known for the methods she developed for the Children's House, for children 3 to 6 years of age. These are the ages of the sensitive periods and the unique power to absorb impressions in such a powerful way. But Montessori also developed fairly detailed programs for the elementary school years (ages 6 to 12) and outlined general ideas for education in the adolescent and young adult years. In recent decades, increasing numbers of elementary schools, middle schools, and even some high schools have developed Montessori programs.

Montessori's philosophical approach to elementary and later education was the same as that with respect to young children. She didn't believe that education should begin with adults' ideas about what children should learn (Lillard, 1996, p. 75). When adult goals dominate, too many lessons have nothing to do with children's own developing needs and interests: "We make them listen when they have no desire to hear, write when they have nothing to say,

---

[3]For a discussion of instruction in music, see Montessori, 1948a, chap. 21.

observe when they have no curiosity" (Montessori, 1917, p. 269). Instead, education should continue to nourish the vital growth forces at work within the child. The growing child has an inner need—indeed a yearning—for certain activities to develop herself, and we should make these activities available.

Elementary Education (ages 6 to 12).   At the age of 6 or 7 years, children's developing needs do undergo a major shift. Before this, their deepest needs were to develop personal capacities such as walking, language, and the senses. Now, they become more intellectual and their focuses turn outward. Children want to learn all there is to know about the world, including the social world and what is right and wrong. They want to understand why things are as they are and gain some mastery over the world. In this, they are quite ambitious. They aren't interested in isolated skills and information, as taught in textbooks and workbooks; rather, they want to understand the world in a full way—to grasp the big picture.

Montessori therefore introduced a series of stories, under the heading of the "cosmic plan," which tells about the beginning of the earth, the origins of life, early humans, the growth of technology, and so on. These stories aren't meant to hand down the ultimate truth, but to excite the child's imagination and stimulate the child to ask questions and do research to find answers. For example, the child might want to know how early peoples made their clothes and what food they ate. As with younger children, the Montessori school respects the child's inner urge to find answers and figure things out for herself (Lillard, 1996, chap. 4; Montessori, 1948a, pp. 4, 15).

Six- to 12-year-olds also wish to explore the world by physically moving away from family and school. To meet this need, Montessori proposed activities she called "going out" expeditions. The child, usually with two or three others, carries out research in the community. The children might visit museums, zoos, a planetarium, ponds, libraries, artists' studios, or botanical gardens. The range is wide. Typically, the children go on their own—without the teacher—although the teacher lets relevant people in the community know the children may be coming. She also may give the children safety instructions and perhaps a letter of introduction. The teacher creates a safe and favorable environment for exploration, but the children choose the expeditions and conduct their investigations on their own (Lillard, 1996, chap. 7).

Secondary School.   Montessori didn't fully develop educational methods for the secondary school years, but she did offer some thoughts (e.g., Montessori, 1948b). She believed that the adolescent has a deep, personal need to improve society, but the young person also is plagued by the self-doubts that characterize this stage. Perhaps the single-best means of gaining confidence, Montessori said, is through real, meaningful work—work in which students engage in cooperative business ventures. Because adolescents still have a feeling for nature, an ideal kind of work is farming, and young people should take as much responsibility for running a farm as possible. As an alternative, teenagers might run a hotel in the countryside. They could figure out expenses, fees, guest schedules, publicity, and so forth. Students can learn a considerable amount of academic material through such economic ventures (e.g., math through hotel accounting), and real work gives adolescents a feeling of worth. In today's Montessori secondary schools, educators make room for business activities such as running salad bars and shops (Coe, 1996).

Montessori definitely favored rustic settings, where young people can breathe pure air, get good exercise, and maintain their feelings for nature. But she also valued technological innovation and wanted teenagers to understand how modern farming techniques and other machinery contribute to civilizations. Indeed, she thought that teenagers can gain feelings of self-esteem by identifying with the technological progress of the human race (Montessori, 1948b, pp. 117–118).

EVALUATION

A cornerstone of developmental or child-centered education is a faith in the child—or, better put, a faith in nature's laws guiding the child from within. Rousseau, Pestalozzi, Gesell, and others made this point. Adults shouldn't constantly set goals and try to influence children; they should try to provide tasks that give children opportunities to pursue their naturally emerging interests. Before Montessori, however, no one knew how much children seem to need such tasks, or how much energy they will pour into them. In the Children's House, 3- to 6-year-olds freely chose certain tasks and worked on them with the deepest concentration. And when they finished, they emerged happy, refreshed, and serene. They seemed at peace because they had been able to develop themselves. This intensity of concentration seems to be especially great in the first 6 years of life, but Montessori believed all education should consider what children themselves are most eager to learn.

How effective is Montessori education? In my experience, people who have visited Montessori schools, or have children in them, are impressed. At the early level (ages 3 to 6 years), people are typically struck by the quiet dignity of the classroom. The atmosphere is often like that of a monastery, with everyone so seriously at work. No teacher is shouting, and the children are respectful of one another. Parents see their children becoming increasingly independent and loving school. With respect to elementary school classes, parents and visitors are again impressed by children's purposefulness.

Psychologists want to know, however, about the empirical research on the effectiveness of Montessori education. Good studies are scarce, and they are not terribly conclusive, but they generally indicate that Montessori preschools advance children's test scores about as well or better than other preschool programs. Montessori children may read and spell particularly well.

But researchers have generally been more impressed by the attitudes that Montessori schools foster—concentration, confidence, and independence (Chattin-McNichols, 1992; Evans, 1975, pp. 270–275; Kahn, 1993, p. 18; Miller & Dyer, 1975). One study that included both 5- and 12-year-olds found that Montessori schools fostered greater creativity as well as greater respect for peers (Lillard & Else-Quest, 2006).

If Montessori were to hear of this pattern of results, she probably would be pleased. Her primary goal was not high scores on achievement tests but positive attitudes. If children in Montessori schools typically learn to read and write at an early age, this is fine, but in terms of her overall philosophy, it is just a fortunate happenstance. Montessori chose to teach writing and reading to 4-year-olds only because they revealed an inner urge to write at this young age. If she had found no such urge until, say, age 10, she would not have taught it until then. She did not want to impose tasks on children just because adults are anxious that they learn them as soon as possible. She cared little about how rapidly children learn standard skills or about advancing them along the ladder of achievement tests. Rather, she was concerned with children's attitudes toward learning. She wanted to unharness their natural love for learning and their capacities for concerted and independent work, which unfold according to an inner timetable. As she once said,

> My vision of the future is no longer of people taking exams and proceeding on that certificate from the secondary school to the University, but of individuals passing from one stage of independence to a higher, by means of their own activity, through their own effort of will, which constitutes the inner evolution of the individual. (Montessori, 1936, cited in Montessori, 1970, p. 42)

Although Montessori is well known as a teacher, she is underestimated as an innovative theoretician. She anticipated much that is current in developmental thinking. For one thing, she was among the first to argue for the possibility of sensitive or critical periods in intellectual development. Even more impressive were her insights into language acquisition. Early on, she suggested that children unconsciously master complex grammatical rules and must possess an innate mechanism that enables them to do so—ideas that anticipated the work of Chomsky (see Chapter 17 in this book).

Montessori also was among the first to call attention to the child's need for contact with nature. She said children are especially attuned to nature and benefit from rich exposure to it. She didn't specify a precise sensitive period when this is so, but she believed children need experience with nature to develop their powers of observation and other qualities, such as a feeling of connection to the living world. Today, we find such thoughts among researchers advancing the "biophilia hypothesis" (Wilson, 1993). These scholars speculate that if by some age children don't develop a feeling for nature, this feeling will never take hold. I should add, though, that the number of scholars and researchers investigating such possibilities is still very small. Most research seems guided by our modern society's general assumption that a feeling for nature isn't terribly important. What counts is the child's social development and the intellectual skills she will need for the indoor high-tech workplace. Montessori was among the few scholars ever to take the child's tie to nature seriously (Crain, 1997).

What are the criticisms of Montessori? Dewey (Dewey & Dewey, 1915) thought the Montessori teacher sometimes limits the child's freedom and creativity. When, in particular, a child finds an apparatus too difficult and therefore plays with it in some new way (e.g., rolling cylinders), the teacher will suggest working on something else. The child is not allowed to innovate. Montessori teachers respond that children inwardly feel inadequate with respect to such tasks and will feel far more creative working on tasks for which they are ready. Still, the teachers hope the times they must intervene are few.

More generally, Montessori had little patience for many of the more expressive, emotional aspects of childhood. She not only discouraged free play in the classroom, but fantasy and free drawing as well. Until the elementary years, even social interactions aren't particularly prominent in the classroom. Early Montessori education has an impersonal, matter-of-fact quality. Children become deeply absorbed in their work, which is extremely meaningful to them, but Montessori might have given more recognition to young children's social, imaginative, and artistic development.

In the case of drawing, Montessori overlooked the remarkable qualities of children's works. Young children's spontaneous drawing goes through phases when it is fresh, lively, and beautifully organized (Gardner, 1980). Montessori recognized the natural impulse to draw in the young child and didn't want to hinder it, but she overlooked its natural blossoming.

I believe Montessori also was wrong about fairy tales. Montessori said that fairy tales and imaginary stories encourage the child to depart from reality. She also believed fairy tales force children into passive listening, a state in which they merely receive impressions from adults. But Bettelheim's (1976) book on fairy tales makes a strong case for a different view. Bettelheim argued that the fairy tales do not really teach children to believe in imaginary happenings because children know the fairy tale is make-believe. The stories themselves make this point with their opening lines—"Once upon a time," "In days of yore and times and tides long ago," and so on (p. 117). Children intuitively understand that the story addresses itself not to real, external events, but to the inner realm of secret hopes and anxieties. For example, "Hansel and Gretel" deals with the child's fear of separation and does so in a way that points to a solution. It indirectly encourages children to become independent and use their own intelligence.

Furthermore, the process of listening to a fairy tale may be much more active than Montessori realized. When children listen to a story, they interpret it in their own way and fill in the scenes with their own images. When a story speaks to an issue with which the child is inwardly struggling, the child wants to hear it over and over, much as Montessori children work repeatedly on external exercises. And, finally, children often emerge from the story in a state of calm and peace, as if they have resolved some issue.[4]

Montessori, then, may have undervalued some components of the childhood years, such as play, drawing, and fairy tales. But whatever Montessori may have overlooked, her oversights are minor in comparison to her contributions. Montessori, as much or more than anyone, demonstrated how the developmental philosophies of Rousseau, Gesell, and others can be put into practice. She showed how it is possible to follow children's spontaneous tendencies and to provide materials that will permit them to learn independently and with great enthusiasm. Montessori was one of history's great educators.

---

[4]The process of listening to a fairy tale seems much more active, for example, than most television watching. Television itself usually supplies the child with all the images.

CHAPTER 5

Werner's Organismic and Comparative Theory

BIOGRAPHICAL INTRODUCTION

Heinz Werner (1890–1964) was born and grew up in Vienna, Austria. He was a studious boy who also loved music, taking up the violin when he was 7 years old. After completing the Gymnasium (roughly the equivalent to our high school), Werner thought briefly about becoming an engineer, but he changed his mind and entered the University of Vienna, hoping to become a composer and a music historian. At the university, however, his interests quickly broadened to include philosophy and psychology. This change began one day when he mistakenly went to the wrong lecture hall. He had thought he was attending a music class but found himself listening to a lecture on the philosophy of Immanuel Kant. Since he thought it would be too embarrassing to walk out, he stayed, and he became so engrossed in the topic that he soon decided to major in philosophy and psychology (the two fields were still combined). Still, Werner's interest in music remained, and he wrote his doctoral dissertation on the psychology of aesthetic enjoyment.

In 1917 Werner joined the Psychological Institute at Hamburg, where he participated in lively discussions about a new psychological movement: Gestalt psychology. Gestalt psychologists argued that when we perceive things, we perceive whole forms, *gestalts*, which cannot be analyzed in terms of their separate elements. In Figure 5.1, for example, we directly perceive circles, and it does not matter whether the circles are comprised of dots or dashes. There is a sense in which the circle is a whole pattern that is more than its parts.

Gestalt psychologists went on to assert that our experience of forms is governed by organizing forces in the central nervous system, and they tried to show the principles by which these forces work.

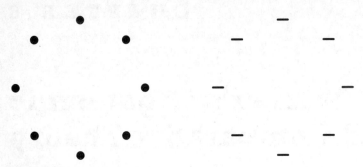

FIGURE 5.1
An example of Gestalt perception: We perceive both forms as circles despite their different elements.

One principle is *closure,* a tendency to complete patterns. Figure 5.2, for example, is not perceived merely as two lines but as a triangle with pieces missing. We tend to perceive it as a whole, meaningful pattern.

Although Werner was strongly influenced by Gestalt psychology, it was not the Gestalt psychology with which we are familiar. That form was brought here by Max Wertheimer, Kurt Koffka, and Wolfgang Kohler, who gave us examples like those just mentioned. These psychologists were sometimes called the Berlin School. Werner identified more closely with the Leipzig School of Felix Krueger, Friedrich Sander, and others—people who are still hardly known in the United States. The Leipzig School agreed with the general Gestalt principles, but it believed the Berlin orientation was not genuinely holistic because it focused too narrowly on perception instead of on the whole, acting, feeling organism. The Leipzig School was also more developmentally oriented. As we shall see, the Leipzig viewpoint had a strong influence on Werner's organismic-developmental writings.

Werner's years at Hamburg were extremely productive, and it was there that he published the first edition (1926) of his famous book, *Comparative Psychology of Mental Development* (2nd edition, 1948). This book was a bold,

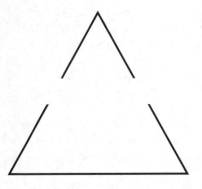

FIGURE 5.2
The Gestalt principle of closure: We tend to close or complete figures into whole patterns.

sweeping venture. In it, Werner tried to show how the concept of development, properly defined, could be used to compare patterns found in humans across various cultures and even between humans and other species.

In 1933 Werner was dismissed from Hamburg by the Nazis because he was Jewish. He spent a few months in Holland and then came to the United States, where he held a number of positions, including that of research psychologist at the Wayne County Training School in Michigan. There, between 1936 and 1943, he did a great deal of research on developmentally delayed and brain-injured children. In 1943 Brooklyn College gave him his first full-time teaching position in the United States, assigning him to what we would now consider the ridiculously low rank of instructor. Werner was simply not recognized here as the great theorist he was.

But he continued with his work, and in 1947 Clark University hired him as a professor of psychology and education. At Clark he found a true intellectual home, working with sympathetic colleagues and inspired students. Former students remember Werner as a formal but kindly man who was extremely open-minded and had a rare ability to draw out the best in his students (Franklin, 2004; Witkin, 1965).[1]

WERNER'S VIEW OF DEVELOPMENT

Werner wanted to tie development to both an organismic and a comparative orientation. We first review his conception of development and then relate it to these two orientations.

Psychologists usually talk about development in loose ways, but Werner believed the concept needed a precise definition. Development, he argued, refers to more than the passage of time; we may grow older but without developing. Furthermore, development refers to more than increases in size; we may grow taller or fatter, but such growth is not necessarily developmental. Development involves changes in structure, which may be defined according to the *orthogenic principle:*

> Whenever development occurs, it proceeds from a state of relative lack of differentiation to a state of increasing differentiation and hierarchic integration. (Werner & Kaplan, 1956, p. 866)

Let us look at these two concepts—differentiation and hierarchic integration—more closely. *Differentiation* occurs when a global whole separates into parts with different forms or functions. For example, the embryo begins as a global unit that separates into different organs, such as the brain, heart,

---

[1]Margery Franklin and Joseph Glick provided helpful comments and recollections for this biographical introduction.

liver, and kidney. Similarly, the fetus's motor activity becomes more differentiated when its limbs and trunk no longer all move together in one "mass action" but move separately.

As behavior becomes differentiated, it also becomes *hierarchically integrated*. That is, behaviors come under the control of higher regulating centers. In the fetus, for example, limb and trunk movements become not only more differentiated but also more fluid and coordinated as they come under the control of higher organizing circuits in the central nervous system (Hofer, 1981, pp. 97–100).

The orthogenic principle describes behavior in many realms. For example, when children begin to draw, they first make the same kinds of back-and-forth movements, producing circular scribbles. Their drawing becomes more differentiated as they experiment with different kinds of strokes. We also see hierarchic organization when their drawing comes under the control of their plans. Instead of drawing away and deciding what it looks like afterward, they start off with a plan or image that guides their strokes.

The orthogenic principle applies to personality development, too. For example, adolescents differentiate between the goals they want to pursue in life and those they do not. The goals they select then assume hierarchical control over much of their daily behavior. A girl who decides to become a doctor, for instance, will organize many of her daily activities with this goal in mind. Until young people do settle on their goals, they often feel their lives lack coherence and structure. They complain they cannot find themselves. They need a purpose to guide them.

A Major Theme: Self-Object Differentiation

Werner wrote extensively on the many applications of the orthogenic principle. However, he was particularly interested in the process of self-object differentiation, the gradual process by which children separate themselves from the environment. This process often seems to progress through three levels. These levels roughly correspond to infancy, childhood, and adolescence, but Werner was not concerned with ages; he was interested only in differing developmental patterns.

Initially, at the *sensorimotor-affective* level, infants hardly experience an outside world apart from (differentiated from) their own immediate actions, sensations, and feelings. They know objects only insofar as they are sucking them, touching them, grasping them, and so on. If, as Piaget (1936b) showed, a young baby loses hold of a toy, the baby will act as if the toy no longer exists. There is little sense of objects existing apart from oneself.

Gradually, children come to function on a more purely *perceptual* level, perceiving things "out there," apart from themselves. They stand back and look at objects, point to them, ask their names, and describe them. They gain a measure of objectivity. Still, their perceptions remain strongly bound up with their actions and feelings. For example, Katz and Katz (cited in Werner, 1948, p. 383) observed that preschool children take a great interest in furniture that can be used for climbing and jumping, as well as houses in which acquaintances live, whereas other furniture and houses hardly seem to enter into their awareness.

The extent to which children's perceptions are colored by their personal needs and actions is sometimes revealed by the words they use. For example, 4-year-old Laura called a certain tree the "resting tree" because she often sat under its cool branches on the way home from school. She called the yard where the "resting tree" was located the "resting place," and the family who lived there "the resting people." Her perceptions were still bound up with her personal needs and activities (Smart & Smart, 1978, p. 89).

To gain the most detached, objective view of the world, we must rise to a *conceptual level* of thought. That is, we must begin to think in very general and abstract dimensions, such as height, volume, and velocity, which lend themselves to precise measurement. For example, the rule "area = height × width" enables us to quantify space objectively, without any reference to our personal feelings about it. Such detached, impersonal analysis has long been the goal of Western science.

Returning to Primitive Levels

Werner believed development is teleological, which means that it directs itself toward mature end-states. Humans, therefore, naturally progress toward abstract, conceptual modes of thought. This does not mean, however, that once we develop these intellectual operations, we must rely on them alone. If we did, our lives would become empty, abstract, and barren. The world would become, in Whitehead's words, "a dull affair, soundless, scentless, colorless" (1929, p. 88). We would long for the kinds of thinking that characterized earlier levels, in which images were tied to feelings, sensations, and actions.

Sometimes, Werner said, adults preserve the rich, earlier kinds of experience to a greater extent than it might initially seem. A biologist might write up her research results in a highly abstract manner, but her research is actually based on direct perceptions of living organisms. Her abstract formulations bring order to her sensory impressions, which remain in the background (Werner, 1948, p. 52).

Werner also said we return to earlier, richer modes of experience in dreams or in states induced by hallucinogenic drugs (1948, p. 82). In his later writings, however, Werner (1957; Werner & Kaplan, 1963) increasingly emphasized a new concept—*microgenesis.*

Microgenesis refers to the developmental process that occurs each time we confront a task, such as perceiving an object or figuring out a problem.

In each instance, our mental process goes through the same sequences that characterize development during the life span. That is, we begin with vague, global impressions that are fused with feelings and bodily sensations. These impressions give way to more differentiated perceptions, which finally become integrated into a coherent whole. Microgenesis, then, is a self-renewing process in which we continually begin at undifferentiated levels.

Microgenesis often occurs so rapidly that we are unaware of the process, but we may become aware of it at times, as when we find ourselves in new, unfamiliar settings. Imagine, for example, that we enter a foreign city. At first our perception is likely to be global, diffuse, and heavily colored by feelings. We are struck by the strange sounds, lights, odors, shapes, and colors. We feel disoriented, vaguely wondering if we are safe and how we are going to find anything. Soon, however, our picture of the city becomes more differentiated; we identify a hotel, a restaurant, a bus route. And finally we may begin to see how the various parts of the city are interrelated; we form a more conceptual map of the city. Thus, within a fairly short time, our knowledge of the city goes through a developmental process similar to that which characterizes development during childhood.

Werner suggested that people differ in the extent to which they engage in the microgenetic process. Some people have greater *microgenetic mobility;* they can regress farther back and fully utilize both primitive and advanced forms of thinking. Above all, this ability to regress characterizes the creative person, the person who is willing to start anew. Many creative scientists, for example, have admitted that they begin thinking about problems on a pre-conceptual level, starting out with vague intuitions, hunches, dreamlike images, and gut-level feelings (Dubos, 1961). As a group, the ethologists make a special point of forming rich perceptions of animals with whom they feel a certain empathy before detaching themselves and moving on to a formal, con-ceptual plane (Lorenz, 1981; Tinbergen, 1977).

Some thinking, in contrast, is distinctly lacking in microgenetic mobil-ity. Schizophrenic patients regress to primitive forms of thought, but they get stuck there and their thinking remains disorganized. Conversely, many of us seem to shift too quickly to conventional, rational modalities, so our thinking lacks richness and creativity. In general, Werner said, "[T]he more creative the person, the wider his range of operations in terms of developmental level, or in other words, the greater his capacity to utilize primitive as well as advanced operations" (1957, p. 145).

The Organismic Orientation

We have seen how mental processes such as perception and cognition emerge from contexts in which they are fused with actions, sensations, and feelings. This occurs in the development of the child, and it keeps recurring, microge-netically, in us as adults. For Werner, this conception of development coincided with a position to which he was deeply committed—the holistic or organismic position. Essentially, this position maintains that we should, as far as possible, study psychological processes as they occur within the whole acting, feeling, striving organism. We should not, for example, study perceptual activities in isolation, but as they emerge from the more primitive matrices of action and feeling in which they are embedded.

Despite Werner's appeals, the organismic orientation has been more the exception than the rule in psychology. Researchers usually study processes such as perception, cognition, language, and memory as if they were self-contained activities. This compartmentalized approach, Werner noted (1948, p. 49), is convenient, and it does not strike us as too inappropriate when studying adults because adult functioning has become fairly differentiated. For example, as adults we can usually distinguish between our thoughts and our feelings, so we believe it is all right to study thinking as an isolated activity. But even adults do not become disembodied minds. We still need to know how cognitive processes are related to the rest of the organism. Here, the concept of microgenesis is helpful. Microgenesis indicates how cognitive processes, even in adults, continually emerge from physical, emotional, and sensory experiences.

Compartmentalized research becomes most problematic when we turn to children, for whom the various psychological processes are far less differentiated. The child's perception, for example, is strongly fused with motor action and emotion. A child, upon seeing a wooden triangle, does not see it as we do, as simply a geometric form. Because it looks sharp, it is something one might dig with, or something that is threatening. When we examine and measure the child's "form perception" as an isolated activity, as is usually done, we miss out on the chance to see how it is distinctive in the child's experience. We examine form perception as if it were already differentiated from action and emotion, which it is not (see Wapner, Kaplan, & Cohen, 1973).

The Comparative Approach

Werner wanted to study development not only from an organismic viewpoint but also from a comparative viewpoint. That is, he wanted to show how the orthogenic principle enables us to compare developmental patterns across many diverse areas, including various cultures, species, and pathological states.

Werner was particularly interested in parallels between humans and cultures in their early phases of development. In many ways, he argued, the mental lives of children and indigenous peoples have underlying similarities. Werner said, for example, that the thought of both is often characterized by a lack of differentiation between the self and the external world. Both children and indigeneous peoples may perceive trees, clouds, and wind expressing emotions that they themselves experience. We will discuss such parallels, but as Baldwin (1980) has demonstrated, it is first useful to point to some misunderstandings concerning Werner's purpose.

First, Werner was not trying to show that children and indigenous peoples think in completely identical ways. The thinking of children in industrialized cultures, for example, is not nearly as rich, complex, and fully formed as that of adults in small tribal cultures. Children may have some impressions of the emotions and forces expressed by the natural elements, but they have nothing resembling the complex mythologies of early peoples.

Second, Werner was not advancing a theory of recapitulation (such as that proposed by Rousseau or Haeckel). That is, he did not believe that children resemble indigenous peoples because children are repeating the evolutionary history of the species. He believed that the recapitulation theory takes the similarities between children and people in early tribal societies too literally, ignoring the differences between them.

Werner, moreover, was not interested in evolutionary history itself. That is, he was not interested in *when* behavior appeared, but in its developmental status in a *formal* sense, as defined by the orthogenic principle. In some instances, the thinking of extinct cultures may have been more differentiated than that found in some contemporary cultures. In any event, when Werner used terms such as *primitive, early,* or *advanced,* he was referring to developmental status in terms of a formal, theoretical model.

The greatest problem with Werner's comparative theory is that it seems to have political overtones. When Werner described indigenous peoples as primitive and compared them to children, he seemed to be implying they are inferior.

Werner wanted to avoid such value judgments. He noted (1948, p. 34) that in earlier stable environments, primitive modes of thought were highly adaptive. And, as we saw in our discussion of microgenesis, even Western adults may need to return to primitive levels to think in creative ways. Furthermore, as we shall later see, artists still develop primitive forms of experience and thereby enrich our lives. For Werner, the term "primitive" hardly need carry any negative connotations.

SOME COMPARATIVE STUDIES

Pictorial Imagery

Werner said that children, compared to Western adults, often think in pictures. We can sometimes see this when we ask them to define words. If a 5-year-old is asked to define the word *girl,* he might say, "She has long hair and a dress. She's pretty." The boy's definition is based on a specific pictorial image.

The boy does not yet define the term in broad, conceptual categories ("a young female member of the human species").

Werner observed that pictorial imagery is so dominant in young children that many possess *eidetic* imagery, or what we commonly call photographic memory. Children can describe a scene in such vivid detail that we are amazed to find they are no longer looking at it. Strong forms of eidetic imagery seem to be present in only a minority of children, but many children possess some form of it, and it is very rare in Western adults (Haber, 1969; Werner, 1948, p. 143).

Werner believed that indigenous peoples commonly have had eidetic imagery, but this is difficult to document. In any case, their languages indicate a preference for pictorial images over general categories. There are often few general terms, but many words, that evoke specific images. In one Bantu language, for example, there is no general term "to go," but many specialized words for different kinds of walking. There is a word that means "to walk along slowly and carefully with a convalescent man" and another one that means "to hop across earth seared by great heat" (Werner, 1948, p. 267). One anthropologist observed that the Solomon Islanders would never say anything so general and abstract as, "Five people arrived." They might say, "A man with a large nose, an old man, a child, a man with a skin disease, and a little fellow are waiting outside" (p. 288).

Social scientists have long debated the capacity of indigenous peoples to think in abstract terms. I believe that whenever we look closely at the matter, we find the tribe or society has the capacity to use abstract categories but doesn't always see the point to it. To indigenous peoples, it is frequently much more important to describe objects and events in precise detail. They use words in the way many Western poets and writers do—to depict the world in vivid, picturelike images.

Physiognomic Perception

If there was a single topic on which Werner wrote with the deepest feeling, it was physiognomic perception. We perceive stimuli physiognomically when we react to their dynamic, emotional, expressive qualities. For example, we might perceive a person as happy and energetic or sad and tired. Werner called this perceptual mode physiognomic because it is the physiognomy—the face—that most directly conveys emotion to us, although we may also perceive emotion in other ways—for instance, through a person's posture.

Physiognomic perception is contrasted with *geometric-technical* perception. Here, we perceive objects in terms of shape, length, hue, width, and other objective, measurable properties. Geometric-technical perception is more realistic and matter-of-fact. It is the perceptual modality of the scientist and technician.

As rational adults, we believe physiognomic perception is appropriate only when stimuli are animate. We feel it is silly to perceive emotions in rocks, sticks, cups, and other inanimate objects. Occasionally, of course, we wax poetic and respond to the physical environment physiognomically, as when we say a landscape is majestic or subdued. Usually, however, we perceive the physical environment in a more impersonal, matter-of-fact manner (Werner, 1956).

For children the situation is very different. Children, lacking clear self/environment boundaries, perceive the whole world as full of life and emotion. A child, seeing a cup lying on its side, might say the cup is tired. Watching a stick being broken in two, the child might feel that the stick is being hurt. Or, looking at the number 5, the child might say the number is angry or mean, finding a facial expression in it. Children, Werner (1948) argued, quite naturally experience the inanimate world in terms of the same forces and emotions they feel within themselves (pp. 67–82; see Figure 5.3).

FIGURE 5.3
A 5-year-old's drawing reveals physiognomic perception (the sun is smiling).

Like children, indigenous peoples have felt a strong unity with the rest of the world, and they too have displayed a greater degree of physiognomic perception than adults in modern society. Native Americans, for example, typically grew up feeling that they were one with nature and that everything around them—the wind, the trees, even the stones—possessed life and feeling (Lee, 1959, p. 61). Consequently, they were often shocked at the white people's indifference toward the environment. As an old Wintu woman said,

> We don't chop down the trees. We only use dead wood. But the White people plow up the ground, pull up the trees, kill everything. The tree says, "Don't. I am sore. Don't hurt me." But they chop it down and cut it up. The spirit of the land hates them. . . . The White people destroy all. They blast rocks and scatter them on the ground. The rock says, "Don't. You are hurting me." But White people pay no attention. . . . Everywhere the White man has touched it, the earth is sore. (Lee, 1959, pp. 163–164)

This old woman's attitude is completely different from the geometric-technical approach of the engineer or surveyor. She perceives the environment physiognomically, as teeming with life and emotion.

In advanced cultures, dramatic examples of physiognomic perception may be found in the reports of schizophrenic patients who regress to primitive mental states. These patients may lose their sense of detachment from physical objects and experience them as dangerously alive. One patient looked fearfully at some swinging doors and exclaimed, "The door is devouring me!" (Werner, 1948, p. 81).

So far I have probably managed to convey the impression that physiognomic perception is something fairly strange and unusual—something that most of us have long overcome. And to an extent this is true. As we develop, Werner (1956) said, physiognomic perception is superseded by a geometric-technical outlook. We increasingly come to view the world through the eyes of the engineer or technician. We evaluate things in terms of their measurable properties and practical uses. Even people become categorized in terms of impersonal, quantifiable dimensions. We define them in terms of their IQ, age, income, property holdings, number of dependents, and so on.

Nevertheless, we never lose our capacity for physiognomic perception, and it too develops within us, if at a slower rate than geometric-technical perception. Werner and others have devised some simple demonstrations to show that we can still perceive physiognomic properties in supposedly impersonal forms. Figure 5.4 shows two lines: Which is happy and which is sad? Most adults immediately report that the upwardly moving line expresses gaiety and the downward sloping line conveys sadness. We can see that simple lines—which, of course, are merely inanimate figures—do express feelings through their dynamic patterns.

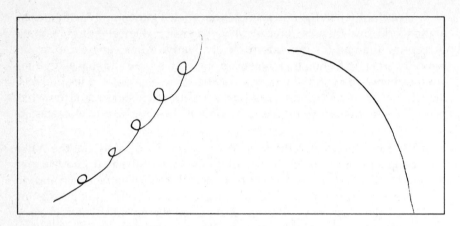

FIGURE 5.4
Lines express feelings. Which is happy and which is sad?

Most of all, we are aware of physiognomic qualities when we perceive them aesthetically, through the eyes of the *artist*. For in modern industrial cultures, it is primarily painters, poets, musicians, and others who alert us to the expressive features of forms, colors, sounds, and movements. They help us experience the sad posture of a willow tree, the anger of thunder, the caress of a tonal pattern, the smile of a sunny sky, and the upward striving of a geometric column (Arnheim, 1954; Werner, 1956).

The extent to which artists develop physiognomic sensitivities is suggested by the painter Wassily Kandinsky:

> On my palette sit high, round rain-drops, puckishly flirting with each other, swaying and trembling. Unexpectedly they unite and suddenly become thin, sly threads which disappear in amongst the colors, and roguishly slip about and creep up the sleeves of my coat. . . . It is not only the stars which show me faces. The stub of a cigarette lying in an ash-tray, a patient, staring white button lying amidst the litter of the street, a willing, pliable bit of bark—all these have physiognomies for me. (Werner, 1948, p. 71)

Because artists like Kandinsky have developed physiognomic capacities, our world is a richer place.

The Unity of the Senses

Physiognomic perception, as we have noted, is based on a unity between oneself and objects. That is, we perceive objects as full of the same dynamic forces we feel within ourselves. Physiognomic perception is also based on *synesthesia,* the syncretic unity of the senses. Sounds, for example, may simultaneously involve several of our senses. A sad tone may seem dark and heavy. A cheerful tone may strike us as bright, clear, and light in weight.

Werner believed that intersensory experiences are developmentally primitive; they exist prior to the differentiation of the senses into separate modalities. If this is so, synesthesia might be especially prominent in children, and Werner offered several anecdotes to this effect. For example, a 4-year-old girl says, "Father talks . . . boom boom boom! As dark as night . . . ! But we talk light, like the daytime . . . bim bim bim!" (Werner, 1948, p. 262). There is also some experimental evidence that synesthesia, especially color hearing, is more common in children than in adults (Marks, 1975; Werner, 1948, pp. 89–91).

Intersensory modes of experience are often well developed among indigenous peoples. In West African languages, for example, a *high pitch* may express something that is fine, pointed, alert, fresh, energetic, loud of color, sharp of taste, quick, or agile. A *low pitch* may express something big, plump, awkward, muggy, dull, colorless, stupid, or slow (Werner, 1948, pp. 259–260).

Intersensory experiences also become prominent in contemporary Western adults who regress to primitive states in psychosis or under the influence of hallucinogens. One subject experimenting with mescaline said, "I think that I hear noises and see faces, and yet everything is one and the same. I cannot tell whether I am seeing or hearing. I feel, taste, and smell the sound. It's all one. I, myself, am the tone" (p. 92).

Intersensory experiences, finally, are the special domain of the artist. The painter Kandinsky, for example, wrote that for him even geometric shapes have "inner tones" and "their own inimitable fragrances" (Werner, 1956, p. 4). And through his great paintings, colors affect us as warm or cold, sharp or soft, and so on. Fine music, too, affects us through many senses, as when tones seem golden or pale, bright or dull, sweet or harsh, sharp or soft, light or heavy.

When we have truly intersensory experiences, Werner added, we do not experience colors or sounds objectively, as "out there," but feel them within our bodies. Colors and sounds invade us or envelop us or fill us up. Werner believed the various senses influence one another through general bodily feelings because "they develop out of a common primitive level . . . that is bodily, motoric, and affective" (Werner, 1934, p. 164).

SYMBOL FORMATION: AN ORGANISMIC VIEW

Although Werner wrote many articles, he published only two books. The first was the *Comparative Psychology of Mental Development* (1948), which I have been summarizing. The other, *Symbol Formation* (Werner & Kaplan, 1963), was on language.

The study of language has mushroomed in recent years, but from Werner's perspective the general approach has been nonorganismic. That is, researchers have focused on the elements of speech and grammar as if these developed in a vacuum, unrelated to a living, acting, feeling organism. Werner believed, in contrast, that language initially emerges out of an undifferentiated matrix that includes bodily, gestural, and affective (emotional) processes. Language does eventually become a relatively separate activity, but it never completely loses touch with its rich organismic grounding.

As the title *Symbol Formation* suggests, Werner's focus was on the formation of symbols. A symbol is a word, image, or action that represents something else—some other object, concept, or event. For example, the word *tree* symbolizes a tree. When we use symbols, we implicitly recognize that the symbol is different from its referent (e.g., the word *tree* is different from the tree itself).

How are symbols formed? Probably the most common view is what might be called the label theory. We simply learn our culture's labels for things. We learn the word *tree* goes with trees, *cup* with cups, and so on. In this view, the connections between symbols and things are purely arbitrary. They are mere conventions handed down to us by our culture.

Werner viewed the process quite differently. He acknowledged, of course, that children do learn the culture's labels, but he argued that symbolic activities initially emerge out of *bodily-organismic* activities—motoric actions, physical and vocal gestures, and feelings. The process of referring to things, for example, begins with the physical act of *pointing*. The child points to an object of interest and says something like "da," inviting the mother to look at it too (Werner & Kaplan, 1963, pp. 70–71).

Many of the child's first "natural" symbols are *motoric imitations*. Children might flutter their eyelids to depict the flickering of lights, or they might tremble their hands to portray the agitation of water stirred by a boat (p. 89).

Most of the child's early symbols, like ours, are sounds they make. These, too, initially emerge out of bodily-emotional actions, such as expressions of pleasure, cries, and calls. For example, a baby in a high chair might call out for a doll that has dropped to the floor. At first she might just cry out, but on later occasions she might say her word for the doll, too (e.g., "Bappa"!).

Babies' first names for objects often center on their actions toward the objects. For example, an 11-month-old girl used the same word for a pin, a breadcrumb, and a caterpillar—apparently because they are all things to be picked up gingerly with one's fingers (p. 118).

Among the most active, dynamic aspects of the world are the sounds animals and things make. It's no surprise, then, that many of the child's own "baby talk" words are *onomatopoeic*—imitations of the sounds. A child might refer to a dog as "wfff," a coffee grinder as "rrrr," and a hammer as "boom" (p. 46).

A bit later, children use expressive intonation to capture other qualities of objects. A girl might speak of tiny objects in a high, peeping voice and large objects in a deep, gruff voice. Or she might say something rapidly or slowly to indicate how fast an object is moving. Werner called such speech *physiognomic* because it depicts the active, expressive aspects of things.

Underlying the child's symbolic activities—her pointing, naming, imitating, and expressing—is a supporting emotional context. This is the presence or availability of the mother (or other loving adult). Without this, the child wouldn't feel safe in the world and could not take a lively interest in describing it (p. 71).

It is clear that children do not feel that their natural symbols are related to objects in an arbitrary manner. The symbol "wfff," for instance, conveys the most striking property of a dog.

When, however, children begin using conventional language, the connection between symbols and referents would seem to dissolve. What, after all, is the inner relationship between the word *hammer* and a hammer? For a while, children may preserve the tie by using combinations of their own natural symbols and conventional words, as when they say "boom-hammer" or "bah-sheep." But with the shift to purely conventional speech, any felt similarity between symbol and referent would seem to disappear.

But Werner believed the tie is never completely broken. In his studies, he found that adults can still respond to words as physiognomic forms that directly express the dynamic, expressive qualities of objects. One man reported that when he said the word *hammer*, the short "ha" seemed to come down sharply on the "mmm," evoking the sensation of hammering (p. 130). Another subject, looking at the German word *wolle* (wool), spoke of the dull, stringy quality of the "ll" (p. 209).

Readers might wonder if these subjects weren't simply giving Werner the responses he wanted to hear. However, writers and poets have also tried to get us to see that words have physiognomic properties. Balzac, for instance, asked us to consider how the sound of an abstract word like *vrai* (true) expresses the feeling-tone of truth itself. Is there not, he asked, in the word

> a fantastic strength of honesty? Does one not find in the short sound which it commands a vague image of modest nakedness, of the inherence of the truth in everything? This syllable breathes forth an indefinable freshness. (Werner, 1948, pp. 257–258)

According to Werner, we may perceive words physiognomically more frequently than we realize. We may do so whenever we first try to recognize them (during the early microgenetic phases of word perception). To investigate this possibility, Werner presented words for a very short time, without giving subjects a chance to recognize them fully, and he found that their impressions were dominated by feelings and bodily reactions. Subjects said that although they couldn't make out a word, it felt "warm," "heavy," "distressing," and so on—qualities they later said corresponded to the word's meaning for them (Werner & Kaplan, 1963, p. 215).

In summary, then, Werner argued that even conventional words are not merely empty, arbitrary labels. They seem to be such only when we examine their external structure in a purely objective manner. Inwardly, we may perceive words as expressive forms that resonate with life and feeling, evoking the same emotional and bodily reactions as their referents. An inner, organismic tie between symbol and referent is maintained.

THEORETICAL ISSUES

We have now reviewed Werner's writing on several topics, including physiognomic perception and the development of language. But Werner was never just interested in particular topics; he was also concerned with the larger theoretical issues that the topics addressed.

The Multilinear Nature of Development

One of Werner's theoretical concerns was whether development is unilinear or multilinear, whether it proceeds along a single line or along many separate lines (Werner, 1957). A consideration of physiognomic perception helped him answer this question.

Physiognomic perception, as we have seen, is attuned to the dynamic and expressive qualities of things. It is an early form of perception, dominant in children, and in our culture is superseded by a more geometric-technical outlook. We may sometimes revert to physiognomic modes, as in moments of creative regression, but we generally rely on more logical, rational modes of thought.

If this were the whole story, we could conclude that development is unilinear; one cognitive mode follows another. Yet physiognomic perception itself develops. In most of us, to be sure, it develops only modestly, since we do not nurture it, but in artists it becomes quite advanced. So we must conceive of development as a multilinear branching-out process, with separate lines following their own course. Figure 5.5 attempts to diagram this conception of development.

The Discontinuity Issue

An even more fundamental issue is whether development is continuous or discontinuous. Basically, when we say change is continuous, we are proposing that we can measure it along a single *quantitative* dimension. Just as we can

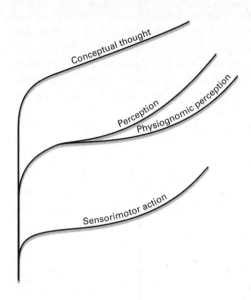

FIGURE 5.5
Werner thought that different lines of development branch out. (Adapted from J. Langer, *Theories of Development.* New York: Holt, Rinehart & Winston, 1969, p. 153.)

measure a child's height with a tape measure, we can measure a child's vocabulary, attention span, memory capacity, and a host of other psychological variables along one quantitative scale. A vast amount of research in developmental psychology has assumed that change is measurable in this manner. To many, the concept of continuous, quantifiable measurement seems to be the essence of science.

Actually, biologists in particular have long recognized that many changes are discontinuous, involving *qualitative* transformations. Early forms emerge into new forms that are different in kind; they have different patterns and modes of functioning. Particularly dramatic examples of qualitative changes are metamorphoses, such as the emergence of a caterpillar into a butterfly. In such cases, many quantitative comparisons become meaningless. It makes no sense, for instance, to measure the speed with which caterpillars can fly. They have their own mode of locomotion.

Since Rousseau, developmentalists have been more like the biologists who emphasize qualitative change. The transformations from childhood to adulthood may not be as dramatic as the metamorphoses, but, as Rousseau argued, "Childhood has its own way of seeing, thinking, and feeling" (1762b, p. 54). If this position is correct, we cannot measure children in terms of an adult yardstick without missing what is unique to the child.

Werner, taking the broadest possible perspective, noted that both quantitative and qualitative changes occur. Like Rousseau, however, he really believed that the most important changes are qualitative. The adult's abstract thought, for example, differs *in kind* from the child's perceptual-motor-affective thinking.

In many respects, comparing the child to the adult is like comparing the artist to the scientist. The child, like the artist, approaches the world through a physiognomic, intersensory, vividly pictorial style. Especially between the ages of about 2 and 7 years, children love to draw, sing, and engage in make-believe (theatric) play, and their activities are energetic and imaginative. Howard Gardner (1980) has shown how children's drawings reach a special kind of perfection. Between the ages of about 5 and 7, they routinely produce drawings that are fresh, lively, and beautifully balanced; the drawings express gaiety, playfulness, and a strong sense of life. Indeed, many great artists have said that they have tried to recapture the artistic qualities of the young child (Gardner, 1973, p. 20). Gardner (1980, p. 99) has called this the "golden period" of artistic development. Then, at about the age of 8 years or so, children's drawings undergo a major change; they become more precise and geometric (Gardner, 1980, chap. 6). It seems that geometric-technical thinking is taking over. The fresh liveliness of the young child is lost (see Figures 5.6 and 5.7).

Young children, to be sure, do not just demonstrate artistic exuberance; they reveal the beginnings of scientific skills as well. There is continuity with later orientations. But young children's dominant outlook seems more naturally

FIGURE 5.6
A 6-year-old boy's drawing of a girl jumping rope (left) expresses liveliness and balance. Howard Gardner (1980) compares it to a work by the master Paul Klee (right), although the child's work is livelier.
(From *Artful Scribbles* by Howard Gardner. Copyright © 1980 by Howard Gardner. Reprinted by permission of Basic Books, a Division of HarperCollins Publishers, Inc. The Klee work is reprinted by permission of the Artists Rights Society.)

Andy, age 6   Andy, age 9

FIGURE 5.7
Andy's drawings illustrate the shift from a livelier to a more
geometric style.

artistic, and it seems almost beside the point to persist in evaluating them in terms of the rational, logical skills of adults, although this is what researchers usually do.

Developmentalists, then, emphasize that development is often discontinuous—that it involves a qualitative change. Such changes need not be sudden. Abstract thinking, for example, may differ in quality from earlier thinking but emerge gradually. Discontinuity only means the change involves a qualitative shift; the suddenness of the change is another matter (Werner, 1957).

Phenomenology

A school of thought with which Werner was very familiar was phenomenology. Phenomenologists believe the first thing we should do when studying children (or anyone else) is to abandon our preconceptions about them. We cannot assume children think as we do; we need to take a fresh look at children themselves. Above all, we need to learn about children's subjective experiences of things. We need to explore their *phenomenal* world—how it appears to them.

Most developmentalists have been phenomenological only up to a point (see Chapter 18). They have believed we should suspend any preconceptions that the child thinks as we do, but they have generally analyzed the child's thinking from the outside instead of trying to see things through the child's eyes. Werner, too, usually described thinking from an external viewpoint (e.g., as differentiated). Still, he provided some fine insights into children's subjective experiences, suggesting, for instance, that they tend to perceive objects physiognomically.

Werner (1948, chap. 12) also wrote enthusiastically about the phenomenological research of his colleagues Jacob von Uexküll and Martha Muchow. Von Uexküll was an ethologist who tried to show how different the environment looks to different species. By analyzing the reactions of a fly, for example, he indicated how a room must look very different to her than it does to us. Muchow, following von Uexküll's lead, thought everyday scenes might appear different to children from the way they do to adults. She therefore observed children and adults in some everyday settings, including a canal dock in Hamburg, and inferred how these settings might appear to them (Wohlwill, 1984).

The dock was at the bottom of a steep slope, and to get to it one could walk down a narrow path that was fenced in. This is what adults did. Children, however, ignored the path. Instead, they spent their time climbing and swinging on the fence and rolling and sliding down the grassy slopes beside it. Because the children were so much more motorically inclined, they seemed to perceive the entire scene very differently from the adults. To them, the fence and the slopes—mere background elements for the adults—were the main features.

A second setting was a large new department store in the city. The youngest children (ages 6 to 9) did not approach the store as we do. They paid little attention to the merchandise, rushing instead to areas that provided opportunities for action and games. They were particularly attracted to the stairs, elevators, and escalators, on which they liked to run up and down in the wrong direction. Here again, Muchow inferred, young children experienced the setting very differently from adults.

Muchow, who died at an early age, did not develop her research as fully as we might have wished. She inferred children's perceptions from their behavior alone; we would like other evidence, such as drawings, to show how they viewed the scenes. Still, she made a beginning effort to depict the child's phenomenal world.

PRACTICAL APPLICATIONS

Werner was first and foremost a theoretician, and he wrote very little on the practical applications of his work. He offered scant advice on child rearing, education, or therapy. Nevertheless, his writing has practical relevance in a number of settings.

Clinical Settings

In the treatment of schizophrenia, psychoanalysts such as Searles (1965) have found Werner's concepts to be of great value. Searles believes we cannot understand most schizophrenic patients without appreciating the undifferentiated quality of their experience. These patients have little sense of themselves as separate from inanimate objects or other people. They may feel they are actually part of a room or the therapist. The therapist's recognition of this can in itself be beneficial, because one thing that helps patients is their sense that someone else understands what life is like for them. Searles discusses such points and many specific ways in which Werner's concepts guide his therapeutic interventions.

Werner's own work with patients was pioneering diagnostic research on children suffering from brain injuries. Between 1937 and 1945, he and Alfred Strauss carried out a number of studies comparing the cognitive behavior of these children to that of children with a diagnosis of mental retardation (Barten & Franklin, 1978, part 3). They found that whereas children diagnosed with mental retardation often thought in ways that seemed simple, vague, and global, children diagnosed with brain injuries exhibited special kinds of disorganization. When copying designs, for example, they were often unable to concentrate on the main figure because they were so distracted by background details. They were, in Werner's terms, stimulus-bound; everything jumped out at them. They could not stand back from a design and differentiate between the main figure and the background details. Today many children Werner called "brain injured" would receive different labels (e.g., "attention deficit/hyperactivity disorder"). But Werner's insights into figure/background problems are still fundamental, and educators often try to keep rooms and backgrounds simple and uncluttered so distractible children can focus on the tasks at hand.

The Push for Early Literacy

Werner composed no treatises on mainstream education, but his general orientation has become quite relevant today. Our nations' educational policymakers are pressing for formal academic instruction at younger and younger ages. They are calling for instruction in literacy—in reading and writing—even in preschool. But from Werner's holistic perspective, we shouldn't focus on any specific intellectual process, such as literacy, without considering the broader context out of which it develops. In this case, we need to consider how literacy can develop out of rich experiences with oral language and other symbolic activities.

Werner described how children's oral language develops out of actions and feelings. Before children learn many conventional words, they create their own words that resonate with the sounds and actions of life around them, as when they refer to a dog as "rfff" and a hammer as "boom." Additional research reveals that much early language is also melodic; babies like to play with the rhythms and rhymes of sounds, and parents join them in their melodic cooing, babbling, and baby talk. As children grow, they continue to engage in wordplay as they run, climb, jump, and play, saying things such as, "Up a lup a dup, up a dup I go." They also create lovely poems. In the preschool and early elementary school years, they are eager to hear and tell stories, and they engage in a good deal of make-believe play, using dolls, sticks, and other objects to symbolize the people and things in their dramas. They also love to draw, which involves further symbols, and when they become absorbed in drawing they often make up songs and stories (Crain, 2003). Through all such experiences, children develop a love of language—of its rhythms and beauty and its power to convey excitement and adventure. These experiences with oral language, in turn, enrich and energize their writing and reading. They want to read books to gain access to the riches that books contain, and they are eager to write their own stories, jokes, poems, and important messages.

However, early academic instruction is crowding out these rich early experiences. Today's kindergartens (and even many preschools) are so dominated by formal academic instruction that there's little time for children to make up rhymes or engage in make-believe play, or to draw, sing, or swap stories. Instead, adults rush in and teach them literacy skills in an abstract, mechanistic manner. The children do not look forward to books and writing to further the joys and adventures of oral language, for they haven't had a chance to experience these joys and adventures. Werner did not specifically address such literacy instruction, but his holistic and organismic orientation asks us to pay much more attention to the variety of experiences out of which literacy more naturally emerges.

Adult Education

Werner also offered a concept that may prove of considerable importance for the education of adults. This is the concept of *microgenetic mobility*. Werner, you will recall, proposed that the most creative thinking does not restrict itself to advanced, rational analysis, but it begins with the full use of preconceptual processes—global impressions fused with bodily sensations, intuitions, and so on. If so, educators in many fields, including the arts and sciences, medicine, and architecture, may wish to broaden the range of the thinking they try to nurture and enhance in their students.

A case in point is the education of physicians, where there is a growing effort to teach strictly rational problem-solving skills. Young doctors are encouraged to make diagnostic evaluations in a purely logical, step-by-step fashion, often employing decision trees, flow charts, and other devices derived from computer-based theories of cognition. Werner's concept of microgenetic mobility, however, suggests that doctors make fuller clinical judgments when they begin at preconceptual levels, with the impressions, sensations, and feelings that patients arouse in them.

Following Werner's lead, my wife (a pediatrician) and I (Crain & Crain, 1987) asked pediatricians at different levels of competence to report their thoughts and impressions as they examined infants with fevers who had come to the emergency room of a large urban hospital. Analyses of the tape recordings revealed that the beginning doctors tried to think about the patients in a purely objective, logical manner throughout the examination. In contrast, the most experienced and esteemed pediatricians initially engaged the babies in informal interactions, trying to get a global sense of the baby's health through the sensations and feelings the baby evoked in them. Their approach demonstrated greater microgenetic mobility; they initially engaged in more primitive, intuitive processes before advancing to a conceptual approach. Thus educators who stress a purely rational approach to medical decision making may be overlooking the rich preconceptual ground from which the most mature clinical judgments emerge.

EVALUATION

Today many consider Werner a historical relic. People vaguely remember him as someone who constructed a theory similar to Piaget's—both began writing in the 1920s—but it was Piaget, not Werner, who became the dominant figure in developmental psychology. Werner, to be sure, did contribute his well-known definition of development (the orthogenic principle), and he did influence some important people. But by and large, he has receded into the background.

Let us look first at some possible reasons for this neglect and then consider the need to take him seriously once again.

Werner has been overlooked partly because his theory is so abstract and difficult. Moreover, on major issues he was often vague and noncommittal. One thing we would like to know of any developmental theorist is his or her view of developmental change. To what extent does the writer see change as an innate maturational process? Or as a product of environmental influences? Werner's biological model is that of a maturationist (Baldwin, 1980), but if we look to Werner for a clear statement, we look in vain. Instead, we find statements such as, "Developmental psychology directs its efforts not toward the solution of the tricky problems of innate versus acquired function, but only the establishment and description of . . . types of mental activity" (Werner, 1948, p. 18). He simply skirted a basic issue.

In a similar vein, we might like to know the extent to which Werner believed that the child spontaneously creates his or her ideas, as opposed to absorbing the ideas of adults. Again, Werner was surprisingly noncommittal.

Symbol Formation (1963), for example, extensively describes early symbols that are so different from ours that they must be spontaneous creations, yet Werner and Kaplan said, "In our opinion the problem of free 'inventions' has been unduly stressed in the literature" (p. 102). Here again, Werner took no stand, saying he was only interested in the pattern of the child's thought.

Werner may seem noncommittal partly because he was a tolerant man who tried to see the value in all points of view. He also believed a degree of theoretical looseness was a good thing. He wanted to keep his concepts general and tentative so others would feel free to specify the details in their particular areas of investigation (Glick, 1983). So, for example, he never committed himself to any single set of levels or stages. He proposed some levels (sensorimotor, perceptual, and conceptual), but he hoped others would feel at liberty to find their own.

Complaints about Werner's vagueness, then, may be unfair because they ignore his purpose. But the fact remains that Werner has been generally neglected, and a major reason is that he failed to give us much we can sink our teeth into. If he had proposed a set of clear-cut stages, as Piaget did, researchers could test them and try to prove him right or wrong. This he didn't do.

But no matter how vague and difficult, Werner's theory is becoming increasingly important. The reason has to do with broad trends in our culture, of which psychology is a part.

If social critics such as Theodore Roszak (1972) are correct, our culture has steadily become dominated by science and technology. That is, we have come to view the world almost exclusively through the mental categories of logic, number, and mechanistic connection. Taking the computer as our model, we have translated mental life into flow charts and decision trees, and we have made precision, objectivity, and rationality our ultimate goals. In the process, Roszak says, we have lost touch with nonrational modes of experience. We have cut ourselves off from the fluid world of dreams, emotions, and intuitions and the organic rhythms of the body. Simultaneously, we have lost our feeling for nature, reducing her to mere physical matter to be exploited and controlled. Employing our great technological powers, we have turned the organic world into an artificial environment "as lifeless and gleamingly sterile as the glass and aluminum, stainless steel and plastic of the high-rise architecture and its interiors that now fill the urban-industrial world" (p. 89). We have, Roszak says, pressed technology forward against the natural world to such an extent that we are startled when anxious ecologists remind us that our survival still depends on air, water, soil, plants, and animals (p. 10).

Developing this theme, David Abram's book *The Spell of the Sensuous* (1996) calls attention to how we have lost connection to nature through our language. The oral languages of the indigenous peoples, Abram says, resonate with the sounds and forms of the animate landscape. The Kaluli of New Guinea still sing along with the birds, insects, frogs, and tumbling waterfalls. Like other indigenous peoples, the Kaluli's names for animals are often onomatopoeic, imitating the animals' sounds and activities. But modern industrial societies, which are driving indigenous peoples out of existence, emphasize literacy. And literacy insulates us from nature. To learn to read, we must shut out the sights and sounds of the out-of-doors and concentrate on the printed page. As literate individuals, we no longer see language as something we share with animals, trees, and the wind, but as a distinctly human form of communication. Written language is abstract and cerebral. And so we encase ourselves in buildings, using computer technology to send written messages to anywhere in the world, insulated from the breezes and birdsongs just outside.

Still, Abram argues, linguistic connections to the natural world cannot be entirely severed. In its depths, language remains a physical process that has been nourished by nature's sounds, and we still use words that echo nature. "It is not by chance," Abram says, "that when hiking in the mountains, the English terms we spontaneously use to describe the surging waters of the nearby river are words like 'rush,' 'splash,' 'gush,' 'wash'" (p. 82). Abram hopes we can recover our connections to the "varied contours and rhythms of a more-than-human earth" (p. 272).

Abram covers much of the same theoretical ground as Werner did. Werner, too, wrote about how speech, at its foundations, resonates with the expressive and dynamic features of the world. Like Abram, Werner saw this expressive speech as being stronger among indigenous peoples than among us in technological, literacy-based societies.

Werner, in addition, indicated that this speech is strong in children. He observed how children's initial symbols are often onomatopoeic, imitating the sounds of animals and objects. He also described how children physiognomically perceive the expressive qualities in the outer world and how this perception is developed by artists. Poets, painters, and other artists convey the joy of a flower at sunrise, the whisper of the wind in the trees, and the explosiveness of thunder.

Whether flowers, wind, and thunder really possess these qualities is open to debate. But in our technologically advanced society, in which so many of us have lost our sensitivity to the natural world, Werner showed where this sensitivity is to be found.

CHAPTER 6

Piaget's
Cognitive-Developmental
Theory

BIOGRAPHICAL INTRODUCTION

In all psychology, few theorists are as important as Jean Piaget (1896–1980), who forged the single-most comprehensive and compelling theory of intellectual development.

Piaget was born in Neuchâtel, a small college town in Switzerland where his father was a medieval historian at the university. Piaget (1952) described his father as a careful and systematic thinker. His mother, in contrast, was highly emotional, and her behavior created tensions within the family. Piaget adopted his father's studious ways and found refuge from the family's conflicts in solitary research.

Piaget showed promise as a scientist from the start. At the age of 10 he published an article on an albino sparrow he had seen in the park. While he was still in high school, his research on mollusks brought invitations to meet with foreign colleagues and a job offer to become the curator of a museum—all of which he turned down because of his age.

At 15 years of age, Piaget experienced an intellectual crisis when he realized his religious and philosophical convictions lacked a scientific foundation. He therefore set out to find some way of bridging philosophy with science. He read widely and worked out his new ideas in writing, even though the writing was intended for no one but himself. This search did not occupy all his time—he still managed to earn his doctorate in the natural sciences at the age of 21—but Piaget's broader quest did at times leave him confused and exhausted. Finally, at the age of 23, he settled on a plan. He would first do scientific research in child psychology, studying the development of the mind. He then would use his findings to answer broader questions in epistemology, philosophical questions concerning the origin of knowledge. He called this new enterprise "genetic epistemology" (Ginsburg & Opper, 1988, pp. 2–3; Piaget, 1952).

Piaget decided to study children in 1920 while working in the Binet Laboratory in Paris. There, his assignment was to construct an intelligence test for children. At first he found this work very boring—he had little interest in scoring children's answers right and wrong, as intelligence testing requires. However, Piaget soon became interested in the younger children's responses, especially their *wrong* answers. Their mistakes, he found, fit a consistent pattern that suggested their thinking might have a character all its own. Young children, Piaget speculated, might not simply be "dumber" than older children or adults, but might think in an entirely different way (Ginsburg & Opper, 1988, p. 3).

In order to learn about children's potentially unique ideas, Piaget abandoned the standardized tests, which forced children's responses into "artificial channels of set question and answer," and devised a more open-ended clinical interview that "encourages the flow of spontaneous tendencies" (Piaget, 1926, p. 4). He also spent many hours observing children's spontaneous activities. The point was to suspend his own adult preconceptions about children's thinking and to learn from the children themselves.

While in Paris, Piaget published two studies based on his new approach, but he did most of this new research at the Rousseau Institute in Geneva, where he settled in 1921. He primarily interviewed children between the ages of 4 and 12 years, and he found that the younger children, before the age of 7 or so, do indeed think in a qualitatively different way about dreams, morals, and many other topics.

In 1925 Piaget's first child, Jacqueline, was born—an event that initiated an important series of studies on the cognitive behavior of infants. Piaget and his wife, Valentine Châtenay, made very careful observations of Jacqueline's behavior, as they also did of their next two babies, Lucienne and Laurent.

Beginning about 1940 Piaget returned to the study of children, and adolescents as well, but he changed his research focus. Whereas his earlier investigations covered such topics as dreams, morality, and other matters of everyday interest to the child, his new studies focused on the child's understanding of mathematical and scientific concepts—a focus that dominated his work until the end of his life (Ginsburg & Opper, 1988, pp. 15–16).

In the 1950s Piaget finally turned to philosophical questions in epistemology, although he continued to study children's cognitive development. In this book I will say little about Piaget's epistemological theory; rather, our task is to gain some understanding of his developmental theory.

Piaget's research has evoked different responses from psychologists at different times. His first work caught the attention of psychologists in many parts of the world. After this initial enthusiasm, however, interest in Piaget declined, especially in the United States. For one thing, psychologists had difficulty understanding his orientation. They also objected to his methodology.

Piaget sometimes changed his questions during an interview if he thought this might help him understand a particular child's thinking; this, many psychologists pointed out, violates the canon of standardized interviewing. Piaget also ignored such matters as reports on his sample sizes and statistical summaries of his results. He seemed to regard such matters as less important than rich, detailed examples of children's thinking (Flavell, 1963, pp. 10–11, 431; Ginsburg & Opper, 1988, p. 6).

By and large, Piaget's research suffered from the same methodological shortcomings throughout his career, but the 1960s saw a remarkable revival of interest in his work. In the decades that followed, growing numbers of psychologists recognized the stature and importance of his theory. Many have been skeptical of his claims, and many have tried to prove him wrong, but they have recognized Piaget's theory as something to be reckoned with. Today there is hardly a study of children's thinking that does not refer to Piaget.

OVERVIEW OF THE THEORY

Although Piaget's research changed over the years, each part of it contributes to a single, integrated stage theory. The most general stages, or periods, are listed in Table 6.1.

Before we examine these stages in detail, it is important to note two theoretical points. First, Piaget recognized that children pass through his stages at different rates, and he therefore attached little importance to the ages associated with them. He did maintain, however, that children move through the stages in an *invariant sequence*—in the same order.

Second, as we discuss the stages, it is important to bear in mind Piaget's general view of the nature of *developmental change*. Because he proposed

TABLE 6.1   The General Periods of Development

Period I.	Sensorimotor Intelligence (birth to 2 years). Babies organize their physical action schemes, such as sucking, grasping, and hitting, for dealing with the immediate world.
Period II.	Preoperational Thought (2 to 7 years). Children learn to think—to use symbols and internal images—but their thinking is unsystematic and illogical. It is very different from that of adults.
Period III.	Concrete Operations (7 to 11 years). Children develop the capacity to think systematically, but only when they can refer to concrete objects and activities.
Period IV.	Formal Operations (11 to adulthood). Young people develop the capacity to think systematically on a purely abstract and hypothetical plane.

an invariant stage sequence, some scholars (e.g., Bandura & McDonald, 1963) have assumed he was a maturationist. He was not. Maturationists believe stage sequences are wired into the genes, and stages unfold according to an inner timetable. Piaget, however, did not think his stages are genetically determined. They simply represent increasingly comprehensive ways of thinking. Children are constantly exploring, manipulating, and trying to make sense out of the environment, and in this process they actively construct new and more elaborate structures for dealing with it (Kohlberg, 1968).

Piaget did make use of biological concepts, but only in a limited way. He observed that infants inherit reflexes, such as the sucking reflex. Reflexes are important in the first month of life but have much less bearing on development after this.

In addition, Piaget sometimes characterized children's activities in terms of biological tendencies that are found in all organisms. These tendencies are assimilation, accommodation, and organization. *Assimilation* means taking in, as in eating or digestion. In the intellectual sphere, we have a need to assimilate objects or information into our cognitive structures. For example, adults assimilate information by reading books. Much earlier, a baby might try to assimilate an object by grasping it, trying to take it into her grasping scheme.

Some objects do not quite fit into existing structures, so we must make *accommodations*, or changes in our structures. For example, a baby girl might find that she can grasp a block only by first removing an obstacle. Through such accommodations, infants begin constructing increasingly efficient and elaborate means for dealing with the world.

The third tendency is *organization*. For example, a 4-month-old boy might have the capacity to look at objects and to grasp them. Soon he will try to combine these two actions by grasping the same objects he looks at. On a more mental plane, we build theories. We seem to be constantly trying to organize our ideas into coherent systems.

So, even though Piaget did not believe that stages are wired into the genetic code, but constructed by children themselves, he did discuss the construction process in terms of biological tendencies (Ginsburg & Opper, 1988, pp. 16–19).

If Piaget was not a maturationist, he was even less a learning theorist. He did not believe children's thinking is shaped by adult teachings or other environmental influences. Children must interact with the environment to develop, but it is they, not the external environment, who build new cognitive structures.

Development, then, is not governed by internal maturation or external teachings. It is an *active construction process*, in which children, through their own activities, build increasingly differentiated and comprehensive cognitive structures.

PERIOD I. SENSORIMOTOR INTELLIGENCE (BIRTH TO 2 YEARS)

Piaget's first developmental period consists of six stages.

Stage 1 (birth to 1 month)[1]: The Use of Reflexes

When Piaget talked about the infant's action-structures, he used the term *scheme* or *schema* (e.g., Piaget, 1936a, p. 34). A scheme can be any action pattern for dealing with the environment, such as looking, grasping, hitting, or kicking. As mentioned, although infants construct their schemes and later structures through their own activities, their first schemes consist primarily of inborn reflexes. The most prominent reflex is the sucking reflex; babies automatically suck whenever their lips are touched.

Reflexes imply a certain passivity. The organism lies inactive until something comes along to stimulate it. Piaget, however, showed that even a reflex like sucking quickly becomes part of the human infant's self-initiated activity. For example, when his son Laurent was only 2 days old, he began making sucking movements when nothing elicited them. Since he did this between meals, when he wasn't hungry, he seemed to suck simply for the sake of sucking. Piaget said that once we have a scheme, we also have a need to put it to active use (pp. 25–26, 35).

Furthermore, when babies are hungry, they do not just passively wait for the mother to put the nipple into their mouth. When Laurent was 3 days old, he searched for the nipple as soon as his lips touched part of the breast. He groped, mouth open, across the breast until he found it (p. 26).

Babies do not confine themselves to sucking on nipples. Piaget's children sucked on clothes, pillows, blankets, their own fingers—on anything they chanced upon. In Piaget's terms, they assimilated all kinds of objects into the sucking scheme (pp. 26, 32, 34).

Although assimilation is the most prominent activity during stage 1, we also can detect the beginnings of accommodation. For example, babies must learn to adjust their head and lip movements to find the breast and nurse. Such adjustments also demonstrate the beginnings of organization; babies organize their movements so that nursing becomes increasingly smooth, rapid, and efficient (pp. 29–31, 39).

---

[1]The age norms for this period follow those suggested by Flavell (1963). I use the stage headings suggested by Ginsburg and Opper (1988).

Stage 2 (1 to 4 months):
Primary Circular Reactions

A circular reaction occurs when the baby chances upon a new experience and tries to repeat it (Piaget, 1936a, p. 55). A prime example is thumb-sucking. By chance, the hand comes into contact with the mouth, and when the hand falls the baby tries to bring it back. For some time, however, babies cannot do this. They hit the face with the hand but cannot catch it, or they fling their arms wildly, or they chase the hand with the mouth but cannot catch it because the whole body, including the arms and hands, moves as a unit in the same direction. In Piaget's language, they are unable to make the accommodations necessary to assimilate the hand to the sucking scheme. After repeated failures, they organize sucking and hand movements and master the art of thumb-sucking.

As with thumb-sucking, most of the primary circular reactions involve the organization of two previously separate body schemes or movements. For example, when we see a baby girl repeatedly bring her hand next to her face and look at it, she is exercising a primary circular reaction. She is coordinating looking with hand movements (pp. 96–97).

These circular reactions provide a good illustration of what Piaget means by intellectual development as a "construction process." The baby actively "puts together" different movements and schemes. It is important to emphasize the amount of work involved; the baby manages to coordinate separate movements only after repeated failures.

Stage 3 (4 to 8 months):
Secondary Circular Reactions

The developments of the second stage are called *primary* circular reactions because they involve the coordination of parts of the baby's own body. *Secondary* circular reactions occur when the baby discovers and reproduces an interesting event *outside* herself (Piaget, 1936a, p. 154). For example, one day when Piaget's daughter Lucienne was lying in her bassinet, she made a movement with her legs that stirred the dolls hanging overhead. She stared at the dolls a moment and then moved her legs again, watching the dolls move again. In the next few days, she repeated this scene many times, kicking her legs and watching the dolls shake, and she often would squeal with laughter at the sight of the moving dolls (pp. 157–159).

Piaget sometimes referred to secondary circular reactions as "making interesting sights last" (p. 153). He speculated that infants smile and laugh at the recognition of a moderately novel event. At the same time, it seems they are enjoying their own power, their ability to make an event happen again and again.

Stage 4 (8 to 12 months):
The Coordination of Secondary Schemes

In stage 3, the infant performs a single action to get a result—for example, kicking to move some dangling dolls. In stage 4, the infant's actions become more differentiated; he or she learns to coordinate two separate schemes to get a result. This new accomplishment is most apparent when infants deal with obstacles. For example, one day Laurent wanted to grab a matchbox, but Piaget put his hand in the way. At first, Laurent tried to ignore the hand; he tried to pass over it or around it, but he did not attempt to displace it. When Piaget kept his hand in the way, Laurent resorted to "storming the box while waving his hand, shaking himself, [and] wagging his head from side to side"—various "magical" gestures (1936a, p. 217). Finally, several days later, Laurent succeeded in removing the obstacle by striking the hand out of the way before he grabbed the box. Thus Laurent coordinated two separate schemes—striking and grabbing—to obtain the goal. One scheme, striking, became a means to an end, grabbing the box.

Such simple observations are very important for our understanding of how children develop the basic categories of experience, of space and time. We cannot talk to babies and ask them about their experiences of space and time, but we can see how these categories are developing through their actions. When Laurent learned to move the hand to get the box, he showed a sense that some objects are *in front of* others in space, and that some events must *precede* others in time (Ginsburg & Opper, 1988, p. 52).

Stage 5 (12 to 18 months):
Tertiary Circular Reactions

At stage 3, infants perform a single action to obtain a single result—to make an interesting sight last. At stage 4, they perform two separate actions to obtain a single result. Now, at stage 5, they experiment with different actions to observe the different outcomes.

For example, one day Laurent became interested in a new table. He hit it with his fist several times, sometimes harder, sometimes more gently, in order to hear the different sounds his actions produced (Piaget, 1936a, p. 270).

Similarly, one day when our son Tom was 12 months old, he was sitting in the bathtub, watching the water pour down from the faucet. He put his hand under the faucet and noticed how the water sprayed outward. He repeated this action twice, making the interesting sight last (stage 3). But he then shifted the position of his hand, sometimes nearer, sometimes farther away from the faucet, observing how the water sprayed out at different angles. He varied his actions to see what new, different results would follow.

It is worth pausing to note that the infants were learning entirely on their own, without any adult teaching. They were developing their schemes solely out of an intrinsic curiosity about the world.

Stage 6 (18 months to 2 years): The Beginnings of Thought

At stage 5, children are little scientists, varying their actions and observing the results. However, their discoveries all occur through direct physical actions. At stage 6, children seem to think out situations more internally, before they act.

The most widely known example of stage 6 behavior involves Lucienne and a matchbox. Piaget placed a chain in the box, which Lucienne immediately tried to recover. She possessed two schemes for getting the chain: turning the box over and sticking her finger in the box's slit. But neither scheme worked. She then did something curious. She stopped her actions and looked at the slit with great attention. Then, several times in succession, she opened and shut her mouth, wider and wider (Piaget, 1936a, p. 338). After this, she promptly opened the box and obtained the chain.

Piaget (p. 344) noted that at stage 5 the child probably would have obtained the chain through a slow trial-and-error process of experimenting with different actions. Because Lucienne stopped acting and thought out the situation, she was able to achieve the result much more quickly. She did not yet have a good grasp of language, so she used motor movements (her mouth) to symbolize the action she needed to perform.

Children's progress at stage 6 can also be seen in their efforts at imitation. Piaget observed that for some time children cannot imitate new models at all; they can only reproduce actions that already exist in their behavioral repertoires. By stage 5, though, they can make the necessary accommodations to imitate new behavior through experimental trial and error. But it is only at stage 6 that children are capable of *deferred imitation*—the imitation of models hours or days after observing them. For example, at 16 months of age Jacqueline

> had a visit from a little boy . . . whom she used to see from time to time, and who, in the course of the afternoon, got into a terrible temper. He screamed as he tried to get out of a play-pen and pushed it backwards, stamping his feet. J. stood watching him in amazement, never having witnessed such a scene before. The next day, she herself screamed in her play-pen and tried to move it, stamping her foot lightly several times in succession. The imitation of the whole scene was most striking. (Piaget, 1946, p. 63)

Piaget argued that because Jacqueline's imitation came an entire day later, she must have carried within her some internal representation of the model. Since she lacked the vocabulary to represent his actions in words, she probably used some form of motoric representation. She may have imitated his behavior with very brief muscle movements when she saw it, and these movements served as the basis for her later imitation.

The Development of Object Permanence

We have so far described only some of the main features of the six sensori-motor stages. Piaget studied other developments during this period; he showed how infants construct concepts of permanent objects, time, space, and causality. Because of space limitations, we will briefly review only one important development—that of object permanence.

During stages 1 and 2, babies have no conception of objects existing outside themselves. If a person or an object leaves their field of vision, the most babies do is to continue to look for a moment to where they last saw it. If the object does not reappear, they go on to something else. They make no attempt to search for it. For the baby, out of sight is out of mind (Piaget, 1936b).

At stage 3, new progress is made. As babies increasingly explore and interact with the outer world, they gain a better sense of the permanence of external things. If objects are dropped from their line of vision, they now look to the place where the object has fallen. They also can find partly hidden objects (if, for example, a blanket covers only part of a toy). Also, if they momentarily put an object aside and look elsewhere, they can return their attention to the object and recover it. But they only recover the object when it was related to their own actions. At this stage they cannot find objects that are completely hidden by others.

Stage 4 marks the beginning of a genuine sense of object permanence. Babies can now find completely hidden objects. If we completely cover a toy with a blanket, the baby will lift the blanket and find it.

However, Piaget found an interesting limitation at this stage. When he hid an object at point A, his children could find it, but when he then hid the same object at point B, they again tried to find it at point A—the place of their prior success. In Piaget's terms, they could not follow a series of displacements (movements from hiding place to hiding place).

At stage 5, children can follow a series of displacements, so long as they can see us making them. It is only at stage 6 that infants can follow invisible displacements. For example, it was only at the sixth stage that Jacqueline could recover a ball that rolled under the sofa by making a detour around the sofa. She could do this because she now had the ability to visualize to herself, internally, the ball's trajectory path even when it was invisible.

For Piaget, such detour behavior is very important. It shows that the child has constructed a sense of space that has the characteristics of a mathematical model called a *group*. For example, Jacqueline's detours demonstrate the principle of *associativity*, that one can reach a point through different interconnected paths. She also demonstrates the group principle of *reversibility* by bringing the ball back. Similarly, detour behavior reveals the other principles that define a coherent group structure (Piaget & Inhelder, 1966, pp. 15–17).

Less technically, we can note the tremendous progress that infants make. At the beginning of life, they have no sense of objects existing apart from themselves—from their vision and actions. By the end of the sensorimotor period, objects are separate and permanent. Children have developed a universe containing independent objects, in which they are only one object among many. Along with object permanence, then, they have a clear sense of themselves as independent beings (Piaget, 1936b, pp. 108–109).

PERIODS II AND III. PREOPERATIONAL THOUGHT (2 TO 7 YEARS) AND CONCRETE OPERATIONS (7 TO 11 YEARS)

By the end of the sensorimotor period, the child has developed efficient and well-organized actions for dealing with the immediate environment. The child continues to use sensorimotor skills throughout life, but the next period, that of preoperational thought, is marked by a major change. The child's mind rapidly advances to a new plane, that of symbols (including images and words). As a result, the child must organize her thinking all over again. This cannot be done at once. For some time, during the entire preoperational period, the child's thinking is basically unsystematic and illogical. It is not until the age of 7 or so, the beginning of concrete operations, that thinking becomes organized on a mental plane (Piaget, 1964a, p. 22).

The Growth of Symbolic Activity

Children begin to use symbols when they use one object or action to represent an absent one (Ginsburg & Opper, 1988, p. 70). Actually, as we have seen, children begin to do this during the sixth stage of sensorimotor development. For example, when Lucienne opened her mouth before opening the matchbox, she used her mouth to represent an action she had not yet performed. Piaget emphasized that the first symbols are motoric, not linguistic.

We also see nonlinguistic symbols in children's make-believe play, which also begins toward the end of the sensorimotor period. One day Jacqueline pretended that a piece of cloth was her pillow. She put her head on the cloth and, laughing, pretended to go to sleep. Her play was symbolic because she used one object, a piece of cloth, to represent an absent one, the pillow (Piaget, 1946, p. 96).

As their make-believe play develops, children start adding words. When Jacqueline had just turned 2 years old, she moved her finger along a table and said, "Horse trotting." A few days later, she slid a postcard along the table and said, "Car." Her words, like her finger and the postcard, symbolized objects not present in the immediate situation (Piaget, 1946, p. 124).

Language develops rapidly during the early preoperational years (from about age 2 to 4), and it vastly widens the child's horizons. Through language, the child can relive the past, anticipate the future, and communicate events to others. But precisely because the young child's mind is so rapidly expanding, it initially lacks the properties of a coherent logic. This is apparent in the young child's use of words. He or she does not use words to stand for true classes of objects, but merely as *preconcepts*. For example, when Jacqueline was 3 years old, she said that a daddy is a man who "has lots of Luciennes and lots of Jacquelines" (p. 255). She did not yet possess the concept of a general class, *children*, within which those with the names Lucienne and Jacqueline comprise only a small subset.

Because children lack general classes, their reasoning is frequently *transductive*, shifting from the particular to the particular. At $4\frac{1}{2}$ years Lucienne said, "I haven't had my nap yet so it isn't afternoon" (p. 232). She did not yet understand that afternoons are general time periods that contain many particular events, of which her nap was only one.

Some psychologists believe that children learn to think more logically as they master language. In this view, language provides us with our conceptual categories (see Brown, 1965). Piaget, however, disagreed. Although language is tremendously important—it provides us with a source of shared symbols for communicating with others—it does not itself provide the structure of logical thinking. Logic, instead, stems from actions. Infants develop logically coherent action systems during the sensorimotor period, before they talk, and later logic is simply organized actions of a more internal kind (Piaget & Inhelder, 1966, pp. 86–90). To study how internal actions form logical systems, Piaget gave children various scientific tasks. He usually began such experiments with children at age 4 years, because they could now sit down, focus on the tasks, and communicate with the examiner.

Scientific Reasoning

Conservation of Continuous Quantities (Liquids). This is Piaget's most famous experiment. In one version (Piaget & Szeminska, 1941, p. 17), the child is shown two glasses, A1 and A2, that are filled to the same height (see Figure 6.1). The child is asked if the two glasses contain the same amount of liquid, and the child almost always agrees that they do. Next, the experimenter (or the child) pours the liquid from A2 to glass P, which is lower and wider. The child is asked if the amount of liquid is still the same. At the *preoperational* level, the responses fall into two substages.

At the first substage, the children clearly fail to conserve—that is, they fail to realize that the quantity is the same. Usually, they say that A1 now has more because it is taller. Occasionally, the child says that P now has more because it is wider. In either case, the child "centers" on only one dimension, the height or the width. The child is so struck by a single perceptual dimension—the way it looks—that he or she fails to understand that logically the liquid must remain the same.

FIGURE 6.1
Conservation-of-liquid experiment. A child sees that beakers A1 and A2 contain the same amount of liquid. He then pours A2 into P and claims that now A1 has more because it is taller.

At the second substage, the child takes steps toward conservation but does not achieve it. A boy might at one moment say that A1 has more because it is taller, then change his mind and say that P has more because it is wider, and then become confused. The boy is showing "intuitive regulations"; he is beginning to consider *two* perceptual dimensions, but he does not yet reason about the two dimensions simultaneously and recognize that a change in one dimension cancels out a change in the other. His confusion, however, means he is becoming aware that he is contradicting himself, and it is a good bet that he will soon resolve the contradiction and move on to the stage of conservation.

Children generally achieve conservation of liquids at about 7 years. When they do so, they are entering the stage of *concrete operations*. Basically, children demonstrate conservation by using three arguments. First, the child might say, "You haven't added any or taken any away, so it has to be the same." This is the *identity* argument. Second, the child might say, "This glass is taller here, but the other one is wider here, so they're still the same." This is the argument of *compensation*—that the changes cancel each other out. The child assumes that the changes are part of an organized system—that a change in one dimension is necessarily related to a compensating change in another dimension. Third, the child might say, "They are still the same because you can pour this one back to what it was before." This is the argument of *inversion* (Piaget & Inhelder, 1966, p. 98). Piaget believed the concrete operational child can use all three arguments, although the child might not spontaneously do so on any given task.

Underlying these arguments are logical *operations*—*mental actions* that are *reversible* (p. 96). When the child argues that a change in height is canceled out by a change in width, the child understands that the end result is a return, or reversal, to the original amount. The principle of reversibility is obvious, of course, when the child uses the inversion argument, pointing out that "You can pour it back."

Operations, it is important to note, are mental actions. The child has not actually performed or seen the transformations she is talking about. She is only thinking, for example, about pouring water back. Operations are similar to the actions of the infant (as when an infant places a toy under a blanket and pulls it back out), but operations are on a more mental plane.

People sometimes wonder if young children might fail to conserve simply because of their difficulties with language. They might think that what the experimenter means by "more" is "taller," and therefore they point to the taller glass. One can get around such difficulties by changing one's wording—for example, by asking, "Which one would give you more to drink?" Usually we find that the young child still fails to conserve (Peill, 1975, p. 7, chap. 2).

How does the child learn conservation? The most ready answer is that conservation is taught. However, as we shall see, the teaching of conservation frequently meets with unexpected resistance. The preoperational child does not genuinely believe the adult's explanations.

Piaget argued that children master conservation *spontaneously*. The crucial moment comes at the second substage, when the child first says that one glass has more because it is taller, then says the other has more because it is wider, and then becomes confused. The child is in a state of *internal contradiction*, which she resolves by moving on to a higher stage. Sometimes we can see this change happen before our very eyes. The child says, "This has more . . . no, that one is wider, no, wait. They're both the same. This looks taller, but you've poured it into a wider glass."

Conservation of Number. In one of his experiments Piaget gave children a row of egg cups and a bunch of eggs (Piaget & Szeminska, 1941, pp. 49–56; Inhelder, 1971). Piaget then asked the children to take just enough eggs to fill the cups. Again, the responses at the preoperational period fell into two substages.

At the first substage, the children simply made the rows equal in length, ignoring the number of eggs in the row. When Piaget then asked them to actually put the eggs in the cups, they were surprised to find they had too many or too few eggs.

At the second preoperational stage, the children spontaneously created a one-to-one correspondence, placing one egg beneath each cup (see Figure 6.2). According to Piaget, they used an intuitive approach to achieve a precise perceptual order. However, their success was limited to this simple perceptual arrangement. When Piaget then bunched up (or sometimes spread out) one of the rows, the children claimed that now one had more. As with conservation of liquids, the children failed to conserve because they were more influenced by their immediate perceptions than by logic. Because one row now looked so much longer, they failed to reason that the number must remain the same.

At this stage, in addition, children sometimes begin to waver in their answers. One moment they say that one row has more because it is longer, but the next moment they think the other row has more because it is denser. This state of conflict marks the transition to concrete operations.

At the stage of concrete operations, children realize that the number in each row is the same despite the different appearances in length. They reason that the two rows are the same because "you haven't taken any away or added any" (identity), because "one row is longer here but this one is more bunched in" (compensation), or because "you could make this row long again and make them equal" (inversion).

Other Conservation Experiments. Piaget has studied several other kinds of conservation, such as the conservation of substance, weight, volume, and length. For example, in a conservation-of-substance experiment, the child is shown two equal balls of plasticine or play dough and then watches as one

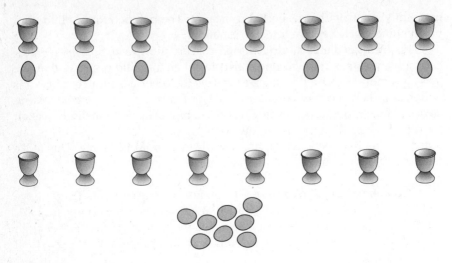

FIGURE 6.2
Conservation of number experiment. Young children can often create two rows of equal number, but if we shorten or bunch up one row, they think that the number has changed.

ball is rolled into a longer, thinner shape, like that of a hot dog. At the preoperational level, the child thinks the two balls now have different amounts of play dough.

We will not describe the various kinds of conservation here, but simply note that they all are thought to involve the mastery of the same logical concepts—identity, inversion, and compensation. Nevertheless, some kinds of conservation appear more difficult than others and are mastered later.[2] Thus the attainment of conservation is a gradual process within the concrete operational period.

Classification.   In a typical classification experiment, Piaget (Piaget & Szeminska, 1941, pp. 161–181) presented children with 20 wooden beads—18 brown and 2 white. Piaget made sure the children understood that although most beads were brown and two were white, they all were made of wood. He then asked the children, "Are there more brown beads or more wooden beads?" At the preoperational level, the children said there were more brown beads. Apparently they were so struck by the many brown beads in comparison to the two white ones that they failed to realize that

---

[2]In fact, the mastery of one series—conservation of substance, weight, and volume—may always occur in the same invariant sequence (Ginsburg & Opper, 1988, pp. 151–153; Piaget & Inhelder, 1966, p. 99).

both brown and white beads are parts of a larger whole—the class of wooden beads. As with conservation, children master such classification tasks during the period of concrete operations, and the same logical operations appear to be involved (p. 178).

Social Thinking

Egocentrism. Piaget believed that at each period there is a general correspondence between scientific and social thinking. For example, just as preoperational children fail to consider two dimensions on conservation tasks, they also fail to consider more than one perspective in their interactions with others. Preoperational children are frequently egocentric, considering everything from their own single viewpoint. This is apparent from young children's conversations (Piaget, 1923). A little girl might tell her friend, "I'm putting this here," oblivious to the fact that the place to which she is pointing is blocked from her friend's vision.

One of Piaget's most widely quoted studies on egocentrism dealt with the child's perception of space. In this study (Piaget & Inhelder, 1948) the child was taken for a walk around a model of three mountains so he or she could see how the model looked from different angles. After the walk, the child was seated on one side of the model, facing a doll that looked at the model from the opposite side. The child was then asked to select from among several photographs the picture that best showed what he or she saw and the picture that showed what the doll saw. All the children could pick the picture that represented their own view, but the youngest children (from about 4 to 6 years) frequently chose the same picture to show the doll's view. Apparently, they did not understand that the doll's perspective differed from their own.

Egocentrism, then, refers to the inability to distinguish one's own perspective from that of others. Egocentrism does not, however, necessarily imply selfishness or conceit. This point can be clarified by an example. One day two boys went shopping with their aunt for a birthday present for their mother. The older boy, who was 7, picked out a piece of jewelry. The younger boy, who was $3\frac{1}{2}$, selected a model car. The younger child's behavior was not selfish or greedy; he carefully wrapped the present and gave it to his mother with an expression that clearly showed that he expected her to love it. However, his behavior was egocentric; he did not consider the fact that his mother's interests were different from his own.

As long as children are egocentric, they tend simply to play alongside one another. For example, two children in the sandbox will build their own structures. As they overcome egocentrism, they learn to coordinate their actions in joint endeavors. Each might dig a tunnel so that the tunnels eventually connect. This requires considering each other's perspective. Such cooperative play occurs at the stage of concrete operations.

Egocentrism also may influence young children's speech, as when they engage in "collective monologues." Two little girls may appear to be holding a conversation while they play, but each girl is actually just talking about what is on her own mind. One girl might talk about a toy house she is building while the other talks about a trip she took, and no connection is ever made. As children overcome egocentrism, they consider the reactions and viewpoints of their listeners.

Much peer interaction, then, is initially egocentric. Nevertheless, Piaget (1923, p. 101; 1932, p. 94) speculated, children overcome egocentrism as they interact less exclusively with adults and more with other children. They discover that whereas grownups seem to understand whatever is on their minds, their peers do not. Consequently, they learn to consider others' viewpoints in order to make themselves understood.

Furthermore, children are less impressed by the authority of other children and feel freer to engage in conflicts with them. They argue with their peers and sometimes reach compromises and cooperate with them. They begin to coordinate alternative viewpoints and interests (Piaget, 1924, p. 205).

Whether children overcome egocentrism primarily through peer interaction or not, the most crucial point for Piaget's theory is that children themselves play an active role in grasping the fact of alternative viewpoints. On this point, I recall an instance in which our son Adam, then 5 years old, seemed actually to make this discovery. He was riding alone in the car with me when, after a few minutes of silence, he said, "You know, Dad, you're not remembering what I'm remembering." I asked him what he meant, and he replied, "Like I was remembering about my shoes, but you can't see what I'm remembering; you can't be remembering what I'm remembering." At that moment he seemed actually to discover, by himself, that others' perspectives differ from his own. He might not have completely surmounted his egocentrism at that instant, but the point is that whatever step he took, he took on his own.

Moral Judgment.   Piaget investigated children's social thought in many areas, including morals. In his classic work, *The Moral Judgment of the Child* (1932), he paid particular attention to how children understood the rules of the game of marbles.

Piaget first observed how children actually played the game, and he found that between the ages of 4 and 7 children typically played in an egocentric manner. If two boys were playing, each would play in his own way. They had little sense of winning—one might exclaim, "I won and you won too!" After the age of about 7 years, children tried to follow common rules and win according to them (pp. 29–46).

Piaget next investigated children's *thinking* about the rules. He was particularly interested in whether children thought the rules could be changed. Here, he found that children for several years—up to the age of 10 or so—believed the rules were fixed and unchangeable. They said the rules came from some prestigious authority, from the government, or from God. The rules could not be changed, they asserted, because then it wouldn't be the real game.

After the age of 10 or so, the children were more relativistic. Rules were seen simply as mutually agreed-upon ways of playing the game. Children no longer considered the rules as fixed or absolute; they said the rules probably had changed over the years, as children invented new rules. And they added that they too could change them, as long as everyone in the game agreed (pp. 50–76).

These different conceptions of rules, Piaget said, reveal two basic moral attitudes. The first, characteristic of the younger children, is moral *heteronomy*, a blind obedience to rules imposed by adults. Children assume there is one powerful law that they must always follow. The second morality—that of the older children—is *autonomy*. This morality considers rules as human devices produced by equals for the sake of cooperation (pp. 401–406).

Piaget believed that moral heteronomy is tied to egocentrism; children view rules from a single perspective, seeing only what powerful adults impose. As a form of egocentrism, moral heteronomy is overcome quite late, at the age of 10 or so, compared to egocentric play, which is usually overcome by age 7. Here, Piaget reminded us that heteronomy is a form of egocentric *thought* and said that thought often lags behind action. Children may need to engage in a good deal of genuinely cooperative play with peers, in which they actually change rules to meet everyone's satisfaction, before they can discuss the relativity of rules on a conscious plane (pp. 94–95).

In their informal play, older children's interest in the formulation of rules can become quite keen. Piaget (1932, p. 50) described how a group of 10- and 11-year-olds, preparing for a snowball fight, spent considerable time debating the rules for voting on a "president" for the game, dividing themselves into teams, deciding the distances of the shots, and discussing the appropriate sanctions for violations of the rules. According to one account of the episode, the boys were called home before they got a chance to begin the actual snowball fight, but all seemed content with their afternoon (Ginsburg & Opper, 1988, p. 98). What really interested them was the discussion of rules. Children at this age are like little lawyers, discussing what is fair and right. In the process, they develop their conceptions of justice.

Animism. Piaget described other ways in which young children's thinking differs from that of older children and adults. Like Werner, Piaget observed that young children do not make the same distinctions between living and nonliving things that adults do. As Werner said, they perceive everything, including physical objects, physiognomically, as full of life and feeling. A loud truck may seem angry and a single cloud lonely. Piaget called this view of the physical world *animistic*.

Although Piaget and Werner were struck by a similar attitude in young children, they studied it somewhat differently. Werner was concerned with children's direct perceptions of objects; Piaget was more interested in their concepts and definitions of life.

At first, Piaget found that children equate life with any kind of activity. For example, one boy was asked,

> Is the sun alive?—*Yes.*—Why?—*It gives light.*—Is a candle alive?—*Yes because it gives light. It is alive when it is giving light, but it isn't alive when it is not giving light.* . . . Is the play-bell alive?—*Yes, it rings.* (Piaget, 1926, p. 196)

Such thinking is common between the ages of 4 and 6 years.

A bit later, between the ages of about 6 and 8, children restrict life to things that move. For example,

> Is a stone alive?—*Yes.*—Why?—*It moves,* . . . How does it move?—*By rolling.*—Is the table alive?—*No, it can't move.* . . . Is a bicycle alive?—*Yes.*—Why?—*It goes.* (p. 196)

Only after 8 years or so do children restrict life to objects that move on their own and, later, to plants and animals.

Piaget found roughly similar stages in thinking about the kinds of objects that have feelings and consciousness. At first, children believe that an object has feelings if it reacts in any way. For example, a stick feels fire because it gets burnt. A bit later, children restrict feelings and consciousness to objects that move, then to objects that move on their own, and finally to animals.

Thus children gradually abandon their animism and come to make the distinctions characteristic of most adults. The fate of animism in Piaget's theory, we might note, differs from that of physiognomic perception in Werner's. For Werner, physiognomic perception, while less dominant in most adults than in young children, nevertheless remains with us and contributes to our artistic and poetic outlooks. For Piaget, animism is simply overcome.

Dreams.   One of Piaget's earliest studies examined children's conceptions of dreams (1926, chap. 3). As with conceptions of life, young children's understanding of dreams seems to follow a specific stage sequence. Since Piaget's first study, others (especially the American psychologist Lawrence Kohlberg, 1966a) have refined Piaget's dream sequence.

At first, children seem to believe that dreams are real. For example, when a 4-year-old girl was asked if the giant in her dream was really there, she answered, "It was really there but it left when I woke up. I saw its footprint on the floor" (Kohlberg, 1966a, p. 6). Soon afterward, children discover that dreams are not real, but they still view dreams quite differently from the way older children or adults view them. They think their dreams are visible to others and that dreams come from the outside (from the night or the sky, or through the window from the lights outside). They also think dreams remain outside themselves while they are dreaming. It is as if they were watching a movie, with the action taking place in their rooms in front of their eyes. Gradually, stage by stage, children realize that dreams not only are unreal but are also invisible, of internal origin, of internal location, and possess the other characteristics that adults assign to them. Children usually complete their discoveries by the age of 6 or 7 years, at the beginning of concrete operations.

How do children learn about dreams? Our first assumption probably is that they learn about them from adults. When children have nightmares, parents reassure them, saying, "Don't worry, it was only a dream. It wasn't real; it was only in your mind." Piagetians, however, maintain that children actually discover the various properties of dreams on their own. Kohlberg (1966a), for example, argued that because children master the dream sequence in an invariant six-stage sequence, it is unlikely that their thinking is the product of adult teachings; adults do not take the trouble to teach children about dreams in such a detailed, precise order. Instead, children arrive at different conceptualizations on their own, in an order of increasing difficulty.

To gather additional information on the role of adult teaching, Kohlberg (1966a) administered the dream interview to children in an aboriginal society in which the adults believe dreams are real (the Atayal on Formosa). Despite the adults' beliefs, these children seem to progress through the stages in the same order as American or Swiss children. That is, they first discover that dreams are unreal, then that they are invisible, and so on. Finally, when they reach the last stage, they feel the impact of the adult views and change their minds, adopting the view that dreams are real after all. Still, they initially progress through the dream sequence in opposition to any adult beliefs, so adult views cannot be the sole determinants of their learnings.

Summary and Conclusion

Piaget argued that children's thinking during the preoperational period is very different from that of older children and adults. Preoperational thinking is characterized by egocentrism, animism, moral heteronomy, a view of dreams as external events, a lack of classification, a lack of conservation, as well as other attributes we have not had the space to cover.

The list is a long one, and you might ask, "What do all these characteristics have in common?" The question is central to Piaget's theory, for it maintains that each developmental stage has a basic unity. Unfortunately, Piaget did not give as much attention to this question as we would like, but most often (e.g., 1964a, pp. 41–60), he tried to link the various preoperational characteristics to the concept of egocentrism.

In speech, children are egocentric when they consider matters only from their own perspective. Animism—the attribution of life to physical objects—also stems from egocentrism; children assume that everything functions just as they do. Similarly, Piaget tried to show that young children's conceptions of dreams are related to egocentrism. As long as children are egocentric, they fail to realize the extent to which each person has private, subjective experiences such as dreams. In the realm of morals, furthermore, egocentrism goes hand in hand with moral heteronomy. Young children regard rules from only one perspective, as absolutes handed down from above. They do not yet see how rules are based on the mutual agreements of two or more actors attempting to coordinate their different objectives in a cooperative way.

There is also a link between egocentrism and children's performances on scientific tasks, such as the experiments on conservation. Just as the egocentric child views things from a single perspective, the child who fails to conserve focuses on only one aspect of the problem. For example, when water is poured from one glass into a shorter, broader one, the child "centers" on a single striking dimension—the difference in height. The child cannot "decenter" and consider two aspects of the situation at once.

Children at the level of concrete operations are able to consider two aspects of a problem simultaneously. In their social interactions, they consider not only what they are saying but also the needs of the listener. When they perform conservation experiments, they consider not only the most visible change but also a compensating change. The coordination of two perspectives forms the basis of both their social and their scientific thinking (Piaget, 1947, pp. 156–166).

PERIOD IV. FORMAL OPERATIONS (11 YEARS TO ADULTHOOD)

At concrete operations, children can think systematically in terms of "mental actions." For example, when water is poured into a new glass, they can tell us about the implications of reversing the process, without actually performing the activity. However, there is a limit to such abilities. They can think logically and systematically only as long as they refer to tangible objects that can be subjected to real activity (Piaget, 1964a, p. 62).

During formal operations, in contrast, thinking soars into the realm of the purely abstract and hypothetical. The capacity for abstract reasoning can be seen in responses to questions such as the following: If Joe is shorter than Bob, and Joe is taller than Alex, who is the tallest? At the level of concrete operations, children can handle this problem only if they actually place people in order and compare their heights; beyond this, they simply guess. At the level of formal operations, however, adolescents can order their thoughts in their minds alone (p. 62).

Piaget was most concerned with the capacity to reason with respect to hypothetical possibilities. In one experiment (Inhelder & Piaget, 1955, pp. 107–122), children were given four flasks containing colorless liquids, labeled 1, 2, 3, and 4. They also were given a small container of colorless liquid, labeled *g*. Their task was to mix these liquids to make the color yellow.

At the level of preoperational intelligence, children typically made a mess. They poured the liquids in and out of the bottles in a haphazard way.

At the level of concrete operations, children's actions showed more organization. A typical strategy was to pour *g* into each flask: *g* into 1, *g* into 2, *g* into 3, and *g* into 4. However, they then gave up. When questioned, these children usually said there wasn't anything more they could do. Thus their actions revealed some organization, as we could have expected from their systematic behavior on conservation tasks, on which they can think in terms of two dimensions at once. But they entertained only a limited range of possibilities.

At the level of formal operations, the adolescents worked systematically in terms of *all possibilities.* Some started out by trying various combinations and then realized they had better make sure that they would include all possible combinations, so they wrote them down before acting any further.

When adolescents think about the various possibilities inherent in a situation beforehand and then systematically test them, they are working like true scientists. For example, a teenage girl might test the effects of a new soil for plants. At the level of formal operations, she does not just put new soil into one pot and old soil into the other and watch the plants grow; she considers other possibilities. Perhaps these two plants would have grown to different heights anyway, because of individual differences, so she obtains several plants and examines the average effects of the different soils. Perhaps the sunlight also has an effect, so she makes sure that all the plants are exposed to the same sunlight. Perhaps the amount of water is also important, so she controls for this variable too. The essence of such reasoning is that one is systematically thinking about hypotheses. One is not just entertaining a new possibility but is isolating one hypothesis by controlling for the effects of other possible variables.

As with the other periods, Piaget introduced logico-mathematical models to describe formal operational thinking. These models are in some respects similar to those that apply to earlier developmental levels, but they also go beyond them. The models are very complex, and we will not attempt to cover them here. It is important to note, however, that at the level of formal operations, thinking reaches its highest degree of equilibrium. This means, among other things, that the various operations are more tightly interrelated and apply to the widest possible field of application—the realm of hypothetical possibilities.

Although Piaget limited most of his research on adolescents to mathematical and scientific reasoning, he did speculate on the role of formal operations in the adolescent's social life (Inhelder & Piaget, 1955, chap. 18). Unlike the concrete-operational child, who lives primarily in the here and now, adolescents begin to think about more far-reaching problems—about their futures and the nature of the society they will enter. In this process, their new cognitive powers can lead to a striking idealism and utopianism. They can now grasp abstract principles and ideals, such as liberty, justice, and love, and they envision hypothetical societies very different from any that presently exist. The adolescent becomes a dreamer, constructing theories about a better world.

Piaget believed that such idealistic and utopian thinking carries with it a new kind of egocentrism. To fully appreciate this new egocentrism, we must review how egocentrism appears whenever the child enters a new realm of intellectual life. At first, infants are egocentric in the sense that they have no conception of the world apart from their own actions. External objects have no permanent existence of their own. Only at the end of the sensorimotor period do children situate themselves in a world of permanent objects, of which they are only one.

At the next level—that of preoperational thought—children enter a new, vastly enlarged world—one that includes language, symbolic representation, and communication with others. Children once again become egocentric and have difficulty considering more than their own immediate perspective. Gradually, they learn to consider alternative perspectives—as long as they are thinking about concrete objects immediately before them.

Finally, adolescents enter a broader world yet—the world of possibilities—and egocentrism reappears. This time egocentrism is seen when adolescents attribute unlimited power to their own thoughts. They dream of "a glorious future or of transforming the world through Ideas" (p. 346), without attempting to test out their thoughts in reality. Young people overcome this final form of egocenrism, in Piaget's view, when they actually take up adult roles. They then learn the limits and resistances to their own thoughts. They learn that a theoretical construction or a utopian vision has value only in relation to how it works out in reality.

THEORETICAL ISSUES

The Stage Concept

Many psychologists use the term *stage* loosely, as merely a convenient device for summarizing their findings. This, however, is not the case with Piaget. As Kohlberg (1968) stressed, the Piagetian stage concept implies several strong positions on the nature of development.

First, in a rigorous stage theory, the stage sequence should be invariant. People proceed through the stages at different rates, and some may not reach the highest of Piaget's stages; but to the extent that they move through them, they proceed in order.

Second, stages imply that growth is divided into qualitatively different periods. If intellectual development were a continuous, quantitative process, any division into separate stages would be arbitrary (Flavell, 1963, p. 19). For example, if knowledge can be scored from 0 to 100, then any division into stages at 40, 50, and 70 makes no more sense than any other series of cutoff points. Piaget, however, believed that thinking at different times is organized along qualitatively different lines. Thinking at concrete operations, for instance, is qualitatively different from that at formal operations. (It is logical insofar as it refers to concrete objects and activities, but it is not yet truly abstract and hypothetical.) Consequently, there is a natural, valid distinction between the two periods.

Third, stages refer to general characteristics. Kohlberg liked to discuss this point by asking the following question: At the age of 4 years, a child cannot copy a diamond. At the age of 5, the child can. Has the child reached the diamond copying stage? Kohlberg explained that this proposal sounds somewhat silly because diamond copying is too specific to be called a stage. If we were to call each particular achievement a stage, we would have thousands of stages. It is more appropriate to say that the child has reached a new *general* stage of perceptual-motor coordination that permits him or her to do many new things. Similarly, Piaget's stages refer to general patterns of thought, and if we know a child is in a particular stage, we should be able to predict behavior across a wide variety of tasks. This is not completely true, for children may be at somewhat different stages in different areas (e.g., in scientific versus social reasoning). Piaget called such irregularities *décalages*. However, there should be a substantial unity in performances at each general period.

Fourth, Piaget (Inhelder & Piaget, 1955) believed his own stages represent hierarchic integrations. That is, the lower stages do not disappear but become integrated into, and in a sense dominated by, new broader frameworks. For example, a teenage boy who begins using formal operations can still use concrete operations—he can still reason systematically about concrete, visible events. However, he now realizes these events are only a part of a wider range of theoretical possibilities, and he will prefer to approach difficult problems with this wider range in mind.[3]

Fifth, Piaget, like other rigorous stage theorists, claimed his stages unfold in the same sequence in all cultures. This proposal frequently puzzles readers. Don't different cultures teach different beliefs, particularly with regard to morals? We will take up this issue in the next chapter, but in general the Piagetian answer is that the theory is not concerned with specific beliefs but

---

[3]Piagetians imply that successive hierarchic integrations characterize development for all the periods except for preoperational thought. The illogical features of this period do not seem to be retained and integrated into any higher structures; they are simply overcome (see Inhelder, 1971).

with underlying cognitive capacities. So young children, regardless of their cultural beliefs on matters such as sex or fighting, will base their views on what they think authority condones or punishes. It is not until adolescence, when young people acquire formal operations, that they will give abstract, theoretical treatises on moral matters, whatever their specific beliefs.

In summary, then, Piaget advanced a rigorous stage theory, which means he believed his stages (1) unfold in an invariant sequence, (2) describe qualitatively different patterns, (3) refer to general properties of thought, (4) represent hierarchic integrations, and (5) are culturally universal.

Movement from Stage to Stage

Piaget devoted a great deal of attention to the structures of his stages and far less attention to the problem of movement through them. Nevertheless, he had definite views on this topic.

He acknowledged (1964b) that biological maturation plays some role in development. For example, children probably cannot attain concrete operations without some minimal maturation of the nervous system. However, Piaget said that maturation alone cannot play the dominant role because rates of development depend so much on where children live. Children who grow up in impoverished rural areas frequently develop at slow rates, apparently because they lack intellectual stimulation. The environment is also important.

However, it is easy to exaggerate the role of the environment, as learning theorists do. Generally speaking, learning theorists believe the child's mind is primarily a product of external reinforcements and teaching. Piagetian concepts, they assume, must be taught by parents, teachers, and others. However, it is not at all clear that this is the case, as we will discuss in the last section of this chapter.

In Piaget's view, the environment is important, but only partly so. The environment nourishes, stimulates, and challenges the child, but children themselves build cognitive structures. As children seek out the environment, they encounter events that capture their *interest*. They are particularly intrigued by events that are moderately novel—events that do not quite correspond to their past experience. Children then adjust their actions to learn about these events, and in the process they build new ways for dealing with the world. For example, I mentioned earlier how our son Tom, at the age of 12 months, was struck by the way water sprayed outward when he placed his hand under it. He then adjusted his hand up and down to learn more about it, and as he did so, he probably learned a little about the efficacy of actively experimenting with different actions to see different results (stage 5 of sensorimotor development). In such behavior, it is not the environment that structures the child's mind, but the child who develops new schemes.

Experiences that promote cognitive development, in addition, are not only interesting, but usually place the child in a state of *conflict*. For example, an infant might be unable to grasp an object because an obstacle is in the way. The child needs to invent a new structure—a means-ends relationship—to obtain the object. The child assimilates new objects by making accommodations that build new cognitive structures.

The concept of conflict is involved in a formal model of developmental change that Piaget called *equilibration* (1964b). We already have discussed the essence of this model, without using its name, when we discussed how children achieve conservation. For example, a little girl sees a ball of clay elongated and initially thinks the amount has increased. After a while, however, she considers the clay's narrow width and thinks the clay has shrunk; she perceives something that *contradicts* her initial view. When she thinks about both the length and the width, she becomes confused. This conflict motivates the child to realize that one change cancels out the other, leading to the discovery of conservation. Piaget's equilibration model tries to assign numerical probabilities to the chances that the child will consider one dimension, then the other, and finally both.

In philosophy, Piaget's equilibration model would be called a dialectical theory. *Dialectical theory* holds that change occurs when our ideas meet with counterevidence that motivates us to formulate new and better ideas.

Another source of new, conflicting information is the social environment. For example, preoperational children overcome egocentrism when they interact with peers, with whom they get into arguments and conflicts. In such interchanges, they learn that others have views different from their own, and they also learn to coordinate different interests to behave in a cooperative fashion. This ability to coordinate viewpoints also contributes to the growth of scientific thinking, where the coordination of dimensions is also important (Piaget, 1947, pp. 156–166).

Piaget, then, tried to indicate different ways in which interesting and conflicting pieces of information lead children to develop new cognitive structures. It is important to emphasize that development is always a spontaneous process. It is the children themselves who assimilate new information, resolve contradictions, and construct new cognitive structures.

IMPLICATIONS FOR EDUCATION

Piaget did not write extensively on education, but he did have some recommendations. Essentially, his overall educational philosophy is similar to that of Rousseau and Montessori. For Piaget, too, true learning is not something handed down by the teacher, but something that comes from the child. It is a process of spontaneous invention and discovery. This is clearly true of infants, who make incredible intellectual progress simply by exploring and manipulating the environment on their own, and it can be true of older children as well. Accordingly, the teacher should not try to impose knowledge on the child but should find materials that will interest and challenge the child and then permit the child to solve problems on her own (Piaget, 1969, pp. 151–153, 160).

Like Rousseau and Montessori, Piaget also stressed the importance of gearing instruction to the child's particular level. He did not agree with Montessori's maturational view of stages, but the general principle still holds: The educator must appreciate the extent to which children's interests and modes of learning are different at different times.

Say, for example, a boy is just entering the stage of concrete operations. He is beginning to think logically, but his thinking is still partly tied to concrete objects and activities. Accordingly, lessons should give him opportunities to deal actively with real things. If, for example, we wish to teach him about fractions, we should not draw diagrams, give him lectures, or engage him in verbal discussions. We should allow him to divide concrete objects into parts (Flavell, 1963, p. 368). When we assume he will learn on a verbal plane, we are being egocentric; we are assuming he learns just as we do. The result will be a lesson that sails over his head and seems unnatural to him.

It might appear that this principle—tailoring education to the child's own stage—is self-evident. Unfortunately, this is not always so. A case in point was the wave of curricular reforms that the United States initiated in the late 1950s and 1960s in response to the Soviet Union's launching of *Sputnik.* To try to catch up with the Russians, educators introduced the "new math," "new science," and other studies designed to teach children abstract, theoretical reasoning at very young ages. Initially, this seemed to be a great idea, but the new curriculum was not very successful. The reason, according to Kohlberg and Gilligan (1971), was that it attempted to teach young children, largely at the level of concrete operations and lower, ideas that assume capacities only attained at formal operations. The curricular reforms began with an adult conception of what children should learn and ignored children's own cognitive levels.

Beginning in the late 1970s and early 1980s, we witnessed a similar trend—a trend that continues today. U.S. leaders, worried that the country was losing its technological leadership to the Japanese, began calling for a new excellence in education. Parents, too, became anxious about their children's future and wanted to give them an early academic start. One result has been more and more academic instruction at younger and younger ages—all the way down to kindergarten and even earlier. David Elkind (1981, 1986), a Piagetian, was one of the first to protest this trend. Five-year-olds, Elkind pointed out, learn primarily through play and direct sensory contact with the environment; formal instruction, including workbooks and worksheets, does not coincide with the young child's natural modes of learning. Early formal instruction primarily teaches young children that learning is stressful and unnatural.

It is not always easy to find the educational experiences that are most natural for a given child. A knowledge of cognitive stages can help, but children are sometimes at different stages in different areas (Piaget, 1969). What is needed is sensitivity and flexibility on the teacher's part—a willingness to look closely at the child's actions, to learn from the child, and to be guided by the child's spontaneous interests (Ginsburg & Opper, 1988, p. 239). For active learning always presupposes interest (Piaget, 1969, p. 152).

Like Rousseau and Montessori, then, Piaget believed learning should be a process of active discovery and should be geared to the child's stage. But Piaget disagreed with Rousseau and Montessori on one point. Piaget saw much greater educational value in social interactions. Children begin to think logically—to coordinate two dimensions simultaneously—partly by learning to consider two or more perspectives in their dealings with others. So interactions should be encouraged, and the most beneficial ones are those in which children feel a basic equality, as they most often do with peers. As long as children feel dominated by an authority who knows the "right" answer, they will have difficulty appreciating differences in perspectives. In group discussions with other children, in contrast, they have a better opportunity to deal with different viewpoints as stimulating challenges to their own thinking (pp. 173–180).

Kamii's Constructivism

Several attempts have been made to bring Piaget's ideas into the classroom, particularly the preschool and the early grades (DeVries & Kohlberg, 1987, chap. 3). Some educators have focused on Piaget's tasks, attempting to teach conservation, classification, and so on. Others have been more concerned with the spirit of Piaget's theory. An inspired proponent of this approach is Constance Kamii.

Kamii begins with the Piagetian premise that real cognitive growth occurs only when children construct their own knowledge. Children need opportunities to figure things out on their own. They will not do this, Kamii has found, if teachers use worksheets and tests. These practices make children so worried about getting the "right answers," the answers that the teacher will mark as correct, that they don't think problems out for themselves. Instead of worksheets and tests, then, teachers need to provide experiences that children will find so interesting and meaningful that they will work on them for their own sake. Such problems, Kamii says, can be found throughout children's daily lives. For example, first-graders will enthusiastically work on arithmetic problems as they come up during card games, keeping score during outdoor games, voting on class decisions, and taking attendance. During such activities, the teacher can ask questions that further stimulate the child's interest in arithmetic. If children are playing softball, the teacher might ask, How many points do you need to reach 11? If a child brings pudding for the class, the teacher might ask, Are there just enough cups for all the children? The teacher's questions set the children's minds in motion, but the teacher always leaves the problem solving to the children themselves. The teacher should even respect the children's "wrong answers." For it is better for children to come up with a wrong answer that is their own than to feel that they must turn to an adult to know what is correct (Kamii, 1985, pp. 119–121, 161–165; Kamii & DeVries, 1977).

As children move into the second and third grades, Kamii adds many dice, card, and board games that stimulate mathematical thinking. She also presents children with standard problems in addition, subtraction, and so on, but she always encourages the children to invent their own solutions. Kamii vehemently opposes the conventional practice of teaching algorithms (e.g., a teacher tells a child to add 18 + 17 by adding the 8 and the 7, carrying the 1, and so on). Algorithms, she points out, teach children to follow mechanical procedures without the slightest understanding of why they are performing them. Children in a constructivist class invent methods that make sense to them (such as, "I'll make this two 10s, with a 7 and an 8 left over."). They create methods for surprisingly difficult problems, and their methods are often quite original (Kamii, 1994, 2004).

Kamii applies her approach to nearly every aspect of school life, including "discipline problems." If some children get into an argument during a card game, the teacher should resist the impulse to step in and solve the problem for them. Instead, the teacher might ask, "Can you think of a way that would be fair to everybody?" (Kamii, 1985, p. 48) In this way, the teacher prompts the children themselves to work on a question of justice.

Piagetian teaching, Kamii (1973) says, often means giving children more time to work on problems than schools usually do. Kamii tells, for example, about lessons in specific gravity. Children in the elementary grades are usually surprised to see that a pin sinks in water, whereas a block of wood (which is larger) floats. And it usually takes children some time to figure out why this is so. Teachers are therefore tempted to explain the answer to their pupils, especially when the teacher wants to move on to a new lesson. But Kamii urges the teacher to wait. It is far better, she says, for the children to keep thinking and wondering about the matter than "to be told the answer and to learn incidentally that the answer always comes from the teacher's head" (p. 225).

Kamii (1985, 1994, 2004) has conducted evaluation research on her method of teaching arithmetic in the early elementary grades. She has found that on traditional standardized tests, her children do almost as well as those taught by conventional methods. But her children demonstrate a far greater understanding of the logic behind their work. They also are much more independently minded. When a teacher tried to help one first-grade girl with a hint, the girl said, "Wait, I have to think it in my own head" (Kamii, 1985, p. 235). To Kamii, such responses are very important. Like Rousseau and

Montessori, Kamii is less interested in the amount of knowledge children gain than in their desire to think for themselves.

EVALUATION

Since about 1960 Piaget has stimulated a vast amount of research and theoretical discussion. We cannot summarize all of it here, but we can look at some trends and issues. I will organize this section around some basic questions.

Has Research Supported Piaget on His Tasks?

As mentioned in the introduction, Piaget's own research has been criticized for its scientific shortcomings. For example, he based some conclusions only on observations of his own three children—hardly a representative sample. Consequently, when Piaget was rediscovered in the early 1960s, many people wanted to see if they could replicate his findings.

Stage Sequences.   On the whole, the replication research using Piaget's own tasks has supported his stage sequence. That is, children do seem to move through the substages, stages, and periods in the order in which Piaget initially found. His stages have held up particularly well for the sensorimotor period and for scientific and mathematical reasoning with respect to the later stages (E. Evans, 1975; Harris, 1983; Lovell, 1968; Neimark, 1975). The results have been somewhat less clear cut for Piaget's stages of social thought, such as animism (Looft & Bartz, 1969), moral judgment (Kohlberg, 1964), and egocentrism (Damon, 1983, pp. 120–121), but in general younger children do differ from older children as Piaget found. This replication research, it should be noted, has typically used Piaget's own tasks. A bit later we will mention some studies that have questioned Piaget's conclusions by modifying his tasks.

Stage Generality.   Although Piaget's sequences have received support, his position that stages are general modes of thought has fared less well. That is, researchers have found rather low correlations among tasks that should tap the same general stages of thinking (Flavell, 1977, p. 248; Gelman & Baillargeon, 1983, pp. 169–172). For example, a child who demonstrates conservation of liquid might not exhibit the grasp of class inclusion that would seem to go along with it. Piaget himself recognized that children will master different tasks at different rates—he called such unevenness *décalage*—but he implied more consistency than has been found.

These largely negative findings have prompted many psychologists (e.g., Bandura, 1986, pp. 484–485) to recommend abandoning Piaget's stages altogether. Children, many say, do not go through general periods when their thinking reflects broad mental structures. Instead, they simply learn numerous task-specific skills. Children learn arithmetic skills, reading skills, communication skills, and so on, and there are no general mental structures underlying them. Even psychologists who are sympathetic to Piaget, such as John Flavell, have at times questioned the existence of general stages (Flavell, 1985, p. 295).

An abandonment of Piaget's stages, however, would be premature. Consider the child from 5 to 7 years of age. Sheldon White (1965, 1970) and others (e.g., Kegan, 1985; Sameroff & Haith, 1996) have accumulated a wealth of evidence that suggests children undergo important psychological changes during this period. The changes involved in this *5- to 7-year shift* go far beyond responses to Piagetian tasks. They include behavior in a variety of learning contexts. Prior to this shift, children are generally impulsive, distractible, and full of fantasy. Afterward, they are more logical, rational, and reasonable. Throughout the world, cultures have chosen this time to begin entrusting children with important responsibilities, including care for the younger ones (Weisner, 1996).

In many ways, the 5- to 7-year shift marks a loss of creativity. Before the age of 7 or 8, children's drawings are full of life and harmony; afterward, their drawings become more geometric and precise. Before the age of 7, children engage in elaborate make-believe play. Many children even create imaginary companions. By the age of 7 or so, this world of make-believe has declined. As in the song *Puff the Magic Dragon,* the imaginary friend must go away because the little boy is growing up and no longer believes in magic. He is becoming logical and realistic (Crain, 2003).

Thus there is strong evidence for a broad stagelike transition occurring at this time. And, as White (1965, 1996) observes, Piaget's theory is one that can help explain it. Children approach life in a more logical, rational way because they are developing concrete operational thought.

There is still the problem, to be sure, of inconsistency across Piaget's tasks. Some researchers believe that higher levels of generality are to be found at certain points within general periods (Siegler & Alibali, 2005, p. 59; Uzgiris, 1964). I think it is more promising to pursue White's (1996) thought that the ultimate validity of the stage theory is to be found in daily life, outside the tabletop universe of tests and tasks. As scholars study Piaget's stages and consider revisions, they might look for the features of his stages that throw the most light on the child's spontaneous activities and thinking in everyday life. What features of concrete operations are related to the decline in make-believe play? What cognitive processes develop when a child questions Santa Claus and magic? What cognitive capacities enable a boy to look competently after his baby sister, rationing her juice for the day and anticipating her unique needs? Piaget's stage theory has the potential to help us understand such broad dimensions of life. It would be foolish to dismiss his stages. In our chapter on Erikson, we will again discuss how Piaget's stages may help us understand very general changes at different points of life.

Do People Reach the Highest Stages?

A rather surprising finding is that most adults do not regularly demonstrate the highest stages of formal operations on Piaget's standard tasks. Most middle-class adults employ formal operations only some of the time (Kuhn et al., 1977; Neimark, 1975), and in many small village and tribal communities, many adults barely use any formal operations at all (Berk, 2009, p. 256; Dasen, 1972). These findings do not necessarily contradict Piaget. There is no theoretical reason why all people must reach Piaget's highest stages; thinking only moves forward when it is sufficiently challenged and stimulated. Nevertheless, the findings are puzzling.

Piaget (1972) attempted to account for these findings. It is likely, he said, that most people attain some degree of formal operational thinking, but primarily in areas of special interest or ability. An automobile mechanic may not think in a formal, theoretical manner about philosophy or physics but does use formal operations when trouble-shooting a car. An eager young law student might not employ formal operations when faced with a problem in chemistry but does so when discussing constitutional issues.

Similarly, Tulkin and Konner (1973) suggest that adults in small tribal societies might fail to demonstrate formal operations on Piagetian tasks of mathematical and scientific reasoning, but they employ them when working on problems of vital importance to them. For example, when the indigenous people of the Kalahari discuss animal tracking, they advance and weigh hypotheses in ways "that tax the best inferential and analytic capacities of the human mind" (p. 35).

Piaget conceded, then, that at the highest stages people will not demonstrate a great deal of consistency across intellectual tasks—certainly not the same degree of consistency that we expect at the earlier stages. Instead, people employ the highest stages of thinking primarily in their areas of strongest interest.

Do Children Really Learn on Their Own?

Perhaps Piaget's most controversial claim is that cognitive development is a spontaneous process. Children, he said, develop cognitive structures on their own, without direct teaching from adults. The most incontestable evidence for spontaneous learning comes from Piaget's observations on infants, who make enormous intellectual progress simply by exploring the environment, before anyone takes the trouble to educate them. Once we begin teaching, in fact, we often seem to stifle the child's natural curiosity. In school, children become disinterested, lazy, rebellious, and frightened of failure. The major task of education, it would seem, would be to liberate the bold curiosity with which children enter life.

When Piaget said children learn on their own, he did not mean they learn in a vacuum. Other children can stimulate and challenge the child's thinking, and it would seem that adults can do the same. As we have seen, Kamii asks children stimulating questions that start them thinking. But Piaget did not believe it is productive to try to teach children right answers or procedures. Instead, real learning comes from experiences that arouse children's curiosity and give them opportunities to work out their solutions on their own.

But many psychologists, particularly American psychologists in the learning-theory tradition, believe adult teaching is more important than Piaget thought. To demonstrate this, they have devised a number of "training studies," most of which have tried to teach conservation to 4- and 5-year-olds.

A major finding is that conservation is surprisingly difficult to teach (E. Evans, 1975; Halford & Andrews, 2006, p. 579; Liebert, Poulos, & Marmor, 1977, pp. 176–179). It is difficult, for example, to teach conservation by simply explaining and reinforcing the right answers. And if one does succeed on one task, the ability does not always generalize to new tasks. Further, the teaching does not always cut very deep. People have told me how they had apparently taught a child to conserve liquids; however, when they then offered the child a choice between liquids he or she liked to drink (e.g., a soft drink), the child insisted on taking the larger glass.

Nevertheless, conservation can be taught. In the first quite successful experiment, Rochel Gelman (1969) taught children to conserve number and length by reinforcing them for attending to the most relevant stimuli—for example, the number of objects in a row rather than the row's length. The training worked, and, furthermore, 60% of the children showed an immediate new ability to conserve substance and liquid. Gelman's training was laborious (it lasted two days and consisted of 192 trials), but others have successfully used similar methods in briefer training (Brainerd, 2003).

Still, we may wonder how accurately the training methods reflect the ways in which children master conservation in their ordinary lives. We also may wonder about the effects of the training methods on children's feelings. When children solve problems on their own, they gain confidence in their abilities to make discoveries. When they undergo the training programs, in which they are consistently told whether they are correct or what to think, they can easily learn to mistrust their own powers of thought.

Piaget (1970) added some additional thoughts that are relevant here. We frequently assume that spontaneous development is undesirable because it is slow; direct teaching seems good because it can speed things up. But Piaget pointed out that when Howard Gruber examined the development of object permanence in kittens, Gruber found that they progressed through the sequences at a much faster rate than human infants do. Yet kittens, Piaget noted, "do not progress any further and one may wonder whether the slower rate of progress does not . . . make for greater progress ultimately" (1970, p. 111). Piaget also observed that it took Darwin a remarkably long time to formulate his basic ideas (in addition to the years he withheld it from publication because it was so controversial), and Piaget speculated that slowness may sometimes be one of the conditions of fruitful invention.

Did Piaget Underestimate the Child's Abilities?

In recent years, dozens of researchers (some of whom have conducted training studies) have tried to show that Piaget underestimated children's capacities—that children are a lot smarter than he gave them credit for.

Sensorimotor Period Capacities.   Some researchers have examined *deferred imitation*, the imitation of events several hours or days after observing them. I mentioned one of Piaget's observations earlier. One day his daughter Jacqueline watched in amazement when a little boy threw a temper tantrum in his playpen. The boy screamed, pushed his playpen backward, and stomped his foot several times. The next day, when Jacqueline was in her playpen, she imitated the little boy precisely, even lightly stomping her foot. Deferred imitation begins in Piaget's sixth stage of sensorimotor development, at about 18 months of age. Piaget said it illustrates the new capacity for symbolic representation; the child must have some way of representing the events internally and carrying the representation over time.

Questioning Piaget's observations, Andrew Meltzoff (1988) found that babies as young as 9 months imitate events after a 24-hour delay. In Meltzoff's experiments, babies saw an adult do things such as shake a small plastic egg to make a rattle sound. Then, 24 hours later, when the babies were presented with the egg, about half the babies imitated the adult's actions.

Meltzoff's study is widely cited as convincing evidence that infants have the capacity for representation at a younger age than Piaget believed. But the infants in Meltzoff's study reproduced very simple actions that were probably familiar to them. The egg, for example, was really another rattle—to be shaken. The infants didn't seem to need to hold many images of new behavior in their minds. Jacqueline, in contrast, behaved like an actor who memorized a detailed action scene. Some of the actions, especially stomping a foot several times, were probably entirely new to her. She carried an internal image of the scene in her mind from one day to the next, and she referred to this image to guide her performance.

More recently, researchers have begun to examine the deferred imitation of more complex events (more like those Jacqueline imitated). The findings suggest that although infants as young as 6 months have some capacity for deferred imitation, they must initially see an action performed many times, and even then they don't reproduce it very fully. Deferred imitation becomes increasingly robust between about 13 and 24 months of age—about the time Piaget saw it emerging (Barr, Dowden, & Hayne, 1996; Bauer, 2006).

Other investigators have tried to show that infants have *object permanence* at younger ages than Piaget observed. Piaget, you will recall, found that babies don't search for completely hidden objects until stage 4 of the sensorimotor period, when they are 8 or 9 months old. If we cover a toy with a blanket, the baby won't continue to search for it. But Renée Baillargeon (1987) speculated that the problem might be that the baby is required to physically reach for hidden objects. If only looking were involved, the baby might demonstrate object permanence earlier.

In Baillargeon's best-known study (1987), babies saw a screen move toward a block. When the screen got near the block, the screen impeded the babies' view of the block. The block was now hidden from their view. The experiment was arranged so that two groups of babies now saw different things. One group saw the screen appear to stop when it made contact with the block. But a second group of babies saw the screen appear to go right through the block—as if the block no longer existed! Baillargeon found that babies as young as $3\frac{1}{2}$ and $4\frac{1}{2}$ months of age looked longer, as if surprised, at the sight of the screen going through the hidden block. This longer "looking time," Baillargeon says, suggests that infants know that hidden objects continue to exist at much earlier ages than Piaget indicated.

Reviewing this and similar experiments, several notable psychologists (e.g., Flavell, Miller, & Miller, 2002; Mandler, 1998) conclude that Piaget underestimated infants' knowledge about objects because his tests relied too heavily on their immature motor systems. When infants need only look at objects—not physically interact with them—they demonstrate knowledge much earlier than Piaget thought possible.

But these critiques of Piaget tend to overlook the essence of his theory. The criticisms often assume that an infant's "motor system" is some trivial matter and distracts us from what really counts—the infant's knowledge. The criticisms overlook Piaget's powerful insight that motor action is the foundation of logic and scientific thinking.

Consider the baby's ability to find a completely hidden object. At the time babies can do this, Piaget showed, they are constantly hiding and finding objects in their everyday life. On one occasion, Piaget's daughter Lucienne hid her feet under a blanket, pulled the blanket off, put it on again, and so on. A few days later, she endlessly repeated hiding a rattle under a rug and retrieving it (Piaget, 1936b, p. 172). Piaget said these physical actions contain the elements of the logical operation of reversal that the child will later carry out on a more mental plane (as in the thought, "I lost five cards so I have to get five new cards to get back to what I had"). For Piaget, all math and logic, even at its most advanced levels, involves action—adding, subtracting, combining, canceling, deducing, and so forth. At an advanced level, the individual carries out these actions more quickly and briefly in her mind, but they are actions nonetheless, and their precursors are found in sensorimotor activity.

Although Piaget didn't *prove* that logic and advanced reasoning grow out of action, he has a particularly strong case with respect to the "active experimenting" of stage 5. At this stage children begin to vary actions to see the different outcomes. For instance, they drop objects from different heights to see the different effects. Many years later, individuals carry out such experiments on a purely mental plane, as when a medical scientist thinks to herself, "I wonder what would happen if I doubled or tripled the dose." It seems very likely that the scientist's experimental approach had its beginnings in her active physical experiments in infancy.

The experiments by Baillargeon and others are widely accepted as demonstrating that infants are "more competent" than Piaget said, providing us with a "more positive" view of them (Flavell et al., 2002, pp. 75, 330). Although most psychologists don't intend their comments to be value judgments, it's easy to conclude that Piaget gave us a negative view of infants. But what could be more inspiring than the sight of infants spontaneously engaged in the intense explorations Piaget described? The baby engrossed in hiding and retrieving objects, or trying out different actions to see the results, is quite an investigator! Piaget suggested, moreover, that these sensorimotor investigations lead to advanced thought. If these investigations take some time, why should we consider this to be negative? As Piaget said, the development of logical and scientific thinking is a monumental enterprise.

The new experiments, to be sure, do indicate that infants have some knowledge at younger ages than Piaget observed. These experiments, in which babies merely sit and look at events, qualify Piaget to some extent. Perhaps there is an innate component to babies' early perceptual knowledge. But the experimenters have only offered speculations on how any such knowledge is related to advanced thought. They have hardly replaced Piaget's richly documented account of the long journey from sensorimotor action to advanced logical operations.

Preoperational Capacities.   Many psychologists have tried to show that Piaget also underestimated the intellectual capacities of the preoperational child. They have looked for ways of altering or simplifying Piaget's tasks with respect to conservation, egocentrism, classification, and other topics to show that 3-, 4-, and 5-year-olds can actually think like older children and adults. Such findings, they say, correct Piaget's picture of the young child as cognitively inept.

In an early study, Borke (1975) suggests that young children are not as egocentric as Piaget implied. Her research indicates that although 3- and 4-year-olds have difficulty on Piaget's mountain task, they can perform less egocentrically on simpler versions of the task. Other researchers have produced similar findings. It seems, for example, that even many 2-year-olds know that the side of a cube they see is different from the side a person facing them sees. (See Gelman & Baillargeon, 1983, and Siegler & Alibali, 2005, pp. 60–61, for summaries of this research.)

In recent years, a popular topic is the child's "theory of mind"—the child's theory of how people think—and many of the findings are relevant to egocentrism. For example, a child is shown a box with pictures of candy on it, guesses that candy is inside, but sees that the box actually contains crayons. Then the child is asked to guess what another person, who hasn't looked inside the box, will believe. Three-year-olds often guess the other person will think the box contains crayons. The 3-year-olds egocentrically assume others will know what they now know. On such tasks, children generally overcome this egocentrism by 4 or 5 years of age, which is sooner than Piaget indicated (Flavell et al., 2002).

Investigators have also tried to demonstrate that young children can think rationally on mathematical and scientific tasks. Gelman (1972), for example, suggests that young children have some capacity to conserve number. Piaget, you will recall, showed that when we shorten or lengthen a row of objects, preoperational children believe the number is changed. They seem more influenced by the perceptual configuration—the way the row looks—than by logic or number. In Piaget's studies, however, the rows often contained as many as eight objects. Gelman, in contrast, presented 3- to 5-year-olds with smaller sets of objects—two, three, or four objects—and found that children ignored changes in length and continued to base their judgments on number alone. They displayed conservation with these small sets.

Gelman's findings, we might note, do not necessarily contradict Piaget. It may be that changing such small rows produces very little perceptual change, so we do not know if young children can ignore perceptual changes in favor of logic or number. More broadly, Graeme Halford and Glenda Andrews (2006) have questioned the extent to which several studies actually refute Piaget with respect to young children's scientific and mathematical reasoning. Rebuttals of Piaget seem stronger with respect to egocentrism. Nevertheless, there is a general consensus among major psychologists that Piaget gave an overly pessimistic and negative picture of children's thinking on scientific and mathematical tasks as well (see, for example, Berk, 2009, p. 243–246; Flavell et al., 2002, p. 174; Miller, 2011, pp. 82–84; Siegler & Alibali, 2005, p. 57).

In the following paragraphs I will reply to this criticism from a strongly developmental perspective, as I imagine Rousseau might have done.

First of all, we may note that Piaget's critics seem to equate a positive and optimistic view of childhood with early and rapid development. We might ask, as Rousseau did, why it is pessimistic to observe that the development of logical structures takes time. Piaget himself made this point with respect to sensorimotor development, and it applies here as well.

Furthermore, Piaget's critics judge young children's thinking to be competent insofar as it is as rational and logical as ours. But this may be an inappropriate yardstick because young children's thinking may be *qualitatively different* from ours. As I suggested in the chapter on Werner (pp. 110–111), the young child's orientation, compared to that of the older child and adult, seems more akin to that of an artist. In fact, two key features of the preoperational period contribute to an artistic orientation. First, on many tasks the preoperational child bases her judgments on her perceptions. Artists, too, place a premium on perception, as when they help us see the beauty of a landscape or a bird in flight. Second, the preoperational child's animistic or physiognomic attitude is one that artists utililze. It helps them capture the dynamic, emotional, expressive qualities of the world (such as the sadness of the sky or the gentleness of a breeze).

Young children reveal their artistic orientation in many ways. They love activities such as drawing, singing, and composing poems, and they develop arresting works. For example, by the age of 6 or 7 years they consistently produce drawings that are fresh, lively, and beautifully organized. Many great artists have said they try to recapture the young child's artistic orientation. After this age their work becomes more geometric, wooden, and lifeless. It seems that logical intelligence is taking over (Gardner, 1973, p. 21; 1980). Moreover, the young child's rich fantasy life and theatrical playfulness also correspond to a mental organization that is more akin to the arts than to logic.

In response to Piaget's critics, then, I would say that each stage has its own distinctive quality, its own perfection. In early childhood, this perfection is more artistic than logical. We don't provide a positive view of the child by showing that she isn't quite so illogical after all, but by considering how preoperational thinking contributes to the child's true strength, which is in the artistic realm.

Unfortunately, Piaget worked himself into a corner where he couldn't make this response. Although he began his career with the goal of understanding the distinctive qualities of each stage, he was never open to the special strength of the preoperational stage. He kept comparing it to the superior logic of older children, and it never measured up. In his writings, the preoperational child "fails to grasp" basic notions, "continues to make the same mistake," and so on (Piaget & Szeminska, 1941, pp. 13, 142). If Piaget had considered preoperational thought on its own terms, he might have seen its affinity to that of the artist.

Conclusion

We see, then, that there are many criticisms of Piaget's theory. In later chapters we will discuss the debates that other major theorists—Bandura, Vygotsky, and Chomsky—have had with Piaget. For the present, though, it is worth noting that nearly everyone pits his or her ideas against Piaget's. This in itself is a testament to the stature of Piaget's theory. And it is a good bet that when all the dust clears, Piaget's theory will still stand. For whatever its weaknesses, it captures essential aspects of development.

CHAPTER 7

Kohlberg's Stages of Moral Development

BIOGRAPHICAL INTRODUCTION

An outstanding example of research in the Piagetian tradition is the work of Lawrence Kohlberg (1927–1987). Kohlberg focused on moral development and provided a stage theory of moral thinking that goes well beyond Piaget's initial formulations.

Kohlberg[1] grew up in Bronxville, New York, and attended Andover Academy in Massachusetts, an academically demanding private high school. He did not go straight to college but instead went to help the Israeli cause, serving as the second engineer on an old freighter carrying European refugees through British blockades to Israel. After this, in 1948, Kohlberg enrolled at the University of Chicago, where he scored so high on admission tests that he only had to take a limited number of courses to earn his bachelor's degree. This he did in one year. He stayed on at Chicago for graduate work in psychology, at first thinking he would become a clinical psychologist. But he soon became interested in Piaget and began interviewing children and adolescents on moral issues. The result was his doctoral dissertation (1958a), the first rendition of his new stage theory. Kohlberg taught at the University of Chicago from 1962 to 1968 and at Harvard University from 1968 until his death in 1987.

Kohlberg was an informal, unassuming man. When he taught, he frequently came to class dressed in a flannel shirt and baggy pants—as if he had thought it was his day off. He usually began asking questions in an off-the-cuff manner. In the first days of the school year, students didn't always know what to make of him. But they soon saw that they were in the presence of a true scholar, a man who had

---

[1]I would like to thank David F. Ricks for his help with this introductory section.

157

thought long and deeply about critical issues in philosophy and psychology, and Kohlberg was inviting them to ponder these issues with him. In his lectures and writings, he did much to help others appreciate the wisdom of the "old psychologists," writers such as Rousseau, John Dewey, and James Mark Baldwin.

Unfortunately, Kohlberg suffered from a tropical disease and bouts of depression that caused him intense pain during the last 20 years of his life. At the age of 59, he ended his life by drowning.

PIAGET'S STAGES OF MORAL JUDGMENT

While he was in graduate school, Kohlberg became deeply impressed by Piaget's studies of moral judgment. Piaget, Kohlberg saw, was talking to children about fundamental matters in moral philosophy and was drawing out their real thinking. At the same time, Piaget's work seemed incomplete.

Essentially, Piaget's findings on moral judgment fit into a two-stage theory. Children younger than 10 or 11 years think about moral dilemmas one way; older children consider them differently. As we have seen, younger children regard rules as fixed and absolute. They believe rules are handed down by adults or by God and cannot be changed. The older child's view is more relativistic. She understands it is permissible to change rules if everyone agrees. Rules are not sacred and absolute but are devices that humans use to get along cooperatively.

At approximately the same time—age 10 or so—children's moral thinking undergoes other shifts. Younger children base their moral judgments more on consequences, whereas older children base their judgments on intentions. When, for example, the young child hears about one boy who made a large ink spot trying to help his dad and another boy who made only a small ink spot when playing around, the young child thinks the first boy did worse. The child primarily considers the amount of damage—the consequences— whereas the older child is more likely to judge wrongness in terms of the motives underlying the act (Piaget, 1932, p. 130).

There are many more details to Piaget's work on moral judgment, but he essentially found a series of changes that occur between the ages of 10 and 12, just when the child begins to enter the general stage of formal operations. Intellectual development, however, does not stop at this point. This is just the beginning of formal operations, which continue to develop at least until age 16. Accordingly, one might expect thinking about moral issues to continue to develop throughout adolescence. Kohlberg therefore interviewed both children and adolescents about moral dilemmas, and he did find stages that go well beyond Piaget's. He uncovered six stages, only the first three of which share many features with Piaget's stages.

KOHLBERG'S METHOD

Kohlberg's (1958a) core sample was comprised of 72 boys from both middle- and lower-class families in Chicago. They were ages 10, 13, and 16. He later added to his sample younger children, delinquents, and boys and girls from other U.S. cities and from other countries (Kohlberg, 1963, 1970).

The basic interview consists of a series of dilemmas such as the following:

Heinz Steals the Drug

In Europe, a woman was near death from a special kind of cancer. There was one drug that the doctors thought might save her. It was a form of radium that a druggist in the same town had recently discovered. The drug was expensive to make, but the druggist was charging ten times what the drug cost him to make. He paid $200 for the radium and charged $2,000 for a small dose of the drug. The sick woman's husband, Heinz, went to everyone he knew to borrow the money, but he could only get together about $1,000 which is half of what it cost. He told the druggist that his wife was dying and asked him to sell it cheaper or let him pay later. But the druggist said: "No, I discovered the drug and I'm going to make money from it." So Heinz got desperate and broke into the man's store to steal the drug for his wife. Should the husband have done that? (Kohlberg, 1963, p. 19)

Kohlberg was not really interested in whether the subject said "yes" or "no" to this dilemma but in the reasoning behind the answer. The interviewer wants to know *why* the subject thinks Heinz should or should not have stolen the drug. The interview schedule then asks new questions that help us understand the child's reasoning. For example, children are asked if Heinz had a right to steal the drug, if he was violating the druggist's rights, and what sentence the judge should give him once he was caught. Once again, the main concern is with the reasoning behind the answers. The interview then goes on to give more dilemmas in order to get a good sampling of a subject's moral thinking.

Once Kohlberg had classified the various responses into stages, he wanted to know whether his classification was *reliable*. In particular, he wanted to know if others would score the protocols in the same way. Other judges independently scored a sample of responses, and he calculated the degree to which all raters agreed. This procedure is called *interrater reliability*. Kohlberg found these agreements to be high, as he did in his subsequent work, but whenever investigators use Kohlberg's interview, they should also check for interrater reliability before scoring the entire sample.[2]

---

[2]For a discussion of other forms of reliability, see Colby, Kohlberg, Gibbs, and Lieberman, 1983.

KOHLBERG'S SIX STAGES

Level I. Preconventional Morality

Stage 1. Obedience and Punishment Orientation.   Kohlberg's stage 1 is similar to Piaget's first stage of moral thought. The child assumes that powerful authorities hand down a fixed set of rules that she must unquestioningly obey. To the Heinz dilemma, the child typically says that Heinz was wrong to steal the drug because "it's against the law" or "it's bad to steal," as if this were all there were to it. When asked to elaborate, the child usually responds in terms of the consequences involved, explaining that stealing is bad "because you'll get punished" (Kohlberg, 1958b).

Although the vast majority of children at stage 1 oppose Heinz's theft, it is still possible for a child to support the action and still employ stage 1 reasoning. A child might say, "Heinz can steal it because he asked first and it's not like he stole something big; he won't get punished" (see Rest, 1973). Even though the child agrees with Heinz's action, the reasoning is still stage 1; the concern is with what authorities permit and punish.

Kohlberg calls stage 1 thinking *preconventional* because children do not yet speak as members of society. Instead, they see morality as something external to themselves—something the big people say they must do (Colby, Kohlberg, & Kauffman, 1987a, p. 16).

Stage 2. Individualism and Exchange.   At this stage children recognize there is not just one right view handed down by the authorities. Different individuals have different viewpoints. "Heinz," they might point out, "might think it's right to take the drug, the druggist would not." Since everything is *relative*, each person is free to pursue his or her *individual* interests. One boy said that Heinz might steal the drug if he wanted his wife to live, but that he doesn't have to if he wants to marry someone younger and better looking (Kohlberg, 1963, p. 24). Another boy said Heinz might steal it because

> maybe they had children and he might need someone at home to look after them. But maybe he shouldn't steal it because they might put him in prison for more years than he could stand. (Colby, Kohlberg, & Kauffman, 1987b, p. 208)

What is right for Heinz, then, is what meets his own self-interests.

You might have noticed that children at both stages 1 and 2 talk about punishment. However, they perceive it differently. At stage 1, punishment is tied up in the child's mind with wrongness; punishment "proves" that disobedience is wrong. At stage 2, in contrast, punishment is simply a risk that one naturally wants to avoid.

Although stage 2 respondents sometimes sound amoral, they do have some sense of right action. There is a notion of *fair exchange* or fair deals. The philosophy is one of returning favors— "If you scratch my back, I'll scratch yours." To the Heinz story, subjects often say Heinz was right to steal the drug because the druggist was unwilling to make a fair deal; he was "trying to rip Heinz off." Or they might say he should steal for his wife "because she might return the favor some day" (Colby et al., 1987c, pp. 16–17).

Respondents at stage 2 are still said to reason at the preconventional level because they speak as isolated individuals rather than as members of society. They see individuals exchanging favors, but there is still no identification with the values of the family or community.

Level II. Conventional Morality

Stage 3. Good Interpersonal Relationships.   At this stage children— who are by now usually entering their teens—see morality as more than simple deals. They believe people should live up to the expectations of the family and community and behave in "good" ways. Good behavior means having good motives and interpersonal feelings such as love, empathy, trust, and concern for others. Heinz, they typically argue, was right to steal the drug because "he was a good man for wanting to save her" and "his intentions were good, that of saving the life of someone he loves." Even if Heinz doesn't love his wife, these subjects often say, he should steal the drug because "I don't think any husband should sit back and watch his wife die" (Kohlberg, 1958b; Colby et al., 1987c, pp. 27–29).

If Heinz's motives were good, the druggist's were bad. The druggist, stage 3 subjects emphasize, was "selfish," "greedy," and "only interested in himself, not another life." Sometimes the respondents become so angry with the druggist that they say he ought to be put in jail (Colby et al., 1987c, pp. 20–33). A typical stage 3 response is that of Don, age 13:

> It was really the druggist's fault, he was unfair, trying to overcharge and letting someone die. Heinz loved his wife and wanted to save her. I think anyone would. I don't think they would put him in jail. The judge would look at all sides, and see that the druggist was charging too much. (Kohlberg, 1963, p. 25)

We see that Don defines the issue in terms of the actors' character traits and motives. He talks about the loving husband, the unfair druggist, and the understanding judge. His answer deserves the label "conventional morality" because it assumes that the attitude expressed would be shared by the entire community—"anyone" would be right to do what Heinz did (p. 25).

As mentioned earlier, there are similarities between Kohlberg's first three stages and Piaget's two stages. In both sequences there is a shift from unquestioning obedience to a relativistic outlook and to a concern for good motives. For Kohlberg, however, these shifts occur in three stages rather than two.

Stage 4. Maintaining the Social Order.   Stage 3 reasoning works best in two-person relationships with family members or close friends, where one can make a real effort to get to know the other's feelings and needs and try to help. At stage 4, in contrast, the respondent becomes more broadly concerned with *society as a whole*. Now the emphasis is on obeying laws, respecting authority, and performing one's duties so the social order is maintained. In response to the Heinz story, many subjects say they understand that Heinz's motives were good, but they cannot condone the theft. What would happen if we all started breaking the laws whenever we felt we had a good reason? The result would be chaos; society couldn't function. As one subject explained,

> I don't want to sound like Spiro Agnew, law and order and wave the flag, but if everybody did as he wanted to do, set up his own beliefs as to right and wrong, then I think you would have chaos. The only thing I think we have in civilization nowadays is some sort of legal structure which people are sort of bound to follow. [Society needs] a centralizing framework. (Colby et al., 1987c, p. 89)

Because stage 4 subjects make moral decisions from the perspective of society as a whole, they think from a full-fledged member-of-society perspective (Colby et al., 1987a, p. 17).

You will recall that stage 1 children also generally oppose stealing because it breaks the law. Superficially, stage 1 and stage 4 subjects are giving the same response, so we see here why Kohlberg insisted that we must probe into the reasoning behind the overt response. Stage 1 children say, "It's wrong to steal" and "It's against the law," but they cannot elaborate any further, except to say that stealing can get a person jailed. Stage 4 respondents, in contrast, have a conception of the function of laws for society as a whole—a conception that far exceeds the grasp of the younger child.

Level III. Postconventional Morality

Stage 5. Social Contract and Individual Rights.   At stage 4, people want to keep society functioning. However, a smoothly functioning society is not necessarily a good one. A totalitarian society might be well organized, but it is hardly the moral ideal. At stage 5, people begin to ask, "What makes for a good society?" They begin to think about society in a very theoretical way, stepping back from their own society and considering the rights and values a society ought to uphold. They then evaluate existing societies in terms of these prior considerations. They are said to take a "prior-to-society" perspective (Colby et al., 1987a, p. 20).

Stage 5 respondents basically believe that a good society is best conceived as a social contract into which people freely enter to work toward the benefit of all. They recognize that different social groups within a society will have different values, but they believe all rational people would agree on two points. First, they would all want certain basic *rights,* such as liberty and life, to be protected. Second, they would want some *democratic* procedures for changing unfair laws and for improving society.

In response to the Heinz dilemma, stage 5 respondents make it clear that they do not generally favor breaking laws; laws are social contracts that we agree to uphold until we can change them by democratic means. Nevertheless, the wife's right to live is a moral right that must be protected. Thus stage 5 respondents sometimes defend Heinz's theft in strong language:

> It is the husband's duty to save his wife. The fact that her life is in danger transcends every other standard you might use to judge his action. Life is more important than property. (Kohlberg, 1976, p. 38)

This young man went on to say that "from a moral standpoint," Heinz should save the life of even a stranger, since, to be consistent, the value of a life means any life. When asked if the judge should punish Heinz, he replied,

> Usually the moral and legal standpoints coincide. Here they conflict. The judge should weight the moral standpoint more heavily but preserve the legal law in punishing Heinz lightly. (Kohlberg, 1976, p. 38)

Stage 5 subjects, then, talk about "morality" and "rights" that take some priority over particular laws. Kohlberg insisted, however, that we do not judge people to be at stage 5 merely from their verbal labels. We need to look at their social perspective and mode of reasoning. At stage 4, too, subjects frequently talk about the "right to life," but for them this right is legitimized by the authority of their social or religious group (e.g., by the Bible). Presumably, if their group valued property over life, they would too. At stage 5, in contrast, people are making more of an independent effort to think out what any society ought to value. They often reason, for example, that property has little meaning without life. They are trying to determine logically what a society ought to be like (Colby et al., 1987c, pp. 53–55; Kohlberg, 1981, pp. 21–22).

Stage 6. Universal Principles.   Stage 5 respondents are working toward a conception of the good society. They suggest that we need to (1) protect certain individual rights and (2) settle disputes through democratic processes. However, democratic processes alone do not always result in outcomes that we intuitively sense are just. A majority, for example, may vote for a law that hinders a minority. Thus Kohlberg believed there must be a higher stage—stage 6—that defines the principles by which we achieve justice.

Kohlberg's conception of justice followed that of the philosophers Immanuel Kant and John Rawls, as well as great moral leaders such as Mohandas Gandhi and Martin Luther King, Jr. According to these people, the principles of justice require us to treat the claims of all parties in an impartial manner, respecting the basic dignity of all people as individuals. The principles of justice are therefore universal; they apply to all. We would not vote for a law that aids some people but hurts others. The principles of justice require an equal respect for every person.

In actual practice, Kohlberg said, we can reach just decisions by looking at a situation through one another's eyes. In the Heinz dilemma, this would mean that all parties—the druggist, Heinz, and his wife—take the roles of the others. To do this in an impartial manner, people can assume a "veil of ignorance" (Rawls, 1971), acting as if they do not know which role they would eventually occupy. If the druggist did this, even he would recognize that life must take priority over property; for he wouldn't want to risk finding himself in the wife's shoes with property valued over life. Thus they would all agree the wife must be saved—this would be the fair solution. Such a solution, we must note, requires not only impartiality but also the principle that everyone is given full and equal respect. If the wife were considered of less value than the others, a just solution could not be reached.

Until 1975 Kohlberg had been scoring some of his subjects at stage 6, but he then stopped doing so. One reason was that he and other researchers had found very few subjects who consistently reasoned at this stage. Also, Kohlberg concluded that his interview dilemmas did not draw out differences between stage 5 and stage 6 thinking. Theoretically, stage 6 has a clearer and broader conception of universal principles (including justice as well as individual rights), but the interview did not draw out this broader understanding. So he dropped stage 6 from his manual, calling it a "theoretical stage" and scoring all post-conventional responses at stage 5 (Colby et al., 1987a, pp. 35–40).

One issue that would distinguish stage 5 from stage 6 is civil disobedience. Stage 5 thinkers would be hesitant to endorse civil disobedience because of their commitment to the social contract and to changing laws through democratic agreements. Only when an individual right is clearly at stake does violating the law seem justified. At stage 6, in contrast, a commitment to justice makes the rationale for civil disobedience stronger and broader. Martin Luther King argued that laws are valid only insofar as they are grounded in justice, and that a commitment to justice carries with it an obligation to disobey unjust laws. King also recognized, of course, the general need for laws and democratic processes (stages 4 and 5), and he was therefore willing to accept the penalties for his actions. Nevertheless, he believed that the higher principle of justice required civil disobedience (Kohlberg, 1981, p. 43).

Summary

At stage 1 children think of what is right as what authority says is right. Doing the right thing is obeying authority and avoiding punishment. At stage 2 children are no longer so impressed by any single authority; they see that there are different sides to any issue. Since everything is relative, one is free to pursue one's own interests, although it is often useful to make deals and exchange favors with others.

At stages 3 and 4 young people think as members of the conventional society, with its values, norms, and expectations. At stage 3 they emphasize being a good person, which basically means having helpful motives toward people who are close to one. At stage 4 the concern shifts toward obeying laws to maintain society as a whole.

At stages 5 and 6 people are less concerned with maintaining society for its own sake, and more concerned with the principles and values that make for a good society. At stage 5 they emphasize basic rights and the democratic processes that give everyone a say, and at stage 6 they define the principles by which agreements will be most just.

A Possible Seventh Stage

Those who have developed conception of justice often work to bring it about, but they also encounter serious setbacks. They go through periods of doubt and despair. Martin Luther King and activists in the civil rights movement of the 1950s and 1960s experienced such periods. Any of us can go through them as well. We might ask ourselves, Why should I act morally when no one else seems to? Why act generously when the world is governed by self-interest? Why should I bother to live when those whom I love the most are dying and suffering and I can do nothing about it?

One answer to these kinds of questions has come from secular existentialists such as Albert Camus (1948, 1955). Camus believed that even though our efforts may be futile, we gain dignity by sticking with them. Although the world offers nothing meaningful, we create meaning by working for what we believe is right.

Kohlberg described an alternative. He observed that answers to despair can come from a spiritual attitude he called stage 7.

Stage 7 isn't a stage of moral reasoning, but rather a stage of spiritual development growing out of personal experiences and reflection. It needn't be tied to organized religion. It doesn't replace stage 6 efforts to rationally consider what is fair or right, but it gives some people emotional support for working for what is right. Essentially, it is a sense of being part of something much larger than oneself—a sense of oneness with life, God, or Nature. Feeling a part of a transcendent whole, one no longer feels futile or hopeless. One even feels courage in the face of death (Kohlberg & Power, 1981).

Martin Luther King expressed his personal view this way: "I am convinced that the universe is under the control of a loving purpose, and that in the struggle for righteousness man has cosmic companionship" (1963, p. 153). No matter what King faced, this "cosmic companionship" kept him going.

Kohlberg based his ideas about stage 7 on the lives of moral leaders as well as James Fowler's research on the development of faith in children and adults. On the basis of very limited data, Kohlberg speculated that stage 7 follows stage 6 of moral reasoning. It comes after stage 6 as an answer to the question of why one should act morally when it feels pointless to do so. If it emerges this late, stage 7 is extremely rare (Kohlberg & Power, 1981). One of Kohlberg's former coworkers, John Gibbs (2003), suggests that stage 7 thinking often occurs earlier and is even fairly common in adolescence. In any event, I want to emphasize that Kohlberg didn't consider stage 7 part of his moral stage sequence. Rather, he thought of it as a type of consciousness through which some individuals gain moral strength (Kohlberg & Power, 1981).

THEORETICAL ISSUES

How Development Occurs

Kohlberg, it is important to remember, was a close follower of Piaget. Accordingly, Kohlberg's theoretical positions, including that on developmental change, reflected those of his mentor.

Kohlberg (e.g., 1968; 1981, chap. 3) said his stages are not the product of maturation—that is, the stage structures and sequences do not simply unfold according to a genetic blueprint.

Neither, Kohlberg maintained, are his stages the product of socialization. That is, socializing agents (e.g., parents and teachers) do not directly teach new forms of thinking. Indeed, it is difficult to imagine them systematically teaching each new stage structure in its particular place in the sequence.

The stages emerge, instead, from our own thinking about moral problems. Social experiences do promote development, but they do so by stimulating our mental processes. As we get into discussions and debates with others, we find our views questioned and challenged and are therefore motivated to come up with new, more comprehensive positions. The stages reflect these broader viewpoints (Kohlberg et al., 1975).

We might imagine, for example, a young man and woman discussing a new law. The man says that everyone should obey it, like it or not, because laws are vital to social organization (stage 4). The woman notes, however, that some well-organized societies, such as Nazi Germany, were not particularly moral. The man therefore sees that some evidence contradicts his view. He experiences some cognitive conflict and is motivated to think about the matter more fully, perhaps moving a bit toward stage 5.

Kohlberg also sometimes spoke of change occurring through role-taking opportunities, opportunities to consider others' viewpoints (e.g., Kohlberg, 1976). As children interact with others, they learn how viewpoints differ and how to coordinate them in cooperative activities. As they discuss their problems and work out their differences, they develop their conceptions of what is fair and just.

Whatever the interactions are specifically like, they work best, Kohlberg said, when they are open and democratic. The less children feel pressured simply to conform to authority, the freer they are to settle their own differences and formulate their own ideas.

The Stage Concept

Piaget, you will recall, proposed that true mental stages meet several criteria. They (1) are qualitatively different ways of thinking, (2) are structured wholes, (3) progress in an invariant sequence, (4) can be characterized as hierarchic integrations, and (5) are cross-cultural universals. Kohlberg took these criteria very seriously, trying to show how his stages meet them all. Let's consider these points one at a time.

1. Qualitative Differences.   It seems fairly clear that Kohlberg's stages are qualitatively different from one another. For example, stage 1 responses, which focus on obedience to authority, sound very different from stage 2 responses, which argue that each person is free to behave as he or she wishes. The two stages do not seem to differ along any quantitative dimension; they seem qualitatively different.

2. Structured Wholes.   By *structured wholes*, Kohlberg meant the stages are not just isolated responses but are *general* patterns of thought that consistently show up across many different kinds of issues. One gets a sense this is true by reading through his scoring manual; one finds the same kinds of thinking reappearing on diverse items. For example, one item asks, Why should a promise be kept? As on the Heinz dilemma, children at stage 1 again speak in terms of obedience to rules, whereas those at stage 2 focus on exchanging favors that are in one's self-interest (e.g., "You never know when you're going to need that person to do something for you"). Similarly, as children proceed through the stages, they keep giving responses that are similar to those to the Heinz dilemma (Colby et al., 1987c, pp. 802–854).

In addition, Kohlberg and his coworkers (Colby et al., 1983) have obtained quantitative estimates of the extent to which subjects respond in terms of one particular stage. Since some subjects might be in transition between stages, one does not expect perfect consistency. Nevertheless, Kohlberg found that subjects scored at their dominant stage across nine dilemmas about two thirds of the time. This seems to be a fair degree of consistency, suggesting the stages may reflect general modes of thought.

3. Invariant Sequence. Kohlberg believed his stages unfold in an invariant sequence. Children always go from stage 1 to stage 2 to stage 3 and so forth. They do not skip stages or move through them in mixed-up orders. Not all children necessarily reach the highest stages; they might lack intellectual stimulation. But to the extent they do go through the stages, they proceed in order.

Most of Kohlberg's evidence on his stage sequence came from *cross-sectional* data. That is, he interviewed different children at various ages to see if the younger ones were at lower stages than the older ones. Figure 7.1

FIGURE 7.1
Use of six types of moral judgments at four ages.
(From Kohlber, L. Use of six types of moral judgments at four ages. *Human Development, 6,* p. 16. Copyright © 1963. Reprinted by permission of S. Karger A.G..)

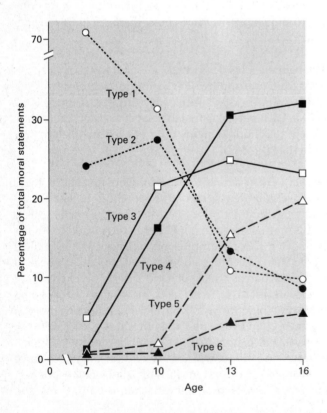

summarizes this data from his first studies. As you can see, stages 1 and 2 are primarily found at the youngest age, whereas the higher stages become more prevalent as age increases. The data support the stage sequence.

Cross-sectional findings, however, are inconclusive. In a cross-sectional study, different children are interviewed at each age, so there is no guarantee that any individual child actually moves through the stages in order. For example, there is no guarantee that a boy who is coded at stage 3 at age 13 actually passed through stages 1 and 2 in order when he was younger. More conclusive evidence must come from *longitudinal* studies, in which the same children are followed over time.

The first two major longitudinal studies (Holstein, 1973; Kohlberg & Kramer, 1969) began with samples of teenagers and then tested them at 3-year intervals. These studies produced ambiguous results. In both, most subjects either remained at the same stage or moved up one stage, but there were also some who might have skipped a stage. Furthermore, these studies indicated that some subjects had regressed, and this finding also bothered Kohlberg because he believed that movement through his stages should always be forward.

Kohlberg's response to these troublesome findings was to revise his scoring method. He had already become uncomfortable with his first (1958b) scoring manual, believing it relied too heavily on the *content* of subjects' answers rather than their underlying *reasoning*. So, in 1975, after these longitudinal findings showed stage-skipping and regression, he decided to develop a more precise scoring system. He and his coworkers created a manual that was more stringent in assigning high scores; high-stage reasoning had to be more clearly demonstrated. It was during this work that Kohlberg decided to drop stage 6 because so few people now fit into it. He and his colleagues then carried out a new longitudinal analysis of his original sample with the new manual, and this time they found no stage skipping and very little regression. Other longitudinal studies obtained similar results (Colby et al., 1983).

Kohlberg's new, longitudinal study changed the earlier picture of moral development in other ways. If we look again at Figure 7.1, which depicts the age changes found in Kohlberg's first studies, we see that stage 4 had become the dominant stage by age 16. In the new scoring system, Kohlberg found that stage 4 did not become dominant until the boys were in their 20s and 30s (Figure 7.2). Stage 5, too, appears only in the mid-20s and never becomes very prevalent.

4. Hierarchic Integration.   When Kohlberg said his stages were hierarchically integrated, he meant that people do not lose the insights gained at earlier stages but integrate them into new, broader frameworks. For example, people at stage 4 can still understand stage 3 arguments, but they now subordinate them to wider considerations. They understand that Heinz had good motives for stealing, but they point out that if we all stole whenever we had

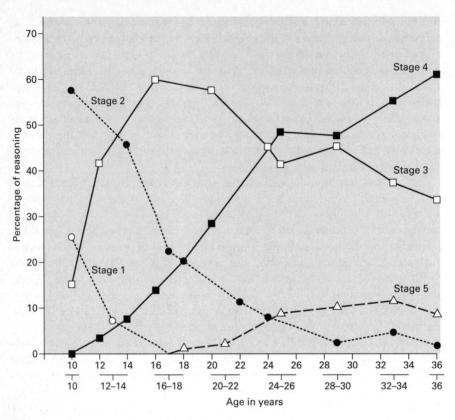

FIGURE 7.2
Mean percentage of moral reasoning at each stage for each age group.
(From Colby, Kohlberg, Gibbs, & Lieberman, A longitudinal study of moral judgment.
Monographs of the Society for Research in Child Development, Serial No. 200, 1983,
p. 46. Copyright © 1983. Reprinted by permission of Wiley-Blackwell.)

a good motive, the social structure would break down. Thus stage 4 subordi-
nates a concern for motives to a wider concern for the society as a whole.

The concept of hierarchic integration was very important for Kohlberg
because it enabled him to explain the direction of his stage sequence. Since he
was not a maturationist, he could not simply say the sequence is wired into
the genes. So he wanted to show how each new stage provides a broader
framework for dealing with moral issues. Stage 4, as mentioned, transcends
the limitations of stage 3 and becomes more broadly concerned with social
organization. Stage 5, in turn, sees the weakness of stage 4; a well-organized
society is not necessarily a moral one. Stage 5 therefore considers the rights and
orderly processes that make for a moral society. Each new stage retains the
insights of the prior stage, but it recasts them into a broader framework. In this
sense, each new stage is more cognitively adequate than the prior stage.

If Kohlberg was right about the hierarchic nature of his stages, we would expect that people would still be able to understand earlier stages but consider them inferior. In fact, when Rest presented adolescents with arguments from different stages, this is what he found. They understood lower-stage reasoning, but they disliked it. What they preferred was the highest stage they heard, whether they fully understood it or not. This finding suggests, perhaps, that they had some intuitive sense of the greater adequacy of the higher stages (Rest, 1973; Rest, Turiel, & Kohlberg, 1969).

5. Cross-Cultural Universality. Kohlberg, like all stage theorists, maintained that his stage sequence is universal; it is the same in all cultures. At first glance, this proposal might be surprising. Don't different cultures socialize their children differently, teaching them very different moral beliefs?

Kohlberg's response was that different cultures do teach different beliefs, but his stages refer not to specific beliefs but to underlying modes of reasoning (Kohlberg & Gilligan, 1971). For example, one culture might discourage physical fighting, while another encourages it more. As a result, children will have different beliefs about fighting, but they will still reason about it in the same way at the same stage. At stage 1, for example, one child might say it is wrong to fight when insulted "because you will get punished for it," while another says that "it is all right to fight; you won't get punished." The beliefs differ, but both children reason about them in the same underlying way—in terms of the physical consequences (punishment). They do so because this is what they can cognitively grasp. Later on, the first child might argue that fighting is bad "because if everyone fought all the time there would be anarchy," while the second child argues that "people must defend their honor, because if they don't everyone will be insulting everyone, and the whole society will break down." Once again, the specific beliefs differ, reflecting different cultural teachings, but the underlying reasoning is the same—in this case it is stage 4, where people can consider something as abstract as the social order. Children, regardless of their beliefs, will always move to stage 4 thinking some time after stage 1 thinking because it is cognitively so much more sophisticated.

Kohlberg, then, proposed that his stage sequence is the same in all cultures, for each stage is conceptually more advanced than the next. He and other researchers have given his interview to children and adults in a variety of cultures, including Mexico, Taiwan, Turkey, Israel, the Yucatan, Kenya, the Bahamas, and India. Most of the studies have been cross-sectional, but a few have been longitudinal. The studies have supported Kohlberg's stage sequence. To the extent that children in different cultures move through the stages, they appear to move in order (Edwards, 1981; Gibbs et al., 2007).

At the same time, people in different cultures seem to move through the sequence at different rates and to reach different end-points. In the United

States most urban, middle-class adults reach stage 4, with a small percentage using some stage 5 reasoning. The picture is fairly similar in urban areas of other countries. But in the isolated villages and tribal communities of many countries, stage 4 is rarer and stage 5 is completely absent (Gibbs et al. 2007; Edwards, 1981).

Kohlberg (Nisan & Kohlberg, 1982) suggested that we can understand these findings in terms of Piagetian theory. Cultural factors, in this theory, do not directly shape the child's moral thought, but they do stimulate thinking. Social experiences can challenge children's ideas, motivating them to come up with new ones. In traditional villages, there may be little to challenge a stage 3 morality; the norms of care and empathy work very well in governing the face-to-face interactions of the group. There is little to stimulate thinking beyond this stage.

When, in contrast, young people leave the village and go off to the city, they witness the breakdown of interpersonal ties. They see that group norms of care and empathy have little impact on the impersonal interactions of city life, and they see the need for a formal legal structure to ensure moral conduct. They also become aware of the need to coordinate a new variety of formal roles, such as manager, foreman, and worker, to keep organizations functioning smoothly. In the city, then, it's natural to think in terms of stage 4 morality. Keniston (1971) also notes that if young people attend the universities, they may take classes in which the teachers deliberately question the unexamined assumptions of their childhoods and adolescences. They are stimulated to think about moral matters in new, postconventional ways.

Nevertheless, the results for traditional village societies are striking and raise the possibility that Kohlberg's stages fail to do justice to non-Western philosophical thought. As an example, Kohlberg's former co-author John Snarey (Gibbs et al., 2007) refers to a 50-year-old man from India who said that the Heinz dilemma illustrates the need to become conscious of the unity of all life, including the lives of animals. This man's thinking was difficult to score according to Kohlberg's manual, but it seemed advanced. Similar unity-of-life thinking also is found in indigenous peoples around the world (Suzuki & Knudston, 1992). It also appears in Kohlberg's stage 7, but Kohlberg kept stage 7 out of his official six-stage moral sequence. Perhaps a more comprehensive, culturally universal stage theory would include this unity-of-life orientation and map out its development.

Moral Thought and Other Forms of Cognition

Kohlberg also tried to relate his moral stages to other forms of cognition. He first analyzed his stages in terms of their underlying cognitive structures and then looked for parallels in purely logical and social thought. For this purpose, he analyzed his own stages in terms of implicit *role-taking capacities*, capacities to consider others' viewpoints (Kohlberg, 1976; see also Rest, 1983; Selman, 1976).

At stage 1, children hardly seem to recognize that viewpoints differ. They assume there is only one right view—that of authorities. At stage 2, in contrast, they recognize that people have different interests and viewpoints. They seem to be overcoming egocentrism, and they see that perspectives are relative to the individual. They also begin to consider how individuals might coordinate their interests in terms of mutually beneficial deals.

At stage 3, people conceptualize role taking as a deeper, more empathic process—one becomes concerned with the other's feelings. Stage 4, in turn, has a broader, society wide conception of how people coordinate their roles through the legal system.

Stages 5 and 6, finally, take a more idealized look at how people might coordinate their interests. Stage 5 emphasizes democratic processes, and stage 6 considers how all parties take one another's perspectives according to the principles of justice.

The moral stages, then, reflect expanded insights into how perspectives differ and might be coordinated. As such, the moral stages might be related to stages of logical and social thought that contain similar insights. So far, the empirical evidence suggests that advances in moral thinking may *rest on* prior achievements in these other realms (Colby et al., 1987a, pp. 12–15). For example, children seem to advance to stage 2, overcoming their egocentrism in the moral sphere, only after they have made equivalent progress in their logical and social thought. If this pattern is correct, we can expect to find many individuals who are logical and even socially insightful but still underdeveloped in their moral judgment.

Moral Thought and Moral Behavior

Kohlberg's scale has to do with moral thinking, not moral action. In many situations, we might have a clear idea about what is right, but we might not act accordingly. We might put self-interest first; or we might feel our action will be futile; or we might lack the courage of our moral convictions. Consequently, we would not expect perfect correlations between moral judgment and moral action. Still, Kohlberg thought there should be some relationship.

As a general hypothesis, he proposed that moral behavior is more consistent, predictable, and responsible at the higher stages (Kohlberg et al., 1975) because the stages themselves increasingly employ more stable and general standards. For example, stage 3 bases decisions on others' approval, which can vary, but stage 4 refers to set rules and laws. Thus we can expect that moral behavior, too, will become more consistent as people move up the sequence. Generally speaking, there is some research support for this hypothesis (e.g., with respect to cheating), but the evidence is not clear cut (Blasi, 1980; Brown & Herrnstein, 1975; Kohlberg & Candee, 1984).

In a socially relevant study, Haan, Smith, and Block (1968) examined the moral reasoning of those who participated in the Berkeley Free Speech Movement in 1964. They wondered if the protestors were motivated by postconventional democratic principles. The researchers did find that the protestors' thinking was more often postconventional than that of a matched sample of nonparticipants, but this finding was not replicated with some other protests, perhaps because moral principles were not as clearly at stake (Keniston, 1971, pp. 260–261).

Overall, then, research has indicated rather modest links between moral thought and moral action (Berk, 2009, pp. 502–503). Kohlberg's adherents are unhappy with the results, believing there must be some stronger relationship that has yet to be found (Walker & Pitts, 1998).

GILLIGAN ON THE FEMININE VOICE

In 1977 Carol Gilligan, one of Kohlberg's associates and coauthors, published an essay that criticized Kohlberg's work as biased against girls and women. Gilligan expanded this article into a book, *In a Different Voice* (1982), which ignited a great deal of controversy and stimulated a considerable amount of new thinking.

Gilligan pointed out that Kohlberg developed his stages exclusively from interviews with boys, and she argued that the stages reflect a decidedly male orientation. For males, advanced moral thought revolves around rules, rights, and abstract principles. The ideal is formal justice, in which one tries to be impartial in evaluating the competing claims of all parties. The individual stands apart from the situation and tries to come up with a moral solution that is fair in some theoretical sense. This conception of morality leaves out the female voice on moral matters.

For women, Gilligan said, morality centers not on rights and rules but on interpersonal relationships and the ethics of compassion and care. The ideal is not impersonal justice but more affiliative and connected ways of living. Women's morality, in addition, is more contextualized; it is tied to real ongoing relationships rather than abstract solutions to hypothetical dilemmas.

Gilligan said that because of these gender differences, men and women frequently score at different stages on Kohlberg's scale. Women more often score at stage 3, with its focus on interpersonal relationships, whereas men more commonly score at stages 4 and 5, which reflect more abstract conceptions of social organization. Thus women score lower than men. If, however, Kohlberg's scale were more sensitive to women's distinctly interpersonal orientation, it would show that women also continue to develop their thinking beyond stage 3.

Several research studies have examined the validity of Gilligan's charge that Kohlberg's stages are biased. By and large, gender differences on Kohlberg's stages appear to be minimal. Girls often reach stage 3 a bit earlier than boys do, but overall, females and males perform at the same levels on Kohlberg's sequence (Berk, 2009, p. 499). The results do not support Gilligan's charge that Kohlberg's stage theory makes females appear inferior.

At the same time, Gilligan has called attention to an ethic of care that seems distinct from the abstract justice orientation that Kohlberg emphasized. And females do seem more drawn to the care orientation. In an early (1983) study, Nora Lyons asked men and women, "What does morality mean to you?" The following gender differences were typical:

> *Male.* "Morality is basically having a reason for a way of knowing what is right, what one ought to do."
>
> *Female.* "Morality is a type of consciousness, I guess, a sensitivity . . . that you can affect someone else's life." (p. 125)

The men's responses were more abstract, whereas the women, employing an ethic of care, more fequently saw themselves in relation to others.

Lyons reported substantial gender differences in the use of the two moral orientations. Subsequent research has found more modest differences, and both males and females usually use both justice and care orientations to at least some extent (Pratt, Skoe, & Arnold, 2004). The two orientations are also subject to cultural influences; some cultures, such as Japan, socialize both boys and girls to adopt care orientations (Berk 2009, pp. 499–450). But all in all, it does appear that there are two moral orientations, with females more generally represented by the care orientation.

Gilligan also sketched out the way women's moral orientation develops. Because she believes that women's conceptions of care and affiliation are embedded in real-life situations (not hypothetical ones), she interviewed women facing a personal crisis—the decision to have an abortion. Through these interviews, Gilligan described how women progressed from preconventional to conventional to postconventional modes of thinking. At the preconventional level, women talked about the issues in terms of what they meant to themselves, in terms of their self-interests. At the conventional level, they adopted the position of a caring, maternal person as defined by others and society at large. At the postconventional level, they formed their own insights based on their cumulative knowledge of human relationships (Gilligan, 1982, p. 74).

Throughout women's discussions, Gilligan says, we hear a concern for what is "selfish" and what is "responsible." At the first level there is an emphasis on the self, which at the conventional level shifts toward socially defined responsibility toward others. At the postconventional level, women develop insights into ways the self and others are actually interdependent. As a woman called Claire put it,

> By yourself, there is little sense to things. It is like the sound of one hand clapping, the sound of one man or one woman, there is something lacking. . . . You have to love someone else, because while you may not like them, you are inseparable from them. In a way, it is like loving your right hand. *They are part of you.* (1982, p. 160, emphasis in original)

Eva Skoe and her colleagues (Skoe & von der Lippe, 1998; Pratt et al., 2004) have begun more systematic studies of developmental changes in the care orientation. These investigators have created a standard interview (which partly allows respondents to talk about real-life dilemmas of their own choosing) and have developed a formal scoring system. Focusing on adolescents and young adults, the researchers have basically found developmental changes similar to those outlined by Gilligan. There is sometimes a slight tendency for females to score higher than males. The researchers have not, however, come across individuals who articulate human interrelatedness with the eloquence of Claire in Gilligan's study (quoted above). Perhaps such insightful responses appear with more frequency in later adulthood.

It would be interesting to know if Claire and those who think like her extend their view of interrelatedness beyond humans and include all life. If so, they may have attained a wisdom associated with non-Western cultures, and Gilligan's care orientation may provide a developmental pathway toward this wisdom.

IMPLICATIONS FOR EDUCATION

Kohlberg wanted to see people advance to the highest possible stage of moral thought. The best possible society would contain individuals who not only understand the need for social order (stage 4) but can entertain visions of universal principles, such as justice and liberty (stage 6) (Kohlberg, 1970).

How, then, can we promote moral development? Turiel (1966) found that when children listened to adults' moral judgments, the resulting change was slight. This is what Kohlberg might have expected, for he believed if children are to reorganize their thinking, they must be more active.

Accordingly, Kohlberg encouraged another student, Moshe Blatt, to lead discussion groups in which children had a chance to grapple actively with moral issues (Blatt & Kohlberg, 1975). Blatt presented moral dilemmas that engaged sixth-graders in a good deal of heated debate. He tried to leave much of the discussions to the children themselves, stepping in only to summarize, clarify, and sometimes present a view himself (p. 133). He encouraged arguments that were one stage above those of most of the class. In general, he tried to implement one of Kohlberg's main ideas on how children move through the stages. They do so by encountering views that challenge their thinking and stimulate them to formulate better arguments (Kohlberg et al., 1975).

Blatt began a typical discussion by telling a story about a man named Mr. Jones who had a seriously injured son and wanted to rush him to the hospital. Mr. Jones had no car, so he approached a stranger, told him about the situation, and asked to borrow his car. The stranger, however, refused, saying he had an important appointment to keep. So Mr. Jones took the car by force. Blatt then asked whether Mr. Jones should have done that.

In the discussion that followed, one child, Student B, felt Mr. Jones had a good cause for taking the car and also believed the stranger could be charged with murder if the son died. Student C pointed out that the stranger violated no law. Student B still felt the stranger's behavior was somehow wrong, even though he now realized it was not legally wrong. So Student B was in a kind of conflict. He had a sense of the wrongness of the stranger's behavior, but he could not articulate this sense in terms that would meet the objection. He was challenged to think about the problem more deeply.

In the end, Blatt gave him the answer. The stranger's behavior, Blatt said, was not legally wrong, but morally wrong—wrong according to God's law (this was a Sunday School class). At this point, Blatt was an authority teaching the "correct" view. In so doing, he might have robbed Student B of the chance to formulate spontaneously his own position. Blatt would have done better to ask a question or to simply clarify the student's conflict (e.g., "So it's not legally wrong, but you still have a sense that it's somehow wrong . . ."). In any case, it seems clear that part of this discussion was valuable for this student.

The Kohlberg-Blatt method of inducing cognitive conflict exemplifies Piaget's equilibration model. The child takes one view, becomes confused by discrepant information, and then resolves the confusion by forming a more advanced and comprehensive position. The method is also the dialectic process of Socratic teaching. The students give a view, the teacher asks questions that get them to see the inadequacies of their views, and they are then motivated to formulate better positions.

In Blatt's first experiment, the students (sixth-graders) participated in 12 weekly discussion groups. Blatt found that over half the students moved up one full stage after the 12 weeks. Blatt and others have tried to replicate these findings, sometimes using other age groups and lengthier series of classes. As often happens with replications, the results have not been quite so successful; upward changes have been smaller—usually a third of a stage or less. Still, it generally seems that Socratic classroom discussions held over several months can produce changes that, although small, are significantly greater than those found in control groups that do not receive these experiences (Rest, 1983).

One of Blatt's supplementary findings was that those students who reported they were most "interested" in the discussions made the greatest amount of change. This finding is in keeping with Piagetian theory. Children develop not because they are shaped through external reinforcements but because their curiosity is aroused. They become interested in information that does not quite fit into their existing cognitive structures and are thereby motivated to revise their thinking. Other investigators (Berkowitz & Gibbs, 1985) have examined actual dialogues to see if those who become most challenged and involved in the tensions of moral debates are also those who move forward. The evidence suggests this is the case.

Although Kohlberg was committed to the cognitive-conflict model of change, he also developed another strategy—the *just community* approach. Here, the focus is not on individuals but on groups. Kohlberg and some of his colleagues (Power & Reimer, 1979) set up a special high school group of about 180 students and encouraged them to function as a democracy and to think of themselves as a community. Initially, little community feeling was present. The group's dominant orientation was stage 2; it treated problems such as stealing as purely individual matters. If a boy had something stolen, it was too bad for him. After a year, however, the group norms advanced to stage 3; the students now considered stealing to be a community issue that reflected on the degree of trust and care in the group. As a result, stealing and other behavior problems sharply declined and the students began helping one another in many ways. Similar projects have produced similar results (Power, Higgins, & Kohlberg, 1989).

The just community approach has troubled some of Kohlberg's followers. Although the students are encouraged to participate in a good deal of democratic decision making, the adults in the program actively state their own positions. When Kohlberg participated, he forcefully urged the students to form a true community. Reimer, Paolitto, and Hersh (1983) wondered if the adults were not practicing indoctrination. After discussing the matter with Kohlberg, they seemed reassured that Kohlberg hadn't abandoned his belief in students' need to think for themselves (p. 251), but there are still grounds for some uneasiness. In his last years, Kohlberg may have departed somewhat from his basic commitment to independent thinking.

Although the just community approach focuses on the moral orientations of groups, researchers have wondered if the programs produce changes in individuals. Power, Higgins, and Kohlberg (1989) found that students who participated in the programs for 2 or 3 years, compared to similar students in ordinary high schools, showed greater advances in their moral judgment scores, but their progress was still modest. Most advanced from stage 2 to stage 3. The researchers advise those who primarily want to promote moral development in individuals to concentrate on academic discussions of hypothetical moral dilemmas. This intervention is easier than trying to change an entire group.

EVALUATION

Kohlberg, a follower of Piaget, offered a new, more detailed stage sequence for moral thinking. Piaget basically found two stages of moral thinking, the second of which emerges in early adolescence; Kohlberg uncovered additional stages that develop well into adolescence and adulthood. He suggested that some people even reach a postconventional level of moral thinking where they no longer accept their own society as given but think reflectively and autonomously about what a good society should be.

The suggestion of a postconventional morality is unusual in the social sciences. Perhaps it took a cognitive-developmentalist to suggest such a thing. Whereas most social scientists have been impressed by the ways in which societies mold and shape children's thinking, cognitive-developmentalists are more impressed by the capacities for independent thought. If children engage in enough independent thinking, Kohlberg suggested, they will eventually begin to formulate conceptions of rights, values, and principles by which they evaluate existing social arrangements.

Kohlberg's theory has provoked sharp criticism. We have reviewed Gilligan's view that it is male-oriented, as well as the cultural critique that Kohlberg's theory contains a Western bias. Both critiques point out that Kohlberg worked in a Kantian tradition that emphasizes abstract rights and principles of justice rather than interconnectedness, a sense of unity with others or with all of life. I believe these critiques have merit.

All the same, we shouldn't minimize the Kantian philosophical tradition in which Kohlberg worked. As Broughton (1983) argues, this morality of justice has inspired battles against repressive state power that other ethical orientations seem less equipped to handle. Gilligan's ethic of care seems to naturally focus on the interpersonal relationships of daily life, not the powerful legal system that Martin Luther King challenged in the name of justice. Similarly, as Albert Schweitzer (1929, pp. 302–304) observed, the Eastern consciousness of the unity of life is more contemplative than action oriented. In the pursuit of an abstract principle of justice, King acted.

Kohlberg gave us a picture of how children, through their own thinking, might work their way toward such principled positions. Few, to be sure, will grapple with moral issues so long and intently that they will come to think about them in the manner of Kant, Socrates, Gandhi, and King. But Kohlberg's stages provide us with an inspiring vision of where moral development might lead.

CHAPTER 8

Learning Theory: Pavlov, Watson, and Skinner

We have discussed theorists in the developmental tradition. These theorists believe that key developments are governed by internal forces—by biological maturation or by the individual's own structuring of experience. In this and the following chapter, we will describe the work of some of the theorists in the opposing, Lockean tradition—learning theorists who emphasize the processes by which behavior is formed from the outside, by the external environment.

PAVLOV AND CLASSICAL CONDITIONING

Biographical Introduction

The father of modern learning theory is Ivan Petrovich Pavlov (1849–1936). Pavlov was born in Ryazan, Russia, the son of a poor village priest. Pavlov himself planned to become a priest until the age of 21, when he decided he was more interested in a scientific career. For many years he devoted his attention to physiological investigations, and in 1904 he won the Nobel Prize for his work on the digestive system. It was just a little before this time, when Pavlov was 50 years old, that he began his famous work on conditioned reflexes. This new interest came about through an accidental discovery about the nature of salivation in dogs. Ordinarily dogs salivate when food touches their tongues; this is an innate reflex. But Pavlov noticed that his dogs also salivated *before* the food was in their mouths; they salivated when they saw the food coming, or even when they heard approaching footsteps. What had happened was that the reflex had become conditioned to new, formerly neutral stimuli.

For a while Pavlov could not decide whether to pursue the implications of his new discovery or to continue with his earlier research. Finally, after a long struggle with himself, he began studying the conditioning process. Still, Pavlov believed that he was working as a physiologist, not a psychologist. In fact, Pavlov required that everyone in his laboratory use only physiological terms. If his assistants were caught using psychological language—referring, for example, to a dog's feelings or knowledge—they were fined (R. Watson, 1968, pp. 408–412).

Basic Concepts

The Classical Conditioning Paradigm.   In a typical experiment (Pavlov, 1928, p. 104), a dog was placed in a restraining harness in a dark room and a light was turned on. After 30 seconds some food was placed in the dog's mouth, eliciting the salivation reflex. This procedure was repeated several times—each time the presentation of food was paired with the light. After a while the light, which initially had no relationship to salivation, elicited the response by itself. The dog had been conditioned to respond to the light.

In Pavlov's terms (1927, lectures 2 and 3), the presentation of food was an *unconditioned stimulus (US)*; Pavlov did not need to condition the animal to salivate to the food. The light, in contrast, was a *conditioned stimulus (CS)*; its effect required conditioning.[1] Salivation to the food was called an *unconditioned reflex (UR)*, and salivation to the light was called a *conditioned reflex (CR)*. The process itself is called *classical conditioning.*

You might have noticed in this experiment that the CS appeared *before* the US; Pavlov turned on the light before he presented the food. One of the questions he asked was whether this is the best order for establishing conditioning. He and his students discovered that it is. It is very difficult to obtain conditioning when the CS follows the US (1927, pp. 27–28). Other studies have suggested that conditioning often occurs most rapidly when the CS is presented about one-half second prior to the US (see Schwartz, 1989, p. 83).

Pavlov discovered several other principles of conditioning, some of which we will briefly describe.

Extinction.   A conditioned stimulus, once established, does not continue to work forever. Pavlov found that even though he could make a light a CS for salivation, if he flashed the light alone over several trials, it began to lose its effect. Drops of saliva became fewer and fewer until there were none at all. At this point, extinction had occurred (Pavlov, 1928, p. 297).

Pavlov also discovered that although a conditioned reflex appears to be extinguished, it usually shows some *spontaneous recovery*. In one experiment (Pavlov, 1927, p. 58), a dog was trained to salivate to the mere sight of food— the CS. (Previously, the dog would salivate only when food was in its mouth.) Next, the CS alone was presented at 3-minute intervals for six trials, and by

---

[1]Pavlov actually used the terms *conditional* and *unconditional*; they were translated *conditioned* and *unconditioned*, the terms psychologists now generally use.

the sixth trial, the dog no longer salivated. The response appeared to have been extinguished. But, after a 2-hour break in the experiment, the presentation of the CS alone once again produced a moderate amount of salivation. Thus the response showed some spontaneous recovery. If one were to continue to extinguish the response, without periodically repairing the CS to the US, the spontaneous recovery effect would also disappear.

Stimulus Generalization. Although a reflex has been conditioned to only one stimulus, it is not just that particular stimulus that elicits it. The response seems to generalize over a range of similar stimuli without any further conditioning (Pavlov, 1928, p. 157). For example, a dog that has been conditioned to salivate to a bell of a certain tone will also salivate to bells of differing tones. The ability of the neighboring stimuli to produce the response varies with the degree of similarity to the original CS. Pavlov believed that we observe stimulus generalization because of an underlying physiological process he called *irradiation*. The initial stimulus excites a certain part of the brain that then irradiates, or spreads, over other regions of the cerebrum (p. 157).

Discrimination. Initial generalization gradually gives way to a process of differentiation. If one continues to ring bells of different tones (without presenting food), the dog begins to respond more selectively, restricting its responses to the tones that most closely resemble the original CS. One can also actively produce differentiation by pairing one tone with food while presenting another tone without food. This would be called an experiment in stimulus discrimination (Pavlov, 1927, pp. 118–130).

Higher-Order Conditioning. Pavlov showed, finally, that once he had solidly conditioned a dog to a CS, he could then use the CS alone to establish a connection to yet another neutral stimulus. In one experiment, Pavlov's student trained a dog to salivate to a bell and then paired the bell alone with a black square. After a number of trials, the black square alone produced salivation. This is called *second-order conditioning*. Pavlov found that in some cases he could also establish third-order conditioning, but he could not go beyond this point (p. 34).

Evaluation

In a sense, Pavlov's basic idea was not new. In the 17th century, Locke had proposed that knowledge is based on associations. Pavlov went beyond Locke, however, and uncovered several principles of association through empirical experiments. He took the theory of learning out of the realm of pure speculation. Pavlov, as we shall see, did not discover everything there is to know about conditioning; in particular, his brand of conditioning seems restricted to a certain range of innate responses. Nevertheless, he was the first to put learning theory on a firm scientific footing.

WATSON

Biographical Introduction

The man most responsible for making Pavlovian principles a part of the psychological mainstream was John B. Watson (1878–1958). Watson was born on a farm near Greenville, South Carolina. He said that in school "I was lazy, somewhat insubordinate, and so far as I know, I never made above a passing grade" (Watson, 1936, p. 271). Nevertheless, he went to college at Furman University and graduate school at the University of Chicago, where he began doing psychological research with animals. After earning his doctorate, he took a position at Johns Hopkins University in Baltimore, where he did his most productive work.

In 1913 Watson made a great impact on psychology by issuing a manifesto, "Psychology as the Behaviorist Views It." In this article he argued that the study of consciousness through introspection has no place in psychology as a science. Psychology should abandon "the terms consciousness, mental states, mind, content, introspectively verifiable, imagery and the like" (Watson, 1913, p. 166). Instead, its goal should be "the prediction and control of behavior" (p. 158). In particular, it should study only stimuli, responses, and the formation of habits. In this way psychology could become a science like the other natural sciences.

A year later he read the works of Pavlov and the Russians on conditioned reflexes and made Pavlovian conditioning the cornerstone of his thinking. Then, in 1916, Watson began research on young children, becoming the first major psychologist to apply principles of learning to the problems of development.

In 1929 Watson's academic career came to an abrupt end. His divorce from his wife became so widely and sensationally publicized that Johns Hopkins fired him. Watson remarried (Rosalie Raynor, a coworker) and entered the business world. In order to get a good sense of business, he worked for a while as a coffee salesman and a clerk at Macy's department store. He continued to write, but now for magazines such as *Cosmopolitan*, *Harper's*, and *McCall's*, in which he advanced his ideas on child development.

Basic Concepts

Environmentalism. Watson was a behaviorist; he said we should study only overt behavior. He also was an environmentalist and made this famous proposal:

> Give me a dozen healthy infants, well-formed, and my own specified world to bring them up in and I'll guarantee to take any one at random and train him to become any type of specialist I might select—doctor,

lawyer, artist, merchant, chief, and yes, even begger-man and thief, regardless of his talents, penchants, tendencies, abilities, vocations, and race of his ancestors. (1924, p. 104)

In the next sentence Watson added that "I am going beyond my facts, and I admit it, but so have the advocates of the contrary and they have been doing it for many thousands of years" (p. 104).

Study of Emotions.   One of Watson's major interests was the conditioning of emotions. He claimed that at birth there are only three unlearned emotional reactions—fear, rage, and love. Actually, all we observe are three different physical responses, but for the sake of simplicity we can call them emotions.

Fear, Watson said (1924, pp. 152–154), is observed when infants suddenly jump or start, breathe rapidly, clutch their hands, close their eyes, fall, and cry. There are only two unconditioned stimuli that elicit fear. One is a sudden noise; the other is loss of support (as when the baby's head is dropped). Yet older children are afraid of all kinds of things—strange people, rats, dogs, the dark, and so on. Therefore it must be that the stimuli evoking most fear reactions are learned. For example, a little boy is afraid of snakes because he was frightened by a loud scream when he saw one. The snake became a conditioned stimulus.

Rage is initially an unlearned response to the restriction of body movement. If we grab a 2-year-old girl, preventing her from going where she wants, she begins to scream and stiffens her body. She lies down stiff as a rod in the middle of the street and yells until she becomes blue in the face (p. 154). Although rage is initially a reaction to one situation—being forcibly held—it later is expressed in a variety of situations; children become angry when told to wash their faces, sit on the toilet, get undressed, take a bath, and so on. Such commands elicit rage because they have been associated with physical restraint in these situations. The child becomes angry when told to get undressed because this order was initially associated with being forcibly held.

Love is initially a response that is automatically elicited by the stroking of the skin, tickling, gentle rocking, and patting. The baby responds by smiling, laughing, gurgling and cooing, and other responses that we call affectionate, good natured, and kindly. Although Watson had no use for Freud, he noted that such responses "are especially easy to bring about by the stimulation of what, for lack of a better term, we may call the erogenous zones, such as the nipples, the lips, and the sex organs" (p. 155).

Infants initially do not love specific people, but they are conditioned to do so. The mother's face frequently appears along with patting, rocking, and stroking, so it becomes a conditioned stimulus that alone elicits the good feelings toward her. Later, other people associated with the mother in some way also elicit the same responses. Thus tender or positive feelings toward others are learned through second-order conditioning.

Actually, much of Watson's writing on the emotions was speculation—and vague speculation at that. He said the three basic emotions become attached to a variety of stimuli and "we get marked additions to the responses and other modifications of them" (p. 165), but he said little about how these further developments occur. Where Watson did become specific was in his experimental work. His major experiment was on the conditioning of fear in an 11-month-old infant he called Albert B.

Conditioning Fear in Little Albert.

Conditioning Fear in Little Albert.   Watson and Raynor (Watson, 1924, pp. 159–164) wanted to see if they could condition Albert to fear a white rat. At the beginning of the experiment Albert showed no such fear. Next, the experimenter on four occasions presented the rat and simultaneously pounded a bar behind Albert's head, producing a startle response. On the fifth trial Albert was shown the rat alone, and he puckered his face, whimpered, and withdrew. He had been conditioned to fear the rat. For good measure, the experimenter combined the rat and the pounding twice more, and on the next trial, when the rat was again presented alone, Albert cried and tried to crawl away as rapidly as he could.

A few days later, Watson and Raynor tested for stimulus generalization. They found that although Albert played with many objects, he feared anything furry. He cried or fretted whenever he saw a rabbit, dog, fur coat, cotton wool, or a Santa Claus mask, even though he previously had not been afraid of these things. Albert's fear had generalized to all furry objects.

Practical Applications.   One of Watson's major practical innovations was a method for deconditioning fears. He was not able to decondition Albert of his new fears, because Albert was an orphan who was adopted and taken out of town before this could be attempted. But Watson advised one of his colleagues, Mary Cover Jones, on procedures for eliminating the fears of another little boy, a 3-year-old called Peter.

Peter seemed active and healthy in every respect except for his fears. He was scared of white rats, rabbits, fur coats, feathers, cotton wool, frogs, fish, and mechanical toys. As Watson noted, "One might well think that Peter was merely Albert B. grown up, but Peter was a different child whose fears were 'home grown'" (1924, p. 173).

Jones tried a variety of methods, including having Peter watch other children play with a rabbit. But the procedure that she and Watson highlighted was the following. Peter was placed in his highchair and given a midafternoon snack. Then a caged white rabbit was displayed at a distance that did not disturb him. The next day, the rabbit was brought increasingly closer, until he showed a slight disturbance. That ended the day's treatment. The same thing was done day after day; the rabbit was brought closer and closer, with the experimenter taking care never to disturb Peter very much. Finally, Peter was able to eat with one hand while playing with the rabbit with the other. By similar means, Jones eliminated most of Peter's other fears as well.

Jones's technique, although anticipated by Locke (Chapter 1), was quite innovative at the time. It is today known as a form of *behavior modification* called *systematic desensitization* (see Wolpe, 1969). The subject is relaxed and gradually introduced to the feared stimulus. The experimenter makes sure that the subject is at no time made to feel too anxious. Gradually, then, the subject learns to associate relaxed feelings, rather than fear, to the object or situation.

Watson did not confine his advice to therapeutic procedures for eliminating fears. He also had much to say on child rearing, which he wanted to turn into a scientific enterprise. Watson recommended, among other things, that parents place babies on rigid schedules, and he insisted they refrain from hugging, kissing, or caressing their babies. For when they do so, their children soon associate the very sight of the parent with indulgent responses and never learn to turn away from the parent and explore the world on their own (Watson, 1928, p. 81). Watson's advice was quite influential in the 1930s, but it was too extreme to last. Under the influence of Spock, Bowlby, and others, parents relaxed their schedules and became more affectionate with their children. Nevertheless, Watson's more general goal—that of placing child training on the firm foundation of scientific learning principles—remains a vital part of child care in the United States.

Evaluation

Largely because of Watson's efforts, the classical conditioning paradigm became a cornerstone of psychological theory. It would seem that many of our reactions to objects and people develop through this conditioning process (see Liebert et al., 1977).

At the same time, we need to note that the model has certain limitations. For one thing, researchers have found it much more difficult to condition infants' responses than Watson implied. This seems particularly true during the first month of life (Lamb & Campos, 1982; Sameroff & Cavanaugh, 1979). Perhaps classical conditioning becomes easier once infants have developed what Piaget calls primary circular reactions. Once they can coordinate sensorimotor actions (e.g., look at what they hear), they might more readily learn to make various associations.

There also seem to be limitations to the kinds of conditioned stimuli humans will learn. When, for example, researchers attempted to classically condition infants to fear objects such as curtains and wooden blocks instead of rats, they had great difficulty. Perhaps humans are innately disposed to fear certain stimuli. There may be biological constraints on the kinds of stimuli we will associate with different responses (Harris & Liebert, 1984, pp. 108–109; Seligman, 1972).

From a learning theory perspective, finally, classical conditioning seems limited to certain kinds of responses. It seems to apply best to the conditioning of reflexes and innate responses (which may include many emotional reactions). It is questionable whether this kind of conditioning can also explain how we learn such active and complex skills as talking, using tools, dancing, or playing chess. When we master such skills, we are not limited to inborn reactions to stimuli, but we engage in a great deal of free, trial-and-error behavior, finding out what works best. Accordingly, learning theorists have developed other models of conditioning, the most influential of which is that of B. F. Skinner.

SKINNER AND OPERANT CONDITIONING

Biographical Introduction

B. F. Skinner (1905–1990) grew up in the small town of Susquehanna, Pennsylvania. As a boy, he liked school and enjoyed building things such as sleds, rafts, and wagons. He also wrote stories and poetry. After graduating from high school, he went to Hamilton College in New York. There, he felt somewhat out of place, but he graduated Phi Beta Kappa with a major in English literature.

Skinner spent the next two years trying to become a writer, but he eventually decided that he could not succeed because "I had nothing important to say" (1967, p. 395). Because he was interested in human and animal behavior, he enrolled in the graduate psychology department at Harvard, where he began doing research and formulating his ideas on learning. Skinner taught at the University of Minnesota (1936–1945), Indiana University (1945–1947), and Harvard University (1947 until his death in 1990).

Despite his successful career as a scientist, Skinner never completely abandoned his earlier interests. For one thing, he continued to display his boyhood enthusiasm for building things. When his first child was born, he decided to make a new, improved crib. This crib, which is sometimes called his "baby box," is a pleasantly heated place that does away with the necessity of excessive clothing and permits freer movement. It is not, as is sometimes thought, an apparatus for training babies. It is simply a more comfortable crib. Skinner's literary interests also reemerged. In 1948 he published a novel, *Walden Two*, which describes a utopian community based on his principles of conditioning.

The Operant Model

Like Watson, Skinner was a strict behaviorist. He believed psychology should dispense with any references to intangible mental states (such as goals, desires, or purposes); instead, it should confine itself to the study of overt behavior. Like Watson, in addition, Skinner was an environmentalist; although Skinner recognized that organisms enter the world with genetic endowments, he was primarily concerned with how environments control behavior.

In contrast to Watson, however, Skinner's primary model of conditioning was not Pavlovian. The responses that Pavlov studied, Skinner said, are best thought of as *respondents*. These are responses that are automatically "elicited" by known stimuli. For example, the ingestion of food automatically elicits salivation, and a loud noise automatically elicits a startle response. Most respondents are probably simple reflexes.

A second class of behavior, which most interested Skinner, is called *operant*. In operant behavior, the animal is not harnessed in, like Pavlov's dogs, but moves freely about and "operates" on the environment. For example, in early experiments by Thorndike (1905), cats in a puzzle box would sniff, claw, and jump about until they hit upon the response—pulling a latch—that enabled them to get food. The successful response would then be more likely to recur. In such cases, we cannot always identify any prior stimulus that automatically elicits the responses. Rather, animals emit responses, some of which become more likely in the future because they have led to favorable *consequences*. Behavior, in Skinner's terms, is controlled by the reinforcing stimuli that follow it (Skinner, 1938, pp. 20–21; 1953, pp. 65–66). The two models, respondent and operant, are diagrammed in Figure 8.1.

To study operant conditioning, Skinner constructed an apparatus that is commonly referred to as a "Skinner box." This is a fairly small box in which an animal is free to roam about (see Figure 8.2). At one end there is a bar (lever) that, when pressed, automatically releases water or a pellet of food. The animal, such as a rat, at first pokes around until she eventually presses the bar, and then she gets the reward. As time goes on, she presses the bar more frequently. The most important measure of learning, for Skinner, is the *rate* of responding; when responses are reinforced, their rates of

FIGURE 8.1
Respondent and operant conditioning. In respondent (Pavlovian) conditioning, stimuli precede responses and automatically elicit them. In operant conditioning, the initial stimuli are not always known; the organism simply emits responses that are controlled by reinforcing stimuli (S_Rs) that follow.

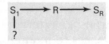

Respondent conditioning   Operant conditioning

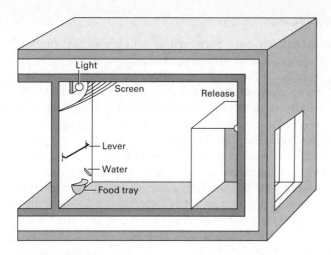

FIGURE 8.2
A Skinner box. One side has been cut away to show the
part occupied by the animal.
(From Skinner, B. F., *The Behavior of Organisms*, p. 49.
Copyright 1938, renewed 1966. Reprinted by permission
of Prentice-Hall, Inc.)

occurrence increase. In Skinner's apparatus, the bar presses are automatically registered on a graph, so the experimenter need not be present much of the time. The data are presented as a learning curve, illustrated in Figure 8.3.

Skinner believed that operant behavior, in comparison to respondent behavior, plays a much greater role in human life. When we brush our teeth, drive a car, or read a book, our behavior is not automatically elicited by a specific stimulus. The mere sight of a book, for instance, does not elicit reading in the same way a bright light automatically elicits an eyeblink. We may or may not read the book, depending on the consequences that have followed in the past. If reading books has brought us rewards, such as high grades, we are likely to engage in this behavior. Behavior is determined by its consequences (Munn, Fernald, & Fernald, 1974, p. 208).

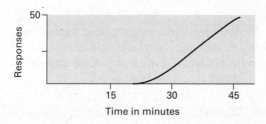

FIGURE 8.3
A typical learning curve.
(From Skinner, B. F. *The Behavior of Organisms,* Copyright 1938. Renewed 1966. Reprinted by permission of Prentice-Hall, Inc.)

Principles of Conditioning

Reinforcement and Extinction.   Skinnerians have performed numerous experiments showing that human behavior, beginning in infancy, can be controlled by reinforcing stimuli. For example, infants increase their rates of sucking when sucking results in sweet, as opposed to nonsweet, liquid (Lipsitt, 1975). Similarly, infants' rates of smiling and vocalization can be increased if the behavior leads to rewards such as the experimenter's smiles, caresses, and attention (Brackbill, 1958; Rheingold, Gewirtz, & Ross, 1959).

In such experiments, one is dealing with different kinds of reinforcers. Some reinforcers, such as food or the removal of pain, are *primary reinforcers;* they have "natural" reinforcing properties. Other reinforcing stimuli, such as an adult's smiles, praise, or attention, are probably *conditioned reinforcers;* their effectiveness stems from their frequent association with primary reinforcers (Skinner, 1953, p. 78).

Operant behavior, like respondent behavior, is also subject to *extinction* (p. 69). For example, because children do things "just to get attention" (p. 78), one can extinguish undesirable behaviors, such as excessive crying or temper tantrums, by consistently withdrawing one's attention whenever they occur (Etzel & Gewirtz, 1967; Williams, 1959).

Operant behavior that has apparently been extinguished may also show *spontaneous recovery.* For example, a little boy whose temper tantrums had been extinguished through the withdrawal of attention began having tantrums once again when placed in a new situation (Williams, 1959). The behavior had to be extinguished further.

Immediacy of Reinforcement.   Skinner (1953, p. 101; 1959, p. 133) found he could initially establish responses at the highest rates when he reinforced them promptly. A rat will begin pressing a bar at a high rate only if she has promptly received a food pellet each time she has done so. As Bijou and Baer (1961, p. 44) point out, this principle has importance for child rearing. If a father shows pleasure immediately after his son brings him the newspaper, the boy is likely to repeat the behavior the next evening. If, however, the father is so engrossed in something else that he delays reinforcing his son's behavior for a few minutes, the boy's behavior will not be strengthened. In fact, what gets strengthened is the boy's behavior at the moment of reinforcement. If he is building blocks at that moment, it is block-building, not newspaper-fetching, that gets reinforced.

Discriminative Stimuli.   We have said that operant conditioning may be described without any reference to initiating stimuli. This is true, but it does not mean such stimuli are unimportant. Stimuli that precede responses may gain considerable control over them.

For example, Skinner (1953, pp. 107–108) reinforced a pigeon each time she stretched her neck. At this point Skinner had no knowledge of any initial stimulus; he simply waited for the pigeon to emit the response and then reinforced it. Next, however, he reinforced the response only when a signal light was on. After a few trials, the pigeon stretched her neck much more frequently when the light was flashing than when it was off. The flashing light had become a *discriminative stimulus.* The light controlled the behavior because it set the occasion upon which the behavior was likely to be reinforced.

Skinner (pp. 108–109) listed numerous examples to show how everyday behavior becomes attached to discriminative stimuli. In an orchard in which red apples are sweet and all others are sour, redness becomes a stimulus that sets the occasion upon which picking and eating will produce favorable outcomes. Similarly, we learn that a smile is an occasion upon which approaching another will meet with a positive response. When others frown, the same approach meets with aversive consequences, such as rebuffs. Insofar as this is true, the facial expressions of others become discriminative stimuli that control the likelihood that we will approach them.

Although discriminative stimuli do exert considerable control, it must be emphasized that this control is not automatic, as in the case of respondent conditioning. In Pavlov's experiments, prior stimuli automatically elicit responses; in operant conditioning, such stimuli only make responses more *likely.*

Generalization.   In operant conditioning, as in respondent conditioning, there is a process of *stimulus generalization* (Skinner, 1953, p. 132). Suppose a little girl has been reinforced for saying "Da da" at the sight of her father, but not when she is looking at her mother or siblings. The father has become a discriminative stimulus. It is not unusual, however, to find the girl saying "Da da" when she sees any man at all, such as strangers on the street. The stimulus has generalized. Her parents must now teach her to make a finer discrimination. They might say, "That's right," when she utters "Da da" in the presence of her father, but not when she looks at any other man.

Similarly, we can observe *response generalization.* It has been shown, for example, that when children are reinforced for using one part of speech, such as plurals, they begin uttering new plurals—even though they haven't received reinforcement for those particular words. Reinforcement influences not only particular responses but those of the same general class (Lovaas, 1977, pp. 112–113).

Shaping.   Operant behavior is not acquired in all-or-nothing packages. It is usually learned gradually, little by little. Even teaching a pigeon to peck a spot on the wall, Skinner (1953, p. 92) showed, must be gradually shaped. If we place a pigeon in a box and wait for her to peck the spot, we may have to wait days or even weeks. Much of the time, the pigeon doesn't even approach the spot. So we must shape her behavior. First, we give the bird food when she turns in the direction of the spot. This increases the frequency of this behavior. Next, we withhold food until she makes a slight movement in the right direction. We then keep reinforcing positions closer and closer to the spot, until the bird is facing it. At this point we can reinforce head movements, first giving food for any forward movement and finally reinforcing the bird only when she actually pecks the spot. Through this procedure we gradually shape the desired response. Shaping is also called the "method of approximations," because reinforcement is made contingent upon better and better approximations of the desired response.

We probably teach many human skills in this bit-by-bit shaping process. When we teach a boy to swing a baseball bat, we first say "Good" when he gets his hands into the right grip. We then say "Right" when he lifts his bat in the correct position over his shoulder. We then work on his stance, a level swing, and so on—gradually shaping the complete behavior.

Behavior Chains.   Although behavior may be shaped bit by bit, it also develops into longer, integrated response chains. For example, batting in baseball involves picking up the bat, getting the right grip and stance, watching for the right pitch, swinging, running the bases, and so on. Skinnerians attempt to examine each step in terms of reinforcements and stimuli. Reaching for the bat is reinforced by obtaining it, which also serves as a stimulus for the next act, getting the right grip. Once the hands are placed on the bat, we get a certain "feel" that we recognize as the proper grip. This "feel" is a reinforcement, and it also signals the next action, pulling the bat over the shoulder. A little later, the sensation of the bat squarely striking the ball is a reinforcement for the swing, and it also signals the next action, running the bases. When a boy or girl has become a good hitter, the entire sequence is often performed in a smooth, integrated fashion (Schwartz, 1989).

Schedules of Reinforcement.   Skinner (1953, p. 99) observed that our everyday behavior is rarely reinforced *continuously*, every time; instead, it is reinforced *intermittently*. We do not find good snow every time we go skiing or have fun every time we go to a party. Accordingly, Skinner studied the effects of different schedules of intermittent reinforcement.

Intermittent reinforcement may be set up on a *fixed-interval* schedule, such that the organism receives a reward for the first response after a specified period of time. For instance, a pigeon receives food after pecking a disc, but must wait 3 minutes before her next peck is rewarded, then 3 more minutes, and so on. The rate of responding on this schedule is generally low. Higher rates are produced by *fixed-ratio* schedules, as when the pigeon gets food after every fifth peck. On both schedules, however, there is a lull in responding immediately after reinforcement. It is as if the organism knows it has a long way to go before the next reinforcement (p. 103). Students often experience this effect immediately after completing a long term paper—it is difficult to get started on another assignment.

The lulls produced by fixed schedules can be avoided by varying reinforcement in unpredictable ways. On *variable-interval* schedules, reinforcement is administered after an average length of time, but the intervals are mixed up. With *variable-ratio* schedules, we vary the number of responses needed to produce a reward. When put on these two schedules, organisms consistently respond at high rates, especially on variable-ratio schedules. They keep responding because a reward might come at any time.

One of Skinner's most important findings is that intermittently reinforced behavior, in comparison to that which is continuously reinforced, is much more difficult to extinguish. This is why many of our children's undesirable behaviors are so difficult to stop. We might be able to resist a child's nagging or demanding behavior most of the time, but if we yield every once in a while, the child will persist with it (Bijou & Baer, 1961, p. 62).

If we wish to begin teaching a desirable form of behavior, it is usually best to begin with continuous reinforcement; this is the most efficient way to get the behavior started. However, if we also wish to make the behavior last, we might at some point switch to an intermittent schedule (Bijou & Baer, 1961, p. 62).

Negative Reinforcement and Punishment.   So far we have been focusing on positive reinforcement. Reinforcement means strengthening a response (increasing its rate), and positive reinforcements strengthen responses by adding positive consequences such as food, praise, or attention. Responses may also be strengthened through *negative reinforcement*, by removing unpleasant or aversive stimuli. Basically, what is strengthened in this way is the tendency to escape, as when a girl standing on a diving board learns to escape the taunts of her peers by diving into the water (Skinner, 1953, pp. 73, 173).

When we *punish*, in contrast, we do not try to strengthen behavior but to eliminate it. Punishment, Skinner said, is "the commonest technique of control in modern life. The pattern is familiar: If a man does not behave as you wish, knock him down; if a child misbehaves, spank him; if the people of a country misbehave, bomb them" (p. 182).

Punishment, however, does not always work. In an early experiment, Skinner (1938) found that when he punished rats for bar pressing (by having the bar swing back and smack them on the legs), he only temporarily suppressed the response. In the long run, punishment did not eliminate the response any faster than did extinction. Other studies (e.g., Estes, 1944) have obtained similar results, and the findings conform to everyday experience. Parents who hit their children get them to behave for a while, but the parents find that the misconduct reappears later on.

Skinner also objected to punishment because it produces unwanted side effects. A child who is scolded in school may soon appear inhibited and conflicted. The child seems torn between working and avoiding work because of the feared consequences. The boy or girl may start and stop, become distracted, and behave in other awkward ways (Skinner, 1953, pp. 190–191).

Some researchers believe Skinner overstated the case against punishment. In some instances punishment will in fact completely eliminate responses. This is especially true when the punishment is extremely painful. Also, punishment can be effective when it is promptly administered, and when the organism can make alternative responses that are then rewarded (Liebert et al., 1977, pp. 138–141). Nevertheless, the effects of punishment are often puzzling and undesirable.

Skinner recommended that instead of punishing children, we try extinction. "If the child's behavior is strong only because it has been reinforced by 'getting a rise out of' the parent, it will disappear when this consequence is no longer forthcoming" (1953, p. 192). Skinnerians often suggest that we combine extinction for undesirable behavior with positive reinforcement for desirable behavior. In one study, teachers simply ignored nursery school children whenever they were aggressive and gave them praise and attention whenever they were peaceful or cooperative. The result was a quieter classroom (P. Brown & Elliott, 1965).

Internal Events:
Thoughts, Feelings, and Drives

Thoughts.   It is sometimes said that Skinner proposed an "empty organism" theory. He examined only overt responses and ignored internal states. This characterization is accurate but slightly oversimplified. Skinner did not deny that an inner world exists. We do have inner sensations, such as the pain from a toothache. We also can be said to think. Thinking is merely a weaker or more covert form of behavior. For example, we may talk to ourselves silently instead of out loud, or we may think out our moves silently in a chess game. However, such private events have no place in scientific psychology unless we can find ways of making them public and measuring them (Skinner, 1974, pp. 16–17, and chap. 7).

Skinner was particularly distressed by our tendency to treat thoughts as the causes of behavior. We say we went to the store because "we got an idea to do so" or that a pigeon pecked a disc because she "anticipated" food. However, we are in error when we speak in this way. We go to stores, and pigeons peck discs, only because these actions have led to past reinforcements. Any discussion of goals or expectations is superfluous. Worse, it diverts us from the true explanation of behavior—the controlling effect of the environment (Skinner, 1969, pp. 240–241; 1974, pp. 68–71).

Feelings.   Skinner acknowledged that we have emotions, just as we have thoughts. However, feelings do not cause behavior any more than thoughts do. We might say we are going to the movies because "we want to" or because "we feel like it," but such statements explain nothing. If we go to the movies, it is because this behavior has been reinforced in the past (Skinner, 1971, p. 10).

Emotional responses themselves can be explained according to learning-theory principles. In our discussion of Watson, we saw how emotional reactions might be learned through classical conditioning. Skinner believes an operant analysis is also useful. Many emotions are the by-products of different reinforcement contingencies. Confidence, for example, is a by-product of frequent positive reinforcement. When we learn to hit a baseball sharply and consistently, we develop a sense of confidence and mastery (Skinner, 1974, p. 58). Conversely, we become depressed and lethargic when reinforcements are no longer forthcoming. On certain fixed-ratio or fixed-interval schedules we find it difficult to get going after receiving a reward because further rewards will not be coming for some time (p. 59).

An operant analysis also helps us understand why various patterns of emotional behavior persist. If a little girl persistently behaves in an aggressive manner, it is important to know the consequences of this behavior. Do her actions succeed in getting attention or other children's toys? If so, her aggressiveness is likely to continue. Similarly, if displays of happiness, meekness, sympathy, fearfulness, and other emotional responses persist, it is because they have produced positive consequences (Bijou & Baer, 1961, pp. 73–74; Skinner, 1969, pp. 129–130).

Skinner believed, then, that we can understand emotions if we look at them as the products of environmental control. It is useless to consider emotions as intrapsychic causes of behavior, as the Freudians do. For example, a Freudian might talk about a man who fears sex because of anticipated punishment from an internal agency, the superego. To Skinner, such discussions get us nowhere. If we wish to understand why a person avoids sex, we must look at the past consequences of his sexual behavior (Skinner, 1974, chap. 10).

Drives.   Skinner's refusal to look for causes of behavior within the organism led to certain difficulties. In particular, he had trouble with the concept of drive. Drives, such as hunger or thirst, would seem to refer to internal states that motivate behavior, and Skinner himself deprived his animals of food and water in order to make reinforcements effective.

Skinner argued that we do not need to conceive of drives as inner states, either mental or physiological. We simply specify the hours we deprive an animal of food or water and examine the effect of this operation on response rates (Skinner, 1953, p. 149).

Still, the drive concept has remained a thorn in the side of Skinnerians, and they have therefore searched for ways of conceptualizing reinforcement without reference to this concept. One interesting proposal has been made by Premack (1961), who suggests we think of reinforcement simply as the momentary probability of a response. Behavior that has a high probability of occurrence at the moment can serve as a reinforcer for behavior with a lower probability. If children are supposed to be eating their dinner but are busy playing instead, playing can be used as a reinforcer for eating. We simply say, "Eat some dinner and then play some more" (Homme & Totsi, 1969). Conceptualized in this way, eating and drinking have no special status as reinforcers. Eating and drinking, like any other actions, may or may not be good reinforcers, depending on their probabilities of occurrence at a particular time.

Species-Specific Behavior

Skinner argued, then, that we need not look inside the organism for the causes of behavior. Behavior is controlled by the external environment. There do seem to be, however, certain limitations to environmental control. As we briefly mentioned in our evaluation of Watson, each species has a particular genetic endowment that makes it easier to teach it some things rather than other things. Operant research has found, for example, that it is hard to teach a rat to let go of objects, and it is hard to shape vocal behavior in nonhuman species (Skinner, 1969, p. 201). There are, as learning theorists increasingly say, biological "constraints" on what a species can learn.

In practice, Skinnerians often deal with species-specific behavior as the *topography* of a response. That is, the experimenter maps out a description of the behavior he or she can work with—for example, vocal behavior in humans. The topography is merely a description and does not constitute the most important part of the analysis, which is the way reinforcements shape and maintain behavior. Nevertheless, the topography is essential (pp. 199–209).

In a larger sense, Skinner argued, even species-specific behavior is a product of environmental contingencies. For such behavior has become, in the course of evolution, part of the species' repertoire because it has helped that species survive in a certain environment. Thus environments selectively reinforce all behavior—not only that in an animal's lifetime but also that in its species' evolutionary past (pp. 199–209).

Practical Applications

Behavior Modification with Children with Autism.   Skinner's research readily lends itself to practical applications. We have seen how Skinnerians might extinguish temper tantrums or get an unruly class to behave. The use of operant techniques to correct behavior problems is a branch of behavior modification. Operant techniques supplement the systematic desensitization procedures first employed by Watson and Jones.

An impressive example of operant therapy is Lovaas's work with children with autism. Autism was first described by Kanner in 1943. It is a severe disorder in which children are extremely isolated. The children also engage in repetitive behavior such as spinning objects or flapping their hands over and over. Many are mute, and others are echolalic—they merely echo what one says. Some engage in self-injurious behavior, such as hitting themselves (Lovaas, 2003; Koegel & Koegel, 2006, p. 34).

Lovaas tries to gain control over the children's behavior so he can change it. He tries to eliminate socially inappropriate behavior and reinforce socially appropriate behavior. If a child engages in echolalia, repetitive behavior, or self-injurious behavior, Lovaas withdraws attention or punishes the child with a loud "No!" or a slap on the thigh. If the child does something more appropriate, such as emitting correct speech, Lovaas gives the child a reward, perhaps a bit of tasty cereal and the word "Good" (Lovaas, 1987).

Frequently, appropriate behavior must be gradually shaped, as when the therapist teaches mute children to imitate words. At first, the therapist reinforces *any* vocalization the child makes, even blowing air out of the mouth. Once the child is regularly making sounds, the therapist says a word such as "baby" and rewards any sound that comes within the next 5 seconds. After that, rewards are made contingent on better and better approximations of "baby" (or other target words) (Lovaas, 1969, 1977).

Initially, some children are so silent that the therapist must elicit sounds by tickling them or pressing their lips together and then letting the air out. These interventions are called *manual prompts*. Strictly speaking, these prompts violate Skinner's operant paradigm; operant conditioning reinforces freely emitted behavior—not behavior forced by the therapist's actions. Prompts are faded as soon as possible (Lovaas, 1977, pp. 36–37).

Lovaas's therapy is intensive. In his first major project, begun in the 1960s, Lovaas and his staff trained children seven hours a day, seven days a week, for one year in a residential treatment setting at UCLA. Most of the children were 5 to 8 years old (Lovaas, 1973, 1977). Many made significant progress, but when they were discharged to state hospitals, they lost all they had gained. In his next major project, in the 1970s and 1980s, Lovaas avoided this discharge problem; he worked with children in their homes and taught parents to help train the children. He also worked with younger children—under the age of 4 years. The children were trained at least 40 hours a week. After 2 to 3 years, nearly half entered first grade as regular students—an achievement that would have once seemed impossible (Lovaas, 1987). A 6-year follow-up study found that almost all of these children still attended a regular school (McEachlin, Smith, & Lovaas, 1993).

Lovaas and his colleagues have described their treatment as *applied behavior analysis,* or *ABA,* a term they apply to any therapy that uses principles of learning in a measurable, scientific manner. Lovaas's ABA methods are still the most widely used, but there are new variations. Robert and Lynn Koegel and their colleagues (2006) have developed a program that focuses less on teaching discrete skills and more on broad areas such as motivation. The Koegels believe that children often have difficulty with Lovaas's tasks and sometimes lose their enthusiasm for learning because reinforcement is infrequent. The Koegels therefore offer reinforcement more frequently—often just for the effort. (They call this *loose shaping*.) They also let the child choose toys and activities. And instead of giving cereal treats, they offer rewards that are important to the child in his or her everyday environment. If a girl wants a shovel to dig in the sand, the therapist asks her to say "Shovel," and if she does, she receives the shovel. If she says, "Swing," she gets a push on the swing. The Koegels have reported success, although their studies aren't nearly as extensive as those by Lovaas.

Compared to Lovaas, the Koegels give children more opportunities to take the lead. But the therapist still maintains control, as when the therapist requires the child to name an object such as a shovel before receiving it. Furthermore, if a child engages in highly repetitive behavior, the therapist actively intervenes to turn the child's attention to other activities. Sometimes the therapist actually stands in front of the object, such as a fan, that stimulates repetitive behavior (Koegel & Koegel, 2006, p. 221). In Chapter 14 we will look at a more thoroughly child-initiated therapy with autistic children—the psychoanalytic therapy of Bruno Bettelheim.

Programmed Instruction. Skinner contributed to the education of normal children through his invention of teaching machines and programmed instruction (Skinner, 1968). The teaching machine was a simple apparatus that permitted one to read a brief passage, answer questions, and then, by turning a knob, see if one was correct. Actually, the machine itself was less important than the programmed material it contained, and today the material is presented in simple booklet form or installed in a computer. To get an idea of how programmed instruction works, read the following material[2] and pretend to fill in the blanks. As you do so, cover the answers on the left side with a piece of paper, sliding it down just far enough to check your answers.

	1. Programmed instruction involves several basic principles of learning. One of these, called the principle of *small steps*, is based on the premise that
small	new information must be presented in _____ steps.
	2. The learner gradually acquires more and more
small steps	information, but always in _____ _____.
	3. Because active readers generally acquire more knowledge than passive readers, programmed instruction also is based on the principle of *active participation*. Writing key words as one is reading
active	involves the principle of _____ participation.

[2]From Munn, N. L., Fernald, L. D., and Fernald, P. S., *Introduction to Psychology*, 3rd ed., Boston: Houghton Mifflin Co., 1974, pp. 249–250. By permission.

4. While reading a book, an uninterested learner may slip into a passive state and discover that he cannot recall what he has just "read." In using programmed instruction the learner is prompted to remain alert by writing the key words, thus utilizing the principle of _____ _____.

active participation

5. In these two techniques of programmed instruction, information is presented in _____ _____, and occasionally key words are missing thus requiring the learner's _____ _____ to complete the statements.

small steps

active participation

6. A third principle, *immediate knowledge of results*, is illustrated when a professor returns quiz papers to his students at the end of the class in which they were written. These students receive almost immediate _____ of results.

knowledge

7. If a student makes an incorrect response at any point in programmed instruction, he discovers his mistake because the correct answer may be seen immediately after the frame, before the next one is considered. Thus, in programmed instruction, the learner receives _____ knowledge _____ _____.

immediate
of results

8. Notice that in programmed instruction, unlike the evaluation of term papers, "immediate" does not mean a week or even a day but rather a few seconds. The reader of the program is continuously informed concerning his progress; he receives _____ _____ _____ _____.

immediate knowledge
of results

9. Let us review the three techniques of programmed instruction already considered. By means of _____ _____, the reader learns new material, which he acquires through _____ _____ followed by _____ _____ _____ _____.

small steps
active participation
immediate knowledge
of results

Programmed instruction embodies several Skinnerian principles. First, it proceeds in small steps, because Skinner has found that the best way to establish new behavior is to shape it bit by bit. Second, the learner is active, because this is the natural condition of organisms. (Recall how Pavlov's dogs, in contrast, were harnessed in and simply reacted to stimuli.) Third, feedback is immediate because Skinner found that learning is most rapid when promptly reinforced. (Reinforcement here is the knowledge that one's answer is correct.)

A sample of programmed reading for children is found in Figure 8.4. In programmed instruction, students work independently and at their own pace. The instruction units are constructed so each student may begin at a level she can easily master. One does not want the student making many errors at first, for then she will lack positive reinforcement for learning. As with shaping, one

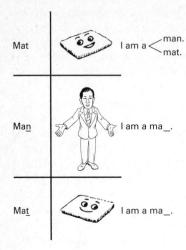

Mat   I am a ⟨man. / mat.⟩

Man   I am a ma_.

Mat   I am a ma_.

FIGURE 8.4
Programmed instruction for children.
(Adapted from Sullivan, M. W., Programmed
learning in reading. In A. D. Calvin, Ed.,
Programmed Instruction: Bold New Venture.
Bloomington: Indiana University Press, 1969,
p. 111. By permission of the publisher.)

begins by reinforcing responses that are within the student's behavioral repertoire and gradually building up from there.

On a technical level, programmed instruction has run into some difficulties. For example, students sometimes rush through the programs without fully mastering the material (Munson & Crosbie, 1998). But the
underlying principles are important and make efforts to solve the problems
worthwhile.

Surprisingly, the principles underlying programmed instruction overlap somewhat with Montessori's. Both Skinner and Montessori wanted to
make learning an individualized, self-paced activity that begins at the student's own level and builds skills gradually. For both, the goal is not to tear
down, through criticism or punishment, but to make learning a consistently
positive experience.

But the two approaches also differ. For one thing, programmed
instruction involves material that young children read (see Figure 8.4),
whereas Montessori materials are largely physical. Even when learning to
read, Montessori children begin with sandpaper letters, metal insets, and so
on. Montessori thought young children find such physical activities more
natural.

More fundamentally, there is the difference in the extent to which the
child's work is free from adult direction. Montessori allowed children to
choose their own tasks and work on them while the teacher steps into the
background. She wanted children to discover for themselves how something is out of place, how cylinders fit, how water is poured, and whatever
else is important to them. In programmed instruction, in contrast, adult
direction is pervasive. Although it might seem that children work

independently on the booklets, in fact an adult (the program developer) has structured each small response. The child follows the adult's lead, repeatedly checking with this social authority to see if she is right. Children probably derive less sense that they are making their own discoveries about the world.

Nevertheless, it is important not to overlook the similarities between the two methods—especially the way both try to make learning a positive experience. One can even imagine Skinner approving Montessori's physical tasks, albeit in his own terms. He would say they work not because they allow for spontaneous discoveries, but because they allow children to make responses that readily result in positive feedback from the physical environment.

EVALUATION

Skinner considerably widened the scope of learning theory. After noting the limitations of classical conditioning, he explored the nature of operant behavior, where the organism acts freely and is controlled by the consequences of its actions. In a brilliant series of studies, Skinner showed how such control is exerted—by schedules of reinforcement, shaping, the influence of discriminative stimuli, and other factors. Furthermore, Skinner amply demonstrated the practical importance of his ideas.

In the process, Skinner stirred up controversies on many fronts. To some, his work lends itself to authoritarian practices—for he suggests ways to control, manipulate, and program others' behavior. Skinner's (e.g., 1974, p. 244) reply was that environments do, in fact, control behavior, and how we use our knowledge of this fact is up to us. We can create environments that suit humane purposes, or we can create ones that do not.

Developmentalists, too, often enter into heated, value-laden debates with Skinnerians. Developmentalists cringe at talk of controlling and changing children's behavior, when we should, instead, try to understand children and give them opportunities to grow on their own. To many Skinnerians, such sentiments are romantic and naive, for children chiefly develop through the molding influence of the external environment.

In a more objective vein, there are essentially three ways in which Skinner and writers in the developmental tradition disagree. First, developmental theorists often discuss *internal* events. Piaget described complex mental structures, even though he did not expect to find direct evidence for all of them in any individual case. Freudians discuss internal events, such as unconscious fantasies, that we cannot directly observe at all. Skinner believed such concepts divert us from scientific progress, which is made when we confine ourselves to the measurement of overt responses and environmental stimuli. But on this point, Skinner is now generally considered too extreme. Since the 1960s, there has been a dramatic new interest in cognition, and even growing numbers of learning theorists have been considering internal, cognitive events, even if the events cannot be directly measured. In the next chapter we will discuss a major example of cognitive learning theory.

Second, developmental theorists and Skinnerians disagree on the meaning and importance of developmental *stages*—periods when children organize experience in very different ways. In Piaget's theory, for example, a child's stage is a crucial variable; it is a predictor of the kind of experience the child can learn from. A child at the sensorimotor level will not learn tasks that involve language, nor will a child beginning to master concrete operations learn much from lectures covering abstract theory.

Skinnerians doubt the validity of stages as general, distinct ways of thinking or behaving; they believe the environment shapes behavior in a gradual, continuous manner (Bijou, 1976, p. 2; Skinner, 1953, p. 91). Skinner did acknowledge that one must note the child's age in any experiment, just as one must note an animal's species and characteristic behavior (Skinner, 1969, p. 89). Age contributes to the "topography" of behavior; it helps describe the behavior that the experimenter sets about to shape or maintain. However, such information is still merely descriptive; it is secondary to environmental variables that control behavior. The question is whether the child's developmental status deserves this secondary role.

A third issue dividing Skinner and developmental theorists is the most important of all. This issue concerns the *source* of behavioral change. Developmentalists contend that in crucial instances a child's thoughts, feelings, and actions develop spontaneously, from within. Behavior is not exclusively patterned by the external environment. Gesell, for example, believed children stand, walk, talk, and so on from inner maturational promptings. Piaget was not a maturationist, but he also looked primarily to inner forces underlying developmental change. In his view, children's behavior is not structured by the environment but by children themselves. Children, out of a spontaneous interest in moderately novel events, construct increasingly complex and differentiated structures for dealing with the world.

Consider, for example, a baby girl who drops a block, hears the sound, and drops it again and again, making this new and interesting sound last. In Skinner's theory, the sound is a reinforcer that controls her behavior. But this reinforcer will soon lose its effectiveness, for she will soon become interested in more complex outcomes (Kohlberg, 1969a). She may, for instance, begin listening for different sounds as she drops objects from different heights. For Piaget, we cannot look to external reinforcements as the determinants of behavior, for these often vary with the child's developing interests. For him, the main variable is the child's spontaneous curiosity about increasingly complex events.

Developmental theorists, then, try to conceptualize ways in which children grow and learn on their own, somewhat independent of others' teachings or external reinforcements. At the same time, no one can deny that environments also reinforce and control behavior to a considerable extent, and often in ways Skinner described. Skinner's theory and research, moreover, have a clarity and elegant simplicity that others would do well to emulate. It is clear that Skinner's enormous contribution to scientific method and theory will be a lasting one.

Bandura's Social Learning Theory

BIOGRAPHICAL INTRODUCTION

The pioneering learning theorists usually developed their concepts by experimenting with animals in physical settings. They watched how animals ran through mazes, solved puzzle boxes, and learned to press levers in Skinner boxes. These situations were not social; there were no other animals present. Skinnerians and others then showed how the same principles apply to human learning in social contexts. Just as rats learn to press levers to get food, people learn to interact with others to obtain social rewards.

In the 1960s, however, Albert Bandura argued that our learning in social situations goes beyond anything Skinner and most learning theorists described. In social settings, Bandura said, we learn a great deal through imitation, and imitation involves *cognitive* processes. We acquire considerable information just by observing models, mentally coding what we see.

In the 1970s Bandura refined his ideas on observational learning and demonstrated the powerful effects models have on our behavior. Beginning in the 1980s he turned more attention to the ways our efforts are influenced by our beliefs in our capacities—our self-efficacy beliefs. Bandura's lifetime of work occupies a central place in modern psychology.

Bandura was born in 1925 in the tiny town of Mundare in the province of Alberta, Canada. His parents had emigrated to Mundare from Eastern Europe as teenagers and had converted a homestead into a farm, which they struggled to maintain against storms and droughts. As a boy Bandura pitched in when he could. Although his parents had no schooling, they valued education and instilled this value in Bandura. After attending a high school with only 20 students, Bandura enrolled in the University of British Columbia, working afternoons in a woodwork plant to help pay the cost (Bandura, 2006; Evans, 1989).

Bandura enrolled in his first psychology class almost by chance. He was commuting to the college with a group of engineering and premed students who took early morning classes, and Bandura had a gap in his schedule. So he signed up for the psychology course and immediately became fascinated by the topic. He majored in it; and after earning his bachelor's degree, he entered the clinical psychology graduate program at the University of Iowa. While he was there he became impressed by the work of Robert Sears and other pioneers of social learning theory, and Bandura began thinking seriously about the role of models in shaping our lives (Bandura, 2006; Evans, 1989; Zimmerman & Schunk, 2003).

Soon after graduate school, Bandura joined the faculty of Stanford University, where he has been ever since. In 1974 he was elected president of the American Psychological Association. Bandura didn't just serve as a titular head; he actively organized the members to fight federal budget cuts to psychological services. Over the years, Bandura has received numerous honors and awards. Former students speak fondly of his wry humor and praise him for the demanding but helpful mentorship he provided (Zimmerman & Schunk, 2003).

BASIC CONCEPTS

Observational Learning

In Skinner's theory, learning often appears to be a gradual process in which organisms must act to learn. Organisms emit responses, which are gradually shaped by their consequences. Bandura (1962), however, argues that in social situations we often learn much more rapidly simply by observing the behavior of others. When, for example, children learn new songs or play house just like their parents, they often reproduce long sequences of new behavior immediately. They appear to acquire large segments of new behavior all at once, through observation alone.

The power of observational learning is well documented in the anthropological literature (Bandura & Walters, 1963, chap. 2; Honigmann, 1967, p. 180). In one Guatemalan subculture, girls learn to weave almost exclusively by watching models. The teacher demonstrates the operations of the textile machine while the girl simply observes. Then, when the girl feels ready, she takes over, and she usually operates it skillfully on her very first try. She demonstrates, in Bandura's (1965a) term, *no-trial learning;* she acquires new behavior all at once, entirely through observation. She does not need to fumble through any tedious process of trial-and-error learning with differential reinforcement for each small response.

When new behavior is acquired through observation alone, the learning appears to be *cognitive.* When the Guatemalan girl watches her teacher and then imitates her perfectly without any practice, she must rely on some inner representation of the behavior that guides her own performance. Bandura, unlike Skinner, believes learning theory must include internal cognitive variables.

Observation also teaches us the probable consequences of new behavior; we notice what happens when others try it. Bandura calls this process *vicarious reinforcement*. Vicarious reinforcement is also a cognitive process; we formulate expectations about the outcomes of our own behavior without any direct action on our part.

We learn from models of many kinds—not only from live models but also from *symbolic* models, such as those we see on television or read about in books. Another form of symbolic modeling is verbal instruction, as when an instructor describes for us the actions for driving a car. In this case the teacher's verbal descriptions, together with a demonstration, usually teach us most of what we need to know. This is fortunate, for if we had to learn to drive exclusively from the consequences of our own actions, few of us would survive the process (Bandura, 1962, pp. 214, 241).

Let us now look more closely at the observational learning process, which Bandura divides into four subprocesses.

The Four Components
of Observational Learning

1. Attentional Processes.   First of all, we cannot imitate a model unless we pay attention to the model. Models often attract our attention because they are distinctive, or because they possess the trappings of success, prestige, power, and other winsome qualities (Bandura, 1971, p. 17). Television is particularly successful at presenting models with engaging characteristics and exerts a powerful influence on our lives (Bandura, 1977, p. 25). Attention is also governed by the psychological characteristics of observers, such as their interests, but less is known about such variables (p. 25).

2. Retention Processes.   Because we frequently imitate models some time after we have observed them, we must have some way of remembering their actions in symbolic form. Bandura (1965a; 1971, p. 17) thinks of symbolic processes in terms of *stimulus contiguity,* associations among stimuli that occur together. Suppose, for example, we watch a man use a new tool, a drill. He shows us how to fasten the bit, plug it in, and so on. Later, the sight of the drill alone arouses many associated images, and these guide our actions.

In the example, the stimuli are all visual. However, we usually remember events, Bandura (1971, p. 18) says, by associating them with verbal codes. When we watch a motorist take a new route, we connect the route with words (e.g., "Route 1, then Exit 12 . . ."). Later, when we try to drive the route ourselves, the verbal codes help us follow it.

Young children, under the age of 5 years or so, are not yet accustomed to thinking in words and probably must rely quite heavily on visual images. This limits their ability to imitate. We therefore can improve on their imitations by directing them to use verbal codes—that is, by asking them to give verbal descriptions of a model's behavior while they are watching it (Bandura, 1971, p. 19; Coates & Hartup, 1969).

On many memory tasks, young children display a striking disregard for their own capacities and limitations. For example, Vygotsky (1931b, p. 71) found that young children approach tasks, no matter how simple or difficult, with the same unbridled enthusiasm. They act as if they can remember anything. In contemporary terms, they lack *metacognitive* awareness; they do not yet observe and assess their own cognitive skills. Between the ages of about 5 and 10 years, children gradually learn to evaluate their memory capacities and learn when to use memory aids such as verbal rehearsals (repeating something to themselves over and over to remember it better). Bandura (1986, p. 89) summarizes experimental evidence that suggests models can help children learn to use verbal rehearsal and other techniques.

3. Motor Reproduction Processes.   To reproduce behavior accurately, the person must have the necessary motor skills. For example, a boy might watch his father use a saw but find he cannot imitate very well because he lacks the physical strength and agility. From observation alone, he picks up a new *pattern* of responses (e.g., how to set up the wood and where to place the saw) but no new physical abilities (e.g., cutting with power). The latter come only with physical growth and practice (Bandura, 1977, p. 27).

4. Reinforcement and Motivational Processes.   Bandura, like cognitive learning theorists before him (Tolman, 1948), distinguishes between the *acquisition* and the *performance* of new responses. We can observe a model, and thereby acquire new knowledge, but we may or may not perform the responses. A boy might hear his neighbor use some profane language, and thereby learn some new words, but the boy might not reproduce them himself.

Performances are governed by reinforcement and motivational variables; we will actually imitate another if we are likely to gain a reward. In part, it is our past history of *direct reinforcements* that matters. If, in our example, the boy has himself received respect and admiration for swearing, he is likely to imitate his neighbor. If, however, he has been punished for swearing, he probably will hesitate to imitate his neighbor.

Performances also are influenced by *vicarious reinforcements,* the consequences one sees accrue to the model. If the boy sees his neighbor admired for swearing, the boy is likely to imitate him. If he sees the neighbor punished, he is less likely to do so (Bandura, 1971, p. 46; 1977, pp. 117–124).

Performances, finally, are partly governed by *self-reinforcements,* the evaluations we make of our own behavior. We will discuss this process in a later section.

Conclusion.   To imitate a model successfully, then, we must (1) attend to the model, (2) have some way of retaining what we have seen in symbolic form, and (3) have the necessary motor skills to reproduce the behavior. If these conditions are met, we probably know how to imitate the model. Still, we might not do so. Our actual performances are governed by (4) reinforcement contingencies, many of which are of a vicarious sort.

In reality, these four components are not totally separate. Reinforcement processes, in particular, influence what we attend to. For example, we often attend to powerful, competent, prestigious models because we have found that imitating them, rather than inferior models, leads to more positive consequences.

SOCIALIZATION STUDIES

Bandura's four-part model gives a fine-grained analysis of imitative learning. On a broader level, one of Bandura's primary, if sometimes implicit, concerns has been the socialization process—the process by which societies induce their members to behave in socially acceptable ways.

Socialization is an inclusive process that influences almost every kind of behavior, even technical skills. Many American teenage boys, for example, feel they will not fit into their social group unless they learn to drive a car. Automobile driving, however, is not something required by all cultures, and there are classes of social behavior that have broader relevance. All cultures seem to try to teach their members when it is acceptable to express aggression. It also is likely that all cultures try to teach people certain modes of cooperation, sharing, and helping. Aggression and cooperative behavior, then, are "targets" of socialization in all cultures (Hetherington & Parke, 1977, p. 231). In the next few sections we sample social learning analyses of some of the target behaviors in the socialization process.

Aggression

Bandura (1967; Bandura & Walters, 1963) believes that the socialization of aggression, as well as other behavior, is partly a matter of operant conditioning. Parents and other socializing agents reward children when they express aggression in socially appropriate ways (e.g., in games or in hunting) and punish children when they express aggression in socially unacceptable ways (e.g., hitting younger children). But socializing agents also teach children a great deal by the kinds of models they present. Children observe aggressive models, notice when they are reinforced, and imitate accordingly. Bandura has examined this process in several experiments, one of which is now considered a classic.

In this study (Bandura, 1965b), 4-year-olds individually watched a film in which an adult male model engaged in some moderately novel aggressive behavior. The model laid a Bobo doll[1] on its side, sat on it, and punched it, shouting such things as, "Pow, right in the nose," and "Sockeroo . . . stay down" (pp. 590–591). Each child was assigned to one of three conditions, which meant that each child saw the same film but with different endings.

1. In the *aggression-rewarded* condition, the model was praised and given treats at the end of the film. A second adult called him a "strong champion" and gave him chocolate bars, soft drinks, and the like (p. 591).
2. In the *aggression-punished* condition, the model was called a "big bully," swatted, and forced to cower away at the end of the film (p. 591).
3. In the third, *no-consequences* condition, the model received neither rewards nor punishments for his aggressive behavior.

Immediately after the film, each child was escorted into a room with a Bobo doll and other toys. The experimenters observed the child through a one-way mirror to see how often he or she would imitate the aggressive model.

The results indicated that those who had seen the model punished exhibited significantly fewer imitations than did those in the other two groups. Thus vicarious punishment reduced the imitation of aggressive responses. There was no difference between the aggression-rewarded and no-consequences groups. This is often the finding with respect to behavior, such as aggression, that is typically prohibited. The observation that "nothing bad happens this time" prompts imitation just as readily as does vicarious reward (Bandura, 1969, p. 239).

The experiment also had a second, equally important phase. An experimenter came back into the room and told each child that he or she would get juice and a pretty sticker picture for each additional response he or she could reproduce. This incentive completely eliminated the differences among the three groups. Now all the children—including those who had seen the model punished—imitated him to the same extent. Vicarious punishment had only blocked the *performance* of new responses, not their *acquisition*. The children in the aggression-punished condition had learned new responses, but had not felt it wise to actually reproduce them until a new incentive was introduced.

One of Bandura's followers, Robert Liebert (Liebert et al., 1977, p. 145), suggests this experiment has implications for aggression in television and movies. Children are frequently exposed to actors who demonstrate clever ways of committing homicides and other crimes. The widespread showing of such films is justified by the fact that the criminals are usually caught in the

---

[1] A large inflated rubber doll.

end. But Bandura's work suggests that children probably learn about criminal behavior nonetheless, and only inhibit such behavior until a time when environmental contingencies clearly favor its occurrence.

In the above experiment, children performed *newly* acquired responses. Models also can influence the performance of *previously learned* behavior of the same general class. For example, a boy might watch a violent movie and then act roughly toward his sister. He does not actually imitate the behavior he saw in the film, but he feels freer to engage in previously learned behavior of the same kind. In such cases, we say the behavior has been *disinhibited*. Models may also *inhibit* previously learned behavior, as when a girl sees a boy punished in class and therefore decides to check her impulse to do something else of a mischievous nature (Bandura & Walters, 1963, p. 72; Liebert et al., 1977, pp. 146–147).

Gender Roles

During socialization, children are taught to behave in gender-appropriate ways. Societies encourage boys to develop "masculine" traits and girls to develop "feminine" traits.

It is possible, of course, that gender traits are also, in part, genetically linked. Social learning theorists do not deny this possibility. But they believe that more is to be gained from the study of socialization processes and the role of imitation in particular (Bandura & Walters, 1963, pp. 26–29; Mischel, 1970).

In the learning of gender roles, the acquisition/performance distinction is especially important (Mischel, 1970). Children frequently learn, through observation, the behavior of both genders; however, they usually perform only the behavior appropriate to their own gender because this is what they have been reinforced to do. Margaret Mead (1964) told how Eskimo boys are encouraged to practice hunting and building snow houses, whereas the girls are not. So, ordinarily only the boys engage in these activities. But the girls watch the boys, and in emergencies they can execute many of the skills. The girls pick up the skills through observation alone (see Figure 9.1).

It is also possible, though, for children to become discouraged with respect to opposite-gender activities. If they don't get much opportunity to practice the skills, and aren't reinforced for them, they might stop paying as careful attention to them. Sex-typed social reinforcement, then, might have a negative effect on observation itself (Grusec & Brinker, 1972; Maccoby & Wilson, 1957).

Prosocial Behavior

Since the 1970s there has been considerable interest in the nature and roots of prosocial behavior—acts of sharing, helping, cooperation, and altruism. Social learning theorists have taken the lead in this area, showing that prosocial

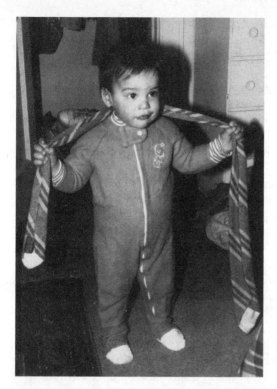

FIGURE 9.1
This young girl is imitating her father. After a while she probably will find that she receives more reinforcement for imitating females. However, she still may learn a good deal about "masculine" skills from observation alone.

behavior can be readily influenced by exposure to the appropriate models. In a typical study (Rushton, 1975), 7- to 11-year-old children watched an adult model play a bowling game and donate some of his winnings to a "needy children's fund." Immediately afterward, these children played the game alone, and they themselves made many donations—far more than did a control group who had not seen the altruistic model. Furthermore, the children who had observed the model still donated more 2 months later, even when placed in a different room with a different experimenter. Evidently, even a relatively brief exposure to a generous model exerts a fairly permanent effect on children's sharing.

Numerous other experiments have shown that models influence not only children's sharing but also their helpfulness toward others in distress, their cooperativeness, and their concern for the feelings of others (Bryan, 1975; Mussen & Eisenberg-Berg, 1977, pp. 79–90). The experimental findings in this area also seem supported by more naturalistic studies, in which parental behavior is linked to their children's altruism (DeHart et al., 2004, p. 353; Mussen & Eisenberg-Berg, 1977, pp. 86–90).

Practicing and Preaching.   Socializing agents teach children not only by behavioral example but also by preaching virtue and telling children how to behave. Such verbal techniques have been most fully explored in research on prosocial behavior, so a brief review might be in order.

First of all, preaching seems ineffective unless it is forceful. If an adult simply says, "It is nice to share," the child will be far more influenced by what the adult actually does. If the adult shares, so will the child—regardless of whether the adult preaches altruism or greed (Bryan & Walbek, 1970). When, however, the preaching becomes stronger, taking the form of long emotional sermons and commands, it can be effective (Mussen & Eisenberg-Berg, 1977, pp. 151–152).

Commands, however, are coercive and may backfire, as found in a study by G. M. White (1972). In this experiment some children took turns bowling with an adult who *told* them to share some of their winnings with needy children. Other children were simply given the opportunity to follow an altruistic example. The immediate result was that the children who were ordered to share did so to a greater extent, even when playing alone. In a posttest, however, these children's sharing decreased sharply, and they displayed a greater incidence of stealing, perhaps reflecting their resentment against the coercive technique.

Self-Regulation

As people become socialized, they depend less on external rewards and punishments and increasingly regulate their own behavior. That is, they establish their own internal standards and reward and punish themselves in accordance with them. For example, a woman might criticize herself for a moral transgression that no one else is even aware of. She punishes herself because her behavior violated her own standards.

Bandura has been very interested in how people evaluate their own performances as they strive for success and achievement. Some people set exceedingly high achievement goals and reward themselves only when they meet them. An artist, for example, might approve of his own work only after he has corrected flaws that others would never detect. Others are satisfied with less perfect work.

How are self-evaluative standards acquired? In part, Bandura believes, they are the product of direct rewards and punishments. For example, parents might give their daughter approval only when she earns very high grades, and after a while she adopts this high standard as her own.

But Bandura's focus, once again, has been on the influence of models. In several experiments, Bandura and his colleagues (Bandura & Kupers,

1964; Bandura, 1986, pp. 341–342) have shown that children and adults adopt the self-evaluative standards they observe in others. For example, if children watch an adult model reward himself with self-praise and candy treats only when he attains a high score in bowling, the children will adopt high self-evaluative standards when it's their turn to bowl. If, in contrast, the children observe a model who displays low self-evaluative standards (and gives himself treats even when he scores poorly), the children will use low standards too.

In ordinary life, the situation is more complicated because children are exposed to a variety of models (e.g., parents, TV characters, and peers), some of whom exemplify high self-evaluative standards and some of whom do not. Which models will children follow?

Bandura (1986, pp. 342–343) says that children tend to adopt the self-evaluative standards of peers rather than adults because children can more easily achieve the lower standards that peers set. But Bandura also points out that we can do things to get children to adopt higher standards. For example, we can encourage children to associate with high-achieving peers (peers who meet high self-evaluative standards). We can also expose children to models who are rewarded for adhering to high standards. We might read children stories about scientists and athletes who settled for nothing short of excellence and who eventually achieved great success and public acclaim.

People who set high self-evaluative standards are generally hard workers, and hard work produces real accomplishments. At the same time, high goals are difficult to achieve, and people who set high goals are prone to disappointment and depression. Such people, Bandura says, can avoid depression by focusing on subgoals. That is, instead of measuring their progress in terms of distant aims, they should set realistically attainable goals for each day and reward themselves when they achieve them (pp. 354, 359–360). Like Locke, Watson, and Skinner before him, Bandura recommends a method of small steps.

SELF-EFFICACY

When we regulate our own behavior, we engage in self-observation. We evaluate our ongoing performances in terms of our standards and goals. On other occasions, we reflect on our general abilities, reaching conclusions such as, "I'm good at algebra" and "I'm a poor swimmer." Bandura calls such general judgments *self-efficacy appraisals* (1986, chap. 9). In recent years, self-efficacy has been a central focus of Bandura's work.

Bandura believes that our self-efficacy appraisals exert powerful effects on our levels of motivation. When we believe we are good at tasks, we work on them vigorously and persist with them despite temporary setbacks. When we doubt our abilities, we work less energetically and are more likely to give up when we encounter difficulties (p. 394).

The importance of perceived self-efficacy was demonstrated in an experiment by Collins (1982, cited in Bandura, 1986, p. 391). Collins divided children into two groups according to their level of ability in mathematics, and he also asked the children about their own opinions of their abilities. Collins then gave all the children some difficult problems. As we would expect, the children in the high-ability group outperformed those in the low-ability group. But perceived self-efficacy also had an effect. Within each ability group, the children who believed they were good at math solved more problems, chose to work on more of the problems they failed, and displayed a more positive attitude toward mathematics.

It is possible, of course, to have too high an estimate of one's abilities. This is especially true when physical injury can result. If we overestimate our ability to ski down a steep slope, we could be seriously hurt. In general, however, Bandura believes it's good to overestimate our capacities and our belief we will succeed. Life is strewn with difficulties—disappointments, setbacks, impediments, inequities. Optimistic self-efficacy is therefore beneficial: "Tenacious strivers believe so strongly in themselves that they are able to exert extraordinary effort and suffer countless reversals in pursuit of their vision" (Bandura, 1998, p. 57).

Sources of Self-Efficacy Appraisals

Bandura (1986, pp. 399–408) suggests that self-efficacy appraisals are based on four sources of information.

1. The most influential source of knowledge is *actual performance*. If we repeatedly succeed at tasks, our sense of efficacy increases. If we repeatedly fail, our sense of efficacy drops. Once we have developed a robust sense of self-efficacy in an area, we are not too troubled by temporary setbacks. We are likely to attribute failures to our lack of effort or to poor tactics and to try again. And if we succeed, our sense of efficacy goes up even higher.

2. Self-efficacy appraisals are also influenced by *vicarious experiences*. If we see others succeed at a task, we infer that we can do it too. This is especially true if we believe others have roughly the same abilities as we do.

3. Another variable is *verbal persuasion*—pep talks. When someone convinces us we can perform a task, we usually do better on it. Pep talks cannot, of course, enable us to accomplish tasks that are far too difficult. But outside encouragement can help, largely because success usually depends more on the effort we put into a task than on any inherent ability.

4. Finally, we judge our abilities partly on the basis of *physiological cues.* For example, we might interpret fatigue or tension as signs that a task is becoming too difficult for us. At the same time, people often react differently to the same bodily cues. One girl, warming up for the 400-meter race, may interpret her anxiety as a sign that she is too tense to do well. Another girl may interpret the same bodily cues as an indication that she is getting "fired up," that her "adrenaline is flowing," and that she is ready to do her best.

Bandura (1994) has sketched out, in a very preliminary way, the development of self-efficacy over the life span. Infants develop a sense of self-efficacy as they explore the environment and get the sense that they can have some control over it. As children grow, their social world widens. They look to peers as models of self-efficacy and also as sources of social comparison. Teenagers evaluate their efficacy in new areas, including dating. Young adults must evaluate new capacities as workers and parents, and older people reassess their abilities as they adjust to retirement and create a new lifestyle. Throughout life, a resilient sense of self-efficacy keeps people moving forward with energy and vitality. When self-efficacy is low, people are prone to depression, resignation, and painful self-doubts.

ABSTRACT MODELING AND PIAGET'S STAGES

In the course of his writing, Bandura has expanded on the meaning of imitation. Ordinarily, Bandura (1971) observes, psychologists think of modeling as a process of exact imitation. Exact imitation occurs, for example, when a child tries to imitate a friend's precise behavior, such as the friend's way of writing the letter *L.* But children also engage in *abstract modeling;* they induce the general rules or principles underlying particular behaviors, and they then use these rules to generate entirely new behavior on their own. For example, English-speaking children induce, from all the language they hear, that the rule for forming the plural is to add the s sound, and they then use the rule to generate countless new sentences. Similarly, Bandura says, children induce the kinds of concepts that Piaget has discussed. By observing a model, a child might induce a new moral rule or the principle of conservation.

To some extent, Bandura views abstract modeling in a Piagetian vein. Like Piaget, Bandura sees the child as an active agent; the child induces rules and grasps concepts. But Bandura's emphasis is much more on the way the external environment—especially models—influences the kinds of concepts children learn. Later we review some of the research by Bandura and his colleagues on how models might influence children's conceptual development. But first, let us compare the theories of Piaget and Bandura a bit more thoroughly.

Bandura and Piaget

Piaget, you will recall, thought that children learn much on their own, from an intrinsic interest in the world. Children are especially curious about stimuli that are moderately novel, that do not quite fit into their existing cognitive structures. When, for example, our son Tom was 11 months old, he could grasp many things with his hands, so he was surprised to discover one day that he couldn't grasp water. He kept trying and failing, intently studying the way the water responded to his actions. Tom was not motivated by adult approval or any other external reinforcement. He was engrossed in the problem itself. And because he was so interested in the problem, he continued to work on it, and over the next several months he invented some ways of holding water.

In Piaget's view, then, children construct their own cognitive structures as they work on intrinsically interesting problems. In the process, their thinking undergoes a series of broad transformations called *stages*. These stages, in turn, indicate the kinds of new problems children will find most interesting; for they continue to be most curious about events and activities that are just beyond their current level. This principle of moderate discrepancy holds for imitation too; children are spontaneously interested in models whose behavior is slightly more complex than their own (Kohlberg, 1966b; 1969a, p. 434; Kuhn, 1974). This is why we often see children tagging along after somewhat older ones, trying to do the same things. Thus Piagetians do not spend much time examining the modeling influences in a child's life; they study, instead, the child's cognitive behavior at each stage, for the child's stage determines the kinds of models the child will seek out.

Bandura, in contrast, is much more of an environmentalist. It is appealing, he says, to imagine children making their own discoveries and creating their own ideas. In reality, however, children's minds are structured by the environment, by the models and the social training practices the environment provides (Bandura, 1977, p. 183; Bandura & Walters, 1963, p. 44).

In some major works (1977, 1986, 1997), Bandura has softened his environmentalism somewhat. He talks about "reciprocal influences" among individuals, their behavior, and the environment. But Bandura is still much more an environmentalist than Piaget, and Bandura continues to raise strong objections to Piagetian theory. Specifically, he disagrees with two basic Piagetian tenets.

First, Bandura doubts that children learn much on their own, out of an intrinsic interest in moderately novel events. He says that if children were motivated to figure out everything that is slightly beyond their grasp, they would be learning all the time. But this is not the case. If we want children to learn, we must motivate them and assist them. We must teach them things, administer rewards and punishments, and provide them with appropriate models. After a while, to be sure, children do become self-motivated learners. But this does not mean they now learn for learning's sake, because of their natural curiosity about the world. Rather, they learn to meet their internal achievement standards (for example, to master 90% of the material on a test). These internal standards, moreover, are themselves the products of social teaching and modeling influences (Bandura, 1986, pp. 340, 480–488; 1989, pp. 8–9, 34–35).

Bandura (1997, p. 219) acknowledges that intrinsic interest does exist. But he says it occurs *after* we meet our achievement standards and develop feelings of self-efficacy. For example, after we do well in biology courses, we begin to enjoy the subject matter itself. But intrinsic interest is not primary.

Second, Bandura questions the validity of Piagetian stages. At first the stages seem plausible because children do often master material in sequences. But this is only because people usually solve easier problems before they solve more difficult ones. There is nothing special about Piaget's stage sequences, and they are not as absolute as he claims.

Moreover, the stage concept implies that thinking becomes organized and reorganized into broad unitary structures that underlie children's thinking across a wide range of tasks. For example, the child at the stage of concrete operations should apply the same logical operations to a wide variety of problems. But stages in this sense, Bandura argues, do not exist. Thinking actually consists of numerous discrete skills that vary from one cognitive domain to the next. For example, reading, writing, and arithmetic all involve many of their own particular skills and subskills. Piagetian stages, which lump children's thinking into broad categories, tell us little about the particular thinking skills in each area (Bandura, 1986, pp. 484–485).

Bandura argues, then, that Piaget's view of development is false. Children do not primarily learn on their own, nor does their thinking undergo broad stage transformations.

Bandura's opposition to Piaget is long standing, and Bandura and his colleagues have conducted some classic studies that were designed to demonstrate the superiority of their theory. In one, Bandura and McDonald (1963) tried to show that modeling influences can alter Piaget's stages of moral reasoning.

Moral Reasoning.   Piaget, you will recall, proposed a two-stage theory of moral judgment, one aspect of which concerns consequences versus intentions. That is, younger children tend to judge wrongdoing in terms of its consequences, whereas older children base their judgments on the intentions behind the act. For example, a young child is likely to say that a boy who made a large ink spot trying to help his dad is naughtier than one who made a small ink spot when playing around. The young child focuses on the consequences—the amount of damage. The older child, in contrast, usually puts more weight on the underlying motive.

Bandura gave 5- to 11-year-old children 12 such items and found the age shift that Piaget and others (Kohlberg, 1969a) have documented. However,

Bandura emphasized, children of all ages evidenced at least some reasoning of both kinds, suggesting the stages are not rigidly demarcated.

Following this pretest, Bandura tried to show that the children's thinking could be altered by modeling influences. In a key part of the experiment, children individually observed an adult model who was praised for giving responses *contrary* to their own dominant mode. If, for example, a child had typically judged wrongdoing in terms of intentions, the model always based her judgment on the consequences. An experimenter presented the model with a moral dilemma, praised her when she gave her answer, and gave the child a turn on a new item. Taking turns in this way, the model and child each responded to 12 new items (different from the pretest items).

This training procedure did have a strong effect. Prior to the training, children gave one type of moral response only about 20% of the time; during the treatment, this number increased to an average of about 50%.

The experiment also included an immediate posttest in which the children responded once again to the pretest items. The results indicated that the children persisted with their new mode of responding (about 38% to 53% of the time).

The study, Bandura says, shows that "the so-called developmental stages were readily altered by the provision of adult models" (Bandura & Walters, 1963, p. 209). There seems to be nothing fixed or invariant about them.

Cognitive developmentalists have viewed the study suspiciously. They acknowledge that modeling can influence cognitive stages, but the influence should be small. This is because stages represent broad, deeply rooted cognitive structures. We cannot, in theory, effortlessly get a child to reason in any way we wish. And when we do produce change, it should be primarily in the direction of the stage sequence—one stage forward. Several experiments have, in fact, found that these are the kinds of changes that do occur when Kohlberg's, rather than Piaget's, stages are used (Gardner, 1982, p. 219). This, Kohlberg (1969a) argued, is because his stages represent broader cognitive structures than Piaget's moral stages do, so his are harder to change. However, as Bandura (1986, pp. 494–496) notes, the modeling influences in these studies were brief and weak.

We can see, then, that Bandura's experiment has stirred up a good deal of controversy. He has presented a serious challenge to cognitive stage theory.

Conservation.   Social learning theorists have also tried to show that conservation can be altered through modeling. In some key experiments, Rosenthal and Zimmerman (1972; Zimmerman & Rosenthal, 1974) reported that 5- and 6-year-olds gained significant mastery of conservation on a battery of tasks (including liquid, number, and weight) after they observed an adult model demonstrate conservation reasoning. However, the investigators found that 4-year-olds gained conservation skills only to a modest degree.

Rosenthal and Zimmerman's interpretation of the results indicates the way researchers' conclusions reflect their theoretical orientations. The researchers concluded that the modeling produced rapid and substantial change in conservation behavior. Conservation skills, they believe, are probably the product of socialization—of the teachings of adults in the child's culture. Developmentalists would be more skeptical and would point to the weaker results with children who were not ready to benefit from the modeling experience.

PRACTICAL IMPLICATIONS

Bandura's work should do a good deal to increase our awareness of the importance of models in child rearing and education. Although most parents and teachers are already somewhat aware of the fact that they teach by example, they probably have also overlooked just how influential modeling can be. A case in point is physical punishment. Many parents try to prevent their children from fighting by spanking them when they fight—only to find, it seems, that their children fight all the more (Bandura & Walters, 1963, p. 129). The likely explanation is that the parents, by spanking, are inadvertently providing a good demonstration of how to hurt others (Bandura, 1967). Similarly, whenever we find that we are unable to rid a child of some distressing bit of behavior, we might ask whether we have been inadvertently modeling the behavior ourselves.

Modeling, according to Bandura, takes many forms. The familiar kind is behavioral modeling; we exemplify an activity by performing it. Modeling may also be done verbally, as when we give instructions or issue commands. Social learning researchers have evaluated the effectiveness of the various kinds of modeling, and their findings should be of importance to parents and educators. Of particular interest are studies such as G. M. White's (1972), which examined the effects of commanding children to share. At first, the commands seemed to work, but their impact diminished over time, and the commands also produced resentment and rebelliousness. In the long run, we may do better simply to model generosity and helpfulness through our own behavior. Then children can follow our example without feeling forced to do so.

Social learning theorists have also shown that behavior is influenced not only by personal or live models but also by those presented in the mass media. Filmed models, in particular, seem to exert a powerful impact, and one major implication is that television, which many children watch for hours on end, is shaping young lives. Social learning theorists have been especially concerned with the effects that televised violence has on children, and there is substantial evidence that it can, in fact, increase children's aggressiveness in their daily lives (Anderson & Gentile, 2008; Kirsh, 2006).

The kinds of models presented in the mass media have been of concern to leaders of historically disenfranchised groups. Civil rights leaders and feminists have pointed out that television and motion pictures have traditionally depicted people of color and women in stereotyped roles, and, by doing so, have restricted people's sense of what they might become in life. Accordingly, activists have tried to get the media to present new kinds of models, such as women and people of color as scientists and environmentalists rather than housewives and criminals. The social learning research suggests that the activists have adopted a good strategy for social change.

Because modeling can have a strong impact on behavior, it has significant promise as a therapeutic device. You might recall that in Mary Cover Jones's (1924) famous experiment, modeling was part of the method used to eliminate Peter's fear of furry objects. Bandura and others have conducted a number of studies that have more systematically shown how modeling can help reduce fears. In one experiment (Bandura, Grusec, & Menlove, 1967), for example, 4-year-olds who were afraid of dogs observed a child calmly play with one, and then the children themselves became less fearful.

Bandura (1986) urges therapists to pay special attention to self-efficacy appraisals when they diagnose and treat their clients. For example, Bandura believes that whatever technique a therapist uses to treat a phobia—whether it is modeling or some other technique—the treatment will work best if it gives the client the sense that he or she has the ability to deal with the feared stimulus. Similarly, techniques for dealing with pain, such as relaxation or guided imagery, work best when they give clients the feeling they are capable of influencing the amount of pain they feel (pp. 425–445).

Pediatricians have found self-efficacy theory valuable in the treatment of children with asthma. Too often, doctors simply tell parents what to do at home, and then the doctors complain that the parents do not adhere to the plan. Doctors have obtained better results when they pay attention to the parents' feelings of self-efficacy. Because the parents often feel helpless with respect to their children's asthma, health-care workers model the ways the parents can remove allergens from the home, give the parents positive feedback, and help them believe they can be effective (Hussain-Rizvi, Kunkov, & Crain, 2009).

Bandura (1994) also has called attention to the social conditions that undermine self-efficacy. He observes that standard school practices such as ranking and competitive grading make many children feel inadequate. It would be better if children worked more cooperatively and could judge their work according to their own individual progress (rather than against that of other pupils). Bandura adds that it is important for teachers to feel self-efficacy as well. When they believe their work will have an effect, their confidence serves as a model for their children.

More broadly, Bandura (1998) is worried about the impersonality of our technological society, and the difficulty any individual has changing it.

Self-efficacy in the modern world, he speculates, must become collective self-efficacy—people working together for change.

EVALUATION

Bandura's work has changed over the years. Initially, he wanted to show how the Skinnerian model, in which one must act to learn, is inadequate. Learning also includes the observation of models, which is a cognitive process. In this early work, Bandura focused clearly on the power of modeling influences, and he and his colleagues devised a series of brilliant experiments to show just how powerful models can be. In 1977 he wrote,

> One can get people to behave altruistically, to volunteer their services, to delay or to seek gratification, to show affection, to behave punitively, to prefer certain foods or apparel, to converse on particular topics, to be inquisitive or passive, and to engage in most any course of action by having such conduct exemplified. (p. 88)

In more recent years, especially since the mid-1980s, Bandura's theory has become increasingly eclectic and wide ranging. In his recent self-efficacy theory, Bandura considers modeling influences to be less powerful than successful performances (in which the person achieves results through hard work), and Bandura speculates about the broad social context in which self-efficacy develops.

Still, the theme of modeling runs throughout his work, and modeling, together with the general social environmental orientation, has presented a significant challenge to the developmental position. It is therefore useful to more fully consider the reaction of developmentalists to his work.

Developmentalists recognize that environments influence behavior, and often in the ways that Bandura has specified. But developmentalists place a high value on the kinds of growth that emerge from within the child—from the child's inner maturational promptings and spontaneous interests in the world. Bandura has generally minimized the importance of such growth.

Among the developmentalists, it has been the Piagetians who have become most embroiled in debates with Bandura. Piagetians believe that children learn from a spontaneous interest in moderately novel events. Bandura (1986, pp. 480–482) has dismissed this suggestion. Children, he says, really learn in order to obtain reinforcements, such as praise, which they eventually come to administer to themselves. But Bandura's own research may contradict his argument. In several experiments, models perform what he calls "moderately novel" or "relatively unique" behaviors (Bandura, 1962, pp. 250, 252; 1965b, p. 116). Models sock Bobo dolls, march about, knock objects off shelves, and engage in other zany physical antics. As Kohlberg (1969a, p. 435) pointed out, these behaviors seem intuitively designed to capture the imagination of 4-year-olds, and in several experiments the children readily imitated the behaviors even though there were no reinforcements available (Bandura, 1965b; Bandura & Huston, 1961; Bandura, Ross, & Ross, 1963). Quite possibly, the children reproduced such behaviors because they found them intrinsically interesting. Reinforcement variables, to be sure, can increase or alter imitation, but a spontaneous interest in moderate novelty might also be at work.

Bandura (1986, pp. 480–482) argues that the principle of moderate novelty does not fit with everyday observations. If people learned from their intrinsic interest in moderately novel events, they would be learning all the time; for they are constantly encountering slightly new information. But, Bandura says, people in general are not eager learners. They usually restrict their learning to one or two areas of life, such as their areas of occupational expertise.

Piagetians (e.g., Kamii, 1980) and other developmentalists (e.g., Montessori, 1936b) would agree that people often seem to be fairly apathetic when it comes to learning. But this observation does not prove that humans have no intrinsic interest in the world. Rather, the observation shows that the child's natural curiosity has been stifled.

Children, in the developmental view, begin life full of enthusiasm for learning, and during the first few years they learn a tremendous amount on their own, without adult instruction. Then adults get hold of them, sending them to schools and taking charge of their learning. Adults provide them with modeling influences and teach them what and how to think. Children feel the pressure to please grownups and try to think in the ways the adults prescribe. As a result, children stop pursuing their spontaneous interests and lose the thrill that comes from making their own discoveries.

Bandura says that he, too, believes in self-motivated learning, but of a different kind. People, in Bandura's view, do not learn out of a spontaneous interest in the world, but to achieve their internal goals and standards. Children internalize external standards and make their own positive self-evaluations contingent on the achievement of these standards. For example, a college student, studying for exams, might only be pleased with herself when she is certain she has mastered enough material to earn straight A's. Bandura (1997, p. 219) says that people enjoy learning for its own sake *after* they start meeting their internal standards and feeling good about their abilities.

I believe Bandura sheds light on the kind of learning that is dominant in our society today. We do seem to constantly set standards and evaluate our progress and abilities. But such extensive self-evaluation is confining and debilitating. We become so wrapped up in ourselves that we lose touch with the childlike delight in the world itself—in nature, other people, art, and the world as we find it.

Piagetians also believe Bandura overlooks the importance of cognitive structures or stages. Bandura acknowledges that cognitive skills set limits on what children can learn and imitate, but he does not believe these skills belong to broad stage structures. Instead, he believes the cognition consists of a large number of specific, isolated skills.

Bandura's position has its supporters, but as we saw discussed in our evaluation of Piaget in Chapter 6, the issue is still very unsettled. Piaget's stages, despite certain problems, are important.

In fact, social learning research itself occasionally suggests that the child's general stage is at work. For example, Liebert and his colleagues (1969) found that 14-year-olds, but not 8- or 6-year-olds, could imitate a new grammatical rule. The oldest subjects were able to figure out the rule underlying the model's behavior because they had capacities for abstract thinking that the younger children lacked. They had, it seems, formal operations.

It might be, then, that Bandura underestimates the importance of developmental variables. He certainly seems to overlook the extent to which children learn on their own, from an intrinsic interest in the world. He might also overlook the extent to which modeling is influenced by cognitive stages. Nevertheless, Bandura has significantly broadened learning theory and contributed enormously to our understanding of how environmental factors shape behavior.

Vygotsky's Social-Historical Theory of Cognitive Development

BIOGRAPHICAL INTRODUCTION

This book focuses on theorists in the developmental tradition—scholars who have seen developmental change primarily in terms of inner forces. For example, Gesell emphasized inner maturational promptings and Piaget saw children making their own discoveries. By way of contrast, we have also examined the ideas of learning theorists, who have emphasized the role of the external environment.

Some of you may be dissatisfied with this theoretical division. Why, you might ask, must we view development in either/or terms? Can't a theory assign major roles to both inner and outer forces?

The construction of such an integrative theory is a worthy goal, but few people have made much progress in attaining it. Bandura, as we saw, pronounces behavior to be multidetermined—to be influenced by various internal and external variables—but he also discredits the developmental perspective on how change comes from within. Later we will discuss the ways Freud and Erikson weave inner and outer forces into their psychoanalytic theories. In the realm of cognitive development, the major theorist who discussed both developmental and environmental forces was the Russian L. S. Vygotsky (1896–1934).

Vygotsky had read the early writings of Gesell, Werner, and Piaget, and he recognized the importance of the kinds of intrinsic development they were addressing. At the same time, Vygotsky was a Marxist who believed that we can understand human beings only in the context of the social-historical environment. So Vygotsky tried to create a theory that allowed for the interplay between the two *lines of development*—the *natural line* that emerges from within and the *social-historical* line that influences the child from without (Vygotsky, 1931a, p. 17).

Vygotsky was only partly successful. He had only sketched out an integrative theory of development when, at the age of 38, his life was cut short by tuberculosis. Nevertheless, many psychologists believe that if we eventually do construct a solid integrative theory, it will build on the start Vygotsky gave us.

Lev Semenovich Vygotsky grew up in Gomel, a port city in western Russia. His father was a banking executive, and his mother was a teacher, although she spent most of her life raising her eight children. The family loved interesting conversation, a trait that rubbed off on the young Vygotsky. As a teenager, he was known among his friends as the "little professor" because he was constantly leading them in discussions, mock trials, and debates. Vygotsky also loved to read history, literature, and poetry (Wertsch, 1985, pp. 3–4).

When he was 17, Vygotsky wanted to attend the University of Moscow, but because he was Jewish he had to struggle with the state's quota system; the university's enrollment was only 3% Jewish. Initially, Vygotsky seemed assured of a spot because he was so bright. But before he completed his oral examinations, the educational ministry shifted to a lottery system for Jewish applicants. Vygotsky felt he had lost all hope, but then he won a position by chance alone.

At the university, Vygotsky specialized in law, but he also took a wide variety of courses in other fields, as well as courses at Shanyavskii People's University, where a number of professors had gone after being expelled from the University of Moscow for anti-czarist leanings. Vygotsky graduated with a law degree from the University of Moscow in 1917 and returned to his home of Gomel (Wertsch, 1985, pp. 5–6).

Between 1917 (the year of the Communist Revolution) and 1924, Vygotsky taught literature in a secondary school and psychology at the local teacher's college, and he became interested in the education of the physically disabled. He also worked on his doctoral dissertation on the psychology of art. During this period he became ill with tuberculosis (Wertsch, 1985, pp. 7–8).

On January 6, 1924, Vygotsky traveled to Leningrad to deliver a lecture on the psychology of consciousness. The clarity and brilliance of his speech— by the unknown young man from the provinces—had an electrifying effect on the young psychologists in the audience. One, A. R. Luria (1902–1977), recommended Vygotsky for a position at the Moscow Institute of Psychology, which Vygotsky received. During his first year of work at the institute, he finished his dissertation and received his doctorate (p. 8).

In Moscow, Vygotsky soon became a commanding presence. When he lectured, students stood outside the packed auditorium and listened through open windows. When he traveled, students wrote poems in honor of his journey. Vygotsky inspired such enthusiasm not only because his ideas were exciting but also because he led a group of young Marxists on a mission—to create a psychology that would help build a new socialist society (p. 10).

Perhaps sensing his life would be short, Vygotsky worked at a breakneck pace. He read, lectured, and conducted research as rapidly as he could, and he also traveled extensively to help clinics working with children and adults with neurological disorders. Vygotsky's daily schedule was often so busy that he did his writing after 2 A.M., when he had a few quiet hours to himself. During the last 3 years of his life, his coughing spells became so severe that he was sometimes left exhausted for days at a time. Nevertheless, he worked until he died at the age of 38 (pp. 12–14).

A few of Vygotsky's writings were published shortly after his death in 1934, but in 1936 the Soviet government banned his work—a ban that lasted until 1956. The primary reason for the ban was that Vygotsky conducted some research with intelligence tests, which the Communist Party condemned. Actually, Vygotsky criticized the conventional use of intelligence tests and employed them in new ways, but such subtleties were lost on the authorities. Fortunately, Vygotsky's colleagues and students kept his work alive, and today his ideas are extremely popular among psychologists and educators throughout the world (Cole & Scribner, 1978; Kozulin, 1986, pp. xxiv–xxv).

MARX'S VIEWS ON HUMAN NATURE

Because Vygotsky tried to create a psychology along Marxist lines, it will be helpful to review briefly some of the ideas of Karl Marx (1818–1883) on human nature before discussing Vygotsky in detail.

Marx's comments on human nature were relatively brief, and they primarily appeared in his early writings (Marx, 1844, 1845; Marx & Engels, 1846). Marx recognized that humans have biological needs, but he emphasized the human capacity for tool use and production. It is by inventing and using tools that humans master their environments, satisfy their needs, and, ideally, fulfill their deepest creative potentials. Production, Marx also emphasized, is an inherently social process. People join together to plant and harvest crops, exchange goods, assemble machines, and so on.

Beyond these general comments, Marx had little to say about human nature. Indeed, he argued that it is a mistake to describe human nature in the abstract, apart from its social-historical context. Although humans are distinguished by their capacity for tool use and technological production, the conditions under which they work and produce change throughout history. The working conditions of the medieval artisan, for example, were quite different from those of the 19th-century factory worker. To understand humans, then, we need to understand history and the dynamics of historical change (Marx, 1845, pp. 107–109; Marx & Engels, 1846, pp. 118–121, 129).

History, in Marx's view, is a *dialectical* process, a series of conflicts and resolutions. New forces of production (e.g., new ways of manufacturing) come into conflict with the existing social system, and a new social system is installed. For example, in 18th- and 19th-century Europe, the creation of new factories gave a rising class of capitalists the opportunity to make vast sums of money, but the ancient feudal system stood in their way. The result of this conflict was the overthrow of the feudal system and the establishment of a new system—the free enterprise system that allowed the capitalists to make as much money as they liked (Marx, 1859; Marx & Engels, 1872, pp. 336–340; Mills, 1962, pp. 82–83).

Marx believed that his own age—the second half of the 19th century—was experiencing a new phase in the dialectic of history. Technological progress was now being impeded by the free enterprise system. The resolution of this conflict would be a communist revolution in which the workers would take over the industries and organize them for the benefit of all.

We have encountered the concept of dialectic—of conflict and resolution—earlier (Chapter 6). Marx, like so many other scholars, adopted the concept from Hegel. However, Marx used the concept in a very different way.

For Hegel, the dialectic of history occurs in the realm of consciousness and ideas; one viewpoint comes into conflict with its opposite, leading to a new synthesis. Marx, in contrast, believed that conflicts in ideas are superficial. The conflicts that really matter are social and economic. In fact, most ideas and values merely justify particular social and economic interests. The medieval lords praised loyalty and honor; the rising capitalists heralded liberty and free competition; and both groups believed they were giving expression to the highest of all values. In reality, both groups were merely spouting opinions that justified their own social and economic interests.

Marx, then, was highly critical of those scholars who analyzed the nature of consciousness—people's ideas, values, and outlooks—as if these had an independent existence. What people think, Marx said, depends on their material life—the ways in which they work, produce, and exchange goods—at a certain point in historical development.

But it is not just the *content* of thinking that depends on historical development. Our species' cognitive *capacities*, too, have changed as a result of historical change, especially technological development. This, at least, was the position of Marx's collaborator Friedrich Engels (1820–1895), who forcefully argued that early technology—early tool use—gave rise to uniquely human traits such as advanced intelligence and speech.

Engels on Tool Use and Human Evolution

According to Engels (1925, pp. 47–49, 238–246), our ancestors became capable of tool use when they came down from the trees and began living on level ground. This new mode of life enabled them to develop an upright posture, which freed the hands for the production of stone implements. Once people began making tools, their minds expanded. They discovered new properties of natural objects, such as the properties of stone and wood that facilitate cutting. They also became aware, however dimly at first, of the scientific principles underlying tool use, principles such as leverage, mass, and force.

Tool use also led to new modes of cooperation and communication. As technologies advanced, people discovered the advantages of working together. For example, they found that they could more effectively build a hut or a boat by joining forces. But they now needed some way of communicating beyond grunts and gestures. People needed to give one another instructions, such as "Turn right," and "Pull harder." "Men in the making," Engels said, "arrived at the point where *they had something to say* to one another" (p. 232), and they developed speech.

More generally, technology promoted a new orientation toward the environment. With tools in hand, humans no longer had to accept the environment as they found it. They could change it. At a certain point, they stopped picking fruit and vegetables wherever they found them; they began clearing land and planting their own crops. This new orientation promoted planning and foresight. Successful farming requires people to plan months and years ahead. Such foresight, Engels observed, has not always been a capacity that humans have exercised as well as they should. Nevertheless, once people saw the power of tools and technology, they began transforming the environment according to their own plans and designs.

VYGOTSKY'S THEORY
OF PSYCHOLOGICAL TOOLS

Vygotsky was deeply impressed by Engels's writing on tool use, and he attempted to extend Engels's insights. Just as people have developed tools to master the environment, Vygotsky proposed, they also have created "psychological tools" to master their own behavior. For example, early peoples used notched sticks and knotted ropes to help them remember events, much as a person might tie a string around his or her finger today. Later, as cultures developed, they created other mental tools. Voyagers began using maps to help them retrace prior routes and plan future expeditions. Vygotsky called the various psychological tools that people use to aid their thinking and behavior *signs,* and he argued that we cannot understand human thinking without examining the signs that cultures provide (Vygotsky, 1930, pp. 39–40; 1931).

Undoubtedly, the single most important sign system is *speech.* Speech serves many functions, but most fundamentally it frees our thought and attention from the immediate situation—from the stimuli impinging on us at the moment. Because words can symbolize things and events that go beyond the present situation, speech enables us to reflect on the past and plan for the future (Luria, 1976, p. 10; Vygotsky, 1930, p. 26).

For example, I know a farming family whose vegetables were being raided by deer. For a while the family members simply reacted to each immediate situation as it occurred. Whenever someone saw a deer eating the vegetables, he or she chased it away. After a while, however, the family sat down and discussed long-term solutions. They talked about building a new fence, how high it should be, and whether a ditch would be useful. One family member shared an idea she heard from a neighbor a few months earlier. By using words to symbolize things and events that were not immediately present—"a fence," "a ditch," "the neighbor's idea"—the family developed a plan. (They decided to build a higher fence.)

When humans use signs, Vygotsky said, they engage in *mediated* behavior. That is, they do not just respond to environmental stimuli; their behavior is also influenced or "mediated" by their own signs. In the present example, the family members did not just respond directly to the environmental stimuli (the deer); they also acted on the basis of a verbally formulated plan ("OK, we've decided to build a 10-foot fence") (Vygotsky, 1930a, pp. 19–40).

The acquisition of speech is of major importance to the growing child; it enables the child to participate intelligently in the social life of his or her group. But speech does more than this. It also facilitates the child's own, individual thinking. By the age of 3 or 4 years, Vygotsky noted, children begin to carry out the kinds of dialogues they had had with others with themselves alone. At first they do this aloud, and we can hear children at play saying things such as, "I wonder where this wheel goes? Does it go here?" After a while, at the age of 6 or 7 years, children begin to carry out such dialogues more inwardly and silently. Vygotsky believed that our ability to talk to ourselves—to think with the help of words—contributes enormously to our powers of thought.

Two other important sign systems are *writing* and *numbering systems*. The invention of writing was a great human achievement; it enabled people to keep permanent records of information. For most children, however, learning to write (and read) is a real struggle because writing forces children to detach themselves from physical, expressive speech, which comes so naturally to them, and to use abstract symbols for words. Learning to write usually requires a good deal of formal instruction (Vygotsky, 1934, p. 181; 1935, p. 105).

Numbering systems have also been of great importance in human evolution. Vygotsky suggested that early peoples created numbering systems because they found they were unable to quantify objects (such as vegetables or cattle) by sight alone. They needed sets of symbols to help them count. For example, the Papaus of New Guinea invented a method of counting that used their fingers and many parts of their bodies to stand for objects. As societies evolved, they developed other numbering systems, such as the abacus and written notation. They also increasingly dealt with quantities in abstract and theoretical ways, apart from particular objects. Algebra, for example, deals with general quantitative categories without even specifying particular numbers. If $a + 10 = b$, then $a = b - 10$, regardless of the particular values of a and b. The mastery of algebra and other theoretical uses of number, like the mastery of reading and writing, usually require formal instruction (John-Steiner & Souberman, 1978).

Vygotsky argued that cultural sign systems have a major impact on cognitive development—an impact overlooked by developmentalists such as Gesell and Piaget. Gesell and Piaget looked at development as if it comes from the child alone, from the child's inner maturational promptings or spontaneous discoveries. Vygotsky acknowledged that such intrinsic development, the "natural line" of development, is important. It may even dominate cognitive development up to the age of 2 years or so (Vygotsky, 1930, p. 24). But after this, the growth of the mind is increasingly influenced by the "cultural line" of development, the sign systems the culture provides. In fact, all our uniquely human powers of thought—those that distinguish us from other species—would be impossible without speech and other sign systems.

Vygotsky speculated, in addition, that the highest levels of thinking—the levels of purely abstract or theoretical reasoning—require instruction in writing, math, and other kinds of abstract concepts. Although children might develop some concepts on their own, in their everyday experience, they will not develop purely abstract modes of thought without instruction in abstract sign systems. And since this instruction is only widespread in technologically advanced societies, we will find purely abstract thinking prevalent only in these societies (Vygotsky, 1934, pp. 103, 206; 1935, p. 90; Luria, 1976, pp. 8, 161).

In 1931 Vygotsky saw a unique opportunity to test this latter hypothesis—that abstract thinking is a product of relatively advanced levels of social-historical development. At this time, there were many remote areas of the Soviet Union, including Central Asia, where peasants still lived a feudal existence. The peasants worked on small farms and were completely dependent on wealthy landowners and feudal lords. Most were illiterate. The new Soviet government, attempting to develop the entire nation into a modern socialist state, instituted collective farming practices, in which peasants met in groups to plan production, measure output, and so on. The government also gave the peasants short courses in writing, reading, and the theoretical uses of number. Because, in 1931, the government was still phasing in the new programs, Vygotsky saw the opportunity to compare the mental processes of those adults who had begun to participate in the modern forms of social life with those who were still living in the old ways.

Actually, Vygotsky himself was too ill to go to Central Asia to conduct fieldwork, but he encouraged Luria and others to do so. In one aspect of the study, the interviewers presented the subjects with syllogisms such as the following:

In the Far North, where there is snow, all bears are white. Novaya is in the Far North. What color are the bears there? (Luria, 1976, p. 108)

The nonliterate subjects refused to deal with the question in a purely theoretical way. They said things such as, "I don't know what color the bears there are, I never saw them" (p. 111). When the interviewer pressed them, asking them to answer "on the basis of my words," the peasants still refused to speak beyond their personal experience. As one said, "Your words can be answered only by someone who was there, and if a person wasn't there he can't say anything on the basis of your words" (p. 109). Those who had been participating in the new programs, in contrast, were willing to deal with the syllogisms on a theoretical plane and they answered them correctly (p. 116).

This study wasn't perfect. Luria gave the impression that the nonliterate subjects not only refused to think in syllogisms but also were incapable of doing so. However on occasion a few subjects, when pressed sufficiently, went against their deep-seated mental habits and answered the questions correctly. They were capable of abstract thinking—they just preferred not to engage in it.

But in general the study did support the Marxist contention that the mind is a product of social-historical change. The study suggested that we cannot meaningfully discuss the "principles of thinking" or "cognitive development" in the abstract, as psychologists usually do. We need to examine the culture into which the child is growing, and the sign systems the culture provides. For, as Vygotsky said, as these tools of thinking change, the mind takes on a different character.

Not all Marxist psychologists, we should note, have enthusiastically endorsed Vygotsky's ideas. Several Marxists have argued that Vygotsky stretched the metaphor of tools too far. Tools, they say, mean real tools—not speech, writing, math, and other "psychological tools" (see Kozulin, 1986, pp. xlviii–l).

But whatever his standing as a Marxist, Vygotsky pointed developmental psychology in a promising new direction. Vygotsky recognized the role of intrinsic forces, but he suggested that a complete understanding of cognitive development requires the study of the psychological tools the culture hands down to the child.

These two forces—intrinsic and cultural—generally seem to be opposed. Perhaps it is for this reason that most scholars have emphasized one force or the other, but not both. Vygotsky, in contrast, was schooled in dialectical theory and was therefore primed to consider the ways in which opposing forces interact and produce new transformations. The growing child, trying to make sense of the world in her own way, encounters a culture that expects her to use its particular psychological tools. These interactions are complex and difficult to study. Vygotsky himself only began to investigate them, and he generally focused on only one side of the dialectic—the impact of culture on the child. In the following sections, we will look at Vygotsky's insights into how some of these psychological tools are acquired.

MEMORY AIDS

Vygotsky suggested that some of humankind's earliest psychological tools were memory aids, and these tools are still very important to us today. Vygotsky and his colleagues conducted various experiments to try to gain insights into the ways in which children acquire them.

In one experiment, Vygotsky (1931a, pp. 70–71) instructed children and adults to respond in different ways when they saw different colors. He told them to lift a finger when they saw red, to press a button when they saw green, and so on. Sometimes he made the task simple, sometimes he made it difficult, and at certain points he offered memory aids.

In such experiments, the youngest children, between the ages of 4 and 8 years, typically acted as if they could remember anything. Whether the task was simple or difficult, they rushed into it as soon as they heard the instructions. When the experimenter offered them pictures and cards "to help you remember," they usually ignored the aids, or used them inappropriately. Young children, Vygotsky concluded, "do not yet know their capacities and limitations" or how to use external stimuli to help them remember things (1931b, p. 71).

Older children, from about 9 to 12 years, typically used the pictures Vygotsky offered, and these aids did improve their performance. Interestingly, the addition of such aids did not always improve the memory of the adults. But this was not because they had become like young children and no longer used memory devices. Rather, it was because they now rehearsed instructions and made mental notes to themselves inwardly, without the need for external cues (Vygotsky, 1930, pp. 41–45).

By today's standards, these experiments were very informal. But they were pioneering investigations into an area that has become a major topic in contemporary psychology. This is *metacognition*, the awareness people have of their own thought processes. (People's specific awareness of their own memory processes is sometimes called *metamemory*.) Like Vygotsky, contemporary psychologists are trying to discover how children become aware of their thinking and how they learn to use psychological tools and strategies to improve it (Flavell et al., 2002, pp. 163–167, 262–263).

SPEECH

The single-most important psychological tool is speech (Vygotsky, 1930, p. 24; 1934, p. 256). Speech frees our thought and attention from the immediate perceptual field. This freedom sets us apart from other species.

To illustrate this difference, Vygotsky called attention to research by Kohler (1925) on the problem solving of apes. Kohler found that if one places a banana within an ape's visual field—but behind some bars so the ape cannot grab it—the ape's attention will be so riveted on the banana that it will hardly consider anything else. The ape won't consider using a stick lying nearby, unless the stick also happens to lie directly in front of the bars. The stick, that is, must also be part of the immediate visual field (Kohler, 1925, pp. 37–38; Vygotsky, 1930, pp. 35–37).

Human thinking, in contrast, can range much more freely beyond the immediate perceptual field, and it is speech that enables it to do so. Because words frequently refer to absent objects, we can, in a situation like that of the ape, ask ourselves, What object might reach that banana? Is there a stick or a pole around here that will reach it? Thus, we use words to contemplate and direct our search for objects not in our visual field.

Vygotsky suggested that the ability to engage in such internal dialogues develops in three steps.

1. Initially, references to absent objects occur in the child's interactions with others. For example, a 2-year-old girl might ask her mother to help her find something. Or the mother might say, "We're going to the park now, so get your pail and shovel," directing the girl's attention to objects she had not been looking at.
2. Next, at the age of 3 years or so, the child begins to direct similar comments to herself. While playing with her toys, she might say, "Where's my shovel? I need my shovel," and begin looking for an object that had not been within her immediate surroundings.

   For a time, this self-guiding speech is said aloud; we frequently hear children talking as they play or work on problems. Then, beginning at about 6 years of age, children's self-directed speech becomes increasingly quiet, abbreviated, and less comprehensible to us.
3. Finally, by age 8 or so, we cannot hear this talk at all. But the child's self-directed speech has not disappeared; it has merely gone underground. It has turned into *inner speech,* the silent dialogue that one has with oneself (Vygotsky, 1934, pp. 29–40).

The general process, then, is one of *internalizing* social interactions. What begins as an interpersonal process, occurring between the parent and the child, becomes an intrapsychic process, occurring within the child. Vygotsky believed that this general progression characterizes the development of all the "higher mental processes," all the forms of thought and attention that depend on cultural signs. In fact, he stated that the progression is a general law:

Any function in the child's cultural development appears on the stage twice, on two planes, first on the social plane and then on the psychological. (1931a, pp. 44–45)

This law, in the view of Vygotsky and his followers, was a cornerstone of a Marxist psychology. A Marxist does not seek the origins of thinking within the individual child, spontaneously sprouting from the child's mind, but in external social existence (Vygotsky, 1930, p. 45). "The child," Vygotsky said, "learns the social forms of behavior and applies them to himself" (1931a, p. 40).

Egocentric Speech

In the process of internalizing social speech, children go through a phase (step 2) in which they spend considerable time talking to themselves aloud. The first person to call attention to this kind of speech was Piaget (1923), who called it *egocentric speech*. Piaget observed, for example, that if two 5-year-old girls are playing in a sandbox, each might talk enthusiastically about topics without considering the fact that the other couldn't possibly know what she was referring to. Piaget called this speech "egocentric" because he thought it reflects the child's general egocentrism; the child doesn't adjust her speech to the perspective of the listener because she egocentrically assumes the listener's perspective is the same as her own. Piaget estimated that between the ages of 4 and 7 years about 45% of all speech is egocentric (1923, p. 51).

Vygotsky agreed that egocentric speech is very prevalent in this age group, but he disagreed with Piaget about its theoretical meaning. In Piaget's view, egocentric speech is basically useless. It merely reflects a deficiency in the child's thinking. Vygotsky, in contrast, emphasized its positive function; it helps the child solve problems. In one of Piaget's studies (1923, p. 14), $6\frac{1}{2}$-year-old Lev says to no one in particular, "I want to do that drawing, there. . . . I want to draw something, I do. I shall need a big piece of paper to do that." In Vygotsky's view, Lev's self-directed talk helps Lev plan and direct his activities (Vygotsky, 1934, p. 29).

Vygotsky also disagreed with Piaget about egocentric speech's ultimate fate. Piaget implied that as children overcome their egocentrism, egocentric speech simply dies out. Vygotsky argued that it doesn't just fade away, but it goes underground and turns into inner speech, the kind of silent dialogue we so often have with ourselves when we try to solve problems. Interpreting the decline of egocentric speech as an indication it is dying, Vygotsky said, "is like saying that the child stops counting when he ceases to use his fingers and starts adding in his head" (1934, p. 230).

Vygotsky argued, then, that egocentric speech is highly useful and an important way station on the road to inner speech. But even if we were to agree with Vygotsky on these points, we would still have to agree with Piaget that there is something puzzling about it. The child seems to be talking to someone, yet doesn't do so in any full way. For example, a child playing alone with Tinkertoys while an adult is silently seated across the room says,

The wheels go here, the wheels go here. Oh, we need to start it all over again. We need to close it up. See, it closes up. We're starting it all over again. Do you know why we wanted to do that? Because I needed it to go in a different way. (Kohlberg, Yaeger, & Hjertholm, 1968, p. 695)

The child seems to be talking to the listener (e.g., asking him, "Do you know why . . . ?"), but the child doesn't wait for the listener to respond.

According to Vygotsky, the child's self-directed speech is puzzling because it is not yet differentiated from social speech. The child is trying to use speech to direct her own activities, but she still casts her speech in the form of social communication. It takes a while for self-directed speech to "differentiate out" and take on its own character. Only gradually does self-directed speech become quieter and more abbreviated and turn into inner speech (Vygotsky, 1934, pp. 229–232).

Research Bearing on the Vygotsky–Piaget Issue.   Vygotsky tried to think of ways to test whether his view of egocentric speech was more correct than that of Piaget. In his most prominent study, Vygotsky reasoned that if egocentric speech serves a problem-solving function, it should increase when tasks become more difficult. Because Piaget saw no positive function to egocentric speech, his theory makes no such prediction.

So Vygotsky did various things to make children's tasks more difficult. "For instance, when a child was getting ready to draw, he would suddenly find that there was no paper, or no pencil of the color he needed. In other words, by obstructing his free activity, we made him face problems" (Vygotsky, 1934, pp. 29–30). In these situations, the proportion of egocentric speech (the amount of egocentric speech compared to all speech) nearly doubled among 5- to 7-year-olds (Luria, 1961, p. 33). The children tried to solve problems by talking to themselves. For example, one child said, "Where's the pencil? I need a blue pencil. Never mind, I'll draw with the red one and wet it with water; it will become dark and look like blue" (Vygotsky, 1934, pp. 29–30). This study suggested, then, that egocentric speech does serve a problem-solving function in young children, as Vygotsky suggested.

This study has been widely replicated, and the results have largely been in agreement with Vygotsky's. There is, however, one qualification. If tasks are made much too difficult for children, they do not engage in self-guiding speech. They just give up and don't say anything. As Laura Berk says, tasks must be "appropriately challenging" (2009, p. 265).

Other research has examined the contrasting positions of Piaget and Vygotsky, and most of it supports Vygotsky. It suggests that egocentric or self-directed speech serves a positive function and turns into inner speech, which continues to guide behavior (Berk, 2009, p. 265; Kohlberg et al., 1968).

Nevertheless, it still seems possible that Piaget was partly correct. Even if some egocentric speech serves the self-guiding function that Vygotsky emphasized, it also seems that *some* egocentric speech might reflect the child's inability to consider the audience's viewpoint. It may be that both Piaget and Vygotsky were correct.[1]

---

[1] In their research reports, contemporary psychologists often refer to both egocentric and vocalized self-directed speech as *private speech*.

Self-Control

So far we have focused on the way children use self-guiding speech to help them solve problems, as when they work on tasks such as drawing and building things with Tinkertoys. But verbal self-regulation also helps people gain emotional self-control, in the sense of overcoming impulses and temptations. In everyday conversations, we speak of this capacity as willpower.

According to Vygotsky, the basic question of willpower is: How is it possible for us to take action in situations in which forces pull us strongly against it? How, for instance, do we stop watching TV and go study instead?

Vygotsky's (1932) answer was that we use words to create artificial stimuli to direct our behavior. If we are watching TV, we might say to ourselves, "OK, I'm going to watch it until 8 o'clock, then I'll study." We create a new, verbal signal to control our behavior.

As usual, Vygotsky argued that we initially acquire such signals through social interactions. When we were young, adults frequently used signals to direct our behavior. They might have told us, "I want you to jump in the water on the count of three" or "You can watch TV until the big hand on the clock reaches the 12." A little later, we began applying similar signals to ourselves, at first aloud and then silently through inner speech.

As Berk observes, we can sometimes hear young children talking to themselves as they try to gain self-control. A toddler who is tempted to touch a light socket says to herself, "Don't touch," and pulls her hand back. A little boy who starts to jump on a sofa says to himself, "No, can't," and climbs down (Berk, 2001, pp. 89, 511). Several psychologists are interested in the process by which children learn to delay gratification, as when they are told to wait before eating a treat. Berk points out that this capacity emerges with the development of language and that one can often overhear young children instructing themselves to wait (2001, p. 89).

Luria's Research on the Verbal Regulation of Behavior

An especially fine-grained analysis of the verbal self-regulation of behavior was provided by Vygotsky's colleague A. R. Luria.

Luria focused on the internalization of adult commands. He wanted to see how the child comes to obey adult commands and then applies those commands to herself. Vygotsky, we should note, did not imply that all self-regulation is limited to the internalization of commands. Children internalize all kinds of dialogue. But Luria focused on commands.

Luria found that a child's ability to follow adult commands develops rather slowly. Suppose a toy fish is lying on a table. If we tell a 14-month-old child, "Bring me the fish," the child will do so. But if we place a shiny toy cat closer to the child and again say, "Bring me the fish," the child will bring us the shiny cat. Our verbal instructions cannot overcome the power of an attractive stimulus (Luria, 1960, p. 360).

There are other difficulties as well. In one experiment, Luria gave a 2-year-old a rubber balloon and told him to press it, which the child did. But Luria noted, "He does not stop his reaction, for he presses a second, a third, and a fourth time" (p. 360). Luria gave the boy only one instruction, but the boy's action *perseverated*—it kept going.

What's more, our commands, which can so easily set a child's behavior in motion, do not have nearly the same power to *inhibit* it. If an experimenter tells a 2-year-old who is pressing a balloon, "That's enough," the command usually has little effect. In fact, in many cases the command only intensifies the child's reaction; the child presses even more energetically (Luria, 1961, p. 53).

By the ages of 3 or $3\frac{1}{2}$, children can follow specific adult commands fairly well (Luria, 1961, p. 70; Slobin, 1966, p. 131). But can they follow their *own* verbal instructions?

In one experiment, Luria told children to say "Press" and press a balloon when they saw one light and to say "Don't press" and to refrain from pressing when they saw another light. But 3- and $3\frac{1}{2}$-year-olds pressed at every light. They said "Press" and pressed, and they said "Don't press" and pressed. Once again, words excite action, but they have a weak inhibiting effect (Luria, 1960, pp. 374–375; 1961, pp. 90–91).

Luria believed that a good part of the difficulty is that young children respond to the *excitatory* function of speech rather than to its *meaning*. The phrase "Don't press" excites action simply because it is a signal, regardless of its meaning.

A number of Luria's experiments suggest that children can verbally regulate much of their own behavior by the age of 5 or 6 years. They can easily handle the kinds of experiments previously described. In fact, an experimenter need only give them instructions at the outset, and they will perform correctly without saying anything to themselves aloud. But Luria believed they are still giving themselves verbal instructions—only now they are doing so silently, through inner speech. To support his interpretation, Luria reported that when he made tasks more complicated or speeded them up, the 5- and 6-year-olds spontaneously began giving themselves instructions aloud once again (Luria, 1961, p. 93).

Self-Regulation and Neurological Functioning.

Luria emphasized the social origins of self-regulation. First, children submit to the commands of others; then they command themselves. At the same time, Luria recognized that the child's ability to regulate her behavior depends on the maturation of the nervous system. In fact, Luria devoted a great portion of his life studying the neurological mechanisms underlying self-regulation and other mental functioning, and he is considered one of history's great neurologists.

Many of Luria's insights came during his work with patients who suffered brain injuries during the Second World War. Luria, like others, found that the kinds of difficulties the patients experienced depended greatly on the specific location of their injuries. The ability to regulate one's own behavior, Luria found, is tied to the frontal lobes, particularly in the left hemisphere. Patients who suffered frontal lobe injuries could still speak and perform simple habitual tasks, such as greeting others and dressing themselves. But in new situations, they were unable to regulate their own behavior and, as a result, they were slaves to environmental stimulation.

For example, one patient was supposed to take a train to Moscow, but when he arrived at the station he stepped onto the first train he saw boarding and traveled in the opposite direction. Apparently the call "All aboard" and the sight of the others getting onto the train was more than he could resist. He couldn't tell himself, "This isn't my train," and use these words to regulate his own behavior.

Patients with severe frontal lobe damage also have problems with perseveration; once they begin an activity, they cannot easily stop it. Luria told about a patient "who began occupational therapy after the war. He was instructed to plane a piece of wood. He planed a board down completely and continued to plane the work bench, being unable to stop" (Luria, 1982, p. 111).

In such cases, we must guess that the patients were unable to use speech to control their behavior. We suppose that they could not effectively tell themselves "Stop" or "Hold it." Some of Luria's other research added more direct support for this speculation. In one study, Luria asked patients to imitate him and raise a finger or a fist whenever he did so. This they could do. But when Luria reversed the instructions, they had difficulty. They could repeat his instructions, but they couldn't apply them to their behavior. A patient would say, "Yours is a fist, so now I must raise my finger," but he still imitated Luria and raised his fist. He couldn't use speech to regulate his actions (p. 112).

Inner Speech

Under ordinary circumstances, adults have developed the capacity to give themselves verbal instructions inwardly and silently, through inner speech. Inner speech, however, is very difficult to investigate. Vygotsky obtained some clues from writers and poets, but he relied primarily on the study of egocentric speech in children. That is, he assumed that the changes we see in egocentric speech just before it goes underground forecast what inner speech is like (Vygotsky, 1934, pp. 226–227).

Inner speech, in comparison to social speech, seems more abbreviated. It omits information that we already know and focuses on that which is new. Sometimes we can observe the same phenomenon in social situations. Vygotsky asked us to imagine several people waiting for a particular bus. "No one will say, on seeing the bus approach, 'The bus for which we are waiting is coming.'" The speaker is likely to say merely, "Coming," or some such expression. She limits her statement to the new information—the bus's arrival (1934, p. 236). When we talk silently to ourselves, we abbreviate our statements in a similar way.

Another characteristic of inner speech is the dominance of *sense* over *meaning*. The sense of the word is the feeling it arouses in us. For example, the word *lion* can evoke feelings ranging from fear to tender sympathy, depending on the context in which we are thinking about the animal. The meaning is the more precise definition, like that found in a dictionary. A word's meaning is important for clear communication, but when we use words to think about something just to ourselves, we are strongly affected by the emotional sense of the words (Vygotsky, 1934, pp. 244–245).

To understand inner speech more fully, Vygotsky (1934, pp. 245–249) said we need to examine its role within a microgenetic process. Microgenesis, you will recall from Chapter 5, is the relatively brief developmental process that occurs every time we form a thought or a perception. The formation of a verbal statement, too, unfolds microgenetically, and inner speech enters this process at a critical point.

The act of making a verbal statement begins with an emotion—a desire, interest, or need. Next comes the dim stirring of a thought, which always includes something of the original feeling. At this point, inner speech comes into play. We engage in inner speech as we try to articulate our thoughts. This process is fluid and dynamic, and both our thoughts and our words undergo several transformations as we struggle to make a clear statement without losing feeling behind our original thought (pp. 249–255).

Sometimes we cannot find words to express our thoughts at all. Vygotsky referred to a novel by Gelb Uspensky, in which "a poor peasant, who must address an official with some life-important issue, cannot put his thoughts into words" (p. 249). The poor man asks the Lord for help, but to no avail.

Even great poets, who are so good with words, experience this difficulty. The poet Afanasey Fet wrote, "If only soul might speak without words!" F. Tiutcheve felt that the process of translating thoughts into words so routinely distorts the original thought that "a thought once uttered is a lie" (Vygotsky, 1934, pp. 251, 254). Vygotsky recognized this danger. Nevertheless, he argued that we need words to develop our thoughts. A thought that fails to realize itself in words remains unfulfilled. A "voiceless thought" as the poet Osip Mandelstam said, "returns to shadow's chambers" (Vygtosky, 1934, p. 210).

PLAY

We have seen that speech frees the child from the immediate physical situation. Using words, the child can talk about objects and events beyond the here and now. The young child also gains freedom from the concrete situation through play. In make-believe play, a piece of wood becomes a person, a stick becomes a horse. The child creates an illusory world where objects take on new meanings. Play is a big step in imaginative thinking.

But Vygotsky (1933) emphasized that the child's play, although spontaneous and imaginative, is not completely free. In the child's mind, there are rules to be followed. When two young girls pretend it is night and they have to go to sleep, they follow an implicit rule that they do not engage in any imaginary activity whatsoever, such as digging in the dirt or riding bikes; they only engage in bedtime activities. Vygotsky told about two girls, ages 5 and 7, who decided to play sisters. They followed an implicit rule that sisters do things the same. They dressed alike and talked alike.

By adhering to the rules implicit in their play, children exhibit more self-control than in the rest of their lives. They behave according to what they think a role requires, not their immediate desires. If three children pretend to be shopkeepers and customers, and let pieces of candy represent money, they don't eat the candy. They use the candy as a prop and stay in their roles.

Vygotsky said that because the child exhibits so much greater self control in play, it's as if he were "a head taller than himself" (1933, p. 102). Yet the child doesn't experience the rules in play as a burden. On the contrary, the child takes pleasure in adhering to them. Play, Vygotsky said, is the prototype for later taking pleasure in following one's guiding idea or moral principle (p. 99).

After the age of 7 or so, children begin playing games that have very set rules. Vygotsky (1934, p. 104) observed that play isn't as free and imaginative as it once was. But we should note that when Vygotsky wrote about older children's play, he was primarily thinking of structured, competitive sports, not more informal children's games, like snowball battles. In their more informal games, children feel freer to create and revise rules, as Piaget observed.

SCHOOLING

Vygotsky noted that children master language quite naturally (1935, p. 105), and he made it sound as if early play springs spontaneously from the child herself. One might ask if speech and play are as much a part of the natural line of development as the cultural line. Unfortunately, Vygotsky didn't say much on this question. But he made it clear that the acquisition of cultural sign systems such as math and writing don't usually come naturally. These are taught in schools, and most children have difficulty with these subjects. Vygotsky was one of the first psychologists to devote considerable attention to the impact of school instruction on the developing child. As was his custom, he developed his ideas by comparing them to the ideas of others, particularly those of Piaget.

Vygotsky versus Piaget

Piaget drew a sharp distinction between development and teaching. Development, he said, is a spontaneous process that comes from the child. It comes from inner maturational growth and, more importantly, from the child's own efforts to make sense of the world. The child, in Piaget's view, is a little intellectual explorer, making her own discoveries and formulating her own positions.

Piaget did not mean that the child develops in isolation, apart from the social world. Other people do have an impact on the child's thinking. But they do not help the child by trying to directly teach her things. Rather, they promote development by stimulating and challenging the child's own thinking. This often occurs, for example, when children get into discussions and debates with friends. If a girl finds that a friend has pointed out a flaw in her argument, she is stimulated to come up with a better argument, and her mind grows. But the girl's intellectual development is an independent process. For it is the girl herself—not an outside person—who must construct the new argument.

As a proponent of independent thinking, Piaget was highly critical of the teacher-directed instruction that occurs in most schools. Teachers try to take charge of the child's learning, acting as if they could somehow pour material into the child's head. They force the child into a passive position. Moreover, teachers often present abstract concepts in math, science, and other areas that are well beyond the child's own grasp. Sometimes, to be sure, children appear to have learned something, but they usually have acquired mere "verbalisms"; they repeat back the teacher's words without any genuine understanding of the concepts behind them. If adults want children to genuinely grasp concepts, they must give children opportunities to discover them on their own (Piaget, 1969).

In Vygotsky's view, spontaneous development is important, but it is not all-important, as Piaget believed. If children's minds were simply the products of their own discoveries and inventions, their minds wouldn't advance very far. In reality, children also benefit enormously from the knowledge and conceptual tools handed down to them by their cultures. In modern societies, this usually occurs in schools. Teachers do, as Piaget said, present material that is too difficult for children to learn by themselves, but this is what good instruction should do. It should march ahead of development, pulling it along, helping children master material that they cannot immediately grasp on their own. Their initial understanding might be superficial, but the instruction is still valuable, for it moves the children's minds forward.

Scientific Concepts

Vygotsky saw particular value in the kinds of abstract concepts that are taught in schools. He called them *scientific concepts,* and he included in this category concepts in math and science (e.g., Archimedes' law) as well as concepts in the social sciences (e.g., class conflict). He contrasted these concepts with the *spontaneous concepts* that children learn on their own. Because children develop most of their spontaneous concepts outside of school, in their everyday lives, Vygotsky also referred to spontaneous concepts as *everyday concepts* (although there is no reason why schools cannot also give children opportunities to make their own discoveries, as Montessori, Dewey, and Piagetians such as Kamii have shown).

In any case, Vygotsky argued that instruction in scientific concepts is very helpful because it provides children with broader frameworks in which to place their spontaneous concepts. For example, a 7-year-old boy might have developed the spontaneous concept of *grandmother,* but his concept is primarily based on his image of his own grandmother. If we ask him to define the term, he might reply, "She has a soft lap." Formal instruction, in which the teacher diagrams abstract "family trees" (which include concepts such as *grandparents, parents,* and *children*) can give the child a broader framework in which to place his spontaneous concept and help him understand what a grandmother really is (Vygotsky, 1930, p. 50).

Vygotsky argued that this kind of formal instruction brings consciousness to the child's thinking. So long as the child thinks of the concept *grandmother* as a particular person, he is not really conscious of the concept. His awareness is directed to the person, not the concept. Only when he sees that *grandmother* is a category within a more general system of categories does he become aware of the concept as such (Vygotsky, 1934, p. 171).

A similar process occurs when children learn to write. Before we are introduced to writing, we have mastered a great deal of spoken language, but our mastery is not at a very conscious level. Speaking is a bit like singing; it is physically expressive and flows rather naturally. Writing, in contrast, uses more formal and abstract systems of symbols and forces us to behave much more consciously and deliberately. When we write, we are constantly making conscious decisions with respect to the proper verb form, the point at which a sentence should end, and so forth. Learning to write takes great effort, but it helps us see how language is structured. Writing, Vygotsky said, "brings awareness to speech" (p. 183).

Support for Vygotsky's views has come from the research of Sylvia Scribner and Michael Cole (1981, pp. 151–156) on the effects of literacy among the Vai people in Liberia. The investigators presented both literate and nonliterate Vai adults with several sentences, some of which were ungrammatical. Both groups were perfectly able to say which sentences were ungrammatical. But the literate Vai were better able to explain why (for example, to explain that the subject and the verb of a sentence didn't agree). Apparently, literacy training had given them a greater conceptual awareness of their speech. In contemporary terms, they had gained *metacognitive* knowledge of their own speech.

To get a better sense of what it feels like to learn on a newly conceptual level, we might recall the experience of studying a foreign language in school. The process probably felt awkward and self-conscious. But we might also have felt we were becoming aware of our native language for the first time because we were seeing it within a broader, abstract framework, as employing one set of rules where other options are possible (Vygotsky, 1934, p. 196). As Goethe said, "He who knows no foreign language does not really know his own" (Vygotsky, 1934, p. 160).

Vygotsky, then, saw much more value in scientific concepts than Piaget did. In Vygotsky's view, both scientific and spontaneous concepts have their own specific virtues. Spontaneous concepts, such as the child's own concepts of *grandmother* and *brother,* are "saturated with experience" (p. 193); they are full of rich personal sensations and imagery. Scientific concepts, such as abstract family lineage systems, are comparatively dry. But scientific concepts give children broader frameworks in which to view their own concepts.

Interactions Between Scientific and Spontaneous Concepts.   In school, the two kinds of concepts typically influence and benefit each other in the following way. Scientific concepts, which the teacher hands down "from above," lead the way. They give cognitive development a new goal, pressing children to think more abstractly than they ordinarily would.

For a while, however, children usually have difficulty understanding the new concepts. That the children understand them at all must be credited to their spontaneous concepts. When, for example, a typical Russian class of third-graders listens to the teacher discuss the concept of *class conflict,* it is only because the children have already developed spontaneous concepts of rich and poor people that they have an inkling of what the teacher is talking about. As the teacher presses on, the children are asked to think about the scientific concepts further, and after a while they may develop some understanding of how their spontaneous concepts fit into a more abstract scheme (Vygotsky, 1934, p. 194).

Instruction, then, propels the mind forward. Instruction, Vygotsky emphasized, does not just add something new to the child's development, like adding clothes to the child's body. Rather, it interacts with development, awakening it, charting new paths for it. Vygotsky said that psychologists should do all they can to learn about this interaction (1935, pp. 80, 91).

Vygotsky himself, however, found that this interaction is difficult to study; the developmental processes stimulated by instruction are largely hidden from view. The one thing that is certain, Vygotsky found, is that development does not follow instruction in any straightforward way. When he plotted the two curves—one for the course of instruction, the other for the child's subsequent mental development—he found that the curves do not coincide. For example, it often happens that three or four steps in instruction produce no change in the child's understanding of arithmetic, and then

> with a fifth step, something clicks; the child has grasped a general principle, and his developmental curve rises markedly. For this child, the fifth operation was decisive, but this cannot be a general rule. The turning points at which a general principle becomes clear to the child cannot be set in advance by the curriculum. (Vygotsky, 1934, p. 185)

Thus the teacher cannot prescribe the manner in which the child learns. The teacher might create a curriculum that progresses in a step-by-step manner, but this doesn't mean the child will develop according to the teacher's plan. Development has its own rhythms. Still, adult teaching is necessary. Without it, the child's mind wouldn't advance very far (1934, p. 185).

The Zone of Proximal Development

Most teachers would probably agree with Vygotsky's general viewpoint. They would agree that it is their job to move the child's mind forward, and to do this they must directly teach children new concepts, not wait for them to make their own discoveries. At the same time, teachers know they cannot teach any concept to any child. They cannot, for example, effectively begin teaching algebra to most first-graders. Teachers need ways of determining the kinds of lessons children are ready for.

Most schools have made such decisions with the help of standardized achievement and intelligence tests. A school might give a third-grade child an achievement test, find that she is doing math at the third-grade level, and assign her to a middle-level math group. Vygotsky argued, however, that the conventional tests are inadequate. They only measure the child's actual level of development, telling us how far she has developed so far. They do not tell us about the child's ability to learn new material beyond her present level.

The reason for this shortcoming, Vygotsky said, is that conventional tests only evaluate what the child can accomplish when working independently. But before children can perform tasks alone, they can perform them in collaboration with others, receiving some guidance or support. To determine a child's potential for new learning, then, we need to see how well the child can do when offered some assistance.

Vygotsky asked us to consider two boys who scored at the 8-year-old level on a conventional intelligence test (Vygotsky, 1934, p. 187). They scored at this level, that is, when working independently, as the test requires. Then, however, the examiner presented some new problems, too difficult for the boys to solve on their own, and offered each some slight assistance, such as a leading question or the first step in a solution. With this help, one boy scored at the 9-year-old level while the other boy scored at the 12-year-old level. Clearly, the boys' potential for new learning was not the same. Vygotsky called the distance that children can perform beyond their current level the *zone of proximal development*. More precisely, he defined the zone as

the distance between the actual developmental level as determined by independent problem solving and the level of potential development as determined through problem solving under adult guidance or in collaboration with more capable peers. (1935, p. 86)

Vygotsky hoped the zone of proximal development would give educators a much better indication of each child's true potential.

Actually, Vygotsky wrote just as enthusiastically about the concept's usefulness to developmental psychology. He discussed the concept as if it provides a new, improved searchlight that illuminates not only those functions that have already matured but also those that are in the process of maturing. By focusing on the activities children can accomplish with assistance, the zone reveals those abilities that are just beginning to develop, such as the ability to walk in an infant who can do so only if she has a hand to hold. The zone of proximal development casts light not so much on "the ripe as the ripening functions"—those that the child can carry out only with assistance today but will be able to perform alone tomorrow (Vygotsky, 1934, p. 188).

But how do we know Vygotsky was correct, that the zone of proximal development does illuminate the stirrings of inner development? When a *slight* amount of assistance quickly enables a child to succeed, we can be fairly certain we are observing a spontaneously developing capacity. The rapid success suggests that the adult aided a capacity that had already been emerging from within.

But Vygotsky also suggested that adults occasionally provide a *great deal* of assistance. He approvingly noted, for example, that a child could use an abstract concept "because the teacher, working with the child, [had] explained, supplied information, questioned, corrected, and made the pupil explain" (1934, p. 191). In this case, the teacher appears to have treated the child like a puppet, and it isn't clear that the teacher has stimulated anything spontaneous within the child.

Perhaps the only way to know if the child's spontaneous development is activated is to watch the child. Is the child enthusiastic, curious, and actively involved? Or does the child look off into space? In fact, some research (e.g., Rogoff, Malkin, & Gilbride, 1984) suggests that adults who teach effectively within the zone of proximal development do continually look for signs of spontaneous interest on the child's part.

PRACTICAL APPLICATIONS

Vygotsky wanted to help build a new society, and he deliberately set out to construct a theory that addressed practical matters. As we have just seen, he tried to show how school instruction can promote child development, and he offered a new concept—the zone of proximal development—to assess each child's potential for new learning. If we want to know what a child is ready to learn, Vygotsky said, we cannot look at what the child can do when working alone; we must see how far ahead she can go when offered some assistance.

The zone of proximal development has captured the interest of a growing number of researchers. Some have evaluated the extent to which the zone does in fact diagnose a child's potential for new learning. The zone's diagnostic value seems promising but in need of refinement; it does not yet predict end-of-the-year achievement better than IQ tests do (Berk, 2001, p. 205).

The zone of proximal development has stimulated much more interest in the teaching process itself—how adults can help a child solve problems or use strategies that are initially beyond the child's independent abilities. Typically, psychologists and educators refer to this process as *scaffolding* (Wood, 1998). The adult (or more competent peer) at first provides a good deal of assistance, but reduces it as the child gets the hang of the activity. The assistance is like a temporary scaffold that comes down when construction is finished. For example, a parent might initially help a child pedal and steer a bicycle, but then step aside as the child seems able to ride it on her own.

Brown and Palinscar (1989) showed how teachers might scaffold reading skills using a method they call *reciprocal teaching*. Initially, the teacher shows children how to summarize and clarify reading passages. Then the children take turns "being the teacher," leading small groups of classmates in the use of the strategies. The teacher continues to guide the process but gradually shifts much of the responsibility to the children. The method has produced positive results (Berk, 2009, p. 269).

Elena Bodrova and Deborah Leong have developed a program called Tools of the Mind to help preschool and kindergarten children learn self-regulation skills such as planning activities, sticking to tasks, and ignoring distractions. Bodrova and Leong began with Vygotsky's observation that children frequently demonstrate remarkable self-regulation in their make-believe play. For example, the preschooler who has difficulty sitting still during circle time can do so when she plays the role of a pupil in a make-believe scene (Bodrova & Leong, 2007, p. 132). Using the Tools of the Mind program, the teacher helps young children initiate and sustain make-believe play.

Teachers introduce children to play themes through videos, field trips, and books. Teachers also ask children to create *play plans.* The children write down their plans (to the best of their abilities) and draw pictures of themselves engaged in the activities. Children are encouraged to make their play plans as specific as possible.

During the planning, the teachers suggest how the children "can try out new roles, add new twists to the play scenario, or think of a way to substitute for missing props" (Bodrova & Leong, 2001, p. 19). Initially, children often believe props must be realistic-looking toys. Teachers wean children away from this idea; they brainstorm with children about the different things a simple object, such as wooden block, might represent. If children have difficulty sustaining their play, the teacher intervenes. She helps them plan and act out a new scenario. If she intervenes a second time, she offers less assistance (as scaffolding requires) (Bodrova & Leong, 2007, p. 151). In general, teachers do a considerable amount of coaching, which they gradually fade out (Tough, 2009, p. 35).

The Tools of the Mind program values both the quality of play—its richness and complexity—and the planning process itself. Planning helps children gain cognitive control over their behavior.

Tools of the Mind also employs Vygotsky's ideas with respect to academic activities such as writing. For example, teachers ask children to use private or self-directed speech while drawing letters. After observing a class, journalists Bronson and Merryman report:

> When the kids are learning the capital C, they all say in unison, "Start at the top and go around" as they start to print. No one ever stops the kids from saying it out loud, but after a few minutes, the Greek chorus ends. In its place is a low murmur. A couple of minutes later, a few kids are still saying it out loud—but most of the children are saying it in their heads. (Bronson & Merryman, 2009, p. 167)

In kindergarten, children and teachers have mini-conferences to evaluate the child's activities during the past week and to plan for the next week (Tough, 2009, p. 35). These conferences, too, are designed to help children gain cognitive control over their behavior. Some research indicates that Tools of the Mind does, in fact, increase children's ability to regulate their behavior (Diamond et al., 2007).

It is interesting to note that Vygotsky didn't write about assisting children's play. He described play as if it's a spontaneous development, coming from children themselves. But Bodrova and Leong are justified in calling their project "Vygotskian" (2001, p. 17) because Vygotsky generally emphasized the way adults or more competent peers advance children's skills.

Indeed, contemporary Vygotskians believe that adults and older peers—not children themselves—initiate the first episodes of make-believe play (Bodrova & Leong, 2007, p. 120; Berk, 2009, p. 268). If a toddler is holding a doll, an adult might say, "Tell your baby to chew her food," helping the child get into the mother role. Vygotskians (Berk, 2009, p. 268; Berk & Winsler, 1995, p. 64) frequently cite two studies to demonstrate the need for parental direction, but I don't believe the studies' results warrant this conclusion.

In one study, Wendy Haight and Peggy Miller (1993) found that mothers tried to get their 1-year-olds started on imaginary play. Then, when the children were studied again at age 2, the children initiated 41% of their play episodes. It might seem that the parents introduced the children to make-believe play, which the children later initiated on their own. But what is overlooked is that the parents' efforts at age 1 had no discernable effect. The children rarely played at that age. So the children who began make-believe episodes a full year later (at age 2) might have acted spontaneously.

In a second study, Miller and Catherine Garvey (1984) found that parents provided props such as dolls for their 2-year-olds' imaginary play. The parents also allowed their children to borrow household objects such as pots and pans for other props. But the children themselves usually began the play episodes. Certainly, parents and older children can support and expand youngsters' imaginary play, but I don't find evidence that their teaching or guidance is necessary for its emergence.

In any case, it will be good to see further research on this question, which highlights a basic disagreement between the Vygotskians and Piagetians. The Vygotskians believe that development always has social origins. The Piagetians believe that development emerges from the child herself. You might remember how Piaget's daughter Jacqueline began make-believe play at about the age of 2 years, as when she moved her finger on a table and said, "Horse trotting." From Piaget's accounts, all her play at this age seemed to be her own creation.

EVALUATION

Vygotsky's work has generated great excitement because it suggests important ways to expand traditional developmental theory. Vygotsky recognized that intrinsic development, as studied by Gesell, Piaget, and others, is important; children do grow and learn from their inner maturational promptings and inventive spirit. But these forces alone, Vygotsky said, will not take children very far. To develop their minds fully, children also need the intellectual tools provided by their cultures—tools such as language, memory aids, numerical systems, writing, and scientific concepts. A major task of developmental theory is to understand how these tools are acquired.

But Vygotsky did more. He suggested we should study how intrinsic developmental and cultural forces interact and produce new transformations. It is the interaction between these conflicting forces that psychology must eventually understand.

Vygotsky's suggestion is more impressive than it might initially sound. Many psychologists have called for eclectic approaches, saying we need to consider a variety of intrinsic and environmental variables when we study development. Such statements sound reasonable, but they overlook the legitimate conflicts between theorists who emphasize one force or the other. Piagetians believe the child grasps a concept on her own; environmentalists believe she learns it from others; how can both be right? There is a logical contradiction.

Vygotsky, as a dialectical theorist, offered a new perspective. According to dialectical theory, life is full of contradictions, and what we need to study is what happens when opposing forces meet. We need to see what happens when the growing child, trying to figure things out for herself, encounters adults who try to teach her things. These interactions, Vygotsky observed, are complex and largely hidden from view. Indeed, Vygotsky frequently used the metaphors of magnifying glasses, X-rays, and telescopes to convey the need to get a better view of them (Cole & Scribner, 1978, p. 12; Vygotsky, 1933, p. 102; 1935, p. 91). But although these interactions are difficult to study, they are very important.

At the same time, Vygotsky's work suffers from one-sidedness. As James Wertsch (1985, pp. 40–49) points out, Vygotsky's accounts about intrinsic or natural development—that which comes from the children themselves—were vague. Moreover, when it came to the interactions between these intrinsic forces and cultural forces, Vygotsky's own research focused largely on cultural forces. For example, he studied the ways in which memory aids, writing, and scientific concepts transform the child's mind, but he didn't examine the ways in which the child's inner, spontaneous development might affect cultural forces. He gave us a good picture of how children internalize their culture, but he told us little about how they might challenge or criticize their culture, as an idealistic adolescent might do.

It is easy to forgive any one-sidedness in Vygotsky's own research. A person can only do so much in his or her research career, and Vygotsky's career was cut tragically short. Others can study the interactions between development and culture in fuller and more balanced ways.

The problem is that Vygotsky did not restrict himself to academic matters. He also tried to shape educational practices, and his educational ideas are rapidly gaining popularity. In this realm, any one-sidedness becomes a more urgent matter, and we need to take a close look at it. In the following comments, I evaluate Vygotsky's educational theory from a strongly developmental perspective—that of writers such as Rousseau, Montessori, and Piaget.

Vygotsky, compared to these developmentalists, was enthusiastic about school instruction. Instruction, he said, gives development a forward thrust. It "does not preclude development, but charts new paths for it" (1934, p. 152).

On a day-to-day basis, the teacher moves the child forward by working within the zone of proximal development. That is, the teacher does not just give children tasks that they can solve by themselves, but more difficult tasks—tasks they can solve only with some assistance. In this way, instruction stimulates capacities that are still in an embryonic state and pushes development forward.

At first glance, this kind of forward-looking instruction would seem desirable. But many developmental scholars have been wary of attempts to accelerate development. One danger is that we can push children forward before we give them the chance to develop their potentials fully at their present stage.

As an example, Vygotskians are attempting to promote goal-directed, self-regulated thinking in 3- to 5-year-olds. Left on their own, children at this age aren't very focused or deliberate in their approach to tasks. They don't screen out irrelevant information, and they don't monitor their progress.

Because these self-regulation skills will be essential for future school success, Vygotskian educators are trying to help children acquire them early on.

But this forward-looking instruction overlooks a potential strength of early childhood—an open-minded receptivity to the world in all its richness and variety. Young children love to wander about without any goal in mind, taking delight in whatever they find. They become enthralled by their discoveries—a shiny rock, a bird, a fish in a shallow brook. The world is full of enchantment. Adult poets, artists, and naturalists try to recapture this fresh openness and sense of wonder. Naturalist Cathy Johnson (1990) says she tries to reduce the narrow, goal-directed approach that we associate with cognitive maturity. Johnson says that if she wants to make serendipitous discoveries, she needs to allow herself to wander about and be open to whatever she encounters. Thus, the young child's unfocused approach to the world has its benefits. If we stress goal-directed behavior too early, we curtail a valuable approach to life. (For more on the young child's openness to the world, see Chapter 15 in this book, as well as Crain, 2003, and Gopnik, 2009.)

Vygotsky's educational philosophy contains a second danger. Instruction, Vygotsky said, propels the child forward because teachers and more capable peers give the child assistance. With the help of others, children can solve problems that are beyond them as individuals. Vygotsky was undoubtedly correct about this, but he overlooked the extent to which outside assistance undermines the child's independence. Developmentalists have repeatedly warned that when we give children assistance and direction, we encourage them to depend on others to know what and how to think, undermining their ability to think for themselves.

Vygotsky, to be sure, usually recommended that we provide children only with slight amounts of assistance (such as a leading question or the first step in a solution). In such cases, the threat to the child's independence does not seem to be too great. But on occasion, Vygotsky implied that we might give the child a great deal of assistance. He implied this, for example, when discussing his research on the concept of *because.*

Vygotsky found that 8-year-olds frequently use *because* correctly when speaking on theoretical topics learned in school before they do so with respect to their everyday concerns. For example, a girl might correctly say, "Planned economy in the USSR is possible because there is no private property" (Vygotsky, 1934, p. 191). The reason for the girl's success, Vygotsky said, is that "the teacher, working with the child, has explained, supplied information, questioned, corrected, and made the pupil explain" (p. 191). So, when the girl responds alone, she speaks correctly because the teacher's help is "invisibly present" (p. 191).

But to those who value independent thinking the girl's correct response is no cause for celebration. When the teacher's assistance is this pervasive, it is difficult to imagine that the girl is in any way thinking for herself. She is more like a toy puppet that is saying what it has been programmed to say.

Vygotsky (1935) had little patience with such objections. Many developmentalists, he said, are so worried about the harmful effects of instruction that they constantly keep it at bay. They introduce instruction only when the child is "ready" for it, which usually means waiting for a capacity to fully mature before adding any relevant instruction. Instruction then becomes superfluous, doing nothing to move the child forward.

Actually, developmental educators in the tradition of Montessori, Dewey, and Piaget believe that children sometimes consolidate current capacities and sometimes move forward. These educators believe that children themselves tell us which tasks they need. They take a keen interest in such tasks and work on them with great energy and concentration. For example, Montessori found that children of 4 years or so become deeply engrossed in cutting vegetables and other practical activities, probably because these activities help them develop their perceptual-motor skills. The teacher's job is to observe the child's interests and inclinations and to provide activities that engage the child in a full way.

Teachers will, of course, be tempted to introduce materials that they know the child will need in the future. But education is most effective when it is geared to the child's own interests and inclinations, not the teacher's goals for the future. And in no case should the teacher present tasks that are so far ahead of the child that the child can solve them only with the teacher's assistance. The teacher should introduce activities that stimulate, challenge, and engage the child, and then let the child solve them on his or her own.

Some of Vygotsky's followers have narrowed the gap between Vygotsky and the strong developmentalists. They point to instruction that pays close attention to the child's interest and enthusiasm as it leads the child through tasks (Griffin & Cole, 1984; Rogoff, 1998). These investigators do not want to squash the child's creativity or participation in the learning process. In fact, in one essay, Vygotsky (1935, pp. 116–119) himself argued that instruction should arouse the child's vital interests and correspond to the child's natural way of learning.

One Vygotskian, Barbara Rogoff (2003, chap. 8), suggests that part of the problem is that Vygotsky focused on schools, where learning is predominantly adult directed. In many non-Western communities, children more frequently learn through participation in work-related activities and take more initiative with respect to the tasks. For example, young Mayan children decide on their own to make tortillas, with mothers giving them any assistance they need. In many communities, children are expected to initially learn adult work through observation, and "children take a leading role in managing their own attention, motivation, and involvement in learning, through their observation and participation in ongoing mature activities" (Rogoff, 2003, p. 301).

Rogoff, then, shares the developmentalists' emphasis on children taking the initiative in their learning. But neither she nor other Vygotskians endorse a really strong developmental position. They particularly object to Piaget. As Bruner (1984, p. 96) has said, they oppose Piaget's "image of human development as a lone venture for the child," in which the child must figure everything out on her own. Instead, society has a responsibility to provide the child with the intellectual tools it has developed, and this means providing her with instruction and assistance. If this assistance forces the child to lean on others for intellectual support, so be it. Children simply cannot discover everything on their own. To develop their minds they need the help of adults and more capable peers.

In the last analysis, then, Vygotsky and the developmentalists disagree over the extent to which development can be entrusted to the child, to the child's own interests and efforts. And this disagreement is likely to continue for a long time. But this may be a good thing. For disagreement can be part of an ongoing dialectic, a series of challenges and responses that keep both sides thinking and coming up with new ideas.

CHAPTER 11

Freud's Psychoanalytic Theory

BIOGRAPHICAL INTRODUCTION

In most of the chapters so far, the primary focus has been on motor or cognitive development. In this chapter we will begin discussing a group of theorists—the psychoanalysts—whose special province has been the inner world of feelings, impulses, and fantasies. The principal founder of psychoanalytic theory was Sigmund Freud (1856–1939).

To an extent, Freud's thinking was similar to developmentalists such as Gesell; Freud believed psychological change is governed by inner forces, especially biological maturation. But Freud also thought that maturation brings with it unruly sexual and aggressive energies, which societies must harness. So, social forces also play a powerful role in Freud's theory.

Freud was born in Freiberg, Moravia (later part of Czechoslovakia). He was the first child of a 20-year-old mother and a 40-year-old father, although his father also had two grown sons from a previous marriage. The father was a wool merchant who never became very successful in business, and financial troubles forced the family to move twice when Freud was young—first to Leipzig, and then, when Freud was 4, to Vienna, where Freud lived until the last year of his life (Jones, 1961, chap. 1).

As a boy, Freud was a brilliant student, and the family encouraged his studies. His parents made sure he had an oil lamp to study by, while the other family members had only candles (Schultz, 1975, p. 302). Freud's intellectual interests covered a wide variety of topics, and when he was old enough to enter the university he had difficulty deciding on an area of study. With some reluctance, he chose medicine, primarily because it gave him an opportunity to do research. In medical school Freud conducted important investigations of the spinal cord of the *Petromyzon,* a type of fish (Jones, 1961, chaps. 3 and 4).

Between the ages of 26 and 35, Freud restlessly searched for a field in which he might make some important discovery. He continued to do research in established areas of neurology, but he was more excited by other possibilities. For a while, he thought he might find revolutionary uses for cocaine, a drug to which he seemed temporarily addicted. Freud also visited Charcot's laboratory in Paris, where Charcot was investigating the mysteries of hysteria. The study of this disorder became the starting point of Freud's great contributions (Jones, 1961, chaps. 5, 6, 10, and 11).

The term *hysteria* is applied to physical ailments as well as to losses of memory for which there is no physiological explanation. A woman might complain of a "glove anesthesia," a loss of feeling in the hand up to the wrist, even though physiologically there is no way she could lose sensation in precisely this part of the body.

Freud's first work on hysteria followed the example of Josef Breuer, who had treated a woman ("Anna O.") by helping her uncover buried thoughts and feelings through hypnosis. It seemed to Breuer and Freud (1895) that hysteric patients had somehow blocked off, or *repressed*, wishes and emotions from awareness. The blocked-off energy had then become converted into physical symptoms. Therapy, then, consisted of uncovering and releasing emotions that had been relegated to a separate part of the mind—the *unconscious*.

Freud's early work with hysteric patients can be illustrated by the case of a woman he called Elizabeth von R. Elizabeth suffered from hysterical pains in her thighs, pains that became worse after walks with her brother-in-law, toward whom she "grew to feel a peculiar sympathy . . . which easily passed with her for family tenderness" (Freud, 1910, p. 23). The sister (his wife) then died, and Elizabeth was summoned to the funeral. As Elizabeth "stood by the bedside of her dead sister, for one short moment there surged up in her mind an idea, which might be framed in these words: 'Now he is free and can marry me'" (p. 23). This wish was totally unacceptable to her sense of morality, so she immediately repressed it. She then fell ill with severe hysterical pains, and when Freud came to treat her, she had completely forgotten the scene at her sister's bedside. Many hours of psychoanalytic work were necessary to uncover this and other memories, for Elizabeth had strong reasons for barring them from consciousness. Eventually, she was able to gain awareness of her feelings, and, to the extent she could accept them, they no longer needed to be redirected into bodily symptoms.

In Freud's work with Elizabeth and many other patients, he did not use hypnosis, the technique Breuer had employed. Freud found that hypnosis, among its other drawbacks, could only be used with some patients, and even with those it often produced only temporary cures. In its place Freud developed the method of *free association*, in which the patient is instructed to let his or her mind go and to report everything just as it occurs, making no effort to order or censor the thoughts in any way.

Freud found, however, that although free association eventually leads to buried thoughts and feelings, it is by no means completely free. Patients strongly resist the process. They block on certain topics, change the topic, insist that their thoughts are too trivial or embarrassing to mention, and so on (Freud, 1920, pp. 249–250). Freud named these interruptions *resistance* and considered resistance new evidence for the power of repression in the mind (Breuer & Freud, 1895, p. 314). That is, Freud saw new evidence for his theory that the patient's mind is at war with itself, that certain wishes are unacceptable to the patient's "ethical, aesthetic, or personal pretensions," and that the wishes therefore need to be repressed (Freud, 1910, p. 22).

As Freud built his theory, he speculated that not only hysterics and other neurotic patients suffer from this kind of internal conflict. We all have thoughts and desires we cannot admit to ourselves. In neurosis, repression and conflict become particularly intense and unmanageable, and symptoms result. Nevertheless, conflict characterizes the human condition (Freud, 1900, p. 294; 1933, p. 121).

Breuer and Freud published a book together—*Studies on Hysteria* (1895)—which became the first classic work in psychoanalytic theory. Afterward, however, Breuer discontinued his work in the area. Breuer's decision was largely influenced by the direction the work was taking. Freud was increasingly finding that the central emotions that hysterics blocked from awareness were sexual ones—a finding that Breuer sensed was true but which he also found personally distasteful and troubling. Moreover, the sexual theory brought ridicule from the scientific community, and this hurt Breuer deeply. Consequently, Breuer left it to Freud to investigate this new area by himself.

As Freud pressed on with the work, he found that his patients' buried memories led farther back into their pasts—into their childhoods. Freud had great trouble understanding what he was finding. His patients repeatedly told stories about how their parents had committed the most immoral sexual acts against them as children—stories that Freud finally concluded must mainly be fantasies. For a while, it seemed his research had gone up in smoke. It was not built on truth, but on fiction. But he then concluded that fantasies, too, govern our lives. Our thoughts and feelings can be as important as actual events (Freud, 1914a, p. 300; Gay, 1988, p. 95).

In 1897, the year in which Freud was puzzling over the truth of his patients' memories, he began a second line of investigation—a self-analysis. Motivated by the disturbance he felt when his father died, he began examining his own dreams, memories, and childhood experiences. Through this analysis, he gained independent confirmation of his theory of childhood sexuality and discovered what he considered his greatest insight: the Oedipus complex in the child. That is, he discovered that he (and presumably all children as well) develop an intense rivalry with the parent of the same sex for the affection of the parent of the opposite sex. Freud first published this theory in the *Interpretation of Dreams* (1900). He called the interpretation of dreams "the royal road to the unconscious" (p. 647).

Freud's self-analysis was not an easy process. He had begun delving into an area—the unconscious—out of which "God knows what kind of beast will creep" (Jones, 1961, p. 213). At times, Freud was unable to think or write; he experienced "an intellectual paralysis such as I have never imagined" (p. 213). And, on top of this, what he was finding—evidence for childhood sexuality—was unacceptable to most of the scientific community. Most of his colleagues believed, with everyone else, that sexuality begins at puberty, not before. Freud's suggestion that innocent children experience sexual desires indicated that he was little more than a perverted sex maniac. In the face of this reaction, Freud felt "completely isolated" and said he often dreaded losing his way and his confidence (Freud, 1914a, p. 302).

About 1901 (when Freud was 45 years old) he finally began to emerge from his intellectual isolation. His work attracted various younger scientists and writers, some of whom began meeting with him for weekly discussions. These discussion groups gradually evolved into a formal psychoanalytic association. Among Freud's early disciples were Alfred Adler and Carl Jung, who, like several others, eventually broke with Freud and established their own psychoanalytic theories.

Freud continued to develop and revise his theory until the end of his life, the last 16 years of which he spent in pain from cancer of the jaw. In 1933 the Nazis burned his books in Berlin, and in 1938 he had to leave Vienna for London, where he lived his last year and died at the age of 83.

THE STAGES OF PSYCHOSEXUAL DEVELOPMENT

We have seen how Freud's work led him to believe that sexual feelings must be active in childhood. Freud's concept of sex, however, was very broad. In his view (1905), "sex" includes not just sexual intercourse but practically anything that produces bodily pleasure. In childhood, in particular, sexual feelings are very general and diffuse. Sexual feelings may be included in activities such as sucking for pleasure, masturbation, the wish to show off one's body or to look at the bodies of others, anal excretion or retention, body movements such as rocking, and even acts of cruelty, such as pinching or biting (pp. 585–594).

Freud had two major reasons for considering such diverse activities as sexual. First, children seem to derive pleasure from them. Babies enjoy sucking even when they are not hungry; they suck their hands, fingers, and other objects because it produces pleasurable sensations on the mucous membranes of the mouth (p. 588). Second, Freud regarded many childhood activities as sexual because they later reemerge in adult sexual activity. Most adults engage in sucking (i.e., kissing), looking, exhibitionism, or cuddling immediately prior to and during sexual intercourse. Sometimes, in the cases of so-called perversions, adults reach orgasm through childhood sexual activities alone (without sexual intercourse). A "Peeping Tom" may reach orgasm simply by looking at the bodies of others. Neurotic adults, too, retain childhood sexual wishes, but they feel so much guilt and shame that they repress them (Freud, 1920, chaps. 20 and 21; 1905, pp. 577–579).

In Freud's theory, the term for one's general sexual energy is *libido*, and any part of the body on which this energy becomes focused is called an *erogenous zone* (Freud, 1905, pp. 585–594, 611). Almost any part of the body can become an erogenous zone, but in childhood the three most important zones are the mouth, the anus, and the genital area. These zones become the center of the child's sexual interests in a specific *stage sequence*. The child's first interests center on the mouth (the oral stage), followed by the anus (the anal stage), and finally the genital region (the phallic stage). Freud thought that this sequence is governed by a *maturational* process—by innate, biological factors (pp. 587, 621). At the same time, the child's *social experiences* also play a decisive developmental role. For example, a child who experiences a great deal of frustration at the oral stage may develop a lasting preoccupation with things having to do with the mouth. Let us now look at Freud's stages in more detail.

The Oral Stage

The First Months.   Freud said that "if the infant could express itself, it would undoubtedly acknowledge that the act of sucking at its mother's breast is far and away the most important thing in life" (Freud, 1920, p. 323). Sucking is vital, of course, because it provides nourishment; the baby must suck to stay alive. But, as mentioned, Freud thought that sucking also provides pleasure in its own right. This is why babies suck on their thumbs and other objects even when they are not hungry. Freud called such pleasure-sucking *autoerotic*; when babies suck their thumbs, they do not direct their impulses toward others but find gratification through their own bodies (Freud, 1905, p. 586).

Autoerotic activities are not confined to the oral stage. Later on, for example, children stimulate their genitals for pleasure, and this too is auto-erotic. However, Freud emphasized the autoerotic nature of the oral stage because he wanted to stress the extent to which babies are wrapped up in their own bodies. Like Piaget, Freud thought that during the first six months or so the baby's world is "objectless." That is, the baby has no conception of people or things existing in their own right. When nursing, for example, young infants experience the comfort of the mother's hold, but they do not recognize the existence of the mother as a separate person. Similarly, when cold, wet, or hungry, babies feel mounting tension and even panic, but they are unaware of any separate person who might relieve the pain. They simply long for a return of pleasurable feelings. Thus, although babies are completely dependent on others, they are unaware of this fact because they do not yet recognize other people's separate existence.

Sometimes Freud described this initial objectless state as one of *primary narcissism* (e.g., Freud, 1915a, p. 79). The term *narcissism* means self-love and is taken from the Greek myth about a boy called Narcissus, who fell in love with his reflection in a pond. As Edith Jacobson (1964, chap. 1) has observed, this term is somewhat confusing because it implies that babies have a clear conception of themselves to love, when they still cannot distinguish themselves from the rest of the world. Still, *narcissism* does convey the idea that at first babies focus primarily inward, on their own bodies. The basic narcissistic state, Freud (1916) said, is sleep, when infants feel warm and content and have absolutely no interest in the outside world.

The Second Part of the Oral Stage.   Beginning at about 6 months of age, babies begin to develop a conception of another being, especially the mother, as a separate, necessary person. They become anxious when she leaves or when they encounter a stranger in her place (Freud, 1936a, p. 99).

At the same time, another important development is taking place: the growth of teeth and the urge to bite. At this point, Karl Abraham (1924a) pointed out, babies dimly form the idea that it is they, with their urge to bite and devour, who can drive their mothers away. Life at this stage, then, becomes increasingly complex and troubling. It is little wonder that we may often unconsciously wish to return to the earlier oral stage, when things seemed so much simpler and more gratifying.

An Illustration: Hansel and Gretel.   Freud was aware of the difficulty in reaching conclusions about the infant's mental life. Babies cannot talk and tell us about their feelings and fantasies. To some extent, we are forced to reconstruct the infant's psychic life from the analyses of adults who seem to revert to early ways of thinking—namely, psychotics. But Freudians also suggest that many myths and fairy tales reveal the child's early fantasies and concerns.

Bruno Bettelheim (1976, pp. 159–166) wrote about the oral themes contained in the story of Hansel and Gretel. Briefly, Hansel and Gretel are two children who are sent into the forest by their parents, especially the mother, because they are careless with food (milk) and there is no longer enough to feed them. In the forest, they discover a gingerbread house, which they proceed to devour. Sensing that it may be dangerous to eat so much of the house, Hansel and Gretel hear a voice that asks, "Who is nibbling at my house?" But they ignore it, telling themselves, "It is only the wind" (The Brothers Grimm, 1972, p. 90). The woman who owns the house then appears, and she is at first completely gratifying. She gives them all kinds of good things to eat and nice beds in which to sleep. But the next day she turns out to be worse than their mother. She is a witch who intends to eat them.

In Bettelheim's analysis, the themes are largely those of t
stage. The story begins with the children experiencing the dr
tion from their caretakers. There is some hint that the childre
urges are at the root of their troubles; they have been reckless with their
mother's milk and they greedily devour the gingerbread house. The children's
wish is to return to the first oral stage, which seemed so blissful. So they meet
the witch, who is temporarily "the original, all-giving mother, whom every
child hopes to find again later somewhere out in the world" (Bettelheim, 1976,
p. 161). However, this proves impossible. Because they are dimly aware of
their own oral destructiveness, they imagine that others will take an oral
revenge, which is what the witch attempts to do.

Bettelheim says that fairy tales facilitate growth by addressing children's
deepest fears while, at the same time, showing them that their problems have
solutions. In this story, Hansel and Gretel finally quit acting solely on the basis
of their oral impulses and use more rational parts of the personality. They
employ reason to outwit the witch and kill her, and they return home as more
mature children.

Fixation and Regression.   According to Freud, we all go through the
oral stage as well as every other stage of psychosexual development. However,
we also can develop a *fixation* at any stage, which means that no matter how
far we have advanced beyond it, we maintain a lasting preoccupation with the
pleasures and issues of the earlier stage. For example, if we are fixated at the
oral stage, we might find ourselves continually preoccupied with food; or we
find that we work most comfortably when we are sucking or biting on objects,
such as pencils; or we gain the most pleasure from oral sexual activities; or we
find ourselves addicted to smoking or drinking partly because of the oral
pleasure involved (Abraham, 1924b; Freud, 1905).

Freud (1920, p. 357) said that he was not certain about the causes of fixation, but psychoanalysts generally believe that fixations are produced by either
excessive gratification or excessive frustration at the stage in question (Abraham, 1924b, p. 357; Fenichel, 1945, p. 65). The baby who receives prolonged
and very satisfying nursing may continue to seek oral pleasures. Alternatively,
the baby who experiences sharp frustrations and deprivations at the oral stage
may act as if he or she is unwilling to give up oral satisfactions or as if there is
a persistent danger that oral needs will not be met. Such a person might, for
instance, become anxious when meals are not served on time and devour the
food as if it might disappear at any moment. In general, it seems that severe
frustrations, rather than excessive gratifications, produce the strongest fixations (White & Watt, 1973, pp. 136, 148, 189; Whiting & Child, 1953).

Sometimes people show few oral traits in their daily lives until they
experience some frustration, and then they *regress* to the oral fixation point. A
little boy who suddenly finds himself deprived of parental affections when his
baby sister is born might regress to oral behavior and once again take up

thumb sucking—something he had previously given up. Or a teenage girl may not be particularly concerned about oral matters until she loses a boyfriend, and then she becomes depressed and finds comfort in eating.

The tendency to regress is determined by both the strength of the fixation in childhood and the magnitude of the current frustration (Freud, 1920, chap. 22). If we have a strong oral fixation, a relatively small frustration in our current life may be sufficient to cause an oral regression. Alternatively, a major frustration might cause a regression to an earlier developmental stage even if the fixation was not particularly strong.

The kinds of regressions we have been discussing might occur in any of us—in relatively "normal" people. We all find life frustrating at times, and now and then we regress to earlier, more infantile, ways of behaving. Such regressions are not pathological, because they are only partial and temporary. For example, the boy who resumes thumb sucking when his baby sister is born usually does so only for a while; in any case, he does not become like an infant in other respects.

Freud also believed, however, that the concepts of fixation and regression can help clarify more serious emotional disorders. In certain forms of schizophrenia, there is a very complete regression to the first developmental stage. The schizophrenic often withdraws from interaction with others and entertains grandiose ideas concerning his or her importance. A patient may think she is God and her ideas affect the whole world. In such a case, the person has undergone a fairly complete regression to a state of primary narcissism, in which the libido is invested solely in the self, and the boundaries between the self and the rest of the world have once again become unstable (Freud, 1920, pp. 422–424).

According to Abraham (1924a), regression to the oral stage is also evident in severe cases of depression. Such depressions frequently follow the loss of a loved one, and a common symptom is the patient's refusal to eat. Perhaps patients are punishing themselves because they unconsciously feel it was their own oral anger that destroyed the love object.

The Anal Stage

During the second and third years of the child's life, the anal zone becomes the focus of the child's sexual interests. Children become increasingly aware of the pleasurable sensations that bowel movements produce on the mucous membranes of the anal region. As they gain maturational control over their sphincter muscles, they sometimes learn to hold back their bowel movements until the last moment, thereby increasing the pressure on the rectum and heightening the pleasure of the final release (Freud, 1905, p. 589). Children also frequently take an interest in the products of their labors and enjoy handling and smearing their feces (Freud, 1913, pp. 88–91; Jones, 1918, p. 424).

It is at this stage that children are first asked to renounce their instinctual pleasures in a fairly dramatic way. Few parents are willing to permit their children to smear and play with feces for very long. Most parents, as well-socialized individuals, feel a certain repugnance over anal matters and soon get children to feel the same way. As soon as their children are ready, if not sooner, parents toilet-train them.

Some children initially fight back by deliberately soiling themselves (Freud, 1905, p. 591). They also sometimes rebel by becoming wasteful, disorderly, and messy—traits that sometimes persist into adulthood as aspects of the "anal expulsive" character (J. F. Brown, 1940; Hall, 1954, p. 108).

Freud, however, was most interested in the opposite reaction to parental demands. He observed that some people develop an excessive stake in cleanliness, orderliness, and reliability (1908a). It seems as if they felt, as children, that it was too risky to rebel against parental demands, and so they anxiously conformed to parental rules. Instead of messing and smearing, they became models of self-control, acquiring a disgust for anything dirty or smelly, and developing a compulsive need to be clean and orderly. Such people, who are sometimes labeled "anal compulsive" characters, also harbor resentment over submitting to authority, but they do not dare express their anger openly. Instead, they frequently develop a passive obstinacy; they insist on doing things according to their own schedule—often while others are forced to wait. They may also be frugal and stingy. It is as if they feel that although they were forced to give up their feces when others demanded it, they will hold on to other things, such as money, and nobody will take these things away.

Toilet training probably arouses sufficient anger and fear to produce some measure of fixation in most children, especially in the United States, where we tend to be strict about this matter (Munroe, 1955, p. 287). Consequently, most people probably develop at least some tendency toward "anal expulsiveness," "anal compulsiveness," or some combination of both. Sometimes these traits have little serious impact on one's life but then emerge in a more pronounced way when one is under stress. For example, writers may be prone to compulsive behavior when they become anxious about their work. A writer may be unable to finish a manuscript because of a compulsive need to check and recheck it for mistakes. To a Freudian, such behavior probably represents a regression to the anal stage, where the individual learned that his or her natural actions met with unexpected disapproval. That is, the writer might have learned that his or her first "productions" were considered dirty and revolting when done spontaneously but prized if done properly. Thus, the writer, anxious about the impact of the manuscript, tries to protect himself or herself by seeing that everything is done precisely as it is supposed to be.

The Phallic or Oedipal Stage

Between the ages of about 3 and 6 years, the child enters the phallic or oedipal stage. Freud understood this stage better in the case of the boy than in the case of the girl, so we begin our discussion with the boy.

The Boy's Oedipal Crisis.   The oedipal crisis begins when the boy starts to take an interest in his penis. This organ, which is "so easily excitable and changeable, and so rich in sensations," fires his curiosity (Freud, 1923, p. 246). He wants to compare his penis to those of other males and of animals, and he tries to see the sexual organs of girls and women. He may also enjoy exhibiting his penis and, more generally, imagines the role he might play as an adult, sexual person. He initiates experiments and spins fantasies in which he is an aggressive, heroic male, frequently directing his intentions toward his primary love object, his mother. He may begin kissing Mommy aggressively, or want to sleep with her at night, or imagine marrying her. He probably does not yet conceive of sexual intercourse per se, but he does wonder what he might do with her.

The boy soon learns, however, that his most ambitious experiments and plans are considered excessive and improper. He learns that he cannot, after all, marry Mommy or engage in any sex play with her. He cannot even touch, hug, or cuddle with Mommy as much as he would like, since he is now a "big boy." At the same time, he notices that Daddy seems to be able to do whatever *he* wants: Daddy seems to kiss and hug Mommy at will, and he sleeps with her all night long (doing with her whatever grownups do at night). So the lines of the Oedipus complex are drawn: The boy sees the father as a rival for the affections of the mother.

The little boy's oedipal wishes are illustrated by Freud's case of Little Hans (Freud, 1909). When Hans was about 5 years old, he asked his mother to touch his penis, and he wanted to cuddle with her at night. His father, however, objected. Soon after, Hans had the following dream:

> In the night there was a big giraffe in the room and a crumpled one; and the big one called out because I took the crumpled one away from it. Then it stopped calling out; and then I sat down on top of the crumpled one. (p. 179)

According to Freud, Hans's dream probably represented his wish to take his mother (the crumpled giraffe) from the father (the big giraffe).

The little boy, of course, cannot realistically hope to carry out his rivalrous wishes; the father is too big. The youngster could still entertain rivalrous fantasies, but these too become dangerous. For one thing, he not only feels jealous of his father but he also loves and needs his father, so he is frightened by his destructive wishes toward him. But more important, the boy begins to consider the possibility of *castration*. In Freud's day, parents often made outright threats of castration when a boy masturbated. Today, parents may discourage masturbation more delicately, but the boy does probably begin to worry about castration when he realizes his sister and other females are missing a penis. He then concludes that they once had one, but it was cut off, and the same thing could happen to him. The oedipal rivalry takes on a new, dangerous dimension, and the boy must escape the whole situation (Freud, 1924, p. 271).

FIGURE 11.1
Drawings by a 5-year-old boy and a 6-year-old girl suggest sexual interests of the phallic stage.

Typically, the boy resolves the oedipal predicament through a series of defensive maneuvers (Freud, 1923; 1924). He fends off his incestuous desires for his mother through *repression;* that is, he buries any sexual feelings toward her deep into his unconscious. He still loves his mother, of course, but he now admits only to a socially acceptable, "sublimated" love—a pure, higher love. The boy overcomes his rivalry with his father by repressing his hostile feelings and by increasing his *identification* with him. Instead of trying to fight the father, he now becomes more like him, and in this way vicariously enjoys the feeling of being a big man. It is as if the boy were to say, "If you can't beat him, join him."

To overcome the oedipal crisis, finally, the boy internalizes a *superego.* That is, he adopts his parents' moral prohibitions as his own, and in this way establishes a kind of internal police officer who guards against dangerous impulses and desires. The superego is similar to what we ordinarily call the *conscience;* it is an inner voice that reprimands us and makes us feel guilty for bad thoughts and actions. Before the child internalizes a superego, he suffers only from external criticism and punishment. Now, however, he can criticize himself, and thus he possesses an inner fortification against forbidden impulses.

The foregoing review suggests the complexity of the Oedipus complex, but it actually is far more complex than we have indicated. The boy's rivalry and love work both ways—he also rivals the mother for the affection of the father (Freud, 1923, pp. 21–24). The situation is also complicated by the presence of siblings, who also become the objects of love and jealousy (Freud, 1920, p. 343), and by other factors, such as the loss of a parent. We cannot begin to go into the limitless variations here, but the interested reader can refer to Fenichel (1945, pp. 91–98).

Typical Outcomes.   Typically, when the boy resolves the Oedipus complex at the age of 6 years or so, his rivalrous and incestuous wishes are temporarily driven underground. As we shall see, he enters the latency period, during which he is relatively free of these worries. Nevertheless, oedipal feelings continue to exist in the unconscious. They threaten to break into consciousness once again at puberty and exert a strong influence on the life of the adult. This influence has many variations, but it typically is felt in two central areas: competition and love.

As the adult male enters into competition with other men, he carries with him the dim knowledge of his first forays into this area. The first time he dared to rival a man, his masculinity suffered a sharp setback. Consequently, he may be apprehensive about rivaling men again. In the back of his mind, he is still a little boy, wondering if he can really be a big man (Fenichel, 1945, p. 391; Freud, 1914b).

The adult may also feel a sense of guilt over competitive urges. The first time he rivaled a man, he wished to do away with his competitor. He repressed these hostile wishes and established a superego to help fend them off, but he still may dimly feel that the wish to become more successful than others is somehow wrong (Freud, 1936b, p. 311).

Oedipal feelings also influence a man's experiences in love. Freud (1905) said that the man "seeks above all the memory-image of the mother" (p. 618). However, this desire has its problems. In the early years, it became associated with castration anxiety and guilt. Consequently, men are sometimes impotent with women who evoke too much of the mother's presence. They become sexually inhibited with women who arouse the deep and tender feelings associated with the mother, and they are most potent with women whom they regard as mere outlets for their physical needs (Freud, 1912).

Freud thought that everyone undergoes an oedipal crisis, so all men have some of these feelings to a certain degree. Severe problems usually stem from excessive fears experienced as a child. Still, oedipal problems are not as serious as those that develop at earlier periods, when the personality is in a more formative stage.

The Girl's Oedipus Complex.

Freud thought there was an Oedipus complex for the little girl too, but he admitted that "here our material—for some reason we do not understand—becomes far more shadowy and incomplete" (1924, p. 274). Freud's views on this topic, in broad outline, were as follows. He noted (1933, pp. 122–127) that the girl, by the age of 5 years or so, becomes disappointed in her mother. She feels deprived because her mother no longer gives her the constant love and care that she required as a baby, and, if new babies are born, she resents the attention they receive. Furthermore, she is increasingly irritated by the mother's prohibitions, such as that on masturbation. Finally, and most upsetting, the girl discovers that she does not have a penis—a fact for which she blames the mother, "who sent her into the world so insufficiently equipped" (Freud, 1925a, p. 193).

The little girl's genital disappointment is illustrated by an anecdote from Ruth Munroe (1955, pp. 217–218), a psychologist who said she was skeptical about Freud's theory until one day when she observed her 4-year-old daughter in a bathtub with her brother. The daughter suddenly exclaimed, "My weewee (penis) is all gone,"—apparently comparing herself with her brother for the first time. Munroe tried to reassure her, but nothing worked, and for some weeks she objected violently even to being called a girl. Thus this little girl felt what Freud called *penis envy*, the wish to have a penis and to be like a boy (Freud, 1933, p. 126).

The little girl does, however, recover her feminine pride. This happens when she begins to appreciate the attentions of her father. The father may have not paid any special attention to his daughter when she was in diapers, but now he may begin to admire her cuteness and growing femininity, calling her his little princess and flirting with her in other ways. Thus inspired, she begins to spin romantic fantasies involving herself and her father. At first her thoughts include a vague wish for his penis, but this soon changes into a wish to have a baby and give it to him as a present.

As with the little boy, the little girl discovers that she lacks sole rights to her new love object. She realizes that she cannot, after all, marry Daddy, nor can she cuddle, hug, or sleep with him as much as she would like. However, the mother seems to be able to do these things, so she becomes the rival for his affections. Freud said that this oedipal situation might be called the *Electra complex* (1940, p. 99).

What most puzzled Freud about the girl's Oedipus complex was the motivation for its resolution. In the case of the little boy, the primary motivation seemed clear: The boy is frightened by the threat of castration. But the little girl cannot fear castration, for she has no penis to lose. Why, then, does she renounce her oedipal wishes at all? In one essay, Freud (1925a, p. 196) said that he simply did not know the answer, but his best guess was that the girl resolves the oedipal crisis because she fears the loss of parental love (1933, p. 87). So she does after all repress her incestuous desires, identify with her mother, and institute a superego to check herself against forbidden impulses and wishes.[1] Still, lacking castration anxiety, her motivation to erect strong defenses against oedipal feelings must be weaker, and, as a result, she must develop a weaker superego. Freud knew that this last conclusion would anger the feminists, but this was where his reasoning led and he argued that women in fact are less rigid about moral issues (p. 129).

Like a boy, then, the little girl entertains and then abandons rivalrous and incestuous fantasies. In some ways, the later consequences of the oedipal experience would seem similar to those for the boy. For example, the girl too may carry within her the dim knowledge that her first attempt at rivaling a woman for a man's love failed, and she may therefore doubt her future prospects. At the same time, though, the girl's oedipal experiences differed from the boy's, so the effects may differ as well. She had less need to resolve the Oedipus crisis, so her oedipal desires may be more open and transparent later in life (p. 129). Furthermore, just before she entered into the oedipal rivalry, she experienced a deep disappointment over being female. This feeling, Freud felt, may lead to a "masculinity complex," in which the woman may avoid intimate relationships with men, since these only remind her of her inferior state, and, instead, try to outdo men by becoming very aggressive and assertive (p. 126).

The Latency Stage

With the establishment of strong defenses against oedipal feelings, the child enters the latency period, which lasts from about age 6 to 11 years. As the name suggests, sexual and aggressive fantasies are now largely latent; they are kept firmly down, in the unconscious. Freud thought that the repression of sexuality at this time is quite sweeping; it includes not only oedipal feelings and memories, but oral and anal ones as well (Freud, 1905, pp. 580–585). Because dangerous impulses and fantasies are now kept underground, the child is not excessively bothered by them, and the latency period is one of relative calm. The child is now free to redirect his or her energies into concrete, socially acceptable pursuits, such as sports and games and intellectual activities.

Some of Freud's followers have argued that sexual and aggressive fantasies do not disappear at this time as completely as Freud implied (Blos, 1962, pp. 53–54). For example, an 8-year-old boy is still interested in girls' bodies, and he typically discovers the real facts of life at about this age. Nevertheless, most Freudians agree that sexual concerns lose their frightening and

---

[1]As with the boy, the girl's Oedipus complex is exceedingly complex. Rivalries develop with both parents and with siblings as well.

overwhelming character. In general, the latency-age child possesses a new composure and self-control.

Puberty (The Genital Stage)

The stability of the latency period, however, does not last. As Erikson said, "It is only a lull before the storm of puberty" (1959, p. 88). At puberty, which begins at about age 11 for girls and age 13 for boys, sexual energy wells up in full adult force and threatens to wreak havoc with the established defenses. Once again, oedipal feelings threaten to break into consciousness, and now the young person is big enough to carry them out in reality (Freud, 1920, p. 345).

Freud said that from puberty onward, the individual's great task is "freeing himself from the parents" (p. 345). For the son, this means releasing his tie to the mother and finding a woman of his own. The boy must also resolve his rivalry with his father and free himself of his father's domination of him. For the daughter, the tasks are the same; she too must separate from the parents and establish a life of her own. Freud noted, however, that independence never comes easily (1905, p. 346). Over the years we have built up strong dependencies on our parents, and it is painful to separate ourselves emotionally from them. For most of us, the goal of genuine independence is never completely attained.

Anna Freud on Adolescence

Although Freud sketched the general tasks of adolescence, he wrote little about the distinctive stresses and behavior patterns of this stage of life. It was his daughter, Anna Freud, who made many of the first contributions to the psychoanalytic study of adolescence.

Anna Freud's starting point was the same as that of her father: The teenager experiences the dangerous resurgence of oedipal feelings. Typically, the young person is most aware of a growing resentment against the parent of the same sex. Incestuous feelings toward the other parent remain more unconscious.

Anna Freud said that when adolescents first experience the welling up of oedipal feelings, their first impulse is to *take flight*. The teenager feels tense and anxious in the presence of the parents and feels safe only when apart from them. Some adolescents actually run away from home at this time; many others remain in the house "in the attitude of a boarder" (A. Freud, 1958, p. 269). They shut themselves up in their rooms and feel comfortable only when they are with their peers.

Sometimes adolescents try to escape their parents by developing a blanket *contempt* for them. Instead of admitting any dependence and love, they take an attitude that is exactly the opposite. It is as if they think they can become free of parental involvement by thinking absolutely nothing of them.

Here, again, teenagers may fancy themselves suddenly independent, but their parents still dominate their lives, for they spend all their energy attacking and deriding their parents (p. 270).

Adolescents sometimes attempt to defend themselves against feelings and impulses altogether, irrespective of the individuals to whom their feelings are attached. One strategy is *asceticism*. That is, the adolescent tries to fend off all physical pleasure. Boys or girls might adhere to strict diets; deny themselves the pleasures of attractive clothes, dancing, or music, or anything else fun or frivolous; or try to master their bodies through exhausting physical exercise.

Another defense against impulses is *intellectualization*. The adolescent attempts to transfer the problems of sex and aggression onto an abstract, intellectual plane. He or she might construct elaborate theories on the nature of love and the family, and on freedom and authority. While such theories may be brilliant and original, they are also thinly disguised efforts to grapple with oedipal issues on a purely intellectual level (A. Freud, 1936).

Anna Freud observed that adolescent turmoil and the desperate strategies and defenses of this period are actually normal and to be expected. She did not usually recommend psychotherapy; rather, she believed that the adolescent should be given time and scope to work out his or her own solution. However, parents may need guidance, for there "are few situations in life which are more difficult to cope with than an adolescent son or daughter during the attempt to liberate themselves" (A. Freud, 1958, p. 276).

THE AGENCIES OF THE MIND

We have now reviewed the stages of development. Freud's theory contains many other concepts, and we cannot review them all. However, an introduction to Freud does require a look at one other cluster of concepts, those pertaining to the agencies of the mind. Freud was continually revising his ideas on this topic, but his best known concepts are those of the id, ego, and superego.

The Id

The *id* is the part of the personality that Freud initially called "the unconscious" (e.g., 1915b). It is the most primitive part of the personality, containing the basic biological reflexes and drives. Freud likened the id to a pit "full of seething excitations," all pressing for discharge (1933, p. 73). In terms of motivation, the id is dominated by the *pleasure principle*; its goal is to maximize pleasure and minimize pain. Pleasure, in Freud's view, is primarily a matter of reducing tension (1920, p. 365). During sexual intercourse, tension mounts and its final release is pleasurable. Similarly, we find that the release of hunger or bladder tensions brings pleasurable relief. In general, the id tries to remove all excitation and to return to a quiet state—namely, that of deep, peaceful sleep.

At first, the baby is almost all id. Babies worry about little besides bodily comfort, and they try to discharge all tensions as quickly as possible. However, even babies must experience frustration. For example, they sometimes must wait to be fed. What the id does then is to *hallucinate* an image of the desired object, and in this way it temporarily satisfies itself. We see such *wish-fulfilling* fantasies at work when a starving person hallucinates an image of food, or when a thirsty dreamer dreams that a glass of water is at hand and therefore does not have to wake up and get one (Freud, 1900, pp. 158, 165). Such fantasies are prime examples of what Freud called *primary process thinking* (p. 535).

In the course of life, many impressions and impulses are repressed into the id, where they exist side by side with the basic drives. In this "dark and inaccessible" region of the mind, there is nothing that corresponds to logic or a sense of time (Freud, 1933, pp. 73–74). Impressions and strivings "are virtually immortal; after the passage of decades they behave as though they had just occurred" (p. 74). Images in the id, furthermore, are very fluid and easily merge into one another. The id is oceanic, chaotic, and illogical. It is completely cut off from the external world. Our best knowledge of this mysterious region comes from the study of dreams.

The id, then, contains basic drives and reflexes, along with images and sensations that have been repressed. So far we have focused on the id's sexual drives and those associated with the preservation of life, such as hunger and thirst. The id also contains aggressive and destructive forces. Freud's views on aggression are complex and underwent drastic revisions, but in a sense we can see how aggression follows the id's basic principle of reducing tension. In the id, any image associated with pain or tension should be instantly destroyed. It does not matter to the id that one may be wishing for the destruction of someone one needs and loves; contradictions such as these have no importance in this illogical region of the mind. The id simply wants a reduction in disturbing tensions immediately.

The Ego

If we were ruled by the id, we would not live for long. To survive, we cannot act solely on the basis of hallucinations or simply follow our impulses. We must learn to deal with reality. For example, a little boy soon learns that he cannot just impulsively grab food from wherever he sees it. If he takes it from a bigger boy, he is likely to get hit. He must learn to consider reality before acting. The agency that delays the immediate impulse and considers reality is called the *ego*.

Freud said that whereas "the id stands for the untamed passions," the ego "stands for reason and good sense" (1933, p. 76). Because the ego considers reality, it is said to follow the *reality principle* (Freud, 1911). The ego tries to forestall action until it has had a chance to perceive reality accurately, to consider what has happened in similar situations in the past, and to make realistic plans for the future (Freud, 1940, p. 15). Such reasonable ways of thinking are called *secondary process thinking* and include what we generally think of as perceptual or cognitive processes. When we work on a math problem, plan a trip, or write an essay, we are making good use of ego functions. At first, though, the ego's functioning is largely bodily or motoric. For example, when a child first learns to walk, she inhibits impulses toward random movement, considers where she is headed to avoid collisions, and otherwise exercises ego controls (p. 15).

The term *ego* is one that we hear a great deal in everyday language. Quite often, we hear that someone has a "big ego," meaning this person has an inflated self-image. Although Freud himself (e.g., 1917) occasionally wrote about the ego in just this way, many Freudians (e.g., Beres, 1971; Hartmann, 1956) contend that we should distinguish between the ego and the self-image. Strictly speaking, they say, the ego refers only to a set of functions—judging reality accurately, regulating impulses, and so on. The self-image, the picture we have of ourselves, is different from the ego itself.

Freud emphasized that although the ego functions somewhat independently from the id, it also borrows all its energy from the id. He likened the ego's relation to the id to that of a rider on a horse. "The horse supplies the locomotive energy, while the rider has the privilege of deciding on the goal and guiding the powerful animal's movement. But only too often there arises between the ego and the id the not precisely ideal situation of the rider being obliged to guide the horse along the path by which it itself wants to go" (1933, p. 77).

The Superego

The ego is sometimes called one of the "control systems" of the personality (Redl & Wineman, 1951). The ego controls the blind passions of the id to protect the organism from injury. We mentioned how a little boy must learn to inhibit the impulse to grab food until he can determine whether it is realistically safe to do so. But we also control our actions for other reasons. We might also refrain from taking things from others because we believe such actions are morally wrong. Our standards of right and wrong constitute the second control system of the personality—the *superego*.

We referred earlier to Freud's view on the origin of the superego: It is a product of the oedipal crisis. Children introject parental standards to check themselves against the dangerous impulses and fantasies of this period. Freud did note, though, that the superego continues to develop after this period as well. Children continue to identify with other people, such as teachers and religious leaders, and to adopt their moral standards as their own (Freud, 1923, p. 27).

Freud wrote about the superego as if it contained two parts (pp. 24–25). One part is sometimes called the *conscience* (Hall, 1954). It is the punitive, negative, and critical part of the superego that tells us what *not* to do and punishes us with feelings of guilt when we violate its demands. The other part is called the *ego ideal*, and this part consists of *positive* aspirations. For example, when a child wants to be just like a famous basketball player, the athlete is the child's ego ideal. The ego ideal may also be more abstract. It may include our positive ideals, such as the wish to become more generous, courageous, or dedicated to principles of justice and freedom.

Levels of Awareness of the Three Agencies

The id, ego, and superego function at differing levels of awareness, as Freud tried to show by means of a diagram (1933, p. 78), reproduced here as Figure 11.2.

The id, at the bottom of the drawing, is completely removed from the region labeled *pcpt.-cs,* from consciousness and the perception of reality. The id is entirely unconscious, which means that its workings can be made conscious only with a great deal of effort.

The ego extends into consciousness and reality; it is the part of the id that develops in order to deal with the external world. The ego, you will note, largely inhabits a region labeled *preconscious.* This term refers to functioning that is below awareness but can be made conscious with relatively little effort.

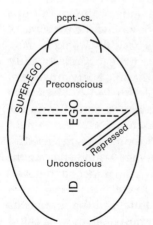

FIGURE 11.2
Freud's sketch of the personality structure.
(Reprinted from *New Introductory Lectures on Psychoanalysis* by Sigmund Freud. Translated by James Strachey. Copyright © 1965, 1964 by James Strachey. Used by permission of W. W. Norton & Co., Inc.)

The ego is also partly unconscious; for example, it represses forbidden thoughts in a completely unconscious way.

The superego is drawn on top of the ego, illustrating its role of criticizing the ego from above. The superego, too, is partly unconscious; although we are sometimes aware of our moral standards, they also frequently affect us unconsciously. For example, we might suddenly become depressed without any idea why, because our superego is punishing us for forbidden thoughts.

The superego also works unconsciously during dreams. Dreams begin as wishes from the id, but many wishes violate the superego's standards, so the superego demands that the wishes undergo distortion or disguise before surfacing into consciousness (Freud, 1940, p. 51). In one of Freud's examples, a little boy was told it was wrong for him to eat very much because of his illness; so one night, when he was especially hungry, he dreamt that someone else was enjoying a sumptuous meal (1900, pp. 301–302). Similarly, many sexual and aggressive wishes must be disguised and distorted before surfacing. Because the dream we remember upon waking has undergone disguise, we cannot interpret it in any simple, straightforward way. In psychoanalysis, the patient is asked to free-associate to the dream, to say whatever comes to mind in connection with each aspect of it. In this way, the unconscious wishes of the id may eventually come to light, and the patient's ego can make some conscious assessment of them.

The Central Role of the Ego

In the last analysis, our ability to deal with life—our mental balance—rests with our ego's ability to meet the various pressures put upon it. More specifically, the ego is the executive agency that must somehow serve three "tyrannical masters"—the id, reality, and the superego (Freud, 1933, p. 78). The ego must eventually meet the biological demands of the id, but in a way that also respects external reality and does not violate the precepts of the superego. The task is difficult because the ego is basically weak; as mentioned, it has no energy of its own, but borrows it from the id. Consequently, the ego is quite prone to anxiety—to the fear it might not satisfy any one of its three dictators. Anxiety arises when we feel helpless to satisfy a basic biological need in the id; when we anticipate moral punishment from the superego; or when we face danger in the external world.

"Thus the ego, driven by the id, confined by the superego, repulsed by reality, struggles to master its economic task of bringing harmony among the forces and influences working in and upon it; and we can understand how it is that so often we cannot suppress a cry: 'Life is not easy!'" (p. 78)

In much of Freud's writing, the ego seems to regard the id and the superego as adversaries, as powerful combatants it must somehow appease and control. But Freud also recognized the vital necessity of the id and superego, and some of Freud's closest followers have elaborated on the positive ways the ego utilizes these agencies. In an important contribution, Kris (1952) described how the ego can utilize the fluid, sensuous, dreamlike imagery of the id as a source of creative thinking. Artists, for example, may temporarily abandon their tight ego controls and realistic thinking in order to delve into the unconscious for its rich imagery and inspirational power. Kris called this process "regression in the service of the ego," and Kris's concept has become very important in Freudian theory. You might recall that Werner (Chapter 5) also emphasized a similar process in his discussions of microgenesis. For both Werner and the Freudians, then, primordial thinking is not just something to be overcome but may continually serve as a rich resource for creative work.

The Ego's Mechanisms of Defense

Although the ego is weak, it can ward off excessive anxiety by employing mechanisms of defense. Freud (1926) thought the central defense mechanism is *repression,* the rejection of thoughts, fantasies, or impulses from conscious awareness. We saw earlier how children repress sexual and aggressive impulses and fantasies as they resolve the Oedipus complex. We also briefly noted repression in the case of one of Freud's patients, Elizabeth von R. At the bedside of her just-deceased sister, Elizabeth had a romantic thought about her brother-in-law: "Now he is free and can marry me." This wish totally violated her moral (superego) standards, and she immediately repressed it, forgetting the thought and the entire scene as well.

For many years, Freud considered repression to be the only defense mechanism. Eventually (1926) he came to include others, some of which I will review below. In her classic work *The Ego and the Mechanisms of Defense* (1936), Anna Freud observed that repression is the most powerful defense mechanism and often used in combination with others. She also made it clear that the ego employs all the defense mechanisms unconsciously (p. 52). So, when a psychoanalytic patient tries to free-associate but tells the therapist that her mind has suddenly gone blank, she isn't necessarily concealing something on purpose. It is likely that her ego is repressing a thought, and the repression occurs unconsciously, below her level of awareness.

A second defense mechanism is *displacement,* the shifting of impulses or feelings from one object onto another. By way of illustration, Anna Freud (1936) described a young female patient who felt intense anger at her mother. However, the girl unconsciously feared it would result in the loss of her mother's love. The girl therefore repressed her anger toward her mother and displaced it onto other females. For many years there was always some other woman she hated with a passion.

Reaction-formation occurs when we turn our feelings into the opposite. Freud (1908a) thought that anal compulsivity reflects an underlying reaction-formation; the person wishes to be messy, but instead becomes a stickler for neatness and cleanliness. Reaction-formation also is involved in the adolescent's blanket contempt for her parents. Instead of acknowledging any feelings of love or tenderness toward her parents, she simply cannot stand them (A. Freud, 1936).[2]

Projection occurs when we attribute our own impulses, feelings, and characteristics onto others. A man might believe he is free of hostile wishes but sees other people as full of hostility. He represses anger in himself and projects it onto others. If Bettelheim (1967) was correct, projection is implicit in the story of Hansel and Gretel. The children's own oral greed and wishes to devour are projected onto the wicked witch.

Most defense mechanisms deal with anxiety-producing impulses, fantasies, and emotions that emerge from within, as when we repress a forbidden desire. *Denial* addresses the outside; it defends against reality by denying the facts (A. Freud, 1936). Denial is often necessary in severe circumstances, as when a child whose mother has died says, "My mommy is coming today." Elizabeth Kubler-Ross (1969) found that terminally ill patients usually go through an initial stage of denying the evidence that they have the illness.

Anna Freud (1936) tentatively suggested that the defense mechanisms are also tied to specific developmental stages. Repression is characteristic of the oedipal stage, reaction-formation of the anal stage. Projection and denial are primitive mechanisms that may be characteristic of the oral stage. But this association between defenses and stages is somewhat sketchy.

Following Freud's (1926) suggestion, many psychoanalysts have examined how different defenses are at work in different emotional disorders. For example, they have found that displacement plays a major role in many phobias, including school phobias. A young child who starts attending school might develop an extraordinary fear of it, and the fear is especially intense because the child displaces her anxiety over separation from her mother onto the school (White & Watt, 1973).

While not necessarily denying the value of such analyses, several contemporary scholars seek to cast defense mechanisms in a more positive light. They ask us to consider some defenses as healthy coping strategies. These scholars are exploring an important area—constructive coping—but they often overextend the concept of a defense mechanism. For example, Valliant (2000) calls *suppression* a healthy defense mechanism. But suppression is a fairly conscious effort to avoid interfering thoughts, whereas the classic defense mechanisms operate unconsciously.

---

[2]In her discussion of adolescence, which we reviewed earlier, Anna Freud described several ways young people try to ward off sexual and aggressive impulses welling up at this time. Two of the strategies, asceticism and intellectualization, are technically considered mechanisms of defense in standard psychoanalytic texts (e.g., Waelder, 1960).

In traditional psychoanalytic theory, the healthiest defense mechanism is *sublimation*. This is the process by which the ego redirects impulses into socially acceptable pursuits. For example, people might channel their aggressive energies into competitive sports. Or they might sublimate their sexual interests into artistic activities, writing fiction or painting pictures on the topic of romantic love.

The Ego's Development

In the years after Freud's death, many of his followers addressed the process by which the ego develops. Freud wrote little on this subject. His main suggestion (1911) was that the ego develops because the drives are frustrated. As long as babies are gratified, they have no reason for dealing with reality. But they do experience frustration. At first they try to reduce tensions through hallucinations, but these do not work for long. So they must seek need-gratifying objects in reality.

The difficulty with Freud's proposal is that it implies the ego acts only when the id activates it. Construed in this way, the ego is weak. It only serves the id.

Hartmann's Revision.   One of Freud's most influential followers, Heinz Hartmann, suggested that Freud's theory might permit a different picture of the ego—one that gives it more autonomy. Hartmann (1939, 1950) noted that Freud wondered whether the ego might not have genetic roots of its own. If so, ego functions such as motility (body movement), language, perception, and cognition might develop according to their own *maturational timetable*. Children, then, might begin to walk, talk, grasp objects, and so on, from inner promptings that are biologically governed but are also independent of the instinctual drives. Children have a maturational need to develop ego functions when the id is at rest, when life is "conflict free." Thus the ego might develop independently from the id. Hartmann's proposal is widely considered a major breakthrough in the study of ego development.

Ego Development and Object Relations.   Freudians have also studied the kind of environment most conducive to ego growth. When Freudians talk about the environment, they usually are speaking not about the physical world but the world of other people. They call interactions with others *object relations*.

According to Hartmann (Hartmann, Kris, & Lowenstein, 1946), Benedek (1938), and others, the optimal interpersonal environment at first is a consistently gratifying one. When caretakers are consistently loving, babies become interested in them and learn about the external world of people. Consistent care seems especially important for the development of one essential ego function—the ability to postpone gratification. As Benedek says, when the mother is consistent and loving, the baby gains *confidence* in her. The baby does not grow unduly impatient the minute his or her needs are not met but learns to wait. The baby knows care is forthcoming.

As psychoanalysis has developed, a number of people have moved object relations to the forefront. Some analysts have given object relations priority over everything else—over the instinctual drives, libidinal zones, and ego functions. What people really want, these writers say, is not to relieve instinctual tensions or to engage in ego functions for their own sake, but to develop mature interpersonal relationships (see Greenberg & Mitchell, 1983, especially chap. 6). In the next two chapters, we discuss two theories—those of Erikson and Mahler—that have moved psychoanalytic theory in the direction of object relations while maintaining a commitment to classical Freudian concepts.

PRACTICAL IMPLICATIONS

It is impossible to make any sharp distinctions between Freudian theory and practice. Freud's theory emerged from the clinical treatment of patients, and his followers continue to use therapy as a main source of data. In this chapter we have focused on Freud's theory of normal growth and development, rather than pathology and treatment, but we still have found it necessary to mention topics in the latter areas (e.g., hysteria).

A description of Freud's therapeutic work is well beyond our scope. What we can say here is that a major goal of psychoanalysis is to recover repressed or blocked-off experience. We saw how this was necessary in the case of Elizabeth von R. Elizabeth had repressed sexual feelings toward her brother-in-law, and these feelings, far from disappearing, became diverted into painful bodily symptoms. The only solution, Freud thought, is for us to become more conscious of our thoughts and feelings so that, instead of their controlling us, we can gain a measure of control over them. As he put it, "Where id was, there ego shall be" (1933, p. 80).

Therapy with children usually proceeds somewhat differently from that with adults, for children are not given to verbal discussions and recollections. Instead, they learn to express, accept, and master feelings and fantasies through play. In the Bettelheim chapter (Chapter 14), we will discuss a therapeutic approach with extremely disturbed children.

It is important to note that Freud never believed that psychoanalysis can completely cure our problems. Because we all live in society, which demands some repression of our instinctual urges, we all suffer to some extent. Further, Freud saw the therapist's role as limited. A psychiatrist was once asked by Freud if he was really able to cure. The psychiatrist replied, "In no way, but one can, as a gardener does, remove some impediments to personal growth." "Then," Freud answered, "we will understand each other" (Ellenberger, 1970, p. 461).

The practical implications of Freud's ideas extend far beyond the treatment of patients. His ideas have influenced practically every area of life, including the practice of law, art, literature, religion, and education. The area of most interest to us here is education. Freud's thoughts on education were not as radical as it is sometimes supposed. He believed societies will always exact some instinctual renunciation, and he said it would be unfair to send children into the world expecting they can do just as they please (1933, p. 149). On the other hand, Freud thought discipline is usually excessive; it makes children feel unnecessarily ashamed and guilty about their bodies and their natural functions. Freud was particularly emphatic on the need for sex education. He recommended that sex education be handled by the schools, where children could learn about reproduction in their lessons on nature and animals. They themselves would then draw the necessary conclusions with respect to humans (Freud, 1907).

Freudian ideas have motivated some more adventurous experiments in education. For example, at Summerhill, A. S. Neill (1960) gave children a great deal of liberty of all kinds, including sexual freedom. However, such radical innovations are rare, and Freud's influence is more typically found in the general attitude a teacher takes toward children. This attitude is particularly evident when a teacher refrains from automatically disciplining some unwanted behavior and instead tries to understand the emotional reasons behind it (Russell, 1971). When a teacher takes a closer look at a child's life, the teacher may discover that the angry or sullen child is not really mad at the teacher but is finding something at home, such as the neglect of a parent, deeply frustrating. Or the teacher may discover that the seemingly lazy teenager is actually brooding endlessly over sex or social failure (White & Watt, 1973, p. 34). The teacher may not always be able to correct such problems, or even feel it is prudent to discuss them with the student, for the student may need his or her privacy in certain matters. Nevertheless, a measure of understanding can help. For the teacher is then not so quick to criticize or punish but has a reason for being patient and encouraging—attitudes that have helped many a child.

EVALUATION

Freud was one of the great thinkers of modern times. Before Freud, some poets, artists, and philosophers may have known about the unconscious and early sexual fantasies, but it was Freud's remarkable work that made us take these matters seriously. At the same time, Freud was more bitterly attacked than any other psychological theorist before or since. Even today many consider his ideas scandalous.

It is not surprising, then, that Freud and his followers have sometimes reacted dogmatically and defensively. At times they have behaved like members of a religious sect, isolating themselves from other scientists and gathering in their own groups to reaffirm the truth of their own beliefs. At other times, Freudians have resorted to *ad hominem* arguments—arguments directed not against others' ideas, but against their personalities. In one essay (1925b), Freud argued that his critics objected to his ideas because of their own resistances and repressions.

In the midst of such emotionally charged debates, several criticisms of psychoanalysis have been offered that have merit, and some Freudians have tried to face them openly and to correct the weaknesses in the theory.

Some of the most important criticisms of Freud have come from anthropologists who have argued that Freud's theory is culture bound. In the 1920s, Malinowski and others zeroed in on Freud's theory of the Oedipus complex, pointing out that it is not nearly as universal as Freud imagined. Malinowski noted that the family constellation on which this complex is based—the nuclear triangle of mother, father, and child—is not found in all cultures. Among the Trobriand Islanders, Malinowski found, the child's chief disciplinarian was not the father but the maternal uncle. Further, the strongest incest taboo was not between children and parents but between brothers and sisters. In this situation, Malinowski pointed out, repressed fears and longings were very different. "We might say that in the Oedipus complex there is a repressed desire to kill the father and marry the mother, while in the . . . Trobriands the wish is to marry the sister and to kill the maternal uncle" (Malinowski, 1927, pp. 80–81). The oedipal situation is by no means just as Freud described.

But Malinowski did not wish to dispense with Freud altogether. On the contrary, he was indebted to Freud for the insight that repressed wishes emerge in projections such as dreams, magic, and folklore. This insight provided him with an important theoretical tool. Malinowski's argument was that such projections vary with the cultural setting. Among the Trobriand Islanders, he found no oedipal myths or dreams, but many that centered on their own strongest temptations and taboos—especially brother-sister relations. For example, although they themselves never admitted to incestuous wishes toward siblings, they told stories about how magic originated long ago when a brother and sister did commit incest.

At the time of Malinowski's writings, Freud and his followers resisted anthropological modifications of psychoanalytic theory. However, later Freudians (e.g., Erikson, 1963; Kardiner, 1945) have tried to combine psychoanalytic and anthropological insights.

Freud has also been sharply criticized for cultural bias on the topic of women. Psychoanalytically oriented writers such as Clara Thompson (1950) and modern feminists have charged that Freud's views on women reflect his own unexamined Victorian attitudes. Freud's limitations, Thompson said, are most evident in his concept of penis envy. She agreed that girls envy boys, but not for the reasons Freud thought. Freud assumed that penis envy is based on a real biological inferiority—a view that fit well with his society's prejudice. Actually, she said, penis envy is much more of a cultural problem; girls feel inferior to boys because girls lack the same privileges in a male-dominated society. That is, they lack the opportunities for adventure, independence, and success. Freud ignored women's legitimate desire for social equality.

Writers have also accused Freud of cultural bias in his discussions of women's sense of morality. Freud thought that girls, not fearing castration, have less need to internalize a strong superego. As evidence he pointed to women's greater emotionality and flexibility in moral matters. Such observations, his critics contend, simply reflect his own cultural stereotypes.

Empirical evidence does suggest that Freud would have done well to question his theory on superego formation. Most evidence suggests that children do not acquire an initial sense of morality because they fear harm, whether castration or some other physical punishment. The child who only fears physical punishment simply tries to avoid getting caught (and perhaps learns to hate the punisher). A sense of morality, instead, appears to develop when the child experiences love and wishes to keep it. The child who receives love tries to behave properly to gain parental approval (Brown, 1965, pp. 381–394; White & Watt, 1981, pp. 359–360.) So, if a girl is loved as much as a boy, she should develop an equally strong conscience.

Several contemporary feminist psychoanalysts say that Freud's theory is too individualistic. Nancy Chodorow (1978) and Jessica Benjamin (1988) argue that we cannot understand people as isolated individuals with their drives and ego functions. We must focus on object relations—interactions with others. In the view of both prominent feminists and object relations theorists, humans don't merely seek gratification of erotic needs; they seek relationships (Greenberg & Mitchell, 1983, chap. 6).

Freud has also been criticized on scientific grounds. Although his theory hinges on universal childhood developments, his evidence came primarily from adults—from the memories and fantasies of adults in treatment. Freud did not investigate his hypotheses in an unbiased way with representative samples of normal children.

Some psychologists think Freud's theory is of little scientific value because it is so hopelessly opaque and complex. Sometimes, in fact, the theory predicts equally probable but contradictory outcomes. For example, children who experience frustration at the anal stage might develop habits of orderliness, cleanliness, and obedience, or they might develop the opposite characteristics, rebelliousness and messiness. How do we predict which set of traits any given child will develop?

Finally, there is the unnerving experience of never seeming able to disconfirm Freud's hypotheses. If, for instance, we do a study that finds no relationship between weaning and later oral behavior, we can be sure some Freudians will say we failed to understand Freud's thoughts in sufficient depth.

But despite the difficulties, an enormous amount of research on Freud's ideas has been done and will continue, and investigators will eventually sort out the valid and invalid propositions. Researchers will continue to struggle with Freud's theory and to test it the best they can because they sense that Freud was basically on the right track. As Hall, Lindzey, and Campbell (1998) say, his theory has a fundamental appeal because it is both broad and deep:

> Over and above all the other virtues of his theory stands this one: It tries to envisage full-bodied individuals living partly in a world of reality and partly in a world of make-believe, beset by conflicts and inner contradictions, yet capable of rational thought and action, moved by forces of which they have little knowledge and by aspirations which are beyond their reach, by turn confused and clear-headed, frustrated and satisfied, hopeful and despairing, selfish and altruistic; in short, a complex human being. For many people, this picture of the individual has an essential validity. (p. 77)

Erikson and the Eight Stages of Life

BIOGRAPHICAL INTRODUCTION

Among the advances in the psychoanalytic theory of development, none has been more substantial than that made by Erik H. Erikson (1902–1994). Erikson has given us a new, enlarged picture of the child's tasks at each of Freud's stages. Beyond this, he has added three new stages—those of the adult years—so the theory now encompasses the entire life cycle.

Erikson was born to Danish parents in Frankfurt, Germany, the child of an extramarital union he and his mother kept secret ("Erik Erikson," 1994). Erikson was raised by his mother alone until he was 3 years old, when she married again, this time to a local pediatrician, Dr. Homburger. His mother and Dr. Homburger were Jewish, but Erikson looked different—more like a tall, blond, blue-eyed Dane. He was even nicknamed "the goy" (non-Jew) by the Jewish boys (Coles, 1970, p. 180).

Young Erikson was not a particularly good student. Although he excelled in certain subjects—especially ancient history and art—he disliked the formal school atmosphere. When he graduated from high school, he felt lost and uncertain about his future place in life. Instead of going to college, he wandered throughout Europe for a year, returned home to study art for a while, and then set out on his travels once again. He was going through what he would later call a *moratorium,* a period during which young people take time out to try to find themselves. Such behavior was acceptable for many German youth at the time. As Erikson's biographer, Robert Coles (1970), says, Erikson "was not seen by his family or friends as odd or 'sick,' but as a wandering artist who was trying to come to grips with himself" (p. 15).

Erikson finally began to find his calling when, at the age of 25, he accepted an invitation to teach children in a new Viennese school founded by Anna Freud and Dorothy Burlingham. When Erikson wasn't teaching, he studied child psychoanalysis with Anna Freud and others, and he was himself analyzed by her.

At the age of 27, Erikson married Joan Serson and started a family. Their life was disrupted in 1933 when the rise of Hitler forced them to leave Europe. They settled in Boston, where Erikson became the city's first child analyst.

But the urge to travel seemed firmly implanted in Erikson's nature. After 3 years in Boston, he took a position at Yale University, and 2 years later he made another trip—to the Pine Ridge Reservation in South Dakota, where he lived with and learned about the Lakota (Sioux). Erikson then moved on to San Francisco, where he resumed his clinical practice with children and participated in a major longitudinal study of normal children at the University of California. He also found time to travel up the California coast to study another Indian tribe, the Yurok fishermen. We can see that Erikson was exploring areas that Freud had left uncharted—the lives of normal children and of children growing up in different cultural contexts.

In 1949, during the McCarthy era, Erikson came into conflict with his employer, the University of California. The university demanded a loyalty oath of all its employees, which Erikson refused to sign. When some of his colleagues were dismissed, he resigned. Erikson took a new job at the Austin Riggs Center in Stockbridge, Massachusetts, where he worked until 1960. He was then given a professorship at Harvard University, even though he had never earned a formal college degree, and he taught at Harvard until his death.

Erikson's most important work is *Childhood and Society* (1950; 2nd ed. 1963). In this book he maps out his eight stages of life and illustrates how these stages are played out in different ways in different cultures. Two other highly influential books are *Young Man Luther* (1958) and *Gandhi's Truth* (1969), which bridge psychoanalytic insights with historical material.

ERIKSON'S STAGE THEORY

General Purpose

Freud, you will recall, postulated a sequence of psychosexual stages that center on body zones. As children mature, their sexual interest shifts from the oral to the anal to the phallic zone; then, after a latency period, the focus is once again on the genital region. Freud presented a completely new way of looking at development.

At the same time, Freud's stage theory is limited. In particular, its focus on body zones is too specific. As you will recall from Chapter 6, a rigorous stage theory describes *general* achievements or issues at different periods of life. For example, we do not call shoe tying a stage because it is too specific. Similarly, the focus on zones also tends to be specific, describing only parts of the body. Even though it is interesting to note that some people become fixated on these zones—and, for example, find the mouth the main source of pleasure in life—there is more to personality development than this.

Freud's writings, of course, were not limited to descriptions of body zones. He also discussed crucial interactions between children and significant others. Erikson tried to do this more thoroughly. At each Freudian stage, Erikson introduced concepts that gradually led to an understanding of the most decisive, general encounter between the child and the social world.

1. The Oral Stage

Zones and Modes.   Erikson first tried to give the Freudian stages greater generality by pointing out that for each libidinal zone, we can also speak of an ego mode. At the first stage, the primary zone is the mouth, but this zone also possesses a mode of activity, *incorporation,* a passive yet eager taking in (Erikson, 1963, p. 72). Further, incorporation extends beyond the mouth and characterizes other senses as well. Babies not only take in through the mouth but also through the eyes; when they see something interesting, they open their eyes eagerly and widely and try to take the object in with all their might. Also, they seem to take in good feelings through their tactile senses. And even a basic reflex, the grasp reflex, seems to follow the incorporative mode; when an object touches the baby's palm, the fist automatically closes around it. Incorporation describes a general mode through which the baby's ego first deals with the external world.

Freud's second oral stage is marked by the eruption of teeth and aggressive biting. According to Erikson, the mode of *biting* or *grasping,* like incorporation, is a general one that extends beyond the mouth. With maturation, babies can actively reach out and grasp things with their hands. Similarly, "the eyes, first part of a relatively passive system of accepting impressions as they come along, have now learned to focus, to isolate, to 'grasp' objects from a vaguer background, and to follow them" (p. 77). Finally, the organs of hearing conform to the more active mode of grasping. Babies can now discern and localize significant sounds and can move their heads and bodies so as to actively take them in. Thus the mode of biting or grasping—of active taking—is a general one that describes the central way in which the ego now deals with the world.

The Most General Stage: Basic Trust versus Mistrust.   The most general stage at each period consists of a general encounter between the child's maturing ego and the social world. At the first stage, as babies try to take in the things they need, they interact with caretakers, who follow their own culture's ways of giving to them. What is most important in these interactions is that babies come to find some consistency, predictability, and reliability in their caretakers' actions. When they sense that a parent is consistent and dependable, they develop a sense of basic trust in the parent. They come to sense that when they are cold, wet, or hungry, they can count on others to relieve their pain. Some parents come promptly while others minister on schedules, but in either case babies learn the parent is dependable and therefore trustworthy. The alternative is a sense of mistrust, the feeling that the parent is unpredictable and unreliable, and may not be there when needed (Erikson, 1963, p. 247).

Babies must also learn to trust themselves. This problem becomes particularly acute when babies experience the rages of teething and hurt the nursing mother with their sharp bites and grasps. When babies learn to regulate their urges—to suck without biting and to hold without hurting—they begin to consider themselves "trustworthy enough so that the providers will not need to be on guard lest they be nipped" (p. 248). For her part, the mother needs to be careful not to withdraw too completely or to wean too suddenly. If she does, the baby will feel that her care is not dependable after all, for it may be suddenly taken away.

When babies have developed a sense of trust in their caretakers, they show it in their behavior. Erikson said the first sign of trust in a mother comes when the baby is willing "to let her out of sight without undue anxiety or rage" (p. 247). The word *undue* is probably important here, for we saw in the discussion of Bowlby that most babies experience some separation anxiety. Nevertheless, if parents are dependable, babies can learn to tolerate their absences. If caretakers are undependable, babies cannot afford to let them go and panic when they begin to do so.

Trust is similar to what Benedek called confidence (see p. 276 in the preceding chapter). It is a basic faith in one's providers. Erikson said he preferred the term *trust* because "there is more naiveté and more mutuality in it" (p. 248). But trust results in the same attitude that Benedek was concerned about—the calm patience that comes from the certainty that one's providers will be there when needed.

Trust, then, is the sense that others are reliable and predictable. At the same time, however, Erikson implied that trust ultimately depends on something more. Ultimately, he said, trust depends on the *parents' own confidence*, on their sense they are doing things right. Parents "must be able to represent to the child a deep, an almost somatic conviction that there is a meaning to what they are doing" (p. 249). This sense of meaning, in turn, requires cultural backing—the belief that the "way we do things is good for our children."

At first glance, Erikson's emphasis on the caretaker's own confidence is puzzling. What does the parent's confidence have to do with the baby? Erikson might have had in mind thoughts similar to those of the psychiatrist H. S. Sullivan. Sullivan (1953) believed that in the first months of life the infant has a special kind of physical empathy with the mother figure such that the baby automatically feels the mother's state of tension. If the mother feels anxious, the baby feels anxious; if the mother feels calm, the baby feels calm. It is important that parents feel reasonably confident and self-assured, so babies will not become too wary of interpersonal contact. Babies need to feel that it is basically good and reassuring to be close to others.

Erikson (1959, p. 64) observed that it is not always easy for U.S. parents to have an inner confidence in their child-rearing practices. Whereas parents in simpler, more stable cultures follow practices that have been handed down over the generations, the modern American parent has fewer traditions to fall back on. Modern parents receive all kinds of advice on newer, "better" child-rearing techniques, and the advice is by no means uniform.

In this situation, Erikson believed books such as Spock's (1946) are helpful. Throughout his book, Spock encourages parents to trust themselves. He tells parents that they know more than they think and they should follow their impulses to respond to their babies' needs. It is almost as if Spock had read Erikson and understood the importance of parents possessing an inner assurance.

Beyond reading Spock, Erikson said, parents can gain an inner security from religion. Their own faith and inner assurance will be transmitted to the child, helping the child feel the world is a trustworthy place. If parents are without religion, they must find faith in some other area, perhaps in fellowship, or the goals of their work, or in their social ideals (Erikson, 1959, pp. 64–65).

Erikson has sometimes given readers the impression that babies should develop trust but not mistrust. But he did not mean this. He saw each stage as a vital conflict or tension in which the "negative" pole is also necessary for growth. In the present case, infants must experience both trust and mistrust. If they only developed trust, they would become too gullible. "It is clear," Erikson said, "that the human infant must experience a goodly measure of mistrust in order to learn to trust discerningly" (1976, p. 23).

At the same time, it is critical that infants emerge from this stage with a favorable balance of trust over mistrust. If they do, they will have developed the core ego strength of this period: *hope*. Hope is the expectation that despite frustrations, rages, and disappointments, good things will happen in the future. Hope enables the child to move forward into the world and take up new challenges (Erikson, 1982, p. 60).

Conclusion.   We see, then, that Erikson considerably broadened Freud's description of the oral stage. Erikson showed that it is not just the oral zone that is important, but the corresponding ego modes of dealing with the world. The infant incorporates and later grasps things in the world through the various senses. The infant's maturing ego, in turn, meets the social world—in this case, the caretakers—in a general, decisive encounter. The critical issue is that of trust versus mistrust. The baby needs to know that the caretakers are predictable and to sense their inner assurance. If the baby can develop a favorable balance of trust over mistrust, the baby develops the core ego strength of this period: hope. Hope enables the child to move forward and enthusiastically confront the world despite current and past frustrations.

Issues of trust, mistrust, and hope are, of course, with us throughout our lives. Erikson recognized this. But he also claimed that the struggle between trust and mistrust reaches its own particular crisis and is the dominating event in the first year of life. And the way in which infants resolve this first crisis, with or without a firm sense of hopefulness, determines the energy and vitality they bring to subsequent stages.

2. The Anal Stage

Zones and Modes.   In Freud's second stage, which occurs during the second and third years, the anal zone comes into prominence. With the maturation of the nervous system, children gain voluntary control over their sphincter muscles; they can now retain and eliminate as they wish. They often hold on to their bowel movements to maximize the sensations of the final release.

Erikson agreed with Freud that the basic modes of this stage are retention and elimination, of holding on and letting go. However, Erikson also pointed out that these modes encompass more than the anal zone. For example, children begin to use their hands to hold stubbornly on to objects and, just as defiantly, to throw them away. Once they can sit up easily, they carefully pile things up one moment, only to discard them the next. With people, too, they sometimes hold on, snuggling up, and at other times insist on pushing the adult away (Erikson, 1959, pp. 82, 86).

The General Stage: Autonomy versus Shame and Doubt.   Amidst these contradictory impulses—holding on one moment and expelling the next—the child is primarily trying to exercise a choice. Two-year-olds want to hold on when they want and to push aside when they do not. They are exercising their will, their sense of autonomy (see Table 12.1).

Table 12.1   The Stages of Freud and Erikson

AGE	FREUD'S STAGE	ERIKSON'S GENERAL STAGE
Birth to 1	Oral	Trust vs. Mistrust: *Hope*
1 to 3	Anal	Autonomy vs. Shame, Doubt: *Will*
3 to 6	Phallic (Oedipal)	Initiative vs. Guilt: *Purpose*
6 to 11	Latency	Industry vs. Inferiority: *Competence*
Adolescence	Genital	Identity vs. Role Confusion: *Fidelity*
Young Adulthood		Intimacy vs. Isolation: *Love*
Adulthood		Generativity vs. Self-Absorption, Stagnation: *Care*
Old Age		Ego Integrity vs. Despair: *Wisdom*

In other ways, too, maturation ushers in a sense of autonomy during the second and third years. Children can now stand up on their own two feet, and they begin to explore the world on their own. They also insist on feeding themselves, even if this means exercising their right to make a mess. Their language, too, reveals a new-found autonomy and sense of selfhood; they repeatedly use the words *me* and *mine*. Most of all, they express their autonomy in a single word—*no*. Two-year-olds seem unable to say "Yes," as if any agreement means a complete forfeiture of their independence. Through the strong and insistent "No," children defy all external control.

As children seem so much more in control of themselves and reach peaks of willfulness, societies, through parents, decide it is time to teach them the right ways to behave. As Freud observed, parents do not permit their children to enjoy their anality in any way they please; instead, they train them to behave in the socially proper way. Parents quite often toilet-train children by making them feel ashamed of messy and improper anal behavior. Children may resist training for some time, but they eventually submit to it.

Erikson agreed that the "battles of the toilet bowl" are important. But he also is suggesting that the battles of this time—between the child's autonomy and the society's regulations—take place in a number of arenas. For example, when children insist on feeding themselves and making a mess, parents try to regulate their behavior. Similarly, parents sooner or later decide their 2-year-olds cannot say "No" to every single request. Two-year-olds, like everyone else, must live in society and respect others' wishes. Thus the conflict at this stage is a very general one.

Erikson defined the conflict as that of autonomy versus shame and doubt. Autonomy comes from within; biological maturation fosters the ability to do things on one's own—to control one's own sphincter muscles, to stand on one's own feet, to use one's hands, and so on. Shame and doubt, in contrast, come from an awareness of social expectations and pressures. Shame is the feeling that we do not look good in others' eyes. For example, a little girl who wets her pants becomes self-conscious, worried that others will see her in this state. Doubt stems from the realization that one is not so powerful after all, that others can control one and perform actions much better.

It is hoped that children can learn to adjust to social regulations without losing too much of their initial sense of autonomy. Some parents try to assist the child with this. They gently try to help the child learn social behavior without crushing the child's independence. Other parents are not so sensitive. They may shame children excessively when they have a bowel accident; they may try to break their children of any oppositional behavior; or they may ridicule their children's efforts to do things on their own. In such instances, children can develop lasting feelings of shame and doubt that override their impulses toward self-determination.

To the extent that children resolve this second crisis in a positive way, with a favorable ratio of autonomy over shame and doubt, they develop the ego strength of rudimentary *will*. "Will," Erikson said, is "the unbroken determination to exercise free choice as well as self-restraint" (1964, p. 119). Erikson includes self-restraint in his definition because he believes it is important for children to learn to control their impulses and to renounce what is not worth doing (or cannot be done). Still, it is the child—not external powers—who is in charge.

3. The Phallic (Oedipal) Stage

Zone and Modes.   During Freud's third stage (between about 3 and 6 years of age), the child's concern with the anal zone gives way to the primacy of the genital zone. Children now focus their interest on their genitals and become curious about the sex organs of others. They also begin to imagine themselves in adult roles and even dare to rival one parent for the love of the other. They enter the oedipal crisis.

Erikson called the primary mode at this stage *intrusion*. By this term, he hoped to capture Freud's sense of the child as now exceedingly daring, curious, and competitive. The term *intrusion* describes the activity of the boy's penis, but as a general mode it refers to much more. For both sexes, the maturation of physical and mental abilities impels the child forward into a variety of intrusive activities. "These include the intrusion into other bodies by physical attack; the intrusion into other people's ears and minds by aggressive talking; the intrusion into space by vigorous locomotion; the intrusion into the unknown by consuming curiosity" (Erikson, 1963, p. 87).

The General Stage: Initiative versus Guilt.   Initiative, like intrusion, connotes forward movement. The child with a sense of initiative makes plans, sets goals, and perseveres in attaining them. I noted, for example, some of the activities of our son Adam when he was 5 years old. In a single day, he decided to see how high he could build his blocks, invented a game that consisted of seeing who could jump the highest on his parents' bed, and led the family to a new movie containing a great deal of action and violence. His behavior had taken on a goal-directed, competitive, and imaginative quality.

The crisis comes when children realize their biggest plans and fondest hopes are doomed for failure. These ambitions, of course, are the oedipal ones—the wish to possess one parent and rival the other. The child finds out that these wishes violate deep social taboos and are far more dangerous than imagined. Consequently, the child internalizes social prohibitions— a guilt-producing superego—to keep such dangerous impulses and fantasies in check. The result is a new form of self-restriction. Forever after, the individual's naive exuberance and daring will be offset by self-observation, self-control, and self-punishment (see Figure 12.1).

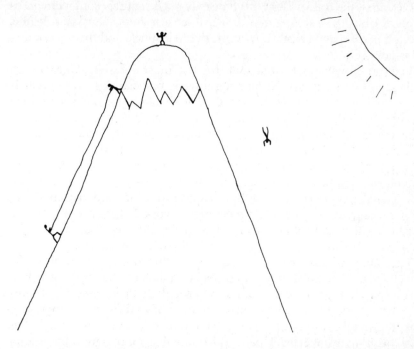

Figure 12.1
A boy's drawing expresses daring initiative and disaster. There is a resemblance to the myth of Icarus, about a boy who went too far—too near the sun. This drawing, by a 9-year-old, may also suggest the industry theme of the next stage: The climbers on the left are engaged in skillful cooperation.

In Erikson's view, the creation of a superego constitutes one of the great tragedies in life. Although the superego is necessary for socialized behavior, it stifles the bold initiative with which the child met life at the phallic stage. Still, Erikson was not completely pessimistic. He observed that 3- to 6-year-old children are, more than at any other time, ready to learn quickly and avidly, and they are willing to find ways of channeling their ambition into socially useful pursuits (1963, p. 258). Parents can help this process by easing their authority somewhat and by permitting children to participate with them as equals on interesting projects. In this way, parents can help children emerge from the crisis of this stage with a strong sense of *purpose*, "the courage to envisage and pursue valued goals," unimpaired by guilt and inhibition (Erikson, 1964, p. 122).

4. The Latency Stage

In Freud's theory, the resolution of the Oedipus complex brings about a latency period, lasting from about age 6 to 11. During this period the sexual and aggressive drives, which produced crises at earlier periods, are temporarily dormant. There is no libidinal (sexual) zone for this stage.

Of course, the child's life at this time may not be entirely conflict free. For example, the birth of a sibling may arouse intense jealousy. But as a rule, this is a period of calm and stability. In terms of the instincts and drives, nothing much is going on.

Erikson, however, showed that this is a most decisive stage for ego growth. Children master important cognitive and social skills. The crisis is *industry versus inferiority*. Children forget their past hopes and wishes, which were often played out within the family, and eagerly apply themselves to learning the useful skills and tools of the wider culture. In indigenous societies, children learn to track, find food, and make utensils. In these cultures, learning is often informal, and much of it comes from older children. In modern technological societies such as ours, children go to school, where they are asked to master more cerebral skills—reading, writing, and arithmetic. In either case, they are learning to do meaningful work and are developing the ego strengths of "steady attention and persevering diligence" (Erikson, 1963, p. 259). They also are learning to work and play with their peers.

The danger of this stage is an excessive feeling of inadequacy and inferiority (1963, p. 260). Most of us can probably remember the hurts of failure in the classroom or on the playground. A particularly deep sense of inferiority may have various roots. Sometimes children have difficulty at this stage because they have not successfully resolved the conflicts at earlier stages. For example, a girl may have developed more doubt than autonomy at the second stage, so she is unsure of herself as she tries to master new tasks. At other times, school and community attitudes may hinder the development of a sense of industry. An African American boy may learn that the color of his skin counts for more than his wish and will to learn. And all too often schools fail to discover and encourage the individual's special talents (p. 260).

Good teachers (who often are those who feel trusted and respected by the community) can help children at this time. Erikson (1959, p. 87) said he had repeatedly observed that in the lives of inspired and gifted people just one teacher made a difference by encouraging the individual's talent.

In any case, the successful resolution of this stage leads to the ego strength Erikson called *competence,* the free exercise of intelligence and skill in the completion of tasks, unimpaired by excessive feelings of inferiority (1964, p. 124).

5. Puberty (The Genital Stage)

According to Sigmund and Anna Freud, adolescence is a turbulent stage because of the dramatic physiological changes occurring at this time. Sexual and aggressive drives, which were dormant during the latency stage, now threaten to overwhelm the ego and its defenses. The genital zone, in particular, is infused with tremendous sexual energy, and the adolescent is once again troubled by oedipal fantasies. The teenager may find it difficult simply to be around his or her parents.

Erikson agreed that the great increase in drive energy is disruptive at adolescence, but he saw this as only part of the problem. Adolescents also become disturbed and confused by new *social* conflicts and demands. The adolescent's primary task, Erikson believed, is establishing a new sense of *ego identity*—a feeling for who one is and one's place in the larger social order. The crisis is one of *identity versus role confusion.*

The upsurge of instinctual drives certainly contributes to the adolescent's identity problems. Adolescents suddenly feel as if their impulses have a will of their own, that they are no longer one with themselves. Also, the rapid physical growth at puberty creates a sense of identity confusion. Young people begin to grow so quickly and to change in so many ways that they barely recognize themselves. It is probably for this reason that teenagers spend so much time looking in mirrors and pay so much attention to their appearance.

But identity problems are as much, if not more, a social matter. It is not physical growth or sexual impulses per se that trouble young people, but it is the thought that one might not look good to others or meet others' expectations. And, even more than this, young people begin to worry about their future place in the larger social world. Adolescents, with their rapidly expanding mental powers, feel overwhelmed by the countless options and alternatives before them.

Because adolescents are so uncertain about who they are, they anxiously tend to identify with in-groups. They can "become remarkably clannish, intolerant, and cruel in their exclusion of others who are 'different'" (Erikson, 1959, p. 92). In their hurry to find some identity, they stereotype "themselves, their ideals, and their enemies" (p. 92). They often put themselves and others to a "loyalty test." Some young people align themselves to political or religious ideologies. In all this, we can detect young people's search for values to which they can be true.

To understand identity formation, it is important to recognize that it is a lifelong process. In part, we form our identities through identifications. Although we are not necessarily aware of it, we identify with those who appeal to us and therefore become like them. Each person's identity, then, is partly a synthesis of various partial identifications (1959, pp. 112–113).

We also develop a sense of identity through our accomplishments. The ability to stand up, walk, run, play ball, draw, read, and write all contribute to a sense of ego identity. We come to see ourselves as "one who can do these things." Such accomplishments become part of a positive and lasting sense of identity when they have importance for the culture (1959, pp. 89–90).

Still, even though identity formation is a lifelong process, the problem of identity reaches its crisis at adolescence. It is at this time that so many inner changes are taking place, and so much in terms of future commitment is at stake. During adolescence one's earlier identity seems inadequate for all the choices and decisions one must make.

Erikson (1959, p. 123) asked us to consider, for example, a young college girl from a conservative background. When she goes to college she meets people of very different backgrounds, among whom she must choose her friends. She also must decide what her attitude toward sex will be and what occupational goals she is willing to compete for. At this point, her previous identity and identifications offer little help. Each decision seems to affirm some aspect of her past while repudiating others. If she decides to become sexually active, she may violate her family's spoken values, while identifying with some of their hidden wishes. If she chooses to compete in a male-dominated field such as politics or surgery, she ventures beyond certain family values but aligns herself with others. As she makes decisions and commitments, she reworks prior identifications and forms a new identity. Her task is to forge for herself some "central perspective and direction, some working unity, out of the effective remnants of [her] childhood and the hopes of [her] anticipated adulthood" (Erikson, 1958, p. 14).

Identity formation is a largely unconscious process. Still, young people are often painfully aware of their inability to make lasting commitments. They feel there is too much to decide too soon, and that every decision reduces their future alternatives (Erikson, 1959, pp. 124–126). Because commitment is so difficult, they sometimes enter a *psychosocial moratorium*, a kind of "time out" period for finding oneself. Some young people, for example, drop out of college to travel or experiment with various jobs before making any final decisions. However, many young people have trouble achieving a free moratorium state. Until they know who they are and what they will do in life, they often experience a sense of isolation, a feeling that time is passing them by, an inability to find meaning in any kind of activity, and a feeling that life is simply happening to them. As Biff puts it in Arthur Miller's *Death of a Salesman*, "I just can't take hold, Mom, I can't take hold of some kind of life" (Erikson, 1959, p. 91).

Nevertheless, the adolescent frequently postpones commitments anyway, because of an inner need to avoid *identity foreclosure*, a premature acceptance of compartmentalized social roles. And although a protracted identity search can be painful, it can also eventually lead to a higher form of personal integration and to genuine social innovations. As we have seen, many of the theorists in this book resisted the temptation to settle into conventional occupational identities. Piaget, Freud, and Erikson, among others, spent some time searching for their true callings. And their search, while not always pleasant for them, eventually led to new ways of understanding and meaningful changes in their professions.

The adolescent's central task, then, is to find some way of life to which he or she can make a permanent commitment. The struggles of this stage lead to the new ego strength of *fidelity*, the ability to sustain one's freely pledged loyalties (Erikson, 1964, p. 125).

6. Young Adulthood

Erikson is the first Freudian and one of the few developmental writers of any persuasion to propose separate stages for the adult years. If, then, his thoughts seem sketchy, we should remember that he was writing about an uncharted area.

Erikson's stages of adult development describe steps by which people widen and deepen their capacities to love and care for others. The *adolescent* is preeminently self-centered. Adolescents are concerned with who they are, how they appear in the eyes of others, and what they will become. They do become sexually attracted to others and even fall in love, but such attachments most often are really efforts at self-definition. In their interactions, young people try to find out who they are by endlessly talking about their true feelings, their views of each other, and their plans, hopes, and expectations (Erikson, 1959, p. 95).

The adolescent, then, is too preoccupied with who he or she is to take up the task of young adulthood—the attainment of *intimacy*. Real intimacy is only possible once a reasonable sense of identity has been established (1959, p. 95). Only one who is secure with one's identity is able to lose oneself in true mutuality with another. The young man, for example, who is worried about his masculinity will not make the best lover. He will be too self-conscious, too worried about how he is performing, to abandon himself freely and tenderly with his sexual partner. To the extent that people fail to attain genuine mutuality, they experience the opposite pole of this stage—*isolation*.

Erikson observed that some young people marry before they have established a good sense of identity. They hope they will be able to find themselves in their marriage. Such marriages, however, rarely work out. The partners sooner or later begin to feel hemmed in by their obligations as mates and parents. They soon complain that others are not giving them the opportunity to develop themselves. Erikson noted that a change in mate is rarely the answer. What the individual needs is some "wisely guided insight" into the fact that one cannot expect to live intimately with another until one has become oneself (p. 95).

In his discussions of intimacy, Erikson, as a respectable Freudian, spoke glowingly of the experience of orgasm: It is a supreme experience of mutual regulation that takes the edge off the inevitable bitterness and differences between two people (1963, p. 265). He added, though, that the "Utopia of genitality" is by no means a purely sexual matter. True intimacy means that two people are willing to share and mutually regulate all important aspects of their lives (p. 266).

As with the other stages, no one develops only the positive pole of this stage. No couple experiences total intimacy. Because people are different (sexually and otherwise), there is inevitably a degree of antagonism between partners that leads to periodic isolation. Ideally, however, intimacy is stronger than isolation. If so, young adults develop the ego strength of mature *love*— the "mutuality of devotion forever subduing the antagonisms" between them (Erikson, 1964, p. 129).

7. Adulthood

Once two people have established some measure of intimacy, their interests begin to expand beyond just the two of them. They become concerned with raising the next generation. In Erikson's terms, they enter the stage of *generativity versus self-absorption and stagnation* (Erikson, 1982, p. 67). *Generativity* is a broad term that refers not only to the creation of children but also to the production of things and ideas through work. But Erikson focused primarily on the former—the generation of children.

The mere fact of having children, of course, does not guarantee generativity. Parents must do more than produce offspring; they must protect and guide them. This means that parents must often sacrifice their own needs. They must overcome temptations to self-indulgence, which lead to an unproductive stagnation. To the extent they can positively cope with this conflict, they develop their ability to *care* for the next generation.

Some people, Erikson noted, develop generativity and care without having children of their own. Nuns and priests, for example, forgo the right to raise their own children, as do others who apply their special gifts to other areas. Such persons can still teach and guide the next generation "by working with other people's children or helping to create a better world for them" (Erikson in Evans, 1969, p. 51). Such adults must, to be sure, withstand a certain amount of frustration. This is especially true of women, whose bodies are built for nurturing and nourishing offspring. But a sense of care and generativity is still possible.

On the other hand, there are many people who marry but lack generativity. In such cases, the couples often regress to a kind of "pseudointimacy" or "begin to indulge themselves as if they were their one and only child" (Erikson, 1959, p. 97). Erikson might have been thinking of couples who endlessly analyze their relationship in terms of how much each person is getting from the other. The individuals seem more concerned with their own needs than those of their children.

There are several possible reasons for an inability to develop at this stage. Sometimes the parent's own childhood was so empty or frustrating that the parent cannot see how it is possible to do more for his or her children. In other cases, the difficulty seems more cultural. In the United States in particular, our values emphasize independent achievement to such an extent that people can become too exclusively involved in themselves and their successes and neglect the responsibility of caring for others (Erikson, 1959, p. 97).

8. Old Age

The psychological literature on old age, which is still sparse, typically views this period as one of decline. The elderly, it is repeatedly pointed out, must cope with a series of physical and social losses. They lose their physical strength and health; they lose their jobs and much of their income through retirement; and, as time goes by, they lose their spouses, relatives, and friends. Equally damaging, they suffer the inevitable loss of status that accompanies being old, inactive, and "useless" in America (see Gitelson, 1975; Havighurst, 1952, 1968). Some psychologists have tried to paint a more optimistic picture. While acknowledging the many problems and losses, these psychologists say that old age can be satisfying and can provide new experiences—"so long as one actively engages the environment" (Cole & Cole, 1993, p. 671; see also Newman & Newman, 2003, pp. 445, 470-472).

Erikson's insights went in a very different direction. He wasn't primarily concerned with the older person's activity, usefulness, or involvement in external affairs. Instead, he focused on the *inner* struggle of this period—a struggle that involves painful feelings but has potential for inner growth and wisdom. He called this struggle *ego integrity versus despair.*

As older people face death, Erikson implied, they engage in what has been called a *life review* (Butler, 1963). They look back on their lives and wonder whether they were worthwhile. In this process, they confront the ultimate despair—the feeling that life was not what it should have been, but now time has run out and there is no chance to try alternative lifestyles. Frequently, disgust hides despair. Many older people are disgusted by every little thing; they have no patience for the struggles and failings of others. Such disgust, Erikson said, really signifies their contempt for themselves (1959, p. 98).

As the older person faces despair, he or she is trying to find a sense of ego integrity. Ego integrity, Erikson said, is difficult to define but includes the sense that there is an order to one's life and "the acceptance of one's one and only life cycle as something that had to be and that, by necessity, permitted of no substitutions" (1963, p. 268). Integrity, it would seem, expresses the feeling that, "Yes, I made mistakes, but given who I was at the time and the circumstances, the mistakes were inevitable. I accept them, along with the good things in my life." Integrity is a feeling that also extends beyond the self and even transcends national and ideological boundaries. The older person, on some level, has a feeling of companionship "with the ordering ways of distant times and different pursuits, so expressed in the simple products and sayings of such times and pursuits" (p. 268).

Erikson (1976) told us that the crisis of old age is most admirably illustrated by Ingmar Bergman's film *Wild Strawberries.* The film, in Erikson's words,

> records an old Swedish doctor's journey by car from his place of retirement to the city of Lund. There, in the ancient cathedral, Dr. Isak Borg

is to receive the highest honor of his profession, a Jubilee Doctorate marking fifty years of meritorious service. But this journey by car on marked roads through familiar territory also becomes a symbolic pilgrimage back into childhood and deep into his unknown self. (p. 1)

The film begins with Borg writing in his diary, in which he expresses a self-satisfied view of what life has to offer. The film then plunges into a terrifying dream symbolizing his fear of death. Upon awakening, Borg decides to travel to Lund by car instead of by airplane and to take along his daughter-in-law, Marianne, who is in the midst of a marital crisis with which Borg has so far refused to help. As soon as they are in the car, they begin to quarrel, and Marianne tells him that "even though everyone depicts you as a great humanitarian . . . you are an old egotist, Father" (Bergman, 1957, p. 32). Along the journey, Borg engages in other encounters with Marianne and others, and he is visited by vivid dreams and memories about the past. These dreams and memories are extremely humiliating to him. He comes to realize that throughout his life he has been an isolated onlooker, moralistically aloof, and in many ways incapable of love. We see, then, that Borg's initial sense of integrity was superficial; as he imagines death and reviews his life, he confronts its many failures.

In the end, however, Borg's insights do not lead to a final despair but to a new acceptance of the past. While he is receiving his Jubilee Doctorate, which by now has become a rather trivial event, he begins to see "a remarkable causality" in the events of his life—an insight that sounds remarkably similar to Erikson's statement that ego integrity includes a sense of the inevitable order of the past. Equally impressive, though, is a change in character. At the end of the film, Borg expresses his love for Marianne and offers to help her and his son.

Through this film, we see why Erikson emphasized the importance of both the positive and negative poles of his crises. Borg's initial sense of integrity was superficial and unconvincing. He acquired a more meaningful sense of integrity only after confronting his life thoroughly and answering to some existential despair (Erikson, 1976, p. 23).

Erikson and Bergman, then, are pointing to an inner struggle that we are apt to miss when we look at older people. We are aware of their many physical and social difficulties, and we may deplore the fact that older people seem so "useless." We may then try to correct our perceptions by finding examples of older people who are more "useful," energetic, and engaged in external affairs. But we are still evaluating the elderly on the basis of external behavior. We fail to consider the *inner* struggle. We fail to see that the quiet older person may be grappling in some way with the most important of all questions: Was my life, as I face death, a meaningful one? What makes a life meaningful?

This inner struggle tends to make the older person something of a philosopher, and out of the struggle grows the ego strength of *wisdom*. Wisdom may be expressed in many ways, but it always reflects a thoughtful, hopeful effort to find the value and meaning of life in the face of death (Erikson, 1976, p. 23; 1982, pp. 61–62).

THEORETICAL ISSUES

Why Erikson's Theory Is a Stage Theory

In Chapters 6 and 7 we saw that Piaget and Kohlberg believed that cognitive stages should meet several criteria. Erikson's stages deal more with emotional development, but they basically meet the same criteria. That is, the stages (1) describe qualitatively different behaviors, (2) refer to general issues, (3) unfold in an invariant sequence, and (4) are culturally universal. Let us examine these points in turn.

1. The Stages Refer to Qualitatively Different Behavior Patterns. If development were just a matter of gradual quantitative change, any division into stages would be arbitrary. Erikson's stages, however, give us a good sense of how behavior is qualitatively different at different points. Children at the autonomy stage sound very different from those at the trust stage; they are much more independent. Children at the initiative stage are different again. Whereas children who are establishing a sense of autonomy defy authority and keep others out, children with a sense of initiative are more daring and imaginative, running vigorously about, making big plans, and initiating new activities. Behavior has a distinctive flavor at each stage.

2. The Stages Describe General Issues. As I have emphasized, stages refer to general characteristics or issues. Erikson went beyond Freud's relatively specific focus on body zones and attempted to delineate the general issues at each period. At the oral stage, for example, he showed that it is not just the stimulation of this zone that is important but the general mode of taking in and, more generally still, the development of a sense of trust in one's providers. Similarly, at each stage Erikson tried to isolate the most general issue faced by the individual in the social world.

3. The Stages Unfold in an Invariant Sequence. All stage theories imply an invariant sequence, and Erikson's is no exception. He said that each stage is present in some form throughout life, but each reaches its own crisis at a specific time and in a specific order.

Erikson's claim is based on the assumption that his sequence is partly the product of *biological maturation*. As he put it, the child obeys "inner laws of development, namely those laws which in his prenatal period had formed one organ after another and which now create a succession of potentialities for significant interaction with those around him" (Erikson, 1963, p. 67). At the second stage, for example, biological maturation ushers in a sense of autonomy. Because of maturation, children can stand on their own two feet, control their sphincter muscles, walk, use words such as *me, mine,* and *no,* and so on. At the third stage, maturation prompts a new sexual interest, along with capacities for imaginative play, curiosity, and vigorous locomotion.

At the same time, *societies* have evolved such that they invite and meet this inner, maturational succession of potentialities. When, for example, the child at the autonomy stage demonstrates a new degree of self-control, socializing agents consider the child ready for training. For example, they begin toilet training. The result is the battle of wills, between child and society, which creates the crisis of this period. Similarly, when children become recklessly ambitious with respect to sexual matters, societies decide it is now time to introduce their particular sexual prohibitions, creating the core conflict at the third stage. Thus the succession of crises is produced by inner maturation on the one hand and social forces on the other.

4. The Stages Are Cultural Universals.   Erikson believed his stages can be applied to all cultures. You might see how the stages would be universal to the extent they are maturationally governed, but you may still be skeptical, for you know how widely cultures differ.

Erikson, too, was aware of the vast differences among cultures. In fact, he wanted to show readers how cultures handle the stages differently according to their different value systems. For example, the Lakota provide their children with a long and indulgent period of nursing; one of their goals is to get children to trust others and to become generous themselves (1963, pp. 134–140). Our society, in contrast, discourages dependency. Compared to other cultures, we wean our infants very early. We do not seem to want our children to learn to depend on or trust others too much, but to become independent. Independence and free mobility seem part of our cultural ethos, from the pioneer days to the present time (chap. 8).

What Erikson did claim is that all cultures address themselves to the *same issues.* All cultures try to provide their children with consistent care, regulate their extreme wish to do everything their own way, and instill incest taboos. And, as children grow, all cultures ask them to learn the tools and skills of their technology, to find a workable adult identity, to establish bonds of intimacy, to care for the next generation, and to face death with integrity. All cultures attempt to achieve these tasks because culture itself is a part of the evolutionary process; in the course of evolution, those groups that failed in these tasks had less chance of surviving. Unless, for example, cultures could get their members to sacrifice some of their independence for the needs of others (at the autonomy stage), to begin to learn the skills and tools of the society (at the industry stage), and to care for the next generation (at the generativity stage), they probably did not endure.[1]

The Question of Hierarchic Integration.   Piagetians, you may recall, define their stages in terms of a fifth point; they view them as hierarchic integrations. This concept has been used somewhat differently by different writers, but in a stage theory it basically means earlier structures are reintegrated into new, dominant structures. In Erikson's theory, such a process does occur at certain stages, such as adolescence. As young people achieve a new sense of identity, they reorganize a good deal of their personality in the pursuit of dominant goals or life plans. But the concept of hierarchic integration does not apply to all the stages. For example, the issues at the stage of autonomy versus shame and doubt are not reorganized or reintegrated into the next stage, initiative versus guilt. The new stage simply raises new concerns, leaving the earlier stage in the background, in much the same form as before. Thus the concept of hierarchic integration does not seem to characterize development at all of Erikson's stages (see Kohlberg, 1969a, p. 353).

Must We Go Through All the Stages?

We sometimes hear that if we don't achieve a good measure of success at one of Erikson's stages, we may be unable to go on to the next stage. This is wrong. In Erikson's theory, we must, if we live long enough, go through all the stages. The reason has to do with the forces that move us from stage to stage: biological maturation and social expectations. These forces push us along according to a certain timetable, whether we have been successful at earlier stages or not.

Consider, for example, a boy who has been unable to attain much of a sense of industry. When he reaches puberty, he must grapple with the issues of identity even though he is not really ready to do so. Because of biological changes, he finds himself troubled by an upsurge of sexual feelings and by a rapidly changing body. At the same time, social pressures force him to cope with problems of dating and to start thinking about his future occupation. It matters little to the larger society that he is still unsure about his own skills. His society has its own timetable, and by the time he is 20 or so, he will feel pressure to decide on a career. In the same way, he will find himself confronting each new stage in the sequence.

Each of us, then, must go through all the stages, whether we have traversed the earlier stages well or not. What is true is that success at earlier stages affects the chances of success at later ones. Children who developed a firm sense of trust in their caretakers can afford to leave them and

---

[1]Darwin had a similar view, as discussed in Chapter 3.

independently explore the environment. In contrast, children who lack trust—who are afraid to let caretakers out of sight—are less able to develop a sense of autonomy. (Conceptualized slightly differently, it is the child who has developed a favorable balance of trust over mistrust who ventures into the world full of *hope* and anticipation, energetically testing new powers of independent action.) In a similar way, a favorable outcome at each stage affects the chances of a positive outcome at the subsequent stage. But whatever the outcomes, maturational and social forces require the child to face the issues at each new stage.

Comparison with Piaget

We have now reviewed the two most influential stage theories in the developmental literature: Piaget's cognitive-developmental theory and Erikson's psychoanalytic theory. In many respects, the theories are different, as briefly noted before. Broadly speaking, the most basic differences are these.

Erikson's theory describes a variety of feelings we bring to tasks; Piaget's theory focuses on intellectual development. This development, for Piaget, is not motivated by biological maturation and social forces, but by the child's efforts to solve cognitive problems. As children encounter problems they cannot handle with their existing cognitive structures, they become challenged and curious and construct more elaborate structures. Since the driving force is the child's curiosity, there is no reason why the child must go through all the stages; if a child is not curious about an area (e.g., mathematics), he or she may never reach the highest stages in that area. Thus, where maturation and social pressures drive us through all of Erikson's stages, ready or not, we only go through Piaget's stages to the extent we are intellectually motivated to build new structures.

Such differences seem large. Nevertheless, both Erikson and Piaget gave us stage theories, attempting to describe the most general qualitative shifts in behavior. Moreover, they often seemed to be presenting different perspectives on the same basic developments. Let us look at how this is so.

1. *Trust.* As Erikson (1964, pp. 116–117) observed, both Piaget and he were concerned with the infant's development of a secure image of external objects. Erikson discussed the child's growing reliance on the predictability and dependability of people, whereas Piaget documented the developing sense of permanent things. Thus both were concerned with the child's growing faith in the stability of the world.[2]

2. *Autonomy.* As children develop a sense of trust in their caretakers, they become increasingly independent. Secure in their knowledge that others will be there when needed, they are free to explore the world on their own.

---

[2]For research exploring these parallels, see Bell, 1970; Flavell, 1977, p. 54; and Gouin-Décarie, 1965.

Piaget pointed to a similar process. As children gain the conviction that objects are permanent, they can act increasingly independently of them. For example, when his daughter Jacqueline's ball rolled under the sofa, she was no longer bound to the spot where she last saw it. She now knew that the object was permanent, even if hidden, and could therefore try out alternative routes for finding it.

3. *Initiative.* At this stage, between about 3 and 6 years, Erikson and the Freudians emphasize the child's consuming curiosity, wealth of fantasy, and daring imagination. As Erikson said, "Both language and locomotion permit him to expand his imagination over so many things that he cannot avoid frightening himself with what he has dreamed and thought up" (1959, p. 75).

Piaget's view of the thinking at this period was remarkably similar. As Flavell says,

The preoperational child is the child of wonder; his cognition appears to us naive, impression-bound, and poorly organized. There is an essential lawlessness about his world without, of course, this fact in any way entering his awareness to inhibit the zest and flights of fancy with which he approaches new situations. Anything is possible because nothing is subject to lawful constraints. (1963, p. 211)

For Piaget, then, the fantasy and imagination of the phallic-age child owes much to the fact that the child is in the preoperational period—a time in which thoughts run free because they are not yet tied to the systematic logic the child will develop at the next stage.

4. *Industry.* For Erikson and the Freudians, the fantasies and fears of the oedipal child are temporarily buried during the latency stage, which lasts from about age 6 to 11 years. Frightening wishes and fantasies are repressed, and the child's interests expand outward; the child intently tries to master the realistic skills and tools of the culture. In general, this is a relatively calm period; children seem more self-composed.

Piaget, too, would lead us to believe the 6- to 11-year-old is more stable, realistic, and organized than the younger child. For Piaget, this change is not the result of the repression of emotions and dangerous wishes; rather, it comes about because, intellectually, the child has entered the stage of concrete operations. The child can now separate fact from fancy, can see different perspectives on a problem, and can work logically and systematically on concrete tasks. Intellectually, then, the child is in a stage of equilibrium with the world, and this contributes to his or her overall stability and composure. Erikson himself seemed to have concrete operations in mind when he described this period: He said that at this time the child's "exuberant imagination is tamed and harnessed by the laws of impersonal things" (1963, p. 258).

5. *Identity.* In Erikson's view, the calm of the preceding period gives way to the turbulence and uncertainty of adolescence. Adolescents are confused by physical changes and pressures to make social commitments. They wonder who they are and what their place in society will be.

Piaget had little to say about physical changes in adolescence, but his insights into cognitive development help us understand why this can be an identity-searching time. During the stage of concrete operations, the child's thought was pretty much tied to the here and now. But with the growth of formal operations, the adolescent's thought soars into the distant future and into the realm of the purely hypothetical. Consequently, adolescents can now entertain limitless possibilities about who they are and what they will become. Formal operational capacities, then, may contribute to the self-questioning of this period (see Inhelder & Piaget, 1955, chap. 18).

PRACTICAL IMPLICATIONS

Clinical Work: A Case Illustration

Clinical psychologists and other mental health workers have found Erikson's concepts very useful. We can get a sense of this from Erikson's own work with one of his cases, a 4-year-old boy he called Peter.

Peter suffered from a psychogenic megacolon, an enlarged colon that resulted from Peter's emotionally based habit of retaining his fecal matter for up to a week at a time. Through conversations with Peter and his family, Erikson learned that Peter developed this symptom shortly after his nurse, an Asian girl, had been dismissed. Peter, it seems, had begun "attacking the nurse in a rough-housing way, and the girl had seemed to accept and quietly enjoy his decidedly 'male' approach" (Erikson, 1963, p. 56). In her culture, such behavior was considered normal. However, Peter's mother, living in our culture, felt there was something wrong about Peter's sudden maleness and the way the nurse indulged it. So she got rid of the nurse. By way of explanation, the nurse told Peter she was going to have a baby of her own, and that she preferred to care for babies, not big boys like Peter. Soon afterward, Peter developed the megacolon.

Erikson learned that Peter imagined that he himself was pregnant, a fantasy through which he tried to keep the nurse by identifying with her. But, more generally, we can see how Peter's behavior regressed in terms of stages. Initially, he had begun displaying the attacking, sexual behavior of the initiative stage, but he found that it led to a tragic loss. So he regressed to an anal mode. He was expressing, through his body, his central need: *to hold on*. When Erikson found the right moment, he interpreted Peter's wishes to him, and Peter's symptom was greatly alleviated.

Sometimes students, when hearing of Peter's behavior, suggest his symptom was a means of "getting attention." This interpretation is used frequently by the behaviorists. We note, however, that Erikson's approach was different. He was concerned with the meaning of the symptom for Peter, with what Peter was trying to express through it. Through his body, Peter was unconsciously trying to say, "I need to hold on to what I've lost." Erikson and other psychoanalysts believe that instead of changing a child's behavior through external reinforcements such as attention, it is best to speak to the child's fears and to what the child may be unconsciously trying to say.

Thoughts on Child Rearing

Over the years, Erikson applied clinical insights to many problems, including those in education, ethics, and politics. He also had a special interest in child rearing.

As we briefly mentioned in our discussion of trust, Erikson was concerned with the problem facing parents in our changing society. Modern parents are often unable or unwilling simply to follow traditional child-rearing precepts; they would like to bring up their children in more personal, tolerant ways, based on new information and education (Erikson, 1959, p. 99). Unfortunately, modern child-rearing advice is often contradictory and frightens the new parent with its accounts of how things can go wrong. Consequently, the new parent is anxious and uncertain. This is a serious problem, Erikson believed, for, as we have seen, it is important that the parent convey to the child a basic security, a feeling the world is a calm and secure place.

Erikson suggested that parents can derive some inner security from religious faith. Beyond this, he suggested parents heed their fundamental "belief in the species" (1963, p. 267). By this, Erikson meant something similar to Gesell. Parents should recognize that it is not all up to them to form the child; children largely grow according to an inner, maturational timetable. As Erikson said, "It is important to realize that . . . the healthy child, if halfway properly guided, merely obeys and on the whole can be trusted to obey inner laws of development" (p. 67). So it is all right for parents to follow their inclination to smile when their baby smiles, make room for their child to walk when he or she tries to, and so on. They can feel secure that it is all right to follow the baby's own biological ground plan.

Erikson also hoped that parents can recognize the basic inequality between child and adult. The human child, in contrast to the young of other species, undergoes a much longer period of dependency and helplessness. Parents, therefore, must be careful to resist the temptation to take out their own frustrations on the weaker child. They must resist, for example, the impulse to dominate the child because they themselves feel helpless with others. Parents should also be careful to avoid trying to shape the child into the person they wanted to become, thereby ignoring the child's own capacities and inclinations. Erikson said, in conclusion, "If we will only learn to let live, the plan for growth is all there" (1959, p. 100).

EVALUATION

Erikson certainly broadened psychoanalytic theory. He delineated the most general issues at each of Freud's stages and enlarged the stage sequence so it now covers the entire life cycle. Erikson also gave us a new appreciation of how social factors enter into the various stages. For example, he showed that adolescents are struggling not just to master their impulses but to find an identity in the larger social world.

Erikson, finally, gave Freudian theory new insights into the possibilities for healthy development. He did this primarily by making wider use of the concept of maturation than Freud did. In Freud's view, maturation directs the course of the instinctual drives, which must undergo a good measure of repression. For Erikson, maturation also promotes the growth of the ego modes and the general ego qualities such as autonomy and initiative.[3] Erikson, to be sure, discussed the difficulties in attaining these qualities, but he did give us a better picture of how ego growth is possible. By suggesting that healthy development is tied to a maturational ground plan, Erikson moved Freudian theory in the developmental direction of Rousseau, Gesell, and others.

Erikson's theory has also met with various criticisms. Robert White (1960) argued that Erikson tried too hard to link the various aspects of ego development to Freud's libidinal zones. Erikson said that for each zone, there is a characteristic ego mode of interaction with the world. However, White argued, these modes fail to capture many of the child's activities. For example, many of the young child's efforts to achieve autonomy—such as the child's loud "no's" and vigorous walking—seem unrelated to the anal modes of retention and elimination. White himself proposed we think of ego growth as a general tendency toward competence—a tendency that includes locomotion, exploration, and autonomous action without any necessary connection to Freud's zones.

In a different vein, we might fault Erikson for a degree of conceptual vagueness. He wrote in a beautiful, flowing prose, but he left many conceptual matters unclear. For example, he provided new insights for the potential for growth in old age, when people examine their lives and search for wisdom, but he did not clearly indicate how this is part of the maturational process. It may be that there is a biological tendency to review one's life (Butler, 1963),

---

[3]Erikson's suggestion that ego growth has maturational roots follows the lead of Hartmann, discussed in the preceding chapter.

but Erikson was not explicit on this matter. Similarly, he failed to spell out how maturation contributes to the other stages of adulthood.

Erikson was aware of his general vagueness. As he once said, "I came to psychology from art, which may explain, if not justify, the fact that the reader will find me painting contexts and backgrounds where he would rather have me point to facts and concepts" (1963, p. 17).

Erikson's conceptual vagueness may partly explain why empirical research on his theory has been slow to emerge, although there have been some solid efforts. Most notably, James Marcia (1966) has constructed measures of different identity states, and these measures are related to other variables. For example, young people with foreclosed identities—who have simply accepted handed-down occupational goals and values without themselves struggling with alternatives—seem to be most often found at the level of conventional thought on Kohlberg's scale. In contrast, those who have achieved a sense of identity after a personal struggle are more often represented by postconventional moral thinking (Podd, 1972; Kroger 2007, p. 105). Those who have found their identity after a personal exploration also feel more independent and in control of their lives (Berk, 2009, p. 467).

Researchers also have been examining the family contexts that best allow young people to find their own identities (Kroger, 2007, p. 77). All such research is encouraging. Erikson's work is so rich and profound that it deserves energetic scientific investigation.

CHAPTER 13

Mahler's Separation/ Individuation Theory

BIOGRAPHICAL INTRODUCTION

Erikson developed a grand, sweeping theory that gave Freudian thought a much more social and cultural emphasis. Such broad theories are impressive, but it's also possible to advance theory by focusing on a more limited set of details. A striking example of this is Mahler's long and careful study of mother/infant interactions. She showed how babies become separate people within a relationship, and in the process Mahler cast light on universal dimensions of human life.

Margaret S. Mahler (1897–1985) was born in the small town of Sopron, Hungary, a short distance from Vienna, Austria. In her memoirs, she described her mother, a homemaker, as a beautiful, narcissistic, and unhappy woman who didn't want Mahler as a baby. As a result, Mahler was grateful for the interest her father, a physician, took in her. "I became very much my father's daughter," Mahler said. "It was to my father's world, the world of the intellect, of science, of medicine, that I turned" (1988, pp. 4, 7).

When Mahler was 4 years old, her mother gave birth to another girl, to whom her mother devoted more affection. Mahler was completely fascinated by this tender care and spent hours silently observing the mother/baby interactions. In fact, Mahler said, "I do not think it an exaggeration to say that my own mother and sister represented the first mother-child pair that I investigated" (p. 5).

Mahler described herself as a very insecure teenager and young woman. But she also showed early academic promise, and at the age of 16 became only the second girl from her town to seek higher education, which was considered the province of males. She went to a school in Budapest, where she became best friends with a girl whose family was part of a group of pioneering psychoanalysts. They treated Mahler as if she were part of the family, and after some indecision, Mahler decided to pursue a career in medicine followed by psychoanalysis. (Her friend, Alice Balint, also became a distinguished psychoanalyst.)

Mahler received her medical degree from the University of Jena in 1922. During the next several years, she practiced pediatrics and child psychiatry and completed psychoanalytic training. In 1936 she married Paul Mahler, and in 1938 the couple came to the United States to escape the Nazis. They settled in New York City, where Mahler's work on emotional disorders of childhood resulted in several appointments, including a professorship at the Albert Einstein College of Medicine. She also spent years commuting to Philadelphia to teach at its Psychoanalytic Institute.

On a personal level, Mahler retained a considerable amount of insecurity throughout her life, and she sometimes acted in demanding or mistrustful ways. But many sensitive and creative people were committed to working with her because they found her insights so valuable.

OVERVIEW OF CONCEPTS AND METHODS

During the 1940s and 1950s, two striking advances were made in the conceptualization of childhood psychoses—the most severe emotional disorders. The first advance was made by Leo Kanner (1943), who suggested that many strange symptoms fit into a syndrome he called *early infantile autism*. This is a disorder in which children are extremely isolated and aloof. They often avoid eye contact or seem to look right through you. Children with autism also display other symptoms, including problems with language. Many are mute, and those who do talk often engage in echolalia, the meaningless repetition of sounds. If you ask the child, "What's your name?" the child answers, "What's your name?" (Lovaas, 1973). If health workers are alert to the disorder, they can often diagnosis it very early—before the second year of life.

A second diagnostic advance was made by Mahler. Beginning with a footnote in a 1949 paper, Mahler conceptualized a disorder that usually appears in the third or fourth year of life or a bit later. In these cases, the children have formed a relationship with caretakers but are afraid to separate themselves out of it. They cling to their mother, afraid to move out into the world. Using the biological term *symbiosis* as a metaphor, Mahler called this disorder *symbiotic psychosis* (see Mahler, 1968, pp. 72–75).

In Mahler's view, these disturbances aren't simply bizarre occurrences but rather as deviations from normal development. As we can see in Table 13.1, Mahler suggested that normal development begins with a normal autistic phase; the baby is inwardly focused and wards off many stimuli. Next, the baby progresses to a normal symbiotic phase; the baby now attends more fully to outer sensations, but with the illusion of being at one with the mother. Then, with the support of the mother, the baby becomes increasingly independent, especially as she becomes a toddler.

TABLE 13.1   Mahler's Phases

AGE	PHASE	HIGHLIGHTS
Birth to 1 month	Normal Autism	Baby focuses on inner physiological state
1 to 5 months	Normal Symbiosis	Baby responds more to outer stimuli but is under the illusion that she and mother are one
5 to 9 months	Differentiation	On mother's lap, pulls back to study her and world—has "hatched" look
9 to 12 months	Early Practicing	Uses mother as base to explore
12 to 15 months	Practicing	Explores world with bold exhilaration
15 to 24 months	Rapprochement	Realizes she needs mother after all—but still seeks independence
24 to 30 months	Beginnings of Object Constancy	Creates an internal image of mother and can function apart from her

In the case of autism, Mahler suggested, the child doesn't get very far out of the normal autistic phase. In the case of symbiotic psychosis, the child does go through the symbiotic phase; however, she doesn't derive bedrock feelings of comfort and support from the relationship. As she becomes more independent, she experiences some separations as so upsetting that she desperately tries to regain the illusion of symbiotic union with the mother. Mahler suggested that the symbiotic psychosis, appearing later than autism, is more varied, and symbiotic psychotic children sometimes regress to an autistic state (1968, pp. 14–22, 71–81).

A special aspect of Mahler's work was her continuous effort to formulate and revise her ideas on the basis of research on ongoing mother/infant relationships. She developed many of her thoughts on symbiotic psychosis as a result of her work with Manuel Furer in a therapeutic nursery for mothers and disturbed children. Mahler's concept of normal development, which is our focus in this chapter, also drew heavily on observations of mothers and their infants in a nursery setting. Between 1959 and 1968, Mahler and her staff observed and interacted with 38 normal mother/infant pairs in an indoor play area. The space included an area for the mothers to sit, read, sip coffee, and talk to one another—and from which they had a full view and free access to their children at play. The babies typically entered the project when they were between 2 and 5 months of age and left when they were 3 years old. The observations (which included films, family interviews, and home visits) were analyzed somewhat informally—largely through staff discussions—rather than statistically. The observations also focused primarily on the phases during which the child normally moves out of symbiosis and achieves independence, rather than symbiosis itself. Mahler's thinking about the earlier phases, normal autism and symbiosis, drew more heavily on her work with disturbed children and adults and the observations of other investigators (Bergman, 1999, p. 6; Mahler, Pine, & Bergman, 1975, pp. 39, 233–271).

The observations of the normal babies and mothers were extremely rich and were summarized in her 1975 book, *The Psychological Birth of the Human Infant* (coauthored by Fred Pine and Anni Bergman). The book tells the story of how the baby naturally emerges out of symbiosis and becomes a separate individual. Let us now look at Mahler's full sequence of phases in more detail.

PHASES OF NORMAL DEVELOPMENT

Mahler suggested that the phases of normal development overlap, and in some ways the emotional qualities of each persist throughout the life cycle. But the developmental achievement of each phase normally occurs at a certain time in infancy and early childhood (Mahler et al., 1975, pp. 3, 48).

The Normal Autistic Phase
(birth to 1 month)

Mahler said the newborn (the baby up to the age of 1 month) "spends most of his day in a half-sleeping, half-waking state"; he wakes primarily when hunger or other tensions arouse him from within (p. 41). During this time, the newborn infant is achieving a new physiological balance, and it's the baby's inner physiological state—not the outside world—that holds the most interest for him. In fact, the newborn seems protected from the outside by what Freud called a *stimulus barrier,* a kind of shell that keeps out extremes in stimuli. Mahler recognized there are also brief periods when the newborn is quietly alert to his surroundings. But for the most part, the newborn acts as if his inner sensations, not outer sensations, matter.

In recent years, a number of researchers, using advanced film technology, have suggested that infants are more responsive to their mothers than is apparent to the naked eye. According to Mahler's coworker Anni Bergman (1999), Mahler was aware of these findings and privately expressed doubts about the autistic phase. But it still may mark something important in development.

The Normal Symbiotic Phase (1 to 5 months)

At about 1 month of age, the baby starts taking more pleasure in stimuli from the mother—from certain touches, smells, tones of voice, and ways of being held. But the baby doesn't know these sensations are separate from him. He still lives in a twilight state in which he is still under the illusion that he and the mother are one. Mahler said that this undifferentiated state, which we can only infer, is what she meant by "symbiosis" (1975, pp. 8, 44).

The first clear sign that the baby now takes pleasure in outer sensations—which are mainly experiences of the mother—is the baby's social smile. Sometime during the second month, the baby starts staring at the mother's face, and, after doing so over a period of several days, the baby looks into her eyes and bursts into the first social smile. The mother's face isn't the only one that elicits a gaze or smile, but she is likely to be the one who gazes and smiles back. She also talks to the baby in the baby's high-pitched voice and imitates the baby's coos. The deep mutual gaze seems to be the kind that is shared by people in love. It is the kind that melts down boundaries. The mutual gazing, together with the mutual smiles and the mother's imitations of the baby's sounds, all reinforce the baby's illusion of oneness (L. Kaplan, 1978, p. 111; Mahler et al., 1975, p. 45).

According to Mahler, the baby's symbiotic state is marked by a sense of omnipotence, a sense that the world is in perfect harmony with his wishes. The mother fosters this illusion through her empathic sensitivity to the baby's cues. She senses that the baby is hungry and makes the nipple available; she senses his need to rest and allows his body to mold into hers. As he melts into her body, he apparently has a feeling that the world is in complete harmony with his needs.

Anni Bergman adds that although we can't know what the baby actually experiences, mothers often report that they feel a sense of union with their babies. They say that they "lose their usual way of being in the world. They have eloquently articulated something like a symbiotic state in themselves that parallels the state that has been postulated in the baby" (Bergman, 1999, p. 8).

Mahler recognized that mothers cannot be perfectly empathic; no mother can read her baby's every need. To an extent, babies themselves learn to help her; they learn that certain cues, such as the mother's silences, mean that they must let her know what they need. But there are times when all babies must simply suffer cold, bad tastes, tension, hunger, loud noises, dust, bright lights, and so on. Inevitably, then, babies not only mold comfortably into their mothers' bodies, but sometimes stiffen as they react to noxious stimuli. And stiffening has its uses. It's an early way of moving apart from the mother—differentiating from her (L. Kaplan, 1978, pp. 100–104; Mahler et al., 1975, p. 53).

On balance, though, the baby needs a responsive, comforting mother. Mahler said that the baby doesn't need a perfect mother, but, borrowing phrases from D. W. Winnicott, the baby needs a "good enough" mother or an "ordinarily devoted" mother. Mahler thought good mothering is a biologically rooted necessity. The human infant, in comparison to other species, is more helpless and dependent for a much longer time and needs a mother to ward off intrusive stimuli and protect the baby's well-being (1975, pp. 7, 45, 49).

Nurturant mothering is also necessary for the baby's psychological development. Mahler said that the symbiotic phase is important for the initial development of what Erikson called a sense of trust. The baby needs to feel enough consistent comfort and relief of tensions to develop faith in the world as a good place. Moreover, the sense of pleasurable symbiosis—of unity with the mother—provides the growing baby with a sense of what Mahler called a "safe anchor." As the baby emerges from the symbiotic state and turns increasingly outward, she doesn't feel adrift and alone. The baby feels there is a safe anchor of goodness and comfort (1975, pp. 45, 59, 110).

The Separation/Individuation Process

The Differentiation Subphase (5 to 9 months).   The symbiotic state sounds like it can be a period of blissful unity. Why, then, would a child want to leave it? Mahler believed the baby is maturationally driven to develop independent functioning and explore the wider world. Powerful inner forces prompt the baby to scan the surroundings, to try to roll over, to sit up by oneself, to reach out to grab things, and so on.

By 5 months, the baby has already been looking at the surroundings outside the mother and knows the mother is different from others. The baby now smiles at the mother and familiar people, but not others. But this awareness has developed gradually and almost passively. At 5 months, the baby's investigations become more focused, prolonged, and active. Now, even while nursing, babies spend considerable time looking at things besides the mother. When they finish nursing, they turn away to look at objects in the environment. At about 6 months of age, they pull their bodies away from the mother to get a better look at her. (This pulling back is in sharp contrast to the earlier molding.) As babies look at the mother, they touch her face and body and grab things she is wearing, such as glasses or a pin, to inspect them. They also start a "checking back" pattern, actively comparing the mother to other people; first they look at the mother, then at the other person, then back at the mother again. All in all, the baby is no longer merged with the mother. The baby is more of an independent person who is actively studying her mother and the outside world. Mahler said the baby has *hatched* (pp. 53–56).

During this period, babies also inspect strangers tactilely and visually. They usually do so in a very sober mood, which is different from the happier way in which they examine their mothers. Mahler, borrowing a term from Sylvia Brody, called this behavior "customs inspection" (p. 56). At some point, usually at about 7 months of age, many babies, but not all, exhibit *stranger anxiety.* In some babies, stranger anxiety is very acute and they cry. Mahler found this was most common in children whose symbiotic period had been most strained. These babies hadn't developed the beginnings of basic trust and didn't anticipate goodness in interpersonal relationships.

The children who had enjoyed harmonious symbiotic phases typically showed little fear of strangers, looking at them with wonderment and curiosity (pp. 57–58).

As we saw in our discussion of Bowlby (Chapter 3), babies at this time also show *separation anxiety*. They become upset, for example, when the mother leaves them alone. Mahler found that separation anxiety at this time primarily takes the form of low-keyedness—a general lowering of mood. The speculation is that the baby turns inward in an effort to hold on to the image of the absent mother (Bergman, 1999, p. 13).

During this phase, then, the baby is moving out and away from the mother, finding interesting things in the world and experiencing fears as well. Mahler said that technically, two processes are underway. One is separation, which is mainly increased physical distance from the mother. The other is individuation, which includes the ego functions involved in exploring the world perceptually, remembering where the mother and things are, and developing an image of one's powers (Mahler et al., 1975, pp. 63–64).

Early Practicing (9 to 12 months).   The practicing phase is ushered in by the baby's ability to crawl. As the baby moves about on all fours, and then stands and coasts along while holding things, she becomes quite enthusiastic about exploring the wider world. She often moves some distance away from the mother, using her mother as a *home base*. As Ainsworth observed (see Chapter 3), the baby explores new things in her environment, often becoming very absorbed in them, then checks to make sure the mother is present (or even returning to her for "refueling") before venturing forth again.

During these explorations, the mother's attitude is very important. Many mothers—including those who had difficulty with the constant closeness and intimacy of the earlier months—enjoy the baby's new independence. They sense that what the baby needs as the baby explores the world is just the mother's stable presence—her quiet availability. Other mothers become anxious or ambivalent about the child's explorations and have trouble serving as a secure home base. They might try to interrupt the child's activities or communicate their anxiety to the child. In such cases, the child's enthusiasm for moving out into the world is dampened.

The Practicing Subphase Proper (12 to 15 months).   Mahler emphasized the power of the innate drive toward locomotion and exploration, and babies' pleasure in these activities becomes intense once they can walk. The baby, who is now a real toddler, becomes exhilarated by her new ability to move about and explore the world and takes pure delight in the discoveries she makes. Everything she comes across, animate or inanimate, is a source of wonder. The toddler acts as if the entire world was made for her investigations—that when it comes to exploration, "the world is my oyster" (Mahler et al., 1975, p. 71). Knocks and falls don't bother her in the least, and she often seems impervious to the mother's presence as well. The child does, to be sure, occasionally look back to check on the mother's presence, to make sure the mother is still available. But the striking feature of this phase is the way the child becomes so thrilled and absorbed in her explorations. This is a period when the child "has a love affair with the world" (p. 74).

Mahler said this is a precious time when the child's exuberance can overcome emotional fragility. Only in cases when the mother is too intrusive or unavailable is enthusiasm greatly diminished. Ordinarily, the child's pleasure in vigorous locomotion and exploration is immense.

Rapprochement (15 to 24 months). Mahler and her colleagues observed that at 15 or 16 months, the toddlers in the nursery underwent a major shift. Whereas they had been joyfully walking, running, jumping, and playing without much regard to the mother, they now became very aware of her. They began bringing her objects they had found in their explorations—a piece of cookie, a toy, a bit of cellophane, a rock, a tricycle. They also began monitoring her whereabouts and were no longer so impervious to knocks and falls. Now they felt the pain and wanted the mother to come over and ease the pain. In short, they became keenly aware of the mother and their need for her (Bergman, 1999, pp. 18–20). It's as if the toddler, who during the practicing phase adventured into the world with a sense of omnipotence, suddenly thinks, "Hey, where's my mother? What am I doing out here all by myself; I need her."

Mahler believed the change is brought about by the kind of cognitive development described by Piaget. During all their explorations of the outer world, as well as their quiet play, the toddlers have been becoming increasingly aware of how objects exist and function apart from themselves. It's just a matter of time before they think about their mother as a separate person and all she does for them. Thus it dawns on the toddlers that the world is *not* their oyster, that they are in fact "relatively helpless, small and separate individual[s]" (Mahler et al., 1975, p. 78). In Erikson's stage theory, the child begins to experience doubt.

During the next several months, the child enters something of a crisis. She is torn between conflicting aims. She wants to maintain and exert her autonomy, but she also wants her mother. At one moment she emphatically says, "No," to every parental demand or request, asserting her refusal to submit to any authority. At the next moment, she clings to the mother or follows her about, demanding the mother's constant attention. She woos her mother with gifts and objects such as books, knowing the mother believes in reading to her. Many children enjoy a darting-away game in which the parent chases and catches them. The game seems fun because the child feels suddenly autonomous, running away, but also is reunited in the catching.

Sometimes the child is overcome by indecision. For example, in the nursery, children would sometimes stand on the threshold of a new playroom, uncertain whether or not to enter it. Standing on the threshold seemed to symbolize their conflict—whether to venture into a new room and leave the mother, or to stay with her (p. 96).

This is a difficult time for the mother. The child's behavior is often disturbing and demanding, and the child herself doesn't always seem to know what she wants. Mahler again stressed the importance of the mother's quiet patience and emotional availability (p. 79). If the mother can understand that the child's behavior is a natural development that will run its course—the to-be-expected "terrible twos"—the mother can be patient. She can avoid getting caught up in power struggles or withdrawing in retaliation. Then the child will feel freer to work out things for herself, knowing that her own will is respected.

Beginnings of Emotional Object Constancy (24 to 30 months). The child in the rapprochement crisis seems to be in quite a predicament, and we might wonder, "Just how will the child get over it? How can the child resolve the conflicting needs for autonomy and the mother's care?" In good part, the child does so by developing a positive internal image of the mother that the child can evoke in her absence. Then, even though the child may feel some longing for her, he can go on functioning independently without her. This internal image is called *emotional object constancy* (Mahler et al., 1975, p. 109).

Mahler said the attainment of object constancy has two prerequisites. First, the child must have developed object permanence in Piaget's sense. That is, the child must know that objects (including people) exist even when they are out of sight.

The second prerequisite is what Erikson called basic trust—the sense of the mother as a reliable and predictable person who will be there for the child (1975) when needed. The baby began developing this trust as early as the symbiotic phase and developed it further in the differentiation, practicing, and rapprochement phases (1975, p. 110).

Now, in the present phase, the child needs to internalize the image of a good mother. The internalization process is complex, but the child carries it out largely through make-believe play. In her play, the child lets objects represent parents, other people, and herself and consolidates an image of the mother in her psychic structure. This is not always easy to do because the child may be experiencing some strain with the mother. The child experiences separations and frustrations (including toilet training and perhaps early oedipal issues) and may be angry at the mother. It then becomes difficult for the child to imagine the mother as a whole person who values the child despite the tensions between them. But if positive experiences are sufficient, emotional object constancyemerges. This development is open ended; it is subject to change in the years that follow. But the development of object constancy in this phase is crucial.

PRACTICAL APPLICATIONS

Although our focus is on Mahler's theory of normal development, I would like to note how much her work has helped mental health workers. In the early 1970s, when I began working in a partial hospitalization program, I remember how Mahler's ideas cast light on puzzling psychiatric phenomena. One man told me that when his mother died, he became confused and was taken to a hospital where the intake worker asked him "an incomprehensible question: She asked me to tell her something about myself. I didn't have a clue as to what she meant by 'myself.' I could tell her about my mother and me, but I had never thought about myself as a separate person." This man was describing a symbiotic attachment. Numerous stories like this one convinced me and many others that significant insights into the mysterious roots of psychosis are to be found in Mahler's work.

Mahler's work is most directly relevant to therapists treating disturbed children. Prior to Mahler, it was almost taken as an axiom that therapists should try to treat the child alone in a playroom. Mahler, instead, began working with infants and their mothers, trying to facilitate a more harmonious and pleasurable symbiotic experience. For autistic children, her goal was to move them forward into a symbiotic phase. For symbiotic psychotic children, too, she wanted to foster a more complete and harmonious symbiosis. To many people, this seems puzzling. Shouldn't the goal be for these children to become independent? But Mahler found that these children hadn't experienced the pleasurable union and trust that enabled them to move away from the mother. Instead, with the maturation of motor and cognitive functions, they found themselves separating before they felt emotionally ready. They felt prematurely alone and vulnerable, and new separation experiences (such as beginning nursery school or the birth of a sibling) caused them to fall apart and to cling desperately to their mothers. What they needed was not new encouragement to separate, but to build a sense of the mother as a secure anchor so they could more confidently move out into the world.

When it comes to ordinary child rearing, Mahler repeatedly spoke about the mother's "emotional availability." The normal period of symbiosis gives the baby a feeling of being anchored in a place of comfort and safety, but as the baby becomes a separate individual, she needs to be reassured of her mother's continued availability. The most dramatic example is the way the crawling baby uses her mother as a secure base from which to explore. The child ventures out to investigate the world, checking back and sometimes actually returning to her mother before venturing forth again. The mother's calm, stable presence gives the child the courage to explore the world on her own.

There are numerous other ways that the baby uses the mother's stable presence to learn things on his or her own. If a mother is holding a 6-month-old baby boy, the mother's quiet, calm presence allows him to examine her with his eyes and hands. He gets a chance to learn about her in his own way.

This quality of the caretaker, this unobtrusive presence, is a quality we find highlighted by other theorists. Ainsworth emphasized the baby's use of the mother as a secure base. Montessori, too, spoke on several occasions about the ways the adult's patient presence gives the child opportunities for independent learning. Montessori mentioned, for example, how this can occur when a parent takes a child for a walk. If a father is walking with his 2-year-old daughter in a park, he may adjust to the toddler's own rhythms, stopping when the girl stops to examine things, standing patiently by while she investigates a stick, rock, or puddle of water. As he stands by, he may enjoy the delight she takes in examining the object. The father's presence is necessary for the child's security, but the father doesn't have to teach the child. All he needs to do is be quietly present and available, and the child can learn on her own.

EVALUATION

Many contemporary psychoanalysts, including feminist psychoanalysts (e.g., Benjamin, 1988), have criticized Freudians for focusing too exclusively on the internal dynamics of the isolated individual. Mahler has moved Freudian theory in an interpersonal direction.[1] She has given us a vivid account of how the baby achieves a sense of selfhood within an interpersonal relationship. The baby hatches from a state of merger, becomes increasingly independent, and then struggles with the realization of how dependent she actually is. This back-and-forth process, in which the child deals with needs for both relatedness and separateness, seems to capture universal tensions and conflicts within all human life.

Mahler's theory also has met with some strong criticisms, two by the highly respected psychoanalyst and infant researcher Daniel Stern (1985). First, Stern criticizes Mahler for "pathologizing" infancy. That is, Mahler began with an attempt to understand pathological states (autism and symbiosis) and looked for them in normal infancy. This approach, Stern says, distorts our view of normal development. It would have been better if she had studied normal infant and child development on its own terms. In my view, this criticism has some merit, but it is hardly fatal. The ultimate test of her theory is not its origins, but how well it captures the essence of the child's development.

Stern also argues that Mahler's early phases, especially the autistic phase, are in error. The autistic phase, with its hypothesized stimulus barrier, makes it sound as if the newborn primarily shuts herself off from the outer

---

[1]In psychoanalytic terms, Mahler is said to have contributed to object relations theory; see Greenberg and Mitchell (1983).

world. In fact, Stern points out, growing laboratory research and fine-grained film analyses of mother/infant interactions show that the newborn has a strong interest in external reality and an ability to make sense out of it.

This criticism is a serious one. It apparently stimulated Mahler, in her last years, to consider modifying her concept of normal autism (Bergman, 1999, p. 5). But I believe any major change is still premature. For one thing, capacities elicited in the laboratory don't always reflect typical behavior in normal life. The same is true of high-tech film analyses. Moreover, a considerable amount of research tends to support the autistic concept—the view that babies *are* more focused on inward stimuli than on the outer world. Newborns sleep a great deal and defend themselves firmly against high-intensity stimuli; and although they are interested in the world for brief periods of time, they respond to a rather limited range of stimuli (Fogel, 2009, pp. 212–213).

It's possible to raise other objections to Mahler's work—or point to areas where we need more information. For one thing, Mahler often wrote as if the mother is the only person in the infant's life; we need to know more about the baby's interactions with fathers, children, and others. In addition, Mahler focused more on separation than the formation of new capacities for love and mutuality, so more information is needed on this subject as well.

As psychologists extend Mahler's work into new areas, they are especially interested in how Mahler's concepts might cast light on adolescence. Jane Kroger (2007, p. 96) refers to adolescence as "the second separation-individuation process." It's a time when young people often feel the need to break away from parents and find their own identities, yet they are still emotionally tied to their parents and, after a while, they may develop new and more mature relationships with them. It will be interesting to see how well Mahler's ideas provide a framework for understanding these processes.

I would like to suggest another extension of Mahler—the possibility that children develop a oneness not only with their mothers but also with the natural world. As I mentioned in the chapter on Montessori, the child's experience of nature has received almost no attention in psychology. But in her beautifully written book on Mahler (*Oneness and Separateness*, 1978), Louise Kaplan briefly suggests that the child's attachment to nature is important. When the toddler enters the practicing phase, Kaplan says, the child not only plants his feet "solidly on the earth," but, running through open spaces, "haughtily ignores his mother in the flesh, . . . having discovered a more exciting mother in the world of visible space through which his body glides." He "molds his body to its invisible contours, imagining yet again that he is one with the universe" (p. 169).

The few studies on children in natural settings provide evidence that children do develop feelings of oneness with nature. In a rural New England town, Hart (1979) observed that children (between 3 and 12 years) liked to sit or kneel beside brooks and ponds, staring quietly into the water in a day-dreamlike state, seeming to feel a fluid connection between themselves and the water—a oneness with the world. In Berkeley, California, where the community took up a half acre of asphalt and replaced it with a nature area of ponds, wooded areas, and meadows, the children described a new sense of connection and belonging. The nature area made them "feel at home," like being part of "one big happy family." "Being alone doesn't bother me now" (Moore, 1989, pp. 201–203).

A study of adults' autobiographies produced similar results. Chawla (1990) found that those authors who said they benefited from childhood experiences with nature most commonly referred to a lasting sense of root-edness in the world. The African American minister Howard Thurman said that he was a rather lonely boy who found comfort in the woods and the ocean. Sometimes when he walked along the seashore at night and the ocean was still,

> I had the sense that all things, the sand, the sea, the stars, the night, and I were one lung through which all of life breathed. Not only was I aware of a vast rhythm enveloping all, but I was part of it and it was part of me. (Chawla, 1990, p. 21)

Such early feelings with nature, Thurman said,

> gave me a certain overriding immunity against much of the pain with which I would have to deal in the years ahead when the ocean was only a memory. The sense held: I felt rooted in life, in nature, in existence. (Chawla, 1990, p. 21)

This sense of oneness and rootedness is also expressed in William Wordsworth's great ode (1807). Lamenting the loss of the exquisite attune-ment to nature we had as children, Wordsworth said that we can nevertheless take heart:

> Though nothing can bring back the hour
> Of splendour in the grass, of glory in the flower;
> We will grieve not, rather find
> Strength in what remains behind;
> In the primal sympathy
> Which having been must ever be.

This "primal sympathy," this feeling of "rootedness," is what Mahler thought the mother provides in the early months of life and continues to reinforce, through her availability, as the child becomes separate. Thurman and

Wordsworth are suggesting that the growing child also can find a sense of belonging in nature. Today, of course, we so thoroughly enclose children in an artificial world of computers, TVs, videos, and synthetic materials that they may never develop any such feelings at all. This is a problem we must address, for the early feelings of oneness with nature, like oneness with the mother, may fortify the growing child against feeling too alone in the world.

CHAPTER 14

A Case Study in Psychoanalytic Treatment: Bettelheim on Autism

BIOGRAPHICAL INTRODUCTION

In this chapter I will give a fuller description of psychoanalytic treatment. Such treatments vary of course, and I will not attempt to review the variations here. I have selected Bettelheim's work with children diagnosed with autism because it provides an unusually rich account of child therapy that is within the Rousseauist developmental tradition.

In some respects Bettelheim's work is more classic than contemporary. Today, the most popular therapy for children with autism is Lovaas's adaptation of B. F. Skinner's principles (summarized on pages 196–198 of this book). Even the institution that Bettelheim directed until 1973, the Orthogenic School in Chicago, has since added a mix of new techniques to his core principles. But I believe Bettelheim's treatment exemplifies a philosophical approach that will always guide many thoughtful therapists.

Bruno Bettelheim (1903–1990) grew up and became interested in psychoanalysis in Vienna, Austria. In 1932 Bettelheim and his wife took into their home and began caring for a girl who later would have been diagnosed as suffering from *autism* (Kanner, 1943)—a mysterious condition in which children are totally unresponsive to people. But in 1938 Hitler's invasion of Austria disrupted this home treatment, along with everything else (Goleman, 1990). From 1938 to 1939 Bettelheim was a prisoner in the concentration camps of Dachau and Buchenwald. He wrote detailed accounts of this experience (e.g., 1960) and drew on it in all of his work. After his release, Bettelheim came to the United States and, in 1944, took over the direction of the Orthogenic School in Chicago with the hope that if it was possible to build prison camps powerful enough to destroy human personalities, perhaps it was also possible to create environments that can foster their rebirth (Bettelheim, 1967, p. 8). In this special school and home for children, Bettelheim and his staff treated a wide variety of emotional disorders, but Bettelheim always had a special interest in children with autism and he wrote movingly about his school's treatment of them in *The Empty Fortress* (1967). Bettelheim retired as director of the school in 1973, but he continued to write on many topics, including fairy tales (Bettelheim, 1976) and reading instruction (Bettelheim & Zelan, 1981). He died at the age of 86, taking his own life.

Bettelheim was a complex man. In his writings, he emphasized the need for a warm, accepting environment in which even the most disturbed children would feel free to develop according to their inner promptings. This is the philosophy that his staff at the Orthogenic School followed. Yet Bettelheim himself was an autocratic man who sometimes insulted his students and staff. And soon after he died, former patients from the school wrote that he sometimes lost his temper and hit them and humiliated them (e.g., Jatich, 1990). Richard Pollak (1997) published a best-selling book that was scathing in its criticism of Bettelheim. Bettelheim has his defenders (e.g., Bernstein, 1990), but there was definitely a contradiction between his philosophy and his behavior.

Still, we do not study Bettelheim because of his personal attributes. We study him because of his ideas and insights.

THE AUTISTIC SYNDROME

For decades, autism was considered to be very rare. But the diagnosis of autism rose dramatically over the past two decades (Parritz & Troy, 2011). It isn't clear if the trend is due to greater awareness of the disorder or if the rising incidence is real. In any case, autism is the earliest of the severe personality disturbances, usually showing up by the second year of life. Children with autism tend to be physically healthy, but they are isolated and aloof, rebuffing human interaction. They seem to look through people. Often they do not speak, and when they do speak, they engage in echolalia, simply echoing what others say. They also show a variety of other disturbances, such as highly repetitive behavior (e.g., endlessly spinning objects). In a minority of cases, they engage in self-destructive behavior, such as hitting their heads, especially when they are physically moved (Koegel & Koegel, 2006, p. 34; Lovaas, 1973, 2003, pp. 3–7).

The cause of autism is still unknown. Because the onset is so early, most mental health workers believe it is a product of some inborn defect, perhaps a brain dysfunction. Bettelheim believed it is the outcome of early interactions with the social environment, with parents or caretakers. Specifically, he proposed that autistic children fail to develop a sense of autonomy, a sense they can have an effect on the environment.

In normal development, Bettelheim said, babies begin developing autonomy early on. When they nurse, they get the sense that it's their actions— their search for the nipple and their vigorous sucking—that produces the desired result. Or when they cry and people respond, they get the sense that their signals make a difference. But in the case of autism, the babies develop the sense that their actions are more likely to result in indifference, anxiety, or retaliation. As a result, the children begin to give up autonomous action. But more than this, Bettelheim speculated, the children sense, rightly or wrongly, that they are unwanted, that their caretakers would rather they didn't exist, and that any action might be the last straw that results in their destruction. In this respect, children with autism may feel something like the prisoners in concentration camps, for whom any action risked death. Thus the children with autism give up assertiveness. Through a monumental act of will, they decide to do nothing and to be nothing, or to limit their actions to the small world they can control (for example, endlessly spinning a saucer, oblivious to the happenings in the rest of the room).

Bettelheim was often accused of blaming autism on parents. He said this was not his intention. Although he attributed the disorder to parent/infant interactions, he believed innate temperamental differences between parent and child also might play a large role. For example, a fast, hyperactive boy might be out of tune with a slower mother, and the boy will have difficulty finding appropriate feedback from her (Bettelheim, 1967, p. 29).

THERAPY

For a long time, autism was considered essentially untreatable. Then Bettelheim (1967) and a few others (especially Lovaas, 1969) reported some success. In the Orthogenic School, the treatment for all children is on a residential basis; the children live in the school full time. When Bettelheim was its director, the school generally housed 45 to 50 children, but it never attempted to treat more than 6 or 8 children with autism at a time (Bettelheim, 1967, p. 90; 1974, p. 5). The treatment for these children usually lasted at least 5 years. Bettelheim's therapeutic principles emerge from his detailed descriptions of three case studies (1967).

Love and Care

A crucial part of the school's environment, in Bettelheim's day and today, is the provision of a tremendous amount of love, care, and protection—a nurturance that probably counteracts any feelings by the children with autism that others wish their destruction. The school's counselors are extremely devoted to the children, and after a while this loving care seems to register with them. For example, Joey, a 9-year-old boy who had given up on people and had made himself into a machine, seemed to like being bathed,

> though for a long time this too was a mechanical procedure. In the tub he rocked hard, back and forth, with the regularity of an engine and without emotion, flooding the bathroom. If he stopped rocking, he did that too, like a machine. . . . Only once, after months of being carried to bed from his bath, did we catch a slight puzzled pleasure on his face and he said, in a very low voice, "They even carry you to your bed here." This was the first time we heard him use a personal pronoun. (Bettelheim, 1967, p. 255)

Autonomy

Apart from this care, though, there is a sense in which Bettelheim believed the staff cannot do things for children with autism—for the most important thing that the children must develop is autonomy, and if autonomy is to be genuine, the children must gain it on their own. All the staff can do is create the right conditions of love and respect for the children and then hope the children will begin to trust them sufficiently to take the first steps on their own.

The way in which love and care set the stage for autonomous action is illustrated by an incident with Laurie, a girl who came to the school at the age of 7 years. Although Laurie was pretty and well dressed, she was completely inert and withdrawn. She had not uttered a word in more than 4 years. She also ate and drank very little and for months had kept her mouth slightly open, which parched her lips. Laurie's counselor tried to

> wet her lips and also to oil them, to make her more comfortable. Her counselor rubbed her lips softly, and then gently put a finger in her mouth and on her tongue. . . . At first Laurie barely reacted, but later she seemed to like it, and for an instant she touched the finger with her tongue, may even have licked it for a moment. (Bettelheim, 1967, p. 100)

Thus the counselor's loving care seemed to inspire Laurie to take a small, but spontaneous, initial action on her own.

Usually the children's first efforts at self-assertion occurred around the issue of elimination, which is what happened, for example, in the case of Marcia. When Marcia came to the school at the age of $10\frac{1}{2}$ years, she was completely unresponsive to people or objects, and she spoke only in single words that had some personal meaning to her alone. A central problem in her life was her constipation; she had stopped moving her bowels on her own after her mother had begun training her at age 2. Since then, her parents had given her repeated enemas, an experience which, her doll play later revealed, represented for her the feeling of being completely overpowered by huge adults. The staff's attitude toward her constipation illustrates the importance they put on the concept of autonomy. Bettelheim wrote,

> From the moment Marcia came we were convinced that if we were to force her to do anything, to give anything up, we could never help her out of her isolation. Nothing seemed more important than her acquiring the feeling that she was at least in charge of her own body. So from the beginning we assured her that we would not force her to move her bowels, that at the school she would never be given enemas, or any laxatives, and that in regard to elimination she could do as she wished. (1967, p. 70)

She did not have to defecate in the toilet, "but could do it wherever and whenever it was easiest for her" (1967, p. 172). Soon Marcia began to soil, and the first place she defecated with any regularity was in the bathtub, the place where she seemed to feel the most relaxed and comfortable. After defecating in the tub, she frequently played with her stools. "After about a year and again in her own good time—though we occasionally made tentative suggestions—she began to eliminate in the toilet" (1967, p. 172).

The children's progress continued when they made initial attempts to relate to others. After a year at the school, Marcia invited her counselor Inge to play a chasing game, exclaiming, "Chase!" However, Inge always had to maintain a certain distance, and Marcia never chased Inge in turn. Bettelheim speculated that through this game, in which Marcia was never caught, she was trying to master her feelings of being overpowered by adults. That is, she may have been trying to establish "through thousands of repetitions of the game that never again would anyone get hold of her and overpower the now barely emerging 'me'" (1967, p. 179). Thus Bettelheim interpreted Marcia's initial attempts to relate to others in terms of her need to establish autonomy. The counselors respected her wishes and always played the game on her own terms. Their attitude, in turn, seemed to win Marcia's trust to the point where she then tried new ways of relating to them.

The three cases suggest, finally, that progress in relating gave the children the courage to begin a new phase: Through symbolic play, they attempted to reexperience and master conflicts at the earliest developmental stage, the oral stage. For Marcia, it took some time before she could engage in purely oral play. For days, she repeatedly forced water in and out of a baby doll's mouth and rectum in exactly the same manner. Apparently, she first had to free herself of the death grip that enemas had on her total experience before she could work on feeding as a separate function (1967, p. 208). Finally, she separated the two activities by performing them in different rooms. When, however, her play did take on distinctively oral themes, she revealed that orality was fraught with its own grave dangers, as when, for example, she viciously beat a toy dog for daring to drink some milk (p. 224). Marcia seemed to believe oral intake was bad and could bring about the severest retaliation. Gradually, though, she was able to experiment with pleasurable ways of drinking in doll play and even to enjoy drinking itself.

The course of therapy, it should be noted, was not something Bettelheim determined beforehand. The children took the lead in acting and exploring their problems, and the staff supported them the best it could. This was often difficult. Marcia's water play, for example, flooded the floors and required enormous work mopping up. But the staff members usually tolerated such behavior, for the children were trying to master their experience (pp. 204, 217).

Marcia eventually made a partial recovery. After 5 years in the school, she was talking to others and seemed capable of the full range of emotional expression. Her intellectual abilities, however, lagged behind; she was only reading at the fourth-grade level. Perhaps she had entered the school at too late an age ($10\frac{1}{2}$ years) to permit a full recovery. Still, when she returned home, after 7 years in the school, she was able to take care of herself and perform useful tasks. More importantly, she was no longer the frozen child she once had been.

Attitude toward Symptoms

One of the most radical aspects of Bettelheim's philosophy was his attitude toward symptoms. For most mental health workers, symptoms (e.g., self-stimulation and peculiar gestures) are to be directly eliminated, or, at best, tolerated. Bettelheim, however, pointed out that the symptoms are what the children have spontaneously developed to gain some relief from, and even some mastery over, their tensions. They represent the child's greatest spontaneous achievement to date. Accordingly, they deserve our respect. If, instead, we disparage the symptoms—if, for example, we encourage the child to drop them—we cannot convey our respect for the child, either (Bettelheim, 1967, p. 169).

The staff's attitude toward symptoms is illustrated by its approach to Marcia's behavior in the dining room. When Marcia first came to the school, she ate only candy, and in the dining room she plugged her ears with her forefingers and her nose with her little fingers, apparently to protect herself from something dangerous in the situation. This habit made it impossible for her to eat with her hands. The staff thought about telling her it was OK to unplug her ears and nose, but they realized this communication would fall woefully short; for if it were OK for her to unplug them she would do it herself. Similarly, they did not feel that an offer to feed her themselves would convince her they understood her plight; if she could trust anyone to feed her, she would not need to plug herself up.

Our solution was to offer to plug the ears for her; then she could have some fingers free to eat with. Hearing our offer, Marcia promptly plugged her nose with her forefingers and with her other fingers brought food to her mouth by bending as close to the plate as she could—a performance that astonished both the other children and all adults present. (1967, pp. 169–170)

Many professionals would consider the staff's approach completely wrong; what they did was reinforce the psychotic behavior. However, they were trying to show a respect for the child's own devices for handling frightening feelings.

Sometimes the autistic symptoms included self-destructive behavior; the children tried to hurt and damage themselves. In these cases, the staff did step in; they had to protect the children (e.g., 1967, p. 268). However, other symptoms were respected as far as possible, for they were the children's autonomous constructions.

Phenomenology

Bettelheim's work has a phenomenological orientation. As a philosophy, phenomenology is exceedingly complex, but in psychology it generally means suspending our preconception that others think in some customary way and trying to enter into the other's unique world from the inside. It means putting oneself in the other's shoes (Ellenberger, 1958).

The school's phenomenological approach is illustrated by the attitude toward Marcia's plugging of her ears and nose. Although the *staff members* knew it was OK for Marcia to unplug herself, they guessed this was not *Marcia's* experience. Thus they tried to see the world in terms of Marcia's unique inner experience and to act accordingly.

Bettelheim said that children with autism will never leave their defensive positions as long as adults are simply interested in getting them to see the world as they (adults) see it.

This is exactly what the psychotic child cannot do. Instead, our task . . . is to create for him a world that is totally different from the one he abandoned in despair, and moreover a world he can enter right now, as he is. This means, above all, that he must feel we are with him in his private world and not that he is once more repeating the experience that "everyone wants me to come out of my world and enter his." (1967, p. 10)

The phenomenological task is especially difficult in the case of children with autism for two reasons. First, because we have become fairly well adjusted to the external world, we have difficulty understanding the horror with which the autistic child regards it. Second, these children in many ways have never transcended the experiential modalities of the infant—modalities that are largely preverbal and foreign to us as adults.

Summary

In Bettelheim's view, then, therapy should include (1) a great deal of love and care for the children with autism, which (2) enables them to trust others to the point where they will dare to take steps toward autonomous action. Bettelheim also believed (3) that the children will make progress only if they are given full respect as human beings, including respect for their symptoms as their greatest efforts to date to relieve their suffering. Finally (4), they will move out of the autistic position only if the staff somehow communicates to them that it does not simply want them to enter its own world, but that it is trying to understand the children's own unique experience.

EVALUATION

Bettelheim tried to evaluate the school's success with 40 of the children with autism that the school treated up to 1967 (Bettelheim, 1967, pp. 414–416). He believed the school had good success with four fifths of these children. That is, about this number were able to make a decent adjustment to society, including meaningful relationships with others. Of these, about half, for all intents and purposes, were cured; although they sometimes showed some personality quirks, they were doing well in their studies or were earning a living on their own. It is difficult to evaluate such statistics, however, because there are no reports on the reliability of these judgments. We do not know, that is, if neutral observers would have agreed with Bettelheim's assessments. Nevertheless, Bettelheim's case reports and films indicate that the children did make substantial progress, so we can have some confidence in his impressions.

Bettelheim's success is, for our purposes, important because his school took a decidedly developmental approach. Unlike most mental health institutions, the school did not actively try to change the children's behavior. The staff was, in a sense, more passive. It assumed that if it established the right conditions of love and care, the children would begin to take the steps toward health on their own. The staff allowed the children to take the lead. Bettelheim's school, working in the developmental tradition, had faith that even in these very disturbed children there were inner forces toward growth and autonomy that would emerge in the right environment.

Rousseau, Gesell, and other developmentalists distinguish between autonomous growth and socialization. If we actively try to change children's behavior, we usually become socializers. We adopt socially appropriate behavior as our goal and try to teach children accordingly. The behaviorist Lovaas (1973, 1987), for example, tries to reinforce socially appropriate behavior, such as language, while eliminating socially inappropriate behavior, such as peculiar psychotic gestures. Bettelheim, in contrast, put such a high premium on autonomous development that he frequently tolerated socially "deviant" acts. We saw how he respected many psychotic symptoms, for they are the child's autonomous creations. We also saw how the staff permitted Marcia to move her bowels in the bathtub and to flood the floors. It did so because she was taking steps on her own and exploring her problems. Bettelheim said that "too often children's progress is viewed not in terms of a move toward autonomy but of the convenience of a society that cares less about autonomy than conformity, and of parents who prefer not to clean their children's underclothes, no matter what" (1967, p. 294). The real question, he says, is "when, and for what gains, we ought to strip away social adjustment for the sake of personal development" (p. 293).

I have implied that Bettelheim's approach differs not only from the behaviorists' but from that of most mental health workers. At the same time, a number of child psychoanalysts would substantially agree with his approach. Most child analysts, of course, work with less disturbed children and therefore do not need to become active caretakers. Nevertheless, they often share Bettelheim's developmentalist orientation. That is, they do not try to get children to behave in the "correct" ways, but they try to create a climate of acceptance and understanding that will enable children to take the initiative in exploring their problems.

CHAPTER 15

Schachtel on Childhood Experiences

BIOGRAPHICAL INTRODUCTION

Freud, Erikson, Mahler, and Bettelheim share the developmentalist concern for how growth might occur from inner forces, from the organism itself. Although I have made somewhat less a point of it, they also share the developmentalist view that thought and behavior are qualitatively different at different stages. A writer who provided special insights into the unique qualities of early experiences was Ernest Schachtel.

Ernest Schachtel (1903–1975) was born and grew up in Berlin. His father wanted him to become a lawyer, which he did, even though he was more interested in philosophy, sociology, and literature. Schachtel practiced law for 8 years until 1933, when the Nazis had him jailed and then sent to a concentration camp. After his release he worked on family research in England and Switzerland and then in 1935 came to New York, where he received psychoanalytic training. Schachtel worked as a psychoanalyst the rest of his life, with a special interest in Rorschach (inkblot) testing. However, Schachtel was always something of a maverick among psychoanalysts, a man with his own ideas on development (Wilner, 1975).

BASIC CONCEPTS

Schachtel was most specifically interested in the problem of *infantile amnesia*, our inability to remember most of the personal events of our first 5 or 6 years of life. We can, to be sure, remember words and common objects. What's missing is our *autobiographical* memory, our memories for our personal experiences (Schachtel, 1959, p. 286). This curious memory gap was first noted by Freud, who pointed out that as infants we had many intense experiences—loves, fears, angers, jealousies—and yet our recall for them is very fragmentary. Freud's explanation was that this amnesia is the product of repression. Early sexual and aggressive feelings became linked to shame, disgust, and loathing, and therefore were repressed into the unconscious (Freud, 1905, pp. 581–583).

Schachtel believed Freud was partly right, but he pointed out two problems with the repression hypothesis. First, childhood amnesia is quite pervasive; we forget not only the sexual and hostile feelings that we might have had cause to repress, but almost all the rest of our personal experiences as well. Second, even psychoanalytic patients, who sometimes can get beneath the repression barrier, are still unable to remember much of their first few years. So childhood amnesia must have an additional source (Schachtel, 1959, p. 285).

Schachtel suggested that childhood amnesia primarily has to do with *perceptual modes of experience.* Most adult experience and memory is based on verbal categories. We look at a painting and say to ourselves, "That is a picture by Picasso," and this is how we remember what we have seen (see Slobin, 1979, pp. 155–156). Childhood experience, in contrast, is largely preverbal. It is, as Rousseau said, more directly based on the senses. As a result, it cannot be tagged, labeled—and later recalled—through verbal codes, and it is therefore lost to us as we grow up.

Schachtel divided childhood experience into two stages: infancy and early childhood. Let us look at the modes of perception during these two stages and compare them with the orientations of the adult.

Infancy (birth to 1 year)

In infancy we rely on certain senses in particular. One vital sense is *taste.* Babies, who take many things into their mouths, have more taste buds than adults do and probably can make rather fine discriminations through this modality (Schachtel, 1959, pp. 138, 300). Babies also experience objects and people by their *smells.* Since babies are often held, they probably have greater exposure to others' odors than adults do, and they frequently recognize an object such as a blanket or a shirt by its odor (p. 138). Infants, Schachtel said, know what the mother tastes and smells like long before they know what she looks like. They probably can tell when she is tense or calm through these senses (p. 299). Babies are also very sensitive to *touch* and react, for example, to the state of the mother as revealed by her relaxed or tense hold. Babies, finally, react sensitively to temperature through the *thermal sense* (p. 92).

Schachtel called these senses *autocentric*—the sensations are felt in the body. When we taste or smell food, our sensations are felt in the mouth or in the nostrils. Similarly, the experiences of hot and cold, and of being held and touched, are felt in or on the body. The autocentric senses are distinguished from the predominantly *allocentric* senses—*hearing* and especially *sight*. When we use these sensory modalities, our attention is directed to the outside. When we look at a tree, we usually focus outward, on the object itself (1959, pp. 81–84, 96–115).

The autocentric senses are intimately bound up with feelings of pleasure and unpleasure, of comfort and discomfort. Good food, for example, produces a feeling of pleasure; rancid food produces disgust. The allocentric senses, in contrast, are usually more neutral. We experience no keen pleasure or disgust, for instance, in looking at a tree. The baby's predominantly autocentric experience, then, is tied to the pleasure principle, as Freud said.

Adult memory categories—which are predominantly verbal—are poorly suited for the recall of autocentric experience. We have a fair number of words for describing what we see but very few for describing what we smell, taste, or feel. "A wine," for example, "is said to be dry, sweet, robust, fine, full, and so on, but none of these words enables one to imagine the flavor and bouquet of the wine" (1959, pp. 298–299). Poets can sometimes create vivid images of visual scenes, but they are unable to do so with respect to smells and tastes. The world of the infant, then, which is so much a world of smells, tastes, and bodily sensations, is not subject to verbal codes and recall.

Schachtel called special attention to the sense of smell. Western cultures practically outlaw discriminations based on this sense. If, upon being introduced to a man, I were to go up and sniff him, I would be considered extremely uncouth (although it is perfectly acceptable to inspect him visually at a distance). In English, to say "He smells" is synonymous with saying "He smells bad." We do, of course, use perfumes and are aware of some fragrances, but on the whole our discriminations based on this sense are very limited.

Schachtel said the taboo on smell is probably related to the fact that odor is the primary quality of fecal matter. Babies seem to enjoy the smell of their feces, but socializing agents teach them otherwise. The result is that children repress specific anal experiences. But it is more than this. Children quit making fine discriminations based on this sense altogether. Consequently, their early experiences are lost, for they do not fit into the accepted categories of experience (Schachtel, 1959, pp. 298–300).

Early Childhood (1 to 5 years)

During infancy we do not generally welcome changes in internal or external stimulation. Sudden changes—such as sharp hunger pains, shivering cold, or the loss of bodily support—can be quite threatening. The infant would like to remain embedded in a warm, peaceful, protective environment, much like the womb (Schachtel, 1959, pp. 26, 44–68).

At about 1 year of age, however, the child's basic orientation undergoes a change. Children become relatively less concerned about their security; under maturational urging, they take a much more active and persistent interest in new things. To some extent they still rely on the autocentric senses, as when they put objects into their mouths. But they now increasingly utilize the pure allocentric senses—hearing and especially sight. They examine and explore new objects by looking at them.

The young child's attitude is one of openness to the world. The child has the capacity to take everything in, no matter how small or insignificant to us, in a fresh, naive, and spellbound manner. A little girl, coming across an insect, will stop and examine it intently. To her, the insect is full of new and fascinating possibilities. She perceives each new object with a sense of wonder and awe.

This openness contrasts markedly with the predominant attitude of adults. Most adults simply label objects—for example, "That is an ant"—and then go on to something else. Adults use the same allocentric senses—sight and hearing—but not in a fully allocentric way, not with an openness to things themselves. As adults, our greatest need is not to explore the world in all its richness but to reassure ourselves that everything is familiar, as accustomed and expected.

It is not easy to understand why adults are in such a hurry to name, label, and classify things, but the answer probably has to do with the process of socialization. As children grow up, they find that grownups and peers have standard, conventional ways of describing the world, and the pressure is great to adopt them. The older child and the adult become afraid of looking at things in any way that might be different from others. There is always the threat of feeling odd, ignorant, or alone. Just as infants need the security of caretakers, adults need the security of belonging and conforming to their cultural group. Consequently, they come to see what others see, to feel what everyone feels, and to refer to all experiences with the same clichés (Schachtel, 1959, pp. 204–206, 176–177). They then think they know all the answers, but they really only know their way around the conventional pattern, in which everything is familiar and nothing a cause for wonder (p. 292).

What the adult becomes capable of remembering, then, is that which fits into conventional categories. For example, when we take a trip, we see all the sights we are supposed to see, so we can be sure to remember exactly what everybody else remembers, too. We can tell our friends that we saw the Grand Canyon, that we stopped at six IHOP restaurants, and that the desert looked beautiful at sunset (just like in the postcards). We cannot, however, give any real idea of what the country was like. The trip has become a mere collection of clichés (p. 288).

Similarly, our journey through life is remembered in terms of conventional signposts. A man can tell us about his birthdays, his wedding day, his jobs, the number of children he had and their positions in life, and the recognitions he received. But he will be unable to tell us about the truly special qualities of his wife, of his job, or of his children, for to do so would mean opening himself to experiences that transcend the conventional categories of perception (p. 299).

Among adults, Schachtel said, it is primarily the sensitive poet and artist who have retained the young child's capacity to view the world freshly, vividly, and openly. Only they still experience things with the young child's sense of wonder at watching an insect walk; at the way a ball squeezes, bounces, and responds to the hand; or at the way water feels and looks as it is poured. For most of us, unfortunately, "the age of discovery, early childhood, is buried deep under the age of routine familiarity, adulthood" (p. 294).

In summary, then, neither the autocentric experiences of the infant nor the allocentric experiences of the young child fit into the adult's way of categorizing and remembering events. The infant's world of tastes, smells, and touch, as well as the young child's fresh and open experience of things in all their fullness, are foreign to the adult and not subject to recall.

IMPLICATIONS FOR EDUCATION

Most of Schachtel's thoughts on child rearing and education concerned the child as he or she begins actively to explore the world. Schachtel wanted us to preserve and encourage the young child's bold curiosity. Unfortunately, we usually stifle it.

For example, when babies begin to handle and examine everything they see, parents often become overly anxious. Parents, as Montessori observed, are afraid their children are acting too rough, that they might break things or hurt themselves. Actually, it is usually simple enough to childproof a house—to remove all breakable and dangerous objects—and then permit the child to explore. Nevertheless, parents often become anxious at this point, and the result is that children learn it's dangerous to become too curious about the world (Schachtel, 1959, p. 154).

Adults may also discourage children's curiosity by the way they name, label, and explain things to children. For example, when a child becomes curious about something, the adult often simply tells the child the object's name, implying there is nothing more to know about it (p. 187). If a little girl shouts, "Da!" and points excitedly at a dog, the father says, "Yes, that's a dog," and then urges her to continue on with their walk. He teaches her that the conventional category—the word—"explains" the object. Instead, he might say, "Yes, that's a dog!" and stop and observe it with her. In this way, he respects and encourages her active interest in the world.

Schachtel, on the whole, told us more about how parents, teachers, and peers stifle the child's curiosity than how we might protect and encourage it. Like Rousseau, he implied that the most important thing is to avoid negative influences. If we can lessen our tendency to close off their world, children themselves will take an open, active interest in it, from their own spontaneous tendencies.

EVALUATION

Freud thought that the great tragedy of life is that in order for us to live in society, we repress so much of ourselves. Freud had in mind the repression of instinctual drives. Erikson elaborated on this theme, suggesting that positive potentials for autonomy, initiative, and other strengths usually become somewhat curtailed in the course of socialization. Schachtel's contribution is an enlarged conception of just how much we do lose. It is not just that we repress our drives, or even that ego strengths such as autonomy are restricted, but that we lose touch with entire modes of experience. The baby who is in direct contact with objects through the senses of smell, taste, and touch and the child who is openly curious about the world grow into well-socialized adults who view the world through very narrow, verbal, conventional schemes.

Schachtel called special attention to infantile amnesia, the adult's inability to remember personal events before the age of 5 or 6 years. The primary reason for this memory gap, Schachtel said, is that adults rely on conventional verbal categories that cannot capture the rich nonverbal experiences of the early years.

Schachtel didn't cite empirical research demonstrating the existence of infantile amnesia. At the time he wrote, little such-research existed. But since the 1980s, many psychologists have examined the topic.

Investigators have consistently found that adults in Western societies rarely remember any personal experiences before the age of 3 years. The average age of the earliest memory is $3\frac{1}{2}$. In addition, adults recall significantly fewer experiences before the age of 5 than one would expect simply because of the passage of time (Pillemer & White, 1989; Pillemer, Picariello, & Pruett, 1994). Hayne and MacDonald (2003) recorded early memories among the Maori, the indigenous people of New Zealand, who place a great value on telling stories about the past. The average age of the Maori adults' first memories was slightly earlier—just under 3 years, compared to $3\frac{1}{2}$ in the West. All in all, the evidence indicates that infantile amnesia certainly exists, although the ages for completely forgotten experiences are generally earlier than Schachtel suggested.

As psychologists discuss explanations of infantile amnesia, they typically mention Schachtel in a rather cursory manner. However, the most common explanation is in agreement with Schachtel's ideas. Briefly put, the explanation is this. Very young children—under the age of 2 years—are capable of remembering things. As we saw in the chapter on Piaget (Chapter 6), they can imitate events after time delays. But young children are best at reproducing events nonverbally, through their physical actions. Even at the age of 4 years, their verbal recall lags behind (Simcock & Hayne, 2003). It appears, then, that in order to preserve memories, children must learn to put their experiences into linguistic forms, especially the forms their various cultures value. Then children can readily share their memories with others, thereby strengthening the memories in their minds and rendering the memories more accessible to them as adults (Flavell et al., 2002; Nelson, 2003; Wang, 2004).

Many psychologists also believe that parents help children put experiences into words by providing what Vygotskians call *scaffolding*. That is, the parents at first provide a good deal of assistance, helping their children describe what happened. This assistance serves as a kind of scaffold until the child can engage in verbal recall on her own (Flavell et al., 2002; Nelson, 2003).

This, then, is a prevalent interpretation of childhood amnesia, and it accords fairly well with Schachtel's views. He, too, believed that societies teach children to put their experiences into verbal categories, which is why their early, nonverbal experiences are not preserved. (Schachtel didn't write about the method of scaffolding, but I'm sure he would have agreed that this is a way parents teach children to use verbal categories.)

But while there is broad agreement on *what* occurs, there is sharp disagreement on the *benefits* of the process. To my knowledge, every contemporary psychologist who has written on the child's increasing reliance on verbal recall has viewed it in a purely positive light. Schachtel did not. Let us look at an example from the research of Reese and Fivush (1993), in which a mother helps her 3-year-old son, Michael, remember a visit to the aquarium.

Parent:	Did we see any big fishes? What kind of big fishes?
Child:	Big, big, big.
Parent:	And what's their names?
Child:	I don't know.
Parent:	You remember the names of the fishes. What we called them. Michael's favorite kind of fish. Big mean ugly fish.
Child:	Yeah.
Parent:	What kind is it?
Child:	Um, ba.
Parent:	A ssshark?
Child:	Yeah.
Parent:	Remember the sharks?
Child:	Yeah.
Parent:	Do you? What else did we see in the big tank at the aquarium?
Child:	I don't know.

Parent:	Remember when we first came in . . . the aquarium? And we looked down and there were a whole bunch of birdies in the water? Remember the names of the birdies?
Child:	Ducks!
Parent:	Nooo! They weren't ducks. They had on little suits. Penguins. Remember, what did the penguins do?
Child:	I don't know.
Parent:	You don't remember?
Child:	No.
Parent:	Remember them jumping off the rocks and swimming in the water?
Child:	Yeah.
Parent:	Real fast. You were watching them jump in the water, hm.
Child:	Yeah. (p. 606)

Flavell, Miller, and Miller have reprinted this dialogue in their influential book *Cognitive Development* (2002, pp. 241–242) to illustrate how scaffolding promotes recall. But from Schachtel's perspective, the mother also is teaching Michael that his own experience matters less than labels. For example, when Michael gives his enthusiastic impression of the sharks—"Big, big, big"—she replies, "And what's their names?" Also, because Michael doesn't himself come up with the name "shark," the mother even doubts he remembers them:

Parent:	Remember the sharks?
Child:	Yeah.
Parent:	Do you? . . .

If Schachtel was correct, the mother's emphasis on words and labels is shared by Western society as a whole—but at a great cost. The sensual, nonverbal realm of experience is drowned out. Schachtel said that conventional verbal labels protect us from the "precarious and lonely struggle with the unknown" (1959, p. 192). He urged us to dare to transcend linguistic categories and encounter the world in all its mystery. This is the world in which young children reside.

Although Schachtel wrote less than the other theorists in this book, his work is especially important in another way. He demonstrated the value of the phenomenological approach to childhood. He provided glimpses of how the infant's world might appear from the inside, to the infant herself, and how her experience might differ from ours because different senses are dominant. The phenomenological approach deserves wider application in developmental psychology.

At the same time, Schachtel's work suffered from oversimplification. In particular, he gave a somewhat one-sided picture of language. Although conventional words and labels restrict experience, language also can be creative, as we shall see in Chapter 17 on Chomsky.

Still, Schachtel did much to keep us mindful of the value of the radical Rousseau-like way of thinking. He pointed out how very different the child's world is from ours and how much human potential for fresh, creative experience may be lost in the process of becoming a well-adjusted member of the conventional social order.

CHAPTER 16

Jung's Theory
of Adulthood

BIOGRAPHICAL INTRODUCTION

We have noted that few theorists have concerned themselves with development during the adult years. Erikson was one notable exception. Another was C. G. Jung (1875–1961), whose psychoanalytic theory dealt primarily with the issues of adulthood and aging.

Jung was born in Kesswil, a village in northeastern Switzerland. His childhood was mostly unhappy. He experienced the tensions of his parents' marital difficulties and was usually quite lonely. School bored him and even precipitated fainting spells when he was 12 years old (Jung, 1961, p. 30). Because his father was a pastor, Jung went to church, but he disliked it and got into bitter religious arguments with his father. Jung's primary enjoyments during childhood and adolescence were exploring nature and reading books of his own choosing— drama, poetry, history, and philosophy.

Despite his problems, Jung did well in high school and went on to earn a medical degree. He then began practicing psychiatry in Zurich, where he quickly developed a lasting interest in psychotic disorders. Jung's work—including his invention of the word-association test—suggested the importance of Freud's ideas. His colleagues warned him that any alignment with Freud would jeopardize his career, but he went ahead and indicated the importance of Freud anyway (Jung, 1961, p. 148). Freud, of course, appreciated Jung's support, and when the two men met they found they had much in common. For some time, Freud treated Jung like a son and chosen disciple. Jung, however, disagreed with aspects of Freud's theory, particularly with the attempt to reduce all unconscious events to sexual drives. Jung believed the unconscious contains many kinds of strivings, including religious and spiritual ones. In 1912 Jung decided to develop his own ideas, and in 1913 the two men severed ties.

After parting with Freud, Jung lost his footing. He began having uncanny, deeply symbolic dreams and experienced frightening visions during his waking hours. In one vision he saw the Alps grow and then saw mighty yellow waves drown thousands of people and turn into a sea of blood. Since World War I broke out the next year, he believed his vision carried a message that related to events far beyond himself (Jung, 1961, pp. 175–176).

Jung realized he was on the brink of psychosis, but he nevertheless decided to submit to the unconscious—to whatever was welling up and calling him from within. It was his only chance of understanding what was happening to him. Thus he embarked on a terrifying inner journey in which he frequently felt himself descending into lower and lower depths. At each region, he saw archaic symbols and images, and he communicated with demons, ghosts, and strange figures from the distant historical past. During this period, his family and professional practice served as bases of support in the outer world. Otherwise, he was certain, the images welling up from within would have driven him completely out of his mind (1961, p. 189).

Gradually, after about 4 years, he began to find the goal of his inner quest. This happened when he increasingly found himself drawing geometrical figures, symbols composed of circles and squares that he would later call *mandalas* (see Figure 16.1). The drawings represented some basic unity or wholeness, a path to the center of his being. Jung said that during his psychotic state

> I had to let myself be carried along by the current, without knowing where it would lead me. When I began drawing mandalas, however, I saw that everything, all the paths I had been following, all the steps I had taken, were leading back to a single point—namely to the midpoint. It became increasingly clear to me that the mandala is the center. (1961, p. 196)

Thus Jung began to understand his break as a necessary inner journey that led to a new personal integration. Support for this, however, came some 8 years later, when he dreamed of a curiously Chinese-looking mandala, and the next year he received a book in Chinese philosophy that discussed the mandala as the expression of the unity of life. Jung then believed that his own experience partook of an unconscious universal quest for psychic wholeness.

Jung made the exploration of the unconscious and its symbols the center of his research for the rest of his life. He continually explored his own dreams and fantasies and those of his patients. He also extensively studied the myths and art of numerous cultures, finding in these productions the expression of universal, unconscious yearnings and tensions.

FIGURE 16.1
A Tibetan mandala.
(Source: Jung, C.G., *Collected Works of C. G. Jung.* © 1977
Princeton University Press. Reprinted by permission of Princeton
University Press.)

PERSONALITY STRUCTURE

Although Jung was most concerned with the nature of the unconscious, he developed a theory of personality that encompasses various systems of personality functioning. We will first describe Jung's ideas on personality structure, and then discuss his views on how the personality develops.

The Ego.   The ego is roughly equivalent to consciousness. It includes our awareness of the external world as well as our consciousness of ourselves (Jung, 1933, p. 98; Whitmont & Kaufmann, 1973, p. 93).

The Persona.   The persona is the ego's mask, the image we present to the outer world. Our personas vary with our roles. People present one image to business associates, another to their children. Some people develop their personas to the exclusion of deeper parts of the personality. At some point they, or others, sense there is little of substance beneath the superficial front (Jung, 1961, p. 385). It also is true, however, that we need this part of the personality to deal effectively with others. It is often necessary, for example, to convey an image of confidence and decisiveness if we want others to listen to us (Jacobi, 1965, p. 37). To the extent the personality is balanced, the persona will be developed, but not to the exclusion of other parts.

The Shadow.   The shadow consists of those traits and feelings we cannot admit to ourselves. It is the opposite of our ego or self-image; it is the Mr. Hyde of Dr. Jekyll. In dreams, the shadow is projected onto people of the same gender, as when we dream about evil and sadistic people who are the same gender as ourselves. In our daily lives, our shadow often shows when we are in awkward situations and, for example, suddenly blurt out a hostile remark that "doesn't sound like me at all." We also see the projections of our shadows when we complain about "the one thing I cannot stand in people," for such vehemence suggests that we are really defending against an awareness of this quality in ourselves (Von Franz, 1964, p. 174).

In most cases the shadow is largely negative, for it is the opposite of our positive self-image. However, to the extent that our conscious self-image contains negative elements, the unconscious shadow will be positive (Jung, 1961, p. 387). A young woman who considers herself unattractive may dream about a beautiful lady. She considers this lady somebody else, but it may really represent her own beauty wishing to emerge. Whether the shadow is positive or negative, it is important to get in touch with it. Insight into the nature of one's shadow is the first step toward self-awareness and the integration of the personality (Jung, 1933, p. 33).

The Anima and Animus.   Chinese Taoists speak of the yin and the yang, the feminine and the masculine sides of our personalities. According to Jung, the feminine principle includes capacities for nurturance, feeling, and

art, and a oneness with nature. The masculine principle includes logical thinking, heroic assertion, and the conquest of nature (Jung, 1961, pp. 379–380;
Whitmont & Kaufmann, 1973, p. 94). We are all biologically bisexual, and we
all identify with people of both genders, so we all possess both masculine and
feminine traits. However, there are also genetic gender differences, which
socialization pressures exaggerate, forcing women to overdevelop their feminine side and men to overemphasize their masculine nature. The result is
that the "other side" is repressed and weak. Men tend to become one-sidedly
independent, aggressive, and intellectual; they neglect capacities for nurturance and relatedness to others. Women develop their nurturant and feeling sides but neglect their capacities for self-assertion and logical thought.
Nevertheless, the neglected aspects do not disappear but remain active and
call out to us from the unconscious. In men, the feminine side emerges in
dreams and fantasies as "the woman within," the *anima*. In women, the "man
within" is called the *animus* (Jung, 1961, p. 380).

The Personal Unconscious.   Jung thought that the unconscious consists of two layers. The first is the personal unconscious, which contains all the
tendencies and feelings we have repressed during our lifetime (p. 389). Much
of the shadow is in the personal unconscious. It might include, for example,
a man's tender feelings toward his father that, as a child, he needed to repress.
The anima and animus are also partly, but not completely, found in this unconscious region. A woman may have repressed her experiences of her father as
seductive—experiences that then contribute to her animus and reside in her
personal unconscious.

The Collective Unconscious.   Each individual's personal unconscious
is unique, for each person has repressed different thoughts and feelings during his or her lifetime. However, Jung also believed there exists, at the deepest layer of the psyche, a collective unconscious that is inherited and shared
by all humankind. The collective unconscious is made up of innate energy
forces and organizing tendencies called *archetypes* (see Figure 16.2). We can
never know the archetypes directly, but we can learn about them through
archetypal images found in the myths, art, dreams, and fantasies of peoples
throughout the world. Through these images, people try to express their deepest inner yearnings and unconscious tendencies. They include the image of the
Earth Mother, the wise old woman, the wise old man, animals, rebirth, death,
the trickster, the witch, and God.

The archetypes also influence the nature and growth of the other parts
of the personality. For example, a woman's animus results not only from her
experiences with her father and other men but also from unconscious male
aggressive energies that may appear in dreams as wild beasts.

Different cultures express archetypal themes in somewhat different ways,
but humans everywhere have always been fascinated and impressed by them.

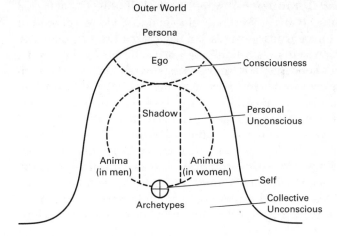

FIGURE 16.2
The psyche in Jung's theory.

Jung said,

> The concept of the archetype . . . is derived from the repeated observation that, for instance, the myths and fairytales of world literature contain definite motifs which crop up everywhere. We meet these same motifs in the fantasies, dreams, deliria, and delusions of individuals living today. . . . They have their origin in the archetype, which in itself is an irrepresentable unconscious, pre-existent form that seems to be part of the inherited structure of the psyche and can therefore manifest itself spontaneously anywhere, at any time. (1961, p. 380)

Although Jung said archetypes are essentially unknowable, he also likened them to instincts in animals—for example, a bird's innate schema of the parent (Jung, 1964, p. 58). Perhaps archetypes can also be likened to the innate perceptual tendencies Gestalt psychologists talk about (Arnheim, 1954; R. Watson, 1968, chap. 19). For example, we may have an inner sense of what constitutes a harmonious form. Mandalas probably strike us as beautiful because they correspond to our senses of proportion, balance, and good organization.

The Self. The most important archetype is that of the Self, our unconscious striving for centeredness, wholeness, and meaning (Jung, 1961, p. 386). The Self is an inner urge to balance and reconcile the opposing aspects of our personalities. It is represented throughout the world in drawings of mandalas, figures in which all sides are perfectly balanced around a center point. The Self is also expressed by our search for God, the symbol of wholeness and ultimate meaning (p. 382).

Introversion and Extroversion.   Although the Self is the ultimate goal in life, no one ever fully attains it. We all develop in one-sided ways. Most of us, for example, develop our consciousness and neglect our unconscious lives. Women neglect their masculine side, and men neglect their feminine side. Jung developed other concepts to describe opposite tendencies, of which we develop one to the exclusion of the other. One such polarity is introversion-extroversion. The extrovert confidently engages in direct action; the introvert hesitates and reflects on what may happen. At a party, an extroverted young woman immediately walks over to others and strikes up a conversation with them. The introverted woman hesitates; she is caught up in her inner state, her fears, hopes, and feelings. The extrovert moves outward, toward the world; the introvert is more secure in his or her inner world and takes more pleasure in activities such as reading and art. We all have both tendencies but are predisposed toward one, leaving the other underdeveloped and unconscious (Jung, 1945).

THEORY OF DEVELOPMENT

The First Half of Life

The personality develops along different lines during the first and second halves of the life cycle. The first period, until the age of 35 or 40, is a time of outward expansion. Maturational forces direct the growth of the ego and the unfolding of capacities for dealing with the external world. Young people learn to get along with others and try to win as many of society's rewards as possible. They establish careers and families, and they do what they can to advance up the social ladder of success. To do so, women usually experience social pressure to develop their feminine traits, and men their masculine traits.

During this phase, Jung thought, a certain degree of one-sidedness is necessary; young people need to dedicate themselves to the mastery of the outer world. It is not especially advantageous for young people to be too preoccupied with their self-doubts, fantasies, and inner natures (Jung, 1933, p. 109); their task is to meet the demands of the external environment confidently and assertively. As we can imagine, extroverts, rather than introverts, have an easier time of it during this period (Jacobi, 1965, p. 42).

The Midlife Crisis

At about age 40 the psyche begins to undergo a transformation. The individual feels that the goals and ambitions that once seemed so eternal have lost their meaning. Quite often the person feels depressed, stagnant, and incomplete, as if something crucial is missing. Jung observed that this happens even among people who have achieved a good measure of social success, for "the achievements which society rewards are won at the cost of a diminution of personality. Many—far too many—aspects of life which should have been experienced lie in the lumber-room among dusty memories" (1933, p. 104).

The psyche itself provides the way out of this crisis. It urges the person to turn inward and examine the meaning of his or her life. This turning inward is prompted by the unconscious, the region in which all the repressed and unlived aspects of the self have grown and now clamor to be heard. The unconscious calls out for recognition in order to bring about psychic balance and harmony (1933, pp. 17–18, 62–63).

The unconscious speaks to us primarily through dreams. For example, early in his analysis, a man who was depressed and felt that his life was meaningless had the following dream:

> I am standing totally perplexed, in the midst of a Casbah-like city with serpentine and winding small streets, not knowing where to turn. Suddenly I see a young, mysterious woman whom I had never seen before, pointing with her hand the direction out. It had a very awesome quality to it. (Whitmont & Kaufmann, 1973, p. 95)

The dream's message is that the man must pay attention to his anima (the mysterious young woman) for the direction out of his impasse. For it is this side of himself that he has so far failed to appreciate and develop.

As adults examine their lives and listen to unconscious messages, they sooner or later encounter images of the Self, the symbols of wholeness and centeredness. For example, a middle-aged man, a highly successful executive who had been increasingly experiencing tension and a suicidal depression, had a dream in which a water devil attacked him and maneuvered him to the edge of an abyss. The creature then rescued him and gave him a drill, which the dreamer was supposed to use to dig to the center of the earth. In Jungian terms, the dream's key figure, the water devil, is initially evil, for it represents elements in the unconscious that the conscious ego has considered inadmissible—destructive urges. Yet the devil turns into a helper, indicating that the man must confront the negative aspects of himself if he is ever to become whole and find his true center (Whitmont, 1969, pp. 224–225).

As the dream continued, the man found himself in a secret chamber where a meeting was in progress around a square table. Presiding were a splendid knight and a Lord Mayor. However, the dreamer was led to the table by a delinquent boy and a dirty, tramplike man who looked like a friar. They sat at the table and gave him some repulsive food, which he ate anyway. He then pushed his drill into the ground, and flowers grew around the drill, and the drill was transformed into a blossoming tree.

According to a Jungian analysis, the splendid knight and the Mayor represent the heroic and authoritative aspects of the personality that the man had consciously realized as a business administrator. The delinquent and the ragged friar stand for the neglected, devalued aspects of the self—elements he has so far repressed. In particular, this man had regarded his religious inclinations as soft and escapist, as tendencies that would undermine his manhood. But it is the monk and the delinquent—repressed shadow figures—who lead him to the square table, the symbol of psychic unity. There he eats repulsive food— for no one likes looking into the repressed parts of the personality—but in so doing he sees that new growth (the blossoming tree) will emerge (Whitmont, 1969, pp. 224–227).

You will notice that the Jungian approach to dreams differs from that of the Freudians. Freud considered dreams to be the end products of distortion and disguise. Jung, in contrast, believed that dreams express unconscious meanings fairly directly (Jung, 1933, p. 13). In the dream just cited, the delinquent and the monk are interpreted, quite literally, as symbols for the delinquent and religious aspects of the personality. Further, the unconscious, the source of dreams, is not just a seething pit of base impulses and desires, as it was for Freud. Rather, the unconscious, as a part of nature, can be a creative force, directing us out of our current stalemates, as the above dreams illustrate. Dreams tell us which aspects of the personality we have neglected and must get in touch with (Jung, 1933, pp. 62–63). This does not mean we should actually live out our evil tendencies. But it does mean we should learn about them, so we can control them, rather than the other way around (Whitmont, 1969, pp. 227–230).

The road toward health and growth—toward the unattainable goal of the Self—is called *individuation* (Jung, 1933, p. 26). Individuation involves not only achieving a measure of psychic balance but also separating ourselves from our ordinary conformity to the goals and values of the mass culture. It means finding one's individual way. Each person's true nature partakes of universal archetypes, but it is also based on unique experiences and potentials that must be discovered (Jung, 1961, p. 383; Jacobi, 1965, pp. 83–87).

The middle of life, then, is marked by a transformation in the psyche. We are prompted to begin turning our energy away from the mastery of the external world and to begin focusing on our inner selves. We feel inner urgings to listen to the unconscious to learn about the potentials we have so far left unrealized. We begin to raise questions about the meaning of our lives, which, after all, are now half over.

Although the focus from middle age onward becomes increasingly inward, the middle-aged adult still has the energy and resources for making changes in his or her external situation. In middle age, adults quite often take up long-neglected projects and interests and even make seemingly incomprehensible career changes. Men and women, Jung observed (1933, p. 108), begin giving expression to their opposite sexual sides. Men become less aggressively ambitious and become more concerned with interpersonal relationships. As an older colleague once told me, "As you get older you find that achievement counts for less and friendship counts for far more." Women, in contrast, become more aggressive and independent. If, for example, a man loses interest in the family business, the wife may willingly take it over. The woman, like the man, is becoming increasingly inner directed as she ages, but her enthusiasm for aggressive pursuits may temporarily counterbalance or stall this general inner orientation.

The changes of life in middle age can create marital problems. A wife might tire of her husband's intellectual condescension, for she will no longer restrain her own thinking side. The husband may feel oppressed by his wife's tendency to treat him emotionally like a child. He no longer simply wants to be calmed and pampered for his moodiness, but he wants to explore the realm of feelings and relationships in a more mature manner. Changes such as these can disturb the marital equilibrium (Jung, 1931).

Although growth during the second half of life creates tensions and difficulties, the greatest failures come when adults cling to the goals and values of the first half of life (Jung, 1933, p. 109). Middle-aged people may try desperately to maintain the attractiveness of their youth or may talk incessantly about their past athletic glories. In such cases, adults miss out on further development, which can emerge only when they risk a confrontation with the neglected parts of themselves.

Old Age

Jung said that "with increasing age, contemplation, and reflection, the inner images naturally play an ever greater part in man's life. . . . In old age one begins to let memories unroll before the mind's eye" (1961, p. 320). The old person tries to understand the nature of life in the face of death (p. 309).

Jung believed we cannot face death in a healthy way unless we have some image of the hereafter. If "I live in a house which I know will fall about my head within the next two weeks, all my vital functions will be impaired by this thought; but if on the contrary I feel myself to be safe, I can dwell there in a normal and comfortable way" (Jung, 1933, p. 112). When Jung recommended that the aged entertain thoughts of an afterlife, he did not feel that he was simply prescribing some artificial tranquilizer. He believed that the unconscious itself has an archetype of eternity that wells up from within as death nears.

Jung could not say, of course, whether our archetypal image of the hereafter is valid, but he believed it is a vital part of psychic functioning, and he therefore tried to get some picture of it. He based his picture on his own last dreams and those of others near death. The archetypal image of eternity, in Jung's view, is not of some hedonistic paradise. Instead, he pictured the souls of the dead to be like a spellbound audience listening to a lecture, seeking information from the newly deceased on the meaning of life. Apparently they know only what they knew at the moment of death—"hence their endeavor to penetrate into life in order to share in the knowledge of men. I frequently have the feeling that they are standing directly behind us, waiting to hear what answer we will give them, and what answer to destiny" (Jung, 1961, p. 308). They continue to strive to attain in death that share of awareness they failed to win in life.

In Jung's view, then, life after death is a continuation of life itself. The dead, like the aged, continue to struggle with the questions of existence; they wonder what it is that makes a life whole and gives it meaning—they search, in Erikson's term, for integrity.

PRACTICAL IMPLICATIONS

As with the Freudians, Jung's theory is inseparable from its practical applications. Much of Jung's theory came out of his work with patients who helped him understand the nature of the unconscious and the kinds of experiences that were necessary to integrate their lives. Jungian psychoanalysis is most applicable to adults and older people. In fact, over two thirds of Jung's own clients were in the second half of their lives (Whitmont & Kaufmann, 1973, p. 110).

Jung's ideas would also seem of value even to those who never find their way to the analyst's office. Most adults, at one time or another, probably experience the special problems that come with growing older. Some knowledge of the kinds of changes that typically occur may help them get their bearings. For this reason, adults seem to derive benefits from a book such as *Passages* (Sheehy, 1976), which discusses the expectable crises of adulthood. Since this book popularizes ideas of Levinson (1977, 1978), and Levinson, in turn, owes much to Jung, we ultimately may find the deepest rewards from Jung himself.

Jung's relevance for psychology and psychiatry extends beyond his special insights into adult development. Because he considered religious questions vital and meaningful in their own right, ministers, priests, and others, who themselves must often work with emotionally distressed people, have found that Jung provides a valuable bridge between the religious and psychiatric professions.

Jung's writings, furthermore, anticipated bold thinking on the nature of psychotic disorders, especially the thinking of R. D. Laing (1967). Laing argued that it is wrong to view psychotic experiences as simply abnormal and bizarre. This attitude characterizes technological cultures that refuse to admit the validity of the inner world and, instead, make outer adjustment the sole objective. Laing contended that the psychotic experience, for all its pain, can be a meaningful inner voyage and a healing process. In this voyage, the therapist can serve as a guide, helping the patient understand his or her inner symbols. Jung's view was somewhat similar, and a knowledge of Jung would seem essential for anyone who wishes to understand psychosis.

EVALUATION

Jung occupies an unusual place in contemporary psychology. For many psychologists his ideas are too mystical. He not only posited a collective unconscious but he also believed in ESP and related phenomena (e.g., Jung, 1961, p. 190). Sometimes, in addition, he seemed unnecessarily determined to keep his concepts shrouded in mystery. For example, he said that the archetypes are unknowable, yet he compared them to instincts in animals—a topic certainly open to scientific investigation.

Jung also annoys scholars by his use of categories. In particular, feminists—even Jungian feminists—note that Jung sometimes wrote about his feminine and masculine categories as if they were essential truths. It would have been better if he had handled the concepts more tentatively, recognizing that they are just ways of describing tendencies. Indeed, Susan Rowland (2002, p. 41) points out that a more tentative approach to gender concepts would correspond to the fluid androgyny of many archetypal images.

Despite these problems, psychologists in general, and developmentalists in particular, increasingly recognize the importance of Jung's ideas. Developmentalists, as we have seen, have long been concerned with how we seem to lose so much of ourselves and our potentials as we become socialized, as we become adjusted to the external world. Jung agreed this happens, but he saw new opportunities for individual growth in the adult years.

Moreover, some very significant empirical research lends support to Jung's ideas. In a major study of adult men, Daniel Levinson (1977, 1978) interpreted his findings in a Jungian context. Levinson found that the vast majority of his subjects underwent a crisis at about age 40 or 45, during which they began to experience "internal voices that have been silent or muted for years and now clamor to be heard" (1977, p. 108). Levinson concluded that the life structure of the 30s necessarily gives high priority to certain aspects of the self, those oriented toward social adjustment and achievement. But in the 40s, "the neglected parts of the self urgently seek expression and stimulate a man to reappraise his life" (p. 108). In a follow-up study, Levinson (1996) reported that for women, too, middle age is a period in which the individual becomes dissatisfied with outer roles and wants to make new connections to the inner self.

The studies of Bernice Neugarten and her colleagues at the University of Chicago also lend support to Jung's insights. Neugarten reports that for both genders, the 40s and 50s mark a "movement of energy away from an outer-world to an inner-world orientation" (1964, p. 201). Introspection, contemplation, and self-evaluation increasingly become characteristic forms of mental life (Neugarten, 1968, p. 140). Furthermore, men "become more receptive to their own affiliative, nurturant, and sensual promptings; while women seem to become more responsive toward, and less guilty about, their own aggressive, egocentric impulses" (Neugarten, 1964, p. 199). Some cross-cultural research suggests these shifts may become even more common and pronounced in old age (Gutman, 1987). Thus the work of Neugarten and her associates, like that of Levinson, supports some of the personality changes Jung outlined.

These shifts, it is important to note, seem to occur consistently before external situations demand them (Havighurst, Neugarten, & Tobin, 1968, p. 167). Adults seem to turn inward before they might be forced to do so by external losses, such as retirement, reduced income, or the loss of a spouse. There seems to be an intrinsic developmental process at work. Adults may have an inherent need to take stock, to resist the pressures of conventional roles, and to concern themselves with the neglected and unrealized aspects of the personality.

CHAPTER 17

Chomsky's Theory of Language Development[1]

BIOGRAPHICAL INTRODUCTION

In 1949 Montessori tried to get us to see that the child's mastery of language is an amazing achievement. It was not the learning of words that impressed her, but the acquisition of grammar or syntax—a system of rules for creating and understanding correct sentences. Grammatical rules are so complex and so deeply buried within spoken language that adults are hardly aware of them, yet children somehow unconsciously master most of them by the age of 6 years. Developmental psychology must understand how this happens.

Psychologists might have agreed with Montessori, but for a long time they were handicapped by their own ignorance of grammatical rules and structures. They were largely limited to counting children's nouns and verbs. Then, in 1957, Chomsky published *Syntactic Structures*, in which he described some of the operations we use to form and transform sentences. Researchers then had an idea of the kinds of operations to look for in children's speech, and the whole new field of developmental psycholinguistics emerged.

Noam Chomsky was born in 1928 in Philadelphia. Growing up, he learned a little about linguistics from his father, a respected Hebrew scholar. Chomsky attended a progressive school run by Temple University, which he describes (2003) as a wonderful place that promoted creative activities. Because the school eschewed grades and competition, Chomsky didn't even know he was a good student until high school. At the age of 16 he entered the University of Pennsylvania, full of anticipation, but found himself so bored that he was ready to drop out

---

[1]This chapter was written in collaboration with Stephen Crain.

after two years. Fortunately, the linguist Zellig Harris invited Chomsky to take his graduate course and to explore other fields. Chomsky earned both his B.A. and Ph.D. from the University of Pennsylvania, although he spent several graduate school years in a special program at Harvard University that permitted him to work on whatever he wanted. Chomsky's new theory, a combination of mathematics and linguistics, was so different from anything that had been done before that the universities had no place for him within their traditional departments. His only job offer came from the Massachusetts Institute of Technology (MIT), where he has been since 1955 (Chomsky, 1977, p. 80).

Chomsky is not only a linguist; he is also an expert on foreign affairs. He was one of the first intellectuals to speak out against the U.S. war in Vietnam, and he opposed American military interventions in Afghanistan and Iraq. Many of his academic colleagues disagree with his radical politics, but they almost unanimously recognize his accomplishments as a linguist. He has been awarded numerous honorary doctorate degrees and is widely considered one of the great minds of our time.

BASIC CONCEPTS

The Importance of Rules

Prior to Chomsky, most people probably believed what Roger Brown called the "storage bin" theory of language learning. Children imitate others and acquire a large number of sentences they store in their heads. They then reach in for the appropriate sentence when the occasion arises (Brown & Herrnstein, 1975, p. 444).

Chomsky has shown this view is incorrect. We do not simply learn a set number of sentences, for we routinely create new ones. As I write this book, I use the same words over and over, but I create a novel sentence practically every time. We all do the same thing when we speak or write. We can do this because we have internal *rules* that enable us to decide which sentences are grammatical and convey our intended meanings. If we could use only sentences that we had already heard and memorized, our language would be severely limited. Because we have a system of rules—a grammar—we can invent and understand sentences we have never heard before (Chomsky, 1959, p. 56).

The Child's Remarkable Grasp of Rules

Chomsky has focused on the rules for making transformations, as when we transform a statement into a question. For example, we might turn the sentence "The dog bit the lady" into the question "Did the dog bite the lady?" Chomsky has shown that the rules for making transformations can be quite complex, and he therefore considers it remarkable that they are routinely mastered by children.

Chomsky himself has observed children only informally. However, we can illustrate the child's linguistic capacities with some findings by Roger Brown (1973), whom Chomsky inspired. Brown unobtrusively tape-recorded a few children's spontaneous speech over a number of years and found, among other things, how they begin making a transformation called *tag questions*. Here are some tag questions produced by a boy called Adam (see Figure 17.1) one day when he was $4\frac{1}{2}$ years old.

> Ursula's my sister, isn't she?
>
> I made a mistake, didn't I?
>
> Diandros and me are working, aren't we?
>
> He can't beat me, can he?
>
> He doesn't know what to do, does he?

The "tags" are the little questions on the end (Brown & Herrnstein, 1975, p. 471).

The first thing we might notice is the creative nature of Adam's speech. These do not seem to be sentences he has heard, but sentences he is making up. He can create new sentences that are grammatical because he is following rules.

Yet the rules are complex. First of all, to create the tags, Adam must reverse the negative or affirmative statement in the first part of the sentence. When Adam says, "I made a mistake," an affirmative statement, the tag must be negative, "Didn't I?" When he begins with a negative statement, such as "He can't beat me," the tag must be positive, "Can he?" Adam does this correctly every time.

Also, Adam must locate the subject of the sentence and then convert it into the correct pronoun in the tag question. In the sentence, "Diandros and me are working, aren't we?," Adam correctly sees that the subject is the noun phrase "Diandros and me," and he converts it into "we."

In addition, Adam implicitly recognizes there are specific times when one must move the auxiliary verb to the front in the question. Note, however, that in the sentence "I made a mistake, didn't I?," the auxiliary "did" is not

Figure 17.1
Adam.
Reprinted by permission of the publisher from *A First Language: The Early Stages* by Roger Brown. Cambridge, Mass.: Harvard University Press, Copyright © 1973 by the President and Fellows of Harvard College.

present in the statement. So Adam creates it, following an abstract rule no one was even aware of until Chomsky (1957) discovered it.

Thus Adam is simultaneously employing several operations, and these are only some of them. It is truly remarkable that he can produce correct tag questions at age $4\frac{1}{2}$, yet he is not unusual in this respect (Brown & Herrnstein, 1975, p. 471).

An interesting aspect of Adam's verbal record is the frequency distribution of these sentences over time. Adam produced no tag questions at all until he was $4\frac{1}{2}$ and then he suddenly burst out with them. In one hour he created 32 such questions, whereas the average adult frequency is 3 to 6. His behavior is reminiscent of Piaget's circular reactions and Montessori's repetitions. Children seem to have an inner need to solidify new capacities through repeated exercise.

In any case, the development of tag questions illustrates Chomsky's point: Children master complex linguistic rules and procedures in a very short time. They seem to master most of the intricacies of grammars by the age of 6 or so, and the rest by puberty. This is not to say they become consciously aware of grammatical rules; even Chomsky is still trying to make them explicit. But they gain a working knowledge of them on an intuitive level. They rapidly learn the rules of their own language—and, if need be, those of a second language as well. It is a common observation, Chomsky says, that a young child of immigrant parents may learn a second language in the streets, from other children, with amazing rapidity, and the child will speak the new language as fluently as the other children (1959, p. 42).

Chomsky acknowledges that everyone's speech, including that of adults, contains errors, slips, false starts, and interrupted fragments. These mistakes are caused by such factors as carelessness, fatigue, and memory lapses. These deficits in *performance*, however, are far outweighed by an underlying *competence*, which is best revealed by an ability to distinguish between poorly formed and well-formed sentences (Chomsky, 1962, p. 531).

The Innateness Hypothesis

Chomsky says the linguistic accomplishments of the ordinary child are too great to be explained in terms of any kind of input from the environment. Children hear only a limited body of speech, much of which is poorly formed, yet they rapidly and uniformly develop an intricate system of rules for creating an unlimited number of sentences. Their knowledge extends far beyond their experience. One can only conclude, Chomsky says, that children do not build grammars primarily from the evidence they hear, but according to an inner design—a genetic program (Chomsky, 1972, p. 171; 1980, pp. 232–234).

But there is a problem. Languages vary considerably from culture to culture, and the language a child learns depends on the culture in which he or she is raised. How, then, can an innate language-learning process be at work?

Chomsky's proposal (1986, pp. 145–150) is this: When children master a grammar, they are guided by an innate knowledge of *Universal Grammar*; they automatically know the general form any language must take. But Universal Grammar (UG) has holes in it; it leaves certain parameters open. For example, one principle of UG is that all sentences must contain a subject, but some languages allow speakers to routinely leave the subject implicit; the speakers do not have to voice it. In Italian one can simply say "Went" where in English one must say "She went" (Hyams, 1986). So children need information from the environment to set this parameter, to determine which rule their particular language follows.[2]

Usually, Chomsky (1986, pp. 146–152) speculates, setting parameters is a simple matter, like setting a switch + or −. Furthermore, the number of switches that a child must set might be fairly small. If so, grammar acquisition can be quick and efficient.

It is not yet clear that this parameter-setting model actually describes the way children learn their particular grammars. Chomsky himself is constantly thinking of new models. But Chomsky is committed to the general theory of Universal Grammar. Regardless of how children pick up the details of their particular grammars, they must have an innate knowledge of the general form that all languages must take. As they put words together, they must intuitively know certain combinations are possible and others are not. If children lacked this knowledge, if they had to learn grammar primarily from experience, they could never master such a complex system in so short a time.

The child's capacity to learn languages, Chomsky also postulates, is species-specific (found only in humans) and a highly specialized faculty within the human mind. That is, it is quite unlike the faculty for learning science, music, and so on. It has its own genetic design (Chomsky, 1980, chap. 6; 1983, p. 37).

Innate Constraints

What, precisely, are the genetically determined aspects of language? We are a long way from knowing for sure. We cannot have an innate knowledge of many of the rules for creating tag questions, for these are not universal.

On a universal level, Chomsky believes we are probably disposed to construct languages out of certain building blocks, such as nouns and verbs. Primarily, however, Chomsky argues that our minds possess built-in *constraints* that limit the rules we will even consider. As children learn languages, these constraints tell them, in effect, "Don't waste your time

---

[2]The idea of UG with gaps filled in by experience reminds one of the imprintinglike process by which some species of birds learn songs (see Chapter 3). However, Chomsky has not suggested this analogy.

considering such-and-such rules; these are wrong." Such constraints free the child of the predicament of the scientific linguist, who must entertain and rule out all conceivable grammatical systems and rules. Children already know that grammars must be of a certain type (Chomsky, 1972, p. 113).

A major innate constraint is that all transformational rules must be *structure dependent*. To get an idea of what this means, let us consider transforming the following sentences into yes/no questions.

> (1) The man is tall.—Is the man tall?
> The book is on the table.—Is the book on the table?
> I can go.—Can I go?

What is the rule for forming these questions? Chomsky says that a neutral scientist, looking at these questions for the first time, would doubtlessly infer that the rule is to read from left to right until we come across the first verbal element (*is, can,* etc.) and then to move it to the front of the sentence. We can call this Hypothesis 1, and it works almost every time with sentences of this type. It is a simple, straightforward rule, one we would use if we were programming a computer. But look what happens when we apply it to the following sentence:

> (2) The man who is tall is in the room.—Is the man who tall is in the room?

The sentence is ungrammatical. Hypothesis 1 is therefore wrong, and our scientist would be surprised.

When we correctly transform sentences, we first analyze them into abstract phrases (e.g., the noun phrase and the verb phrase). The phrases are called abstract because nothing marks off their boundaries; our sense of them is intuitive. Then we locate the first verbal element (*is, can,* etc.) *after the first noun phrase*, and it is this verbal element that we move to the front of the sentence. Thus (to use a diagram suggested by Aitchison, 1976),

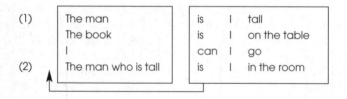

In this way, then, we correctly transform Sentence 2, creating the sentence, "Is the man who is tall in the room?" In Chomsky's terms, we follow a structure-dependent rule; we do not operate on strings of single words, but we analyze the structure of the phrases before making transformations. And

we always keep the first noun phrase (in this case, "the man who is tall") intact (Chomsky, 1975, pp. 30–32).

Chomsky claims that the ordinary child, unlike our imaginary scientist, will never even consider Hypothesis 1. This is because structure dependence is an innate mode of organizing experience, not something derived from evidence. In fact, Chomsky says, people may go through a considerable part of their lives without hearing any evidence that would enable them to choose between Hypothesis 1 and structure dependence, and yet the very first time they must transform a sentence like Sentence 2 they will unhesitatingly use the structure-dependent rule (1975, p. 32).

Several scholars (e.g., Pullum & Scholz, 2002; Tomasello, 2003, p. 288) have challenged Chomksy's claim. Unlike Chomsky, these scholars speculate that children might hear numerous adult questions that resemble "Is the man who is tall in the room?" For example, a teacher might ask children, "Is the boy who was crying still here?" Adult questions of this kind could inform children about the structure that the questions must take.

However researchers have found that questions of this kind are extremely rare in the data bases of speech that children hear from adults (S. Crain & Thornton, 2006). It's possible that some children never hear this kind of question before the age of 5 years. Yet a study by Stephen Crain and Mineharu Nakayama (1987) suggests that 3- to 5-year olds consistently know that questions of this kind must be structure dependent.

In this study, 30 children questioned a doll about various matters, such as whether "the boy who is watching Mickey Mouse is happy." The children sometimes had difficulty framing their questions to the doll—their questions were sometimes awkwardly expressed—but the children always adhered to the principle of structure dependence. They always kept the noun phrase ("the boy who is watching Mickey Mouse") intact. The children seemed to know intuitively that structure dependence must be respected.[3] When, moreover, we consider the fact that all languages, so far as we know, employ only structure-dependent rules, it begins to appear that structure dependence is indeed an innate property of the human mind.

Structure dependence, then, is submitted as an innate constraint that restricts the kinds of transformational rules children must learn. Children growing up in different cultures will learn somewhat different transformational rules, but they will automatically know that all the rules must be structure dependent. The great task of linguistics, Chomsky believes, is to discover what principles, such as structure dependence, set limits on the kinds of rules we automatically follow. Such principles will tell us much about how the mind works.

---

[3]Ambridge, Rowland, and Pine (2008) challenged these results, reporting that 3- to 7-year-olds in their own study violated structure dependence 5 percent of the time. But their study might have contributed to the errors by tiring the children; and, in any case, a 5 percent error rate is small.

Surface and Deep Structure

To help understand how we transform sentences, Chomsky introduced the concepts of deep and surface structure. The deep structure is the basic structure on which we perform various operations to create new sentences. Consider the following sentences:

(3) Susan ate the apple.

(4) The apple was eaten by Susan.

(5) Susan did not eat the apple.

(6) What did Susan eat?

(7) Susan ate the apple, didn't she?

Of these sentences, Sentence 3 is the most straightforward. It is a simple, active, declarative sentence and follows a subject-verb-object word order. In English, Sentence 3 contains the basic form of the abstract deep structure. Using Sentence 3, one could perform certain operations to generate all the other sentences. One could not take any other sentence—say Sentence 4—and derive a clear set of operations for creating the others (Chomsky, 1957, pp. 45, 91; 1965, pp. 138–141).

When Chomsky introduced the term *deep structure*, he created a good deal of confusion. The word *deep* conjures up images of an underlying universal grammar. But deep structure is not universal, largely because languages differ with respect to the word order they treat as basic. Some languages, such as English, treat the subject-verb-object (SVO) word order as basic and use it for performing transformations. Other languages use other word orders. For example, Japanese uses SOV. To avoid confusion, Chomsky has tried replacing *deep* and *surface structure* with different terms. He has even considered abandoning the concepts altogether. But many linguists consider the concepts very useful.

NOTES ON THE GROWTH OF GRAMMAR

As indicated, Chomsky has not himself studied children, and his views on development are rather vague and inconsistent. In general, he suggests we begin with the assumption that development is "instantaneous," that children instantly develop the grammatical structures of the adult. But this is just an initial working assumption—a way to get research started. For Chomsky also realizes that grammatical capacities, like any biological system, do mature and may even undergo qualitatively different stages (Chomsky, 1972, pp. 88–90; 1975, pp. 119–123).

In any case, Chomsky's work has inspired many researchers—psycholinguists—to study children's language development in great detail. The following notes summarize some of the main findings.[4]

---

[4]This summary follows a phase sequence suggested by Cairns and Cairns, 1976, pp. 193–197.

Early Language

Right at birth, babies are tuned in to language. Careful film analyses suggest that they make very slight body movements in response to speech, and their movements vary with the boundaries of sounds and words (Condon & Sander, 1974). Newborns are also very sensitive to the rhythms and pitches of speech (Fogel, 2009, p. 242).

At about 1 month of age, babies begin gurgling and cooing, and by 6 months or so they are usually making babbling sounds such as "ba ba ba" and "da da da" (Sachs, 1976). They like to play with such sounds, and their babbling often has a musical quality, too (Crain, 2003, p. 92).

One-Word Utterances

At about 1 year, babies begin producing single words. Some researchers believe they are trying to use single words to express entire sentences. For example, "cookie" might mean "I want a cookie" or "There is a cookie," depending on the context. There is a danger, however, of reading too much into the baby's speech (Sachs, 1976).

Two-Word Utterances

Beginning at about $1\frac{1}{2}$ years, children put two words together, and their language takes on a definite structure. Researchers have disagreed widely, however, about how best to characterize this structure. Table 17.1 lists some typical two-word utterances, as characterized by some psycholinguists.

In the table, notice how, in utterances 6 through 8, children are separating out agents, actions, and objects. Some people (e.g., McNeill, 1966) have proposed that children possess an underlying knowledge of subject-verb-object

TABLE 17.1   Some Typical Two-Word Utterances

TYPE	EXAMPLE
1. Naming	that doggie
2. Repetition	more jump
3. Negation	allgone ball, no wet
4. Possession	my truck
5. Attribution	big boy
6. Agent-action	Johnny hit
7. Action-object	hit ball
8. Agent-object	Mommy bread (meaning, "Mommy is cutting the bread")

Adapted from Brown and Herrnstein (1975, p. 478) and Slobin (1979, pp. 86–87).

relationships. This, however, is not certain. When children employ agents, they are not necessarily using subjects. An agent is a limited semantic (word-meaning) category; it refers to something that takes action. A subject is a broader syntactic category that refers to parts of sentences that may or may not be taking action (e.g., there is no action in "He is tall"). Thus researchers who infer adult syntax in children's speech may once again be reading too much into it (Gardner, 1982, pp. 168–170).

Developing Grammar

Between 2 and 3 years of age, children typically begin putting three and more words together, saying things such as "I making coffee." Occasionally they say things like "Eve is girl" (Brown, 1973, p. 314), now apparently using subjects and verbs that go beyond agents and actions (Eve isn't *doing* anything). English-speaking children usually follow the subject-verb-object word order, which is integral to deep structure in our language (Brown, Cazden, & Bellugi-Klima, 1969, p. 42).

As soon as children begin putting three or more words together, they indicate a sense of structure dependence—that *noun phrases* are whole units. They reveal this, for example, by their pauses, as when a child says, "Put . . . the red hat . . . on," rather than "Put the . . . red hat . . . on." The child knows the phrase "the red hat" functions as a unit that is not to be broken up (Brown & Bellugi, 1964, p. 150). Later, when children begin making transformations, they will respect the integrity of these units.

During this phase children also begin making use of *word endings*, and when they do, they *overregularize*, saying things like "I runned," "It goed," and "She doed it." A similar process occurs with respect to plurals; children routinely say things such as "foots," "mans," and "mouses" (Ervin, 1964; Slobin, 1972).

Interestingly, children do not begin with overregularizations, but first use correct irregular forms. For example, a child says "went" before saying "goed." But after a month or so children begin to overregularize word endings and continue to do so well into the elementary school years (Siegler & Alibali, 2005, p. 212).

What children seem to be doing, most psycholinguists believe, is formulating rules. They discover that the rule for forming the past tense is to add the *-ed* sound, which they then apply to all cases, assuming the language is more consistent than it actually is. Similarly, they induce that the rule for creating plurals is to add the *-s* sound, which they then apply across the board.

As mentioned earlier, psycholinguists sometimes seem to be looking for adult syntax in children's speech. Developmentalists in the Rousseauist tradition, in contrast, would be interested in the ways children's speech might be qualitatively different from that of adults. Overregularizations do give children's speech a unique flavor. However, children are actually overregularizing adult rules. Consequently, we would like to know if children sometimes also formulate their own rules.

This possibility struck Klima and Bellugi (1966) when examining children's *negatives*. Initially children act as if their rule is: Put the negative in front of the whole sentence (or after it). For example, they say, "No play that," "No want stand head," and "Car go no."

A bit later children seem to form a new rule: Put the negative after the first noun phrase and before everything else. They say things like "He no bite you" and "I no want envelope."

At different stages, then, children structure negatives in their own ways. As Klima and Bellugi (1966) say, "It has seemed to us that the language of children has its own systematicity, and that the sentences of children are not just an imperfect copy of those of an adult" (p. 191).

Transformations

Between about 3 and 6 years, children's grammar rapidly becomes quite complex; most notably, children begin making transformations. Bellugi-Klima (1968) has studied how children form *Where, What,* and *Why* questions, which are transformations of their deep-structure representations. For example, "Where can I put it?" is essentially a transformation of "I can put it where."

Children do not master the transformational operations all at once, and they seem to go through stages somewhat like those with respect to negatives. For example, they go through a period where they say things like, "Where I can put it?" and "What he wants?" They move the *why* or *what* to the front of the sentence, but leave the rest of the sentence alone (retaining the subject-verb-object word order). Even when they are asked to imitate, they commonly stick to their own way of speaking. For example,

> *Adult:*   "Adam, say what I say: Where can I put them?"
> *Adam:*   "Where I can put them?" (Slobin, 1979, p. 96)

Near Adult Grammar

Although children master most aspects of grammar by the age of 5 or 6 years, they still need time to master some sentence constructions. For example, English-speaking children have difficulty understanding a sentence such as, "The doll is easy to see." They think the doll is the one who sees, apparently because of their penchant for subject-verb-object word order. Ages 5 to 10 may be important for the acquisition of the subtlest and most complex grammatical skills (C. Chomsky, 1969).

Universals

As indicated, many psycholinguists believe there may be universals in the developmental process. So far the evidence is strongest for the earliest phases. Children everywhere probably proceed from babbling to one-word to two-word utterances. Early babbling and two-word structures, in particular, appear to be highly similar throughout the world (Brown & Herrnstein, 1975, pp. 477–479; DeHart et al., 2004, p. 239).

The search for syntactic universals after the two-word phase becomes very difficult, and the search has really just begun. Some evidence suggests that children everywhere may initially handle negatives in the same manner, and they may overregularize some parts of speech (Slobin, 1973, 1985). By the time children are mastering transformations, they are clearly using rules that differ somewhat from language to language. Still, there may be universal constraints, such as structure dependence, which limit the rules they will form.

CHOMSKY AND LEARNING THEORY

Chomsky suggests that language is something structured by children themselves. Hearing only a fragmentary body of speech, they nevertheless discover its rules, guided by an innate sense of what the rules must be like. Learning theorists, in contrast, believe we must look to the social environment for the source of linguistic patterning. Language, in their view, is shaped primarily by others through operant conditioning or through modeling influences.

Operant Conditioning

The Skinnerian view of early language learning, which we have already discussed to some extent (Chapter 8), is sometimes called the "babble-luck" theory. Babies babble away until, by luck, they hit on a sound that resembles a word, and it is reinforced. For example, they say "da da" in the presence of Daddy, and the parents show their approval. Gradually, parents make their approval contingent upon increasingly accurate and complex utterances.

Skinner (1957) and his followers (e.g., Lovaas, 1977) have recognized that such meticulous shaping of each utterance would be too slow a process to account for the rapid development of language. Accordingly, they have pointed out that when children are taught specific linguistic behaviors, they may rapidly generalize their learning to new situations. For example, a child who has been taught to pluralize a word may automatically pluralize new words without any further training. Because children generalize, they readily produce entirely new expressions—behavior that Chomsky considers so important.

The principle of generalization would seem to explain overregularizations (e.g., "mans"). However, the picture is complicated because, as you may recall, children initially emit correct irregular forms (e.g., "men"), which are presumably reinforced. Clearer demonstrations of operant principles have come from laboratory research, most of which has been done with children with developmental delay or disturbed children who are behind in their speech. Such children have been taught plurals, prepositions, and other relatively simple grammatical elements, which they have rapidly generalized to new situations (Lovaas, 1977, pp. 110–116). However, it has not yet been shown that operant techniques can produce anything like complex grammatical transformations.

Furthermore, research by Brown and Hanlon (1970) suggests that typically developing children would have great difficulty learning language on the basis of parental conditioning, because parents are such poor language teachers. These investigators found that parents correct surprisingly few ungrammatical utterances. Instead, they concentrate on the truthfulness of their children's remarks. For example, when one girl, Sarah, said, "Her curl my hair," her mother said, "That's right," because that was what she was doing. The mother ignored Sarah's grammatical error. When, however, Sarah said, "There's the animal farmhouse," a grammatically impeccable sentence, her mother corrected her, because it was a lighthouse (p. 202). Thus it is unlikely that Sarah learned grammar as a consequence of her parents' effective use of approval and disapproval.

Perhaps it is not parental approval, but some other form of feedback that constitutes effective reinforcement. Perhaps children learn to use increasingly correct grammar because parents can comprehend and respond accurately to it. However, Brown and Hanlon also failed to find that well-formed utterances met with any better understanding than poorly formed utterances. Brown and Hanlon's data were based on only three children, but these three seemed to learn correct grammar despite the poorest kind of direct reinforcement from their parents.

Bandura and Modeling

Bandura emphasizes the influence of models. He recognizes that modeling does not always work through a process of exact imitation, for children produce novel utterances that they have never heard. For example, children's overregularizations (e.g., "mans") cannot be exact imitations, for adults do not talk this way.[5] However, Bandura contends that modeling is still at

---

[5]It is conceivable that overregularizations are exact imitations of the speech of other children, but it is unlikely. Overregularizations occur in all children, including 2-year-old firstborns whose primary linguistic models are their parents (Slobin, 1979, p. 94).

work; the process is one of "abstract modeling." Children imitate the rules they hear (e.g., add the *s* sound to form the plural), which they imitate too well (Bandura, 1977, p. 175).

Some laboratory research supports Bandura's position. For example, Whitehurst, Ironsmith, and Goldman (1974) showed that the careful modeling of passive sentences produced passives in children's speech. The children did not just copy the model's exact words, but they picked up the general structure of passive sentences and created new sentences of this type.

Chomsky has not commented directly on Bandura's proposal, but we can imagine what his response would be. In the real world, models may sometimes exemplify rules with sufficient clarity for children to infer them on this basis. By and large, however, models present children with a limited body of speech that is frequently degenerate. Much adult speech is full of errors, slips, false starts, and so on. Thus, although children do pick up rules from the speech they hear, they can do so only because they are guided by an innate sense of what the rules are. Instead of focusing on the behavior of models, then, we should study the processing mechanisms of the child.

A good deal of research has challenged Chomsky's view of the quality of speech children hear (Snow, 1979; DeHart et al., 2004, pp. 258–259). Although speech between adults may be full of errors, adults commonly talk to children in a very simple, clear, and grammatical fashion. Such speech is called *child-directed speech* or *motherese* and is illustrated by the following early record of it (Brown & Bellugi, 1964, p. 135):

Adam:	See truck, Mommy. See truck.
Mother:	Did you see the truck?
Adam:	No I see truck.
Mother:	No, you didn't see it? There goes one.
Adam:	There go one.
Mother:	Yes, there goes one.

The mother's speech is short, and it is perfectly grammatical. It is simple enough for Adam to imitate, which he does at one point, saying, "There go one." The mother follows with an *expanded imitation*—"Yes, there goes one." That is, she imitates Adam's sentence and expands a bit on it. Perhaps expanded imitations gradually lead the child toward new grammatical forms.

The discovery of motherese, then, suggests that models may be far more effective than Chomsky implies. If adults model speech in simple, clear, and correct forms, children can learn it from them.

However, we cannot yet draw any firm conclusions about the impact of modeling influences. For one thing, we do not yet know how important motherese is. Current evidence suggests that motherese can speed up some language acquisition a bit, but children can certainly learn language without it. The adults in some cultures, such as the Kulali in New Guinea, do not believe in using simplified speech, yet their children learn language at roughly the same rate as U.S. children (DeHart et al., 2004, pp. 258–259; Tomasello, 2003, pp. 108–109).

Furthermore, even if simplified speech can accelerate language learning slightly, it still may be uninformative on key points. It probably doesn't provide children with the information they would need to know that all rules must be structure dependent by the age they know this. This knowledge, as Chomsky says, may be innate, a part of the mind's natural way of organizing linguistic experience.

There is, finally, another kind of evidence that must caution us against placing too much emphasis on the role of modeling influences. Children sometimes create grammatical structures that are quite unlike those of adults. For example, we noted earlier how children initially put the "no" at the beginning or the end of the rest of the sentence—something that adults never exemplify. Adam does this in the preceding excerpt, saying, "No I see truck." We also saw earlier that when Adam began making transformations, he said things like "Where I can put them?" (retaining SVO word order). Adults don't talk this way, but children do. For some time, Chomsky and his coworkers (e.g., Lightfoot, 1982, p. 184) minimized the significance of children's unique structures, emphasizing instead the early acquisition of adult grammar. But they have more recently begun to appreciate children's unique structures, which suggest that children do not just imitate adult rules but organize speech in their own ways (see Lightfoot, 1999, p. 72).

Pidgins and Creoles

So far we have discussed the views of Chomsky and others on the acquisition of English and traditional languages. The linguist Derek Bickerton (1984, 1999), whose position is close to Chomsky's, believes we can also learn a great deal from the study of pidgins and creoles.

Sometimes adults from diverse linguistic backgrounds have been suddenly thrown together, as happened on slave plantations. To communicate, the workers developed *pidgins*—choppy strings of words that lack most of the qualities of true grammar. For example, pidgins lack rules for making transformations. In conversations, the speakers often become confused.

A *creole* comes about when a population turns a native pidgin into a full, elegant grammar. But, according to Bickerton, it's not the adults who perform this feat. It's the children.

Bickerton (1984, 1999) has presented evidence on how children created a creole in Hawaii at the turn of the 20th century. By that time, slave plantations no longer existed, but adults from various countries came to Hawaii to harvest the crops for a booming sugar industry. There, the adults created a typically choppy pidgin. Their children heard the pidgin and turned it into an elegant creole in a single generation.

Bickerton points out that creoles are highly similar throughout the world. It's therefore reasonable to hypothesize, he says, that children create creoles on the basis of a universal blueprint—a universal grammar. Thus linguists who want to know what universal grammar looks like can get a good idea from the study of creoles.

Bickerton further asserts that children everywhere speak in something like creole grammar before they adjust to the languages they hear from adults (such as English or Spanish). For example, when English-speaking children say things such as "He no bite you," they are uttering sentences that are grammatical in creoles and reveal a universal blueprint.

If Bickerton is right, modeling cannot explain the development of creole grammars. The pidgins with which children must work are too degenerate to serve as models. The Hawaiian children, Bickerton says, didn't draw on other adult grammars (e.g., Spanish or Korean), either.

But how can children create a full creole on the basis of a universal grammar alone? In Chomsky's theory, Universal Grammar would be insufficient; children need some input from the adult languages to discover key facts, such as the language's basic word order and the transformational rules. In Hawaii and elsewhere, the children couldn't obtain this information from the pidgin. In such situations, Bickerton (1999) proposes, the universal grammar frequently provides the children with default solutions. The universal grammar says, in effect, "If you don't hear what transformations are like, use option A."

Bickerton worked with historical records that are far from perfect and his claims are controversial (Tomasello, 2003, p. 287). To many, his account is simply too amazing to believe. How can children, on the basis of an impoverished pidgin, create a full grammar? But such a feat need not come as a complete surprise. Chomsky pointed out that young immigrant children acquire a second language with amazing rapidity, off the streets and playgrounds, while older children and adults struggle with the task. Normal language development, too, points to a special power in children, as we saw in our discussion of tag questions. Children's ability to create a creole confirms this power.

Teaching Language to Chimpanzees

Chomsky (1980, p. 239) has claimed that syntax is a uniquely human capacity. However, many researchers have tried to teach animals, especially chimpanzees, to speak. Chimpanzees do not have human vocal chords, so, beginning in the 1960s, many researchers attempted to teach them sign language. Whenever the chimp gave the correct sign, the experimenter gave the animal a reward such as a toy or piece of fruit. Initially, the results seemed promising. The chimps not only learned individual words, but spontaneously put them together to make statements such as "Gimme tickle" and "More eat" (Gardner

& Gardner, 1969, p. 671; Terrace, Petito, Sanders, & Bever, 1979, p. 894). The researchers were enthusiastic.

However in 1979 Herb Terrace and his coauthors made a strong case that chimpanzees couldn't advance farther than the two-word stage. When the chimps put more than two words together, they merely repeated themselves. Terrace's critique had a devastating effect on research in this field. It suggested that chimps cannot learn human language after all. But not everyone abandoned the effort.

The most eye-opening recent work is that of Sue Savage-Rumbaugh. Savage-Rumbaugh explored new methods with a different kind of chimpanzee—the bonobo. Bonobos, who were only recognized as a separate species in 1929, are smaller than the common chimpanzee and they seem more humanlike. Their walk is more upright and they have a high degree of empathy with us (Savage-Rumbaugh, Shanker, & Taylor, 1998, pp. 4, 8).

Savage-Rumbaugh's star pupil is a bonobo named Kanzi. Kanzi came to Savage-Rumbaugh's research lab in Georgia in 1980 with his mother, Matata, when Kanzi was 6 months old. The staff's initial focus was on Matata, whom they tried to teach symbols on a keyboard that lit up when a symbol was pressed. The keyboard had symbols for bananas, juice, and other objects of interest to Matata. During her training sessions, Kanzi frequently played on Matata's lap, climbed on her shoulders, and performed gymnastics on her head. Matata tolerated Kanzi's antics and was still able to concentrate on her learning tasks, but she didn't have much success (Rumbaugh & Washburn, 2003, p. 129; Savage-Rumbuagh et al., 1998, pp. 3, 15–18).

Then one day, when Kanzi was $2\frac{1}{2}$ years old, the center from which Matata came decided to temporarily take her back for breeding. On the first day of her absence, Kanzi astonished everyone by his extensive use of symbols. He produced 120 different utterances using 12 different symbols. He had been watching Matata all along and suddenly demonstrated what he had learned.

Savage-Rumbaugh was so impressed that she decided to abandon direct instruction with Kanzi. She asked Kanzi's teachers to simply talk about the things in which he expressed an interest, especially on walks in the forest that is part of the research center. The teachers also carried a small keyboard so they could present its symbols as they spoke, and they let Kanzi talk back on the keyboard if he wished. But other than trying to present a language-rich environment, they simply let Kanzi pick up language on his own. Savage-Rumbaugh believes this is how ordinary human children learn language (Rumbaugh & Washburn, 2003, p. 131; Savage-Rumbaugh & Lewin, 1994, p. 177).

Kanzi's initial use of symbols supports Bandura's theory of observational learning. Kanzi learned a lot by simply observing his mother. He didn't perform language until his mother's temporary absence, but he had acquired it (illustrating Bandura's acquisition/performance distinction).

At the same time, Kanzi didn't just imitate what he saw and heard. When he began putting together two-word utterances, he sometimes departed from standard English and created his own word-order rules (Savage-Rumbaugh et al., 1998, p. 64).

But what's striking about Kanzi's language isn't what he produces, but what he comprehends. In production, Kanzi basically seems to use two-word combinations; his ability to comprehend what others say is much greater. At the age of 8 years, he showed by his actions that he understood spoken requests such as, "Put the raisins in the shoe" as well as more complicated sentences such as, "Show me the ball that's on TV" (Savage-Rumbaugh et al., 1998, p. 68-71).

Kanzi even understood Savage-Rumbaugh when she said, "Kanzi, if you give Austin [another chimp] your monster mask, I'll let you have some of Austin's cereal." Kanzi promptly got his monster mask, gave it to Austin, and then pointed to the cereal (Savage-Rumbaugh & Lewin, 1994, p. 170).

Savage-Rumbaugh estimates that at age 9 Kanzi's comprehension was equivalent to that of a $2\frac{1}{2}$ year old human child (1998, pp.67–69). Since human children's comprehension also outpaces their production, this is a significant achievement. When I showed my wife Ellen a YouTube video of Savage-Rumbaugh talking to Kanzi (Savage-Rumbaugh, 2007) Ellen exclaimed, "Wow! He understands English!"

Savage-Rumbaugh acknowledges that Kanzi's linguistic achievements do not match those of humans, but she insists that it's sufficient to refute Chomsky's claim that the capacity for syntax is unique to our species. A bonobo can learn some of it—enough to say that there is a continuity, not a sharp difference, between bonobo and human (Savage-Rumbaugh & Lewin, 1994, pp. 156, 163).

We might note, finally, that discussions of syntax in chimpanzees use *human* syntax as the standard. Perhaps there will come a day when researchers look into the possibility that nonhuman species have their own forms of syntax—forms that may be more sophisticated than we had ever imagined.

CHOMSKY AND PIAGET

Chomsky has primarily pitted his theory against environmentalism, but he also has discussed differences between his theory and that of Piaget. In fact, he met with Piaget in 1975 for a series of debates (Piatelli-Palmarini, 1979).

Piaget and Chomsky, to be sure, have much in common. Both argue that children are not molded by the external environment, but spontaneously create mental structures. But Chomsky is much more nativistic than Piaget. Chomsky believes that children will, when receiving rather minimal input, automatically create grammatical forms according to the genetic design. Piaget, in contrast, placed much less emphasis on genetically controlled development. In his view, cognitive structures emerge simply from the child's own efforts to deal with and make sense of the world.

Another difference concerns the specificity or the autonomy of language development. For Chomsky, language is a highly specialized mental faculty that develops fairly independently from other forms of cognition. Piaget and his followers, in contrast, have viewed language as more closely related to general cognitive development.

In support of his position Piaget (1983) noted that children begin using language as symbols (to represent absent things and events) at about 2 years of age, when they also begin using physical actions as symbols. In fact, the child starts using physical symbols a bit earlier. For instance, Jacqueline playfully used a piece of cloth to represent a pillow before she added words to her make-believe play. Thus, linguist symbols are part of the same general symbolizing process that has its origins in physical activity.

Piagetians (e.g., Sinclair, 1971) have speculated that there are other ways that syntax rests on cognitive achievements, but we can only take the Piagetian view so far. Piaget argued that between the ages of about 2 and 6 years (the preoperational period), thinking is basically illogical and unsystematic. Yet this is the time when language acquisition is so rapid and impressive. The development of language, especially syntax, seems to have its own special time of astonishing progress. Still, it seems unlikely that research will show that language development is as completely divorced from other cognitive activities as Chomsky suggests.

IMPLICATIONS FOR EDUCATION

Chomsky says that children learn an intricate grammatical system almost entirely on their own. All they need is to hear a language spoken, and they will master it. Thus Chomsky proposes no special instructional programs. But this does not mean his work has no practical value. It can help change our attitudes and deepen our appreciation of the child's mind. The teacher who considers the child's linguistic accomplishments will realize how ridiculous it is to focus on the child's shortcomings. Whatever the child may lack, it is trivial in comparison to the complex grammatical system he or she has mastered. The teacher, upon meeting each new elementary school child, will think, "This child has developed a remarkable grasp of linguistic structures. This mind deserves my greatest respect." One can only wonder about the effect such an attitude would have.

Despite Chomsky's work, many psychologists cannot accept the possibility that children really learn language on their own. Instead, they believe it is up to us to teach children a proper grammar. For example, Bandura (1977, p. 175) implies we should correct children's overregularizations (e.g., "We digged the hole"). Chomsky's work suggests otherwise. What children are doing is searching for underlying rules, a search that will eventually lead to the mastery of an intricate grammar. It is wrong to interfere with this process. By correcting children's mistakes, we only confuse them and undermine their confidence. Their mistakes will correct themselves in time.

Nevertheless, many psychologists and educators continue to explore ways of facilitating and accelerating children's speech (Berk, 2009, p. 388). Some of these efforts include the use of expanded imitations—something many parents naturally do. For example, we noted how one of Roger Brown's subjects, Adam, said, "There go one," and his mother responded, "Yes, there goes one." Children then sometimes imitate their parents' expansions. Many parents seem naturally to talk to children in this way, and children may enjoy such conversations. But it is not at all clear that expanded imitations can help the acquisition of syntax in any major way (Berk, 2009, p. 388; Cole & Cole, 2001, p. 326; Dale, 1976).

Others are interested in increasing children's vocabulary, and in this case the results are clearer. Hart and Risley (2003) have found that when parents talk a great deal to their babies and toddlers, the parents can boost their children's vocabularies at age 3 years. These gains, in turn, are associated with elevated IQ and reading scores in elementary school. On the basis of these findings, many authorities, including the American Academy of Pediatrics, encourage parents to talk to their young children as much as possible (Camp, 2002).

However, this "chatty parent" movement is worrisome. As Schachtel emphasized, young children are eager to explore their world nonverbally, through their senses. I have often seen a young child intently absorbed in examining an object—a leaf, a wooden toy, a puddle of water—only to have the parent interrupt the investigation by getting the child to name it. Schachtel noted that poets and artists try to recapture the young child's fresh, nonverbal impressions. We should give children the chance to experience them.

Vocabulary enthusiasts point out that increasing the word power of low-income children can raise their academic achievement. This is a worthy goal. But it's also important to keep vocabulary in perspective. Although the average child spontaneously learns many new words a day, the child's vocabulary growth is minor in comparison to her mastery of a sophisticated and abstract syntax. The ordinary child, whether from a low- or a high-income neighborhood, is really a linguistic genius. Indeed, many children in low-income neighborhoods are recent immigrants who master not one language but two. So while it might be good to increase a child's vocabulary, it would be very wrong to treat the child as if she has some deficit. When it comes to language, every child deserves our admiration.

Some educators have felt it is important to teach children with African American dialects the standard English form. These educators have commonly assumed African American dialects are inferior to standard English, which they are not (Labov, 1970). The likely outcome is that the African American child is made to feel deficient.

In most schools, teachers describe the parts of speech, writing the familiar tree diagrams on the blackboard. Chomsky's work suggests that children already have an implicit grasp of almost everything the teacher is explaining by the age of 6 years. Tree diagrams, to be sure, can make children more *conscious* of their language, a point Vygotsky emphasized. Since tree diagrams are abstract, they probably benefit children primarily after the age of 11 or 12, when the capacity for abstract thinking begins. Before this age, tree diagrams just baffle the child.

In general, the lesson to be gained from Chomsky's work is this: Since children independently master an intricate system of grammatical rules, we should respect their independent efforts. It is presumptuous of us to try to structure the child's learning, and our attempts to do so are likely to lead only to their loss of faith in their own intuitions. Although it is good to talk to children in ways they find enjoyable, it is not necessary to do anything that undermines their nonverbal explorations or deprecates their immense linguistic accomplishments.

EVALUATION

It is remarkable that Chomsky, who is more of a linguist or even a philosopher than a psychologist, has inspired so much psychological research. This research is a testament to the importance of his ideas.

We have focused on the descriptive studies of children's emerging grammar. Chomsky's nativistic theory also has stimulated other lines of investigation. Some researchers have been exploring the possibility that there is a neurologically based sensitive period for language learning. Once the brain has completed a certain degree of maturation—perhaps at the onset of puberty—it may be difficult for children to acquire language with anything like the ease with which they do so before this time. This may be why children seem better able to learn some aspects of a second language more readily when they are young. Similarly, children who are hearing impaired may more readily learn sign language at a young age. There is some evidence that a sensitive period for rapid language acquisition ends even prior to puberty, perhaps at the age of 7 years. There is much to be learned about the sensitive period hypothesis, but we can see how Chomsky's strongly biological theory has inspired new research (Johnson & Newport, 1989; Newport, 1990; Pinker, 1994; Siegler & Alibalil, 2005, pp. 212–214).

The criticisms we might make of Chomsky are primarily from a developmental perspective. First, Chomsky promoted a kind of revival of preformationism. His comments on the "instantaneous" emergence of mature grammar made it sound as if children are miniature adults as far as their language is concerned. More recently, Chomsky's followers have been more sensitive to the ways that children's speech, like their thought, might sometimes possess a quality of its own, but they still seem determined to find adult structures in children's language (see Lightfoot, 1999, p. 72; S. Crain & Thornton, 2006).

The second developmental criticism is one Werner might make. Chomsky contends that grammar can be studied separately from other psychological processes. He even suggests this is the scientific way to proceed, since biologists study organs such as the heart and the lungs apart from one another (Chomsky, 1983, p. 35). However, biologists recognize that organs and systems differentiate out of more primitive and global configurations, and this may be true of language as well. Early language, for example, may be difficult to classify either in terms of syntactic or action categories because these two systems are still undifferentiated (see Hass, 1975). Indeed, at the outset, it's not always easy to separate the baby's speech from her singing. So while we may disagree with Piagetians over the extent to which language rests on prior cognitive achievements, we still need to consider the ways in which language is initially bound up with various actions, feelings, and perceptions.

These criticisms notwithstanding, we can only marvel at the excitement and energy Chomsky has generated. Earlier, a few writers, such as Montessori, indicated that language development merits special study because children are mastering so many complex rules so soon, but it was not until Chomsky began to specify the nature of these rules that the research really got underway.

CHAPTER 18

Conclusion: Humanistic Psychology and Developmental Theory

In this concluding chapter, we will discuss the emergence of humanistic psychology and indicate the extent to which developmental theorists have shared the humanists' concerns.

HUMANISTIC PSYCHOLOGY

Psychology and the Humanistic Revolt

For centuries, psychology was a topic within philosophy. The term *psychology* derives from the Greek word *psyche*, which means soul or life principle. But many Western philosophers, especially since the 16th century, were actually more interested in what we would today call the mind. They discussed how people perceive objects, form memories, associate ideas, and make judgments (Gregory, 1987; Munn et al., 1974).

Psychology began to separate from philosophy in the later part of the 19th century, when Wilhelm Wundt tried to make psychology a scientific discipline. Wundt and his colleagues deeply admired the accomplishments of physics, chemistry, and the other natural sciences. They felt that if psychology could only follow in the example of these sciences, it also could accomplish great things. Psychology, too, should strive for the objective, quantitative measurement of isolated variables and the formulation of abstract laws. Wundt tried to analyze consciousness into its basic elements, just like physicists and chemists had done with respect to matter, and he inspired numerous researchers to adopt his approach.

After a few decades, however, the investigations of consciousness seemed to lose their promise. By the end of the 1920s, the scientific banner had been taken over by another group, the behaviorists.

The behaviorists argued we should confine ourselves to the measurement of overt behavior and the way it is controlled by the observable stimuli in the external environment. Mental processes, they said, cannot be directly observed and therefore have no place in scientific psychology; to study them just opens psychology back up to souls and all kinds of mysticism (Heidbreder, 1933, p. 235). What's more, the behaviorists pointed out, the study of overt behavior and environmental control has enormous practical value. As we have seen, the behaviorists have introduced a variety of techniques—a "technology of behavior" (Skinner, 1971, p. 3)—to improve learning and to alleviate fears, temper tantrums, and other problems. Skinner even wrote a novel, *Walden Two* (1948), which described the way one could create a total environment to produce greater human happiness.

Early on, however, some psychologists had misgivings about the behavioristic brand of science. During the first half of the 20th century, Gordon Allport, Carl Rogers, Abraham Maslow, and others argued that behaviorism, whatever its merits, was producing a very one-sided picture of human nature. Humans, they argued, do not consist of only overt responses, nor are they completely controlled by the external environment. People also grow, think, feel, dream, create, and do many other things that make up the human experience. The behaviorists and others, in their emulation of the physical sciences, were ignoring most aspects of life that make humans unique and give them dignity. These humanists were not at all opposed to scientific investigation, but they argued that psychology should address itself to the full range of human experience, not just the aspects that are most readily measurable and under environmental control. For some time, these writers were calling out in the wilderness; their views were far removed from the mainstream in U.S. psychology. But in the 1950s their writings began to attract increasing attention, and a humanistic movement in psychology was born (Misiak & Sexton, 1973, pp. 108–109).

Modern humanistic psychology, then, developed primarily in reaction to behavioristically oriented approaches. Humanistic psychology's relationship to the second main branch of psychology, psychoanalysis, has been more ambivalent. Many humanists have appreciated the psychoanalytic attempt to explore the inner world at its deepest levels. However, humanists have also felt the psychoanalysts have been too pessimistic about human capacities for growth and free choice. Whereas the behaviorists have seen people as exclusively controlled by the external environment, psychoanalysts have viewed people as dominated by irrational forces in the unconscious. Perhaps, humanists have suggested, psychoanalytic theory has been too colored by the study of patients with crippling emotional disorders. Humanists have proposed that people, to a much greater extent than has been realized, are free and creative beings, capable of growth and self-actualization (Maslow, 1962, pp. 189–197).

The humanistic psychology movement that started gaining momentum in the 1950s, then, was a reaction against two mainstream forces: behaviorism and psychoanalysis. Because of this, one of the movement's leaders, Abraham Maslow, dubbed humanistic psychology "The Third Force" (1962, p. ix). Since the 1970s, however, the psychological mainstream has increasingly moved in a new direction, turning its attention to cognitive processes.

The cognitive revolution was largely inspired by advances in computer technology. Psychologists, like people everywhere, were enormously impressed by the achievements of high-speed computers, and they quickly saw similarities between computers and human thinking. Both computers and humans, psychologists noted, encode, store, and retrieve information, and psychologists began thinking of the mind itself as an "information-processing device." Behaviorists, too, have increasingly included cognitive variables in their theories, and computer-inspired models of human intelligence have captured the interest of scholars in a wide variety of academic disciplines. Philosophers, mathematicians, linguists, computer scientists, and neurologists have all joined the cognitive psychologists, working under the banner of "cognitive science." Some scholars, to be sure, have stuck more closely to computer models than others, but the general upshot has been a great emphasis on the kinds of thinking that computers facilitate—thinking that is rational and task oriented. Many of today's top scholars assume that we think best when we clearly define the task, select strategies for solving it, avoid distractions, and self-consciously monitor our progress each step of the way (see, for example, Palinscar & Brown, 1989; Siegler & Alibali, 2005; Wood, 1998).

But to humanistic psychologists, the new cognitive models are nearly as one-sided as the old behaviorism. Cognitive models describe thinking as a highly rational and cerebral affair. They leave little room for the emotional aspects of thinking—for empathy, wonder, imagination, and inspiration. The new models also leave out the kinds of experience that phenomenologists highlight—the immediate experience of the world just at it reveals itself to us, before we put it into mental categories (including the categories that allow it to be processed as data by a computational machine).

To recap, *psychology* means the study of the soul, but most 19th-century scientific psychologists were more interested in the workings of the mind. Then, in the early 20th century, behaviorism became the dominant force and discouraged the study of the mind. This sequence of events prompted the joke, "First psychology lost its soul. Then it lost its mind" (Munn et al., 1974, p. 187).

But since the 1970s, psychology has returned its full attention to the study of cognitive processes; it has clearly regained its mind. Now the challenge for humanistic psychology is to somehow stimulate mainstream psychology to regain its soul, in the sense of paying attention to inner feelings, creative promptings, and a sense of the wonder of life.

To get a fuller understanding of humanistic psychology, let's look briefly at the life and work of the man who is considered its father, Abraham Maslow.

Maslow

Biographical Introduction.   Abraham Maslow (1908–1970) was born
in Brooklyn, New York, the son of poor Russian immigrant parents. He was
a shy, unhappy boy. Although he liked high school, he had trouble adjusting
to college. He attended the City College of New York, Cornell University, and
finally the University of Wisconsin, where he earned his B.A. and stayed on
for graduate work in psychology. Maslow began his career squarely within the
scientific mainstream. He received rigorous experimental training under
E. L. Thorndike and Harry Harlow and wrote a standard textbook on abnormal psychology (Wilson, 1972, pp. 115–134). In fact, Maslow said that early in
his career he was sold on behaviorism (Goble, 1970, p. 11) and in a sense he
never repudiated it; he always realized that people are subject to conditioning from the external environment. What increasingly annoyed him was
behaviorism's one-sidedness; people also have an inner life and potentials
for growth, creativity, and free choice.

Maslow taught at Brooklyn College from 1937 to 1951 and at Brandeis
University from 1951 to 1969. During his career, he also saw clients as a clinical psychologist and even spent a summer doing anthropological fieldwork
among the Blackfoot Indians in Alberta, Canada (Goble, 1970, p. 12).
Maslow's colleagues have described him as full of curiosity and wonder,
chuckling warmly over new ideas (Manuel, 1972). As his work developed,
it became increasingly broad and inclusive. He wanted psychology to go
beyond rational science and incorporate various ways of knowing, including those of Eastern philosophies. Thus, although Maslow died in 1970,
before the cognitive revolution really got under way, he spelled out alternatives to the rational, task-oriented model of thinking that dominates
cognitive theory.

Maslow's Ideas.   Maslow's first step in the direction of a humanistic
psychology was the formulation of a new theory of motivation (1943). According to this theory, there are six kinds of needs: physiological needs, safety
needs, belongingness needs, love needs, self-esteem needs, and, at the highest level, self-actualization needs. These needs are arranged in a hierarchical
order such that the fulfillment of lower needs propels the organism on to the
next highest level. For example, a man who has a strong physiological need,
such as hunger, will be motivated by little else, but when this need is fulfilled,
he will move on to the next level, that of safety needs, and when these are
satisfied, he will move on to the third level, and so on.

In his major works, Maslow was most interested in the highest need—
the need for self-actualization. Self-actualization, a concept borrowed from
Goldstein (1939), refers to the actualization of one's potentials, capacities, and
talents. To study it, Maslow examined the lives and experiences of the most
healthy, creative people he could find. His sample included contemporaries
and acquaintances, such as the anthropologist Ruth Benedict, as well as public

and historical figures, such as Thomas Jefferson and Eleanor Roosevelt (Maslow, 1954, pp. 202–203).

Maslow's key finding was that the self-actualizers, compared to most people, have maintained a certain independence from their society. Most people are so strongly motivated by needs such as belongingness, love, and respect that they are afraid to entertain any thought that others might disapprove of. They try to fit into their society and do whatever brings prestige within it. Self-actualizers, in contrast, are less conforming. They seem less molded and flattened by the social environment and are more spontaneous, free, and natural. Although they rarely behave in unconventional ways, they typically regard conventions with a good-natured shrug of the shoulders. Instead, they are primarily motivated by their own inner growth, the development of their potentials, and their personal mission in life (Maslow, 1954, pp. 223–228).

Because self-actualizers have attained a certain independence from their culture, they are not confined to conventional, abstract, or stereotyped modes of perception. When, for example, most people go to a museum, they read the name of the artist below the painting and then judge the work according to the conventional estimate. Self-actualizers, in contrast, perceive things more freshly, naively, and as they really are. They can look at any painting—or any tree, bird, or baby—as if seeing it for the first time; they can find miraculous beauty where others see nothing but the common object (Maslow, 1966, p. 88). In fact, they seem to have retained the creative, open approach that is characteristic of the young child. Like the child, their attitude is frequently "absorbed, spellbound, popeyed, enchanted" (p. 100). Unfortunately, most children lose this approach to life as they become socialized.

When such perception is intense, it can be called a "peak experience." The individual becomes overcome with awe and wonder at the object—a forest, a lover, a baby—and becomes so absorbed and poured into the experience that she loses all self-consciousness. She may even feel a mystical sense of communion with a transcendent beauty and perfection. In any case, there is no effort to name or categorize the object, or use it for any purpose. There is pure delight in what is (Maslow, 1966, chap. 6; 1971, pp. 333–334).[1]

In many ways, self-actualizers seem like good phenomenologists. Whether or not their perceptions reach the level of peak experiences, they can suspend or go beyond conventional ways of ordering experience. They savor the concrete, raw experience (Maslow, 1966, p. 87). Maslow also likened the self-actualizers' approach to a "Taoistic letting be," to a receptive, open appreciation of objects without interfering with them or attempting to control them (Maslow, 1962, p. 86).

---

[1]Peak experiences are not restricted to the perception of beauty but may occur during other activities, such as athletics, dance, or the act of love. During peak experiences, people lose themselves in the moment and everything seems to flow naturally (Maslow, 1968, chaps. 6 and 7).

Maslow believed psychologists and other scientists could learn much from self-actualizers' phenomenological and Taoistic approaches. It's widely assumed that science must proceed in an intellectual, goal-directed manner. As scientists, we must clearly define the purpose of our study and then collect data that help solve the problem or test the hypothesis. In the process, we filter out all the rich experiences of people and things that are outside the purpose of our study. Maslow suggested that before we get caught up in our purposes, hypotheses, and generalizations, we open ourselves to the world on a sensory, prerational, experiential level. We should try to experience the world more freshly and receptively, surrendering ourselves to what moves us and enchants us, like a child does. We will then come up with insights that can later inform our rational, goal-directed work (Maslow, 1966; 1968, p. 184).

Maslow reworked his ideas over the years and was not always systematic in the process. But by and large, his overall position was as follows:

1. Humans possess an essential biological, inner nature, which includes all the basic needs and the impulses toward growth and self-actualization (1968, p. 190; 1971, p. 25).

2. This inner core is partly specieswide and partly idiosyncratic, for we all have special bents, temperaments, and abilities (1968, p. 191).

3. Our inner core is a positive force that presses toward the realization of full humanness, just as an acorn may be said to press toward becoming an oak tree. It is important to recognize it is our inner nature, not the environment, that plays the guiding role. The environment is like sun, food, and water; it nourishes growth, but it is not the seed. Social and educational practices should be evaluated not in terms of how efficiently they control the child or get the child to adjust, but according to how well they support and nourish inner growth potentials (1968, pp. 160–161, 211–212).

4. Our inner nature is not strong, like instincts in animals. Rather, it is subtle, delicate, and in many ways weak. It is easily "drowned out by learning, by cultural expectations, by fear, by disapproval, etc." (1968, p. 191).

5. The suppression of our inner nature usually takes place during childhood. At the start, babies have an inner wisdom with respect to most matters, including food intake, amount of sleep, readiness for toilet training, and the urges to stand up and to walk. Babies will also avidly explore the environment, focusing on the particular things in which they take delight. Their own feelings and inner promptings guide them toward healthy growth. However, socializing agents frequently lack respect for children's choices. Instead, they try to direct children, to teach them things. They criticize them, correct their errors, and try to get them to give the "right" answers. Consequently, children quit trusting themselves and their senses and begin to rely on the opinions of others (1968, pp. 49–55, 150, 198–199).

6. Even though our inner core, with its urge toward self-actualization, is weak, it rarely disappears altogether—even in adulthood. It persists underground, in the unconscious, and speaks to us as an inner voice waiting to be heard. Inner signals can lead even the neurotic adult back to buried capacities and unfulfilled potentials. Our inner core is a pressure we call the "will to health," and it is this urge on which all successful psychotherapy is based (1968, pp. 192–193).

7. There are a few people—"self-actualizers"—who have remained deeply responsive to their inner natures and urges toward growth. These people are less molded and flattened by cultural pressures and have preserved the capacity to look at the world in a spontaneous, fresh, childlike manner (1968, pp. 207–208).

DEVELOPMENTALISTS AS HUMANISTS

If Maslow's ideas sound familiar, they are. Maslow and the modern humanistic psychologists have, without making much note of it, drawn heavily on the developmental tradition that began with Rousseau. Since Rousseau, many developmental theorists have been preoccupied with the same basic problem as Maslow: Children, as they become socialized, quit relying on their own experience and judgments; they become too dependent on conventions and the opinions of others. Thus developmentalists, like the humanists, have been searching for an inner force that will guide the individual toward a healthier, more independent development.

Intrinsic Growth Forces

Where Maslow speaks of a biological core that directs healthy growth, developmentalists refer to *maturation*. Maturation is an internal mechanism that prompts children to seek out certain experiences at certain times. Under maturational urging, children regulate their cycles of sleep and eating; learn to sit up, walk, and run; develop an urgent need for autonomy; master language; explore the widening environment; and so on. According to Gesell and others, children, following their own inner schedule and timing, are eminently wise regarding what they need and can do. So, instead of trying to make children conform to our own set schedules and directions, we can let them guide us and make their own choices—as Maslow proposed.

Nevertheless, as Maslow observed, it is often difficult for us to trust children and the growth process. We seem to have particular difficulty believing children can really learn on their own, without our direction and supervision. But developmentalists have tried to show they can. Montessori, in particular, tried to show that if we will open-mindedly observe children's spontaneous interests, they will direct us to the tasks on which they will work independently and with the greatest concentration and sense of fulfillment. They will become absorbed in such tasks because the tasks meet inner needs to perfect certain capacities at certain points in development. So we are not forced to take charge of children's learning, to choose tasks for them, to motivate them by our praise, or to criticize their mistakes—practices that force them to turn to external authorities for guidance and evaluation. Instead, we can trust their maturationally based urges to perfect their own capacities in their own ways. Maslow might have pointed to Montessori as an educator who was thoroughly humanistic in her faith in children's intrinsic creative powers.

Not all developmentalists, of course, are as nativistic as Gesell or Montessori. As we have seen, Piaget, Kohlberg, and the cognitive-developmentalists doubt that biological maturation directly governs the stages of cognitive development. But these theorists also look to children's independent activities, rather than to external teachings, as the source of developmental change. Children, in their view, are intrinsically curious about the world and reach out for new experiences that lead them to reorganize their cognitive structures. In this sense, the cognitive-developmentalists also share the humanists' faith in intrinsic capacities for self-directed learning.

Interestingly, Maslow's thoughts on adulthood were also foreshadowed by earlier developmental theorists—especially by Jung. Maslow pointed out how the well-socialized adult, whose inner potentials for self-actualization lie dormant, will still hear inner voices calling for attention. Jung used nearly identical language to describe the crisis of middle life. Prior to middle age, the individual typically concentrates on adjusting to the external, social world, trying to do things that bring social success and prestige and developing those parts of the personality that are suited for this goal. In middle life, however, social success loses its importance, and inner voices from the unconscious direct one to attend to the previously neglected and unrealized parts of the self. The individual increasingly turns inward and considers the discovery and rounding out of the personality more important than social conformity.

Thus developmental theorists, like the modern humanistic psychologists, have tried to uncover intrinsic growth factors that stand apart from pressures toward social conformity. At the same time, however, some developmental theorists have been more pessimistic than the humanists about the chances for any substantial improvement based on intrinsic forces. In particular, the Freudians have felt that because maturation brings with it unruly sexual and aggressive impulses, a good measure of social repression will always be necessary. Erikson viewed maturational growth somewhat more positively than Freud, calling attention to the maturation of autonomy, initiative, industry, and so on, but he too felt that the other sides of these qualities—shame, doubt, guilt, inferiority, and so on—are inevitable. No child, for example, can become completely autonomous, for societies will always need to regulate the child to some extent. Still, Erikson hoped we can raise children so they can gain as much autonomy, initiative, and as many other virtues as possible.

Furthermore, Freudian therapy relies heavily on inner growth forces. Recall how Freud once asked a psychiatrist if he could really cure. When the psychiatrist responded that he could not—that he could only remove some impediments to growth as a gardener removes some stones or weeds—Freud said they would then understand each other. The psychoanalyst's reliance on intrinsic growth processes is quite evident in Bettelheim's school. Bettelheim did not try to make disturbed children behave in normal ways, but he tried to provide certain conditions—love, acceptance, empathy—that will enable children to feel it is safe to take steps toward growth on their own. The physician treats patients in essentially the same way. The doctor does not actually heal a cut but only cleans and stitches the wound. The rest is up to nature. Any cure, in psychotherapy or in medicine, partly relies on forces toward health that are out of the doctor's control. The doctor puts his or her faith in innate forces toward health.

Thus developmental theorists, like the humanists, have tried to discover the nature of intrinsic growth forces and to devise educational and therapeutic methods based on them. And, to a considerable extent, developmental writers had been working on these tasks long before the modern humanistic movement in psychology even began.

Romanticism

Theories that extol the virtues of nature and biological forces, as opposed to society, are often called Romantic. In this sense, Maslow, as well as Rousseau and the maturationists, are strongly Romantic. Rousseau, in fact, is often credited with the origin of Romantic thought.

Another aspect of Romanticism is a fondness for the past. This attraction is quite evident in Maslow; he looked upon infancy and childhood as times when we were more closely in touch with our natural urges and possessed a more spontaneous and creative outlook. As children, he said, we perceived the world more freshly, directly, and imaginatively than we typically do as well-socialized adults. Maslow recognized the value of mature, adult thought, but he also saw the need to learn to regress temporarily to more childlike modes of experience.

Rousseau, too, "romanticized the past." He suggested that we were happier and more independent as savages, and he saw childhood as a potentially happy and innocent time in which we live in close harmony with nature.

In modern developmental theory, perhaps the most thoroughgoing Romantic was Schachtel, who contrasted the richly sensuous experiences of infancy and the open curiosity of childhood with the stereotyped, conventional thought of most adults.

Neither Rousseau nor Schachtel, however, clearly specified ways in which we, as adults, might recapture childlike modes of experience. For such a conceptualization, we are particularly indebted to Werner. Werner suggested that we continually engage in a process called *microgenesis*, beginning each new thought or perception at primitive levels before moving on to more advanced forms of cognition. Thus the primitive modes of experience are continually available to us. Ordinarily, Werner observed, we do not engage in primitive imagery in a very full way, but we do so when we are most creative, when we truly begin anew. At these moments our impressions become particularly rich and sensuous; for primitive images are fused with emotion, sensation, and imaginative qualities. Creative thinking, of course, does not stop with such images; it goes on to articulate and structure them. Nevertheless, Werner emphasized, creativity begins with a responsiveness to early forms of experience—a view shared by the psychoanalysts who speak of "regressions in the service of the ego."

Not all writers in the developmental tradition, we should note, have been Romantic. The cognitive-developmentalists, in particular, have generally been unimpressed by the distinctive virtues of childlike thinking. Piaget observed that we continue to use early sensorimotor schemes and cognitive operations, but he saw nothing special in the imaginative, fanciful thinking of the preoperational child, and he never suggested that creative people regress to it. Similarly, Kohlberg never seemed impressed by the concept of regression. In his view, stages of moral reasoning simply reflected increasing levels of cognitive adequacy, so there was no point to regressing to earlier stages.

Not all developmentalists, then, have placed a special premium on childlike modes of thought. Most, to be sure, have argued that childhood thinking has unique qualities, but not all have been so enamored with these qualities that they have urged us to recapture them. Still, a Romantic attraction to childhood is one theme that runs through a good deal of humanistic psychology and developmental theory.

Phenomenology

Another central component of modern humanistic psychology is a phenomenological orientation. This orientation or method includes what may be called a "phenomenological suspension." One tries to suspend one's theoretical preconceptions and customary categories and tries to see people and things as openly and freshly as possible—to see them as they really are. This approach, as we have seen, was the starting point of Rousseau's developmental philosophy. Rousseau argued that children have their own ways of seeing, thinking, and feeling, and that we know nothing about these; we therefore must refrain from investing children with our own thoughts and take the time to simply observe them, listen to them, and let them reveal their unique characteristics to us. Later, Piaget and Montessori emphasized the same point. The ethologists, too, may be said to employ a phenomenological suspension. Before an ethologist forms any hypothesis or builds any theory, he or she first simply tries to learn about and describe as much about a particular species as possible. To do this, ethologists believe, we must observe animals in their natural habitats, not in the laboratory.

In psychology, phenomenology usually implies a second step. Phenomenological psychologists usually suspend preconceptions in order to enter into the *inner* world of the other. They try to open themselves to the other's direct experience, to see things through the other's eyes.

Developmental theorists have been less consistent in taking this second step. Those who have worked the hardest to learn about children's inner worlds are Schachtel and the psychoanalysts. Schachtel tried to gain insight into the infant's unique modes of perception, and the psychoanalyst Bettelheim, for example, constantly asked himself, "How does the world look and feel to this child?" Other writers, however, have been less interested in perceiving the world through the child's eyes. Gesell wanted us to be open to children's own needs and interests, but he primarily observed their external motor behavior. Werner gave us insights into how the world might look to the child—how, for instance, it might appear full of life and feeling—but he mostly discussed the child's mental life from the *outside*, analyzing it in terms of concepts such as differentiation and integration. Similarly, Piaget provided valuable insights into the young child's unique experiences—how objects change with momentary perceptions, how dreams seem real, how morals seem imposed by authorities, and so forth—but Piaget, too, primarily examined the young child's thought from the outside, analyzing it in terms of logical structures. The ethologists also primarily look at behavior from an external point of view.

A knowledge of how the world looks to children (and adults) at different stages will not be easy to come by. Young children are not sufficiently verbal to tell us how the world appears to them, and infants cannot tell us anything at all. One approach may be the study of spontaneous interests. For example, Montessori showed how young children attend to minute details and are concerned about anything out of place. These observations give us two clues concerning the young child's perceptual world. Young children also seem to perceive life where we do not, and they may be particularly interested in objects, such as cars, balls, or balloons, which, with a little imagination, take on human qualities. It would seem important to record every aspect of the environment that children find uniquely interesting. To structure such studies, we might follow the lead of Martha Muchow (discussed in Chapter 5), who observed how children of different ages responded to typical settings in their everyday environments, including a landing dock and a department store. By noting the things that children find particularly interesting, as well as those that they ignore, we can begin to form a picture of how the world appears to the child at different phases of life.

Universals

Those of you who have already learned something about developmental psychology will notice this book neglects or skims over certain topics. We have barely mentioned, for example, differences among children or adults on IQ tests. Other topics that have received only minor coverage include cultural differences in personality development and gender differences. The various differences among people, which are partly the product of environmental factors, are tremendously important.

However, the differences among people have not been the primary concern of writers in the developmental tradition. Instead, they have searched for growth forces and sequences common to all people. This search, as Chomsky suggests (1975, pp. 130–133), probably reflects, as much as anything, an ethical orientation. Developmentalists, like humanists, are trying to show how, at the deepest levels, we are all the same. Writers in the developmental tradition are especially reluctant to investigate ways in which one person is better than another. The writers' focus, instead, is on our common humanity (Maslow, 1962, p. 185). They want to show that, at bottom, we all have the same yearnings, hopes, and fears, as well as the same creative urges toward health and personal integration. Hopefully, an appreciation of the strivings that we all share can help in the building of a universal human community.

A Developmental Perspective on the Standards Movement

Developmental theorists, from Rousseau to Gesell and Piaget, have been strongly concerned about practical matters—especially child rearing and education. So we might wonder how they would view the standards movement that dominates contemporary education. I will consider this movement from the strongly developmental or Rousseauist perspective, which is at the heart of this book.

THE STANDARDS MOVEMENT

The United States has generally been proud of its schools, but certain historical events have shaken its confidence in them. In particular, the Soviet Union's launching of *Sputnik* in 1957 provoked a wave of self-criticism and curricular reform. The Russians had taken the lead in the space race, and in order to regain supremacy, our political and educational leaders called for a concerted effort to teach much more advanced math and science at much younger ages. The new curriculum, however, sailed over children's heads and was generally abandoned during the 1960s.

The 1970s saw new challenges to U.S. superiority—not in the space race, but in the economic world. Japan, West Germany, and other nations began to outperform us in the automotive and high-tech industries. In response, U.S. political and corporate leaders once again looked primarily to the schools (rather than their own policies) as the source of the problem. Our schools, they charged, weren't producing a sufficiently skilled and educated workforce to compete in the global economy.

The loudest warning came from a U.S. Department of Education report entitled *A Nation at Risk*, published in 1983, which said our schools had succumbed to a "rising tide of mediocrity that threatens our very future as a Nation and a people" (p. 5). The report called for higher academic expectations for all students and offered specific proposals such as a longer school day and school year.

An endless array of similar reports followed. In 1989 the first President Bush and the nation's governors put the standards movement into high gear, calling for world-class standards and rigorous assessments. The Clinton administration followed suit, placing special emphasis on high achievement in math and science. By 2000 nearly every state in the nation had developed new curriculum goals and standardized tests to measure students' progress. In an effort to hold students accountable, a majority of the states also had made advancement to certain grades (e.g. from 3rd to 4th grade) or high school graduation contingent on specific test scores ("Quality Counts," 2001).

In 2002 the federal government weighed in more strongly than ever. Congress overwhelmingly approved the new George W. Bush administration's No Child Left Behind Act (NCLB), which mandates yearly standardized testing in reading and math in grades 3 through 8. The law includes numerous accountability measures. For example, a school district that fails to improve its test scores each year must transfer some funds to private or public agencies for supplemental instruction. Eventually, "failing" schools are subject to state takeover.

As NCLB was implemented it met with increased criticism. Some schools felt they were already performing well and were unfairly penalized for not making yearly progress. Other schools felt that the pressure to raise test scores in reading and math shortened the time they could devote to other areas, such as social studies.

Apart from specific complaints, by 2009 it became apparent that NCLB wasn't significantly increasing academic achievement. One of its goals has been to erase the achievement gap between white students and students of color, but progress has been disappointing (Hahnel, 2009). Nor has NCLB produced strong gains in student achievement in general. According to one measure, less than a third of U.S. students are proficient in math and reading ("Quality Counts," 2009).

In 2010, the Obama administration announced a preliminary proposal to remedy some of the law's weaknesses. For example, it would no longer subject high-performing schools to penalties. But the proposal does not depart from NCLB in a radical way. It continues to mandate standardized testing, and the Obama administration strongly supports the general thrust of the standards movement. In an effort to make all students "college- and career ready," the Obama administration intends to distribute major funds to only those states that adopt a new, national set of K-12 curriculum standards (Dillon, 2010; Klein, 2010).

As the standards movement has swept through the country, academic instruction has moved down to earlier and earlier grades. Kindergarten is no longer a playful introduction to formal schooling. A study sponsored by the Alliance for Childhood found that full-day kindergarten classes in California and New York typically devoted two to three hours a day to math and literacy instruction. Of that time, 20 to 30 minutes per day was used for standardized testing and test preparation. The kindergarten classes generally allowed less than 30 minutes per day—and often no time at all—for play or choice time (Miller & Almon, 2009). Anecdotal reports suggest that children are baffled by the academic instruction, and the tests are especially upsetting. The children don't know what to do with their test booklets because they cannot yet read. Some cry and wet their pants (Kozol, 2005, p. 114). But standards advocates believe it's never too early to get children started on the academic skills they will need for future success. In fact, the federal government is poised to make preschools much more academic, too (E. Brown, 2009).

In their more theoretical writings, the standards movement's leaders claim they are bringing a badly needed dose of clearheaded rationality to America's muddled educational system. Educational reform, they say, must begin with clear educational goals; before we do anything else, we must define what students will "need to know and be able to do" in tomorrow's global economy (Ravitch, 1995, pp. 54, 133). Then we can create specific goals for each school grade. In addition, adults must motivate children to work harder. Adults must get children to buckle down and stretch themselves so they will be prepared for college and the 21st century workplace (Carnegie Corporation, 1996, p. 95; Rosenbaum, 2004).

Some parents and teachers have had reservations about the standards movement, but they have had difficulty challenging it. This is largely because the movement uses language that seems so obviously correct. Who can be opposed to high standards and clear goals? Who doesn't want children prepared for the future? But developmental theorists, beginning with Rousseau, have challenged the assumptions on which the standards movement rests.

A DEVELOPMENTAL CRITIQUE

Are We Too Focused on Our Goals for Children?

The standards movement asserts that we must set clear goals for children, which almost always focus on preparation for college and the competitive workplace. But as Rousseau first warned, a preoccupation with our own goals can blind us to the ways children naturally grow and develop. At different stages, children are naturally motivated to develop different capacities. When we focus too exclusively on what we, as adults, think children need for the future, we can overlook the capacities they are ready and eager to develop at their present stage.

Today our hurry to prepare children for the future is having a particularly harmful effect on young children. As we rush in with instruction that will put them on the road to academic success, we not only are putting them under considerable stress; we also are robbing them of the chance to develop the special strengths of their own phase of life. I will point to three areas in which we are restricting their development.

Play.   Children have a spontaneous urge to play, but educational policymakers typically regard play—especially free, unstructured play—as frivolous. It appears to have little to do with the serious business of academic work. But play is vital for the child's development. Piaget observed that make-believe play is one of the first means by which toddlers create symbols. When a 2-year-old uses sticks to represent people, she develops her capacity for symbolic thought.

If children are given the opportunities, their make-believe play flourishes during the next few years. It is often highly creative; children invent elaborate dramas. Many children—perhaps one third to one half—even invent imaginary companions, whose adventures can bring excitement and humor to the whole family (Crain, 2003). This play seems to be an important for the development of the imagination (Hirsh-Pasek et al., 2009, pp. 42–43).

Vygotsky suggested that make-believe play also promotes self-control. Young children might be impulsive and distractible in their ordinary lives, but they stick to the rules implicit in their make-believe roles. When playing the role of a caring mother, the child acts with the appropriate patience.

At the age of 6 or 7 years, make-believe play diminishes and children become more interested in social games with rules, such as tag, hide-and-seek, kickball, and baseball. Piaget observed that when children play games informally, without adult direction, they frequently discuss and debate the rules. In the process, they learn to consider others' perspectives and develop conceptions of what is fair and right.

But today's schools are so concerned with academic achievement that they leave little time for free play. As mentioned, play has almost disappeared from kindergartens. In addition, many school districts have eliminated or greatly reduced recess in the elementary grades (Ginsburg, 2007). Schools further cut into children's playtime by assigning lots of homework—often beginning in kindergarten. Because of these changes, today's children lack opportunities to develop their imaginations through make-believe play and to develop their conceptions of fairness though social games.

It is not schools alone that restrict free play. The electronic media also exert an effect. Instead of playing outdoors, many children spend hours watching television. They also play video games. Video games are a form of play, but the games are highly programmed. They do not encourage children to use their own imaginations or engage in free give-and-take with other children. Competitive youth sports also restrict free play. In youth leagues, adults make most of the decisions. Children are no longer free to discuss rules and settle their own disputes in the ways Piaget considered so valuable. So various factors limit free play today. Nevertheless, the standards movement, by greatly reducing time for play, is a major factor.

The Arts. As mentioned in the chapters on Werner and Piaget (Chapters 5 and 6), children between the ages of about 3 and 8 years love to sing, dance, draw, and compose poems. During this period, moreover, their talents routinely blossom in breathtaking ways. Between the ages of about 5 and 7 years, for example, children produce drawings that are fresh, lively, and beautifully organized. Then the drawings change. They lose their freshness and lively harmonies. They become more precise, geometric, and carefully planned. It would seem that rational intelligence is taking over, and doing so at about the age at which Piaget believed children naturally become more rational and logical in their thinking.

Both kinds of artwork—the younger child's lively, harmonious drawings and the older child's more geometric productions—can be beautiful, but it is the art of the younger child that has caught the eye of modern masters. Several masters have said they try to recapture the flavor of it (Gardner, 1980; Crain, 2003). So it might seem that education officials would recognize the remarkable nature of the young child's art and give it every opportunity to flourish. But our schools have never found adequate time for the arts, and today's push for early academic achievement is crowding out the arts at younger and younger ages—sometimes even in kindergarten (Miller & Almon, 2009). As a result, young children increasingly struggle with academic lessons they can barely fathom, while they have fewer opportunities to develop their astonishing creativity at their own phase of life.

Nature. The standards movement also makes it nearly impossible for children to have rich contact with nature. Sensitive preschool and elementary school teachers have long recognized that young children have an unusually strong interest in animals, water, plant life, rocks, and soil. Montessori shared this impression and made room for nature in her Children's House and elementary schools. She also began to articulate ways in which contact with nature helps children develop, suggesting it increases children's powers of observation and gives them a sense of unity with the world. A small but growing body of research suggests Montessori was correct. The research also indicates that nature fosters children's creativity. In natural settings, children love to build hideouts and shelters, and nature inspires children's artwork and nearly all their best poetry (Crain, 2003).

Sadly, nature doesn't play much of a role in education today. To my knowledge, no leading educational policymaker—and certainly no leader of the standards movement—has argued for the value of nature in children's lives. Instead, the focus is always on the knowledge and skills that children will need for the future, which is envisioned as a high-tech, indoor (computer-driven) workplace. With this goal in mind, there's little point in giving children lots of time exploring nature's outdoors, leisurely rambling through meadows and streams, climbing trees, building hideouts, watching fish and birds, collecting rocks and leaves. The life of Huckleberry Finn is a thing of the past.

Admittedly, only two developmentalists in this book—Rousseau and Montessori—called attention to the child's affinity to nature. But in its truest spirit, the developmental approach opens us to an appreciation of this aspect of childhood. The developmental approach asks us, as adults, to observe children with a very open mind, even a certain naiveté. It asks us to stop thinking exclusively in terms of our goals for children. Instead, we should entertain the possibility that the child comes to us with an inner wisdom about the experiences she needs right now, at her own stage, to develop well. So we should watch the child closely and openly, trying to see what her own deepest interests and ways of learning are. I believe if we followed the true developmental spirit in this way, we would find that children practically yearn for rich contact with nature, and this contact contributes significantly to their full development as persons.

Will More External Pressures Help?

As the standards movement presses forward with its agenda, it constantly raises the issue of students' motivation—or, more precisely, students' lack of motivation. There's broad agreement, inside and outside the standards movement, that most students don't like schoolwork very much and don't work very hard at it. But standards advocates don't urge schools to look for tasks that students find more intrinsically meaningful and motivating (Damon, 1995). Instead, standards advocates ask us to assign more difficult ("challenging") work and to apply external pressures and incentives. They urge us to push and prod children, talking to them about the value of "stretching themselves" and "self-discipline" (Carnegie Corporation, 1996, p. 95). They also urge real consequences, such as holding students back in their current grade if they don't meet a set standard on a standardized test.

In the developmental or child-centered view, pressuring students to do more difficult work won't help. Students might memorize more abstract concepts to pass their tests, but they won't necessarily understand them, and they will come to dislike school even more than they do now. Indeed, pediatricians worry that school-related stress and school avoidance are on the rise (Ginsburg, 2007).

To developmental educators, it is far better to base education on intrinsic motivation, to provide children with tasks that they eagerly perform for their own sake. We saw how Montessori found that if we provide the right environment—an environment with tasks that enable children to develop their naturally emerging capacities—they will become interested in them and work on them with incredible energy, concentration, and perseverance. And when finished, they are often happy and at peace, for the activity helped them develop something vital within themselves. In such circumstances, there is no need to try to motivate children through praise, threats, exhortations, or negative consequences.

Other child-centered educators share this belief in gearing education to children's inner desire to learn. This is true of Piagetian constructivists, Waldorf educators inspired by Rudolf Steiner, and progressive educators following in the footsteps of John Dewey. For example, progressive educators have pointed out that whereas students find the math in workbooks and textbooks abstract and pointless, they eagerly learn the math that enables them to carry out concrete projects such as cooking, carpentry, and gardening. In these activities, they want to learn the math because it enables them to fulfill their creative impulses.

The Issue of Independence

To developmental educators, there is another problem with the standards movement's persistent call to "raise the bar" and pressure students to perform more challenging work. As Rousseau pointed out, overly difficult work can undermine children's independence. When, for example, we give children math or science problems that are over their heads, they have no recourse but to turn outside themselves, to the teacher or others, for help. And because they don't fully understand the solutions, they must accept on faith whatever the "smarter" person (or the textbook) says is true. Children learn to depend on external authority rather than thinking for themselves.

Developmental educators, as we have seen, have suggested ways of stimulating independent thinking. Rousseau suggested the use of stimulating questions. That is, we can ask children questions they find intrinsically interesting and then let them solve them on their own. For example, Rousseau said he would ask Emile which ladder in the barn would reach the cherries on a tree. Emile would then consider the distance and see for himself if his estimate was correct. A contemporary master at this approach is the Piagetian constructivist Constance Kamii. Kamii suggests all kinds of math questions a teacher might ask children while they are engaged in activities they enjoy, such as playing ball. A teacher might ask a first-grade girl how many points her team needs before reaching the winning score. The child will probably find this question meaningful, and the teacher can then let the child spontaneously find a way of solving it. The method of stimulating questions, like other child-centered methods (for example, Montessori's) creates situations in which children can think for themselves.

Don't We Need to End Social Promotion?

Standards advocates rail against social promotion. It's unfair to students, they say, to promote them if they haven't mastered the material in the prior grade. Grade retention—holding students back—is necessary.

For developmental or child-centered educators, the central issue is the policy's emotional impact. The threat of holding students back creates a classroom of chronic fear. If students are, in fact, held back, they suffer great humiliation—an experience that contributes to high dropout rates (Heubert & Hauser, 1999; Herszenhorn, 2004). Real learning cannot occur in this emotional climate. Students must be free to throw themselves enthusiastically into activities. When they become deeply absorbed in activities, they think deeply and creatively and their minds expand. The child's enthusiasm for learning is precious.

On an institutional level, the issue of social promotion is actually an artifact of our schools' traditional factory-style setup. Children are expected to meet the same standards each year, year after year, as if they were on a conveyor belt. In the Montessori classroom, social promotion is not really an issue. In classrooms of mixed ages, each child chooses from a variety of tasks and proceeds at his or her own pace. There are no uniform end-of-year objectives.

Not all developmentally oriented schools mix the ages, but many encourage children to work individually or in small groups on the tasks they are ready for. If we visit an open-education or progressive-education classroom, we might see some children working on individual math projects, others reading books of their own choice, and a group of three or four students building a model canal system. There are no uniform, predetermined schedules. Children work at their own pace on tasks designed to meet their own individual needs. The issue of social promotion rarely comes up.

The Promise of Computers

I have said that the standards movement is making learning a joyless affair. Students are pressured to do increasingly difficult work that has little to do with their spontaneous interests and precludes the pleasure of figuring something out for oneself. While this characterization is basically true, there is one exception. The standards movement vigorously promotes computer-based technology, which promises to make even difficult learning fun.

There is no doubt that computers have considerable appeal. They give us feelings of almost magical power. Just by pressing a few buttons, we can instantly perform complex calculations and produce attractive graphics and stores of information. Through the Internet, computers connect us with people, videos, audiotapes, and other sources of information that extend well beyond the boundaries of our local libraries and resources.

In addition, experts such as Seymour Papert (1980) believe that when children learn to program computers with languages such as Logo, they learn high-order thinking skills. They learn to think in a systematic, goal-directed manner and evaluate their own progress. And because of the computer setup, each student can work at his or her own pace.

However, computer technology has yet to deliver on the educational benefits its promoters have promised (Bauerlein, 2009, pp. 120–124; Oppenheimer, 2003, pp. 22, 84). And computers present their own special problems—none more basic than the computer's physical environment. The child at the computer monitor is locked into a sterile, artificial environment. There is nothing but plastic and metal. As John Davy has said, there is "no wind or birdsong . . . no connection with soil, water, sunlight, warmth, no real ecology" (1984, p. 12). The sterility of the computer environment is particularly worrisome for young children, who are in the process of developing their senses and their connections to the natural world.

There also are problems concerning what the child does learn. The computer monitor presents only symbols—words, pictures, numbers, and graphs. The child is exposed to a great deal of information, but the child receives it on a purely secondhand, mental level. What does it mean to learn biology strictly from words, pictures, and other symbols, without first having rich, personal experience with plant and animal life? Or to learn principles of physics—principles such as velocity, force, and balance—without lots of experience throwing, hammering, seesawing, and climbing? The child learns symbols, but without the personal, bodily, sensory experiences that make the symbols meaningful. The danger is that the child who is learning a great deal for the first time at the computer terminal is learning at too cerebral a level. The child is becoming a disembodied mind.

When I have mentioned this problem to colleagues, they have often said, "Yes, but it doesn't have to happen this way. Why can't children learn from the computer and *also* spend a good deal of time playing outdoors, building things, exploring nature, and gaining physical and sensory experience?" In theory, this is possible. But in reality, children are spending more and more time indoors. When they are not in school or doing homework, they are watching TV, surfing the Internet, playing video games, and talking to their friends via e-mail and text messages (Bauerlein, 2009, chap. 3; Juster, Ono, & Stafford, 2004). As a result, children are spending most of their time in relatively sterile environments and aren't developing the rich, sensory foundations of knowledge.

In view of this problem, it is wise to limit computer-based learning in the elementary school years, when children are still learning heavily through the senses and concrete activities with things and people. Many Waldorf schools don't bring computers into the classrooms until the 8th grade. Few schools will wish to be this restrictive, but educators and parents should set some limits on computer use in the early years, making sure computers aren't substituting purely symbolic learning for rich and direct experience in the world.

The Tyranny of Testing

Ultimately, the standards movement rests on standardized tests. Tests inform federal, state, and municipal officials on how well students are meeting their goals and standards. Largely on the basis of test scores, officials reward some school districts and close down other districts, evaluate teachers and principals, and sometimes determine if students can advance to the next school grade and graduate from high school. Because standardized tests have become so important, teachers often find themselves "teaching to the test."

As tests drive the curriculum, child-centered teachers in particular are finding their autonomy and flexibility curtailed. They have little opportunity to tailor education to the child's own deepest interests. For example, a primary school teacher can hardly afford to give young children ample opportunities to develop their artistic creativity and explore nature when rigorous academic tests are looming. Similarly, a middle school teacher might find that she can teach a good deal of math through a carpentry project, and a high school teacher might observe that students are learning enthusiastically during a mock trial, but such projects and activities take time that simply isn't available under the pressures of high-stakes testing.

Teachers of all orientations are discovering that testing makes children very unhappy. The bulk of test preparation is tedious drill. What's more, children fear the tests. Early in the school year, they are already anxious about them. As the testing dates approach, their anxiety intensifies. Many cannot sleep and feel sick to their stomachs because they are afraid they will fail. When grade promotion depends on test scores, the children's anxiety is even greater. Teachers would like to calm the children down, but there's little the teacher can do when the children's fear is based on reality. To anyone who wants learning to be an exciting, positive experience, test-driven education is a disaster (Crain, 2003, pp. 2–4).

Many standards advocates—especially No Child Left Behind proponents—have argued that testing promotes civil rights. Tests provide an objective measure of how all students are performing, and the public can therefore see how well schools are reducing achievement gaps between minority and nonminority students. In theory, this might be correct. But in practice, it has meant that students of color are given an even heavier diet of tedious test preparation than other students. They also have been more likely to experience the humiliation of grade retention due to their test scores. If government officials really want to help low-income children, they will fund their schools on par with those of middle-class children and bring about equity in terms of class sizes, teacher salaries, lab equipment, books, and comfortable physical environments.

From a developmental perspective, we must reduce the tyranny of testing and put testing into a broader perspective. Tests provide useful information, but there are more basic considerations. Is education in accord with the child's basic growth tendencies—does she have opportunities to pursue interests and develop capacities that seem most important to her at her own phase of development? Does she love learning and have time to make her own discoveries? Is she curious, confident, and able to think for herself? Ultimately, the answers to these questions, not test scores, matter most.

REFERENCES

Abraham, K. (1924a). A short study of the development of the libido viewed in light of mental disorders. *Selected papers of Karl Abraham.* New York: Basic Books, 1927.

Abraham, K. (1924b). The influence of oral eroticism on character formation. *Selected papers of Karl Abraham.* New York: Basic Books, 1927.

Abram, D. (1996). *The spell of the sensuous.* New York: Vintage.

Ainsworth, M. D. S. (1967). *Infancy in Uganda: Infant care and the growth of love.* Baltimore: Johns Hopkins University Press.

Ainsworth, M.D.S. (1973). The development of infant and mother attachment. In. B. M. Caldwell & H. M. Ricciuti (Eds.), *Review of child development research* (Vol. 3). Chicago: University of Chicago Press.

Ainsworth, M. D. S. (1982). Attachment: Retrospect and prospect. In C. M. Parkes & J. Stevenson-Hinde (Eds.), *The place of attachment in human behavior.* New York: Basic Books.

Ainsworth, M. D. S., Bell, S. M., & Stanton, D. S. (1971). Individual differences in strange-situation behavior of one-year-olds. In H. R. Schaffer (Ed.), *The origins of human social relations.* New York: Academic Press.

Ainsworth, M. D. S., Blehar, M. C., Waters, E., & Wall, S. (1978). *Patterns of attachment.* Hillsdale, NJ: Erlbaum.

Ainsworth, M. D. S., & Bowlby, J. (1991). An ethological approach to personality development. *American Psychologist, 46,* 333–341.

Aitchison, J. (1976). *The articulate mammal: An introduction to psycholinguistics.* New York: University Books.

Als, H. (1978). Assessing an assessment: Conceptual considerations, methodological issues, and a perspective on the future of the Neonatal Behavioral Assessment Scale. In A. J. Sameroff (Ed.), *Organization and stability of newborn behavior: A commentary on the Brazelton Neonatal Behavior Assessment Scale. Monographs of the Society for Research in Child Development, 43,* Serial No. 177.

Ambridge, D., Rowland, C.F., & Pine, M. (2008). Is structure dependence an innate constraint? Experimental evidence from children's complex question production. *Cognitive Science, 32,* 222–255.

Ames, L. B. (1971). Don't push your preschooler. *Family Circle Magazine, 79,* 60.

Anderson, C., & Gentile, D. (2008). Media violence, aggression, and public policy. In E. Borgida & S. Fiske (Eds.), *Beyond common sense: Psychological science in the courtroom.* Malden, MA: Blackwell.

Appleton, T., Clifton, R., & Goldberg, S. (1975). The development of behavioral competence in infancy. In F. D. Horowitz (Ed.), *Review of child development research* (Vol. 4). Chicago: University of Chicago Press.

Ariès, P. (1960). *Centuries of childhood: A social history of family life* (R. Baldick, trans.). New York: Knopf, 1962.

Arnheim, R. (1954). *Art and visual perception.* Berkeley: University of California Press.

Ausubel, D. P. (1958). *Theories and problems in child development.* New York: Grune & Stratton.

Baerends, G., Beer, C., & Manning, A. (1975). *Function and evolution in behavior.* Oxford, UK: Clarendon Press.

Baillargeon, R. (1987). Object permanence in $3^1/_2$- and $4^1/_2$-year-old infants. *Developmental Psychology, 22,* 655–664.

Balcombe, J. (2006). *Pleasurable kingdom.* London: Macmillan.

Baldwin, A. L. (1980). *Theories of child development* (2nd ed.). New York: John Wiley.

Balinsky, B. I. (1981). *An introduction to embryology* (5th ed.). Philadelphia: Saunders.

Ball, G. F., & Hulse, S. H. (1998). Birdsong. *American Psychologist, 53,* 37–58.

Bandura, A. (1962). Social learning through imitation. In M. R. Jones (Ed.), *Nebraska symposium on motivation.* Lincoln: University of Nebraska Press.

Bandura, A. (1965a). Vicarious processes. A case of no-trial learning. In L. Berkowitz (Ed.), *Advances in experimental social psychology* (Vol. 2). New York: Academic Press.

Bandura, A. (1965b). Influence of model's reinforcement contingencies on the acquisition of imitative responses. *Journal of Personality and Social Psychology, 1,* 589–595.

Bandura, A. (1967). The role of modeling processes in personality development. In W. W. Hartup & W. L. Smothergill (Eds.), *The young child: Reviews of research.* Washington, DC: National Association for the Education of Young Children.

Bandura, A. (1969). Social-learning theory of identificatory processes. In D. A. Goslin (Ed.), *Handbook of socialization theory and research.* Chicago: Rand McNally.

Bandura, A. (1971). Analysis of modeling processes. In A. Bandura (Ed.), *Psychological modeling.* Chicago: Atherton, Aldine.

Bandura, A. (1977). *Social learning theory.* Englewood Cliffs, NJ: Prentice-Hall.

Bandura, A. (1986). *Social foundations of thought and action: A social cognitive theory.* Englewood Cliffs, NJ: Prentice-Hall.

Bandura, A. (1989). Social cognitive theory. In R. Vasta (Ed.), *Annals of Child Development, 6,* 1–60.

Bandura, A. (1994). Self-efficacy. In V. S. Ramachadraun (Ed.), *Encyclopedia of human behavior* (Vol. 4). New York: Academic Press.

Bandura, A. (1997). *Self-efficacy.* New York: W. H. Freeman.

Bandura, A. (1998). Personal and collective efficacy in human adaptation and change. In J. G. Adair, D. Belanger, & K. L. Dion (Eds.), *Advances in psychological science* (Vol. 1). Hove, UK: Psychology Press.

Bandura, A. (2006). Autobiography. In M.G. Lindzey & W. M. Runyan (Eds.), *A history of psychology in autobiography* (Vol. IX). Washington, DC: American Psychological Association.

Bandura, A., Grusec, J. E., & Menlove, F. L. (1967). Vicarious extinction of avoidance behavior. *Journal of Personality and Social Psychology, 5,* 16–23.

Bandura, A., & Huston, A. C. (1961). Identification as a process of incidental learning. *Journal of Abnormal and Social Psychology, 63,* 311–318.

Bandura, A., & Kupers, C. J. (1964). The transmission of patterns of self-reinforcement through modeling. *Journal of Abnormal and Social Psychology, 69,* 1–9.

Bandura, A., & McDonald, F. J. (1963). Influence of social reinforcement and the behavior of models in shaping children's moral judgments. *Journal of Abnormal and Social Psychology, 67,* 274–281.

Bandura, A., Ross, D., & Ross, S.A. (1961). Transmission of aggression through imitation of aggressive models. *Journal of Abnormal and Social Psychology, 63,* 575–582.

Bandura, A., & Walters, R. H. (1963). *Social learning and personality development.* New York: Holt, Rinehart & Winston.

Barr, R., Dowden, A., & Hayne, H. (1996). Developmental changes in deferred imitation by 6– to 24–month-old infants. *Infant Behavior and Development, 19,* 159–170.

Barten, S. S., & Franklin, M. B. (Eds.). (1978). *Developmental processes: Heinz Werner's selected writings* (Vols. 1 and 2). New York: International Universities Press.

Bateson, P. (1990). Is imprinting a special case? *Philosophical Transactions of the Royal Society, 329,* 125–131.

Bateson, P. (1991). Principles of behavioral development. In P. Bateson (Ed.), *The development and integration of behavior.* Cambridge, UK: Cambridge University Press.

Bauer, P. J. (2006). Event memory. In D. Kuhn & R. S. Siegler (Eds.), *Handbook of child psychology* (6th ed.) (Vol. 2), New York: Wiley.

Bauerlein, M. (2009). *The dumbest generation.* New York: Jeremy P. Tarcher/Penguin.

Baumrind, D. (1967). Child care practices anteceding three patterns of preschool behavior. *Genetic Psychology Monographs, 75,* 43–88.

Baumrind, D. (1989). Rearing competent children. In W. Damon (Ed.), *Child development today and tomorrow.* San Francisco: Jossey-Bass.

Bell, S. M. (1970). The development of the concept of object as related to infant-mother attachment. *Child Development, 41,* 291–311.

Bell, S. M., & Ainsworth, M. D. S. (1972). Infant crying and maternal responsiveness. *Child Development, 43,* 1171–1190.

Bellugi-Klima, U. (1968). Linguistic mechanisms underlying child speech. In E. M. Zale (Ed.), *Proceedings of the conference on language and language behavior.* Englewood Cliffs, NJ: Prentice-Hall.

Belsky, J., & Fearon, R. M. P. (2008). Precursors of attachment security. In J. Cassidy & P. R. Shaver (Eds.), *Handbook of attachment* (2nd ed.). New York: Guilford.

Benedek, T. (1938). Adaptation to reality in early infancy. *Psychoanalytic Quarterly, 7,* 200–215.

Benjamin, J. (1988). *The bonds of love.* New York: Pantheon.

Beres, D. (1971). Ego autonomy and ego pathology. *Psychoanalytic Study of the Child, 26,* 3–24.

Bergman, A. (1999). *Ours, yours, mine: Mutuality and the emergence of the separate self.* Northvale, NJ: Jason Aronson.

Bergman, I. (1957). *Wild Strawberries* [filmscript] (L. Malmstrom & D. Kushner, trans.). New York: Simon & Schuster.

Berk, L. E. (2001). *Awakening children's minds: How parents and teachers can make a difference.* Oxford, UK: Oxford University Press.

Berk, L. E. (2009). *Child development* (8th ed.). Boston: Pearson.

Berk, L.E. & Winsler, A. (1995). *Scaffolding children's learning: Vygotsky and early childhood education.* Washington, D.C.: National Association for the Education of Young Children.

Berkowitz, M. W., & Gibbs, J. C. (1985). The process of moral conflict resolution and moral development. In M. W. Berkowitz (Ed.), *Peer conflict and psychological growth.* San Francisco: Jossey-Bass.

Berman, M. (1970). *The politics of authenticity.* New York: Antheum.

Bernstein, R. (1990, November 4). Accusations of abuse haunt the legacy of Dr. Bruno Bettelheim. *New York Times,* Week in Review.

Bettelheim, B. (1960). *The informed heart: Autonomy in a mass age.* New York: Free Press.

Bettelheim, B. (1967). *The empty fortress: Infantile autism and the birth of the self.* New York: Free Press.

Bettelheim, B. (1974). *A home for the heart.* New York: Knopf.

Bettelheim, B. (1976). *The uses of enchantment: The meaning and importance of fairy tales.* New York: Knopf.

Bettelheim, B., & Zelan, K. (1981). *On learning to read.* New York: Random House.

Bickerton, D. (1984). The language biogram hypothesis. *The Behavioral and Brain Sciences, 7,* 173–221.

Bickerton, D. (1999). Creole languages, the language biogram hypothesis, and language acquisition. In W. C. Ritchie & T. K. Bhatia (Eds.), *Handbook of child language acquisition.* San Diego: Academic Press.

Bijou, S. W. (1976). *Child development: The basic stage of early childhood.* Englewood Cliffs, NJ: Prentice-Hall.

Bijou, S. W., & Baer, D. M. (1961). *Child development* (Vol. 1). Englewood Cliffs, NJ: Prentice-Hall.

Blasi, A. (1980). Bridging moral cognition and moral action: A critical review of the literature. *Psychological Bulletin, 88,* 593–637.

Blatt, M. M., & Kohlberg, L. (1975). The effects of classroom moral discussion upon children's level of moral judgment. *Journal of Moral Education, 4,* 129–161.

Blos, P. (1962). *On adolescence.* New York: Free Press.

Bodrova, E., & Leong, D. J. (2001). *Tools of the mind.* UNESCO. International Bureau of Education. www.ibe.unesco.org/publications/innodata/inno07.pdf

Bodrova, E. & Leong, D. J. (2007). *Tools of the mind: The Vygotskian approach to early childhood education* (2nd ed.). Upper Saddle River, NJ: Pearson/Merrill Prentice-Hall.

Borke, H. (1975). Piaget's mountains revisited: Changes in the egocentric landscape. *Developmental Pyschology, 11,* 240–243.

Bower, T. G. R. (1982). *Development in infancy* (2nd ed.). San Francisco: W. H. Freeman.

Bower, T. G. R. (1989). *The rational infant.* New York: W. H. Freeman.

Bowlby, J. (1965). *Child care and the growth of love.* Baltimore: Penguin Books.

Bowlby, J. (1973). *Attachment and loss* (Vol. 2). *Separation.* New York: Basic Books.

Bowlby, J. (1979). *The making and breaking of affectional bonds.* London: Tavistock Publications. BowlbBB

Bowlby, J. (1980). *Attachment and loss* (Vol. 3). *Loss.* New York: Basic Books.

Bowlby, J. (1982). *Attachment and loss* (Vol. 1). *Attachment* (2nd ed.). New York: Basic Books.

Bowlby, J. (1988). *A secure base.* New York: Basic Books.

Brackbill, Y. (1958). Extinction of the smiling response in infants as a function of reinforcement schedule. *Child Development, 29,* 115–124.

Brainerd, C. J. (2003). Piaget, learning research, and American education. In B. J. Zimmerman & D. H. Schunk (Eds.), *Educational psychology: A century of contributions.* Mahwah, NJ: Erlbaum.

Bretherton, I., Ridgeway, D., & Cassidy, J. (1990). Assessing internal working models of the attachment relationship: An attachment story completion task for 3-year-olds. In M. T. Greenberg, D. Cicchetti, & E. Mark Cummings (Eds.), *Attachment in the preschool years.* Chicago: University of Chicago Press.

Breuer, J., & Freud, S. (1895). *Studies on hysteria* (A. A. Brill, trans.). New York: Nervous and Mental Disease Publishing Co., 1936.

Bronson, P., & Merryman, A. (2009) *Nurture shock.* New York: Twelve.

Broughton, J. M. (1983). Women's rationality and men's virtues: A critque of gender dualism in Gilligan's theory of moral development. *Social Research, 50,* 597–642.

Brown, A. L., & Palinscar, A. S. (1989). Guided cooperative learning and individual knowledge acquisition. In L. B. Resnick (Ed.), *Knowing, learning, and instruction.* Hillsdale, NJ: Erlbaum.

Brown, E. (2009, November 21). Debate on playtime's value grows. *Washington Post.*

Brown, J. F. (1940). *The psychodynamics of abnormal behavior.* New York: McGraw-Hill.

Brown, P., & Elliott, R. (1965). Control of aggression in a nursery school class. *Journal of Experimental Child Psychology, 2,* 103–107.

Brown, R. (1965). *Social psychology.* New York: Free Press.

Brown, R. (1973). *A first language: The early stages.* Cambridge, MA: Harvard University Press.

Brown, R., & Bellugi, U. (1964). Three processes in the child's acquisition of syntax. *Harvard Educational Review, 34,* 133–151.

Brown, R., Cazden, C., & Bellugi-Klima, U. (1969). The child's grammar from I to III. In J. P. Hill (Ed.), *Minnesota symposia on child psychology* (Vol. 2). Minneapolis: University of Minnesota Press.

Brown, R., & Hanlon, C. (1970). Derivational complexity and order of acquisition in child speech. In R. Brown (Ed.), *Psycholinguistics: Selected papers.* New York: Free Press.

Brown, R., & Herrnstein, R. J. (1975). *Psychology.* Boston: Little, Brown.

Bruner, J. (1984). Vygotsky's zone of proximal development: The hidden agenda. In B. Rogoff & J. Wertsch (Eds.), *Children's learning in the "zone of proximal development."* San Francisco: Jossey-Bass.

Bryan, J. H. (1975). Children's cooperation and helping behaviors. In E. M. Hetherington (Ed.), *Review of child development research* (Vol. 5). Chicago: University of Chicago Press.

Bryan, J. H., & Walbek, N. (1970). Preaching and practicing generosity: Children's action, and reactions. *Child Development, 41,* 329–353.

Bryant, P. E. (1974). *Perception and understanding in young children: An experimental approach.* New York: Basic Books.

Butler, R. N. (1963). The life review: An interpretation of reminiscence in the aged. *Psychiatry, 26,* 65–76.

Cairns, H. S., & Cairns, C. E. (1976). *Psycholinguistics: A cognitive view of language.* New York: Holt, Rinehart & Winston.

Caldwell, B. M. (1964). The effects of infant care. In M. L. & L. W. Hoffman (Eds.), *Review of child development research* (Vol. 1). New York: Russell Sage Foundation.

Camp, B. (2002). *Language power: 12 to 24 months.* Denver: Bright Beginnings.

Campbell, N. A., & Reece, J. B. (2005). *Biology* (7th ed.). San Francisco: Pearson/Benjamin Cummings.

Camus, A (1948). *The plague.* (S. Gibert, trans.). New York: Vintage.

Camus, A. (1955). *The myth of Sisyphus and other essays.* (J. O'Brien, trans.). New York: Knopf.

Carnegie Corporation of New York. (1996). *Years of Promise: A comprehensive learning strategy for America's children.*

Carroll, S.B. (2009). *Remarkable creatures.* Boston: Houghton Mifflin Harcourt.

Chattin-McNichols, J. (1992). *The Montessori controversy.* Albany, NY: Delmar.

Chawla, L. (1990). Ecstatic places. *Children's Environments Quarterly, 3,* 34–41.

Chodorow, N. (1978). *The reproduction of mothering.* Berkeley: University of California Press.

Chomsky, C. (1969). *The acquisition of syntax in children from 5 to 10.* Cambridge, MA: MIT Press.

Chomsky, N. (1957). *Syntactic structures.* The Hague: Moulton.

Chomsky, N. (1959). A review of *Verbal behavior* by B. F. Skinner. *Language, 35,* 26–58.

Chomsky, N. (1962). Explanatory models in linguistics. In E. Nagel, P. Suppes, & A. Tarshi (Eds.), *Logic, methodology and philosophy of science*. Stanford: Stanford University Press.

Chomsky, N. (1965). *Aspects of the theory of syntax*. Cambridge, MA: MIT Press.

Chomsky, N. (1968). Recent contribution to the theory of innate ideas. In R. S. Cohen & M. W. Wartofsky (Eds.), *Boston studies on the philosophy of science* (Vol. 3). Dordrecht, Holland: D. Reidel.

Chomsky, N. (1972). *Language and mind*. New York: Harcourt Brace Jovanovich.

Chomsky, N. (1975). *Reflections on language*. San Diego: Pantheon.

Chomsky, N. (1977). Interview. In D. Cohen (Ed.), *Psychologists on psychology*. New York: Taplinger.

Chomsky, N. (1980). *Rules and representations*. New York: Columbia University Press.

Chomsky, N. (1983). Interview. In R. W. Reiber & G. Voyat (Eds.), *Dialogues on the psychology of language and thought*. New York: Plenum.

Chomsky, N. (1986). *Knowledge of language: Its nature, origin, and use*. New York: Praeger.

Chomsky, N. (2003, June 1). Interview on C-SPAN's *In Depth* [Television broadcast]. Washington, DC: National Satellite Cable Corporation.

Clarke-Stewart, K. A. (1989). Infant day care: Maligned or malignant? *American Psychologist, 44*, 266–273.

Coates, B., & Hartup, W. W. (1969). Age and verbalization in observational learning. *Developmental Psychology, 1*, 556–562.

Coe, B. (1996, Spring). Montessori and middle school. *Montessori Life, 8*, 26–29.

Colby, A., Kohlberg, L., Gibbs, J., & Lieberman, M. (1983). A longitudinal study of moral judgment. *Monographs of the Society for Research in Child Development* (Serial No. 200).

Colby, A., Kohlberg, L., & Kauffman, K. (1987a). Theoretical introduction to the measurement of moral judgment. In A. Colby & L. Kohlberg (Eds.), *The measurement of moral judgment* (Vol. 1). Cambridge, UK: Cambridge University Press.

Colby, A., Kohlberg, L., & Kauffman, K. (1987b). Instructions for moral judgment interviewing. In A. Colby & L. Kohlberg (Eds.), *The measurement of moral judgment* (Vol. 1). Cambridge, UK: Cambridge University Press.

Colby, A., Kohlberg, L., Speicher, B., Hewer, A., Candee, D., Gibbs, J., & Power, C. (1987c). *The measurement of moral judgment* (Vol. 2). Cambridge, UK: Cambridge University Press.

Cole, M., & Cole, S. R. (1993). *The development of children* (2nd ed.). New York: Scientific.

Cole, M., & Cole, S. R. (2001). *The development of children* (4th ed.). New York: Freeman.

Cole, M., & Scribner, S. (1978). Introduction. In M. Cole, V. John-Steiner, S. Scribner, & E. Souberman (Eds.), *L. S. Vygotsky: Mind in society*. Cambridge, MA: Harvard University Press.

Coles, R. (1970). *Erik H. Erikson: The growth of his work*. Boston: Little, Brown.

Condon, W. S., & Sander, L. W. (1974). Neonate movement is synchronized with adult speech: Interactional participation and language acquisition. *Science, 183*, 99–101.

Crain, S., & Nakayama, M. (1987). Structure dependence in children's language. *Language, 63*, 522–543.

Crain, S., & Thornton, R. (2006). Acquisition of syntax and semantics (2nd ed) . In M. Traxler & M. Gernsbacher (Eds.), *Handbook of psycholinguistics*. London, UK: Elsevier.

Crain, W. (1993). Technological time values and the assault on healthy development. *Holistic Education Review, 6*, 27–34.

Crain, W. (1997, Spring). How nature helps children develop. *Montessori Life, 9*, 41–43.

Crain, W. (2003). *Reclaiming childhood: Letting children be children in our achievement-oriented society*. New York: Holt.

Crain, W., & Crain, E. F. (1987). Can humanistic psychology contribute to our understanding of medical problem-solving? *Psychological Reports, 61*, 779–788.

Cranston, M. (1982). *Jean-Jacques: The early life and work of Jean-Jacques Rousseau 1712–1754*. Chicago: University of Chicago Press.

Dale, P. S. (1976). *Language development: Structure and function* (2nd ed.). Hinsdale, IL: Dryden Press.

Damon, W. (1983). *Social and personality development*. New York: W. W. Norton.

Damon, W. (1995). *Greater expectations*. New York: Free Press.

Darwin, C. (1859). *The origin of species*. New York: Modern Library.

Darwin, C. (1874). *The descent of man* (2nd ed.). Amherst, NY: Prometheus Books.

Darwin, C. (1887). *The autobiography of Charles Darwin*. New York: W. W. Norton.

Dasen, P. R. (1972). Cross-cultural Piagetian research: A summary. *Journal of Cross-Cultural Psychology, 3*, 23–39.

Davy, J. (1984). Mindstorms in the lamplight. In D. Sloan (Ed.), *The computer in education: A critical perspective.* New York: Teachers College Press.

DeHart, G. B., Sroufe, L. A., & Cooper, R. G. (2004). *Child development: Its nature and course* (5th ed.). Boston: McGraw Hill.

DeVries, R., & Kohlberg, L. (1987). *Constructivist early education: Overview and comparison with other programs.* Washington, DC: National Association for the Education of Young Children.

Dewey, J., & Dewey, E. (1915). *Schools for tomorrow.* New York: Dutton.

Diamond, A., Barnett, W. S., Thomas, J., & Munro, S. (2007). Preschool program improves cognitive control. *Science, 318,* 1387–1388.

Dillon, S. (2010, Jan. 13). Obama proposes sweeping change in education law. *The New York Times,* 1.

Dozier, M., & Rutter, M. (2008). Challenges to the development of attachment relationships faced by young children in foster and adoptive care. In J. Cassidy & P. R. Shaver (Eds.), *Handbook of attachment* (2nd ed.). New York: Guilford.

Dubos, R. J. (1961). *The dreams of reason.* New York: Columbia University Press.

Edwards, C. P. (1981). The comparative study of the development of moral judgment and reasoning. In R. L. Munroe, R. Munroe, & B. B. Whiting (Eds.), *Handbook of cross-cultural development.* New York: Garland.

Ehrlich, P. R., & Holm, K. W. (1963). *The process of evolution.* New York: McGraw-Hill.

Eisen, G. (1990). *Children and play in the Holocaust.* Amherst, MA: University of Massachusetts Press.

Elkind, D. (1981). *The hurried child.* Reading, MA: Addison-Wesley.

Elkind, D. (1986, May). Formal education and early childhood education: An essential difference. *Phi Delta Kappan,* 631–636.

Ellenberger, H. F. (1958). A clinical introduction to psychiatric phenomenology and existential analysis. In R. May, E. Angel, & H. F. Ellenberger (Eds.), *Existence: A new dimension in psychiatry and psychology.* New York: Basic Books.

Ellenberger, H. F. (1970). *The discovery of the unconscious.* New York: Basic Books.

Engels, F. (1925). *Dialectics of nature* (C. Dutt, trans.). Moscow: Foreign Languages Publishing House, 1954.

"Erik Erikson." (1994, May 13). Obituary, *New York Times.*

Erikson, E. H. (1958). *Young man Luther.* New York: W. W. Norton.

Erikson, E. H. (1959). Identity and the life cycle. *Psychological Issues, 1,* 1.

Erikson, E. H. (1963). *Childhood and society* (2nd ed.). New York: W. W. Norton.

Erikson, E. H. (1964). *Insight and responsibility.* New York: W. W. Norton.

Erikson, E. H. (1969). *Gandhi's truth.* New York: W. W. Norton.

Erikson, E. H. (1976). Reflections on Dr. Borg's life cycle. *Daedalus, 105,* 1–28.

Erikson, E. H. (1982). *The life cycle completed.* New York: W. W. Norton.

Ervin, S. M. (1964). Imitation and structural change in children's language. In E. H. Lenneberg (Ed.), *New directions in the study of language.* Cambridge, MA: MIT Press.

Estes, W. K. (1944). An experimental study of punishment. *Psychological Monographs, 57,* 94–107.

Etzel, B. C., & Gewirtz, J. L. (1967). Experimental modification of care-taking maintained high-rate operant crying in a 6- and 20-week-old infant (*infans tyrannotearus*): Extinction of crying with reinforcement of eye contact and smiling. *Journal of Experimental Child Psychology, 5,* 303–317.

Evans, E. (1975). *Contemporary influences in early childhood education* (2nd ed.). New York: Holt, Rinehart & Winston.

Evans, R. I. (1969). *Dialogue with Erik Erikson.* New York: Dutton.

Evans, R. I. (1989). *Albert Bandura: The man and his ideas—A dialogue.* New York: Praeger.

Feeney, J. A. (2008). Adult romantic attachment: Developments in the study of couple relationships. In J. Cassidy & P. R.Shaver (Eds.), *Handbook of attachment* (2nd ed.). New York: Guilford.

Fenichel, O. (1945). *The psychoanalytic theory of neurosis.* New York: W. W. Norton.

Flavell, J. H. (1963). *The developmental psychology of Jean Piaget.* New York: Van Nostrand Reinhold.

Flavell, J. H. (1977). *Cognitive development.* Englewood Cliffs, NJ: Prentice-Hall.

Flavell, J. H. (1985). *Cognitive development* (2nd ed.). Englewood Cliffs, NJ: Prentice-Hall.

Flavell, J. H., Botkin, P. T., Fry, C. L., Wright, J. W., & Jarvis, P. E. (1968). *The development of role-taking and communication skills in children.* New York: John Wiley.

Flavell, J. H., Miller, P. H., & Miller, S. A. (2002). *Cognitive development* (4th ed.). Upper Saddle River, NJ: Prentice-Hall.

Fogel, A. (2009). *Infancy: Infant, family, and society* (5th ed.). Cornwell-on-Hudson, NY: Sloan.

Franklin, M. B. (2004). Prologue to Werner, H. *Comparative psychology of mental development.* Clinton Corners, NY: Percheron Press.

Freedman, D. G. (1971). An evolutionary approach to research on the life cycle. *Human Development, 14,* 87–99.

Freedman, D. G. (1974). *Human infancy: An evolutionary perspective.* New York: John Wiley.

Freud, A. (1936). *The ego and the mechanisms of defense.* New York: International Universities Press, 1946.

Freud, A. (1958). Adolescence. *Psychoanalytic Study of the Child, 13,* 255–278.

Freud, S. (1900). *The interpretation of dreams* (J. Strachey, trans.). New York: Basic Books (Avon), 1965.

Freud, S. (1905). Three contributions to the theory of sex. *The basic writings of Sigmund Freud* (A. A. Brill, trans.). New York: Modern Library.

Freud, S. (1907). The sexual enlightenment of children (J. Riviere, trans.). *Collected papers* (Vol. 2). New York: Basic Books, 1959.

Freud, S. (1908a). Character and anal eroticism (J. Riviere, trans.). *Collected papers* (Vol. 2). New York: Basic Books, 1959.

Freud, S. (1908b). On the sexual theories of children (J. Riviere, trans.). *Collected papers* (Vol. 2). New York: Basic Books. 1959.

Freud, S. (1909). Analysis of a phobia in a five-year-old boy (A. & J. Strachey, trans.). *Collected papers* (Vol. 3). New York: Basic Books, 1959.

Freud, S. (1910). *The origin and development of psychoanalysis.* New York: Henry Regnery (Gateway Editions), 1965.

Freud, S. (1911). Formulations regarding the two principles of mental functioning (J. Riviere, trans.). *Collected papers* (Vol. 4). New York: Basic Books, 1959.

Freud, S. (1912). Contributions to the psychology of love: The most prevalent form of degradation in erotic life (J. Riviere, trans.). *Collected papers* (Vol. 4). New York: Basic Books, 1959.

Freud, S. (1913). The excretory functions in psychoanalysis and folklore (J. Strachey, trans.). *Collected papers* (Vol. 5). New York: Basic Books, 1959.

Freud, S. (1914a). On the history of the psychoanalytic movement (J. Riviere, trans.). *Collected papers* (Vol. 1). New York: Basic Books, 1959.

Freud, S. (1914b). On narcissism: An introduction (J. Riviere, trans.). *Collected papers* (Vol. 4). New York: Basic Books, 1959.

Freud, S. (1915a). Instincts and their vicissitudes (J. Riviere, trans.). *Collected papers* (Vol. 4). New York: Basic Books, 1959.

Freud, S. (1915b). The unconscious (J. Riviere, trans.). *Collected papers* (Vol. 4). New York: Basic Books, 1959.

Freud, S. (1916). Metapsychological supplement to the theory of dreams (J. Riviere, trans.). *Collected papers* (Vol. 4). New York: Basic Books, 1959.

Freud, S. (1917). Mourning and melancholia (J. Riviere, trans.). *Collected papers* (Vol. 4). New York: Basic Books, 1959.

Freud, S. (1920). *A general introduction to psychoanalysis* (J. Riviere, trans.). New York: Washington Square Press, 1965.

Freud, S. (1922). Medusa's head (J. Strachey, trans.). *Collected papers* (Vol. 5). New York: Basic Books, 1959.

Freud, S. (1923). *The ego and the id* (J. Riviere, trans.). New York: W. W. Norton, 1960.

Freud, S. (1924). The passing of the Oedipus complex (J. Riviere, trans.). *Collected papers* (Vol. 2). New York: Basic Books, 1959.

Freud, S. (1925a). Some psychological consequences of the anatomical distinction between the sexes (J. Strachey, trans.). *Collected papers* (Vol. 5). New York: Basic Books, 1959.

Freud, S. (1925b). The resistance to psychoanalysis (J. Strachey, trans.). *Collected papers* (Vol. 5). New York: Basic Books, 1959.

Freud, S. (1926). *Inhibitions, symptoms, and anxiety* (J. Strachey, trans.). New York: Norton, 1959.

Freud, S. (1931). Female sexuality (J. Strachey, trans.). *Collected papers* (Vol. 5). New York: Basic Books, 1959.

Freud, S. (1933). *New introductory lectures on psychoanalysis* (J. Strachey, trans.). New York: Norton, 1965.

Freud, S. (1936a). *The problem of anxiety* (H. A. Bunker, trans.). New York: The Psychoanalytic Press and W. W. Norton.

Freud, S. (1936b). A disturbance in memory on the Acropolis (J. Strachey, trans.). *Collected papers* (Vol. 5). New York: Basic Books, 1959.

Freud, S. (1940). *An outline of psychoanalysis* (J. Strachey, trans.). New York: W. W. Norton, 1949.

Gardner, H. (1973). *The arts and human development.* New York: John Wiley.

Gardner, H. (1980). *Artful scribbles.* New York: Basic Books.

Gardner, H. (1982). *Developmental psychology: An introduction* (2nd ed.). Boston: Little, Brown.

Gardner, R. A., & Gardner, B. (1969, August 15). Teaching sign language to a chimpanzee. *Science, 165,* 644–672.

Gay, P. (1969). *The enlightenment.* New York: W. W. Norton.

Gay, P. (1988). *Freud: A life for our time.* New York: W. W. Norton.

Gelman, R. (1969). Conservation acquisition: A problem of learning to attend to relevant attributes. *Journal of Experimental Child Psychology, 7,* 167–187.

Gelman, R. (1972). The nature and development of early number concepts. In H. Reese (Ed.), *Advances in child development and behavior* (Vol. 7). New York: Academic Press.

Gelman, R. (1979). Preschool thought. *American Psychologist, 34,* 900–905.

Gelman, R., & Baillargeon, R. (1983). A review of some Piagetian concepts. In P. H. Mussen (Ed.), *Handbook of child psychology* (4th ed.) (Vol. 3, *Cognitive development,* J. H. Flavell & E. M. Markman, Eds.). New York: John Wiley.

Gesell, A. (1945). *The embryology of behavior.* New York: Harper & Row.

Gesell, A. (1946). The ontogenesis of infant behavior. In L. Carmichael (Ed.), *Manual of child psychology* (2nd ed.). New York: John Wiley, 1954.

Gesell, A. (1952a). Autobiography. In E. G. Boring, H. Werner, R. M. Yerkes, & H. Langfield (Eds.), *A history of psychology in autobiography* (Vol. 4). Worcester, MA: Clark University Press.

Gesell, A. (1952b). *Infant development: The embryology of early human behavior.* Westport, CT: Greenwood Press, 1972.

Gesell, A., & Amatruda, C. S. (1941). *Developmental diagnosis: Normal and abnormal child development.* New York: Hoeber.

Gesell, A., & Ilg, F. L. (1943). *Infant and child in the culture of today.* In A. Gesell & F. L. Ilg (Eds.), *Child development.* New York: Harper & Row, 1949.

Gesell, A., & Ilg, F. L. (1946). *The child from five to ten.* In A. Gesell & F. L. Ilg (Eds.), *Child development.* New York: Harper & Row, 1949.

Gesell, A., Ilg, F. L., & Ames, L. B. (1956). *Youth: The years ten to sixteen.* New York: Harper.

Gesell, A., & Thompson, H. (1929). Learning and growth in identical infant twins: An experimental study by the method of co-twin control. *Genetic Psychology Monographs, 6,* 1–124.

Gibbs, J. C. (2003). *Moral development and reality.* Thousand Oaks, CA: Sage.

Gibbs, J. C., Basinger, K. S., Grime, R. L., & Snarey, J. R. (2007). Moral judgment development across cultures: Revisiting Kohlberg's universality claims. *Developmental Review, 27,* 443–500.

Gilligan, C. (1977). In a different voice: Women's conceptions of self and morality. *Harvard Educational Review, 47,* 481–517.

Gilligan, C. (1982). *In a different voice.* Cambridge, MA: Harvard University Press.

Ginsburg, H., & Opper, S. (1988). *Piaget's theory of intellectual development* (3rd ed.). Englewood Cliffs, NJ: Prentice-Hall.

Ginsburg, K. R. (2007). The importance of play in promoting healthy child development and maintaining strong parent-child bonds. *Pediatrics, 119,* 182–191.

Gitelson, M. (1975). The emotional problems of elderly people. In W. C. Sze (Ed.), *Human life cycle.* New York: Jason Aronson.

Glick, J. (1983). Piaget, Vygotsky, and Werner. In S. Wapner & B. Kaplan (Eds.), *Toward a holistic developmental psychology.* Hillsdale, NJ: Erlbaum.

Goble, F. G. (1970). *The third force: The psychology of Abraham Maslow.* New York: Grossman.

Goldberg, S. (1995). Introduction. In S. Goldberg, R. Muir, & J. Kerr (Eds.), *Attachment theory.* Hillsdale, NJ: Analytic Press.

Goldstein, K. (1939). *The organism: A holistic approach to biology derived from pathological data in man.* New York: American Book.

Goleman, D. (1990, March 14). Bruno Bettelheim dies at 86; psychoanalyst of vast impact. *New York Times,* p. D25.

Gopnik, A. (2009, August 16). Your baby is smarter than you think. *New York Times.*

Gouin-Décarie, T. (1965). *Intelligence and affectivity in early childhood.* New York: International Universities Press.

Greenberg, J. R., & Mitchell, S. A. (1983). *Object relations in psychoanalytic theory*. Cambridge, MA: Harvard University Press.

Gregory, R. L. (Ed.). (1987). *The Oxford companion to the mind*. Oxford, UK: Oxford University Press.

Griffin, P., & Cole, M. (1984). Current activity for the future: The Zo-ped. In B. Rogoff & J. Wertsch (Eds.), *Children's learning in the zone of proximal development*. San Francisco: Jossey-Bass.

Grimm, The Brothers (1972). *The complete Grimm's fairy tales*. New York: Random House.

Gruber, H. E. (1981). *Darwin on man* (2nd ed.). Chicago: University of Chicago Press.

Grusec, J. E., & Brinker, D. B. (1972). Reinforcement for imitation as a social learning determinant with implications for sex-role development. *Journal of Personality and Social Psychology, 21*, 149–158.

Gutman, D. (1987). *Reclaimed powers*. New York: Basic Books.

Haan, N., Smith, M. B., & Block, J. (1968). Moral reasoning of young adults: Political-social behavior, family background, and personality correlates. *Journal of Personality and Social Psychology, 10*, 183–201.

Haber, R. N. (1969, April). Eidetic images. *Scientific American, 220*, 36–44.

Hahnel, J. (2009, April–June). No Child Left Behind fails to close the achievement gap. *National Center for Youth and Law*. Retrieved January 27, 2009.

Haight, W. L., & Miller, P. J. (1993). *Pretending at home*. Albany, NY: SUNY Press.

Halford, G. S., & Andrews, G. (2006). Reasoning and problem solving. In D. Kuhn & R. Sielger (Eds.), *Handbook of child psychology* (6th ed.) (Vol. 2, Cognition, perception, and language). Hoboken, NJ: Wiley.

Hall, C. (1954). *A primer of Freudian psychology*. New York: Mentor Books (New American Library).

Hall, C., Lindzey, G., & Campbell, J. B. (1998). *Theories of personality* (4th ed.). New York: John Wiley.

Hanawalt, B. A. (1986). *The ties that bound: Peasant families in medieval England*. New York: Oxford University Press.

Harris, J. R., & Liebert, R. M. (1984). *The child*. Englewood Cliffs, NJ: Prentice-Hall.

Harris, P. L. (1983). Infant cognition. In M. M. Haith & J. J. Campos (Eds.), *Handbook of child psychology* (Vol. 2). New York: Wiley.

Hart, B., & Risley, T. R. (2003, Spring). The early catastrophe. *American Educator, 27*, 4–9.

Hart, R. A. (1979). *Children's experience of place*. New York: Irvington.

Hartmann, H. (1939). *Ego psychology and the problem of adaptation*. New York: International Universities Press, 1958.

Hartmann, H. (1950). Comments on the psychoanalytic theory of the ego. In H. Hartman (Ed.), *Essays on ego psychology*. New York: International Universities Press, 1964.

Hartmann, H. (1956). The development of the ego concept in Freud's work. *International Journal of Psychoanalysis, 37*, 425–438.

Hartmann, H., Kris, E., & Lowenstein, R. M. (1946). Comments on the formation of psychic structure. *Psychoanalytic Study of the Child, 2*, 11–38.

Hass, W. R. (1975). Pragmatic structures of language: Historical, formal, and developmental issues. In K. F. Riegel & G. C. Rosenwald (Eds.), *Structure and transformation*. New York: John Wiley.

Havighurst, R. J. (1952). *Developmental tasks and education*. New York: David McKay.

Havighurst, R. J. (1968). A social-psychological perspective on aging. *The Gerontologist, 8*, 67–71.

Havighurst, R. J., Neugarten, B. L., & Tobin, S. S. (1968). Disengagement and patterns of aging. In B. L. Neugarten (Ed.), *Middle age and aging*. Chicago: University of Chicago Press.

Hayne, H., & MacDonald, S. (2003). The socialization of autobiographical memory in children and adults: The roles of culture and gender. In R. Fivush & C. A. Haden (Eds.), *Autobiographical memory and the construction of a narrative self: Developmental and cultural perspectives*. Mahwah, NJ: Erlbaum.

Heidbreder, E. (1933). *Seven psychologies*. New York: Appleton Century Crofts.

Herszenhorn, D. (2004, April 7). Studies in Chicago fault policy of holding back 3rd graders. *New York Times*, B 1,6.

Hess, E. H. (1962). Ethology: An approach toward the complete analysis of behavior. In *New directions in psychology* (Vol. 1). New York: Holt, Rinehart & Winston.

Hess, E. H. (1973). *Imprinting: Early experience and the developmental psychology of attachment*. New York: Van Nostrand Reinhold.

Hesse, E. (2008). The adult attachment interview: Historical and current perspectives. In J. Cassidy & P. R. Shaver (Eds.), *Handbook of attachment* (2nd ed). New York: Guilford.

Heubert, J. P., & Hauser, R. M. (Eds.). 1999. *High stakes. Testing for tracking, promotion, and graduation.* A report by the National Research Council. Washington, DC: National Academy Press.

Hetherington, E. M., & Parke, R. D. (1977). *Contemporary readings in child psychology.* New York: McGraw-Hill.

Hirsh-Pasek, K., Golinkoff, R. M., Berk, L. E., & Singer, D. G. (2009). *A mandate for playful learning in preschool.* New York: Oxford University Press.

Hofer, M. A. (1981). *The roots of human behavior: An introduction to the psychobiology of early development.* San Francisco: W. H. Freeman.

Hoffman, M. L. (1970). Moral development. In P. H. Mussen (Ed.), *Carmichael's manual of child psychology* (3rd ed.) (Vol. 2). New York: John Wiley.

Holstein, C. B. (1973, March). *Irreversible, stepwise sequence in the development of moral judgment: A longitudinal evaluation.* Paper presented at the biannual meeting of the Society for Research in Child Development.

Holt, J. (1964). *How children fail.* New York: Dell.

Homme, L. E., & Totsi, D. T. (1969). Contingency management and motivation. In D. M. Gelfand (Ed.), *Social learning in childhood: Readings in theory and application.* Belmont, CA: Brooks/Cole.

Honigmann, J. J. (1967). *Personality in culture.* New York: Harper & Row.

Hussain-Rizvi, A., Kunkov, S., & Crain, E. F. (2009). Does parental involvement in pediatric emergency department asthma treatment affect home involvement? *Journal of Asthma, 46,* 729–795.

Hyams, N. M. (1986). *Language acquisition and the theory of parameters.* Dordrecht, Holland: D. Reider.

Inhelder, B. (1971). The criteria of the stages of mental development. In J. M. Tanner & B. Inhelder (Eds.), *Discussions on child development.* New York: International Universities Press.

Inhelder, B., & Piaget, J. (1955). *The growth of logical thinking from childhood to adolescence* (A. Parsons & S. Milgram, trans.). New York: Basic Books.

Jacobi, J. (1965). *The way of individuation* (R. F. C. Hull, trans.). San Diego: Harcourt Brace Jovanovich, 1967.

Jacobson, E. (1964). The self and the object world. *Psychoanalytic Study of the Child, 9,* 75–127.

Jatich, A. M. (1990, October). Repudiating Bettelheim. *University of Chicago Magazine, 83.*

Johnson, C. (1990). *On becoming lost.* Salt Lake City, UT: Gibbs-Smith.

Johnson, J. S., & Newport, E. L. (1989). Critical period effects in second language learning: The influence of maturational state on the acquisition of English as a second language. *Cognitive Psychology, 21,* 60–99.

John-Steiner, V., & Souberman, E. (1978). Afterword. In M. Cole, V. John-Steiner, S. Scribner, & E. Souberman (Eds.), *L. S. Vygotsky: Mind in society.* Cambridge, MA: Harvard University Press.

Jones, E. (1918). Anal-erotic character traits. *Journal of Abnormal Psychology, 13,* 261–284.

Jones, E. (1961). *The life and work of Sigmund Freud* (ed. and abridged by J. Trilling & S. Marcus). New York: Basic Books.

Jones, M. C. (1924). A laboratory study of fear: The case of Peter. *Pedagogical Seminary, 31,* 308–315.

Jung, C. G. (1931). Marriage as a psychological relationship (R. F. C. Hull, trans.). In C. G. Jung, *The collected works of C. G. Jung: Vol. 20. The development of personality.* Princeton, NJ: Princeton University Press, 1953.

Jung, C. G. (1933). *Modern man in search of a soul* (W. S. Dell & C. F. Baynes, trans.). New York: Harvest Book.

Jung, C. G. (1945). The relations between the ego and the unconscious (R. F. C. Hull, trans.). *The collected works of C. G. Jung: Vol. 7. Two essays in analytic psychology.* Princeton, NJ: Princeton University Press, 1953.

Jung, C. G. (1961). *Memories, dreams, reflections* (A. Jaffe, Ed., R. & G. Winston, trans.). New York: Vintage Books.

Jung, C. G. (1964). Approaching the unconscious. In C. G. Jung (Ed.), *Man and his symbols.* New York: Dell.

Justor, F. T., Ono, H., & Stafford, F.P. (2004). *Changing times for American youth: 1981–2003.* www.ns.umich.edu/Releases/2004/Nov04/teen_time_report.pdf

Kagan, J. (1984). *The nature of the child.* New York: Basic Books.

Kahn, D. (1993). *Montessori in the public schools.* Cleveland, OH: Montessori Public School Consortium.

Kamii, C. K. (1973). Piaget's interactionism and the process of teaching young children. In M. Schwebel & J. Raph (Eds.), *Piaget in the classroom.* New York: Basic Books.

Kamii, C. K. (1980). Why use group games? In C. Kamii & R. DeVries (Eds.), *Group games in early education.* Washington, DC: National Association for the Education of Young Children.

Kamii, C. K. (1985). *Young children reinvent arithmetic.* New York: Teachers College Press.

Kamii, C. K. (1994). *Young children continue to reinvent arithmetic: 3rd grade.* New York: Teachers College Press.

Kamii, C. K. (2004). *Young children continue to reinvent arithmetic: 2nd grade* (2nd ed). New York: Teachers College Press.

Kamii, C., & DeVries, R. (1977). Piaget for education. In M. C. Day & R. K. Parker (Eds.), *The preschool in action* (2nd ed.). Boston: Allyn & Bacon.

Kanner, L. (1943). Autistic disturbances of affective contact. *Nervous Child, 2,* 217–250.

Kant, I. (1788). *The critique of practical reason* (L. W. Beck, trans.). New York: Liberal Arts Press, 1956.

Kaplan, L. J. (1978). *Oneness and separateness.* New York: Simon & Schuster (Touchstone).

Kardiner, A. (1945). *The psychological frontiers of society.* New York: Columbia University Press.

Karen, R. (1994). *Becoming attached.* New York: Warner Books (Oxford University Press paperback, 1998).

Kegan, R. (1985). The loss of Pete's Dragon: Developments of the self in the years five to seven. In R. L. Leahy (Ed.), *The development of the self.* New York: Academic Press.

Keniston, K. (1971). The perils of principle. In K. Keniston (Ed.), *Youth and dissent.* San Diego: Harcourt Brace Jovanovich.

Kessen, W. (1965). *The child.* New York: John Wiley.

King, M. L., Jr. (1963). *Strength to love.* Philadelphia, PA: Fortress Press.

Kirsh, S. J. (2006). *Children, adolescents, and media violence.* Thousand Oaks, CA: Sage.

Klein, A (2010, March 2). Standards, Title I link scrutinized. *Education Week.*

Klima, E. S., & Bellugi, U. (1966). Syntactic regularities in the speech of children. In J. Lyons & R. J. Wales (Eds.), *Psycholinguistics papers.* Edinburgh: Edinburgh University Press.

Koegel. R. L., & Koegel, L. K. (2006). *Pivotal response treatments for autism.* Baltimore, MD: Paul H. Brookes.

Kohlberg, L. (1958a). *The development of modes of thinking and choice in the years 10 to 16.* Unpublished doctoral dissertation, University of Chicago.

Kohlberg, L. (1958b). Global Rating Guide with new materials. School of Education, Harvard University.

Kohlberg, L. (1963). The development of children's orientations toward a moral order: I. Sequence in the development of moral thought. *Human Development, 6,* 11–33.

Kohlberg, L. (1964). Development of moral character and moral ideology. In M. L. Hoffman & L. W. Hoffman (Eds.), *Review of child development research* (Vol. 1). New York: Russell Sage Foundation.

Kohlberg, L. (1966a). Cognitive stages and preschool education. *Human Development, 9,* 5–17.

Kohlberg, L. (1966b). A cognitive-developmental analysis of children's sex-role concepts and attitudes. In E. E. Maccoby (Ed.), *The development of sex differences.* Stanford: Stanford University Press.

Kohlberg, L. (1968). Early education: A cognitive-developmental approach. *Child Development, 39,* 1013–1062.

Kohlberg, L. (1969a). Stage and sequence. A cognitive-developmental approach to socialization. In D. A. Goslin (Ed.), *Handbook of socialization theory and research.* Chicago: Rand McNally.

Kohlberg, L. (1969b). *The relations between moral judgment and moral action.* Colloquium presented at the Institute of Human Development. Berkeley: University of California Press.

Kohlberg, L. (1970). *The child as a moral philosopher. Readings in developmental psychology today.* Del Mar, CA: CRM Books.

Kohlberg, L. (1976). Moral stages and moralization: The cognitive-developmental approach. In T. Lickona (Ed.), *Moral development and behavior: Theory, research, and social issues.* New York: Holt, Rinehart & Winston.

Kohlberg, L. (1981). *Essays on moral development* (Vol. 1). New York: Harper & Row.

Kohlberg, L., & Candee, D. (1984). The relationship of moral judgment to moral action. In L. Kohlberg (Ed.), *Essays on moral development* (Vol. II). Cambridge, MA: Harper & Row.

Kohlberg, L., & Elfenbein, D. (1975). The development of moral judgments concerning capital punishment. *American Journal of Orthopsychiatry, 45,* 614–640.

Kohlberg, L., & Gilligan, C. (1971). The adolescent as philosopher. *Daedalus, 100,* 1051–1086.

Kohlberg, L., Kauffman, K., Scharf, P., & Hickey, J. (1975). The just community approach to corrections: A theory. *Journal of Moral Education, 4,* 243–260.

Kohlberg, L., & Kramer, R. (1969). Continuities and discontinuities in childhood and adult moral development. *Human Development, 12,* 93–120.

Kohlberg, L., & Power, C. (1981). Moral development, religious thinking, and the question of a seventh stage. In L. Kohlberg (Ed.), *Essays on moral development* (Vol. 1). New York: Harper & Row.

Kohlberg, L., Yaeger, J., & Hjertholm, E. (1968). The development of private speech: Four studies and a review of theories. *Child Development, 39,* 691–736.

Kohler, W. (1925). *The mentality of apes.* London: Routledge & Kegan Paul.

Kozol, J. (2005). *The shame of the nation.* New York: Random House.

Kozulin, A. (Ed.). (1986). Vygotsky in context. Introductory chapter to L. S. Vygotsky's *Thought and language.* Cambridge, MA: MIT Press.

Kramer, R. (1976). *Maria Montessori: A biography.* New York: Putnam's.

Kris, E. (1952). *Psychoanalytic explorations in art.* New York: International Universities Press.

Kroger, J. (2007). *Identity development* (2nd ed.). Thousand Oaks, CA: Sage.

Kubler-Ross, E. (1969). *On death and dying.* New York: Macmillan.

Kuhn, D. (1974). Inducing development experimentally: Comments on a research paradigm. *Developmental Psychology, 10,* 590–600.

Kuhn, D., Langer, J., Kohlberg, L., & Haan, N. (1977). The development of formal operations in logical and moral judgment. *Genetic Psychology Monographs, 95,* 97–188.

Labov, W. (1970). The logic of nonstandard English. In F. Williams (Ed.), *Language and poverty: Perspectives on a theme.* Chicago: Markham.

Laing, R. D. (1965). *The divided self: An existential study in sanity and madness.* Middlesex, UK: Penguin.

Laing, R. D. (1967). *The politics of experience.* New York: Ballantine Books.

Lamb, M. E., & Campos, J. J. (1982). *Development in infancy.* New York: Random House.

Lamprecht, S. P. (1928). Introduction. In S. P. Lambrecht (Ed.), *Locke: Selections.* New York: Charles Scribner's Sons.

Lee, D. (1959). *Freedom and culture.* Englewood Cliffs, NJ: Spectrum (Prentice-Hall).

Levinson, D. (1977). The mid-life transition. *Psychiatry, 40,* 99–112.

Levinson, D. (1978). *The seasons of a man's life.* New York: Ballantine.

Levinson, D. J. (1996). *The seasons of a woman's life.* New York: Ballantine Books.

Liebert, R. M., Odom, R. D., Hill, J. H., & Huff, R. L. (1969). Effects of age and rule familiarity on the production of modeled language constructions. *Developmental Psychology, 1,* 108–112.

Liebert, R. M., Poulos, R. W., & Marmor, G. S. (1977). *Developmental psychology* (2nd ed.). Englewood Cliffs, NJ: Prentice-Hall.

Lightfoot, D. (1982). *The language lottery: Toward a biology of grammars.* Cambridge, MA: MIT Press.

Lightfoot, D. (1999). *The development of language.* Malden, MA: Blackwell.

Lillard, A., & Else-Quest, N. (2006, September 29). Evaluating Montessori education. *Science, 313,* 1893–1894.

Lillard, P. P. (1972). *Montessori: A modern approach.* New York: Schocken.

Lillard, P. P. (1996). *Montessori today.* New York: Schocken.

Lipsitt, L. P. (1971, December 5). Babies: They're a lot smarter than they look. *Psychology Today,* pp. 70–72, 80–89.

Lipsitt, L. P. (1975). The synchrony of respiration, heart rate, and sucking behavior in the newborn. *Biologic and clinical aspects of brain development,* Mead Johnson Symposium on Prenatal and Developmental Medicine, No. 6. Reprinted in R. C. Smart & M. S. Smart (Eds.), *Readings in child development and relations* (2nd ed.). New York: Macmillan, 1977.

Locke, J. (1689). *Two treatises on government,* P. Laslett (Ed.). Cambridge, UK: Cambridge University Press, 1960.

Locke, J. (1690). *Essay concerning human understanding* (Vol. 1, J. W. Yolton, Ed.). London: J. M. Dent and Sons, 1961.

Locke, J. (1693). *Some thoughts concerning education.* In P. Gay (Ed.), *John Locke on education.* New York: Bureau of Publications, Teacher's College, Columbia University, 1964.

Looft, W. R., & Bartz, W. H. (1969). Animisim revived. *Psychological Bulletin, 71,* 1–19.

Lorenz, K. (1935). Companions as factors in the bird's environment. In K. Lorenz, *Studies in animal and human behavior* (Vol. 1) (R. Martin, trans.). Cambridge, MA: Harvard University Press, 1971.

Lorenz, K. (1937). The establishment of the instinct concept. In K. Lorenz, *Studies in animal and human behavior* (Vol. 1) (R. Martin, trans.). Cambridge, MA: Harvard University Press, 1971.

Lorenz, K. (1952a). The past twelve years in the comparative study of behavior. In C. H. Schiller (Ed.), *Instinctive behavior.* New York: International Universities Press, 1957.

Lorenz, K. (1952b). *King Solomon's ring* (M. K. Wilson, trans.). New York: Thomas Y. Crowell.

Lorenz, K. (1963). *On aggression.* San Diego: Harcourt Brace Jovanovich.

Lorenz, K. (1965). *Evolution and modification of behavior.* Chicago: University of Chicago Press.

Lorenz, K. (1981). *The foundations of ethology.* New York: Touchstone Book (Simon & Schuster).

Lovaas, O. I. (1969). *Behavior modification: Teaching language to autistic children.* [Instructional film, 45 min., 16mm-sound]. New York: Appleton-Century-Crofts.

Lovaas, O. I. (1973). *Behavioral treatment of autistic children.* University Programs Modular Studies. Morristown, NJ: General Learning Press.

Lovaas, O. I. (1977). *The autistic child.* New York: Halstead Press.

Lovaas, O. I. (1987). Behavioral treatment and normal educational and intellectual functioning in young autistic children. *Journal of Consulting and Clinical Psychology, 55,* 3–9.

Lovaas, O. I. (2003). *Teaching individuals with developmental delays.* Austin, TX: PRO-ED.

Lovell, K. (1968, April 5 and 6). *Piaget in perspective: The experimental foundations.* Paper presented to the conference of the University of Sussex, Sussex, England.

Luria, A. R. (1960). Verbal regulation of behavior. In M. A. B. Brader (Ed.), *The central nervous system and behavior.* New York: Josiah Macy Jr. Foundation.

Luria, A. R. (1961). *The role of speech in the regulation of normal and abnormal behavior.* New York: Liveright.

Luria, A. R. (1976). *Cognitive development: Its cultural and social foundations* (M. Lopez-Morillas & L. Solotaroff, trans.). Cambridge, MA: Harvard University Press.

Luria, A. R. (1981). *Language and cognition.* (J. Wertsch, ed.). New York: John Wiley.

Lyons, N. P. (1983). Two perspectives: On self, relationships, and morality. *Harvard Educational Review, 53,* 125–145.

Lyons-Ruth, K., & Jacobivtz, D. (2008). Attachment disorganization: Genetic factors, parenting contexts, and developmental transformation from infancy to adulthood. In J. Cassidy & P.R. Shaver (Eds.), *Handbook of attachment* (2nd ed.). New York: Guilford.

Maccoby, E. E., & Wilson, W. C. (1957). Identification and observational learning from films. *Journal of Abnormal and Social Psychology, 55,* 76–87.

Maccoby, E. E., Wilson, W. C., & Jacklin, C. N. (1974). *The psychology of sex differences.* Stanford, CA: Stanford University Press.

MacFarlane, A. (1981). What a baby knows. In H. E. Fitzgerald (Ed.), *Human development 81/82.* Annual Editions. Guilford, CT: Dushkin.

McCartney, K., Clark-Stewart, A., Owen, M. T., Burchinal, M., Bub, K. L., & Belsky, J. (2010). Testing a series of causal propositions relating time in child care to children's externalizing behavior. *Developmental Psychology, 46,* 1–17.

McEachlin, J. J., Smith, T., & Lovaas, O. I. (1993). Long-term outcome for children with autism who received early intensive behavioral treatment. *American Journal on Mental Retardation, 97,* 259–372.

McNeill, D. (1966). Developmental psycholinguistics. In F. Smith & G. A. Miller (Eds.), *The genesis of language: A psycholinguistic approach.* Cambridge, MA: MIT Press.

Maestripieri, D. (2001). Is there mother-infant bonding in primates? *Developmental Review, 21,* 93–120.

Mahler, M. S. (1968). *On human symbiosis and the vicissitudes of individuation. Vol. 1: Infantile psychosis* (in collaboration with M. Furer). New York: International Universities Press.

Mahler, M. S. (1988). *The memoirs of Margaret S. Mahler* (compiled and edited by P. E. Stepansky). New York: Free Press.

Mahler, M. S., Pine, F., & Bergman, A. (1975). *The psychological birth of the human infant.* London: Hutchinson.

Main, M. (1995). Recent studies in attachment: Overview with selected implications for clinical work. In S. Goldberg, R. Muir, & J. Kerr (Eds.), *Attachment theory.* Hillsdale, NJ: Analytic Press.

Main, M., & Goldwyn, R. (1987). *Interview-based adult attachment classifications: Related to infant-mother and infant-father attachment.* Unpublished manuscript, Department of Psychology, University of California, Berkeley.

Main, M., Goldwyn, R., Kaplan, N., & Cassidy, J. (1985). Security in infancy, childhood, and adulthood: A move to the level of representation. In I. Bretherton & E. Waters (Eds.), *Growing points of attachment theory and research. Monographs of the Society for Research in Child Development, 50* (Serial No. 209).

Malinowski, B. (1927). *Sex and repression in savage society.* San Diego: Harcourt Brace Jovanovich.

Mandler, J. M. (1998). Representation. In D. Kuhn & R. S. Siegler (Eds.), *Handbook of Child Psychology* (5th ed.) (Vol. 2). New York: John Wiley.

Manuel, F. (1972). Comments. In International Study Project, Inc., *Abraham Maslow: A memorial volume.* Monterey, CA: Brooks/Cole.

Marcia, J. E. (1966). Development and validation of ego identity status. *Journal of Personality and Social Psychology, 3,* 551–558.

Marks, L. (1975). On colored-hearing synesthesia. *Psychological Bulletin, 82,* 303–331.

Marler, P., & Tamura, M. (1964). Culturally transmitted patterns of vocal behavior in sparrows. *Science, 146,* 1483–1486.

Marx, K. (1844). *Economic and philosophical manuscripts* (M. Milligan, trans.). In R. C. Tucker (Ed.), *The Marx-Engels reader.* New York: W. W. Norton, 1972.

Marx, K. (1845). Theses on Feuerbach. In R. C. Tucker (Ed.), *The Marx-Engels reader.* New York: W. W. Norton, 1972.

Marx, K. (1859). Preface to *A contribution to the critique of political economy.* In R. C. Tucker (Ed.), *The Marx-Engels reader.* New York: W. W. Norton, 1972.

Marx, K., & Engels, F. (1846). *The German ideology* (S. Ryazanskaya & W. Lough, trans.). In R. C. Tucker (Ed.), *The Marx-Engels reader.* New York: W. W. Norton, 1972.

Marx, K., & Engels, F. (1872). *Manifesto of the Communist Party.* In R. C. Tucker (Ed.), *The Marx-Engels reader.* New York: W. W. Norton, 1972.

Maslow, A. (1943). A dynamic theory of human motivation. *Psychological Review, 50,* 370–396.

Maslow, A. (1954). *Motivation and personality* (2nd ed.). New York: Harper & Row, 1970.

Maslow, A. (1966). *The psychology of science: A reconnaissance.* Chicago: Henry Regnery (Gateway), 1969.

Maslow, A. (1968). *Toward a psychology of being* (2nd ed.). New York: Van Nostrand Reihold.

Maslow, A. (1971). *The farther reaches of human nature.* New York: Viking.

Mead, M. (1964). *Continuities in cultural evolution.* New Haven, CT: Yale University Press.

Meltzoff, A. N. (1988). Infant imitation and memory: Nine-month-olds in immediate and deferred tests. *Child Development, 59,* 217–225.

Miller, E., & Almon, J. (2009). *Crisis in the kindergarten: Why children need play in school.* College Park, MD: Alliance for Childhood.

Miller, L. B., & Dyer, J. L. (1975). Four preschool programs: Their dimensions and effects. *Monographs of the Society for Research in Child Development, 40* (Serial No. 162).

Miller, P., & Garvey, C. (1984). Mother-baby role play: Its origins in social support. In I. Bretherton (Ed.), *Symbolic play.* Orlando, FL: Academic Press.

Miller, P. H. (2011). *Theories of developmental psychology* (5th ed.). New York: W. H. Freeman.

Miller, R. (1990). *What are schools for? Holistic education in American culture.* Brandon, VT: Holistic Education Press.

Mills, C. W. (1962). *The Marxists.* New York: Dell.

Mischel, W. (1970). Sex-typing and socialization. In P. H. Mussen (Ed.), *Carmichael's manual of child psychology* (3rd ed.) (Vol. 2). New York: John Wiley.

Misiak, H., & Sexton, V. S. (1973). *Phenomenological, existential, and humanistic psychologies: A historical survey.* New York: Grune & Stratton.

Montessori, M. (1909). *The Montessori method* (A. E. George, trans.). New York: Schocken, 1964.

Montessori, M. (1917). *The advanced Montessori method: Vol. 1. Spontaneous activity in education* (F. Simmonds, trans.). Cambridge, MA: Robert Bentley, 1964.

Montessori, M. (1936a). *The child in the family* (N. R. Cirillo, trans.). Chicago: Henry Regnery, 1970.

Montessori, M. (1936b). *The secret of childhood* (M. J. Costelloe, trans.). New York: Ballantine Books, 1966.

Montessori, M. (1948a). *The discovery of the child* (M. J. Costelloe, trans.). Notre Dame, IN: Fides Publishers, 1967.

Montessori, M. (1948b). *From childhood to adolescence* (A. M. Joosten, trans.). New York: Schocken, 1973.

Montessori, M. (1949). *The absorbent mind* (C. A. Claremont, trans.). New York: Holt, Rinehart & Winston, 1967.

Montessori, M. (1970). *Maria Montessori: A centenary anthology, 1870–1970.* Koninginneweg, Amsterdam: Association Montessori Internationale.

Moore, R. C. (1989). Before and after asphalt. In M. N. Bloch & A. D. Pellegrini (Eds.), *The ecological context of children's play.* Norwood, NJ: Ablex.

Munn, N. L. (1974). *The growth of human behavior* (3rd ed.). Boston: Houghton Mifflin.

Munn, N. L., Fernald, L. D., & Fernald, P. S. (1974). *Introduction to psychology* (3rd ed.). Boston: Houghton Mifflin.

Munroe, R. (1955). *Schools of psychoanalytic thought.* New York: Henry Holt.

Munson, K. J., & Crosbie, J. (1998). Effects of response cost in computerized programmed instruction. *The Psychological Record, 48,* 233–250.

Murphy, M. J. (2007, May 20). My dear fellow species. *New York Times.*

Mussen, P. H., & Eisenberg-Berg, N. (1977). *Roots of caring, sharing, and helping.* San Francisco: W. H. Freeman.

Muuss, R. E. (1975). *Theories of adolescence* (3rd ed.). New York: Random House.

National Institute of Child Health and Human Development. (2003). Does the amount of time spent in child care predict socioemotional adjustment during the transition to kindergarten? *Child Development, 74,* 976–1005.

Needham, J. (1959). *A history of embryology* (2nd ed.). Cambridge, UK: Cambridge University Press.

Neill, A. S. (1960). *Summerhill: A radical approach to child rearing.* New York: Hart.

Neimark, E. D. (1975). Longitudinal development of formal operations thought. *Genetic Psychology Monographs, 91,* 171–225.

Nelson, K. (2003). Narrative and self, myth and memory: Emergence of the cultural self. In R. Fivush & C. A. Haden (Eds.), *Autobiographical memory and the construction of a narrative self: Developmental and cultural perspectives.* Mahwah, NJ: Erlbaum

Neugarten, B. L. (1964). A developmental view of adult personality. In J. E. Birren (Ed.), *Relations of development and aging.* Springfield, IL: Charles C Thomas.

Neugarten, B. L. (1968). Adult personality: Toward a psychology of the life cycle. In B. L. Neugarten (Ed.), *Middle age and aging.* Chicago: University of Chicago Press.

Newman, B. M., & Newman, P. R. (2003). *Development through life* (8th ed.). Belmont, CA: Wadsworth.

Newport, E. (1990). Maturational constraints on language learning. *Cognitive Science, 14,* 11–28.

Nisan, M., & Kohlberg, L. (1982). Universality and variation in moral judgment: A longitudinal and cross-sectional study in Turkey. *Child Development, 52,* 865–876.

Oppenheimer, T. (2003). *The flickering mind.* New York: Random House.

Palinscar, A. S., & Brown, A. L. (1989). Instruction for self-regulated reading. In L. B. Resnick & L. E. Klopfer (Eds.), *Toward the thinking curriculum.* Alexandria, VA: Association for Supervision and Curriculum Development.

Papert, S. (1980). *Mindstorms.* New York: Basic Books.

Parritz, R. H., & Troy, M. F. (2011). *Disorders of childhood.* Belmont, CA: Wadsworth.

Pavlov, I. P. (1927). *Conditioned reflexes* (G. V. Anrep, trans.). London: Oxford University Press.

Pavlov, I. P. (1928). *Lectures on conditioned reflexes* (Vol. 1, W. H. Gantt, trans.). New York: International Publishers.

Peill, E. J. (1975). *Invention and discovery of reality.* London: John Wiley.

Pheardon, T. P. (1952). Introduction. In T. P. Pheardon (Ed.), *John Locke: The second treatise of government.* New York: Liberal Arts Press.

Piaget, J. (1923). *The language and thought of the child* (M. Gabain, trans.). London: Routledge and Kegan Paul, 1959.

Piaget, J. (1924). *Judgment and reasoning in the child* (M. Warden, trans.). Savage, MD: Littlefield, Adams, 1972.

Piaget, J. (1926). *The child's conception of the world* (J. & A. Tomlinson, trans.). Savage, MD: Littlefield, Adams, 1963.

Piaget, J. (1932). *The moral judgment of the child* (M. Gabain, trans.). New York: Free Press, 1965.

Piaget, J. (1936a). *The origins of intelligence in children* (M. Cook, trans.). New York: International Universities Press, 1974.

Piaget, J. (1936b). *The construction of reality in the child* (M. Cook, trans.). New York: Ballantine Books, 1954.

Piaget, J. (1946). *Play, dreams and imitation in childhood* (C. Gattegno & F. M. Hodgson, trans.). New York: W. W. Norton, 1962.

Piaget, J. (1947). *The psychology of intelligence* (M. Piercy & D. E. Berlyne, trans.). Savage, MD: Littlefield, Adams, 1973.

Piaget, J. (1952). Autobiography. In E. Boring, H. S. Langfeld, H. Werner, & R. M. Yerkes (Eds.), *A history of psychology in autobiography* (Vol. 4). Worcester, MA: Clark University Press.

Piaget, J. (1964a). *Six psychological studies* (A. Tenzer & D. Elkind, trans.). New York: Vintage Books, 1968.

Piaget, J. (1964b). Development and learning. In R. Ripple & V. Rockcastle (Eds.), *Piaget rediscovered*. Ithaca, NY: Cornell University Press, 1969.

Piaget, J. (1969). *Science of education and the psychology of the child* (D. Coltman, trans.). New York: Viking, 1970.

Piaget, J. (1970). Piaget's theory. In P. H. Mussen (Ed.), *Handbook of child psychology* (4th ed.) (Vol. 1, W. Kessen, Ed.). New York: John Wiley, 1983.

Piaget, J. (1972). Intellectual evolution from adolescence to adulthood. *Human Development 15*, 1–12.

Piaget, J. (1983). Jean Piaget's views on the psychology of language and thought. In R. W. Rieber (Ed.), *Dialogues on the psychology of language and thought*. New York: Plenum.

Piaget, J., & Inhelder, B. (1948). *The child's conception of space* (F. J. Langdor & J. L. Lunzer, trans.). London: Routledge & Kegan Paul, 1956.

Piaget, J., & Inhelder, B. (1966). *The psychology of the child* (H. Weaver, trans.). New York: Basic Books, 1969.

Piaget, J., & Szeminska, A. (1941). *The child's conception of number* (C. Cattegno & F. M. Hodgson, trans.). New York: W. W. Norton.

Piatelli-Palmarini, M. (Ed.). (1979). *Language and learning: The debate between Jean Piaget and Noam Chomsky*. Cambridge, MA: Harvard University Press, 1980.

Pillmemer, D. B., Picariello, M. L., & Pruett, J. C. (1994). Very long-term memories of a salient preschool event. *Applied Cognitive Psychology, 8*, 95–106.

Pillemer, D. B., & White, S. H. (1989). Childhood events recalled by children and adults. In H. W. Reese (Ed.), *Advances in child development and behavior* (Vol. 21). San Diego: Academic Press.

Pinker, S. (1994). *The language instinct*. New York: HarperPerennial.

Podd, M. (1972). Ego identity status and morality. *Developmental Psychology, 6*, 497–507.

Pollak, R. (1997). *The creation of Dr. B.* New York: Simon & Schuster.

Power, C., & Reimer, J. (1979). Moral atmosphere: An educational bridge between moral judgment and action. In W. Damon (Ed.), *New directions for child development* (Vol. 2). San Francisco: Jossey-Bass.

Power, F. C., Higgins, A., & Kohlberg, L. (1989). *Lawrence Kohlberg's approach to moral education*. New York: Columbia University Press.

Pratt, M. W., Skoe, E. A., & Arnold, M. L. (2004). Care reasoning development and family socialization patterns in later adolescence: A longitudinal analysis. *International Journal of Behavioral Development, 28*, 139–147.

Premack, D. (1961). Predicting instrumental performance from the independent rate of the contingent response. *Journal of Experimental Psychology, 61*, 161–171.

Pullum, G., & Scholz,B. (2002). Empirical assessment of stimulus poverty arguments. *Linguistic Review, 19*, 8–50.

Quality counts. (2001, January 11). *Education Week, 20*.

Quality counts. (2009, January 8). *Education Week, 28*.

Quick, R. H. (1880). Introduction. In R. H. Quick (Ed.), *Some thoughts concerning education by John Locke*. London: C. J. Clay & Sons.

Ravitch, D. (1995). *National standards in American education*. Washington, DC: The Brookings Institution.

Rawls, J. (1971). *A theory of justice*. Cambridge, MA: Harvard University Press.

Redl, F., & Wineman, D. (1951). *Children who hate*. New York: Free Press.

Reese, E., & Fivush, R. (1993). Parental styles of talking about the past. *Developmental Psychology, 29*, 596–606.

Reiber, R. W., & Voyat, G. (1983). *Dialogues on the psychology of language and thought*. New York: Plenum.

Reimer, J., Paolitto, D. P., & Hersh, R. H. (1983). *Promoting moral growth* (2nd ed.). New York: Longman.

Rest, J. (1973). The hierarchical nature of moral judgment: The study of patterns of preference and comprehension of moral judgments made by others. *Journal of Personality, 41,* 86–109.

Rest, J. (1983). Morality. In P. H. Mussen (Ed.), *Handbook of child psychology* (4th ed.) (Vol. 3, J. H. Flavell & E. M. Markman, Eds.). New York: John Wiley.

Rest, J., Turiel, E., & Kohlberg, L. (1969). Relations between level of moral judgments and preference and comprehension of the moral judgment of others. *Journal of Personality, 37,* 225–252.

Reynolds, C. S. (1968). *A primer of operant conditioning.* Glenview, IL: Scott, Foresman.

Rheingold, H. L., Gewirtz, J. L., & Ross, H. W. (1959). Social conditioning of vocalizations in the infant. *Journal of Comparative and Physiological Psychology, 52,* 68–73.

Riegel, K. F. (1975). Toward a dialectical theory of development. *Human Development, 18,* 50–64.

Riess, B. F. (1954). Effect of altered environment and of age on the mother-young relationships among animals. *Annals of the New York Academy of Science, 57,* 606–610.

Robertson, J. (1952). *A two year old goes to hospital* [16 mm, B & W film]. London: Tavistock Clinic. New York: New York University Film Library.

Rogoff, B. (1998). Cognition as a collaborative process. In D. Kuh & R. S. Siegler (Eds.), *Handbook of child psychology* (5th ed.) (Vol. 2, Cognition, perception, and language). New York: Wiley.

Rogoff, B. (2003). *The cultural nature of development.* Oxford, UK: Oxford University Press.

Rogoff, B., Malkin, C., & Gilbride, K. (1984). Interaction with babies as guidance and development. In B. Rogoff & J. Wertsch (Eds.), *Children learning in the "zone of proximal development."* San Francisco: Jossey-Bass.

Rosenbaum, J. E. (2004, Spring). It's time to tell the kids: If you don't do well in high school, you won't do well in college (or on the job). *American Educator, 28,* 8–15, 41–42.

Rosenthal, T. L., & Zimmerman, B. J. (1972). Modeling by exemplification and instruction in training conservation. *Developmental Psychology, 6,* 392–401.

Roszak, T. (1972). *Where the wasteland ends.* Garden City, NY: Anchor (Doubleday), 1973.

Rousseau, J. J. (1750). Discourse on the sciences and arts. In R. D. Masters (Ed.), *The first and second discourses* (R. D. & J. R. Masters, trans.). New York: St. Martin's Press, 1964.

Rousseau, J. J. (1755). Discourse on the origin and foundations of inequality. In R. D. Masters (Ed.), *The first and second discourses* (R. D. & J. R. Masters, trans.). New York: St. Martin's Press, 1964.

Rousseau, J. J. (1762a). *The social contract* (G. Hopkins, trans.). New York: Oxford University Press, 1962.

Rousseau, J. J. (1762b). *Emile, or education* (B. Foxley, trans.). London: J. M. Dent and Sons, 1948.

Rousseau, J. J. (1788). *The confessions of Jean Jacques Rousseau.* New York: Modern Library, 1945.

Rowland, S. (2002). *Jung: A feminist revision.* Cambridge, UK: Polity.

Rumbaugh, D. M., & Washburn, D. A. (2003). *Intelligence of apes and other rational beings.* New Haven, CT: Yale University Press.

Rushton, J. P. (1975). Generosity in children: Immediate and long term effects of modeling, preaching, and moral judgment. *Journal of Personality and Social Psychology, 31,* 459–466.

Russell, B. (1945). *A history of Western philosophy.* New York: Simon & Schuster.

Russell, B. (1971). *Education and the social order.* London: George Allen and Unwin.

Sachs, J. S. (1976). Development of speech. In E. C. Carterette & M. P. Friedman (Eds.), *Handbook of perception* (Vol. 7). New York: Academic Press.

Sahakian, W. S., & Sahakian, M. L. (1975). *John Locke.* Boston: Twayne.

Savage-Rumbaugh, S., & Lewin, R. (1994) *Kanzi.* New York: Wiley.

Savage-Rumbaugh, S., Shanker, S. G., & Taylor, T. J. (1998). *Apes, language, and the human mind.* New York: Oxford University Press.

Savage-Rumbaugh, S. (2007, May 17). *Savage-Rumbaugh: Apes that write, start fires, and play pac man.* YouTube, TED. www.youtube.com/watch?v=a8nDJaH-fVE

Schachtel, E. G. (1959). *Metamorphosis.* New York: Basic Books.

Schultz, D. P. (1975). *A history of modern psychology* (2nd ed.). New York: Academic Press.

Schwartz, B. (1989). *Psychology of learning and behavior* (3rd ed.). New York: W. W. Norton.

Schweitzer, A. (1929). *The philosophy of civilization* (T. C. Campion, trans.). Amherst, NY: Prometheus, 1987.

Scribner, S., & Cole, M. (1981). *The psychology of literacy.* Cambridge, MA: Harvard University Press.

Searles, H. F. (1965). *Collected papers on schizophrenia and related subjects.* New York: International Universities Press.

Seligman, M. E. P. (1972). Phobias and preparedness. In M. E. P. Seligman & J. L. Hager (Eds.), *Biological boundaries of learning.* New York: Appleton-Century-Crofts.

Selman, R. K. (1976). Social-cognitive understanding: A guide to educational and clinical practice. In T. Lickona (Ed.), *Moral development and behavior.* New York: Holt, Rinehart & Winston.

Shahar, S. (1990). *Childhood in the middle ages.* London: Routledge.

Sheehy, G. (1976). *Passages: Predictable crises of adult life.* New York: Dutton.

Siegler, R. S. & Alibali, M. W. (2005). *Children's thinking* (4th ed.). Upper Saddle River, NJ: Prentice-Hall.

Sigel, I. E. (1968). Reflections. In I. E. Sigel & F. H. Hooper (Eds.), *Logical thinking in children: Research based on Piaget's theory.* New York: Holt, Rinehart & Winston.

Simcock, G., & Hayne, H. (2003). Age-related changes in verbal and nonverbal memory during early childhood. *Developmental Psychology, 39,* 805–814.

Sinclair, H. (1971). Sensorimotor action patterns as a condition for the acquisition of syntax. In R. Huxley & E. Ingram (Eds.), *Language acquisition: Methods and models.* New York: Academic Press.

Skinner, B. F. (1938). *The behavior of organisms.* Englewood Cliffs, NJ: Prentice-Hall.

Skinner, B. F. (1948). *Walden two.* New York: Macmillan.

Skinner, B. F. (1953). *Science and human behavior.* New York: Macmillan.

Skinner, B. F. (1957). *Verbal behavior.* Englewood Cliffs, NJ: Prentice-Hall.

Skinner, B. F. (1959). *Cumulative record.* Englewood Cliffs, NJ: Prentice-Hall.

Skinner, B. F. (1967). Autobiography. In E. G. Boring & G. Lindzey (Eds.), *A history of psychology in autobiography* (Vol. 5). Englewood Cliffs, NJ: Prentice-Hall.

Skinner, B. F. (1968). *The technology of teaching.* Englewood Cliffs, NJ: Prentice-Hall.

Skinner, B. F. (1969). *Contingencies of reinforcement.* Englewood Cliffs, NJ: Prentice-Hall.

Skinner, B. F. (1971). *Beyond freedom and dignity.* New York: Bantam.

Skinner, B. F. (1974). *About behaviorism.* New York: Knopf.

Skoke, E. E. A., & von der Lippe, A. L., (1998). *Personality development in adolescence.* London: Routledge.

Slobin, D. I. (1966). Soviet psycholinguistics. In N. O'Connor (Ed.), *Present-day Russian psychology: A symposium by seven authors.* Oxford: Pergamon.

Slobin, D. I. (1972). They learn the same way all around the world. *Psychology Today, 6,* 71–82.

Slobin, D. I. (1973). Cognitive prerequisites for the development of grammar. In C. A. Ferguson & D. I. Slobin (Eds.), *Studies of child language development.* New York: Holt, Rinehart & Winston.

Slobin, D. I. (1979). *Psycholinguistics* (2nd ed.). Glenview, IL: Scott, Foresman.

Slobin, D. I. (1985). Introduction. In D. I. Slobin (Ed.), *The crosslinguistic study of language acquisition* (Vol. 1). Hillsdale, NJ: Erlbaum.

Smart, M. S., & Smart, R. C. (1978). *Preschool children* (2nd ed.). New York: Macmillan.

Snow, C. E. (1979). Conversations with children. In P. Fletcher & M. Garman (Eds.), *Language acquisition.* Cambridge, UK: Cambridge University Press.

Spock, B. (1946). *Baby and child care.* New York: Pocket Books, 1968.

Spinka, M., Newberry, R. C., & Bekoff, M. (2001). Mammalian play: Training for the unexpected. *The Quarterly Review of Biology, 76,* 141–168.

Stern, D. N. (1985). *The interpersonal world of the infant.* New York: Basic Books.

Sullivan, H. S. (1953). *The interpersonal theory of psychiatry.* New York: W. W. Norton.

Suzuki, D., & Knudtson (1992). *Wisdom of the elders.* New York: Bantam.

Taylor, M., & Carlson, S. M. (1997). The relation between individual differences in fantasy and theory of mind. *Child Development, 68,* 436–455.

Terrace, H.S., Petito, L.A., Sanders, R.J., & Bever, T.G. (1979, November 23). Can an ape create a sentence? *Science, 206,* 891-902.

Thain, M., & Hickman, M. (1994). *The Penguin dictionary of biology* (9th ed.). London: Penguin.

Thompson, C. (1950). Cultural pressures in the psychology of women. In P. Mullahy (Ed.), *A study of interpersonal relations.* New York: Hermitage Press.

Thorndike, E. L. (1905). *The elements of psychology.* New York: Seiler.

Tinbergen, N. (1951). *The study of instinct.* Oxford: Clarendon Press.

Tinbergen, N. (1965). The shell menace. In T. E. McGill (Ed.), *Readings in animal behavior.* New York: Holt, Rinehart & Winston.

Tinbergen, N. (1977). Interview. In D. Cohen (Ed.), *Psychologists on psychology*. New York: Taplinger.

Tolman, E. C. (1948). Cognitive maps in rats and man. *Psychological Review, 55,* 189–208.

Tomasello, M. (2003). *Constructing a language*. Cambridge, MA: Harvard University Press.

Tough, P. (2009, September 27). The make-believe solution. *The New York Times Magazine,* 31–35.

Tulkin, S. R., & Konner, M. J. (1973). Alternative conceptions of intellectual functioning. *Human Development, 16,* 33–52.

Turiel, E. (1966). An experimental test of the sequentiality of developmental stages in the child's moral judgments. *Journal of Personality and Social Psychology, 3,* 611–618.

U.S. Department of Education. (1983). National Commission on Excellence in Education, *A nation at risk*. Washington, DC: Government Printing Office.

Uzgiris, I. C. (1964). Situational generality of conservation. *Child Development, 35,* 831–841.

Valliant, G. E. (2000). Adaptive mental mechanisms: Their role in a positive psychology. *American Psychologist, 55,* 89–98.

Van IJzendoorn, M. H., & Sagi-Schwartz, A. (2008). Cross-cultural patterns of attachment: Universal and contextual dimensions. In J. Cassidy & P. R. Shaver (Eds.), *Handbook of attachment* (2nd ed.). New York: Guilford.

Vaughn, B. E., Bost, K. K., & van IJzendoorn, M. H. (2008). Attachment and temperament: Additive and interactive influences on behavior, affect, and cognition during infancy and childhood. In J. Cassidy & P. R. Shaver (Eds.), *Handbook of attachment* (2nd ed.). New York: Guilford.

Von Franz, M. L. (1964). The process of individuation. In C. G. Jung (Ed.), *Man and his symbols*. New York: Dell.

Vygotsky, L. S. (1930). Tool and symbol in children's development (A. R. Luria & M. Cole, trans.). In M. Cole, V. John-Steiner, S. Scribner, & E. Souberman (Eds.), *L. S. Vygotsky: Mind in society*. Cambridge, MA: Harvard University Press, 1978.

Vygotsky, L. S. (1931a). Development of higher mental functions. In *Psychological research in the U.S.S.R.* Moscow: Progress Publishers, 1966.

Vygotsky, L. S. (1931b). The history of the development of the higher mental functions (M. Cole, trans.). Excerpt in M. Cole, V. John-Steiner, S. Scribner, & E. Souberman (Eds.), *L. S. Vygotsky: Mind in society*. Cambridge, MA: Harvard University Press, 1978.

Vygotsky, L. S. (1932). The problem of will and its development in childhood. In R. W. Rieber & A. S. Carton (Eds.), *The collected works of L. S. Vygotsky* (Vol. 1, N. Minick, trans.). New York: Plenum, 1987.

Vygotsky, L. S. (1933). The role of play in development (M. Lopez-Morillas, trans.). In M. Cole, V. John-Steiner, S. Scribner, & E. Souberman (Eds.), *L. S. Vygotsky: Mind in society*. Cambridge, MA: Harvard University Press, 1978.

Vygotsky, L. S. (1934). *Thought and language* (A. Kozulin, trans.). Cambridge, MA: MIT Press, 1986.

Vygotsky, L. S. (1935). Mental development of children and the process of learning (M. Lopez Morillas, trans.). In M. Cole, V. John-Steiner, S. Scribner, & E. Souberman (Eds.), *L. S. Vygotsky: Mind in society*. Cambridge, MA: Harvard University Press, 1978, chaps. 7–8.

Wade, N. (2009, February 10). Darwin: Ahead of his time, is still influential. *New York Times*.

Waelder, R. (1960). *Basic theory of psychoanalysis*. New York: International Universities Press.

Walker, L. S., & Pitts, R. G. (1998). Naturalistic conceptions of morality. *Developmental Psychology, 34,* 403–419.

Wang, Q. (2004). The emergence of cultural self-constructions: Autobiographical memory and self-description in European American and Chinese children. *Developmental Psychology, 40,* 3–15.

Wapner, S., Kaplan, B., & Cohen, S. B. (1973). An organismic-developmental perspective for understanding transactions of men and environments. *Environment and Behavior, 5,* 255–289.

Watson, J. B. (1913). Psychology as the behaviorist views it. *Psychological Review, 20,* 158–177.

Watson, J. B. (1924). *Behaviorism*. New York: W. W. Norton, 1970.

Watson, J. B. (1928). *Psychological care of infant and child*. New York: W. W. Norton.

Watson, J. B. (1936). Autobiography. In C. Murchison (Ed.), *A history of psychology in autobiography* (Vol. 3). Worcester, MA: Clark University Press.

Watson, R. I. (1968). *The great psychologists from Aristotle to Freud* (2nd ed.). Philadelphia: Lippincott.

Weinfield, N. S., Sroufe, L. A., Egeland, B., & Carlson, E. (2008). The nature of individual differences in infant-caregiver attachment. In J. Cassidy & P. R. Shaver (Eds.), *Handbook of attachment* (2nd ed.). New York: Guilford.

Weisner, T. S. (1996). The 5 to 7 transition as an ecocultural project. In A. J. Sameroff & M. M. Haith (Eds.), *The five to seven year shift.* Chicago: University of Chicago Press.

Weiss, R. S. (1982). Attachment in adult life. In C. M. Parkes & J. Stevenson-Hinde (Eds.), *The place of attachment in human behavior.* New York: Basic Books.

Werner, H. (1934). The unity of the senses. In S. S. Barten & M. B. Franklin (Eds.), *Developmental processes: Heinz Werner's selected writings* (Vol. 1). New York: International Universities Press, 1978.

Werner, H. (1948). *Comparative psychology of mental development* (2nd ed.). New York: Science Editions.

Werner, H. (1956). On physiognomic perception. In G. Kepes (Ed.), *The new landscape.* Chicago: Theobald.

Werner, H. (1957). The concept of development from a comparative and organismic point of view. In D. B. Harris (Ed.), *The concept of development.* Minneapolis: University of Minnesota Press.

Werner, H., & Kaplan, B. (1956). The developmental approach to cognition: Its relevance to the psychological interpretation of anthropological and ethnolinguistic data. *American Anthropologist, 58,* 866–880.

Werner, H., & Kaplan, B. (1963). *Symbol formation.* New York: John Wiley.

Wertsch, J. V. (1985). *Vygotsky and the social formation of mind.* Cambridge, MA: Harvard University Press.

White, G. M. (1972). Immediate and deferred effects of model observation and guided and unguided rehearsal on donating and stealing. *Journal of Personality and Social Psychology, 21,* 139–148.

White, R. W. (1960). Competence and the psychosexual stages of development. In M. Jones (Ed.), *Nebraska symposium on motivation.* Lincoln: University of Nebraska Press.

White, R. W. (1963). Sense of interpersonal competence: Two case studies and some reflections on origins. In R. R. White (Ed.), *The study of lives.* New York: Atherton Press.

White, R. W., & Watt, N. F. (1973). *The abnormal personality* (4th ed.). New York: Ronald Press.

White, R. W., & Watt, N. F. (1981). *The abnormal personality* (5th ed.). New York: Wiley.

White, S. (1965). Evidence for a hierarchical arrangement of learning processes. In L. P. Lipsitt & C. C. Spiker (Eds.), *Advances in child development and behavior* (Vol. 2). New York: Academic Press.

White, S. (1970). Some general outlines of the matrix of developmental changes between five and seven years. *Bulletin of the Orton Society, 20,* 41–57.

White, S. H. (1996). The child's entry into the "age of reason." In A. J. Sameroff & M. M. Haith (Eds.), *The five to seven year shift.* Chicago: University of Chicago Press.

Whitehead, A. N. (1929). *Science and the modern world.* New York: Macmillan.

Whitehurst, G. J., Ironsmith, M., & Goldman, M. (1974). Selective imitation of the passive construction through modeling. *Journal of Experimental Child Psychology, 17,* 288–302.

Whiting, J. W. M., & Child, I. L. (1953). *Child training and personality: A cross-cultural study.* New Haven, CT: Yale University Press.

Whitmont, E. C. (1969). *The symbolic quest: Basic concepts of analytical psychology.* New York: Putnam's.

Whitmont, E. C., & Kaufmann, Y. (1973). Analytic psychotherapy. In R. Corsini (Ed.), *Current psychotherapies.* Itasca, IL: F. E. Peacock.

Williams, C. D. (1959). The elimination of tantrum behavior by extinction procedures. *Journal of Abnormal and Social Psychology, 5,* 269.

Wilner, W. (1975, Winter). Schachtel: A life. *William Alanson White Newsletter,* pp. 3–4.

Wilson, C. (1972). *New pathways in psychology: Maslow and the post-Freudian revolution.* New York: Mentor Books.

Wilson, E. O. (1993). Biophilia and the conservation ethic. In S. R. Kellert & E. O. Wilson (Eds.), *The biophilia hypothesis.* Washington, DC: Island Press.

Winner, E. (1982). *Invented worlds.* Cambridge, MA: Harvard University Press.

Witkin, H. (1965). Heinz Werner. *Child Development, 30,* 307–328.

Wohlwill, J. F. (1984). *Martha Muchow and the life-space of the urban child.* Paper presented to the Society for Research in Child Development, Ann Arbor, Michigan.

Wolpe, J. (1969). *The practice of behavior therapy.* New York: Pergamon.

Wood, D. (1998). *How children think and learn* (2nd ed.). Oxford, UK: Blackwell.

Wordsworth, W. (1807). Ode: Intimations of immortality from recollections of early childhood. In W. E. Williams (Ed.), *Wordsworth*. London: Penguin, 1985.

Zelazo, P. R., Zelazo, N. A., & Kolb, S. (1972). "Walking" in the newborn. *Science, 176,* 314–315.

Zimmerman, B. J., & Rosenthal, T. L. (1974). Conserving and retaining equalities and inequalities through observation and correction. *Developmental Psychology, 10,* 260–268.

Zimmerman, B. J., & Schunk, D. H. (2003). Albert Bandura: The scholar and his contributions to educational psychology. In B. J. Zimmerman & D. H. Schunk (Eds.), *Educational psychology: A century of contributions.* Mahwah, NJ: Erlbaum.

SUBJECT INDEX